The African-American Odyssey

Media Research Update

VOLUME TWO: SINCE 1865

SECOND EDITION

Darlene Clark Hine
Michigan State University

William C. Hine
South Carolina State University

Stanley Harrold
South Carolina State University

UPPER SADDLE RIVER, NEW JERSEY 07458

To Carter G. Woodson & Benjamin Quarles

Vice President/Editorial Director: Charlyce Jones Owen
Senior Acquisitions Editor: Charles Cavaliere
Senior Media Editor: Deborah O'Connell
Associate Editor: Emsal Hasan
Editor-in-Chief of Development: Rochelle Diogenes
Development Editor: Gerald Lombardi
Director of Production and Manufacturing: Barbara Kittle
Production Editors: Joseph Scordato, Jan Schwartz
Page Formatting & Layout: Joh Lisa, Rosemary Ross, Scott Garrison, and John Jordan
Manufacturing Manager: Nick Sklitsis
Prepress and Manufacturing Buyer: Sherry Lewis
Marketing Director: Beth Mejia
Marketing Managers: Claire Rehwinkel, Heather Shelstad
Creative Design Director: Leslie Osher
Cover and Interior Design: Anne DeMarinis
Editorial Assistant: Shannon Corliss
Cover Art: Aaron Douglas, *Philosophy,* 1930, oil on canvas, Fisk University Galleries, Nashville, Tennessee.
Photo Research Supervisor: Beth Boyd
Photo Researcher: Jane Sanders
Image Coordinator: Tara Gardner

Credits and acknowledgments for materials borrowed from other sources and reproduced, with permission, in this textbook, appear on pages C-1 to C2.

This book was set in 10/12 New Baskerville and was printed and bound by R. R. Donnelly and Sons, Inc. The cover was printed by Phoenix Color Corp.

A Pearson Education Company
Upper Saddle River, New Jersey 07458

Printed in the United States of America

10 9 8 7 6 5 4 3 2 1

ISBN 0-13-189930-9

Pearson Education Ltd.
Pearson Education Australia Pty. Ltd.
Pearson Education Singapore, Pte. Ltd.
Pearson Education North Asia Ltd.
Pearson Education Canada Ltd.
Pearson Educación de Mexico, S.A. de C.V.
Pearson Education – Tokyo, Japan
Pearson Education Malaysia, Pte. Ltd.

Brief Contents

12 The Meaning of Freedom: The Promise of Reconstruction, 1865–1868 258

13 The Meaning of Freedom: The Failure of Reconstruction, 284

PART IV Searching for Safe Spaces 306

14 White Supremacy Triumphant: African Americans in the South in the Late Nineteenth Century 308

15 Black Southerners Challenge White Supremacy 334

16 Conciliation, Agitation, and Migration: African Americans in the Early Twentieth Century 364

17 African Americans and the 1920s 400

PART V The Great Depression and World War II 426

18 The Great Depression and The New Deal 428

19 Black Culture and Society in the 1930s and 1940s 454

20 The World War II Era and Seeds of a Revolution 480

PART VI The Black Revolution 510

21 The Freedom Movement, 1954–1965 512

22 The Struggle Continues, 1965–1980 542

23 Modern Black America, 1980 to Present 576

Epilogue: "A Nation Within a Nation" 608

Contents

Preface xi

The Meaning of Freedom: The Promise of Reconstruction, 1865–1868 258

The End of Slavery 260
Differing Reactions of Former Slaves 260 Reuniting Black Families 260
Land 261
Special Field Order #15 261 The Port Royal Experiment 262
The Freedmen's Bureau 262
VOICES **A Freedmen's Bureau Commissioner Tells Freed People What Freedom Means** 263
Southern Homestead Act 264 **Sharecropping** 264 **The Black Church** 264 **Education** 267
Black Teachers 267
VOICES **A Northern Black Woman on Teaching Freedmen** 268
Black Colleges 269 Response of White Southerners 270
PROFILE **Charlotte E. Ray** 271
Violence 271 **The Crusade for Political and Civil Rights** 272
PROFILE **Aaron A. Bradley** 273
Presidential Reconstruction under Andrew Johnson 274 **Black Codes** 274 **Black Conventions** 274 **The Radical Republicans** 276
Radical Proposals 276 The Freedmen's Bureau Bill and the Civil Rights Bill 276 Johnson's Vetoes 276
The Fourteenth Amendment 277 **Radical Reconstruction** 277
Universal Manhood Suffrage 278 Black Politics 278 Sit-Ins and Strikes 278
The Reaction of White Southerners 278
Conclusion 279
Recommended Reading 280 Additional Bibliography 281
Retracing the Odyssey 282 Review, Research & Interact 283

The Meaning of Freedom: The Failure of Reconstruction 284

Constitutional Conventions 286 **Elections** 287 **Black Political Leaders** 287 **The Issues** 288
Education and Social Welfare 288
PROFILE **The Gibbs Brothers** 289
Civil Rights 290
Economic Issues 290
Land 290 Business and Industry 291
Black Politicians: An Evaluation 291 **Republican Factionalism** 291 **Opposition** 291
PROFILE **The Rollin Sisters** 292
The Ku Klux Klan 293
VOICES **An Appeal for Help Against the Klan** 295
The Fifteenth Amendment 295 **The Enforcement Acts** 296 **The North Loses Interest** 297 **The Freedmen's Bank** 297 **The Civil Rights Act of 1875** 298
VOICES **Black Leaders Support the Passage of a Civil Rights Act** 299
The End of Reconstruction 299
Violent Redemption 300 The Shotgun Policy 300 The Hamburg Massacre 300 The Compromise of 1877 301
Conclusion 302
Recommended Reading 302 Additional Bibliography 303
Retracing the Odyssey 303 Review, Research & Interact 304

PART IV Searching for Safe Spaces 306

White Supremacy Triumphant: African Americans in the South in the Late Nineteenth Century 309

Politics 310
Black Congressmen 311 Democrats and Farmer Discontent 311 The Colored Farmers' Alliance 313 The Populist Party 313
Disfranchisement 314
Evading the Fifteenth Amendment 314 Mississippi 314 South Carolina 315 The Grandfather Clause 315
Segregation 315
Jim Crow 316 Segregation on the Railroads 316 *Plessy v. Ferguson* 316
VOICES **Majority and Dissenting Opinions on *Plessy v. Ferguson*** 317

Streetcar Segregation 318 Segregation Proliferates 318
Racial Etiquette 318 **Violence** 319
Washington County, Texas 319 The Phoenix Riot 319 The Wilmington Riot 319 The New Orleans Riot 319 Lynching 320 Rape 321
PROFILE **Ida Wells Barnett** 322
Migration 323
The Liberian Exodus 323 The Exodusters 323 Migration within the South 324
Black Farm Families 324
Sharecroppers 324 Renters 325 Crop Liens 325 Peonage 326
VOICES **Cash and Debt for the Black Cotton Farmer** 326
Black Landowners 326 White Resentment of Black Success 327
PROFILE **Johnson C. Whittaker** 328
African Americans and Southern Courts 329
Segregated Justice 329 The Convict Lease System 329
Conclusion 330
Recommended Reading 331 Additional Bibliography 332
Retracing the Odyssey 332 Review, Research & Interact 333

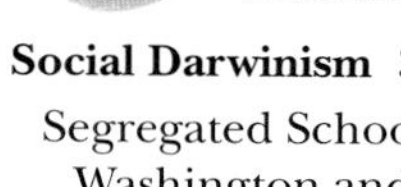

Black Southerners Challenge White Supremacy 334

Social Darwinism 336 Education and Schools 336
Segregated Schools 337 The Hampton Model 338 Washington and the Tuskegee Model 338 Critics of the Tuskegee Model 340
VOICES **Thomas E. Miller and the Mission of the Black Land-Grant College** 340
Church and Religion 341
The Church as Solace and Escape 343 The Holiness Movement and the Pentecostal Church 343
PROFILE **Henry McNeal Turner** 344
Roman Catholics and Episcopalians 345
Red versus Black: The Buffalo Soldiers 345
Discrimination in the Army 345 The Buffalo Soldiers in Combat 346 Civilian Hostility to Black Soldiers 346 Brownsville 346
African Americans in the Navy 347 **The Black Cowboys** 347 **The Spanish-American War** 347
Black Officers 348 A Splendid Little War 349 After the War 349
VOICES **Black Men in Battle in Cuba** 350
The Philippine Insurrection 351
Would Black Men Fight Brown Men? 351
Black Businesspeople and Entrepreneurs 351
PROFILE **Maggie Lena Walker** 352
African Americans and Labor 353
Unions 353 Strikes 354
Black Professionals 355
Medicine 355 The Law 356
Music 356
Ragtime 356 Jazz 357 The Blues 357
Sports 358
Jack Johnson 358 Baseball 359 Basketball and Other Sports 359 College Athletics 359
Conclusion 360
Recommended Reading 360 Additional Bibliography 361
Retracing the Odyssey 362 Review, Research & Interact 363

16 Conciliation, Agitation, and Migration: African Americans in the Early Twentieth Century 364

Race and the Progressive Movement 366 **Booker T. Washington's Approach** 366
Washington's Influence 367 The Tuskegee Machine 368 Opposition to Washington 369
W. E. B. Du Bois 369
VOICES **W. E. B. Du Bois on Being Black in America** 370
The Niagara Movement 371 **The NAACP** 372
Using the System 372 Du Bois and *The Crisis* 372 Washington versus the NAACP 373
The Urban League 374 **Black Women and the Club Movement** 374
The NACW: "Lifting as We Climb" 374 Phillis Wheatley Clubs 374
PROFILE **Mary Church Terrell** 375
Anna Julia Cooper and Black Feminism 376 Women's Suffrage 376
The Black Elite 376
The American Negro Academy 376
PROFILE **Lewis Latimer, Black Inventor** 377
The Upper Class 378 Fraternities and Sororities 378
Presidential Politics 378
Frustrated by the Republicans 378 Woodrow Wilson 378
PROFILE **George Washington Carver and Ernest Everett Just** 379
Black Men and the Military in World War I 380

The Punitive Expedition to Mexico 380 World War I 381 Black Troops and Officers 381 Discrimination and Its Effects 381 Du Bois's Disappointment 383
Race Riots 383
Atlanta 1906 384 Springfield 1908 385 East St. Louis 1917 385 Houston 1917 386 Chicago 1919 387 Elaine 1919 387 Tulsa 1921 387 Rosewood 1923 388
The Great Migration 388
Why Migrate? 388 Destinations 390
VOICES **A Migrant to the North Writes Home** 390
Northern Communities 391
Chicago 392 Harlem 392
Families 393
Conclusion 394
Recommended Reading 395 Additional Bibliography 395
Retracing the Odyssey 397 Review, Research & Interact 399

17 African Americans and the 1920s 400

Strikes and the Red Scare 402 **Varieties of Racism** 402
Scientific Racism 403 *The Birth of a Nation* 403 The Ku Klux Klan 404
Protest, Pride, and Pan-Africanism: Black Organizations in the Twenties 404 **The NAACP** 404
VOICES **The Negro National Anthem: "Lift Every Voice and Sing"** 405
PROFILE **James Weldon Johnson** 406
"Up You Mighty Race": Marcus Garvey and the UNIA 407
VOICES **Marcus Garvey Appeals for a New African Nation** 408
Pan-Africanism 410
Labor 411
The Brotherhood of Sleeping Car Porters 412 A. Philip Randolph 412
The Harlem Renaissance 413
Before Harlem 414 Writers and Artists 415 White People and the Harlem Renaissance 417
Harlem and the Jazz Age 418
PROFILE **Bessie Smith** 419
Song, Dance, and Stage 420
Sports 420
Rube Foster 421 College Sports 421
Conclusion 421
Recommended Reading 422 Additional Bibliography 423
Retracing the Odyssey 424 Review, Research & Interact 425

PART V
The Great Depression and World War II 426

18 The Great Depression and the New Deal 428

The Cataclysm, 1929–1933 430
Harder Times for Black America 430 Black Businesses in the Depression: Collapse and Survival 431
The Failure of Relief 433 **African Americans and the New Deal** 434
Roosevelt and the First New Deal, 1933–1935 434 Black Officials in the New Deal 435
VOICES **A Black Sharecropper Details Abuse in the Administration of Agricultural Relief** 436
Black Social Scientists and the New Deal 437
PROFILE **Mary McLeod Bethune** 438
African Americans and the Second New Deal 439
Black Protest During the Great Depression 441
The NAACP and Civil Rights Struggles 441 Du Bois Ignites a Controversy 441 Challenging Racial Discrimination in the Courts 442 Black Women and Community Organizing 443
Organized Labor and Black America 444 **The Communist Party and African Americans** 445
The International Labor Defense and the "Scottsboro Boys" 445
PROFILE **Angelo Herndon** 446
Debating Communist Leadership 447 The National Negro Congress 448
The Tuskegee Study 448
VOICES **Hoboing in Alabama** 449
Conclusion 450
Recommended Reading 450 Additional Bibliography 451
Retracing the Odyssey 452 Review, Research & Interact 453

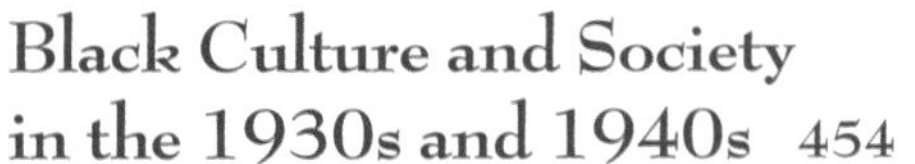

19 Black Culture and Society in the 1930s and 1940s 454

Black Culture in a Midwestern City 456 **The Black Culture Industry and American Racism** 457 **The Music Culture from Swing to Bebop** 457

PROFILE **Charlie Parker** 458

Popular Culture for the Masses: Comic Strips, Radio, and the Movies 460

The Comics 460 Radio and Race 460 Race, Representation, and the Movies 461

The Black Chicago Renaissance 463

PROFILE **Langston Hughes** 464

Jazz in Chicago 465 Gospel in Chicago: Thomas Dorsey 466 Chicago in Dance and Song: Katherine Dunham and Billie Holiday 466

VOICES **Margaret Walker on Black Culture** 467

PROFILE **Billie Holiday, 1915–1959 and "Strange Fruit"** 469

Black Graphic Art 470 **Black Literature** 470

Richard Wright's *Native Son* 471 James Baldwin Challenges Wright 471 Ralph Ellison and *Invisible Man* 472

African Americans in Sports 472

Jesse Owens and Joe Louis 473 Breaking the Color Barrier in Baseball 473

Black Religious Culture 474

The Nation of Islam 474 Father Divine and the Peace Mission Movement 474

CONCLUSION 475
RECOMMENDED READING 475 ADDITIONAL BIBLIOGRAPHY 476
RETRACING THE ODYSSEY 478 REVIEW, RESEARCH & INTERACT 479

20 The World War II Era and Seeds of a Revolution 480

On the Eve of War, 1936–1941 482

African Americans and the Emerging World Crisis 483 A. Philip Randolph and the March on Washington Movement 483 Executive Order #8802 485

Race and the U.S. Armed Forces 485

Institutional Racism in the American Military 485 The Costs of Military Discrimination 486 Soldiers and Civilians Protest Military Discrimination 487 Black Women in the Struggle to Desegregate the Military 487

VOICES **William H. Hastie Resigns in Protest** 488

The Beginning of Military Desegregation 489

VOICES **Separate but Equal Training for Black Army Nurses?** 490

PROFILE **Mabel K. Staupers (1890–1989)** 491

The Tuskegee Airmen 491 The Transformation of Black Soldiers 492

Black People on the Home Front 493

Black Workers: From Farm to Factory 493 The FEPC during the War 494 Anatomy of a Race Riot: Detroit, 1943 494 Old and New Protest Groups on the Home Front 495

PROFILE **Bayard Rustin** 496

The Transition to Peace 497 **The Cold War and International Politics** 497

African Americans in World Affairs: W. E. B. Du Bois and Ralph Bunche 498 Anticommunism at Home 498 Paul Robeson 498 Henry Wallace and the 1948 Presidential Election 499 Desegregating the Armed Forces 499

The Road to Brown 500

Constance Baker Motley and Black Lawyers in the South 500 *Brown* and the Coming Revolution 502

CONCLUSION 506
RECOMMENDED READING 506 ADDITIONAL BIBLIOGRAPHY 506
RETRACING THE ODYSSEY 508 REVIEW, RESEARCH & INTERACT 509

PART VI
The Black Revolution 510

21 The Freedom Movement, 1954–1965 512

The 1950s: Prosperity and Prejudice 514

Brown II 514 Massive White Resistance 514 The Lynching of Emmett Till 515

New Forms of Protest: The Montgomery Bus Boycott 515

The Roots of Revolution 516

VOICES **Letter of the Montgomery Women's Political Council to Mayor W. A. Gayle** 517

Rosa Parks 517

PROFILE **Rosa Loiuse McCauley Parks (1913–)** 518

Montgomery Improvement Association 519 Martin Luther King, Jr. 519 Walking for Freedom 520 Friends in the North 520 Victory 521

No Easy Road to Freedom: 1957–1960 521

Martin Luther King and the SCLC 521 Civil Rights Act of 1957 521 Little Rock, Arkansas 522

Black Youth Stand Up by Sitting Down 522
Sit-ins: Greensboro, Nashville, Atlanta 523 The Student Nonviolent Coordinating Committee 524 Freedom Rides 524
A Sight to be Seen: The Movement at High Tide 525
The Election of 1960 525
PROFILE **Robert Parris Moses** 526
The Kennedy Administration and the Civil Rights Movement 527 Voter Registration Projects 527
The Albany Movement 528
VOICES **Bernice Johnson Reagon on How to Raise a Freedom Song** 528
The Birmingham Confrontation 529 A Hard Victory 530
The March on Washington 530 The Civil Rights Act of 1964 531 Mississippi Freedom Summer 533 The Mississippi Freedom Democratic Party 533
PROFILE **Fannie Lou Hamer** 534
Selma and the Voting Rights Act of 1965 535
Conclusion 536
Recommended Reading 536 Additional Bibliography 537
Retracing the Odyssey 540 Review, Research & Interact 541

22 The Struggle Continues, 1965–1980 542

The Fading Dream of Racial Integration: White Backlash and Black Nationalism 544
Malcolm X 545 Malcolm X's New Departure 545 Stokely Carmichael and Black Power 545 The National Council of Churches 546
The Black Panther Party 547
Police Repression and the FBI's COINTELPRO 547
VOICES **The Black Panther Party Platform** 548
Prisoners' Rights 549
The Inner-City Rebellions 549
Watts 550 Newark 550 Detroit 550 The Kerner Commission 551
Difficulties in Creating the Great Society 551 **Johnson and the War in Vietnam** 552
Black Americans and the Vietnam War 553 Project 100,000 553
Johnson: Vietnam Destroys the Great Society 554
VOICES **They Called Each Other "Bloods"** 555
PROFILE **Muhammad Ali** 556
King: Searching for a New Strategy 557
King on the Vietnam War 557 King's Murder 557
The Black Arts Movement and Black Consciousness 558
Poetry and Theater 559 Music 560
The Second Phase of the Black Student Movement 561
The Orangeburg Massacre 561 Black Studies 561
The Election of 1968 562 **The Nixon Presidency** 563
The "Moynihan Report" and FAP 563 Busing 564 Nixon and the War 564 Nixon's Downfall 565
The Rise of Black Elected Officials 565
The Gary Convention and the Black Political Agenda 566 Black People Gain Local Offices 567
Economic Downturn 567 **Black Americans and the Carter Presidency** 567
Black Appointees 567
PROFILE **Eleanor Holmes Norton** 568
Carter's Domestic Policies 569
Conclusion 569
Recommended Reading 572 Additional Bibliography 572
Retracing the Odyssey 573 Review, Research & Interact 575

23 Modern Black America, 1980 to Present 576

Progress and Poverty 578
The Growth of the Black Middle Class 578
PROFILE **Oprah Winfrey: World's Richest Black Woman** 579
The Persistence of Black Poverty 580
Ronald Reagan and the Conservative Reaction 580
Dismantling the Great Society 581 Black Conservatives 581 The Thomas–Hill Controversy 581 Debating the "Old" and the "New" Civil Rights 582 Affirmative Action 582
VOICES **Black Women in Defense of Themselves** 583
The Backlash 584
Ronald Reagan and the Conservative Reaction 585
The King Holiday 586 TransAfrica and the Antiapartheid Movement 586
Jesse Jackson and the Rainbow Coalition 587 **Policing the Black Community** 588
Human Rights in America 589 Police Director Hubert Williams of Newark 590
The Election of 1992 590
"It's The Economy, Stupid!" 591 Clinton Signs the Welfare Reform Act 592
PROFILE **Spike Lee, A Voice of Protest** 593
African-American Cultural and Intellectual Movements at the End of the Millennium 594
Black Feminism 594

Black Intellectuals 595 Afrocentricity 595 Louis Farrakhan and the Nation of Islam 597 The Million Man March 598 The Million Woman March 599 Black Christianity on the Front Lines 599 The Hip-Hop Nation 600

2000 and Beyond 600

The 2000 Census and Black America 601 Reparations 601 September 11, 2001 603

CONCLUSION 604

RECOMMENDED READING 604 ADDITIONAL BIBLIOGRAPHY 604

RETRACING THE ODYSSEY 606 REVIEW, RESEARCH & INTERACT 607

Epilogue: "A Nation Within a Nation" 608

Appendix A–1

Credits C–1

Index I–1

Contents of Documents CD-ROM M–1

Contents of *Living Words* Audio CD M–3

Maps

12-1 The Effect of Sharecropping on the Southern Plantation: The Barrow Plantation, Oglethorpe County, Georgia 265
12-2 The Location of Black Colleges Founded before and during Reconstruction 270
12-3 Congressional Reconstruction 278
13-1 Dates of Readmission of Southern States to the Union and Reestablishment of Democratic Party Control 300
13-2 The Election of 1876 302
16-1 Major Race Riots, 1900–1921 384
16-2 The Great Migration and the Distribution of the African-American Population in 1920 391
16-3 The Expansion of Black Harlem, 1911–1930 394
21-1 Major Events of the Civil Rights Movement 516
21-2 The Effect of the Voting Rights Act of 1965 537

Figures and Tables

FIGURES

14-1 African-American Representation in Congress, 1867–1900 311
14-2 Lynching in the United States, 1889–1932 320
14-3 Black Farm Owners in Alabama, Arkansas, Florida, Georgia, Louisiana, Mississippi, South Carolina, and Texas, 1870–1910 327
15-1 Black and White Illiteracy in the United States and the Southern States, 1880–1900 337
15-2 Church Affiliation among Southern Black People, 1890 341
17-1 Black Workers by Major Industrial Group, 1920 411
17-2 Black and White Workers by Skill Level, 1920 412
18-1 Unemployment, 1925–1945 430

TABLES

13-1 African–American Population and Officeholding during Reconstruction in the States Subject to Congressional Reconstruction 287
14-1 Black Members of the U.S. Congress, 1870–1901 312
15-1 South Carolina's Black and White Public Schools, 1908–1909 337
16-1 Black Population Growth in Selected Northern Cities, 1910–1920 389
18-1 Median Income of Black Families Compared to the Median Income of White Families for Selected Cities, 1935–1936 431
23-1 Median Income of Black and White Households, 1992 and 1997 578
23-2 Black and White Children and the Conditions Contributing to Poverty 580

PREFACE

"One ever feels his two-ness,—an American, a Negro; two souls, two thoughts, two unreconciled strivings; two warring ideals in one dark body." So wrote W. E. B. Du Bois in 1897. African-American history, Du Bois maintained, was the history of this double-consciousness. Black people have always been part of the American nation that they helped to build. But they have also been a nation unto themselves, with their own experiences, culture, and aspirations. African-American history cannot be understood except in the broader context of American history. American history cannot be understood without African-American history.

Since Du Bois's time our understanding of both African-American and American history has been complicated and enriched by a growing appreciation of the role of class and gender in shaping human societies. We are also increasingly aware of the complexity of racial experiences in American history. Even in times of great racial polarity some white people have empathized with black people and some black people have identified with white interests.

It is in light of these insights that *The African-American Odyssey* tells the story of African Americans. That story begins in Africa, where the people who were to become African Americans began their long, turbulent, and difficult journey, a journey marked by sustained suffering as well as perseverance, bravery, and achievement. It includes the rich culture—at once splendidly distinctive and tightly intertwined with a broader American culture—that African Americans have nurtured throughout their history. And it includes the many-faceted quest for freedom in which African Americans have sought to counter white oppression and racism with the egalitarian spirit of the Declaration of Independence that American society professes to embody.

Nurtured by black historian Carter G. Woodson during the early decades of the twentieth century, African-American history has blossomed as a field of study since the 1950s. Books and articles have appeared on almost every facet of black life. Yet this survey is the first comprehensive college textbook of the African-American experience. It draws on recent research to present black history in a clear and direct manner, within a broad social, cultural, and political framework. It also provides thorough coverage of African-American women as active builders of black culture.

The African-American Odyssey balances accounts of the actions of African-American leaders with investigations of the lives of the ordinary men and women in black communities. This community focus helps make this a history of a people rather than an account of a few extraordinary individuals. Yet the book does not neglect important political and religious leaders, entrepreneurs, and entertainers. And it gives extensive coverage to African-American art, literature, and music.

African-American history started in Africa, and this narrative begins with an account of life on that continent to the sixteenth century and the beginning of the forced migration of millions of Africans to the Americas. Succeeding chapters present the struggle of black people to maintain their humanity during the slave trade and as slaves in North America during the long colonial period.

The coming of the American Revolution during the 1770s initiated a pattern of black struggle for racial justice in which periods of optimism alternated with times of repression. Several chapters analyze the building of black community institutions, the antislavery movement, the efforts of black people to make the Civil War a war for emancipation, their struggle for equal rights as citizens during Reconstruction, and the strong opposition these efforts faced. There is also substantial coverage of African-American military service, from the War for Independence through American wars of the nineteenth and twentieth centuries.

During the late nineteenth century and much of the twentieth century, racial segregation and racially motivated violence that relegated African Americans to second-class citizenship provoked despair, but also inspired resistance and commitment to change. Chapters on the late nineteenth and early twentieth centuries cover the great migration from the cotton fields of the South to the North and West, black nationalism, and the Harlem Renaissance. Chapters on the 1930s and 1940s—the beginning of a period of revolutionary change for African Americans—tell of the economic devastation and political turmoil caused by the Great Depression, the growing influence of black culture in America, the racial tensions caused by black participation in World War II, and the dawning of the civil rights movement.

The final chapters tell the story of African Americans during the second half of the twentieth century. They relate the successes of the civil rights movement at its peak during the 1950s and 1960s and the efforts of African Americans to build on those successes during the more conservative 1970s and 1980s. Finally, there are portrayals of black life during the concluding decades of the twentieth century and of the continuing impact of African Americans on life in the United States.

In all, *The African-American Odyssey* tells a compelling story of survival, struggle, and triumph over adversity. It will leave students with an appreciation of the central place of black people and black culture in this country and a better understanding of both African-American and American history.

The Second Edition

With the generous assistance and advice of many colleagues, we have enhanced, strengthened, and updated this Second Edition. We have added material on stateless societies in West Africa and on contacts between peoples of African and American Indian descent. There is new information on Africans at Jamestown as well as those who were in Spanish

Florida and French Louisiana. There is more coverage of the underground railroad and on black homesteaders. Anna Julia Cooper and black feminism, the American Negro Academy, the 1900 New Orleans riot, and the elimination of Rosewood, Florida in 1923 are new to this edition.

We have expanded coverage of religion with more information on black Roman Catholics and black Episcopalians. There is a fresh discussion of the impact of black Christianity on the civil rights movement

There are new biographical profiles of Billie Holiday, Mabel Staupers, Rosa Parks, Eleanor Holmes Norton, and a new dual profile of nineteenth century black entrepreneurs Stephen Smith and William Whipper.

There is an analysis of the Clinton presidency and coverage of the 2000 election as well as the 2000 census. The odyssey of African Americans has been extended into the twenty-first century with discussions of racial profiling, reparations for slavery, and the events of September 11, 2001.

Special Features

The many special features and pedagogical tools integrated within *The African-American Odyssey* are designed to make the text accessible to students. They include a variety of tools to reinforce the narrative and help students grasp key issues.

- Outlines provide students with a brief overview of the material they are about to read.
- Introductory quotations set the theme for each chapter.
- **NEW** – Part-opening Timelines thematically organize events in African-American history.
- "Voices" boxes provide students with first-person perspectives on key events in African-American history. Brief introductions and study questions help students analyze these primary source documents and relate them to the text.
- The biographical sketches in the "Profiles" boxes highlight the contributions and personalities of both prominent individuals and ordinary people, illuminating common experiences among African Americans at various times and places.
- Brief chronologies provide students with a snapshot of the temporal relationship among significant events.
- End-of-chapter Timelines establish a chronological context for events in African-American history by relating them to events in American history and in the rest of the world.
- Review questions encourage students to analyze the material they have read and to explore alternative perspectives on that material.
- The recommended reading and additional bibliography lists direct students to more information about the subject of each chapter.
- **NEW** – Retracing the Odyssey sections guide instructors and students to educational sites that explore the diverse dimensions of African-American history.
- **NEW** – Map Explorations in many chapters allow students to interact with maps in a dynamic fashion on the book's ***Companion Website***™.
- Maps, charts, and graphs help students visualize the geographical context of events and grasp significant trends.
- **NEW** – Review, Research & Interact sections organize the text's Media Resources into a single study unit at the end of each chapter.

Supplementary Instructional Materials

The extensive package of both traditional and electronic supplements that accompanies *The African-American Odyssey* provides instructors and students with an array of resources that combine sound scholarship, engaging content, and a variety of pedagogical tools to enrich the classroom experience and students' understanding of African-American history.

Instructor's Manual with Tests The Instructor's Manual with Tests provides summaries, outlines, learning objectives, lecture and discussion topics, and audio/visual resources for each chapter. Test materials include multiple choice, essay, identification and short-answer, chronology, and map questions.

Prentice Hall Custom Test This commercial-quality, computerized test management program, available for Windows and Macintosh environments, allows instructors to select from testing material in the Instructor's Manual with Tests and design their own exams.

Study Guide (Volumes I and II) This student study aid includes a summary for each chapter, reviews key points and concepts, and provides multiple choice, essay, chronology, and map questions.

Documents Set (Volumes I and II) The *Documents Set* supplements the text with additional primary and secondary source material covering the social, cultural, and political aspects of African-American history. Each reading includes a short historical summary and several review questions.

The African-American Odyssey *Companion Website*™ The *Companion Website (www.prenhall.com/hine)* works with the text to provide students with additional study materials—including questions and map labeling exercises—and directs them to appropriate sources on African-American history available on the Internet. A Faculty Module provides instructors with downloadable material from both the Instructor's Manual and the text to aid in course organization.

Living Words: An Audio CD of African-American Oral Tradition Every new copy of *The African-American Odyssey* includes an audio CD that presents the rich oral tradition of the African-American experience. Speeches, songs, stories, and poetry expose students to the African roots of African-American culture, connect them to the rhythms of a musical tradition that has left an indelible stamp on American history, and expose them to the urgency of a political struggle that continues today. Extensively revised to accompany the Second Edition of *The African-*

American Odyssey, eleven new tracks have been added, including excerpts of speeches by Frederick Douglass and Ida B. Wells, and excerpts from World War II-era music. To achieve tighter integration between the audio CD and *The African-American Odyssey*, each of the forty-three tracks on the audio CD is now denoted by a special icon at appropriate places in the text.

Instructor's CD-ROM for *The African-American Odyssey* New to the Second Edition, this ancillary contains PowerPoint™ presentations directly linked to the text; maps and graphs from *The African-American Odyssey*; lecture outlines; and other instructional material.

Prentice Hall and Penguin Bundle Program Prentice Hall and Penguin are pleased to provide adopters of *The African-American Odyssey* with an opportunity to receive significant discounts when orders for *The African-American Odyssey* are bundled together with Penguin titles in American history. Please contact your local Prentice Hall representative for details.

Acknowledgments

In preparing *The African-American Odyssey* we have benefited from the work of many scholars and the help of colleagues, librarians, friends, and family.

Special thanks are due to the following scholars for their substantial contributions to the development of this textbook: Hilary Mac Austin, *Chicago, Illinois*; Brian W. Dippie, *University of Victoria*; W. Marvin Dulaney, *College of Charleston*; Sherry DuPree, *Rosewood Heritage Foundation*; Peter Banner-Haley, *Colgate University*; Robert L. Harris Jr., *Cornell University*; Wanda Hendricks, *University of South Carolina*; Rickey Hill, *DePauw University*; William B. Hixson, *Michigan State University*; Barbara Williams Jenkins, *South Carolina State University*; Earnestine Jenkins, *University of Memphis*; Hannibal Johnson, *Tulsa, Oklahoma*; Wilma King, *University of Missouri, Columbia*; Karen Kossie-Chernyshev, *Texas Southern University*; Frank C. Martin, *South Carolina State University*; Jacqueline McLeod, *Western Illinois University*; Freddie Parker, *North Carolina Central University*; Christopher R. Reed, *Roosevelt University*; Linda Reed, *University of Houston*; Mark Stegmaier, *Cameron University*; Robert Stewart, *Trinity School, New York*; Matthew Whitaker, *Arizona State University*; Andrew Workman, *Mills College*; Deborah Wright, *Avery Research Center, College of Charleston.*

We are grateful to the reviewers who devoted valuable time to reading and commenting on *The African-American Odyssey*. Their insightful suggestions greatly improved the quality of the text: Abiodun Goke-Pariola, *Georgia Southern University*; Claude A. Clegg, *Indiana University*; Delia Cook, *University of Missouri at Kansas City*; Mary Ellen Curtin, *Southwest Texas State University*; Roy F. Finkenbine, *Wayne State University*; John H. Haley, *University of North Carolina at Wilmington*; Ebeneazer Hunter, *De Anza College*; Joseph Kinner, *Gallaudet University*; Kenneth Mason, *Santa Monica College*; Andrew T. Miller, *Union College*; John David Smith, *North Carolina State University at Raleigh*; Marshall Stevenson, *Ohio State University*; Harry Williams, *Carleton College*; Andrew Workman, *Mills College*.

We also wish to thank the reviewers who helped us prepare the Second Edition: Carol Anderson, *University of Missouri, Columbia*; Jennifer L. Baszile, *Yale University*; Caroline Cox, *University of the Pacific*; Henry Vance Davis, *Ramapo College of NJ*; Robert Gregg, *Richard Stockton College of NJ*; Keith Griffler, *University of Cincinnati*; Robert V. Hanes, *Western Kentucky University*; Wali Rashash Kharif, *Tennessee Technological University*; John F. Marszalek, *Mississippi State University*; Diane Batts Morrow, *University of Georgia*; Walter Rucker, *University of Nebraska, Lincoln*; Manisha Sinha, *University of Massachusetts, Amherst*; Betty Joe Wallace, *Austin Peay State University*; Vernon J. Williams, Jr., *Purdue University*.

Many librarians provided valuable help tracking down important material. They include Aimee Berry, Ruth Hodges, Doris Johnson, Minnie Johnson, Barbara Keitt, Andrew Penson, and Mary L. Smalls, all of Miller F. Whittaker Library, South Carolina State University; James Brooks and Jo Cottingham of the interlibrary loan department, Cooper Library, University of South Carolina; and Allan Stokes of the South Caroliniana Library at the University of South Carolina. Kathleen Thompson and Marshanda Smith provided important documents and other source material.

Seleta Simpson Byrd of South Carolina State University and Linda Werbish and Marshanda Smith of Michigan State University provided valuable administrative assistance.

Each of us also enjoyed the support of family members, particularly Barbara A. Clark, Robbie D. Clark, Emily Harrold, Judy Harrold, Carol A. Hine, Peter J. Hine, Thomas D. Hine, and Alma J. McIntosh.

Finally, we gratefully acknowledge the essential help of the superb editorial and production team at Prentice Hall: Charlyce Jones Owen, Vice President and Editorial Director for the Humanities, whose vision got this project started and whose unwavering support saw it through to completion; Charles Cavaliere, Acquisitions Editor, who kept us on track; Editorial Assistant, Adrienne Paul; Susanna Lesan, Editor in Chief of Development, and Gerald Lombardi, who provided valuable organizational, substantive, and stylistic insights; Leslie Osher, Creative Design Director; Anne DeMarinis, who created the book's handsome design; Joseph Scordato, Production Editor, who saw it efficiently through production; Jane Sanders, our photo researcher, who skillfully tracked down the book's many illustrations, some of them from obscure sources; Claire Rehwinkel, Marketing Manager, who provided valuable insight into the history textbook market; Emsal Hasan, Assistant Editor, who pulled together the book's supplementary material; and Nick Sklitsis, Manufacturing Manager, Sherry Lewis, Manufacturing Buyer, and Jan Stephan, Managing Editor, who kept the whole team on schedule.

HIGHLIGHTS OF *THE AFRICAN-AMERICAN ODYSSEY, MEDIA AND RESEARCH UPDATE*

Documents and Activities in African-American History. Bound with every new copy of *The African-American Odyssey*, this new CD-ROM includes over 150 primary-source documents in African American history. Formatted in easily navigable PDF files, each document is accompanied by essay questions that allow students to read important sources in African American history. Also included on the CD-ROM are Learning Activities that explore key episodes and developments in American history. These media-rich activities combine primary sources, illustrations, graphs, audio clips, interactive maps, and video to explore important topics indepth. Map Explorations from each chapter reside on the CD-ROM as well. These dynamic maps help students see the spatial dimensions of African-American history and to explore concepts interactively. Documents, Learning Activities, and Map Explorations each contain essay questions which are linked to the Companion Website™ for *The African-American Odyssey*, allowing students to respond online.

TRACK 4

Living Words: An Audio CD of African-American Oral Tradition. Every new copy of *The African-American Odyssey, Media and Research Update* includes an audio CD that presents the rich tradition of the African American experience.

Research Navigator.com RESOURCES FOR COLLEGE RESEARCH ASSIGNMENTS **Research Navigator** activities, located at the end of each chapter, guide students through the many resources available on Research Navigator, a powerful research tool that includes ContentSelect, *The New York Times*, and Best of the Web Link Library. An access code to Research Navigator is included with the Evaluating Online Resources booklet packaged with all new copies of *The African-American Odyssey, Media and Research Update.*

Living Words

An Audio CD of African-American Oral Traditions

Kevin Everod Quashie & Stuart L. Twite

OVERVIEW

Oral traditions are a vital component of the study of African-American life. It is in such traditions—represented by speeches, songs, stories, and poems—that connections between African-American culture and the cultures of Africa and other peoples of the diaspora, like those of the Caribbean, become most readily evident. And it is through oral traditions that the particular rhythms and urgency of the texts come alive. On this audio CD, we aim to capture a general sense of the rich oral legacy of African Americans. The selections are a suitable companion to the history of African Americans told in the pages of this text.

This CD opens with a piece of Ghanian drum music. Ghana is both metaphorically and genealogically an African-American homeland. The drum rhythms on this track closely parallel similar rhythms in music of the Caribbean and the United States, as reflected in the next track, the spiritual "I Just Come from the Fountain." It was through music that Africans, speaking many languages and deprived of access to education, sustained their traditions in slavery.

The spiritual was one of the earliest African-American musical forms and influenced many others. Spirituals in this collection include "Go Down Moses" (perhaps the most famous spiritual), sung by Bill McAdoo; "Come By Hyar," sung by Bernice Reagon; "Swing Low Sweet Chariot," sung by Paul Robeson; "I Couldn't Hear Nobody Pray," sung by the Fisk Jubilee Singers; and "I Sing Because I'm Happy," sung by Mahalia Jackson. As spirituals have been handed down from generation to generation, they have given voice to the political and social concerns of the times. Marian Anderson's stirring rendition of "He's Got the Whole World in His Hands" inspired the crowds at the historic March on Washington in 1963, and "Wade in the Water" became a civil rights movement standard.

Spirituals have influenced and been influenced by the blues and work song traditions. The use of repetition in a classic work song like "Pick a Bale of Cotton" (sung here by Pete Seeger) reflects the rhythms of daily work and echoes the similar use of repetition in spirituals. Leadbelly's performance of "Backwater Blues" reveals the intimate relationship between blues and spirituals, especially the way both traditions describe everyday events as sacred.

Spirituals and Blues have always had a political element, which is represented here by two songs from WWII performed by Buster Ezell and the Georgia Singers.

The last track, "Zum Zum," recorded in New York by Six Boys in Trouble, is an early expression of the dub poetry and beats that later emerged in rap and hip hop music. Its vocal and drum rhythms echo the rhythms of the Ghanian drum music that opens the CD, demonstrating the strong continuities linking contemporary African-American musical traditions to those of the past.

Lucy Terry, probably the earliest African-American poet, is represented here in a reading by Harlem Renaissance poet Arna Bontemps of her only surviving poem, "Bars Fight." Phillis Wheatley, another eighteenth-century poet, is represented by her elegant meditation, "On Being Brought from Africa to America," read by Jean Brannon. Turning to the late-nineteenth and early-twentieth centuries, the CD includes a reading of Paul Laurence Dunbar's "Dawn" and James Weldon Johnson's epic piece "The Creation," both read by Bontemps. Representing the Harlem Renaissance, Claude McKay is heard reading his own poem, "If We Must Die," and Langston Hughes delivers his own "I've Known Rivers" and "I Too." Pulitzer Prize winner Gwendolyn Brooks reads her wonderful piece "Song of the Front Yard." Of more contemporary poets, there is Sonia Sanchez reading "liberation/poem" and Nikki Giovanni delivering "Woman."

The prose works on this CD capture many key moments in African-American history. In the first two selections, former slaves recount their experiences. In "The Rebirth of Sojourner Truth," Jean Brannon draws from aspects of Truth's life story to produce a stirring reflection on her name and identity. Brannon also constructs a glimpse at Harriet Tubman's life from documents about her. "What if I Am a Woman," a speech by the orator Maria W. Stewart, the first woman to address a mixed audience of men and women, is brought back to life in a reading by Ruby Dee. Ossie Davis similarly brings new life to Frederick Douglass's "If There is No Struggle, There is No Freedom." Also by Douglass is an appraisal of John Brown.

The post-Civil War condition of African-American life is represented in a sermon by S.B. Wallace calling for unity and by discussions on labor, while Mary Church focuses on the issues faced by women. A monologue on post-bellum experiences is given by Wallace Quarterman, the effects of the Black Laws are related and Ida B. Wells analyzes lynching. Controversies over the direction of education are represented as well. We hear Booker T. Washington delivering an excerpt from his famous "Address at the Atlanta Exposition" and a talk about the Hampton vision for education.

Political movements are included, with "A Republican Textbook for Colored Voters" and with comments by W.E.B. DuBois in an interview talking about the creation of the N.A.A.C.P. A recording of a speech by Martin Luther King, Jr. to a mass meeting at the height of the civil rights movement conveys the widespread commitment to political action of the period. And Angela Davis voices her protest in an interview from prison.

The CD reflects the diversity of the African-American oral tradition. The rhythms, the words, the history, the politics, the urgency . . . they are all here.

12

The Meaning of Freedom: The Promise of Reconstruction, 1865–1868

Hundreds of black churches were founded across the South following the Civil War, and they grew spectacularly in the decades that followed. This illustration shows a congregation crowded into Richmond's First African Baptist Church in 1874.

AS the great day grew nearer, there was more singing in the slave quarters than usual. It was bolder, had more ring, and lasted later into the night. Most of the verses of the plantation songs had some reference to freedom. True, they had sung those same verses before, but they had been careful to explain that the "freedom" in these songs referred to the next world, and had no connection with life in this world. Now they gradually threw off the mask, and were not afraid to let it be known that the "freedom" in their songs meant freedom of the body in this world.

—Booker T. Washington, Up from Slavery

CHAPTER OUTLINE

The End of Slavery
- Differing Reactions of Former Slaves
- Reuniting Black Families

Land
- Special Field Order #15
- The Port Royal Experiment

The Freedmen's Bureau
- Southern Homestead Act
- Sharecropping

The Black Church

Education
- Black Teachers
- Black Colleges
- Response of White Southerners

Violence

The Crusade for Political and Civil Rights

Presidential Reconstruction under Andrew Johnson

Black Codes

Black Conventions

The Radical Republicans
- Radical Proposals
- The Freedmen's Bureau Bill and the Civil Rights Bill
- Johnson's Vetoes

The Fourteenth Amendment

Radical Reconstruction
- Universal Manhood Suffrage
- Black Politics
- Sit-Ins and Strikes

The Reaction of White Southerners

Conclusion

What did freedom mean to a people who had endured and survived two hundred fifty years of enslavement in America? What did the future hold for nearly four million African Americans in 1865?

Freedom meant many things to many people. But to most former slaves, it meant that families would stay together. Freedom meant that women would no longer be sexually exploited. Freedom meant learning to read and write. Freedom meant organizing churches. Freedom meant moving around without having to obtain permission. Freedom meant that labor would produce income for the laborer and not the master. Freedom meant working without the whip. Freedom meant land to own, cultivate, and live on. Freedom meant a trial before a jury if charged with a crime. Freedom meant voting. Freedom meant citizenship and having the same rights as white people.

Years after slavery ended, a former Texas slave, Margrett Nillin, was asked if she preferred slavery or freedom. She answered unequivocally: "Well, it's dis way, in slavery I owns nothin' and never owns nothin'. In freedom I's own de home and raise de family. All dat causes me worryment and in slavery I has no worryment, but I takes freedom."

The End of Slavery

With the collapse of slavery, many black people were quick to inform white people that whatever loyalty, devotion, and cooperation they might have shown as slaves had never been a reflection of their inner feelings and attitudes. Near Opelousas, Louisiana, a Union officer asked a young black man why he did not love his master, and the youth responded sharply. "When my master begins to lub me, den it'll be time enough for me to lub him. What I wants is to get away. I want to take me off from dis plantation, where I can be free."

TRACK 14

In North Carolina, planter Robert P. Howell, was deeply disappointed that a loyal slave named Lovet fled at the first opportunity. "He was about my age and I had always treated him more as a companion than a slave. When I left I put everything in his charge, told him that he was free, but to remain on the place and take care of things. He promised me faithfully that he would, but he was the first one to leave . . . and I did not see him for several years."

Emancipation was a traumatic experience for many former masters. A Virginia freedman remembered that "Miss Polly died right after the surrender, she was so hurt that all the negroes was going to be free." Another former slave, Robert Falls, recalled that his master assembled the slaves to inform them that they were free. "I hates to do it, but I must. You all ain't my niggers no more. You is free. Just as free as I am. Here I have raised you all to work for me, and now you are going to leave me. I am an old man, and I can't get along without you. I don't know what I am going to do." In less than a year, he was dead. Falls attributed his death to the end of slavery. "It killed him."

Differing Reactions of Former Slaves

Other slaves bluntly displayed their reaction to years of bondage. Aunt Delia, a cook with a North Carolina family, revealed that for a long time she had secretly gained retribution for the indignity of servitude. "How many times I spit in the biscuits and peed in the coffee just to get back at them mean white folks." In Goodman, Mississippi, a slave named Caddy learned she was free and rushed from the field to find her owner. "Caddy threw down that hoe, she marched herself up to the big house, then, she looked around and found the mistress. She went over to the mistress, she flipped up her dress and told the white woman to do something. She said it mean and ugly. This is what she said: 'Kiss my ass!' "

On the other hand, some slaves, especially elderly ones, were fearful and apprehensive about freedom. On a South Carolina plantation, an older black woman refused to accept emancipation. "I ain' no free nigger! I is got a marster and mistiss! Dee right dar in de great house. Ef you don' b'lieve me, you go dar an' see."

Reuniting Black Families

As slavery ended, the most urgent need for many freed people was finding family members who had been sold away from them. Slavery had not destroyed the black family. Husbands, wives, and children went to great lengths to reassemble their families after the Civil War. For years and even decades after the end of slavery, advertisements appeared in black newspapers appealing for information about missing kinfolk. The following notice was published in the *Colored Tennessean* on August 5, 1865:

> Saml. Dove wishes to know of the whereabouts of his mother, Areno, his sisters Maria, Neziah and Peggy, and his brother Edmond, who were owned by Geo. Dove of Rockingham County, Shenandoah Valley, Va. Sold in Richmond, after which Saml. and Edmond were taken to Nashville, Tenn., by Joe Mick; Areno was left at the Eagle Tavern, Richmond. Respectfully yours, Saml. Dove, Utica, New York.

In North Carolina a northern journalist met a middle-age black man "plodding along, staff in hand, and apparently very footsore and tired." The nearly exhausted freedman explained that he had walked almost six hundred miles looking for his wife and children who had been sold four years earlier.

There were emotional reunions as family members found each other after years of separation. Ben and Betty Dodson had been apart for twenty years when Ben found her in a refugee camp after the war. "Glory! glory! hallelujah," he shouted as he hugged his wife. "Dis is my Betty, shuah. I foun' you at las'. I's hunted and hunted till I track you up here. I's boun' to hunt till I fin' you if you's alive."

Other searches had more heart-wrenching results. Husbands and wives sometimes learned that their spouses had remarried during the separation. Believing that his wife had died, the husband of Laura Spicer remarried—only to learn after the war that Laura was still alive. Sadly, he wrote to her but refused to meet with her. "I would come and see you but I know I could not bear it. I want to see you and I don't want to see you. I love you just as well as I did the last day I saw you, and it will not do for you and I to meet."

Tormented, he wrote again pledging his love. "Laura I do not think that I have change any at all since I saw you last—I thinks of you and my children every day of my life. Laura I do love you the same. My love to you never have failed. Laura, truly, I have got another wife, and I am very sorry that I am. You feels and seems to me as much like my dear loving wife, as you ever did Laura."

One freedman testified to the close ties that bound many slave families when he replied bitterly to the claim that he had had a kind master who had fed him and never used the whip. "Kind! yes, he gib men corn enough, and he gib me pork enough, and he neber gib me one lick wid de whip, but whar's my wife?—whar's my chill'en? Take away de pork, I say; take away de corn, I can work and raise dese for myself, but gib me back de wife of my bosom, and gib me back my poor chill'en as was sold away."

Land

As freed people embraced freedom and left their masters, they wanted land. Nineteenth-century Americans of virtually every background associated economic security with owning land. Families wanted to work land and prosper as self-sufficient yeomen. Former slaves believed that their future as a free people was tied to the possession of land. But just as it had been impossible to abolish slavery without the intervention of the U.S. government, it would not be possible to procure land without federal assistance. At first, federal authorities seemed determined to make land available to freedmen.

Special Field Order #15

Shortly after his army arrived in Savannah—after having devastated Georgia—Union General William T. Sherman announced that freedmen would receive land. On January 16, 1865, he issued Special Field Order #15. This military directive set aside a 30-mile-wide tract of land along the Atlantic coast from Charleston, South Carolina, 245 miles south to Jacksonville, Florida. White owners had abandoned the land, and Sherman reserved it for black families. The head of each family would receive "possessory title" to forty acres of land. Sherman also gave the freedmen the use of army mules, thus giving rise to the slogan, "Forty acres and a mule."

Within six months, 40,000 freed people were working 400,000 acres in the South Carolina and Georgia low country and on the Sea Islands. Former slaves generally avoided the slave crops of cotton and rice and instead planted sweet potatoes and corn. They also worked together as families and kinfolk. They avoided

Former slaves assembled in a village near Washington, D.C. Black people welcomed emancipation, but without land, education, or employment, they faced an uncertain future.

the gang labor associated with slavery. Most husbands and fathers preferred that their wives and daughters not work in the fields as slave women had had to do.

The Port Royal Experiment

Meanwhile, hundreds of former slaves had been cultivating land for three years. In late 1861, Union military forces carved out an enclave around Beaufort and Port Royal, South Carolina, that remained under federal authority for the rest of the war. White planters fled to the interior, leaving their slaves behind. Under the supervision of U.S. Treasury officials and northern reformers and missionaries who hurried south in 1862, ex-slaves began to work the land in what came to be known as the "Port Royal Experiment." When Treasury agents auctioned off portions of the land for non-payment of taxes, freedmen purchased some of it. But northern businessmen bought most of the real estate and then hired black people to raise cotton.

White owners sometimes returned to their former lands only to find that black families had taken charge. A group of black farmers told one former owner, "We own this land now, put it out of your head that it will ever be yours again." And on one South Carolina Sea Island, white men were turned back by armed black men.

The Freedmen's Bureau

As the war ended in early 1865, Congress created the Bureau of Refugees, Freedmen, and Abandoned Lands—commonly called the Freedmen's Bureau. Created as a temporary agency to assist freedmen to make the transition to freedom, the bureau was placed under the control of the U.S. Army and General Oliver O. Howard was put in command. Howard, a devout Christian who had lost an arm in the war, was eager to aid the freedmen.

Freedmen's Bureau agents often found themselves in the middle of angry disputes over land and labor that erupted between black and white Southerners. Too often the Bureau officers sided with the white landowners in these disagreements with former slaves. *Harper's Weekly*, July 25, 1868.

VOICES

A Freedmen's Bureau Commissioner Tells Freed People What Freedom Means

In June 1865, Charles Soule, the commissioner of contracts for the Freedmen's Bureau told a gathering of freedmen in Orangeburg, South Carolina, what to expect and how to behave in the coming year:

You are now free, but you must know that the only difference you can feel yet, between slavery and freedom, is that neither you nor your children can be bought or sold. You may have a harder time this year than you have ever had before; it will be the price you pay for your freedom. You will have to work hard, and get very little to eat, and very few clothes to wear. If you get through this year alive and well, you should be thankful. . . . You cannot be paid in money, for there is no good money in the District, nothing but Confederate paper. Then, what can you be paid with? Why, with food, with clothes, with the free use of your little houses and plots. You do not own a cent's worth except yourselves.

You do not understand why some of the white people who used to own you, do not have to work in the field. It is because they are rich. If every man were poor, and worked in his own field, there would be no big farms, and very little cotton or corn raised to sell; there would be no money, and nothing to buy. Some people must be rich, to pay the others, and they have the right to do no work except to look out after their property.

Remember that all of your working time belongs to the man who hires you: therefore you must not leave work without his leave not even to nurse a child, or to go and visit a wife or husband. When you wish to go off the place, get a pass as you used to, and then you will run no danger of being taken up by our soldiers.

In short, do just about as the good men among you have always done. Remember that even if you are badly off, no one can buy and sell you: remember that if you help yourselves, GOD will help you, and trust hopefully that next year and the year after will bring some new blessing to you.

QUESTIONS

1. According to Soule, what is the difference between slavery and freedom?
2. Does freedom mean that freedpeople will have economic opportunities equal to those of white people?
3. How should freed people have responded to Soule's advice?

Source: Ira Berlin, Steven Hahn, Steven F. Miller, Joseph P. Reidy, and Leslie S. Rowland, "The Terrain of Freedom: The Struggle over the Meaning of Free Labor in the U.S. South," *History Workshop*, No. 22 (Autumn 1986): 108–130.

The bureau was given enormous responsibilities. It was to help freedmen obtain land; gain an education; negotiate labor contracts with white planters; settle legal and criminal disputes involving black and white people; and provide food, medical care, and transportation for black and white people left destitute by the war. However, Congress never provided sufficient funds or personnel to carry out these tasks.

The Freedmen's Bureau never had more than nine hundred agents spread across the South from Virginia to Texas. Mississippi, for example, had twelve agents in 1866. One agent often served a county with a population of ten thousand to twenty thousand freedmen. Few of the agents were black because few military officers were black. John Mercer Langston of Virginia was an inspector of schools assigned to the bureau's main office in Washington, D.C., while Colonel Martin R. Delany worked with freedmen on the South Carolina Sea Islands.

The need for assistance was desperate as thousands of black and white Southerners endured extreme privation in the months after the war ended. The bureau established camps for the homeless, fed the hungry, and cared for orphans and the sick as best it could. It distributed more than thirteen million rations—consisting of flour, corn meal, and sugar—by 1866. The bureau provided medical care to one-half million freedmen and thousands of white people who were suffering from smallpox, yellow fever, cholera, and pneumonia. Many more remained untreated.

In July 1865, the bureau took a first step toward distributing land when General Howard issued Circular 13 ordering agents to "set aside" forty-acre plots for freedmen. But the allocation had hardly begun when the order was revoked, and it was announced that land already distributed under General Sherman's Special Field Order #15 was to be returned to its previous white owners.

The reason for this reversal in policy was that President Andrew Johnson, who had become president after Lincoln's assassination in April 1865, began to pardon hundreds and then thousands of former Confederates and restore their lands to them. General Howard was forced to tell black people that they had to relinquish the land they thought they had acquired. In a speech before some two thousand freedmen on South Carolina's Edisto Island in October 1865, Howard pleaded with his audience to "lay aside their bitter feelings, and to become reconciled to their old masters." A black man shouted a response, "Why, General Howard, why do you take away our lands? You take them from us who are true, always true to the Government! You give them to our all-time enemies. This is not right!"

A committee rejected Howard's appeal for reconciliation and forgiveness and they insisted that the government provide land.

> You ask us to forgive the land owners of our island. You only lost your right arm in war and might forgive them. The man who tied me to a tree and gave me 39 lashes and who stripped and flogged my mother and my sister and who will not let me stay in his empty hut except I will do his planting and be satisfied with his price and who combines with others to keep away land from me well knowing I would not have anything to do with him if I had land of my own—that man I cannot well forgive.

Howard was moved by these appeals. He returned to Washington and attempted to persuade Congress to make land available. Congress refused, and President Johnson was determined that white people would get their lands back. It seemed so sensible to most white people. Property that had belonged to white families for generations simply could not be given to freedmen. Freedmen saw matters differently. They deserved land that they and their families had worked without compensation for generations. Freedmen believed it was the only way to make freedom meaningful and to gain independence from white people. As it turned out, most freedmen were forced off land they thought should belong to them.

Southern Homestead Act

In early 1866, Congress attempted to provide land for freedmen with the passage of the Southern Homestead Act. More than three million acres of public land were set aside for black people and southern white people who had remained loyal to the Union. Much of this land, however, was unsuitable for farming and consisted of swampy wetlands or unfertile pine woods. More than four thousand black families—three-quarters of them in Florida—did claim some of this land, but many of them lacked the financial resources to cultivate it. Eventually Southern timber companies acquired much of it, and the Southern Homestead Act largely failed.

Sharecropping

To make matters worse, by 1866 bureau officials tried to force freedmen to sign labor contracts with white landowners—putting black people once again under white authority. Black men who refused to sign contracts could be arrested. Theoretically, these contracts were legal agreements between two equals: landowner and laborer. But they were seldom freely concluded. Bureau agents usually sided with the landowner and pressured freedmen to accept unequal terms.

Occasionally, the landowner would pay wages to the laborer. But because most landowners lacked cash to pay wages, they agreed to provide the laborer with part of the crop. The laborer, often grudgingly, agreed to work under the supervision of the landowner. The contracts required labor for a full year; the laborer could neither quit nor strike. Landowners demanded that the laborers work the fields in gangs. Freedmen resisted this system. They sometimes insisted on making decisions involving planting, fertilizing, and harvesting as they sought to exercise independence (see Map 12–1).

Thus, it took time for a new form of agricultural labor to develop. But by the 1870s, the system of sharecropping had emerged and dominated most of the South. There were no wages. Freedmen worked land as families—not in gangs—and not under direct white supervision. When the landowner provided seed, tools, fertilizer, and work animals (mules, horses, oxen), the black family received one-third of the crop. There were many variations on these arrangements, and frequently black families were cheated out of their fair share of the crop.

The Black Church

In the years after slavery, the church became the most important institution among African Americans other than the family. Not only did it fill deep spiritual and inspirational needs, it offered enriching music, provided charity and compassion to those in need, developed community and political leaders, and was free of white supervision. Before slavery's demise, free black

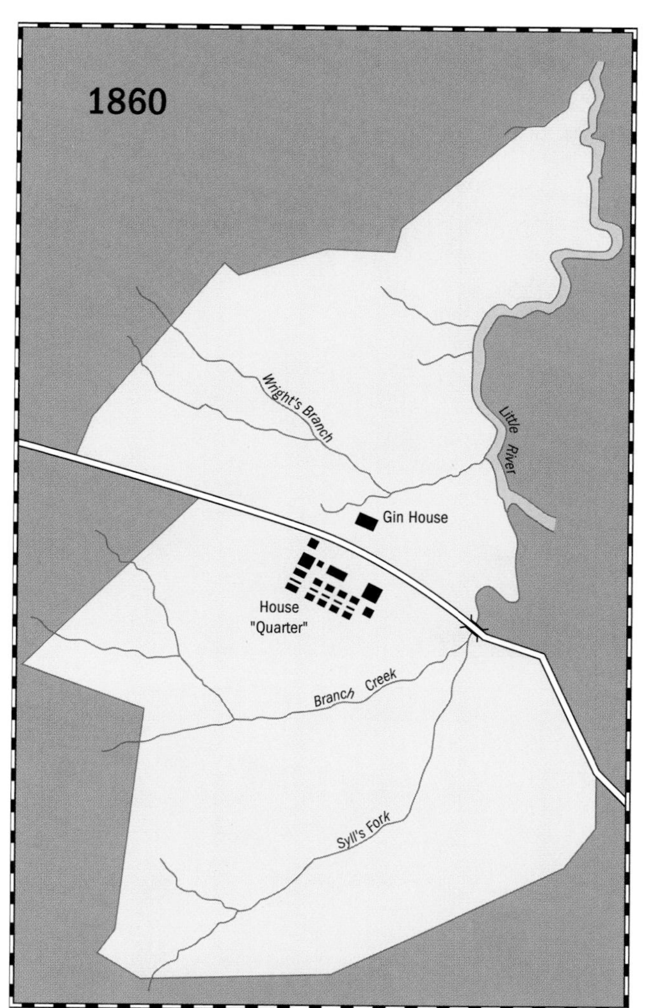

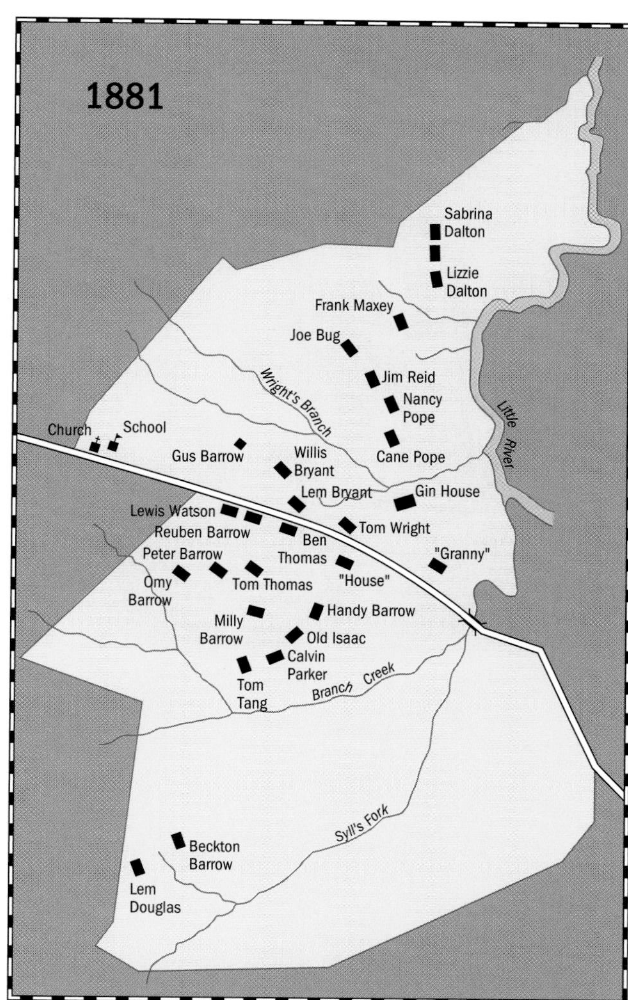

MAP 12–1 The Effect of Sharecropping on the Southern Plantation: The Barrow Plantation, Oglethorpe County, Georgia. With the end of slavery and the advent of sharecropping, black people would no longer agree to work in fields as gangs. They preferred to have each family cultivate separate plots of land, thereby distancing themselves as much as possible from slavery and white supervision.

people and slaves often attended white churches where they were encouraged to participate in religious services conducted by white clergymen and where they were treated as second-class Christians.

Once liberated, black men and women organized their own churches with their own ministers. Most black people considered white ministers incapable of delivering a meaningful message. Nancy Williams recalled, "Ole white preachers used to talk wid dey tongues widdout sayin' nothin', but Jesus told us slaves to talk wid our hearts."

Northern white missionaries were sometimes appalled by the unlettered and ungrammatical black preachers who nevertheless communicated effectively and emotionally with their parishioners. A visiting white clergyman was genuinely impressed and humbled on hearing a black preacher who lacked education, but more than made up for it with devout faith. "He talked about Christ and his salvation as one who understood what he said. . . . Here was an unlearned man, one who could not read, telling of the love of Christ, of Christian faith and duty in a way which I have not learned."

Other black and white religious leaders anguished over what they considered moral laxity and displaced values among the freed people. They preached about honesty, thrift, temperance, and elimination of sexual promiscuity. They demanded an end to "rum-suckers, bar-room loafers, whiskey dealers and card players among the men, and to those women who dressed finely on ill gotten gain."

Church members struggled, scrimped, and saved to buy land and to build churches. Most former slaves

Though superficially similar, these two images provide contrasting perspectives on the lives and circumstances of freedmen. White artist William Aiken in "Life in the South" shows a fairly prosperous, nicely clothed, and contented black family living in a rather large dwelling. They are surrounded by plump chickens, drying laundry, amiable dogs, and gourds that served as bird houses for purple martins. The unidentified photograph depicts the quality of housing that most former slaves inhabited in the decades after the Civil War.

founded Baptist and Methodist churches. These denominations tended to be more autonomous and less subject to outside control. Their doctrine was usually simple and direct without complex theology. Of the Methodist churches, the African Methodist Episcopal (AME) church made giant strides in the South after the Civil War.

In Charleston, South Carolina, the AME church was resurrected after an absence of more than forty years. In 1822, during the turmoil over the Denmark Vesey plot, the AME church was forced to disband and its leader had to flee (see Chapter 8). But by the 1870s, three AME congregations were thriving in Charleston. In Wilmington, North Carolina, the 1,600 members of the Front Street Methodist Church decided to join the AME church soon after the Civil War ended. They replaced the long-time white minister, the Reverend L. S. Burkhead, with a black man.

White Methodists initially encouraged cooperation with black Methodists and helped establish the Colored (now Christian) Methodist Episcopal church (CME). But the white Methodists lost some of their fervor after they tried but failed to persuade the black Methodists to keep political issues out of the CME church, and to dwell solely on spiritual concerns.

The Presbyterian, Congregational, and Episcopal churches appealed to the more prosperous members of the black community. Their services tended to be more formal and solemn. Black people who had been free before the Civil War were usually affiliated with these congregations and remained so after the conflict. Well-to-do free black people in Charleston organized St. Mark's Protestant Episcopal Church when they separated from the white Episcopal church. But they retained their white minister Joseph Seabrook as rector. Poorer black people of darker complexion found churches like St. Mark's decidedly unappealing. Ed Barber visited, but only one time.

> When I was trampin' 'round Charleston, dere was a church dere called St. Mark, dat all de society folks of my color went to. No black nigger welcome dere, they told me. Thinkin' as how I was bright 'nough to git in, I up and goes dere one Sunday, Ah, how they did carry on, bow and scrape and ape de white folks. . . . I was uncomfortable all de time though, 'cause they were too "hifalootin" in de ways, in de singin', and all sorts of carryin' ons.

The Roman Catholic church made modest inroads among black Southerners. There were all-black parishes in St. Augustine, Savannah, Charleston, and Louisville after the Civil War. For generations prior to the conflict large numbers of well-to-do free people of color in New Orleans had been practicing Catholics, and their descendants remained faithful to the church. On Georgia's Skidaway Island Benedictine monks established a school for black youngsters in 1878 that survived for nearly a decade.

Religious differences among black people notwithstanding, the black churches, their parishioners, and clergymen would play a vital role in Reconstruction politics. More than one hundred black ministers were elected to political office after the Civil War.

Education

Freedom and education were inseparable. To remain illiterate after emancipation was to remain enslaved. One ex-slave master bluntly told his former slave, Charles Whiteside: "Charles, you is a free man they say, but Ah tells you now, you is still a slave and if you lives to be a hundred, you'll STILL be a slave, cause you got no education, and education is what makes a man free!"

Almost every freed black person—young or old—desperately wanted to learn. Elderly people were especially eager to read the Bible. Even before slavery ended, black people began to establish schools. In 1861, Mary Peake, a free black woman, opened a school in Hampton, Virginia. On South Carolina's Sea Islands, a black cabinetmaker began teaching openly after having covertly operated a school for years. In 1862 northern missionaries arrived on the Sea Islands to begin teaching. Laura Towne, a white woman, and Charlotte Forten, a black woman, opened a school on St. Helena's Island as part of the Port Royal experiment. They enrolled 138 children and fifty-eight adults. By 1863, there were 1,700 students and forty-five teachers at thirty schools in the South Carolina low country.

With the end of the Civil War, northern religious organizations in cooperation with the Freedmen's Bureau organized hundreds of day and night schools. Classes were held in stables, homes, former slave cabins, taverns, churches, and even—in Savannah and New Orleans—in the old slave markets. Former slaves spent hours in the fields and then trudged to a makeshift school to learn the alphabet and arithmetic. In 1865, black ministers created the Savannah Educational Association, raised $1,000, employed fifteen black teachers, and enrolled six hundred students.

In 1866, the Freedmen's Bureau set aside one-half million dollars for education. The bureau furnished the buildings while former slaves hired, housed, and fed the teachers. By 1869, the Freedmen's Bureau was involved with 3,000 schools and 150,000 students. Even more impressive, by 1870 black people had contributed one million dollars to educate their people.

Black Teachers

While freedmen appreciated the dedication and devotion of the white teachers affiliated with the missionary societies, they usually preferred black teachers. The Reverend Richard H. Cain, an AME minister who came south from Brooklyn, New York, said that black people needed to learn to control their own futures. "We must take into our own hands the education of our race. . . . Honest, dignified whites may teach ever so well, it has not the effect to exalt the black man's opinion of his own race, because they have always been in the habit of seeing white men in honored positions, and respected."

Black men and women responded to the call to teach. Virginia C. Green, a northern black woman felt compelled to go to Mississippi. "Though I have never known servitude they are . . . my people. Born as far north as the lakes I have felt no freer because so many were less fortunate. . . . I look forward with impatience

VOICES

A Northern Black Woman on Teaching Freedmen

Blanche Virginia Harris was born in 1842 in Monroe, Michigan. She graduated from Oberlin College in 1860. She became the principal of a black school in Norfolk, Virginia, attended by 230 students. She organized night classes for adults and a sewing society to provide clothing for impoverished students. Later, she taught in Mississippi, North Carolina, and Tennessee. In the following letter she describes her experiences in Mississippi:

23 January 1866
Natchez, Miss.

I have been in this city now nearly five months. . . . The colored teachers three in number, sent out by the [American Missionary] Association to this city, have been brought down here it is true. And then left to the mercy of the colored people or themselves. The distinction between the two classes of teachers (white and colored) is so marked that it is the topic of conversation among the better class of colored people.

My school is very large, some of them pay and some do not. And from the proceeds I pay the board of my sister and myself, and also for the rent of two rooms; rent as well as board is very high so I have to work quite hard to meet my expenses. I also furnish lights, wood and coal. I do not write this as fault-finding, far from it. I shall be thankful if I can in any way help. I sometimes get discouraged. . . .

I have become very much attached to my school; the interest they manifest in their studies pleases me. I will now tell you how I employ my time. From 8 A.M. until 2 P.M. I teach the children. At 3 P.M. I have a class of adults and at night I have night school.

One afternoon we have prayer meeting, another sewing school. And another singing school. I hope my next letter may be more interesting to you.

Very Respectfully,
Blanche Harris

QUESTIONS

1. Why was the race of the teacher of such concern?
2. What did Harris find difficult about teaching and what did she find rewarding?

Source: Ellen NicKenzie Lawson, ed., *The Three Sarahs: Documents of Antebellum Black College Women*, New York: Edward Mellon Press, 1984.

to the time when my people shall be strong, blest with education, purified and made prosperous by virtue and industry." Hezekiah Hunter, a black teacher from Brooklyn, New York, commented in 1865 on the need for black teachers. "I believe we best can instruct our own people, knowing our own peculiarities—needs—necessities. Further—I believe we that are competent owe it to our people to teach them our speciality." And in Malden, West Virginia, when black residents found that a recently arrived eighteen-year-old black man could read and write, they promptly hired him to teach.

In some areas of the South, the sole person available to teach was a poorly educated former slave equipped primarily with a willingness to teach his or her fellow freedmen. One such teacher explained, "I never had the chance of goen to school for I was a slave until freedom. . . . I am the only teacher because we can not doe better now." Many northern teachers, black and white, provided more than the basics of elementary education. Black life and history were occasionally read about and discussed. Abolitionist Lydia Maria Child wrote *The Freedmen's Book*, which offered short biographies of Benjamin Banneker, Frederick Douglass, and Toussaint L'Ouverture. More often northern teachers, dismayed at the backwardness of the freedmen, struggled to modify behavior and to impart cultural values by teaching piety, thrift, cleanliness, temperance, and timeliness.

Many former slaves came to resent some of these teachers as condescending, self-righteous, and paternalistic. Sometimes the teachers, especially those who were white, became frustrated with recalcitrant students who did not readily absorb middle-class values. Others, however, derived enormous satisfaction from teaching freedmen. A Virginia teacher commented, "I think I shall stay here as long as I live and teach this

Charlotte Forten came from a prominent Philadelphia family of color. She joined hundreds of black and white teachers who migrated South during and after the Civil War to instruct the freed people. Some teachers remained for a few months. Others stayed for a lifetime. Charlotte Forten—shown here in an 1866 photograph—taught on the South Carolina Sea Islands from 1862 to 1864.

people. I have no love or taste for any other work, and I am happy only here with them."

Black Colleges

Northern churches and religious societies established dozens of colleges, universities, academies, and institutes across the South in the late 1860s and the 1870s (see Map 12–2). Most of these institutions provided elementary and secondary education. Few black students were prepared for actual college or university work. The American Missionary Association—an abolitionist and Congregationalist organization—worked with the Freedmen's Bureau to establish Berea in Kentucky, Fisk in Tennessee, Hampton in Virginia, Tougaloo in Alabama, and Avery in South Carolina. The primary purpose of these schools was to educate black students to become teachers.

In Missouri, the black enlisted men and the white officers of the 62nd and 65th Colored Volunteers raised $6,000 to establish Lincoln Institute in 1866, which would become Lincoln University. The American Baptist Home Mission Society founded Virginia Union, Shaw in North Carolina, Benedict in South Carolina, and Morehouse in Georgia. Northern Methodists helped establish Claflin in South Carolina, Rust in Mississippi, and Bennett in North Carolina. The Episcopalians were responsible for St. Augustine's in North Carolina and St. Paul's in Virginia. These and many other similar institutions

MAP 12–2 The Location of Black Colleges Founded before and during Reconstruction. Three black colleges were founded before the Civil War. In Pennsylvania, Cheyney University opened in 1837, and it was followed by the establishment of Lincoln University in 1854. In 1856, Wilberforce University was founded in Ohio. After the Civil War, northern black and white missionary groups fanned out across the South and—frequently with the assistance of Freedmen's Bureau officials—founded colleges, institutes, and normal schools in the former slave states.

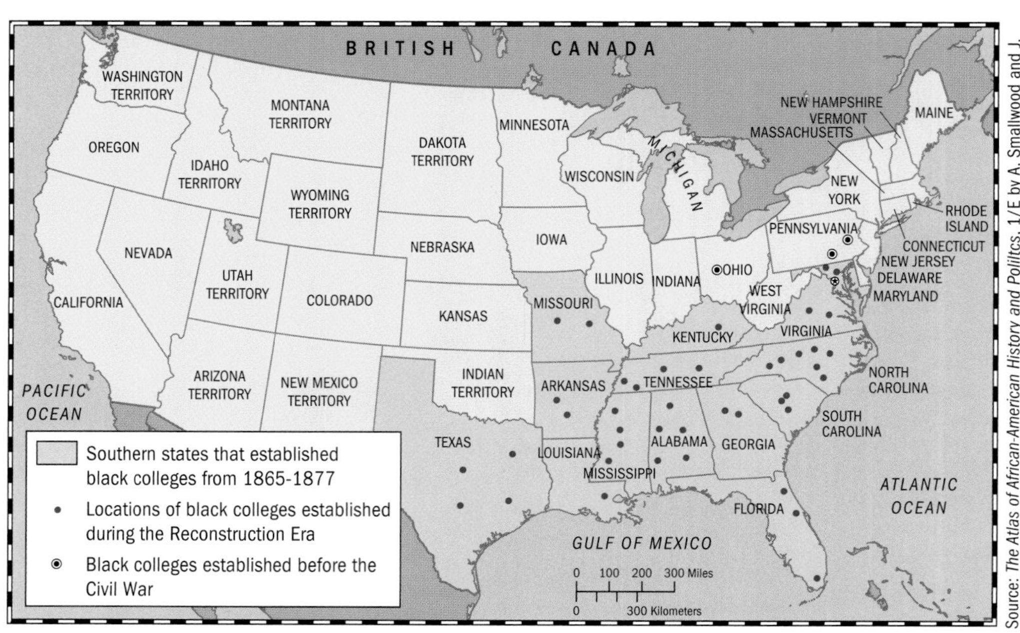

Source: *The Atlas of African-American History and Politics*, 1/E by A. Smallwood and J. Elliot (New York: The McGraw-Hill Companies, 1998).

formed the foundation for the historically black colleges and universities.

Response of White Southerners

White Southerners considered efforts by black people to learn absurd. For generations, white Americans had looked on people of African descent as abjectly inferior. When significant efforts were made to educate former slaves, white Southerners reacted with suspicion, contempt, and hostility. One white woman told a teacher: "I do assure you, you might as well try to teach your horse or mule to read, as to teach these niggers. They can't learn."

Most white people were well aware that black people could learn. Otherwise, the slave codes that pro-

As many as 3000 schools for freedmen opened during and after the Civil War. The Freedmen's Bureau as well as northern churches and missionary societies sponsored most of these educational efforts. Hundreds of enthusiastic black and white teachers—most of them young women—hurried South to provide instruction. Confronting students of almost every age, teachers were sometimes nearly overwhelmed with the immensity of the task. But most found it rewarding and gratifying work.

PROFILE

Charlotte E. Ray

Charlotte E. Ray became the first African American woman to earn a law degree and the first woman admitted to the practice of law in Washington, D.C. She was born on January 13, 1850, in New York City. One of seven children, her parents were the Reverend Charles B. Ray and his second wife, Charlotte Augusta Burroughs Ray. They were firm believers in the rights of African Americans and in their potential for success.

Charlotte attended Myrtilla Miner's Institution for the Education of Colored Youth in Washington, D.C. Myrtilla Miner, a white educator from upstate New York, was determined to demonstrate that black women were as capable of high moral and mental development as white women.

Charlotte completed high school at Miner's in 1869, and she then taught at the Normal and Preparatory Department of recently established Howard University. She also enrolled in law classes at Howard and wrote a thesis analyzing corporations. She graduated from the law school in 1872, and a month later was admitted to the bar in Washington, D.C. She opened an office and planned to practice real estate law. As a real estate lawyer, she could avoid court appearances and the discrimination that women attorneys encountered. She often used her initials, C. E. Ray, so that her clients would not suffer because their legal counsel could be identified as a woman.

Because of the Panic of 1873 and the ensuing economic depression and the difficulties of being a black woman in a white male profession, Ray gave up the practice of law. She supported women's rights and in 1876 attended the annual meeting of the National American Woman Suffrage Association in New York City. By 1879, she had returned to New York and taught school in Brooklyn. Some time before 1886, she had married, but little is known of her husband. Charlotte Ray died of acute bronchitis on January 11, 1911.

hibited educating slaves would have been unnecessary. After slavery's end, some white people went out of their way to prevent black people from learning. Countless schools were burned, mostly in rural areas. In Canton, Mississippi, black people collected money to open a school—only to have white residents inform them that the school would be burned and the prospective teacher lynched if it opened. The female teacher at a freedmen's school in Donaldsonville, Louisiana, was shot and killed.

Other white Southerners grudgingly tolerated the desire of black people to acquire an education. One planter bitterly conceded in 1870, "Every little negro in the county is now going to school and the public pays for it. This is one hell of [a] fix but we can't help it, and the best policy is to conform as far as possible to circumstances."

Most white people adamantly refused to attend school with black people. No integrated schools were established in the immediate aftermath of emancipation. Most black people were more interested in gaining an education than in caring whether white students attended school with them. When black youngsters tried to attend a white school in Raleigh, North Carolina, the white students stopped going to it. For a brief time in Charleston, South Carolina, black and white children attended the same school, but they were taught in separate classrooms.

Violence

In the days, weeks, and months after the end of the Civil War, an orgy of brutality and violence swept across the South. White Southerners—embittered by their crushing defeat and unable to adjust to the end of slave labor and the loss of millions of dollars worth of slave property—lashed out at black people. There were beatings, murders, rapes, and riots—often with little or no provocation.

Black people who demanded respect, wore better clothing, refused to step aside for white people, or asked to be addressed as "mister" or "misses" were attacked. In South Carolina, a white clergyman shot and killed a black man who protested when another black man was removed from a church service. In Texas, one black man was killed because he failed to remove his hat in the presence of a white man and another for refusing to relinquish a bottle of whiskey.

A black woman was beaten for "using insolent language," while a black worker in Alabama was killed for speaking sharply to a white overseer. In Virginia, a black veteran was beaten after announcing that he had been proud to serve in the Union Army.

In South Carolina, a white man asked a passing black man whom he belonged to. The black man replied that he no longer belonged to anybody. "I am free now." With that, the white man roared, "Sas me? You black devil!" He then slashed the freedman with a knife, seriously injuring him. A Freedmen's Bureau agent in North Carolina explained the intense white hostility. "The fact is, it's the first notion with a great many of these people, if a Negro says anything or does anything that they don't like, to take a gun and put a bullet into him, or a charge of shot."

There was also large-scale violence. In 1865, University of North Carolina students twice attacked peaceful meetings of black people. Near Pine Bluff, Arkansas, in 1866, a white mob burned a black settlement and lynched twenty-four men, women, and children. An estimated two thousand black people were murdered around Shreveport, Louisiana. In Texas white people killed one thousand black people between 1865 and 1868.

In May 1866 in Memphis, white residents went on a brutal rampage after black veterans forced local police to release a black prisoner. The city was already beset with economic difficulties and racial tensions caused in part by an influx of rural refugees. White people, led by Irish policemen, invaded the black section of Memphis and destroyed hundreds of homes, cabins, and shacks as well as churches and schools. Forty-six black people and two white men died.

On July 30, 1866, in New Orleans, white people—angered that black men were demanding political rights—assaulted black people on the street and in a convention hall. City policemen, who were mostly Confederate veterans, shot down the black delegates as they fled in panic waving white flags in a futile attempt to surrender. Thirty-four black people and three of their white allies died. Federal troops eventually arrived and stopped the bloodshed. General Philip H. Sheridan characterized the riot as "an absolute massacre."

Little was done to stem the violence. Most Union troops had been withdrawn from the South and demobilized after the war. The Freedmen's Bureau was usually unwilling and unable to protect the black population. Black people left to defend themselves were usually in no position to retaliate. Instead, they sometimes attempted to bring the perpetrators to justice. In Orangeburg, South Carolina, armed black men brought three white men to the local jail who had been wreaking violence in the community. In Holly Springs, Mississippi, a posse of armed black men apprehended a white man who had murdered a freedwoman.

For black people, the system of justice was thoroughly unjust. Although black people could now testify against white people in a court of law, southern juries remained all-white and refused to convict white people charged with harming black people. In Texas in 1865 and 1866, five hundred white men were indicted for murdering black people. Not one was convicted.

The Crusade for Political and Civil Rights

In October 1864 in Syracuse, New York, 145 black leaders gathered in a national convention. Some of the century's most prominent black men and women attended, including Henry Highland Garnet, Frances E. W. Harper, William Wells Brown, Francis L. Cardozo, Richard H. Cain, Jonathan J. Wright, and Jonathan C. Gibbs. They embraced the basic tenets of the American political tradition and proclaimed that they expected to participate fully in it.

Anticipating a future free of slavery, Frederick Douglass optimistically declared "that we hereby assert our full confidence in the fundamental principles of this government . . . the great heart of this nation will ultimately concede us our just claims, accord us our rights, and grant us our full measure of citizenship under the broad shield of the Constitution."

Even before the Syracuse gathering, northern Republicans met in Union-controlled territory around Beaufort, South Carolina, and nominated the state's delegates to the 1864 Republican national convention. Among those selected were Robert Smalls and Prince Rivers, former slaves who had exemplary records with the Union Army. The probability of black participation in postwar politics seemed promising indeed.

But northern and southern white leaders who already held power would largely determine whether black Americans would gain any political power or acquire the same rights as white people. As the Civil War ended, President Lincoln was more concerned with restoring the seceded states to the Union than in opening political doors for black people. Yet Lincoln suggested that at least some black men deserved the right to vote. On April 11, 1865, he wrote, "I would myself prefer that [the vote] were now conferred on the very intelligent, and on those who serve our cause as soldiers." Three days later Lincoln was assassinated.

PROFILE

Aaron A. Bradley

At a time when many white people considered even the most reserved, refined, and well-educated black man holding political office a disgrace, Aaron Bradley's presence in politics was outrageous. White Southerners regarded him as a dangerous revolutionary. White Republicans, who normally would have been his allies, considered him belligerent and uncooperative. But most freedmen admired and supported him. Like him or not, he was a major figure in Georgia politics during Reconstruction.

Bradley was born a slave in about 1815 in South Carolina. His father was probably white. He belonged to Francis W. Pickens, who was South Carolina's governor when the state seceded (see Chapter 10). For a time, Bradley worked as a shoemaker in nearby Augusta, Georgia. At about age twenty, he escaped and went to Boston where he studied law and met black and white abolitionists.

In 1865, after the war, Bradley moved to Savannah where he took up the cause of the freedmen and opened a school. He worked closely with the city's black longshoremen and the low country and Sea Island rice field workers.

Bradley demanded that black families keep the land they had occupied under Sherman's Special Field Order #15. He believed that black people had to have land to prosper. He criticized the Freedmen's Bureau for attempting to force black people off the land and argued that President Johnson should be impeached for supporting Confederate landowners rather than black and white people who were loyal to the union.

Bradley also insisted that black people deserved the rights to vote, testify in court, and have jury trials. After he urged black farmers to defend their land by force, federal authorities charged him with advocating insurrection. He was sentenced to a year's confinement but was soon paroled. Almost immediately, another fiery speech got him in trouble again and he had to leave Georgia.

He returned to Boston and renewed his pleas for land for the freedmen. He wrote the head of the Freedmen's Bureau, General Oliver O. Howard: "My great object is, to give you Back-bone, and as the Chief Justice of 4 millions of Colored people, and Refugees; You can not, and must not, be a Military Tool, in the hands of Andrew Johnson."

In 1867, Bradley returned to Savannah and attacked the system of sharecropping. He complained that freedmen were compelled to work involuntarily and asked that black men be permitted to arm themselves. He also argued that justice would be fairer if the courts included black men. Although the Freedmen's Bureau considered Bradley a troublemaker, he never backed down.

In 1867, black farmers and workers elected Bradley to the state constitutional convention, but he was soon expelled. Then he was elected to the state senate—only to be expelled again along with all the black members of the Georgia legislature.

Meanwhile, Bradley carried on a running battle with Savannah's mayor, a former Confederate colonel affiliated with the Ku Klux Klan. He threatened the "KKK and all Bad Men, . . . if you strike a blow the man or men will be followed, and the house in which he or they shall take shelter, will be burned to the ground."

In 1868, Bradley organized black workers to arm themselves to retain the lands that they believed belonged to them. For a month, black men controlled parts of Chatham County outside Savannah. Eventually, federal authorities jailed one hundred of them. Bradley again fled north.

He returned to Georgia in 1870 and reclaimed his senate seat after Congress forced the legislature to seat its black members. He supported measures to remove Savannah's mayor, reduce taxes on workers, and institute an eight-hour workday.

Democrats regained control of Georgia politics in 1872, and Bradley and the Republicans were swept from power. He ran for Congress in South Carolina in 1874 but lost. He supported black migration to Liberia and Florida, but he moved to St. Louis and died there in 1881.

Aaron Bradley was certainly not a typical Reconstruction leader. He maintained few close ties to black or white politicians. He was constantly embroiled in factional disputes. He did not cooperate with middle-class black leaders and had no ties with local churches and their clergymen—a rarity among black politicians.

He dressed in expensive and flashy clothes. He could be pompous, abrasive, and intemperate. White people universally detested him. Yet Bradley remained exceedingly popular among freedmen.

Presidential Reconstruction under Andrew Johnson

Vice President Andrew Johnson then became president and initially seemed inclined to impose stern policies on the white South while befriending the freedmen. He announced that "treason must be made odious, and traitors must be punished and impoverished." In 1864, he had told black people, "I will be your Moses, and lead you through the Red Sea of War and Bondage to a fairer future of Liberty and Peace." Nothing proved to be further from the truth. Andrew Johnson was no friend of black Americans.

Born poor in eastern Tennessee and never part of the southern aristocracy, Johnson strongly opposed secession and was the only senator from the seceded states to remain loyal to the Union. He had nonetheless acquired five slaves and the conviction that black people were so thoroughly inferior that white men must forever govern them. In 1867, Johnson argued that black people could not exercise political power and that they had "less capacity for government than any other race of people. No independent government of any form has ever been successful in their hands. On the contrary, wherever they have been left to their own devices they have shown a constant tendency to relapse into barbarism."

Johnson quickly lost his enthusiasm for punishing traitors. Indeed, he began to placate white Southerners. In May 1865, Johnson granted blanket amnesty and pardons to former Confederates willing to swear allegiance to the United States. The main exceptions were high former Confederate officials and those who owned property in excess of $20,000, a large sum at the time. Yet even these leaders could appeal for individual pardons. And appeal they did. By 1866, Johnson had pardoned more than 7,000 high-ranking former Confederates and wealthier Southerners. Moreover, he had restored land to those white people who had lost it to freedmen.

Johnson's actions blatantly encouraged those who had supported secession, owned slaves, and opposed the Union. He permitted long-time southern leaders to regain political influence and authority only months after the end of America's bloodiest conflict. As black people and radical Republicans watched in disbelief, Johnson appointed provisional governors in the former Confederate states. Leaders in those states then called constitutional conventions, held elections, and prepared to regain their place in the Union. Johnson merely insisted that each Confederate state formally accept the Thirteenth Amendment (ratified in December 1865, it outlawed slavery) and repudiate Confederate war debts.

The southern constitutional conventions gave no consideration to the inclusion of black people in the political system or to guaranteeing them equal rights. As one Mississippi delegate explained, "'Tis nature's law that the superior race must rule and rule they will."

Black Codes

After the election of state and local officials, white legislators gathered in state capitals across the South to determine the status and future of the freedmen. With little debate, the legislatures drafted the so-called black codes. Southern politicians gave no thought to providing black people with the political and legal rights associated with citizenship.

The black codes sought to ensure the availability of a subservient agricultural labor supply controlled by white people. They imposed severe restrictions on freedmen. Freedmen had to sign annual labor contracts with white landowners. South Carolina required black people who wanted to establish a business to purchase licenses costing from $10 to $100. The codes permitted black children ages two to twenty-one to be apprenticed to white people and spelled out their duties and obligations in detail. Corporal punishment was legal. Employers were designated "masters" and employees "servants." The black codes also restricted black people from loitering or vagrancy, using alcohol or firearms, hunting, fishing, and grazing livestock. The codes did guarantee rights that slaves had not possessed. Freedmen could marry legally, engage in contracts, purchase property, sue or be sued, and testify in court. But black people could not vote or serve on juries. The black codes conceded—just barely—freedom to black people.

Black Conventions

Alarmed by these threats to their freedom, black people met in conventions across the South in 1865 and 1866 to protest, appeal for justice, and chart their future. Men who had been free before the war dominated the conventions. Many were ministers, teachers, and artisans. Few had been slaves. Women and children also attended—as spectators, not delegates—but women often offered comments, suggestions, and criticism. These meetings were hardly militant or radical affairs. Delegates respectfully insisted that white people live up to the principles and rights embodied in the Declaration of Independence and the Constitution.

At the AME church in Raleigh, North Carolina, delegates asked for equal rights and the right to vote. At Georgia's convention they protested against white

Bearing a remarkable resemblance to a slave auction, this scene in Monticello, Florida, shows a black man auctioned off to the highest bidder shortly after the Civil War. Under the terms of most southern black codes, black people arrested and fined for vagrancy or loitering could be "sold" if they could not pay the fine. Such spectacles infuriated many Northerners and led to demands for more rigid Reconstruction policies.

violence and appealed for leaders who would enforce the law without regard to color. "We ask not for a Black Man's Governor, nor a White Man's Governor, but for a People's Governor, who shall impartially protect the rights of all, and faithfully sustain the Union."

Delegates at the Norfolk meeting reminded white Virginians that black people were patriotic. "We are Americans. We know no other country. We love the land of our birth." But they protested that Virginia's black code caused "invidious political or legal distinctions, on account of color merely." They requested the right to vote and added that they might boycott the businesses of "those who deny to us our equal rights."

Two conventions were held in Charleston, South Carolina—one before and one after the black code was enacted. At the first, delegates stressed the "respect and affection" they felt toward white Charlestonians. They even proposed that only literate men be granted the right to vote if it were genuinely applied to both races. The second convention denounced the black code and insisted on its repeal. Delegates again asked for the right to vote and the right to testify in court. "These two things we deem necessary to our welfare and elevation."

They also appealed for public schools and for "homesteads for ourselves and our children." White authorities ignored these and other black conventions and their petitions. Instead they were confident that they had effectively relegated the freedmen to a subordinate role in society.

By late 1865, President Johnson's reconstruction policies had aroused black people. One black Union veteran summed up the situation. "If you call this Freedom, what do you call Slavery?" Republicans in Congress also opposed Johnson's policies toward the freedmen and the former Confederate states.

The Radical Republicans

Radical Republicans, as more militant Republicans were called, were especially disturbed that Johnson seemed to have abandoned the ex-slaves to their former masters. They considered white Southerners disloyal and unrepentant, despite their military defeat. Moreover, radical Republicans—unlike moderate Republicans and Democrats—were determined to transform the racial fabric of American society by including black people in the political and economic system.

Among the most influential radical Republicans were Charles Sumner, Benjamin Wade, and Henry Wilson in the Senate and Thaddeus Stevens, George W. Julian, and James M. Ashley in the House. Few white Americans have been as dedicated to the rights of black people as these men. They had fought for the abolition of slavery. They were reluctant to compromise. They were honest, tough, and articulate, but also abrasive, difficult, self-righteous, and vain. Black people appreciated them; many white people excoriated them. One black veteran wrote Charles Sumner in 1869, "Your name shall live in our hearts forever." A white Philadelphia businessman commented on Thaddeus Stevens. "He seems to oppose any measure that will not benefit the nigger."

Radical Proposals

Stevens, determined to provide freedmen with land, introduced a bill in Congress in late 1865 to confiscate 400 million acres from the wealthiest 10 percent of Southerners and distribute it free to freedmen. The remaining land would be auctioned off in plots no larger than five hundred acres. Few legislators supported the proposal. Even those who wanted fundamental change considered confiscation a gross violation of property rights.

Instead, radical Republicans supported voting rights for black men. They were convinced that black men—to protect themselves and to secure the South for the Republican party—had to have the right to vote.

Moderate Republicans, however, found the prospect of black voting almost as objectionable as the confiscation of land. They preferred to build the Republican party in the South by cooperating with President Johnson and attracting loyal white Southerners.

The thought of black suffrage appalled northern and southern Democrats. Most white Northerners—Republicans and Democrats—favored denying black men the right to vote in their states. After the war, proposals to guarantee the right to vote to black men were defeated in New York, Ohio, Kansas, and the Nebraska Territory. In the District of Columbia, a vote to permit black suffrage lost 6,951 to 35. However, five New England states as well as Iowa, Minnesota, and Wisconsin did allow black men to vote.

As much as they objected to black suffrage, most white Northerners objected even more strongly to defiant white Southerners. Journalist Charles A. Dana described the attitude of many Northerners. "As for negro suffrage, the mass of Union men in the Northwest do not care a great deal. What scares them is the idea that the rebels are all to be let back . . . and made a power in government again, just as though there had been no rebellion."

In December 1865, Congress created the Joint Committee on Reconstruction to determine whether the southern states should be readmitted to the Union. The committee investigated southern affairs and confirmed reports of widespread mistreatment of black people and white arrogance.

The Freedmen's Bureau Bill and the Civil Rights Bill

In early 1866, Senator Lyman Trumball, a moderate Republican from Illinois, introduced two major bills. The first was to provide more financial support for the Freedmen's Bureau and extend its authority to defend the rights of black people.

The second proposal was the first civil rights bill in American history. It made any person born in the United States a citizen (except Indians) and entitled them to rights protected by the U.S. government. Black people would possess the same legal rights as white people. The bill was clearly intended to invalidate the black codes.

Johnson's Vetoes

Both measures passed in Congress with nearly unanimous Republican support. President Johnson vetoed them. He claimed that the bill to continue the Freedmen's Bureau would greatly expand the federal

Federal Reconstruction Legislation, 1865–1867

1865	Freedmen's Bureau established
1865	Thirteenth Amendment passed and ratified
1866	Freedmen's Bureau Bill and the Civil Rights Act of 1866 passed over Johnson's veto
1866	Fourteenth Amendment passed (ratified 1868)
1867	Reconstruction Acts passed over Johnson's veto

bureaucracy and permit too "vast a number of agents" to exercise arbitrary power over the white population. He insisted that the civil rights bill benefited black people at the expense of white people. "In fact, the distinction of race and color is by the bill made to operate in favor of the colored and against the white race."

The Johnson vetoes stunned Republicans. Though he had not meant to, Johnson drove moderate Republicans into the radical camp and strengthened the Republican party. The president did not believe that Republicans would oppose him to support the freedmen. He was wrong. Congress overrode both vetoes. The Republicans broke with Johnson in 1866, defied him in 1867, and impeached him in 1868 (failing to remove him from office by only one vote in the Senate).

The Fourteenth Amendment

To secure the legal rights of freedmen, Republicans passed the Fourteenth Amendment. This amendment fundamentally changed the Constitution by compelling states to accept their residents as citizens and to guarantee that their rights as citizens would be safeguarded.

Its first section guaranteed citizenship to every person born in the United States. This included virtually every black person. It made each person a citizen of the state in which he or she resided. It defined the specific rights of citizens and then protected those rights against the power of state governments. Citizens had the right to due process (usually a trial) before they could lose their life, liberty, or property.

> All persons born or naturalized in the United States, and subject to the jurisdiction thereof, are citizens of the United States and of the State wherein they reside. No State shall make or enforce any law which shall abridge the privileges or immunities of citizens of the United States; nor shall any State deprive any person of life, liberty, or property, without due process of law; nor deny to any person within its jurisdiction the equal protection of the laws.

Eleven years after Chief Justice Roger Taney declared in the Dred Scott decision that black people were "a subordinate and inferior class of beings" who had "no rights that white people were bound to respect," the Fourteenth Amendment vested them with the same rights of citizenship other Americans possessed.

The amendment also threatened to deprive states of representation in Congress if they denied black men the vote. The end of slavery had also made obsolete the three-fifths clause in the Constitution, which had counted slaves as only three-fifths (or 60 percent) of a white person in calculating a state's population and determining the number of representatives each state was entitled to in the House of Representatives. Republicans feared that southern states would count black people in their populations without permitting them to vote, thereby gaining more representatives than those states had had before the Civil War. The amendment mandated that the number of representatives each state would be entitled to in Congress (including northern states) would be reduced if that state did not allow adult males to vote.

Democrats almost unanimously opposed the Fourteenth Amendment. Andrew Johnson denounced it, though he had no power to prevent its adoption. Southern states refused to ratify it except for Tennessee. Women's suffragists felt badly betrayed because the amendment limited suffrage to males. Despite this opposition, the amendment was ratified in 1868.

Radical Reconstruction

By 1867, radical Republicans in Congress had wrested control over Reconstruction from Johnson, and they then imposed policies that brought black men into the political system as voters and office holders. It was a dramatic development, second in importance only to emancipation and the end of slavery.

Republicans swept the 1866 congressional elections despite the belligerent opposition of Johnson and the Democrats. With two-thirds majorities in the House and Senate, Republicans easily overrode presidential vetoes. Two years after the Civil War ended, Republicans dismantled the state governments established in the South under President Johnson's authority. They instituted a new Reconstruction policy.

Republicans passed the First Reconstruction Act over Johnson's veto in March 1867. It divided the South into five military districts, each under the command of a general (see Map 12–3). Military personnel would protect lives and property while new civilian governments

MAP EXPLORATION
To explore this map, go to http://www.prenhall.com/hine/map12.3

MAP 12–3 Congressional Reconstruction. Under the terms of the First Reconstruction Act of 1867, the former Confederate states (except Tennessee) were divided into five military districts and placed under the authority of military officers. Commanders in each of the five districts were responsible for supervising the reestablishment of civilian governments in each state.

were formed. Elected delegates in each state would draft a new constitution and submit it to the voters.

Universal Manhood Suffrage

The Reconstruction Act stipulated that all adult males in the states of the former Confederacy were eligible to vote, except for those who had actively supported the Confederacy or were convicted felons. Once each state had formed a new government and approved the Fourteenth Amendment, it would be readmitted to the Union with representation in Congress.

The advent of radical Reconstruction was the culmination of black people's struggle to gain legal and political rights. Since the 1864 black national convention in Syracuse and the meetings and conventions in the South in 1865 and 1866, black leaders had argued that one of the consequences of the Civil War should be the inclusion of black men in the body politic. The achievement of that goal was due to their persistent and persuasive efforts, the determination of radical Republicans, and, ironically, the obstructionism of Andrew Johnson who had played into their hands.

Black Politics

Full of energy and enthusiasm, black men and women rushed into the political arena in the spring and summer of 1867. Although women could not vote, they joined men at the meetings, rallies, parades, and picnics that accompanied political organizing in the South. For many former slaves, politics became as important as the church and religious activities. Black people flocked to the Republican party and the new Union Leagues.

The Union Leagues had been established in the North during the Civil War, but they expanded across the South as quasi-political organizations in the late 1860s. The Leagues were social, fraternal, and patriotic groups in which black people often, but not always, outnumbered white people. League meetings featured ceremonies, rituals, initiation rites, and oaths. They gave people an opportunity to sharpen leadership skills and gain an informal political education by discussing issues from taxes to schools.

Sit-Ins and Strikes

Political progress did not induce apathy and a sense of satisfaction and contentment among black people. Gaining citizenship, legal rights, and the vote generated more expectations and demands for advancement. For example, black people insisted on equal access to public transportation. After a Republican rally in Charleston, South Carolina, in April 1867, several black men staged a "sit-in" on a nearby horse-drawn streetcar before they were arrested. In Charleston, black people were permitted to ride only on the outside running boards of the cars. They wanted to sit on the seats inside. Within a month, due to the intervention of military authorities, the streetcar company gave in. Similar protests occurred in Richmond and New Orleans.

Black workers also struck across the South in 1867. Black longshoremen in New Orleans, Mobile, Savannah, Charleston, and Richmond walked off the job. Black laborers were usually paid less than white men for the same work, and this led to labor unrest during the 1860s and 1870s. Sometimes the strikers won, sometimes they lost. In 1869, a black Baltimore longshoreman, Isaac Myers, organized the National Colored Labor Union.

The Reaction of White Southerners

White Southerners grimly opposed radical Reconstruction. They were outraged that black people could claim the same legal and political rights that

With the adoption of radical Republican policies, most black men eagerly took part in political activities. Political meetings, conventions, speeches, barbecues and other gatherings also attracted women and children.

they possessed. Such a possibility seemed preposterous to people who had an abiding belief in the absolute inferiority of black people. A statement by Benjamin F. Perry, whom Johnson had appointed provisional governor of South Carolina in 1865, captures the depth of this racist conviction. "The African," Perry declared, "has been in all ages, a savage or a slave. God created him inferior to the white man in form, color and intellect, and no legislation or culture can make him his equal. . . . His hair, his form and features will not compete with the caucasian race, and it is in vain to think of elevating him to the dignity of the white man. God created differences between the two races, and nothing can make him equal."

Some white people, taking solace in their belief in the innate inferiority of black people, concluded they could turn black suffrage to their advantage. White people, they assumed, should easily be able to control and manipulate black voters just as they had controlled black people during slavery. White Southerners who believed this, however, were destined to be disappointed, and their disappointment would turn to fury.

Conclusion

Why were black Southerners able to gain citizenship and access to the political system by 1868? Most white Americans did not suddenly abandon two hundred fifty years of deeply ingrained beliefs that people of African descent were their inferiors. The advances that African Americans achieved fit into a series of complex political developments after the Civil War. Black people themselves had fought and died to preserve the Union,

Timeline

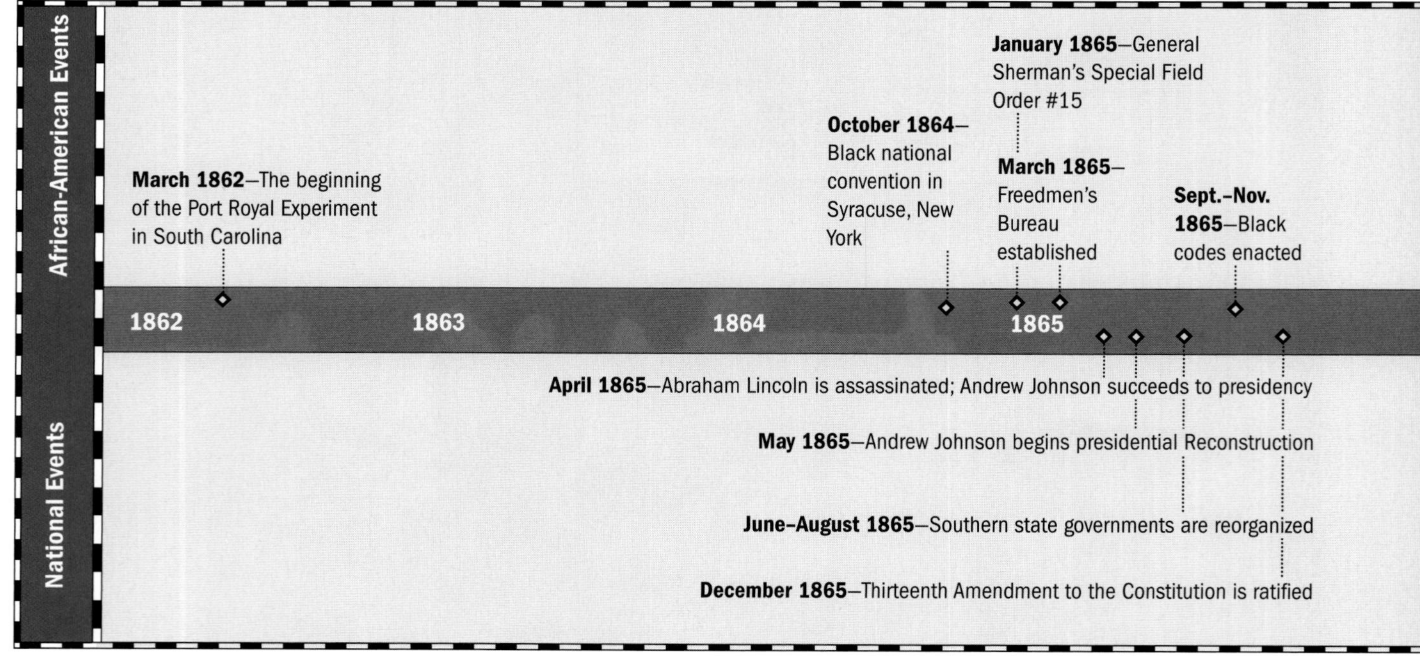

and they had earned the grudging respect of many white people and the open admiration of others. Black leaders in meetings and petitions insisted that their rights be recognized.

White Northerners—led by the radical Republicans—were convinced that President Andrew Johnson had made a serious error in supporting policies that permitted white Southerners to retain pre-Civil War leaders while the black codes virtually made freedmen slaves again. Republicans were determined that white Southerners realize their defeat had doomed the prewar status quo. Republicans established a Reconstruction program to disfranchise key southern leaders while providing legal rights to freedmen. The right to vote, they reasoned, would give black people the means to deal more effectively with white Southerners while simultaneously strengthening the Republican party in the South.

The result was to make the mid to late 1860s one of the few high points in African-American history. During this period, not only was slavery abolished, but black Southerners were able to organize schools and churches, and black people throughout the South acquired legal and political rights that would have been incomprehensible before the war. Yet black people did not stand on the brink of utopia. Most freedmen still lacked land and had no realistic hope of obtaining much if any of it. White violence and cruelty continued almost unabated across much of the South. Still, for millions of African Americans, the future looked more promising than it had ever before in American history.

Recommended Reading

Ira Berlin and Leslie Rowland, eds. *Families and Freedom: A Documentary History of African-American Kinship in the Civil War Era.* New York: Cambridge University Press, 1997. A collection of documents that conveys the aspirations and frustrations of freedmen.

W. E. B. Du Bois. *Black Reconstruction in America: An Essay toward a History of the Part Which Black Folk Played in the Attempt to Reconstruct Democracy in America, 1860–1880.* New York: Russell & Russell, 1935. A classic account of Reconstruction challenging the traditional interpretation that it was a tragic era marked by corrupt and inept black rule of the South.

Eric Foner. *Reconstruction: America's Unfinished Revolution, 1863–1877.* New York: Harper & Row, 1988. The best and most comprehensive account of Reconstruction.

Herbert G. Gutman. *The Black Family in Slavery and Freedom, 1750–1925.* New York: Oxford University Press, 1976. An illustration of how African-American family values and kinship ties forged in slavery endured after emancipation.

Tera W. Hunter. *To 'Joy My Freedom: Southern Black Women's Lives and Labors after the Civil War.* Cambridge, MA: Harvard University Press, 1997. An examination of the interior lives of black women, their work, social welfare, and leisure.

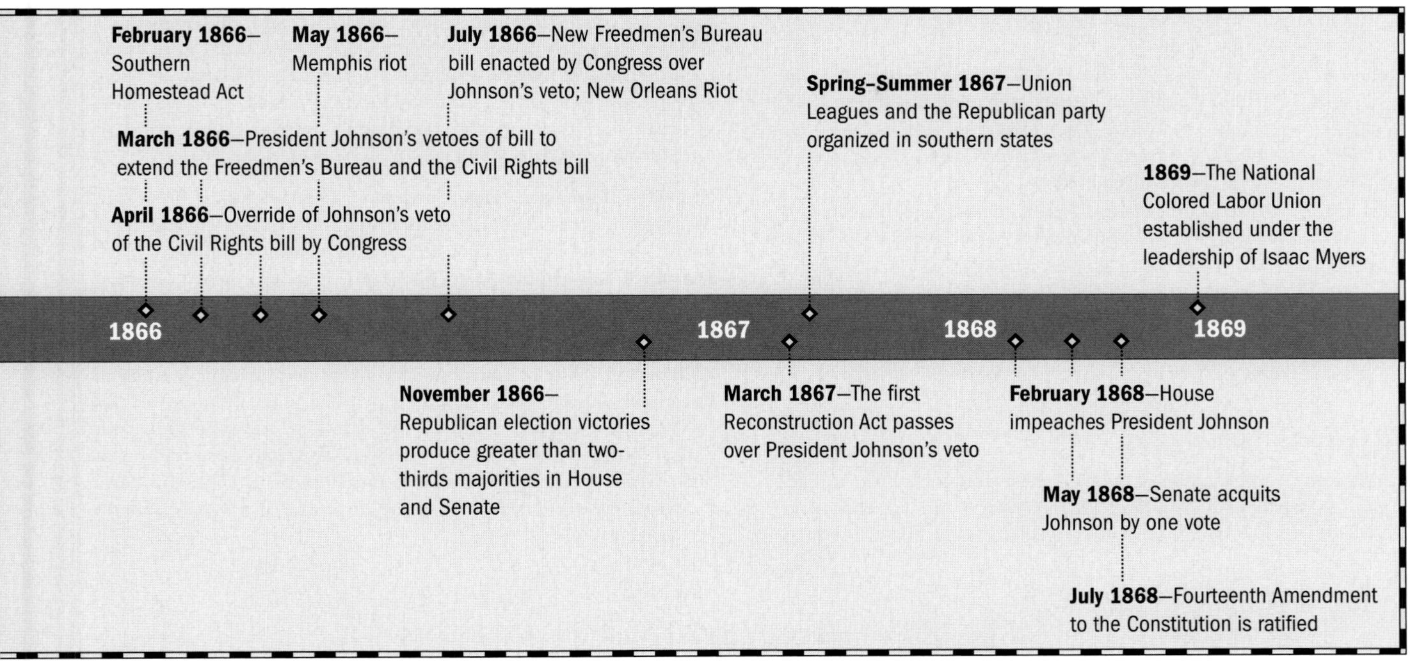

Gerald D. Jaynes. *Branches without Roots: Genesis of the Black Working Class in the American South, 1862–1882.* New York: Pantheon, 1986. The changes in work and labor in the aftermath of slavery.

Leon F. Litwack. *Been in the Storm Too Long: The Aftermath of Slavery.* New York: Alfred A. Knopf, 1979. A rich and detailed account of the transition to freedom largely based on recollections of former slaves.

Additional Bibliography

Education

James D. Anderson. *The Education of Blacks in the South, 1860–1935.* Chapel Hill, NC: University of North Carolina Press, 1988.

Ronald E. Butchart. *Northern Schools, Southern Blacks, and Reconstruction: Freedmen's Education, 1862–1875.* Westport, CT.: Greenwood Press, 1981.

Edmund L. Drago. *Initiative, Paternalism, and Race Relations: Charleston's Avery Normal Institute.* Athens, GA: University of Georgia Press, 1990.

Robert C. Morris. *Reading, 'Riting, and Reconstruction: The Education of the Freedmen in the South, 1861– 1890.* Chicago: University of Chicago Press, 1981.

Joe M. Richardson. *Christian Reconstruction: The American Missionary Association and Southern Blacks, 1861– 1890.* Athens, GA: University of Georgia Press, 1986.

Willie Lee Rose. *Rehearsal for Reconstruction: The Port Royal Experiment.* Indianapolis, IN: Bobbs Merrill, 1964.

Brenda Stevenson, ed. *The Journals of Charlotte Forten Grimke.* New York: Oxford University Press, 1988.

Land and Labor

Barbara J. Fields. *Slavery and Freedom on the Middle Ground: Maryland during the Nineteenth Century.* New Haven, CT: Yale University Press, 1985.

Jacqueline Jones. *Labor of Love, Labor of Sorrow: Black Women, Work and Family, from Slavery to the Present.* New York: Basic Books, 1985.

Edward Magdol. *A Right to the Land: Essays on the Freedmen's Community.* Westport, CT.: Greenwood Press, 1977.

Claude F. Oubre. *Forty Acres and a Mule: The Freedmen's Bureau and Black Landownership.* Baton Rouge, LA: Louisiana State University Press, 1978.

Roger L. Ransom and Richard Sutch. *One Kind of Freedom: The Economic Consequences of Emancipation.* New York: Cambridge University Press, 1977.

Julie Saville. *The Work of Reconstruction: From Slave to Wage Labor in South Carolina, 1860–1870.* New York: Cambridge University Press, 1994.

James D. Schmidt. *Free to Work: Labor, Law, Emancipation, and Reconstruction, 1815–1880.* Athens, GA: University of Georgia Press, 1998.

Leslie A. Schwalm. *A Hard Fight for We: Women's Transition from Slavery to Freedom in South Carolina.* Urbana, IL: University of Illinois Press, 1997.

Black Communities

John W. Blassingame. *Black New Orleans, 1860–1880.* Chicago: University of Chicago Press, 1973.

Cyprian Davis. *The History of Black Catholics in the United States.* New York: Crossroad, 1990.

Robert F. Engs. *Freedom's First Generation: Black Hampton, Virginia, 1861–1890.* Philadelphia: University of Pennsylvania Press, 1979.

William E. Montgomery. *Under Their Own Vine and Fig Tree, The African American Church in the South 1865– 1900.* Baton Rouge, LA: Louisiana State University Press, 1993.

Bernard E. Powers, Jr. *Black Charlestonians: A Social History, 1822–1885.* Fayetteville, AR: University of Arkansas Press, 1994.

Clarence E. Walker. *A Rock in a Weary Land: The African Methodist Episcopal Church during the Civil War and Reconstruction.* Baton Rouge, LA: Louisiana State University Press, 1982.

James M. Washington. *Frustrated Fellowship: The Black Baptist Quest for Social Power.* Macon, GA.: Mercer University Press, 1986.

Retracing the Odyssey

Charleston, South Carolina: The Avery Research Center for African-American History and Culture. In 1865 the American Missionary Association opened a private school for black youngsters that served the Charleston community until 1954. The renovated structure currently contains an archive, a restored classroom, and exhibits devoted to African-American life in the Carolina low country.

Raleigh, North Carolina: Shaw University and St. Augustine's College. These are two of the many black colleges that were established during Reconstruction. The Baptists founded Shaw in 1865, and its impressive Estey Hall has survived almost 130 years. The Episcopal Church and the Freedmen's Bureau collaborated to found St. Augustine's in 1867.

Nashville, Tennessee: Fisk University. The American Missionary Association established Fisk in 1866. Magnificent Jubilee Hall is the nation's oldest building dedicated to the higher education of black students. It was completed in 1876. There is an impressive collection of European and American art on the campus at the Carl Van Vechten Art Gallery.

Wilmington, North Carolina: St. Stephen African Methodist Episcopal Church. Following the Civil War, black members of the Front Street Methodist Church withdrew and founded their own church on Red Cross Street. In 1880, they began construction of the current building. For a time parishioners met in the basement while work continued on the imposing and ornate sanctuary above them.

REVIEW, RESEARCH & INTERACT

REVIEW QUESTIONS

1. How did freedmen define their freedom? What did freedom mean to ex-slaves? How did their priorities differ from those of African Americans who had been free before the Civil War?
2. What did the former slaves and the former slaveholders want after emancipation? Were these desires realistic? How did former slaves and former slaveholders disagree after the end of slavery?
3. Explain why African Americans formed separate churches, schools, and social organizations after the Civil War. What role did the black church play in the black community?
4. Evaluate the effectiveness of the Freedmen's Bureau. How successful was it in assisting ex-slaves to live in freedom?
5. Why did southern states enact black codes?
6. Why did radical Republicans object to President Andrew Johnson's Reconstruction policies? Why did Congress impose its own Reconstruction policies?
7. What factors contributed to passage of laws that enabled black men to vote?
8. Why did black men gain the right to vote but not possession of land?
9. Did congressional Reconstruction secure full legal and political equality for African Americans as American citizens?

Research Navigator.com RESOURCES FOR COLLEGE RESEARCH ASSIGNMENTS **www.researchnavigator.com**

Chapter 12 explores the promise of Reconstruction in the years right after the end of the Civil War. For further research on the early years of Reconstruction, use the tools available to you in Research Navigator.

As you investigate this topic, consider this question: "Who supported Radical Reconstruction? Why?"

- **ContentSelect:** Search in the History database using the search term *reconstruction.*
- **Links Library:** Access the History: U.S. History database and explore the links for *Reconstruction* and *black codes.*
- **New York Times on the Web:** To find more information on the history of Reconstruction, search in the History database using the search term *Andrew Johnson.*

DOCUMENTS AND ACTIVITIES IN AFRICAN-AMERICAN HISTORY

Documents

12-1 Charlotte Forten, Life on the Sea Islands, 1864
12-2 "A Jubilee of Freedom": Freed Slaves March in Charleston, South Carolina, March, 1865
12-3 William Garrison, "The Governing Passion of My Soul," 14 April 1865
12-4 The Freedmen's Bureau Bill, 1865
12-5 Frederick Douglass, Speech to the American Antislavery Society, 1865
12-6 Address of the Colored State Convention to the People of the State of South Carolina, 1865
12-7 The Civil Rights Act of 1866
12-8 President Johnson's Veto of the Civil Rights Act 1866

Interactive Map

Congressional Reconstruction, p. 278
http://www.prenhall.com/hine/map12.3

Learning Activities

Reconstruction: The Struggle to Define the Meaning of Freedom
This activity highlights some of the complexities that faced the nation following the Civil War and the emancipation of nearly four million people who had been held as slaves.

IntegrationQuest: Race Relations and Reconstruction
Take the part of a historian, an educator, or a presidential aide to learn about the mood in America during the Reconstruction years.

13

The Meaning of Freedom: The Failure of Reconstruction

The first seven African Americans to serve in the U.S. Senate and the U.S. House of Representatives. Three of them—Benjamin S. Turner, Josiah T. Walls, and Jefferson H. Long—were former slaves.

LET us with a fixed, firm, hearty, earnest, and unswerving determination move steadily on and on, fanning the flame of true liberty until the last vestige of oppression shall be destroyed, and when that eventful period shall arrive, when, in the selection of rulers, both State and Federal, we shall know no North, no East, no South, no West, no white nor colored, no Democrat nor Republican, but shall choose men because of their moral and intrinsic value, their honesty and integrity, their love of unmixed liberty, and their ability to perform well the duties to be committed to their charge.

From a speech delivered in 1872, by Jonathan J. Wright, Associate Justice of the South Carolina Supreme Court

In 1868 for the first time in American history, thousands of black men would elect hundreds of black and white leaders to state and local offices across the South. Would this newly acquired political influence enable freedmen to complete the transition from slavery to freedom? Would political power propel black people into the mainstream of American society? Equally important, would white Southerners and Northerners accept black people as fellow citizens?

Events in the decade from 1867 to 1877 generated hope that black and white Americans might learn to live together on a compatible and equitable basis. But these developments also raised the possibility that black people's new access to political power would fail to resolve the racial animosity and intolerance that persisted in American life after the Civil War.

CHAPTER OUTLINE

Constitutional Conventions

Elections

Black Political Leaders

The Issues
- Education and Social Welfare
- Civil Rights

Economic Issues
- Land
- Business and Industry

Black Politicians: An Evaluation

Republican Factionalism

Opposition

The Ku Klux Klan

The Fifteenth Amendment

The Enforcement Acts

The North Loses Interest

The Freedmen's Bank

The Civil Rights Act of 1875

The End of Reconstruction
- Violent Redemption
- The Shotgun Policy
- The Hamburg Massacre
- The Compromise of 1877

Conclusion

Constitutional Conventions

Black men as a group first entered politics as delegates to constitutional conventions in the southern states in 1867 and 1868. Each of the former Confederate states, except Tennessee, which had already been restored to the Union, elected delegates to these conventions. Most southern white men were Democrats. They boycotted these elections to protest both Congress's assumption of authority over Reconstruction and the extension of voting privileges to black men. Thus, the delegates to the conventions that met to frame new state constitutions to replace those drawn up in 1865 under President Johnson's authority were mostly Republicans joined by a few conservative southern Democrats. The Republicans represented three constituencies. One consisted of white northern migrants who moved to the South in the wake of the war. They were known as carpetbaggers, because they were said to have arrived in the South with all their possessions in a single carpet bag. A second group consisted of native white Southerners, mostly small farmers in devastated upland regions of the South who hoped for economic relief from Republican governments. This group was known derogatorily as scalawags, or scoundrels, by other southern white people. African Americans made up the third and largest Republican constituency.

Of the 1,000 men elected as delegates to the ten state conventions, 265 were black. Black delegates were a majority only in the South Carolina and Louisiana conventions. In most states, including Alabama, Georgia, Mississippi, Virginia, North Carolina, Arkansas, and Texas, black men made up 10 percent to 20 percent of the delegates. At least 107 of the 265 had been born slaves; about 40 had served in the Union Army. Several were well-educated teachers and ministers; others were tailors, blacksmiths, barbers, and farmers. Most went on to hold other political offices in the years that followed.

From Harper's Weekly, November 16, 1867.

Southern black men cast ballots for the first time in 1867 in the election of delegates to state constitutional conventions. The ballots were provided by the candidates or political parties, and not by state or municipal officials. Most nineteenth-century elections were not by secret ballot.

These delegates produced impressive constitutions. Unlike previous state constitutions in the South, the new constitutions ensured that all adult males could vote, and except in Mississippi and Virginia, they did not disfranchise large numbers of former Confederates. They conferred broad guarantees of civil rights. In several states they provided the first statewide systems of public education. These constitutions were progressive, not radical. Black and white Republicans hoped to attract support from white Southerners for the new state governments these documents created by encouraging state support for private businesses, especially railroad construction.

Elections

Elections were held in 1868 to ratify the new constitutions and elect officials. The white Democratic response varied. In some states, Democrats boycotted the elections. In others, they participated, but voted against ratification, and in still other states they supported ratification and attempted to elect as many Democrats as possible to office. Congress required only a majority of those voting—not a majority of all registered voters—to ratify the constitutions. In each state a majority of those voting eventually did vote to ratify, and in each state, black men were elected to political offices.

Black Political Leaders

Over the next decade, 1,465 black men held political office in the South. Though black leaders individually and collectively enjoyed significant political leverage, white Republicans dominated politics during Reconstruction. In general the number of black officials in a state reflected the size of that state's African-American population. Black people were a substantial majority of the population in just Mississippi and South Carolina, and most of the black office holders came from those two states and Louisiana, where black people were a bare majority. In most states, such as Arkansas, North Carolina, Tennessee, and Texas where black people made up between 25 percent and 40 percent of the population, far fewer black men were elected to office (see Table 13–1).

Initially, black men chose not to run for the most important political offices because they feared their election would further alienate already angry white Southerners. But as white Republicans swept into office in 1868, black leaders reversed their strategy, and by 1870 black men had been elected to many key political positions. No black man was elected governor, but Lieutenant Governor P. B. S. Pinchback served one month (from December 1872 to January 1873) as governor in Louisiana after the white governor was removed from office. Blanche K. Bruce and Hiram Revels represented Mississippi in the U.S. Senate. Beginning with Joseph Rainey in 1870 in South Carolina, fourteen black men served in the U.S. House of Representatives during Reconstruction. Six men served as lieutenant governors. In Mississippi and South Carolina, a majority of the representatives in state houses were black men, and each of these states had two black speakers of the house in the 1870s. Jonathan J. Wright, quoted at the beginning of this chapter, served seven years as a state supreme court justice in South Carolina. Four black men served as state superintendents of education, and Francis L. Cardozo served as South Carolina's secretary of state and then treasurer.

TABLE 13–1
African-American Population and Officeholding during Reconstruction in the States Subject to Congressional Reconstruction

	African-American Population in 1870	African Americans as a Percentage of Total Population	Number of African-American Office Holders during Reconstruction
South Carolina	415,814	58.9	314
Mississippi	444,201	53.6	226
Louisiana	364,210	50.1	210
North Carolina	391,650	36.5	180
Alabama	475,510	47.6	167
Georgia	545,142	46.0	108
Virginia	512,841	41.8	85
Florida	91,689	48.7	58
Arkansas	122,169	25.2	46
Texas	253,475	30.9	46
Tennessee	322,331	25.6	20

Source: Eric Foner, *Freedom's Lawmakers: A Directory of Black Officeholders during Reconstruction* (1993), xiv; The Statistics of the Population of the United States, Ninth Census (1873), xvii.

Harper's Weekly, February 19, 1870

Hiram R. Revels represented Mississippi in the U.S. Senate from February 1870 until March 1871, completing an unexpired term. He went on to serve as Mississippi's secretary of state. He was born free in Fayetteville, North Carolina in 1822. He attended Knox College in Illinois before the Civil War. In 1874 he abandoned the Republican party and became a Democrat. By the 1890s he had acquired a sizable plantation near Natchez.

One hundred twelve black state senators and 683 black representatives were elected during Reconstruction. There were also forty-one black sheriffs, five black mayors, and thirty-one black coroners. Tallahassee, Florida, and Little Rock, Arkansas, had black police chiefs.

Many of these men—by background, experience, and education—were well qualified. Others were not. Of the 1,465 black office holders, at least 378 had been free before the Civil War, 933 were literate, and 195 were illiterate (we lack information about the remaining 337.) Sixty-four had attended college or professional school. In fact, fourteen of the leaders had been students at Oberlin College in Ohio, which began admitting both black and female students before the Civil War.

Black farmers and artisans—tailors, carpenters, and barbers—were well represented among those who held political office. There were also 237 ministers and 172 teachers. At least 129 had served in the Union Army, and 46 had worked for the Freedmen's Bureau.

Several black politicians were wealthy, and a few were former slave owners. Antoine Dubuclet, who became Louisiana's treasurer, had owned more than one hundred slaves and land valued at more than $100,000 before the Civil War. Former slave Ferdinand Havis became a member of the Arkansas House of Representatives. He owned a saloon, a whiskey business, and two thousand acres near Pine Bluff, where he became known as "the Colored Millionaire."

Although black men did not dominate any state politically, a few did dominate districts with sizable black populations. Before he was elected to the U.S. Senate, Blanche K. Bruce all but controlled Bolivar County, Mississippi, where he served as sheriff, tax collector, and superintendent of education. Former slave and Civil War hero Robert Smalls was the political "kingpin" in Beaufort, South Carolina. He served successively in the South Carolina house and senate, and in the U.S. House of Representatives. He was also a member of the South Carolina constitutional conventions in 1868 and 1895. He was a major figure in the Republican party, and served as customs collector in Beaufort from 1889 to 1913.

The Issues

Many, but not all, black and white Republican leaders favored increasing the authority of state governments to promote the welfare of all the state's citizens. Before the Civil War, most southern states did not provide schools, medical care, assistance for the mentally impaired, or prisons. Such concerns—if attended to at all—were left to local communities or families.

Education and Social Welfare

Black leaders were eager to increase literacy and promote education among black people. Republican politicians created statewide systems of public education throughout the South. It was a difficult and expensive task, and the results were only a limited success. Schools had to be built, teachers employed, and textbooks provided. To pay for it, taxes were increased in states still reeling from the war.

In some communities and in many rural areas, schools were not built. In other places, teachers were not paid. Some people—black and white—opposed compulsory education laws, preferring to let parents determine whether their children should attend school or work to help the family. Some black leaders favored a poll tax on voting if the funds it brought in were spent on the schools. Thus, while Reconstruction leaders established a strong commitment to public education, the results they achieved were uneven.

Furthermore, white parents refused to send their children to integrated schools. Though no laws required segregation, public schools during and after

PROFILE

The Gibbs Brothers

Among the many black leaders who emerged during Reconstruction were the Gibbs brothers, who had political careers in two different states, Arkansas and Florida. Mifflin W. Gibbs and Jonathan C. Gibbs grew up in a well-to-do free black family in Philadelphia where their father was a respected Methodist minister. But their paths diverged, and they spent little time together as adults.

Mifflin was born in 1823 and became a building contractor. By the 1840s, he was an active abolitionist. With the discovery of gold in California in 1849, he went west and eventually established California's first black newspaper, *The Mirror of the Times.* He led a protest in 1851 against a provision in the California constitution that denied black men the right to vote. In 1858 he left California for Canada, again because gold had been discovered. He spent more than ten years in Canada and was elected to the Victoria City Council in British Columbia before returning to the United States in 1869. In 1870 he graduated from the law program at Oberlin College.

Mifflin Gibbs was probably the only African American in the nineteenth century elected to political office in two nations. He served as a city councilman in Victoria, British Columbia, in Canada in the late 1860s, and he was elected a judge in Little Rock, Arkansas, in 1873.

Mifflin moved to Arkansas in 1871 and was elected Little Rock Municipal Judge in 1873. Although defeated for reelection, he remained deeply involved in Republican party politics and was a delegate to every Republican national convention from 1876 to 1904. In 1897, Republican president William McKinley appointed him U.S. consul to Madagascar, a French Island colony off the East Coast of Africa, where he served until 1901. He died in 1915. A black high school in Little Rock was named in his honor.

Jonathan, born in 1827 or 1828, also joined the abolitionist movement. Rejected by eighteen colleges because of his color, he finally graduated from Dartmouth in 1852. He then went to Princeton Theological Seminary and became a Presbyterian minister in Troy, New York.

Jonathan attended the 1864 National Black Convention in Syracuse, New York, taught briefly at a freedmen's school in North Carolina, and then spent two years in Charleston, South Carolina. There he joined those black leaders who favored limiting the right to vote to literate men if that restriction were applied both to black and white people.

In 1867, Jonathan moved to Florida, where he became a key Republican leader and the state's highest-ranking black official. He was elected to the 1868 Florida constitutional convention and was appointed secretary of state by the Republican governor. Although defeated for a seat in Congress in 1868, he remained one of Florida's most visible black leaders and was repeatedly threatened by the Ku Klux Klan. In 1873, another Republican governor appointed him state superintendent of education. Jonathan Gibbs died in 1874, but his son Thomas went on to serve in the Florida House of Representatives, where he was instrumental in the establishment of Florida A&M University.

Reconstruction were invariably segregated. Black parents were usually more concerned that their children should have schools to attend than whether the schools were integrated. New Orleans, however, was an exception; it provided integrated schools.

Reconstruction leaders also supported higher education. In 1872, Mississippi legislators took advantage of the 1862 Federal Morrill Land-Grant Act, which provided states with funds for agricultural and mechanical colleges, to found the first historically black state university: Alcorn A&M College. Although the university was named after a white Republican governor, James L. Alcorn, former U.S. Senator Hiram Revels was its first president. The South Carolina legislature created a similar college and attached it to the Methodist-sponsored Claflin University.

Black leaders in the state legislature compelled the University of South Carolina, which had been all white, to admit black students and hire black faculty. Many, but not all, of the white students and faculty left. Several black politicians enrolled in the law and medical programs at the university. Richard Greener, a black Harvard graduate, served on the university's faculty and was its librarian.

Despite the costs, Reconstruction leaders also created the first state-supported institutions for the insane, the blind, and the deaf in the South. Some southern states during Reconstruction began to offer medical care and public health programs. Orphanages were established. State prisons were built. Black leaders also supported revising state criminal codes, eliminating corporal punishment for many crimes, and reducing the number of capital crimes.

Civil Rights

Black politicians were often the victims of racial discrimination when they tried to use public transportation and accommodations such as hotels and restaurants. Rather than provide separate arrangements for black customers, white-owned businesses simply excluded black patrons. This was true in the North, as well as the South. Robert Smalls, for example, the Civil War hero who had commandeered a Confederate supply ship to escape from Charleston in 1862 (see Chapter 11), was unceremoniously ejected from a Philadelphia streetcar in 1864. After protests, the company agreed to accept black riders. In Arkansas Mifflin Gibbs (see Profile: The Gibbs Brothers) and W. Hines Furbish successfully sued a local saloon after they had been denied service. In South Carolina Jonathan J. Wright won $1,200 in a lawsuit against a railroad after he had purchased a first-class ticket but had been forced to ride in the second-class coach.

Black leaders were determined to open public facilities to all people, in the process revealing deep divisions between themselves and white Republicans. In several southern states they introduced bills to prevent proprietors from excluding black people from restaurants, barrooms, hotels, concert halls, and auditoriums, as well as railroad coaches, streetcars, and steamboats. Many white Republicans and virtually every Democrat attacked such proposals as efforts to promote social equality and gain access for black people to places where they were not welcome. The white politicians blocked these laws in most states. Only South Carolina—with a black majority in the house and many black members in the senate—enacted such a law, but it was not effectively enforced. In Mississippi, the Republican governor James L. Alcorn vetoed a bill to outlaw racial discrimination by railroads. In Alabama and North Carolina, civil rights bills were defeated, while Georgia and Arkansas enacted measures that encouraged segregation.

Economic Issues

Black politicians sought to promote economic development in general and for black people in particular. For example, white landowners sometimes arbitrarily fired black agricultural laborers near the end of the growing season and then did not pay them. Some of these landowners were dishonest, but others were in debt and could not pay their workers. To prevent such situations, black politicians secured laws that required laborers to be paid before the crop was sold or at the time when it was sold. Some black leaders who had been slaves also wanted to regulate the wages of laborers, but these proposals invariably failed because most Republicans did not believe that states had the right to regulate wages and prices.

Legislators also enacted measures that protected the land and property of small farmers against seizure for nonpayment of debts. Black and white farmers who lost land, tools, animals, and other property because they could not pay their debts were unlikely ever to recover financially. "Stay laws" prohibited, or "stayed," authorities from taking property. Besides affording financial protection to hard-pressed poor farmers, Republicans hoped these laws would attract political support from white yeomen and draw them away from their attachment to the Democratic party.

Land

Black leaders were unable to initiate programs that would provide land to landless black and white farmers. Many black and white political leaders believed that the state had no right to distribute land. Again, South Carolina was the exception. Its legislature created a state land commission in 1869.

The commission could purchase and distribute land to freedmen. It also gave the freedmen loans on generous terms to pay for the land. Unfortunately, the commission was corrupt, was inefficiently managed, and had little fertile land to distribute. However, despite its many difficulties, the commission enabled more than fourteen thousand black families and a few white families to acquire land in South Carolina. Their descendants still possess some of this land today.

Though some black leaders were reluctant to use the states' power to distribute land, others had no qualms about raising property taxes so high that large landowners would be forced to sell some of their property to pay their taxes. Abraham Galloway of North Carolina explained, "I want to see the man who owns one or two thousand acres of land, taxed a dollar on the acre, and if they can't pay the taxes, sell their property to the highest bidder . . . and then we negroes shall become the land holders."

Business and Industry

Black and white leaders had an easier time enacting legislation to support business and industry. Like most Americans after the Civil War, Republicans believed that expanding the railroad network would stimulate employment, improve transportation, and generate prosperity. State governments approved the sale of bonds supported by the authority of the state to finance railroad construction. In Georgia, Alabama, Texas, and Arkansas, the railroad network did expand. But the bonded debt of these states soared and taxes increased to pay for it. Moreover, railroad financing was often corrupt. Most of the illegal money wound up in the pockets of white businessmen and politicians. Black politicians rarely had access to truly large financial transactions.

So attractive were business profits that some black political leaders formed corporations. They invested modest sums and believed—like so many capitalists—that the rewards outweighed the risks. In Charleston, twenty-eight black leaders (and two white politicians) formed a horse-drawn streetcar line they called the Enterprise Railroad to carry freight between the city wharves and the railroad terminal. Black leaders in South Carolina also created a company to extract the phosphate used for fertilizer from riverbeds and riverbanks in the low country. Neither business lasted long. Black men found it far more difficult than white entrepreneurs to finance their corporations.

Black Politicians: An Evaluation

Southern black political leaders on the state level did create the foundation for public education; for providing state assistance for the blind, deaf, and insane; and for reforming the criminal justice system. They tried, but mostly failed, to outlaw racial discrimination in public facilities. They encouraged state support for economic revival and expansion.

But black leaders could not create programs that significantly improved the lives of their constituents. Because white Republicans almost always outnumbered them, they could not enact an agenda of their own. Moreover, black leaders often disagreed among themselves about specific issues and programs. Class and prewar status frequently divided them. Those leaders who had not been slaves and had not been raised in rural isolation were less likely to be concerned with land and agricultural labor. More prosperous black leaders showed more interest in civil rights and encouraging business. Even when they agreed about the need for public education, black leaders often disagreed about how to finance it and whether or not it should be compulsory.

Republican Factionalism

Disagreements among black leaders paled in comparison to the internal conflicts that divided the Republican party during Reconstruction. Black and white Republicans often disagreed on political issues and strategy, but the lack of party cohesion and discipline was even more harmful. The Republican party in the South constantly split into factions as groups fought with each other. Most disagreements were over who should run for and hold political office.

During Reconstruction, hundreds of would-be Republican leaders—black and white—sought public offices. If they lost the Republican nomination in county or state conventions, they often bolted and formed a competing slate of candidates. Then Republicans ran against each other and against the Democrats in the general election. It was not a recipe for political success.

These bitter and angry contests were based less on race and issues than on the desperate desire to gain an office that would pay even a modest salary. Most black and white Republicans were not well off; public office assured them a modicum of economic security.

Ironically, these factional disputes led to a high turnover in political leadership and the loss of that very economic security. It was difficult for black leaders (and white leaders too) to be renominated and reelected to more than one or two terms. Few office holders served three or four consecutive terms in the same office during Reconstruction. This made for inexperienced leadership and added to Republican woes.

Opposition

Even if black and Republican leaders had been less prone to internecine conflict and more effective in adopting a political platform, they might still have failed to sustain themselves for long. Most white Southerners led by conservative Democrats remained absolutely opposed to letting black men vote or hold office. As a white Floridian put it, "The damned Republican party

PROFILE

The Rollin Sisters

Few women, black or white, were as influential in Reconstruction politics as the Rollin sisters of South Carolina. Although they could not vote or hold political office, the five sisters, and especially Frances and Katherine, were closely associated with the black and white Republican leadership in South Carolina. With their education, knowledge, and charm, these black women affected political decisions and policies.

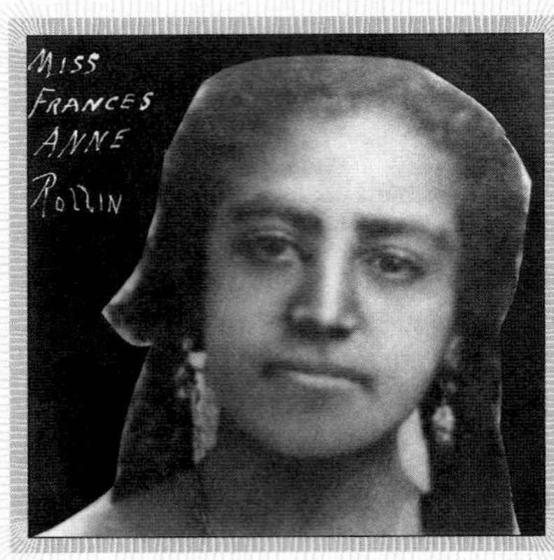

Frances Rollin Whipper was an author, teacher, political activist, wife, and mother. With her sisters, she was deeply involved in Reconstruction politics in South Carolina.

The sisters were born and raised in the elite antebellum free black community in Charleston. Their father, William Rollin, a prosperous lumber dealer, traced his ancestors back to French Catholic families in Haiti. He insisted that his daughters obtain a first-rate education. Frances, who was born in 1844, was sent to Philadelphia to take the "ladies course" at the Quaker's Institute for Colored Youth. At least two of the other sisters attended school in Boston. After the war, Frances joined other members of Charleston's prominent people of color and taught at schools sponsored by the American Missionary Association. She also found time to write the biography of the black abolitionist leader Martin Delany. This was the first major nonfiction work published in America by a black woman, but she felt compelled to identify the author as a male, Frank A. Rollin.

In 1867 and 1868, as black men were entering the political arena, the Rollin sisters also gravitated to politics. Against her father's wishes, Frances married one of Reconstruction South Carolina's most controversial figures, William Whipper, a black attorney from Philadelphia who settled in Beaufort, South Carolina, after the war. He was elected to the state constitutional convention and then the South Carolina House of Representatives. Whipper was a tough, able, shrewd, and not altogether honest politician. He enjoyed an expensive lifestyle. Most white people detested him.

While the legislature was in session, the Whippers and the Rollin sisters took up residence in Columbia, the state capital. There, the sisters were extraordinarily popular. They were well educated, intelligent, refined, and sophisticated. One observer described them as "ravishingly beautiful." Katherine Rollin was frequently seen with white State Senator George W. McIntyre.

The Rollin sisters were enthusiastic proponents of women's rights and women's suffrage. They enlisted the wives of prominent black and white Republican politicians in their cause. Charlotte and Katherine organized a women's rights convention in Columbia in 1870 and formed the South Carolina Branch of the American Women's Suffrage Association.

Charlotte Rollin pleaded for the right to vote.

> We ask suffrage not as a favor, not as a privilege, but as a right based on the grounds that we are human beings and as such entitled to human rights. While we concede that woman's ennobling influence should be confined chiefly to the home and society, we claim that public opinion has had a tendency to limit a woman's sphere to too small a circle and until woman has the right of representation this will last, and other rights will be held by insecure tenure.

Their black and white male allies tried to amend South Carolina's constitution to enable women to vote. After a bitter debate, the legislature rejected women's suffrage.

After the Democrats regained political power in 1877, the Rollin sisters left for the North. Charlotte and Louise settled with their mother in Brooklyn, New York. William and Frances Whipper and their five children moved to Washington, D.C. in 1882, where he practiced law, and she was a clerk in the General Land Office. Three of their children survived to adulthood. Their sole son, Leigh Whipper, was a prominent stage and screen actor in the 1940s and 1950s. Sometime in the 1890s, Frances joined her husband in Beaufort. She died there in 1901.

has put niggers to rule us and we will not suffer it." Of course, because black people voted did not mean that they ruled during Reconstruction, but many white people failed to grasp that. Instead, for most white Southerners, the only acceptable political system was one that excluded black men and the Republican party.

As far as most white people were concerned, the end of slavery and the enfranchisement of black men did not make black people their equals. They did not accept the Fourteenth Amendment. They attacked Republican governments and their leaders unrelentingly. White Southerners blamed the Republicans for an epidemic of waste and corruption in state government. But most of all, they considered it preposterous and outrageous that former slaves could vote and hold political office.

James S. Pike spoke for many white people when he ridiculed black leaders in the South Carolina House of Representatives in 1873:

> The body is almost literally a Black Parliament. . . . The Speaker is black, the Clerk is black, the door-keepers are black, the little pages are black, the chairman of the Ways and Means is black, and the chaplain is coal-black. At some of the desks sit colored men whose types it would be hard to find outside of Congo; whose costume, visages, attitudes, and expression, only befit the forecastle of a buccaneer. It must be remembered, also, that these men, with not more than a half a dozen exceptions, have been themselves slaves, and that their ancestors were slaves for generations.

Pike's observations circulated widely in both North and South.

White Southerners were determined to rid themselves of Republicans and the disgrace of having to live with black men who possessed political rights. White Southerners would "redeem" their states by restoring white Democrats to power. This did not simply mean defeating black and white Republicans in elections; it meant removing them from any role in politics. White Southerners believed that any means—fair or foul—were justified in exorcising this evil.

The Ku Klux Klan

If black men in politics was illegitimate—in the eyes of white Southerners—then it was acceptable to use violence to remove them. This thinking gave rise to militant terrorist organizations, such as the Ku Klux Klan, the Knights of the White Camellia, the White Brotherhood, and the Whitecaps. Threats, intimidation, beatings, rapes, and murder would restore conservative white Democratic rule and force black people back into subordination.

The Ku Klux Klan was founded in Pulaski, Tennessee, in 1866. It was originally a social club for Confederate veterans who adopted secret oaths and rituals—similar to the Union Leagues, but with far more deadly results. One of the key figures in the Klan's rapid growth was former Confederate General Nathan Bedford Forrest, who became its Grand Wizard. The Klan drew its members from all classes of white society, not merely from among the poor. Businessmen, lawyers, physicians, and politicians were active in the Klan as well as farmers and planters.

The Klan and other terrorist organizations functioned mainly where black people were a large minority and where their votes could affect the outcome of elections. Klansmen virtually took over areas of western Alabama, northern Georgia, and Florida's panhandle. The Klan controlled the up country of South Carolina and the area around Mecklenburg County, North Carolina. However, in the Carolina and Georgia low country where there were huge black majorities, the Klan never appeared.

Though the Klan and similar societies were neither well organized nor unified, they did reduce support for the Republican party and helped eliminate its leaders. Often wearing hoods and masks to hide their faces, white terrorists embarked on a campaign of violence rarely matched and never exceeded in American history.

Mobs of marauding terrorists beat and killed hundreds of black people—and many white people. Black churches and schools were burned. Republican leaders were routinely threatened and often killed. The black chairman of the Republican party in South Carolina, Benjamin F. Randolph, was murdered as he stepped off a train in 1868. Black legislator Lee Nance and white legislator Solomon G. W. Dill were murdered in 1868 in South Carolina. In 1870 black lawmaker Richard Burke was killed in Sumter County, Alabama, because he was considered too influential among "people of his color."

As his wife looked on, Jack Dupree—a local Republican leader—had his throat cut and was eviscerated in Monroe County, Mississippi. In 1870, North Carolina Senator John W. Stephens, a white Republican, was murdered. After Alabama freedman George Moore voted for the Republicans in 1869, Klansmen beat him, raped a girl who was visiting his wife, and attacked a neighbor. An Irish-American teacher and four black men were lynched in Cross Plains, Alabama, in 1870.

White men attacked a Republican campaign rally in Eutaw, Alabama, in 1870 and killed four black men and wounded fifty-four other people. After three black leaders were arrested in 1871 in Meridian,

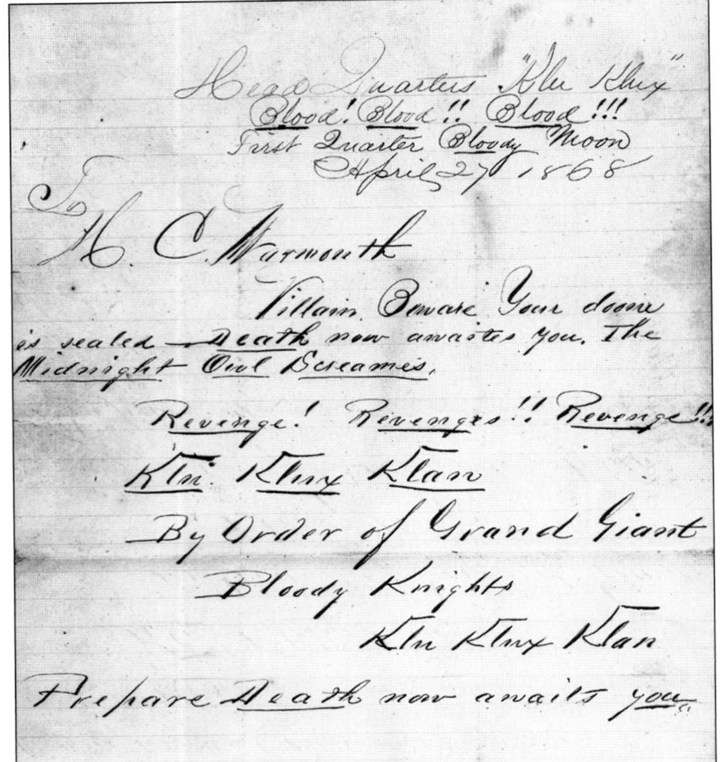

Head Quarters "Klu Klux"
Blood! Blood!! Blood!!!
First Quarter Bloody Moon
April 27 1868

To
H. C. Warmouth

Villain Beware Your doom is sealed — Death now awaits you. The Midnight Owl Screams,

Revenge! Revenge!! Revenge!!!

Klu Klux Klan

By Order of Grand Giant
Bloody Knights
Klu Klux Klan

Prepare Death now awaits you.

The flowing white robes and cone-shaped headdresses associated with the Ku Klux Klan today are mostly a twentieth-century phenomenon. The Klansmen of the Reconstruction era, like these two men in Alabama in 1868, were well armed, disguised, and prepared to intimidate black and white Republicans. The note is a Klan death threat directed at Louisiana's first Republican governor, Henry C. Warmoth.

Mississippi, for delivering what many white people considered inflammatory speeches, shooting broke out in the courtroom. The Republican judge and two of the defendants were killed, and in a wave of violence, thirty black people were murdered, including every black leader in the small community. In the same year, a mob of five hundred men broke into the jail in Union County, South Carolina, and lynched eight black prisoners who had been accused of killing a Confederate veteran.

Nowhere was the Klan more active and violent than in York County, South Carolina. Almost the entire adult white male population joined in threatening, attacking, and murdering the black population. Hundreds were beaten and at least eleven killed. Terrified families fled from their homes into the woods. Appeals for help were sent to Governor Robert K. Scott (see *Voices: An Appeal for Help against the Klan*).

But Scott did not send aid. He had already sent the South Carolina militia into areas of Klan activity, and even more violence had resulted. The militia was made up mostly of black men, and white terrorists retaliated by killing militia officers. Scott could not send white men to York County because most of them sympathized with the Klan. Thus Republican governors like Scott responded ineffectually. Republican-controlled legislatures passed anti-Klan measures that made it illegal to appear in public in disguises and masks, and they strengthened laws against assault, murder, and conspiracy. But enforcement was weak.

A few Republican leaders did deal harshly and effectively with terrorism. Governors in Tennessee, Texas, and Arkansas declared martial law and sent in

VOICES

An Appeal for Help against the Klan

H. K. Roberts, a black lieutenant in the South Carolina State Militia, described Klan terror in York County in late 1870 to Governor Robert K. Scott. Roberts desperately appealed for aid to protect Republicans and defend the black community.

Antioch P.O.
York County
S.C.
Dec. the 6th 1870. To Your Excelency R. K. Scott

Sir I will tell you that on last friday night the 2nd day of this [month] 8 miles from here thier was one of the worst outrages Commited that is on record in the state from 50 to 75 armed men went to the house of Thomas Blacks a colored man fired shots into the house and cald for him he clibed up in the loft of the house they fired up their and he came down jumped out at a window ran about 30 steps was shot down then they shot him after he fell they then draged him about 10 steps and cut his throat from ear to ear their was about 30 bullet holes in his body some 50 to one hundred shots in the house. . . . [They] abused his wife and enquired for one or two more colored men some of the colored people are leaving and a great many lying out in the woods and they reports comes to me evry day that they Ku Kluxs intend to kill us all out and I heard yesterday that they had 30 stands of arms. . . . I wish you would give me 20 or 25 men or let me enroll that many and I will stop it or catch some of them or send some U S Soldiers on for I tell you their must be something don and that quick to for I do believe that they intend to beat and kill out the Radical party in the upper Counties of the state where the vote is close if we was to have the ellection now the Radicals would turn [out] to vote their ticket I leave the matter with you I hope you will wright back to me by return mail and let me heare what you think you can do for us up here I cant tell whether I can hold my own or not I know some men that stay with us at night for safety but if they come as strong as they were the other night they may kill me and all of my men I remain yours truly as ever
H.K. Roberts, Lieut.
Commanding Post
of State Guards Kings Mountain

QUESTIONS

1. What prompted Roberts to write this letter?
2. Would Roberts have had any reason to exaggerate the violence in York County?
3. According to Roberts, what motivated white men to attack?

Source: H. K. Roberts to Governor Robert K. Scott, South Carolina Department of Archives and History.

hundreds of well-armed white and black men to quell the violence. Hundreds of Klansmen were arrested, many fled, and three were executed in Arkansas. But when Governor William W. Holden of North Carolina sent the state militia after the Klan, he succeeded only in provoking an angry reaction. Subsequent Klan violence in ten counties helped Democrats carry the 1870 legislative elections, and the North Carolina legislature then removed Holden from office.

Outnumbered and outgunned, black people in most areas did not retaliate against the Klan, and the Klan was rarely active where black people were in a majority and prepared to defend themselves. In the cause of white supremacy, the Klan usually attacked those who could not defend themselves.

The Fifteenth Amendment

The federal government under Republican domination tried to protect black voting rights and defend Republican state governments in the South. In 1869 Congress passed the Fifteenth Amendment, which was ratified in 1870. It stipulated that a person could not be deprived of the right to vote because of race: "The right of citizens of the United States to vote shall not be denied or abridged by the United States or by any

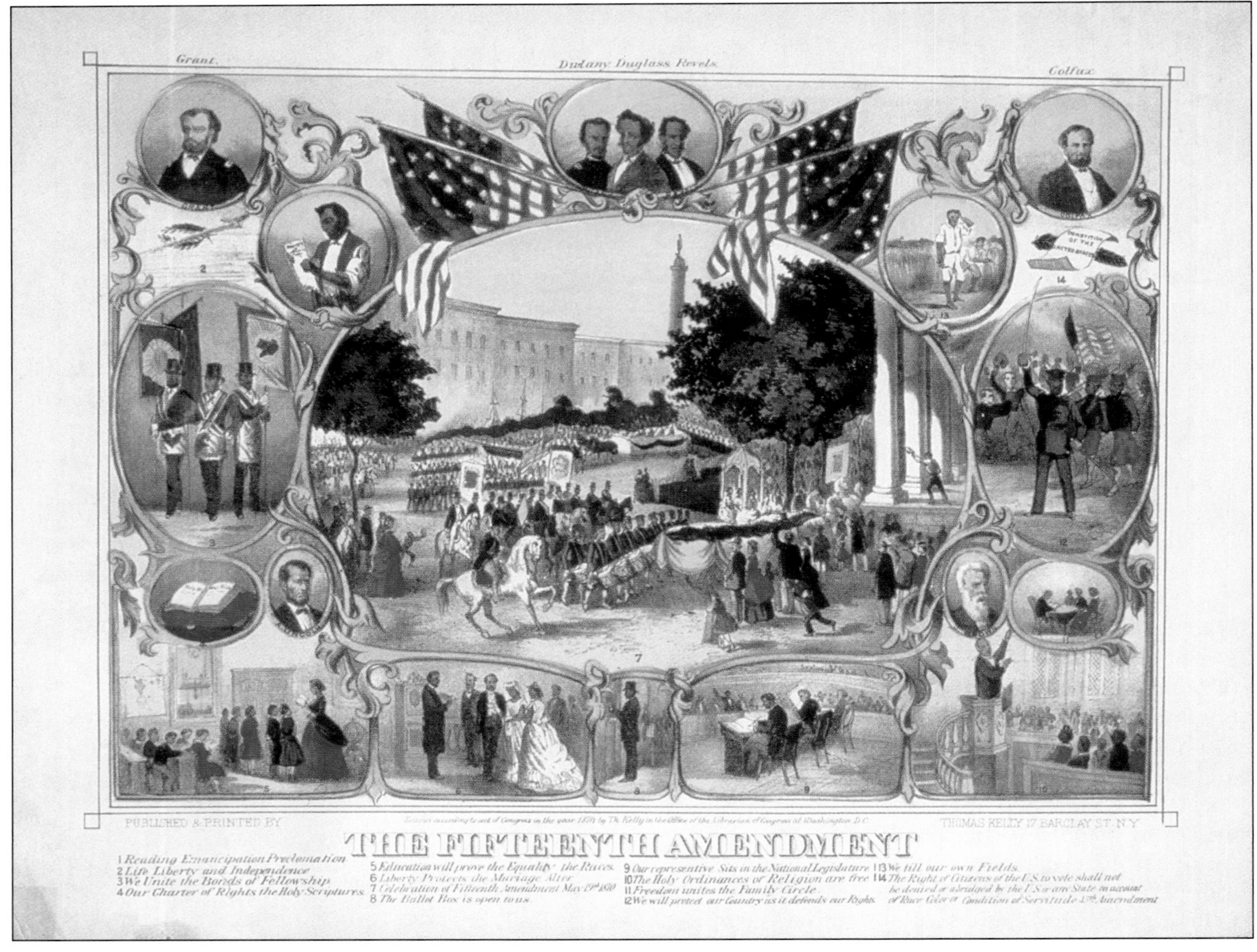

This optimistic 1870 illustration exemplifies the hopes and aspirations generated during Reconstruction as black people gained access to the political system. Invoking the legacy of Abraham Lincoln and John Brown, it suggests that African Americans would soon assume their rightful and equitable role in American society.

State on account of race, color, or previous condition of servitude." Black people, abolitionists, and reformers hailed the amendment as the culmination of the crusade to end slavery and give black people the same rights as white people.

Northern black men were the amendment's immediate beneficiaries because before its adoption, black men could vote in only eight northern states. Yet to the disappointment of many, the amendment said nothing about women voting and did not outlaw poll taxes, literacy tests, and property qualifications that could disfranchise citizens.

Federal Reconstruction Legislation: 1868–1877

1869	**Fifteenth Amendment passed (ratified 1870)**
1870	**Enforcement Act passed**
1871	**Ku Klux Klan Act passed**
1875	**Civil Rights Act of 1875 passed**

The Enforcement Acts

In direct response to the terrorism in the South, Congress passed the Enforcement Acts in 1870 and 1871, and the federal government expanded its authority over the states. The 1870 act outlawed disguises and masks and protected the civil rights of citizens. The 1871 act—known as the Ku Klux Klan Act—

made it a federal offense to interfere with an individual's right to vote, hold office, serve on a jury, or enjoy equal protection of the law. Those accused of violating the act would be tried in federal court. For extreme violence, the act authorized the president to send in federal troops and suspend the writ of habeas corpus. (Habeas corpus is the right to be brought before a judge and not be arrested and jailed without cause.)

Black congressmen who had long advocated federal action against the Klan, endorsed the Enforcement Acts. Representative Joseph Rainey of South Carolina wanted to suspend the Constitution to protect citizens. "I desire that so broad and liberal a construction be placed on its provisions, as will insure protection to the humblest citizen. Tell me nothing of a constitution which fails to shelter beneath its rightful power the people of a country."

Armed with this new legislation, the Justice Department and Attorney General Amos T. Ackerman moved vigorously against the Klan. Hundreds of Klansmen were arrested—seven hundred in Mississippi alone. Faced with a full-scale rebellion in late 1871 in South Carolina's up country, President Ulysses S. Grant declared martial law in nine counties, suspended the writ of habeas corpus, and sent in the U.S. Army. Mass arrests and trials followed, but federal authorities permitted many Klansmen to confess and thereby escape prosecution. The government lacked the human and financial resources to bring hundreds of men to court for lengthy trials. Some white men were tried, mostly before black juries, and were imprisoned or fined. Comparatively few Klansmen, however, were punished severely, especially considering the enormity of their crimes.

The North Loses Interest

While the federal government did reduce Klan violence for a time, white Southerners remained convinced that white supremacy must be restored and Republican governments overturned. Klan violence did not overthrow any state governments, but it gravely undermined freedmen's confidence in the ability of these governments to protect them. Meanwhile, Radical Republicans in Congress grew frustrated that the South and especially black people continued to demand so much of their time and attention year after year. There was less and less sentiment in the North to continue support for the freedmen and involvement in southern affairs.

Many Republicans in the North lost interest in issues and principles and became more concerned with elections and economic issues. By the mid-1870s, there was more discussion in Congress of patronage, veterans' pensions, railroads, taxes, tariffs, the economy, and monetary policy than civil rights or the future of the South. Republicans began to question the necessity for more support for African Americans. Others, swayed by white Southerners' views of black people, began to doubt the wisdom of universal manhood suffrage. Many white people who had nominally supported black suffrage began to believe the exaggerated complaints about corruption among black leaders and the unrelenting claims that freedmen were incapable of self-government. Some white Northerners began to conclude that Reconstruction had been a mistake.

Economic conditions contributed to changing attitudes. A financial crisis—the Panic of 1873—sent the economy into a slump for several years. Businesses and financial institutions failed, unemployment soared, and prices fell sharply. In 1874, the Democrats recaptured a majority in the House of Representatives for the first time since 1860 and also took political control of several northern states.

The Freedmen's Bank

One of the casualties of the financial crisis was the Freedmen's Savings Bank, which failed in 1874. Founded in 1865 when hope flourished, the Freedmen's Savings and Trust Company had been chartered by Congress, but was not connected to the Freedmen's Bureau. However, the bank's advertising featured pictures of Abraham Lincoln, and many black people assumed that it was a federal agency. Freedmen, black veterans, black churches, fraternal organizations, and benevolent societies opened thousands of accounts in the bank. Most of the deposits totaled under $50, and some amounted to only a few cents.

Though the bank had many black employees, its board of directors consisted of white men. They unwisely invested the bank's funds in risky ventures, including Washington, DC, real estate. With the Panic of 1873, the bank lost large sums in unsecured railroad loans. To restore confidence, its directors asked Frederick Douglass to serve as president and persuaded him to invest $10,000 of his own money to help shore up the bank. Douglass lost his money, and African Americans from across the South lost more than one million dollars when the bank closed in June 1874. Eventually about half the depositors received three-fifths of the value of their accounts; but many African Americans believed that the U.S. government owed them a debt, and well into the twentieth century, they wrote to Congress and the president to retrieve their hard-earned money.

The Civil Rights Act of 1875

Before Reconstruction finally expired, Congress made one final—some said futile—gesture to protect black people from racial discrimination when it passed the Civil Rights Act of 1875. Strongly championed by Senator Charles Sumner of Massachusetts, it was originally intended to open public accommodations including schools, churches, cemeteries, hotels, and transportation to all people regardless of race. It passed in the Republican-controlled Senate in 1874 shortly before Sumner died. But House Democrats held up passage until 1875 and deleted bans on discrimination in churches, cemeteries, and schools.

The act stipulated "That all persons . . . shall be entitled to the full and equal enjoyment of the accommodations, advantages, facilities, and privileges of inns, public conveyances on land or water, theaters, and other places of public amusement." After its passage, no attempt was made to enforce these provisions, and in 1883, the U.S. Supreme Court declared it unconstitutional. Justice Joseph Bradley wrote that the Fourteenth Amendment protected black people from discrimination by states but not by private businesses. Black news-

E. Sachse and Company, "The Shackle Broken by the Genius of Freedom," Baltimore, MD; 1874.

On January 6, 1874, Robert Brown Elliott delivered a ringing speech in the U. S. House of Representatives in support of the Sumner Civil Rights Bill. Elliott was responding in part to words uttered the day before by Virginia Congressman John T. Harris who claimed that ". . . there is not a gentleman on this floor who can honestly say he really believes that the colored man is created his equal."

VOICES

Black Leaders Support the Passage of a Civil Rights Act

Black Congressmen Robert Brown Elliott of South Carolina and James T. Rapier of Alabama both spoke passionately in favor of the Sumner Civil Rights Bill in 1874. Both men had been free before the war. Both were lawyers, and though they each accumulated considerable wealth, both died in poverty in the 1880s.

[James T. Rapier]

I must confess it is somewhat embarrassing for a colored man to urge the passage of this bill, because if he exhibit an earnestness in the matter and expresses a desire for its immediate passage, straightaway he is charged with a desire for social equality, as explained by the demagogue and understood by the ignorant white man. But then it is just as embarrassing for him not to do so, for, if he remains silent while the struggle is being carried on around, and for him, he is liable to be charged with a want of interest in a matter that concerns him more than anyone else, which is enough to make his friends desert his cause. So in steering away from Scylla I may run upon Charybdis. But the anomalous, and I may add the supremely ridiculous, position of the Negro at this time, in this country, compel me to say something. Here his condition is without comparison, parallel alone to itself. Just that the law recognizes my right upon this floor as a lawmaker, but that there is no law to secure to me any accommodations whatever while traveling here to discharge my duties as a Representative of a large and wealthy constituency. Here I am the peer of the proudest, but on a steamboat or car I am not equal to the most degraded. Is not this most anomalous and ridiculous?

[Robert Brown Elliott]

The results of the war, as seen in Reconstruction, have settled forever the political status of my race. The passage of this bill will determine the civil status, not only of the Negro but of any other class of citizens who may feel themselves discriminated against. It will form the capstone of that temple of liberty begun on this continent under discouraging circumstances, carried on in spite of the sneers of monarchists and the cavils of pretended friends of freedom, until at last it stands in all its beautiful symmetry and proportions, a building the grandest which the world has ever seen, realizing the most sanguine expectations and the highest hopes of those who in the name of equal, impartial and universal liberty, laid the foundation stone.

QUESTIONS

1. If black men had the right to vote and serve in Congress, why was a civil rights law needed?
2. Exactly who would benefit most from the passage of this bill?
3. What distinction do the two congressmen draw between social discrimination and political rights?

Sources: *Congressional Record*, vol. II, part 1, 43d Congress, 1st session, pp. 565–7; Peggy Lamson, *The Glorious Failure*, p. 181.

papers likened the decision to the Dred Scott case a quarter century earlier.

The End of Reconstruction

Reconstruction ended as it began—in violence and controversy. By 1875, conservative white Democrats had regained control of all the former Confederate states except Mississippi, Florida, Louisiana, and South Carolina (see Map 13–1). Democrats had redeemed Tennessee in 1870 and Georgia in 1871. Democrats had learned two valuable lessons. First, few black men could be persuaded to vote for the Democratic party—no matter how much white leaders wanted to believe that former slaves were easy to manipulate. Second, intimidation and violence would win elections in areas where the number of black and white voters was nearly equal. The federal government had stymied Klan violence in 1871, but by the mid 1870s the government had become reluctant to send troops to the South to protect black citizens.

MAP EXPLORATION To explore this map, go to http://www.prenhall.com/hine/map13.1

MAP 13–1 Dates of Readmission of Southern States to the Union and Reestablishment of Democratic Party Control. Once conservative, white Democrats regained political control of a state government from black and white Republicans, they considered that state "redeemed." The first states the Democrats "redeemed" were Georgia, Virginia, and North Carolina. Louisiana, Florida, and South Carolina were the last. (Tennessee was not included in the Reconstruction process under the terms of the 1867 Reconstruction Act).

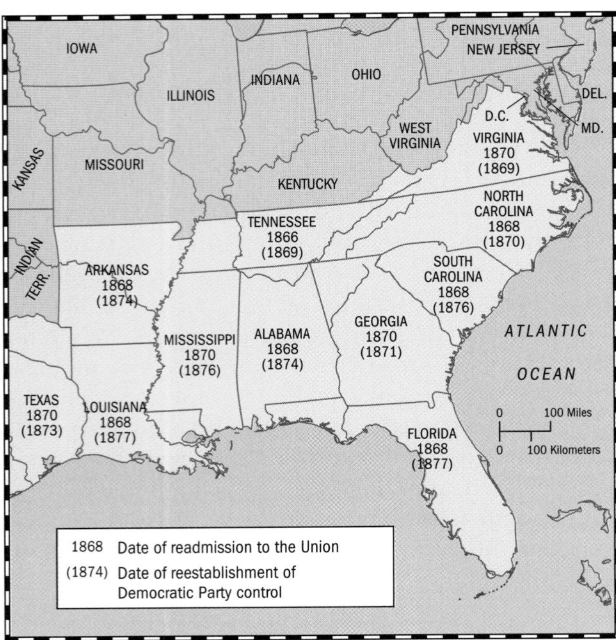

Violent Redemption

In Alabama in 1874, black and white Republican leaders were murdered, and white mobs destroyed crops and homes. On election day in Eufaula, white men killed seven and injured nearly seventy unarmed black voters. Black voters were also driven from the polls in Mobile. Democrats won the election and redeemed Alabama.

White violence accompanied every election in Louisiana from 1868 to 1876. After Republicans and Democrats each claimed victory in the 1872 elections, black people seized the small town of Colfax along the Red River to protect themselves against a Democratic takeover. They held out for three weeks, and then on Easter Sunday in 1873, a well-armed white mob attacked the black defenders, killing 105 in the worst single day of bloodshed during Reconstruction. In 1874 the White League almost redeemed Louisiana in an astonishing wave of violence. Black people were murdered, courts were attacked, and white people refused to pay taxes to the Republican state government. Six white and two black Republicans were murdered at Coushatta. In September, President Grant finally sent federal troops to New Orleans after 3,500 White Leaguers attacked and nearly wiped out the black militia and the Metropolitan Police. But the stage had been set for the 1876 campaign.

The Shotgun Policy

In 1875 white Mississippians, no longer fearful that the national government would intervene in force, declared open warfare on the black majority. The masks and hoods of the Klan were discarded. One newspaper publicly proclaimed that Democrats would carry the election, "peaceably if we can, forcibly if we must." Another paper carried a bold banner: "Mississippi is a white man's country, and by the eternal God we'll rule it."

White Mississippi unleashed a campaign of violence known as the "Shotgun Policy" that was extreme even for Reconstruction. Many Republicans fled and others were murdered. In late 1874, an estimated three hundred black people were hunted down outside Vicksburg after black men armed with inferior weapons had lost a "battle" with white men. In 1875, thirty teachers, church leaders, and Republican officials were killed in Clinton. The white sheriff of Yazoo county, who had married a black woman and supported the education of black children, had to flee the state.

Mississippi Governor Adelbert Ames appealed for federal help, but President Grant refused: "The whole public are tired out with these annual autumnal outbreaks in the South . . . [and] are ready now to condemn any interference on the part of the Government." No federal help arrived. The terrorism intensified, and many black voters went into hiding on election day, afraid for their lives and the lives of their families. Democrats redeemed Mississippi and prided themselves that they—a superior race representing the most civilized of all people—were back in control.

In Florida in 1876, white Republicans noted that support for black people in the South was fading. They nominated an all-white Republican slate, and even refused to renominate black Congressman Josiah Walls.

The Hamburg Massacre

South Carolina Democrats were divided between moderate and extreme factions, but they united to nominate former Confederate General Wade Hampton for governor after the Hamburg Massacre. The prelude to this event occurred on July 4, 1876—the nation's centennial—when two white men in a buggy confronted the black militia that was drilling on a town street in Hamburg, a small, mostly black town. Hot words were exchanged, and days later, Democrats demanded that the militia be disarmed. White rifle club members from around the state arrived in Hamburg and attacked the armory, where forty black members of the militia defended themselves. The rifle companies brought up a cannon and reinforcements from nearby Georgia. After the militia ran low on ammunition, white men captured the armory. One white man was killed, twenty-nine black men were taken prisoner, and the other eleven fled. Five of the black men identified as leaders were shot down in cold blood. The rifle companies invaded and wrecked Hamburg. Seven white men were indicted for murder. All were acquitted.

The Hamburg Massacre incited South Carolina Democrats to imitate Mississippi's "Shotgun Policy." It also forced a reluctant President Grant to send federal troops to South Carolina. In the 1876 election campaign, hundreds of white men in red flannel shirts turned out on mules and horses to support Wade Hampton in his contest against incumbent Republican Governor Daniel Chamberlain and his black and white allies. When Chamberlain and fellow Republicans tried to speak in Edgefield, they were ridiculed, threatened, and shouted down by six hundred Red Shirts, many of them armed.

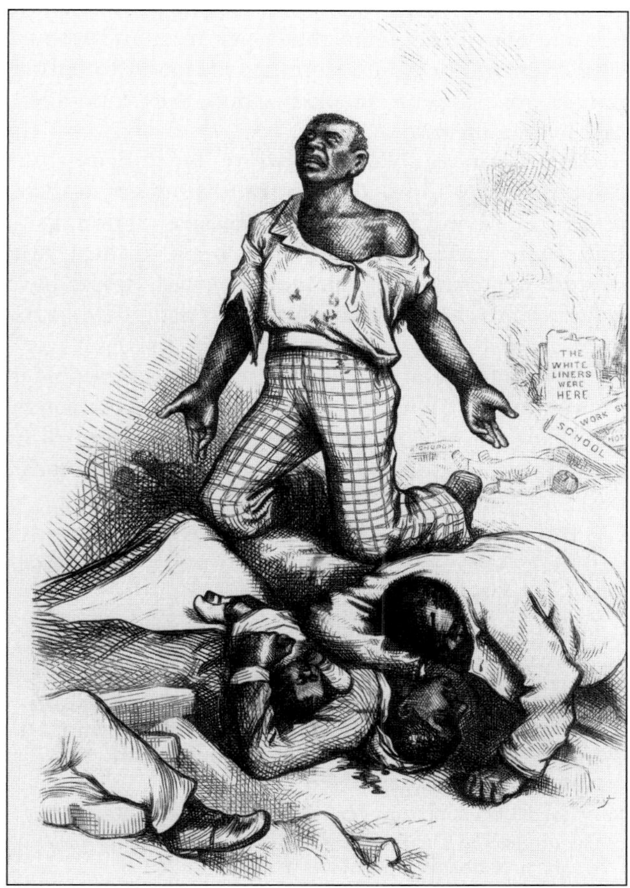

Editorial cartoonist Thomas Nast chronicled the travails of freedmen during the twelve years of Reconstruction in the pages of *Harper's Weekly*. Here Nast deplores the violence and intimidation that accompanied the 1876 election campaign and questions the willingness of white Americans to respect the rights of black Americans.

Democrats attacked, beat, and killed black people to prevent them from voting. Democratic leaders instructed their followers to treat black voters with contempt. "In speeches to negroes you must remember that argument has no effect on them. They can only be influenced by their fears, superstition, and cupidity. . . . Treat them so as to show them you are a superior race and that their natural position is that of subordination to the white man."

As the election approached, black people in the up country of South Carolina knew that it would be exceedingly dangerous if they tried to vote. But in the low country, black people went on the offensive and attacked Democrats. In Charleston, a white man was killed in a racial melee. At a campaign rally at Cainhoy, a few miles outside Charleston, armed black men killed five white men.

A few black men supported Wade Hampton and the Red Shirts. Hampton had a paternalistic view of black people and, although he considered them inferior to white people, promised to respect their rights. Martin Delany believed that Hampton and the Democrats were more trustworthy than unreliable Republicans; Delany campaigned for Hampton and was later rewarded with a minor political post. A few genuinely conservative black men during Reconstruction also supported the Democrats and curried their favor and patronage. Most black people despised them. When one black man threw his support to the Democrats, his wife threw him and his clothes out, declaring that she would prefer to "beg her bread" than live with a "Democratic nigger."

The Compromise of 1877

Threats, violence, and bloodshed accompanied the elections of 1876, but the results were confusing and contradictory. Both Democrats and Republicans claimed to have won in Florida, Louisiana, and South Carolina, the last three southern states that had not been redeemed. This created a stand-off between the two presidential candidates, the Republican Rutherford B. Hayes and the Democrat Samuel J. Tilden. Hayes had won 167 electoral votes. Tilden had 185. Whoever took the nineteen electoral votes of the three contested states would be the next president (see Map 13–2).

The controversy precipitated a constitutional crisis in 1877. Eventually, a compromise was arranged. Democrats accepted a Hayes victory, but Hayes promised southern Democrats that he would not support Republican

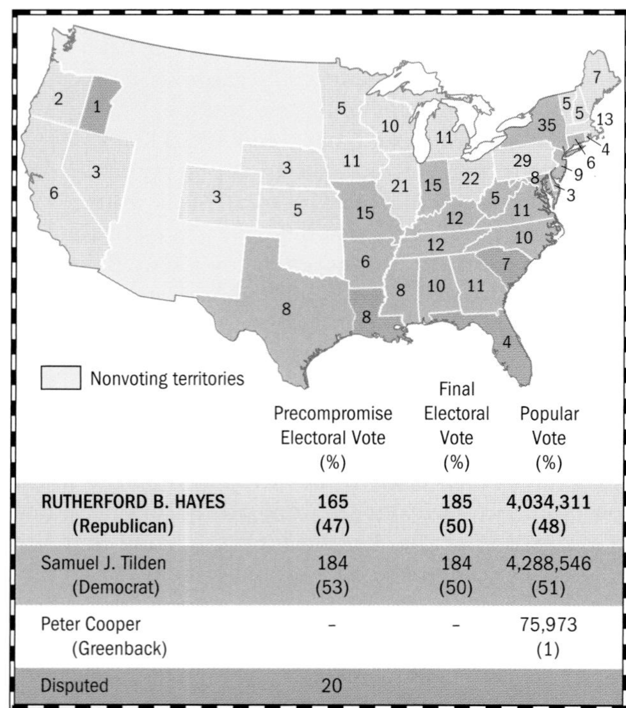

	Precompromise Electoral Vote (%)	Final Electoral Vote (%)	Popular Vote (%)
RUTHERFORD B. HAYES (Republican)	**165 (47)**	**185 (50)**	**4,034,311 (48)**
Samuel J. Tilden (Democrat)	184 (53)	184 (50)	4,288,546 (51)
Peter Cooper (Greenback)	-	-	75,973 (1)
Disputed	20		

MAP 13–2 The Election of 1876. Though Democrat Samuel Tilden appeared to have won the election of 1876, Rutherford B. Hayes and the Republicans were able to claim victory after a prolonged political and constitutional controversy involving the disputed electoral college votes from Louisiana, Florida, and South Carolina (and one from Oregon). In a complex compromise in 1877, Democrats agreed to accept electoral votes for Hayes from those states, and Republicans agreed to permit those states to be "redeemed" by the Democrats. The result was to leave the entire South under the political control of conservative white Democrats. For the first time since 1867, black and white Republicans no longer effectively controlled any former Confederate state.

governments in Florida, Louisiana, and South Carolina. Hayes withdrew the last federal troops from the South, and the Republican administration in those states collapsed. Democrats immediately took control.

Redemption was now complete. Each of the former Confederate states was under the authority of white Democrats. Henry Adams, a black leader from Louisiana, explained what had happened. "The whole South—every state in the South had got into the hands of the very men that held us as slaves."

Conclusion

The glorious hopes that emancipation and the Union victory in the Civil War had aroused among African Americans in 1865 appeared forlorn by 1877. To be sure, black people were no longer slave laborers or property. They lived in tightly knit families that white people no longer controlled. They had established hundreds of schools, churches, and benevolent societies. The Constitution now endowed them with freedom, citizenship, and the right to vote. Some black people had even acquired land.

But no one can characterize Reconstruction as a success. The epidemic of terror and violence made it one of the bloodiest eras in American history. Thousands of black people had been beaten, raped, and murdered since 1865, simply because they had acted as free people. Too many white people were determined that black people could not and would not have the same rights that white people enjoyed. White Southerners would not tolerate either the presence of black men in politics or white Republicans who accepted black political involvement. Gradually most white Northerners and even Radical Republicans grew weary of intervening in southern affairs and became convinced again that black men and women were their inferiors and were not prepared to participate in government. Reconstruction, they concluded, had been a mistake.

Furthermore, black and white Republicans hurt themselves by indulging in fraud and corruption, and by engaging in angry and divisive factionalism. But even if Republicans had been honest and united, white southern Democrats would never have accepted black people as worthy to participate in the political system.

Southern Democrats would accept black people in politics only if Democrats could control black voters. But black voters understood this, rejected control by former slave owners, and were loyal to the Republican party—as flawed as it was.

But as grim a turn as life may have taken for black people by 1877, it would get even worse in the decades that followed.

Recommended Reading

Eric Foner. *Freedom's Lawmakers: A Directory of Black Officeholders During Reconstruction.* New York: Oxford University Press, 1993. Biographical sketches of every known southern black leader during the era.

John Hope Franklin. *Reconstruction after the Civil War.* Chicago: University of Chicago Press, 1961. An excellent summary and interpretation of the post-war years.

William Gillette. *Retreat from Reconstruction, 1869–1879.* Baton Rouge, LA: Louisiana State University Press, 1979. An analysis of how and why the North lost interest in the South.

Thomas Holt. *Black Over White: Negro Political Leadership in South Carolina.* Urbana, IL: University of Illinois Press, 1979. A masterful and sophisticated study of black leaders in the state with the most black politicians.

Michael L. Perman. *Emancipation and Reconstruction, 1862–1879.* Arlington Heights, IL: Harlan Davidson, Inc., 1987. Another excellent survey of the period.

Howard N. Rabinowitz, ed. *Southern Black Leaders of the Reconstruction Era.* Urbana, IL: University of Illinois Press, 1982. A series of biographical essays on black politicians.

Frank A. Rollin. *Life and Public Services of Martin R. Delany.* Boston: Lee and Shepard, 1883. This is the first biography of a black leader by an African American. The author was Frances A. Rollin, but she used a male pseudonym.

Additional Bibliography

Reconstruction in Specific States

Edmund L. Drago. *Black Politicians and Reconstruction in Georgia.* Athens, GA: University of Georgia Press, 1982.

———. *Hurrah for Hampton: Black Red Shirts in South Carolina during Reconstruction.* Fayetteville, AR: University of Arkansas Press, 1998.

Luther P. Jackson. *Negro Officeholders in Virginia, 1865– 1895.* Norfolk, VA: Guide Quality Press, 1945.

Peter Kolchin. *First Freedom: The Responses of Alabama's Blacks to Emancipation and Reconstruction.* Westport, CT.: Greenwood Publishing, 1972.

Merline Pitre. *Through Many Dangers, Toils, and Snares: The Black Leadership of Texas, 1868–1900.* Austin, TX: Eakin Press, 1985).

Joe M. Richardson. *The Negro in the Reconstruction of Florida, 1865–1877.* Tallahassee, FL: Florida State University Press, 1965.

Buford Stacher. *Blacks in Mississippi Politics, 1865–1900.* Washington, DC: University Press of America, 1978.

Ted Tunnell. *Crucible of Reconstruction: War, Radicalism and Race in Louisiana, 1862–1877.* Baton Rouge, LA: Louisiana State University Press, 1984.

Charles Vincent. *Black Legislators in Louisiana During Reconstruction.* Baton Rouge, LA: Louisiana State University Press, 1976.

Joel Williamson. *After Slavery: The Negro in South Carolina: 1861–1877.* Chapel Hill, NC: University of North Carolina Press, 1965.

National Politics: Andrew Johnson and the Radical Republicans

Michael Les Benedict. *A Compromise of Principle: Congressional Republicans and Reconstruction.* New York: Norton, 1974.

Eric L. McKitrick. *Andrew Johnson and Reconstruction, 1865–1867.* Chicago: University of Chicago Press, 1960.

James M. McPherson. *The Struggle for Equality: Abolitionists and the Negro in the Civil War and Reconstruction.* Princeton, NJ: Princeton University Press, 1964.

Hans L. Trefousse. *The Radical Republicans: Lincoln's Vanguard for Racial Justice.* Baton Rouge, LA: Louisiana State University Press, 1969.

Economic Issues: Land, Labor, and the Freedmen's Bank

Elizabeth Bethel. *Promiseland: A Century of Life in a Negro Community.* Philadelphia: Temple University Press, 1981.

Carol R. Bleser. *The Promised Land: The History of the South Carolina Land Commission, 1869–1890.* Columbia, SC: University of South Carolina Press, 1969.

Donald G. Nieman. *To Set the Law in Motion: The Freedmen's Bureau and Legal Rights for Blacks, 1865–1869.* Millwood, NY: KTO, 1979.

Carl R. Osthaus. *Freedmen, Philanthropy and Fraud: A History of the Freedman's Savings Bank.* Urbana, IL: University of Illinois Press, 1976.

Violence and the Ku Klux Klan

George C. Rable. *But There Was No Peace: The Role of Violence in the Politics of Reconstruction.* Athens, GA: University of Georgia Press, 1984.

Allen W. Trelease. *White Terror: The Ku Klux Klan Conspiracy and Southern Reconstruction.* New York: Harper & Row, 1973.

Lou Falkner Williams. *The Great South Carolina Ku Klux Klan Trials, 1871–1872.* Athens, GA: University of Georgia Press, 1996.

Autobiography and Biography

Mifflin Wistar Gibbs. *Shadow & Light: An Autobiography.* Lincoln, NE: University of Nebraska Press, 1995.

Peter D. Klingman. *Josiah Walls.* Gainesville, FL: University Presses of Florida, 1976.

Peggy Lamson, *The Glorious Failure: Black Congressman Robert Brown Elliott and Reconstruction in South Carolina.* New York: Norton, 1973.

Edward A. Miller. *Gullah Statesman: Robert Smalls: From Slavery to Congress, 1839–1915.* Columbia, SC: University of South Carolina Press, 1995.

Loren Schweninger. *James T. Rapier and Reconstruction.* Chicago: University of Chicago Press, 1978.

Okon E. Uya. *From Slavery to Public Service: Robert Smalls, 1839–1915.* New York: Oxford University Press, 1971.

Retracing the Odyssey

Washington, DC: Howard University. The Freedmen's Bureau founded this national university in 1867. Oliver O. Howard, the Commissioner of the Bureau, was Howard's first president from 1868 to 1873. His residence, Howard Hall, is the only building that survives from that era. Also located on the campus is the Moorland-Spingarn Research Center, one of the country's richest archives in African-American history.

Wilberforce, Ohio: Wilberforce University and the National Afro-American Museum and Cultural Center. Wilberforce University opened in 1856, and was named after English abolitionist, William Wilberforce. The AME church took over the school in 1863. The historic campus was nearly destroyed by a 1974 tornado. A new campus was built, and the National Afro-American Museum was erected on the old campus. It contains exhibits, an art gallery, theater, and has a picnic area.

Tallahassee, Florida: Union Bank Building. For a time during Reconstruction, a branch of the Freedmen's Savings and Trust Company was located here. The building, constructed in 1840, originally served as a planters' bank. It failed and so did the Freedmen's bank. For a time in the 1920s, Willis Giles, a black man and graduate of Tuskegee Institute, operated a shoe factory in the building. It is currently part of the Museum of Florida History and includes its African-American History teacher in-service program.

Beaufort, South Carolina: The Robert Smalls Home. The Civil War hero and black political leader bought this house in 1863. The home had belonged to the McKee family, and the McKees had also owned Smalls and his mother Lydia when he was a youngster. He had lived on the premises as a slave, and it remained in his hands until his death in 1915.

TIMELINE

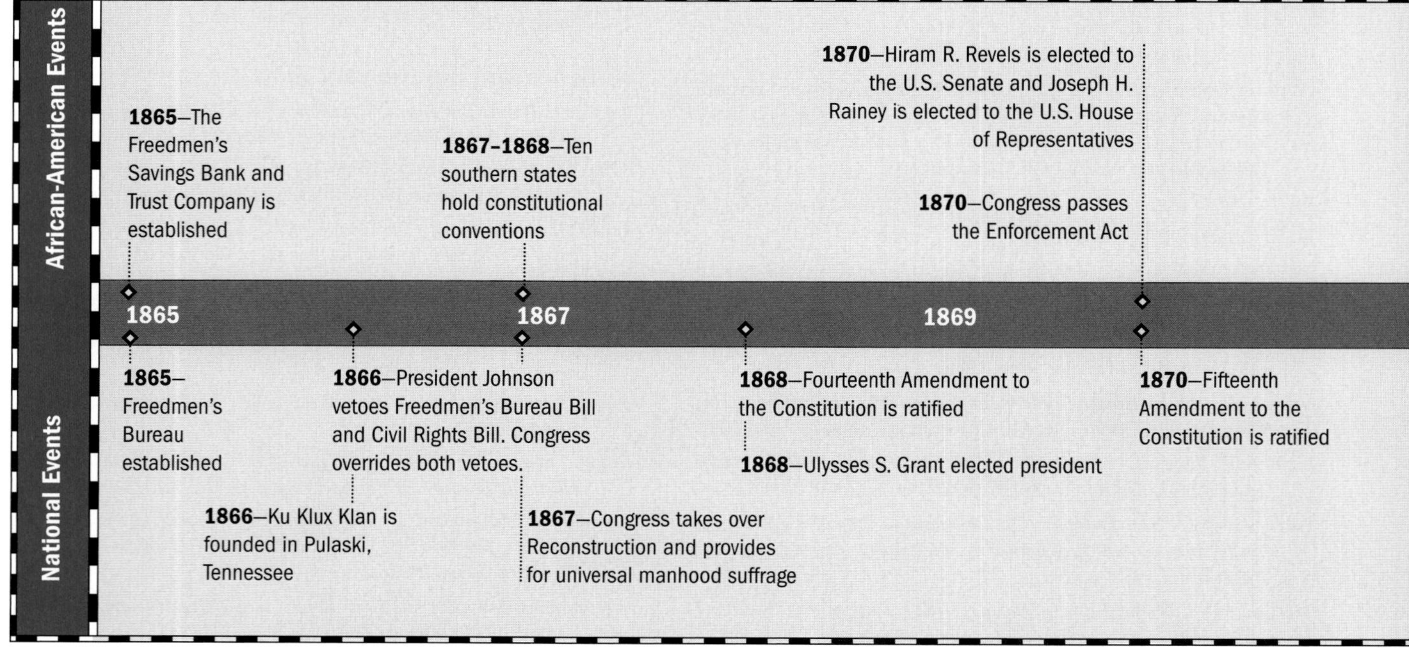

REVIEW, RESEARCH & INTERACT

REVIEW QUESTIONS

1. What issues most concerned black political leaders during Reconstruction?
2. What did black political leaders accomplish and fail to accomplish during Reconstruction? What contributed to their successes and failures?
3. How would you respond to those who argued that black political leaders were unqualified to hold office so soon after the end of slavery?
4. To what extent did African Americans dominate southern politics during Reconstruction? Should we refer to this era as "Black Reconstruction?"
5. Why was it so difficult for the Republican party to maintain control of southern state governments during Reconstruction?
6. What was "redemption?" What happened when redemption occurred? What factors contributed to redemption?
7. How did Reconstruction end? What events marked its conclusion?
8. How would you evaluate Reconstruction? How effective was it in assisting black people to make the transition from slavery to freedom? How effective was it in restoring the southern states to the Union?

Research Navigator.com — RESOURCES FOR COLLEGE RESEARCH ASSIGNMENTS **www.researchnavigator.com**

Chapter 13 looks at the causes and consequences of the failure of Reconstruction. For further research on reasons for this failure, use the tools available to you in Research Navigator.

As you investigate this topic, consider this question: "Why did so many whites in the North lose interest in the situation of blacks in the South?"

- **ContentSelect:** Search in the History database using the search terms *Ku Klux Klan* and *fifteenth amendment.*
- **Links Library:** Access the History: U.S. History database and explore the links for *Compromise of 1877* and *Ku Klux Klan.*

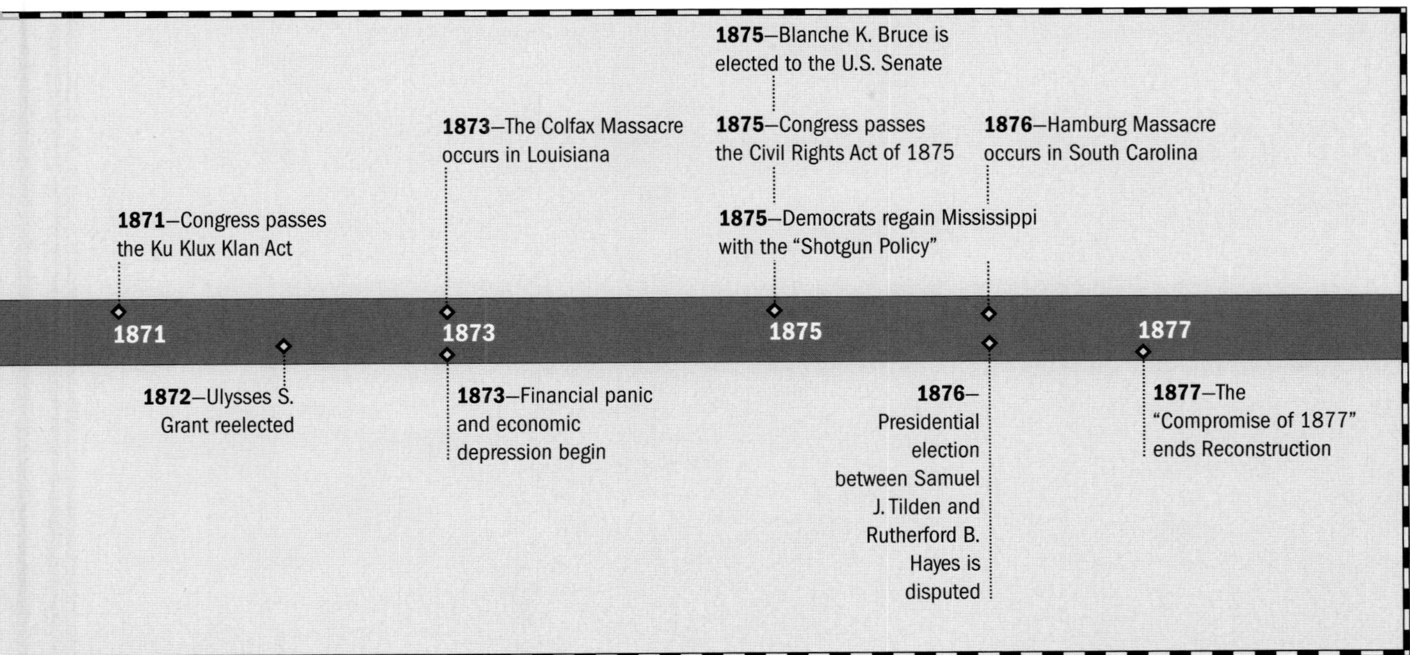

- **New York Times on the Web:** To find more information on the failure of Reconstruction, search the History database using the search term *Civil Rights Act of 1875.*

DOCUMENTS AND ACTIVITIES IN AFRICAN-AMERICAN HISTORY

Documents

13-1 Diary of Joseph Addison Waddell, 1865
13-2 Organization and Principles of the Ku Klux Klan, 1868
13-3 Blanche K. Bruce, Speech in the Senate, 1876
13-4 The New Slavery in the South—An Autobiography
13-5 "When We Worked on Shares, We Couldn't Make Nothing": Henry Blake Talks About Sharecropping after the Civil War

Interactive Map

Dates of Readmission of the Southern States to the Union and Reestablishment of Democratic Party Control, p. 300
http://www.prenhall.com/hine/map13.1

Learning Activity

Did Reconstruction Work for the Freed People?
The war's end was supposed to signal the beginning of a new life for African Americans. How did newly freed slaves attempt to build lives for themselves? What were the principal obstacles they faced?

PART

IV

Searcing for Safe Spaces

RELIGION

1880s–1890s Holiness Movement and Pentecostal churches spread among African Americans

1886 Augustus Tolten ordained first African-American Roman Catholic priest in Rome

1890 Baptist churches count 1,300,000 southern black members, making them the largest African-American denomination

CULTURE

1887 Black players banned from major league baseball

1890s–1920s Emergence of jazz and the Blues among southern blacks

1899 Scott Jopin writes the "Maple Leaf Rag"

1900 James W. Johnson writes "Lift Every Voice and Sing"

1901 Booker T. Washington publishes *Up From Slavery*

1903 W.E.B. DuBois publishes *The Souls of Black Folk*

1905 *The Defender* begins publication in Chicago

1908 Jack Johnson wins heavyweight championship in boxing

1920 Baseball's Negro League organized

1922 Claude McKay publishes *Harlem Shadows*

1924 Jessica R. Faucet publishes *There is Confusion*

1925 Countee Cullen publishes *Color*

Alain Locke publishes *The New Negro*

1926 Carter Woodson organizes Negro History Week

Langston Hughes publishes *The Weary Blues*

1927 James W. Johnson publishes *God's Trombones*

1928 Duke Ellington debuts at the Cotton Club

Claude McKay publishes *Home to Harlem*

1929 Fats Waller's "Ain't Misbehavin" opens on Broadway

1930 James W. Johnson publishes *Black Manhattan*

1933 James W. Johnson publishes his autobiography *Along the Way*

1937 Zora Neale Hurston publishes *Their Eyes Were Watching God*

POLITICS & GOVERNMENT

1869–1889 Four black regiments stationed on the Western frontier

1881 First Jim Crow law segregates trains in Tennessee

1882 South Carolina disenfranchises black voters

1892 Populist Party attracts many black voters

1896 *Plessy v. Ferguson* upholds "separate but equal" doctrine of racial segregation

1898 First black officers command black troops in the Spanish-American War

1899–1901 George H. White serves as the South's last black congressman until 1972

1914 President Woodrow Wilson defends racial segregation

1917–1918 Over 1,000 black men serve as officers in World War I

1920 Nineteenth Amendment grants female suffrage with support from black women

1927 *Nixon v. Herndon* strikes down the white primary laws

SOCIETY & ECONOMY

1867 Independent Order of St. Luke founded

1868 Hampton Institute founded

1870 Howard University Law School founded

1881 Tuskegee Institute founded

1886 Washington County, Texas, race riot

1887 National Colored Farmers' Alliance formed

1892 155 African Americans lynched in the U.S.

1895 Booker T. Washington addresses the Cotton States Exposition in Atlanta

1896 National Association of Colored Women founded

1903 St. Luke Penny Savings Bank established in Richmond

1904 Boule (Sigma Phi Beta) formed

1905 Niagara Movement begins

1906 Brownsville Affair

Atlanta Riot

1908 Springfield Riot

National Association of Colored Graduate Nurses founded

1909 NAACP established

1910 Urban League founded

Negro Fellowship League founded

1914 Universal Negro Improvement Association founded

1915 Reemergence of the Ku Klux Klan

1917 East St. Louis riot

Houston riot

1919 Chicago riot

Elaine, Arkansas riot

Pan-African Congress meets in Paris

Marcus Garvey founds the Black Star Line

1925 National Bar Association founded

A. Philip Randolph founds the Brotherhood of Sleeping Car Porters

NOTEWORTHY INDIVIDUALS

George H. White (1852–1918)

Ida Wells Barnett (1862–1931)

Johnson C. Whittaker (1858–1931)

Booker T. Washington (1856–1915)

W.E.B. Dubois (1868–1963)

William J. Seymour (1870–1922)

C. J. Walker (1867–1919)

Jelly Roll Morton (1890–1941)

W.C. Handy (1873–1958)

Jack Johnson (1878–1946)

Gertrude "Ma" Rainey (1886–1939)

Mary C. Terrell (1863–1954)

Lewis Latimer (1848–1928)

James W. Johnson (1871–1938)

Marcus Garvey (1887–1940)

A. Philip Randolph (1889–1979)

Claude McKay (1890–1948)

Zora Neale Hurston (1901–1960)

Langston Hughes (1902–1967)

Jean Toomer (1894–1962)

Countee Cullen (c. 1903–1946)

Bessie Smith (1894–1937)

Duke Ellington (1899–1974)

Florence Mills (1895–1927)

Paul Robeson (1898–1976)

Carter Woodson (1875–1950)

Scott Joplin (1868–1917)

Fats Waller (1904–1943)

14

White Supremacy Triumphant: African Americans in the South in the Late Nineteenth Century

The Pullman Company manufactured and operated passenger, sleeping, and dining cars for the nation's railroads. The company employed black men to serve and wait on passengers who were usually white people. Black porters and attendants were expected to be properly deferential as they dealt with passengers.

THE supremacy of the white race of the South must be maintained forever, and the domination of the negro race resisted at all points and at all hazards—because the white race is the superior race. This is the declaration of no new truth. It has abided forever in the marrow of our bones, and shall run forever with the blood that feeds Anglo-Saxon hearts.

Henry Grady, Editor of the Atlanta *Constitution*, 1887.

I remember a crowd of white men who rode up on horseback with rifles on their shoulders. I was with my father when they rode up, and I remember starting to cry. They cursed my father, drew their guns and made him salute, made him take off his hat and bow down to them several times. Then they rode away. I was not yet five years old, but I have never forgotten them.

Benjamin E. Mays on his childhood in Epworth, South Carolina, in 1898

Black people struggled against a rising tide of white supremacy in the late nineteenth century. White Southerners—and most white Northerners, for that matter—had long been convinced that as a race they were superior to black people intellectually and culturally. They were certain that black people—because of their inferiority—must play only a subservient role in society. During slavery, white Southerners had taken that subservience for granted. With the Civil War and with slavery's end, black people allied themselves with Radical Republicans during Reconstruction, and they effectively challenged white supremacy as they became citizens and participated in the political system. The federal government established and enforced—though unevenly—the rights of all citizens to enjoy equal protection of the law and due process of law. But the commitment of the Republicans and the federal government wavered, waned, and then largely collapsed by the mid-1870s.

CHAPTER OUTLINE

Politics
- Black Congressmen
- Democrats and Farmer Discontent
- The Colored Farmers' Alliance
- The Populist Party

Disfranchisement
- Evading the Fifteenth Amendment
- Mississippi
- South Carolina
- The Grandfather Clause

Segregation
- Jim Crow
- Segregation on the Railroads
- *Plessy v. Ferguson*
- Streetcar Segregation
- Segregation Proliferates

Racial Etiquette

Violence
- Washington County, Texas
- The Phoenix Riot
- The New Orleans Riot
- Lynching
- Rape

Migration
- The Liberian Exodus
- The Exodusters
- Migration within the South

Black Farm Families
- Sharecroppers
- Renters
- Crop Liens
- Peonage
- Black Landowners
- White Resentment of Black Success

African Americans and Southern Courts
- Segregated Justice
- The Convict Lease System

Conclusion

As memories of the Civil War dimmed and antagonism between white Northerners and Southerners faded, many northern white people who had expressed at least some sympathy for former slaves and hostility toward southern rebels immediately after the war became less concerned with the South. They were increasingly preoccupied with the frontier West or with opportunities presented by the industrial revolution that was so dramatically transforming American society.

Congress, the president, and especially the Supreme Court abandoned the commitment to protect civil and legal rights of African Americans. Political and judicial leaders embraced a laissez-faire approach to social and economic issues. The government would keep hands off the rapidly expanding railroad, steel, and petroleum industries. Neither would government intervene to safeguard the rights of black citizens. The Supreme Court interpreted the Fourteenth Amendment to protect corporations from government regulation, but it failed to protect the basic rights of black people.

As a result, the conservative white Democrats who had regained political power in the South were no more than mildly fearful that the U.S. government or Republicans would intrude as white authority expanded over virtually every aspect of the lives of southern African Americans in the last quarter of the nineteenth century. Between 1875 and 1900, black people in the South were gradually excluded from politics. They were segregated in public life and denied equal, even basic, rights. They were forced to behave in a demeaning and deferential manner to white people. Most of them were limited to doing menial agricultural and domestic jobs that left them poor and dependent on white landowners and merchants. They were often raped, lynched, and beaten. The southern system of justice was systematically unjust.

Unwilling and unable to tolerate such conditions, some African Americans left the South for Africa or the American West. However, most black people remained in the South where many acquired a semblance of education, some managed to purchase land, and a few even prospered.

Politics

In the late nineteenth century, black people remained important in southern politics. Black men served in Congress, state legislatures, and local governments. They received federal patronage appointments to post offices and custom houses. But as southern Democrats steadily disfranchised black voters in the 1880s and 1890s, the number of black politicians declined until the political system was virtually all white by 1900 (see Figure 14–1).

When Reconstruction ended in 1877 and the last Republican state governments collapsed, black men who held major state offices were forced out. In South Carolina, Lieutenant Governor Richard H. Gleaves resigned in 1877, but not without a protest. "I desire to place on record, in the most public and unqualified manner, my sense of the great wrong which thus forces me practically to abandon rights conferred on me, as I fully believe by a majority of my fellow citizens of this State."

For a time, some conservative white Democrats accepted limited black participation in politics as long as no black leader had power over white people and black participation did not challenge white domination. South Carolina's governor Wade Hampton even assured black people that he respected their rights and would appoint qualified black men to minor political offices. Hampton condescendingly told black people in 1878: "We propose to protect you and give you all your rights; but while we do this you cannot expect that we should discriminate in your favor, and say because you are a colored man, you have the right to rule the State. We say to you that we intend to take the best men we can find to represent the State, and you must qualify yourselves to do so before you can expect to be chosen."

Paternalistic Democrats like Hampton did appoint black men to lower-level positions. Hampton, for example, appointed Richard Gleaves and Martin Delany trial justices. In turn, some black men supported the Democrats. A few black Democrats were elected to state legislatures in the 1880s. Some had been Democrats throughout Reconstruction; others had abandoned the Republican party.

Most black voters, however, remained loyal Republicans even though the party had become a hol-

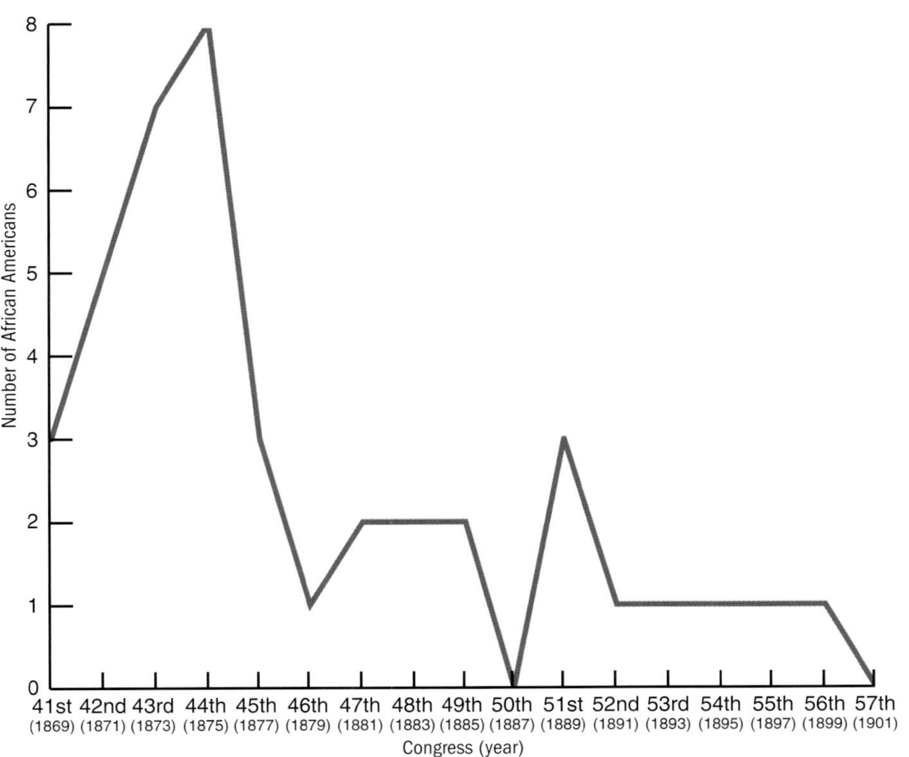

FIGURE 14–1 African-American Representation in Congress, 1867–1900 Black men served in the U.S. Congress from Joseph Rainey's election in 1870 until George H. White's term concluded in 1901. All were Republicans.

DATA EXPLORATION
To explore this data, go to **http://www.prenhall.com/hine/figure14.1**

low shell of what it had been during Reconstruction. Its few white supporters usually shunned black Republicans. The party rarely fielded candidates for statewide elections, limiting itself to local races in regions where Republicans remained strong.

Black Congressmen

Democrats skillfully created oddly shaped congressional districts to confine much of the black population of a state to one district, such as Mississippi's third district, South Carolina's seventh, Virginia's fourth, and North Carolina's second. A black Republican usually represented these districts while the rest of the state elected white Democrats to Congress. This diluted black voting strength, and it reduced the number of white people represented by a black congressman. Thus, Henry Cheatham of North Carolina, John Mercer Langston of Virginia, Thomas E. Miller of South Carolina, and George H. White of North Carolina were elected to the House of Representatives long after Reconstruction had ended (see Table 14–1).

But like their predecessors during Reconstruction, these black men wielded only limited power in Washington. They could not persuade their white colleagues to enact significant legislation to benefit their black constituents. They did, however, get Republican presidents to appoint black men and women to federal positions in their districts—including post offices and custom houses—and they spoke out about the plight of African Americans. North Carolina's George H. White, for example, rebuked white leaders for their readiness to label black people as inferior while denying them the means to prove otherwise. "It is easy . . . to taunt us with our inferiority, at the same time not mentioning the causes of this inferiority. It is rather hard to be accused of shiftlessness and idleness when the accuser . . . closes the avenues for labor and industrial pursuits to us. It is hardly fair to accuse us of ignorance when it was made a crime under the former order of things to learn enough about letters to even read the Word of God."

Democrats and Farmer Discontent

Black involvement in politics survived Reconstruction, but it did not survive the nineteenth century. Divisions within the Democratic party and the rise of a new political party—the Populists—accompanied successful efforts to remove black people entirely from southern politics.

Table 14–1
Black Members of the U.S. Congress, 1870–1901

	Dates	Name	State	Occupation	Prewar Status
1.	1870–1879	Joseph H. Rainey	South Carolina	Barber	Slave, then freed
2.	1870–1873	Jefferson Long	Georgia	Tailor, storekeeper	Slave
3.	1870–1873	Hiram Revels*	Mississippi	Barber, minister, teacher, college president	Free
4.	1871–1877	Josiah T. Walls	Florida	Editor, planter, teacher, lawyer	Slave
5.	1871–1873	Benjamin Turner	Alabama	Businessman, farmer, merchant	Slave
6.	1871–1873	Robert C. DeLarge	South Carolina	Tailor	Free
7.	1871–1875	Robert B. Elliott	South Carolina	Lawyer	Free
8.	1873–1879	Richard H. Cain	South Carolina	AME minister	Free
9.	1873–1875	Alonzo J. Ransier	South Carolina	Shipping clerk, editor	Free
10.	1873–1875	James T. Rapier	Alabama	Planter, editor, lawyer, teacher	Free
11.	1873–1877, 1882–1883	John R. Lynch	Mississippi	Planter, lawyer, photographer	Slave
12.	1875–1881	Blanche K. Bruce*	Mississippi	Planter, teacher, editor	Slave
13.	1875–1877	Jeremiah Haralson	Alabama	Minister	Slave
14.	1875–1877	John A. Hyman	North Carolina	Storekeeper, farmer	Slave
15.	1875–1877	Charles E. Nash	Louisiana	Mason, cigar maker	Free
16.	1875–1887	Robert Smalls	South Carolina	Ship pilot, editor	Slave
17.	1883–1887	James E. O'Hara	North Carolina	Lawyer	Free
18.	1889–1893	Henry P. Cheatham	North Carolina	Lawyer, teacher	Slave
19.	1889–1891	Thomas E. Miller	South Carolina	Lawyer, college president	Free
20.	1889–1891	John M. Langston	Virginia	Lawyer	Free
21.	1893–1897	George W. Murray	South Carolina	Teacher	Slave
22.	1897–1901	George H. White	North Carolina	Lawyer	Slave

*Revels and Bruce served in the Senate and the twenty remaining black legislators served in the House of Representatives.

Militant Democrats stridently opposed the more moderate and paternalistic conservatives who took charge after Reconstruction. In the eyes of the militants, these redeemers seemed too willing to tolerate even limited black participation in politics, while showing little interest in the needs of white yeoman farmers. Dissatisfied independents, "readjusters," and other disaffected white people resented the domination of the Democratic party by former planters, wealthy businessmen, and lawyers who often favored limited government and reduced state support for schools, asylums, orphanages, and prisons while encouraging industry and railroads. Nor did the redeemer and paternalistic Democrats always agree among themselves. Some did favor agricultural education, the establishment of boards of health, and even separate colleges for black students. This lack of redeemer unity permitted insurgent Democrats and even Republicans sometimes to exploit economic and racial issues to undermine Democratic solidarity.

Many farmers felt betrayed as the industrial revolution transformed American society. They fed and clothed America, but large corporations, banks, and railroads increasingly dominated economic life. Wealth was concentrated in the hands of big industrialists and financiers. Farmers were no longer self-sufficient, admired for their hard work and self-reliance. They now depended on banks for loans, were exploited when they bought and sold goods, and found themselves at the mercy of railroads when they shipped their agricultural commodities. As businessmen got richer, farmers got poorer.

Small independent (yeoman) farmers in the South suffered from a sharp decline in the price of cotton between 1865 and 1890. Overwhelmed by debt, many lost their land and were forced into tenant farming and sharecropping. By 1890 most farmers, both black and white—between 58 percent and 62 percent in each state in the deep South—worked land they did not own.

In response to their economic woes and political weakness, farmers organized. In the 1870s they formed the Patrons of Husbandry, or Grange. Initially a social and fraternal organization, the Grange promoted the formation of cooperatives and involvement in politics. Grangers especially favored government regulation of the rates railroads charged to transport crops. By the early 1880s, many hard-pressed small farmers turned to farmers' alliances. The first of these was the Southern Farmers' Alliance, which formed in Texas. Alliances soon spread throughout the South and northward into the states of the Great Plains and westward to the Pacific coast. These organizations further encouraged farmers to buy and sell products cooperatively and to unite politically. They favored railroad regulation, currency inflation (to increase crop prices and ease debt burdens), and support for agricultural education. By 1888 many of them joined in the National Farmers' Alliance.

The Colored Farmers' Alliance

Although the alliances were radical on economic issues, they were conservative on racial issues and did not challenge the racial status quo. The Southern Alliance did not include black farmers, who instead formed their own Colored Farmers' Alliance. It spread from Texas across the South in 1888 and 1889 and claimed over one million members. Even if it did not have that many supporters, the Colored Farmers' Alliance was one of the largest black organizations in American history. When the white alliances met in St. Louis in 1889, so did the black alliance—in a separate convention. The alliances maintained strict racial distinctions but promised to cooperate to resolve their economic woes.

However, black and white alliance members did not always see their economic difficulties from the same perspective. Some of the white farmers owned the land that the black farmers lived on and worked. Black men saw their alliance as a way of getting a political education. In 1891, sixteen black men organized a branch of the Colored Farmers' Alliance in St. Landry Parish in Louisiana. Their purpose was to help their race and their families and to acquire enough information to vote effectively. "This organization is for the purpose of trying to elevate our race, to make us better citizens, better husbands, better fathers and sons, to educate ourselves so that we may be able to vote more intelligently on questions that are of vital importance to our people."

But white people were less certain that they wanted black men to vote at all—intelligently or otherwise. Many white alliance members harbored serious doubts about the right of black men to vote, and they opposed electing black men to office. Paradoxically, they also encouraged black men to vote as long as the black voters supported candidates the alliances backed, and by the late 1880s alliance-backed candidates in the South were elected to state legislatures, to Congress, and to four governorships.

The Populist Party

By 1892, many alliance farmers threw their political support to a new political party—the People's party, generally known as the Populist party—that mounted a serious challenge to the Democrats and Republicans. Convinced that neither of the traditional parties cared about the plight of American farmers and industrial workers, the Populists hoped to wrestle political control of the nation's economy from bankers and industrialists and their allies in the Republican and Democratic parties and to let the "people" shape the country's economic destiny. The Populists favored no less than the government takeover of railroads, telegraph, and telephone companies. The Populists ran candidates for local and state offices and for Congress. In 1892 they nominated James B. Weaver of Iowa for president. The Populists urged southern white men to abandon the Democratic party and southern black men to reject the Republican party and to unite politically to support the Populists.

The foremost proponent of black and white political unity was Thomas Watson of Georgia. He and other Populist leaders believed that economic and political cooperation could transcend racial differences. During the 1892 campaign, Watson explained that black and white farmers faced the same economic exploitation, but that they failed to cooperate with each other because of race. "The white tenant," he said,

> lives adjoining the colored tenant. Their homes are almost equally destitute of comforts. Their living is confined to bare necessities. They are equally burdened with heavy taxes. They pay the same high rent for gullied and impoverished land. . . .
>
> Now the Peoples' Party says to these two men, You are kept apart that you may be separately fleeced of your earnings. You are made to hate each other because upon that hatred is rested the keystone of the arch of financial despotism which enslaves you both. You are deceived and blinded that you may not see how this race antagonism perpetuates a monetary system which beggars both.

Despite such remarks, Watson was not calling for improved race relations. He opposed economic exploitation that was disguised by race, but when Democrats accused him of promoting racial reconciliation, he denied it and bluntly supported segregation to a black audience:

> They say I am an advocate of social equality between the whites and the blacks. THAT IS AN ABSOLUTE FALSEHOOD, and the man who utter[s] it knows it, I have done no such thing, and you colored men know it as well as the men who formulated the slander. It is best for your race and my race that we dwell apart in our private affairs. It is best for you to go to your churches, and I will go to mine; it is best that you send your children to the colored school, and I'll send my children to mine; you invite your colored friends to your home, and I'll invite my friends to mine.

Years after the failure of the Populists, Watson became a racial demagogue who warmly and thoroughly supported white supremacy. But in 1892, Watson and the Populists desperately wanted black and white voters to support Populist candidates. The Populists lost the national election that year and again in 1896, although they did win several congressional and governor's races. Southern Democrats, furious and outraged at the Populist appeal for black votes, resorted again to fraud, violence, and terror to prevail. It is not a coincidence that in 1892, when the Democrats carried every southern state, 235 people were lynched in the United States, more than in any other year in U.S. history.

The Populist challenge heightened the fears of southern Democrats that black voters could tip the balance of elections if the white vote split. But years before the alliances and the Populists emerged, southern Democrats had begun to eliminate the black vote.

Disfranchisement

As early as the late 1870s, southern Democrats had found ways to undermine black political power. Violence and intimidation, so effective during Reconstruction, continued in the 1880s and 1890s. Frightened, discouraged, or apathetic, many black men stopped voting. Black sharecroppers and renters could sometimes be intimidated or bribed by their white landlords not to vote, or to vote for candidates the landlord favored.

There was also simple injustice. In 1890, black congressman Thomas E. Miller ran for reelection and won—or so he thought. But he was charged with using illegal ballots and declared the loser. He appealed to the South Carolina Supreme Court, which ruled that while his ballots were printed on the required white paper, it was "white paper of a distinctly yellow tinge." He did not return to Congress.

Evading the Fifteenth Amendment

More militant and determined Democrats in the South were not content to rely on an assortment of unreliable methods to curtail the black vote. Some "legal" means had to be found to prevent black men from voting. However, the Fifteenth Amendment to the Constitution was a serious obstacle to this goal. It explicitly stated that the right to vote could not be denied on "account of race, color, or previous condition of servitude."

White leaders worried that if they imposed what were then legally acceptable barriers to voting—literacy tests, poll taxes, and property qualifications—they would disfranchise many white, as well as black voters. But resourceful Democrats committed to white supremacy found ways around this problem. In 1882, for example, South Carolina passed the Eight Box Law, a primitive literacy test that required voters to deposit separate ballots for separate election races in the proper ballot box. Illiterate voters could not identify the boxes unless white election officials assisted them.

Mississippi

Mississippi made the most concerted and successful effort to eliminate black voters without openly violating the Fifteenth Amendment. Black men had continued to vote in Mississippi despite hostility and intimidation. In 1889 black leaders from forty Mississippi counties protested the "violent and criminal suppression of the black vote." In response white men called a constitutional convention to do away with the black vote.

With one black delegate and 134 white delegates, the convention adopted complex voting requirements that—without mentioning race—disfranchised black voters. Voting required proof of residency and payment of all taxes, including a two-dollar poll tax. A person who had been convicted of arson, bigamy, or petty theft—crimes the delegates associated with black people—could not vote. People convicted of so-called white crimes—murder, rape, and grand larceny—could vote.

Above all, the new Mississippi constitution required voters to be literate, but with a notable exception. Illiterate men could still qualify to vote by demonstrating that they understood the constitution if the document was read to them. It was taken for granted that white voting registrars would accept almost all white applicants and fail most black applicants seeking to register under this provision.

South Carolina

Black voting had been declining in South Carolina since the end of Reconstruction. In the 1876 election, 91,870 black men voted; in the 1888 election, only 13,740 did. Unhappy that even so few voters might decide an election, U.S. senator Benjamin R. Tillman won approval for a constitutional convention in 1895. The convention followed Mississippi's lead and created an "understanding clause," but not without a vigorous protest from black leaders.

Six black men and 154 white men were elected to the South Carolina convention. Two of the black men—Robert Smalls and William Whipper (see Chapter 13)—had been delegates to the 1868 constitutional convention. The six black men protested black disfranchisement. Thomas E. Miller explained that it was not just a matter of black power, but that the basic rights of citizens were at stake. "The Negroes do not want to dominate. They do not and would not have social equality, but they do want to cast a ballot for the men who make their laws and administer the laws. I stand here pleading for justice to a people whose rights are about to be taken away with one fell swoop."

It was all for naught. Black voters were disfranchised in South Carolina. White delegates did not even pretend that elections should be fair. William Henderson of Berkeley County admitted

> We don't propose to have fair elections. We will get left at that every time. . . . I tell you, gentlemen, if we have fair elections in Berkeley we can't carry it. There's no use to talk about it. The black man is learning to read faster than the white man. And if he comes up and can read you have got to let him vote. Now are you going to throw it out. . . . We are perfectly disgusted with hearing so much about fair elections. Talk all around, but make it fair and you'll see what'll happen.

The Grandfather Clause

In 1898, Louisiana added a new twist to disfranchisement. Its grandfather clause stipulated that only men who had been eligible to vote before 1867—or whose father or grandfather had been eligible before that year—would be qualified to vote. Since virtually no black men had been eligible to vote before 1867—most had just emerged from slavery—the law immediately disfranchised almost all black voters. In Louisiana in 1896, 130,000 black men voted; in 1904, 1,342 voted.

Except for Kentucky and West Virginia, each southern state had enacted elaborate restrictions on voting by the 1890s. As a result, few black men continued to vote, and no black men were elected to office.

The federal government demonstrated a fleeting willingness to protect black voting rights. Republican Senator Henry Cabot Lodge of Massachusetts introduced a bill in 1890 to send federal supervisors to states and congressional districts where election fraud was alleged. But southern Democrats blocked it.

The Spread of Disfranchisement

	State	Strategies
1889	Florida	Poll tax
	Tennessee	Poll tax
1890	Mississippi	Poll tax, literacy test, understanding clause
1891	Arkansas	Poll tax
1893, 1901	Alabama	Poll tax, literacy test, grandfather clause
1894, 1895	South Carolina	Poll tax, literacy test, understanding clause
1894, 1902	Virginia	Poll tax, literacy test, understanding clause
1897, 1898	Louisiana	Poll tax, literacy test, grandfather clause
1899, 1900	North Carolina	Poll tax, literacy test, grandfather clause
1902	Texas	Poll tax
1908	Georgia	Poll tax, literacy test, understanding clause, grandfather clause

Source: Goldfield et al., *The American Journey* (1991, Prentice Hall)

Segregation

When black attorney T. McCants Stewart visited Columbia, South Carolina, in 1885, he told readers of the New York *Age* that he had been pleasantly received and had encountered little discrimination. "I can ride in first class cars on the railroads and in the streets. I can go into saloons and get refreshments even as in New York. I can stop in and drink a glass of soda and be more politely waited upon than in some parts of New England." Stewart's visit occurred before most segregation laws requiring separation of the races in public places had been

TRACK 16

enacted. In fact, the word segregation was almost never used before the twentieth century.

Not that black and white people mingled freely in the 1880s and the 1890s. They did not. Since Reconstruction, schools, hospitals, asylums, and cemeteries had been segregated. Many restaurants and hotels did not admit black people, and many black people did not venture where they felt unwelcome or where they were likely to meet hostility. But what came to be known as "Jim Crow" had not yet become legally embedded in the southern way of life.

Jim Crow

The term Jim Crow originated with a minstrel show routine called "Jump Jim Crow" that a white performer, Thomas "Daddy" Rice, created in the 1830s and 1840s. Rice blackened his face with charcoal and ridiculed black people. How Rice's character came to be synonymous with segregation and discrimination is not clear. What is clear is that by the end of the nineteenth century Jim Crow and segregation were rapidly expanding in the South, greatly restricting the lives of African Americans.

In the decades following slavery's demise, segregation evolved gradually as an arrangement to enforce white control and domination. Many white Southerners resented the presence of black people in public facilities, places of entertainment, and business establishments. If black people were—as white Southerners believed—a subordinate race, then their proximity in shops, parks, and on passenger trains suggested an unacceptable equality in public life.

There were, moreover, many black people who acquiesced in some facets of racial separation. During Reconstruction, people of color formed their own churches and social organizations. Black people were invariably more comfortable around people of their own race than they were among white people. Furthermore, black Southerners often accepted separate seating in theaters, concert halls, and other facilities that previously had been closed to them. Segregation represented an improvement over exclusion.

Segregation on the Railroads

Many white people particularly objected to the presence of black people in the first-class coaches of trains. Before segregation laws, white passengers and railroad conductors sometimes forced black people who had purchased first-class tickets into second-class coaches. In 1889 black Baptists from Savannah bought first-class tickets to travel to a convention in Indianapolis. News was telegraphed ahead, and they were confronted by a white mob at a railroad stop in Georgia where they were threatened and beaten. A white man shoved a pistol into the breast of a black woman who had screamed in fear. He demanded, "You G-d d-d heffer, if you don't hush your mouth and get out of here, I will blow your G-d d-d brains out."

In another instance, a young black woman, Mary Church (later Mary Church Terrell), was traveling alone in a first-class coach when the conductor attempted to move her to the second-class car. She managed to remain, but only after informing the conductor that she would send a telegram to her father telling him that "you are forcing me to ride all night in a Jim Crow car. He will sue the railroad for compelling his daughter who has a first class ticket to ride in a second class car."

The first segregation laws involved passenger trains. Despite the spirited opposition of black politicians, the Tennessee legislature mandated segregation on railroad coaches in 1881. Florida passed a similar law in 1887. The railroads opposed these laws, but not because they wanted to protect the civil rights of black people. Rather, they were concerned about the expense of maintaining separate cars or sections within cars for black and white people. Whether they could pay for a first-class ticket or not, most black passengers found themselves confined to grimy second-class cars crowded with smoking and tobacco-chewing black and white men. Hitched at the head of the train just behind the smoke-belching locomotive, these cars were filthy with soot and cinders.

Plessy v. Ferguson

In 1891 the Louisiana legislature required segregated trains within the state, despite opposition from a black organization, the American Citizens' Equal Rights Association of Louisiana, the state's eighteen black legislators, and the railroads.

In a test case, black people challenged the Louisiana law and hoped to demonstrate its absurdity by enlisting the support of a black man who was almost indistinguishable from a white person. In 1892 Homer A. Plessy bought a first-class ticket and attempted to ride on the coach designated for white people. Plessy, who was only one-eighth black, was arrested for violating the new segregation law.

The case—*Plessy v. Ferguson*—wound its way through the judicial system. Plessy's lawyers argued

VOICES

Majority and Dissenting Opinions on *Plessy v. Ferguson*

The Supreme Court's 8 to 1 decision in Plessy v. Ferguson *sanctioned legal segregation and opened the way for a host of segregation laws throughout the South. The majority opinion ruled that segregation was constitutional so long as both races were provided equal facilities. In practice, of course, the facilities for African Americans were invariably inferior to those for white people.*

From Justice Henry Brown of Michigan's majority opinion:

The object of the [Fourteenth] amendment was undoubtedly to enforce the absolute equality of the two races before the law, but in the nature of things it could not have been intended to abolish distinctions based upon color, or to enforce social, as distinguished from political, equality, or a commingling of the two races upon terms unsatisfactory to either.

We consider the underlying fallacy of the plaintiff's argument to consist in the assumption that the enforced separation of the two races stamps the colored race with a badge of inferiority. If this be so, it is not by the reason of anything found in the act, but solely because the colored race chooses to put that construction upon it. . . . If the two races are to meet on terms of social equality, it must be the result of natural affinities, a mutual appreciation of each other's merits and a voluntary consent of individuals. . . . Legislation is powerless to eradicate racial instincts or to abolish distinctions based upon physical differences. . . . If one race be inferior to the other socially, the Constitution of the United States cannot put them upon the same plane.

From Justice John Marshall Harlan of Kentucky, the lone dissent:

In my opinion, the judgement this day rendered will, in time, prove to be quite as pernicious as the decision made by this tribunal in the Dred Scott Case. . . . But it seems that we have yet, in some of the states, a dominant race, a superior class of citizens, which assumes to regulate the enjoyment of civil rights, common to all citizens, upon the basis of race. The present decision, it may well be apprehended, will not only stimulate aggressions, more or less brutal and irritating, upon the admitted rights of colored citizens, but it will encourage the belief that it is possible, by means of state enactments, to defeat the beneficent purposes which the people of the United States had in view when they adopted the recent amendments of the Constitution, by one which the blacks of this country were made citizens of the United States and of the states in which they respectively reside and whose privileges and immunities, as citizens, the states are forbidden to abridge. . . . What can more certainly arouse race hate, what more certainly create and perpetuate a feeling of distrust between these races, than state enactments which in fact proceed on the ground that the colored citizens are so inferior and degraded that they cannot be allowed to sit in public coaches occupied by white citizens? . . . But in view of the Constitution, in the eyes of the law, there is in this country no superior, dominant, ruling class of citizens. There is no caste here. Our Constitution is color-blind, and neither knows nor tolerates classes among citizens. In respect of civil rights, all citizens are equal before the law.

QUESTIONS

1. What does Justice Brown mean when he distinguishes between political and social equality? How does his position compare to that of Congressmen Rapier and Elliott when they argued for civil rights in 1874? (p. 299)
2. With what arguments does Justice Harlan counter the majority opinion?

Source: 163 U.S. 537 United States Reports: *Cases Adjudged in the Supreme Court* (New York: Banks and Brothers, 1896).

that segregation deprived their client of equal protection of the law guaranteed by the Fourteenth Amendment. But in 1896 the U.S. Supreme Court in an 8 to 1 decision upheld Louisiana's segregation statute. Speaking for the majority, Justice Henry Brown ruled that the law, merely because it required separation of the races, did not deny Plessy his rights, nor did it imply that he was inferior. The lone dissenter from this "separate but equal" doctrine, Justice John Marshall Harlan, whose father had owned slaves, likened the majority opinion to the Dred Scott decision thirty-nine years earlier. Thus with the complicity of the Supreme Court, the Fourteenth Amendment was emasculated. It no longer afforded black Americans equal treatment under the law. After the Plessy decision, southern states and cities passed hundreds of laws that created an American apartheid—an elaborate system of racial separation.

Streetcar Segregation

In the late nineteenth century, before the automobile, the electric streetcar was the primary form of public transportation in American cities and towns. Beginning with Georgia in 1891, states and cities across the South segregated these vehicles. In some communities, the streetcar companies had to operate separate cars for black and white passengers; in other towns they designated separate sections within individual cars. The companies often resisted segregation, citing the expense of duplicating equipment and hiring more employees.

But black people were even more bitterly opposed to Jim Crow streetcars. During Reconstruction, they had fended off streetcar discrimination with boycotts and sit-ins. Thirty years later, they tried the same techniques. There were streetcar boycotts in at least twenty-five southern cities between 1891 and 1910. Black people refused to ride segregated cars in Atlanta, Augusta, Jacksonville, Montgomery, Mobile, Little Rock, and Columbia. They walked or took horse-drawn hacks. Initially, the boycotts succeeded in Atlanta and Augusta, where segregation was briefly abandoned. The boycotts seriously hurt the streetcar companies.

Black people also attempted to form alternative transportation companies in Portsmouth and Norfolk, Virginia, and in Chattanooga and Nashville, Tennessee. In 1905 the black community in Nashville organized a black-owned bus company and committed $25,000 to it. They purchased five buses, but they could not raise enough capital to keep the company going, and it failed after a few months.

Segregation Proliferates

Jim Crow proceeded inexorably. "White" and "colored" signs appeared in railroad stations, theaters, auditoriums, and restrooms and over drinking fountains. Southern white people were willing to go to any length to keep black and white people apart. Courtrooms maintained separate Bibles for black and white witnesses "to swear to tell the truth." By 1915, Oklahoma mandated white and colored public telephone booths. New Orleans attempted to segregate customers of black and white prostitutes, but only achieved mixed results.

Although *Plessy v. Ferguson* required "separate but equal" facilities for black and white people, when facilities were made available to black people, they were inferior to those afforded white people. Often, no facilities at all were provided for people of color. They were simply excluded. Few hotels, restaurants, libraries, bowling alleys, public parks, amusement parks, swimming pools, golf courses, or tennis courts would admit black people. The only exceptions would be black people who accompanied or assisted white people. For example, a black woman caring for a white child could visit a "white only" public park with the child, but she dare not visit it with her own child.

Racial Etiquette

Since slavery, white people had insisted that black people act in an obedient and subservient manner. Such behavior made white dominance clear. After emancipation, white Southerners sought to maintain that dominance through a complex pattern of racial etiquette that determined how black and white people dealt with each other in their day-to-day affairs.

Black and white people did not shake hands. Black people did not look directly into the eyes of white people. They were supposed to stare at the ground when addressing white men and women. Black men removed their hats in the presence of white people. White men did not remove their hats in a black home or in the presence of a black woman. Black people went to the back door, not the front door, of a white house. A black man or boy was never to look at a white woman. A black man in Mississippi observed, "You couldn't smile at a white woman. If you did you'd be hung from a limb." It was a serious offense if a black male touched a white woman, even inadvertently.

White customers were always served first in a store, even if a black customer had been the first to arrive. Black women could not try on clothing in white businesses. White people did not use titles of respect—mister, Mrs., miss—when addressing black adults. They used first names, or "boy" or "girl," or sometimes even "nigger." Older black people were sometimes called "auntie" or "uncle." But black people were expected to use mister, Mrs., and miss when addressing white people, including adolescents. "Boss" or "cap'n" might do for a white man.

Violence

In the late nineteenth century, the South was a violent place. Political and mob violence, so prevalent during Reconstruction, continued unabated into the 1880s and 1890s as Democrats often used armed force to drive the dwindling number of black and white Republicans out of politics.

Washington County, Texas

In 1886 in Washington County in eastern Texas, Democrats were determined to keep the political control that they had only won in 1884 through fraud. Masked Democrats tried to seize ballot boxes in a Republican precinct. But armed black men resisted and, with a shotgun blast, killed one of the white men. Eight black men were arrested. A mob of white men in disguise broke into the jail, kidnapped three of the black men, and lynched them. Three white Republicans fled for their lives, but convinced federal authorities to investigate. The U.S. Attorney twice tried to secure convictions for election fraud. The first trial ended in a hung jury, the second in acquittal. The white Democratic sheriff did not investigate the lynching. But the black man charged with firing the shotgun was sentenced to twenty-five years in prison.

The Phoenix Riot

In the tiny South Carolina community of Phoenix in 1898, a white Republican candidate for Congress urged black men to fill out an affidavit if they were not permitted to vote. This produced a confrontation with Democrats. Words were exchanged, shots were fired, and the Republican candidate was wounded. White men then went on a rampage through rural Greenwood County. Black men were killed—how many is unknown. Others, including Benjamin Mays's father, as related in one of the quotes that opens this chapter—had to humiliate themselves by bowing down and saluting white men.

The Wilmington Riot

While white men roamed Greenwood County in search of black victims, an even bloodier riot erupted in Wilmington, North Carolina. Black men still held political offices in 1898 in Wilmington, including seats on the city council. White Democrats were determined to drive them from power. During the tense campaign, the young editor of a local black newspaper, Alex Manly, published an editorial condemning white men for the sexual exploitation of black women. Manly also suggested that black men had sexual liaisons with rural white women, which infuriated the white community. "Poor white men are careless in the matter of protecting their women, especially on the farms. . . . Tell your men that it is no worse for a black man to be intimate with a white woman than for a white man to be intimate with a colored woman . . . Don't think ever that your women will remain pure while you are debauching ours."

A white mob that included some of Wilmington's business and professional leaders destroyed the newspaper office. Black officials resigned in a vain attempt to prevent further violence. But at least a dozen black men were murdered. Some 1,500 black residents of Wilmington fled. White people then bought up black homes and property at bargain rates. Black congressman George H. White, who represented Wilmington and North Carolina's second district, served the remainder of his term and then moved north. He ruefully remarked, "I can no longer live in North Carolina and be a man." White was the last black man to serve in Congress from the South until the election of Andrew Young in Atlanta in 1972.

The New Orleans Riot

Robert Charles was a 34-year-old literate laborer who had migrated to New Orleans from rural Mississippi. Infuriated by lynching, he was tantalized by the prospect of emigration to Liberia promoted by AME Bishop Henry M. Turner. On July 23, 1900, Charles and a friend were harassed by white New Orleans police officers. One of the officers attempted to beat Charles with a night stick. Failing to subdue the large black man, the officer then drew a gun. Charles pulled out his own gun, and each man wounded the other. Charles fled and for a time evaded authorities. He was tracked down to a rooming house where he had secluded himself with a Winchester rifle with which he proceeded to shoot his tormentors. Eventually, a white mob that numbered as many as twenty thousand gathered. In the meantime, Charles—an expert marksmen—methodically shot twenty-seven white people, killing seven, including four policemen. Finally, burned out of the dwelling, Charles was shot and his corpse stomped beyond recognition by enraged white people. Four days of rioting ensued in which at least a dozen black people were killed and many more injured.

Lynching

Lynching had become common in the South by the 1890s. Between 1889 and 1932, 3,745 people were lynched in the United States (see Figure 14–2). An average of two to three people were lynched every week for thirty years. Most lynchings happened in the South, and black men were usually the victims. Sometimes white people were lynched. In 1891 in New Orleans eleven Italians were lynched for alleged involvement with the Mafia and for the murder of the city's police chief. For black Southerners, violence was an ever-present possibility. Rarely did a sheriff or police officer protect a potential victim, and even if one did, that protection was often not enough.

The people who carried out the lynchings were never apprehended, tried, or convicted. Prominent community members frequently encouraged and even participated in lynch mobs. White political leaders, journalists, and clergymen rarely denounced lynching in public. The Atlanta *Constitution* dismissed lynching as relatively inconsequential. "There are places and occasions when the natural fury of men cannot be restrained by all the laws in Christendom."

There was no such thing as a civilized lynching. Lynchings were barbaric, savage, and hideous. Such mob brutality was another manifestation of white supremacy. Black people were murdered, beaten, burned, and mutilated for trivial reasons—or for no reason. Most white Southerners justified lynching as a response to the raping of white women by black men. But many lynchings involved no alleged rape, and even when they did, the victims often had no connection to the alleged offense.

After a white family was murdered in Statesboro, Georgia, in 1904, Paul Reed and Will Cato were convicted of murder and then seized by a mob that invaded the courtroom. They were burned alive in front of a large crowd. Then the violence spread. Albert Roger and his son were lynched "for being Negroes." A black man named McBride attempted to protect his wife who had had a baby three days earlier. He "was beaten, killed, and shot to death."

Mobs often attacked black people who had achieved economic success. In Memphis, Thomas Moss with two friends opened the People's Grocery Company in a black neighborhood. The store flourished, but it competed with a white-owned grocery. "[T]hey were succeeding too well," one of Moss's friends observed. After the white grocer had had the

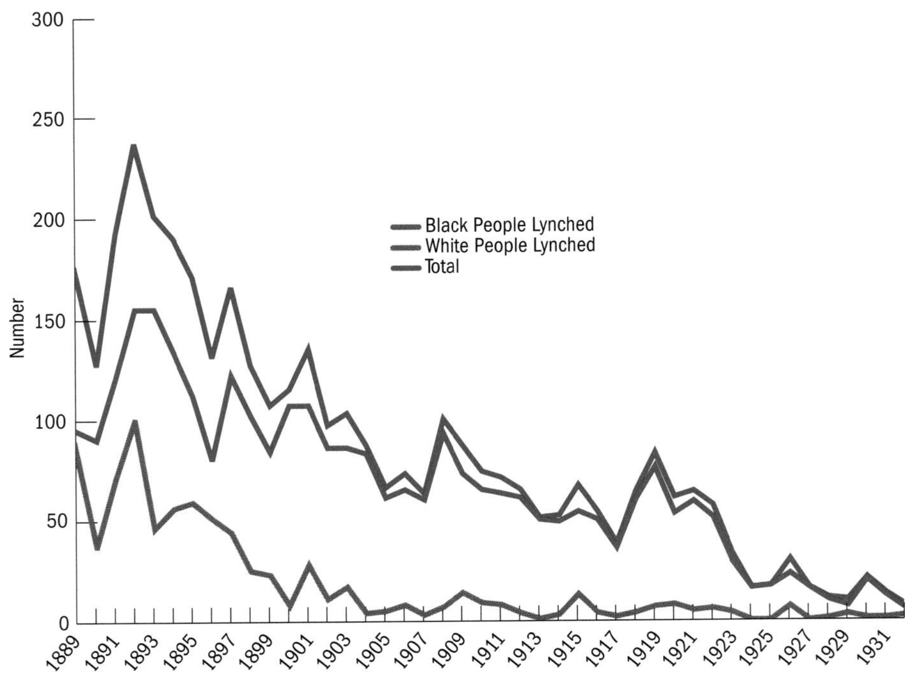

FIGURE 14–2 Lynching in the United States: 1889–1932
Depending on the source, statistics on lynching vary. It was difficult to assemble information on lynching, particularly in the nineteenth century. Not every lynching was recorded.
Source: *The Negro Year Book*, 1931–32, p. 293.

Lynchings were common and public events in the South at the turn of the century. Often hundreds of people took part in and witnessed these gruesome spectacles.

three black men indicted for conspiracy, black people organized a protest and violence followed. The three black men were jailed. A white mob attacked the jail, lynched them, and then looted their store. Ida B. Wells, a newspaper editor and a friend of Moss, was heartbroken. "A finer, cleaner man than he never walked the streets of Memphis." She considered his lynching an "excuse to get rid of Negroes who were acquiring wealth and property and thus keep the race terrorized and keep the nigger down." Responding to the incident in her paper, Wells began a lifelong crusade against lynching. (See *Profile: Ida Wells Barnett.*)

Though less often than men, black women were also lynched. In 1914 in Wagoner County, Oklahoma, seventeen-year-old Marie Scott was lynched because her brother had killed a white man who had raped her. In Valdosta, Georgia, in 1918 after Mary Turner's husband was lynched, she publicly vowed to bring those responsible to justice. Though she was eight months pregnant, a mob considered her determination a threat. They seized her, tied her ankles together, and hanged her upside down from a tree. A member of the mob slit her abdomen, and her nearly full-term child fell to the ground. The mob stomped the infant to death. They then set her clothes on fire and shot her.

Rape

Although white people often justified lynching as a response to the presumed threat black men posed to the virtue of white women, white men routinely harassed and abused black women. There are no statistics on such abuse, but it surely was more common than lynching. Like lynching, rape inflicted pain and suffering, and demonstrated the power of white men over black men and women.

Black men tried to keep their wives and daughters away from white men. They refused to permit black women to work as maids and domestics in homes where white men were present. One black man commented in 1912, "I believe nearly all white men take, and expect to take, undue liberties with their colored female servants, not only the fathers, but in many cases the sons also." A black man could not easily protect a black woman. He might be killed trying to do it, as an Alabama clergyman pointed out. "[W]hite men on the high ways and in their stores and on the trains will insult our women and we are powerless to resent it as it would only be an invitation for our lives to be taken."

Many white people believed that black women "invited" white males to take advantage of them. Black women were considered inferior, immoral, and lascivious. White people reasoned that it was impossible to defend the virtue of black women because they had none. Governor Coleman Blease of South Carolina pardoned black and white men found guilty of raping black women. "I am of the opinion," he said in 1913, "as I have always been, and have very serious doubts as to whether the crime of rape can be committed upon a negro."

PROFILE

Ida Wells Barnett

Ida Wells Barnett began life as a slave in 1862 and grew up during Reconstruction. As a young woman, she saw the worst indignities and cruelties that the Jim Crow South could inflict, but she fought back as a journalist, agitator, and reformer.

Ida Wells was one of eight children born to Jim and Lizzie Wells in Holly Springs, Mississippi. After the Civil War, she attended a school for freed people with her mother, and they learned to read and write. Her parents and one of her brothers died in the yellow fever epidemic of 1878. Sixteen-year-old Ida became mother and father to her five surviving brothers and sisters. She attended Shaw University in Holly Springs (now Rust College) and taught school in Mississippi and Tennessee.

Ida Wells Barnett was born in Mississippi and lived in Memphis until she published an outraged exposé of the lynching of one of her friends, Thomas Moss. Forced to leave Tennessee, she settled in Chicago but remained an anti-lynching crusader. She also supported women's suffrage and women's rights. She was a key figure in the National Association of Colored Women after its founding in 1896.

In 1884, a railroad conductor removed Wells from a first-class car. She sued the railroad and won a $500 settlement. "Dusky Damsel Gets Damages," a Memphis newspaper reported. But a higher court reversed the decision.

Wells then took up journalism and wrote a weekly column for *The Living Way*. In 1889, she bought a one-third interest in the Memphis *Free Speech and Headlight*. She wrote about racial issues and criticized black educators for the quality of black schools. In 1892 her friend Thomas Moss was lynched with two other men for the crime of running a successful grocery store. Wells expressed her rage and horror in a fiery editorial, thus beginning a lifelong crusade against lynching.

Wells blamed the white people of Memphis for her friend's murder and pointed out that more black men were lynched for challenging the myth of white superiority than for allegedly raping a white woman. She angered white people even more by writing that white women could be attracted to black men.

She blamed white clergymen and their parishioners for tolerating lynching. "[O]ur American Christians are too busy saving the souls of white Christians from burning in hell-fire to save the lives of black ones from present burning in fires kindled by white Christians."

Wells moved to Chicago and wrote a pamphlet criticizing the racism at the 1893 World's Fair: *The Reason Why the Colored American is Not in the Columbian Exposition.* In 1895 she married Ferdinand Barnett, the owner of the Chicago *Conservator.*

After a white journalist from Missouri wrote that black women were immoral, "having no sense of virtue and altogether without character," black women including Wells Barnett founded the National Association of Colored Women in 1896.

In 1909, Wells Barnett was one of two black women who supported the founding of the National Association for the Advancement of Colored People (NAACP), although she later broke with the group because of its mostly white board of directors and what she considered its cautious stands. She also helped organize the Negro Fellowship League in 1910.

Wells Barnett became an ardent supporter of black voting rights. She believed that if enough black men and women could vote, their political power would end lynching. In 1913 she helped found the Alpha Suffrage Club, the first black women's suffrage organization in Illinois, and was a delegate to the National American Woman's Suffrage Association meeting in Washington, D.C.

Ever an agitator, she found Booker T. Washington's philosophy too timid. She was influenced by Marcus Garvey and the Universal Negro Improvement Association, in the 1920s, and praised Garvey as a black leader who "made an impression on this country as no Negro before him had ever done."

She continued to write, campaign, speak out, and organize. In 1928 she ran as a Republican for the state Senate. Only death from kidney failure in 1931 ended her efforts to secure justice for black Americans.

Migration

In 1900, AME minister Henry M. Turner despaired for black people in America. "Every man that has the sense of an animal must see that there is no future in this country for the Negro. [W]e are taken out and burned, shot, hanged, unjointed and murdered in every way. Our civil rights are taken from us by force, our political rights are a farce."

It is, therefore, not surprising that thousands of African Americans fled poverty, powerlessness, and brutality in the South. What is perhaps surprising is that more did not leave. In the 1910s, 90 percent of black Americans still lived in the southern states. And of those who left the South, most did not head north along the old underground railroad. The Great Migration to the northern industrial states did not begin until about 1915. Emigrants of the 1870s, 1880s, and 1890s were more likely to strike out for Africa, or move west to Kansas, Oklahoma, and Arkansas, or move from farms to southern towns or cities.

The Liberian Exodus

When white Democrats redeemed Mississippi in 1875 with the "Shotgun Policy," a group of black people from Winona, Mississippi, wrote to Governor Adelbert Ames "to inquire about the possibility of moving to Africa. [W]e the colored people of Montgomery County are in a bad fix for we have no rights in the county and we want to know of you if there is any way for us to get out of the county and go to some place where we can get homes . . . so will you please let us know if we can go to Africa?"

They did not go to Africa, but some black Georgians and South Carolinians did. In 1877, black leaders in South Carolina, including AME minister and congressman Richard H. Cain, Probate Judge Harrison N. Bouey, and Martin Delany urged black people to migrate to Liberia. Many black communities and churches caught "Liberia Fever" while black people in upper South Carolina still felt the trauma of the political terror that had ended Reconstruction.

A white journalist described the situation in Chester County: "At some places in this county the desire to shake off the dust of their feet against this Democratic State is so great, that they are talking of selling out their crops and their personal effects, save what they would need in their new home." They were given promising though sometimes inaccurate information about Liberia: One potato in Liberia, they were told, could feed an entire family.

Several black men organized the Liberian Exodus Joint Stock Steamship Company. They raised $6,000 and hired a ship, the *Azor*, for the trip to Africa. The ship left Charleston in April 1878 with 206 migrants aboard and 175 left behind because there was not enough room for them. With inadequate food and fresh water and no competent medical care, twenty-three migrants died at sea. The ship arrived in Liberia on June 3.

Once settled in Liberia, several of the migrants prospered. Sam Hill established a seven hundred-acre coffee plantation, and C. L. Parsons became the chief justice of the Liberian Supreme Court. But others did less well, and some returned to the United States. The Liberian Exodus Company experienced financial difficulties and could not pay for further voyages.

The Exodusters

In May 1879, black delegates from fourteen states met in a convention in Nashville presided over by Congressman John R. Lynch of Mississippi. The convention resolved to support migration. The delegates declared that "the colored people should emigrate to those States and Territories where they can enjoy all the rights which are guaranteed by the laws and Constitution of the United States." They also asked Congress—in vain—to appropriate $500,000 for this venture.

Nevertheless, black people headed west. Between 1865 and 1880, 40,000 black people known as "Exodusters" moved to Kansas. Several hundred were persuaded to migrate by Benjamin "Pap" Singleton, a charismatic ex-slave from Tennessee. W. R. Hill, a black real estate promoter from Kentucky was instrumental in founding the all-black Kansas town of Nicodemus in 1877. Several all-black towns including Boley, Liberty, and Langston were founded in Indian territory that became Oklahoma. Other black migrants settled in Nebraska, the Dakotas, Colorado and elsewhere on the Great Plains and in the Rocky Mountains.

Many black and white people who moved west after the Civil War took advantage of the 1862 Homestead Act that provided 160 acres of federal land free to those who would settle on it and farm it for at least five years. It was often a bleak, dreary, and lonely existence where trees were few and rain infrequent. People lived in sod houses and relied on cow (or buffalo) chips for heat and cooking as they struggled to endure.

Railroads encouraged migration by offering reduced fares. Some western farmers and agents were eager to sell land, but some of it was of little value. Some of the white residents of Mississippi and South Carolina, which had large black majorities in their population, were glad to see the black people go. Others were alarmed at the loss of cheap black labor.

The Moses Speese family acquired a homestead near Westerville in Custer County, Nebraska. This 1888 photograph shows the extended family assembled in front of their sod house. They have installed a wind mill to provide power to pump water from a well. They also possess two teams of horses.

Some black leaders opposed migration and urged black people to stay put. In 1879, Frederick Douglass insisted that more opportunities existed for black people in the South than elsewhere. "Not only is the South the best locality for the Negro on the ground of his political powers and possibilities, but it is best for him as a field of labor. He is there, as he is nowhere else, an absolute necessity." Robert Smalls urged black people to come to his home county of Beaufort, South Carolina, "where I hardly think it probable that any prisoner will ever be taken from jail by a mob and lynched."

Migration within the South

Many black people left the poverty and isolation of farms and moved to nearby villages and towns in the South. Others went to larger southern cities including Atlanta, Richmond, and Nashville, where they settled in growing black neighborhoods. Urban areas offered more economic opportunities than rural areas. Though black people were usually confined to menial labor—from painting and shining shoes to domestic service—city work paid cash on a fairly regular basis, whereas rural residents received no money until their crops were sold. Towns and cities also afforded more entertainment and religious and educational activities. Black youngsters in towns spent more time in school than rural children, who had to help work the farms.

Black women had a better chance than black men of finding regular work in a town, though it was usually as a domestic or cleaning woman. This economic situation adversely affected the black family. Before the increase in migration, husband and wife headed 90 percent of black families. But with migration, many black men remained in rural areas where they could get farm work while women went to urban communities. Often these women became single heads of households.

Black Farm Families

Most black people did not leave the South or move to towns. They remained poverty-stricken sharecroppers and renters on impoverished land white people owned. They were poorly educated. They lacked political power. They were always in debt. Many rural black families remained precariously close to involuntary servitude in the decades after Reconstruction.

Many black and white people were little better off than medieval serfs. They lived in drafty, leaky cabins without electricity or running water. Outdoor toilets created health and hygiene problems. Medical care was often unavailable. Diets were dreary and unbalanced—mostly pork and cornbread—and deficient in vitamins and protein.

Sharecroppers

Most black farm families (and many white families as well) were sharecroppers. Sharecropping had emerged during Reconstruction as landowners allowed the use of their land for a share of the crop. The landlord also usually provided housing, horses or mules, tools, seed, and fertilizer as well as food and clothing. Depending on the agreement or contract, the landowner received from one-half to three-quarters of the crop.

Sharecropping lent itself to cheating and exploitation. By law, verbal agreements were considered contracts. In any case, many sharecroppers were illiterate and could not have read written contracts. The landowner informed the sharecropper of the value of the product raised—typically cotton—as well as the value of the goods provided to the sharecropping family. Black farmers who disputed white landowners put themselves in peril. Though many sharecroppers were aware that the proprietor's calculations were wrong, they could do nothing about it. Also, cotton brokers and gin owners routinely paid black farmers less than white farmers per pound for cotton. A forlorn ditty circulating among black people in the South in the late nineteenth century captured this inequity:

A naught's a naught, and a figger's a figger—
All fer de white man—none fer de nigger!

Black men were forced to accept the white man's word. One Mississippi sharecropper explained, "I have been living in this Delta thirty years, and I know that I have been robbed every year; but there is no use jumping out of the frying pan into the fire. If we ask any questions we are cussed, and if we raise up we are shot, and that ends it."

Renters

When they could, black farmers preferred renting to sharecropping. As tenants, they paid a flat charge to rent a given number of acres. Payment would be made in either cash—perhaps $5 per acre—or, more typically, in a specified amount of the crop—two bales of cotton per twenty acres. Tenants usually owned their own animals and tools. As Bessie Jones explained, "You see, a sharecropper don't ever have nothing. Before you know it, the man done took it all. But the renter always have something, and then he go to work when he want to go to work. He ain't got to go to work on the man's time. If he didn't make it, he didn't get it."

Crop Liens

In addition to the landowner, many sharecroppers and renters were also indebted to a local merchant for food, clothing, tools, and farm supplies. The merchant advanced the merchandise but took out a lien on the crop. If the sharecropper or renter failed to repay the merchant, the merchant was legally entitled to all or part of the crop once the landowner had received his payment. Merchants tended to charge high prices and high interest rates. They usually

For more than a century—from the early 1800s until the 1920s—cotton was *the* crop across much of the deep South. First as slaves, then as sharecroppers, renters, and land owners, generations of black people toiled in the cotton fields.

VOICES

Cash and Debt for the Black Cotton Farmer

Benjamin E. Mays was born in 1895 in Epworth, South Carolina. He was the youngest and eighth child of parents who had been slaves and whose lives revolved around agriculture. Mays went on to South Carolina State College, to Bates College, and the University of Chicago. He became the president of Morehouse College where he served as a mentor to Martin Luther King Jr. Mays delivered the eulogy at King's funeral in 1968.

As I recall, Father usually rented forty acres of land for a two-mule farm, or sixty acres if we had three mules. The rent was two bales of cotton weighing 500 pounds each, for every twenty acres rented. So the owner of the land got his two, four, or six bales of cotton out of the first cotton picked and ginned.

To make sixteen bales of cotton on a two-mule farm was considered excellent farming. After four bales were used to pay rent, we would have twelve bales left. The price of cotton fluctuated. If we received ten cents a pound, we would have somewhere between five and six hundred dollars, depending on whether the bales of cotton weighed an average of 450, 475, or 500 pounds. When all of us children were at home we, with our father and mother, were ten. We lived in a four-room house, with no indoor plumbing—no toilet facilities, no running water.

We were never able to clear enough from the crop to carry us from one September to the next. We could usually go on our own from September through February; but every March a lien had to be placed on the crop so that we could get money to buy food and other necessities from March through August, when we would get some relief by selling cotton. Strange as it may seem, neither we nor our neighbors ever raised enough hogs to have meat year round, enough corn and wheat to insure having our daily bread, or cows in sufficient numbers to have enough milk. The curse was cotton. It was difficult to make farmers see that more corn, grain, hogs, and cows meant less cash but more profit in the end. Cotton sold instantly, and that was cash money. Negro farmers wanted to feel the cash—at least for that brief moment as it passed through their hands into the white man's hands!

QUESTIONS:

1. What might have led to greater independence for people like the Mays family?
2. Why were southern black and white families so large?

Source: Mays, *Born to Rebel*, pp. 5–6.

insisted that farmers plant cotton before they would agree to a lien. Cotton could be sold quickly for cash.

Peonage

Many farmers fell deeply into debt to landowners and merchants. They were cheated. Bad weather destroyed crops. Crop prices declined. Farmers who were in debt could not leave the land until the debt was paid. If they tried to depart, the sheriff pursued them. This was called peonage, and it amounted to enslavement, holding thousands of black people across the South in a state of perpetual bondage. Peonage violated federal law, but the law was rarely enforced. When landowners and merchants were prosecuted for keeping black people in peonage, white juries acquitted them.

Black Landowners

Considering the incredible obstacles against them, black farm families acquired land at an astonishing rate after the Civil War. Many white people refused to sell land to black buyers, preferring to keep them dependent. Black people also found it difficult to save enough money to purchase land even when they

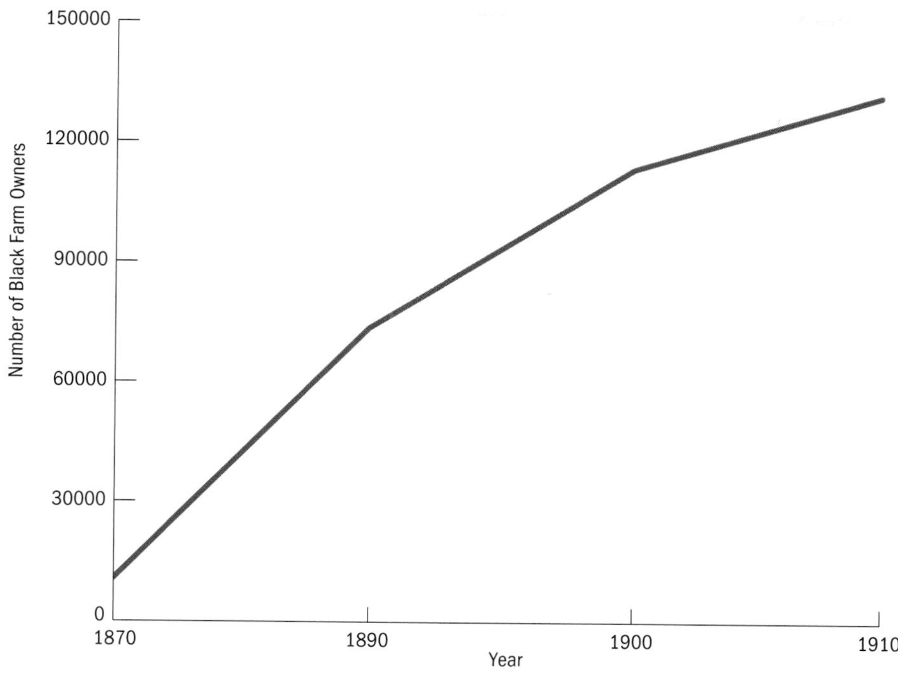

FIGURE 14–3 Black Farm Owners in Alabama, Arkansas, Florida, Georgia, Louisiana, Mississippi, South Carolina, and Texas: 1870–1910 It was very difficult for black families to acquire land. Many former slaves had barely enough money to survive, and saving money to buy land was almost impossible. Moreover, many white people would not sell land to black people. Thus, it is remarkable that so many black families purchased land in the decades after emancipation.

Source: Loren Schweninger, *Black Property Owners in the South, 1790–1915*, p. 164.

could find a willing seller. Still, they steadily managed to accumulate land.

Some black families had kept land that had been distributed in the Carolina and Georgia low country under the Port Royal Experiment and Sherman's Special Field Order #15 (see Chapter 11). In 1880, black people on South Carolina's Sea Islands held ten thousand acres of land worth $300,000.

By 1900, more than one hundred thousand black families owned their own land in the eight states of the deep South (see Figure 14–3). Black land ownership increased more than 500 percent between 1870 and 1900. Most black people possessed small farms of about twenty acres. In many cases these small plots of land were subsequently subdivided among sons and grandsons, making it more difficult for their families to prosper. But some black farmers owned impressive estates. Prince Johnson had 360 acres of excellent Mississippi Delta land. Freedman Leon Winter was the richest black man in Tennessee, with real estate worth $70,000 in 1889. Florida farmer J. D. McDuffy had an eight hundred-acre farm near Ocala and raised cantaloupes, watermelons, cabbages, and tomatoes. Texas freedman Daniel Webster Wallace had a ten thousand-acre cattle ranch. Few black people inherited large estates. Most of these landowners had been born into slavery. In the decades after emancipation, they managed to accumulate land—usually just a few acres at a time.

White Resentment of Black Success

Many white Southerners found it difficult to tolerate black economic success. They resented black progress and lashed out at those who had achieved it. When one rural black man built an attractive new house, local white people told him not to paint it—lest it look better than theirs. He accepted the advice and left the dwelling bare.

When automobiles arrived in the early twentieth century, Henry Watson, a well-to-do black farmer in Georgia, drove a new car to town. Enraged white people surrounded the car, forced Watson and his daughter out at gunpoint, and burned the vehicle. Watson was told, "From now on, you niggers walk into town, or use that ole mule if you want to stay in this city."

In 1916, Anthony Crawford, the owner of 427 acres of prime cotton land in Abbeville, South Carolina, secretary of the Chapel AME Church, a married man with sixteen children, was arrested and then released after he quarreled with a local white merchant over the price of cotton seed. But a mob, infuriated that Crawford spoke so bluntly to a white man, went after him. "When a nigger gets impudent we stretch him out and paddle him a bit," exclaimed one

PROFILE

Johnson C. Whittaker

Shortly after 6 A.M. on April 6, 1880, West Point's lone black cadet, Johnson C. Whittaker, was found lying unconscious on the floor of his room in the barracks. He was splattered with blood. His hands were tied together, and his feet were tied to the bed. In the months that followed, Whittaker's case attracted nationwide attention.

Whittaker was born a slave in 1858 on Mulberry Plantation near Camden, South Carolina, the son of a house slave and a free man. In 1876 white Republican congressman Solomon L. Hoge nominated Whittaker to West Point.

During his first year at the Academy, Whittaker roomed with the only other black cadet, Henry O. Flipper. But Flipper graduated in 1877—the first black man to graduate from the Academy—and Whittaker spent the next four years completely ostracized as the only remaining black cadet. White cadets refused to associate or room with him. Quiet and studious, he established a creditable academic record, but when he failed an exam in 1878, he was required to repeat a year.

Johnson C. Whittaker was the sole black cadet at West Point in 1880. Ostracized and shunned by white cadets, he was court martialed and convicted of conduct unbecoming an officer. Though the conviction was overturned by President Chester Arthur, Whittaker was dismissed from the Military Academy in 1882.

When he was found bloody and bound, Whittaker claimed he had been assaulted by three masked men after receiving a warning note the day before. A Court of Inquiry, however, declared that he had mutilated himself. Whittaker then insisted on a court martial to prove his innocence. In February 1881, that court martial convened in New York City.

Whittaker was charged with conduct unbecoming an officer and with lying. After four months of testimony, the court found him guilty. The court determined that Whittaker was "shamming"—making it all up to avoid failing an exam. Major Asa Bird Gardiner told the court: "Negroes are noted for their ability to sham and feign." Gardiner maintained that Whittaker was unfit. "By his own story the accused has shown himself a coward without one redeeming quality. . . . his mental attitude [was] inferior to the average Anglo-Saxon."

The court ordered Whittaker dishonorably discharged, fined one dollar, and sentenced to a year's hard labor. But the controversy did not end. In March 1882, President Chester Arthur overturned the verdict. But on the same day, the secretary of war, Robert Lincoln (Abraham's son), ordered Whittaker discharged from West Point.

Whittaker spent most of the rest of his life working with young black people at South Carolina State College and at Douglass High School in Oklahoma City. He died in South Carolina in 1931 at age 72. Whittaker had two sons. Both were commissioned officers and served in all-black units in World War I.

Whittaker summed up the meaning of his experience at West Point in a speech after the court martial found him guilty.

> West Point has tried to take from me honor and good name, but West Point has failed. I have honor and manhood still left me. I have an education which none can take from me. That education has come to me at fearful cost. The government may not wish me to use it in her service, but I shall use it for the good of my fellow men and for the good of those around me. . . . Poverty and sneers can never crush manhood. With God as my guide, duty will be my watchword, I can, I must, I will win a place in life!

In July 1995, President Bill Clinton posthumously awarded Johnson C. Whittaker his commission in the United States Army.

white man. But Crawford resisted and crushed the skull of a white attacker. The mob then stabbed and beat Crawford before the sheriff rescued him and put him in jail. Several hours later, a second mob broke into the jail and beat him to death. His body was left hanging at the fairgrounds. After his first beating, Crawford had told a friend, "I thought I was a good citizen." The coroner's jury ruled that his death had occurred at the hands of persons unknown.

African Americans and Southern Courts

The southern criminal justice systems yielded nothing but injustice to black people who ran afoul of it. Southern lawmakers worried incessantly about what they considered the growing black crime problem, and they worked diligently to control the black population. They enacted laws and ordinances to regulate the behavior of black people. Vagrancy laws made it easy to arrest any idle black man or one who was passing through a community. Contract evasion laws ensnared black people who attempted to escape peonage and perpetual servitude.

Segregated Justice

The legal system also became increasingly white after Reconstruction. Black police officers were gradually eliminated, and white policemen acquired a deserved reputation for brutality. Fewer and fewer black men served on juries, which were all white by 1900. (No women served on southern juries.) When black men were accidentally called for jury duty, they were rejected. In Alabama, a black man called for a local grand jury insisted on serving until he was beaten and forced to step down. Judges were white men. Most attorneys were white. The few black lawyers faced daunting hurdles. Some black defendants believed—correctly—that they would be found guilty and sentenced to a longer term if they retained a black attorney rather than a white one. Court personnel treated black plaintiffs, defendants, and witnesses with contempt, referring to them as "niggers," "boy," and "gal." Black people were rarely "mister" or "misses" in court proceedings.

A black defendant could not get justice. Black men and women were more often charged with crimes than white people. They were almost always convicted, regardless of the strength of the evidence or the credibility of witnesses. In one of the few instances when a black man was found not guilty of killing a white man, the defendant's attorney advised him to leave town because local white people were unlikely to accept the verdict. He fled, but returned twenty years later and was castrated by two white men.

Race was always the priority with jurors. Even when black people were the victims of crime, they were punished. In 1897, in Hinds County, Mississippi, a white man beat a black woman with an axe handle. She took him to court only to have the justice of the peace rule that he knew of "no law to punish a white man for beating a negro woman."

Juries rarely found white people guilty of crimes against black people. In a Georgia case in 1911, the evidence against several white people for holding black families in peonage was so overwhelming that the judge virtually ordered the jury to return a guilty verdict. Nonetheless, after five minutes of deliberation, the jury found the defendants not guilty. Many black and white people were, therefore, astonished in 1898 in Shreveport, Louisiana, when a jury actually found a white man guilty of murdering a black man. He was sentenced to five years in prison.

Black people could receive leniency from the judicial system, but it was not justice. They were much less likely to be charged with a crime against another black person, like raping a black woman, than against a white person. Black people often were not charged with crimes such as adultery and bigamy because white people considered such offenses typical of black behavior.

Black defendants who had some personal or economic connection to a prominent white person were less likely to be treated or punished the same way as black people who had no such relationship. In Vicksburg, Mississippi, a black woman watched as the black man who had murdered her husband was acquitted because a white man intervened. Those black people known as "a white man's nigger" had a decided advantage in court.

Black people received longer sentences and larger fines than white people. In Georgia, black convicts served much longer sentences than white convicts for the same offense—five times as long for larceny, for example. An eighty-year-old black preacher went to prison "for what a white man was fined five dollars." In New Orleans, a black man was sentenced to ninety days in jail for petty theft. According to a local black newspaper, it was "three days for stealing and eighty-seven days for being colored."

The Convict Lease System

Conditions in southern prisons were indescribably wretched. Black prisoners—many incarcerated for

Timeline

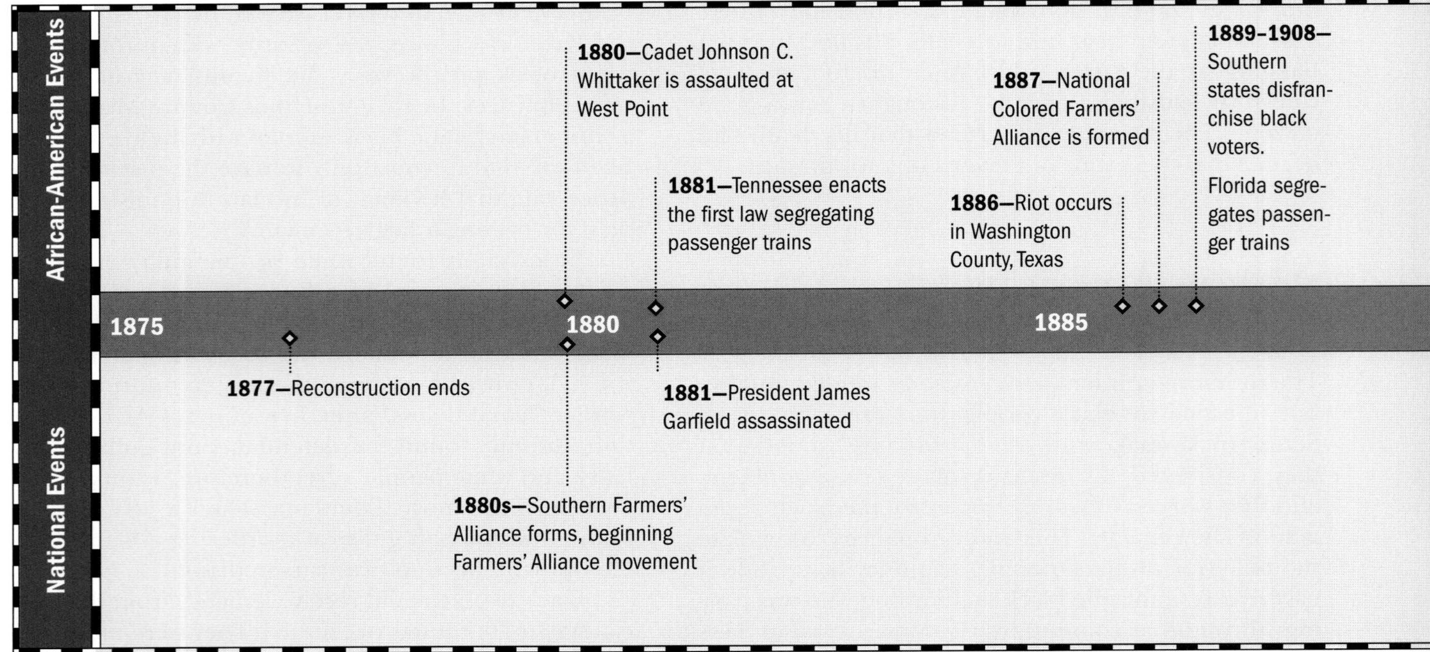

vagrancy, theft, disorderly conduct, and other misdemeanors—spent months and years in oppressive conditions and were subjected to the unrelenting abuse of white authorities. But conditions could and did get worse.

Southern politicians devised the convict lease system in the late nineteenth century. Businesses and planters leased convicts from the state to build railroads, clear swamps, cut timber, tend cotton, and work mines. The company or planter had to feed, clothe, and house the prisoners. Of course, the convicts were not paid. The state and local community was not only freed of the burden of maintaining prisons and jails, but also received revenue. For example, South Carolina was paid three dollars per month per prisoner. Some states and counties found this so remunerative that law-enforcement officials were encouraged to charge even more black men with assorted crimes so they could contribute to this lucrative enterprise.

Leased convicts endured appalling treatment and conditions. They were shackled and beaten. They were overworked and underfed; they slept on vermin-infested straw mattresses and received little or no medical care. They sustained terrible injuries on the job and at the hands of guards; diseases proliferated in the camps. Hundreds died, meaning that they had, in effect, been sentenced to death for their petty crimes.

Businessmen and planters found such cheap labor almost irresistible, and black prisoners found it "nine kinds of hell." It was worse than slavery because these black lives had no value to either the government or the businesses involved in this sordid system. As one employer explained in 1883, "But these convicts; we don't own em. One dies, get another." The inhumanity of convict leasing became such a scandal that states outlawed it by the early twentieth century. Convicts were returned to state-operated penitentiaries.

Conclusion

With the end of the Civil War and slavery in 1865, more than four million Americans of African descent had looked with hope and anticipation to the future. Four decades later, there were more than nine million African Americans, and more than eight million of them lived in the South. The crushing burden of white supremacy increasingly limited their hopes and aspirations. The U.S. government abandoned black people to white Southerners and their state and local governments. The federal government that had assured their rights as citizens during Reconstruction ignored the legal, political,

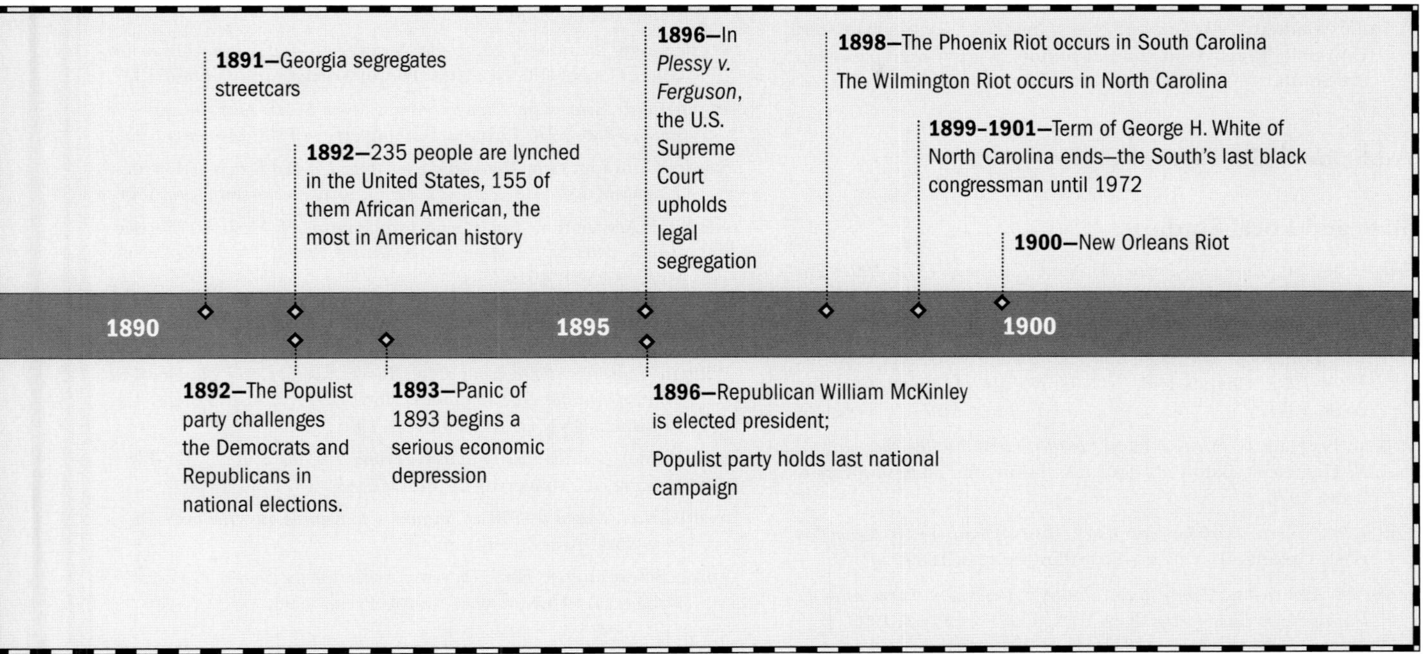

and economic situation that entrapped most black Southerners.

Although the Thirteenth Amendment abolished slavery, thousands of black people were hopelessly trapped in peonage; thousands of others labored as sharecroppers and renters, indebted to white landowners and merchants. Yet, more than 100,000 black families managed to acquire farms of their own by 1900. Many black farmers had also organized and participated in the Colored Farmers' Alliance and the Populist party, though it brought few tangible benefits.

The Fourteenth Amendment had guaranteed the rights of citizenship that included due process of law. No state could deprive a person of life, liberty, or property without a court proceeding. The amendment also ensured each citizen equal protection of the law. But the Supreme Court had ruled that racial segregation in public places did not infringe on the right to equal protection of the law. And as for the right to life, hundreds of black people had lost their lives at the hands of lynch mobs by the early 1900s.

The Fifteenth Amendment stipulated that race could not be used to deprive a man of the right to vote. Nevertheless, southern states circumvented the amendment with poll taxes, literacy tests, and the grandfather clause. Thus, by 1900, after black men had held political offices across the South for the previous thirty years, no black person served in any elected political position in any southern state.

White people clearly regarded black Americans as an inferior race not entitled to those rights that the Constitution so emphatically set forth. What could black people do about the intolerance, discrimination, violence, and powerlessness that they had to endure? What strategies, ideas, and leadership could they use to overcome the burdens that they were forced to bear? What realistic chances did they have of overcoming white supremacy? How could black people organize to gain fundamental rights that were guaranteed to them?

Recommended Reading

Edward L. Ayers. *The Promise of the New South: Life after Reconstruction.* New York: Oxford University Press, 1992. An excellent overview of how people lived in the late nineteenth-century South.

Leon Litwack. *Trouble in Mind: Black Southerners in the Age of Jim Crow.* New York: Alfred A. Knopf, 1998. In moving words and testimony, black people describe what life was like in a white supremacist society.

Rayford Logan. *The Negro in American Life and Thought: The Nadir, 1877–1901.* New York: Dial Press, 1954. Explorations of the contours and oppressiveness of racism.

Benjamin E. Mays. *Born to Rebel: An Autobiography*. New York: Charles Scribner, 1971. Eloquent and graphic recollection of what it was like to grow up black in the rural South at the turn of the century.

C. Vann Woodward. *The Strange Career of Jim Crow*. New York: Oxford University Press, 1955. The evolution of legal segregation in the South.

Additional Bibliography

State and Local Studies

Eric Anderson. *Race and Politics in North Carolina, 1872–1901: The Black Second*. Baton Rouge, LA: Louisiana State University Press, 1981.

Helen G. Edmonds. *The Negro and Fusion Politics in North Carolina, 1894–1901*. Chapel Hill, NC: University of North Carolina Press, 1951.

William Ivy Hair. *Carnival of Fury: Robert Charles and the New Orleans Riot of 1900*. Baton Rouge, LA: Louisiana State University Press, 1976.

Neil R. McMillen. *Dark Journey: Black Mississippians in the Age of Jim Crow*. Urbana, IL: University of Illinois Press, 1989.

David M. Oshinsky. *"Worse than Slavery": Parchman Farm and the Ordeal of Jim Crow Justice*. New York: The Free Press, 1999.

George B. Tindall. *South Carolina Negroes, 1877–1900*. Columbia, SC: University of South Carolina Press, 1952.

Vernon Wharton. *The Negro in Mississippi, 1865–1890*. Chapel Hill, NC: University of North Carolina Press, 1947.

Biographies and Autobiographies

Albert S. Broussard. *African-American Odyssey: The Stewarts, 1853–1963*. Lawrence, KS: University Press of Kansas, 1998.

Alfreda Duster, ed. *Crusade for Justice: The Autobiography of Ida B. Wells*. Chicago: University of Chicago Press, 1972.

Henry O. Flipper. *The Colored Cadet at West Point*. New York: Arno Press, 1969.

John F. Marszalek, Jr. *Court Martial: The Army vs. Johnson Whittaker*. New York: Scribner, 1972.

Linda McMurry. *To Keep the Waters Troubled: The Life of Ida B. Wells*. New York: Oxford University Press, 1998.

Patricia A. Schechter. *Ida B. Wells-Barnett and American Reform, 1882–1930*. Chapel Hill, NC: University of North Carolina Press, 2001.

Politics and Segregation

Grace Hale. *Making Whiteness: The Culture of Segregation in the South, 1890–1940*. New York: Pantheon Books, 1998.

J. Morgan Kousser. *The Shaping of Southern Politics: Suffrage Restriction and the Establishment of the One-Party South, 1880–1910*. New Haven, CT: Yale University Press, 1974.

Michael Perman. *Struggle for Mastery: Disfranchisement in the South, 1888–1908*. Chapel Hill, NC: University of North Carolina Press, 2001.

Lynching

James Allen, Hinton Als, John Lewis, and Leon F. Litwack. *Without Sanctuary: Lynching Photography in America*. Santa Fe, NM: Twin Palms Books, 2000.

W. Fitzhugh Brundage, ed. *Under Sentence of Death: Lynching in the South*. Chapel Hill, NC: University of North Carolina Press, 1997.

W. Fitzhugh Brundage. *Lynching in the New South: Georgia and Virginia, 1880–1930*. Urbana, IL: University of Illinois Press, 1993.

Sandra Gunning. *Race, Rape, and Lynching: The Red Record of American Literature, 1890–1912*. New York: Oxford University Press, 1996.

National Association for the Advancement of Colored People. *Thirty Years of Lynching in the United States, 1889–1918*. New York: NAACP, 1919.

Migration, Mobility, and Land Ownership

William Cohen. *At Freedom's Edge: Black Mobility and the Southern White Quest for Racial Control, 1861–1915*. Baton Rouge, LA: Louisiana State University Press, 1991.

Pete Daniel. *The Shadow of Slavery: Peonage in the South, 1901–1969*. Urbana, IL: University of Illinois Press, 1972.

Nell Painter. *Exodusters: Black Migration to Kansas after Reconstruction*. New York: Alfred A. Knopf, 1977.

Loren Schweninger. *Black Property Owners in the South, 1790–1915*. Urbana, IL: University of Illinois Press, 1990.

Retracing the Odyssey

Omaha, Nebraska: Great Plains Black Museum. Located in the former Webster Telephone Exchange building, this thirty-seven-room museum contains information and artifacts on black homesteaders and on the role that black women played in migration and settlement on the Plains.

Nicodemus, Kansas: Nicodemus National Historic Site. W.R. Hill was a black real estate agent who founded Nicodemus in 1877. By 1887 there were over 250 people living in the town. The absence of a railroad led to a prolonged decline of what had been a small, thriving community. Most of the town's original structures have not survived.

Langston, Oklahoma and Langston University. Langston was one of the many all-black towns established after the Civil War. In 1897 the town set aside forty acres to create a black land-grant university. The town and university are named for John Mercer Langston, a prominent nineteenth-century black leader and congressman from Virginia.

Boley, Oklahoma: Historic District. Boley was an all-black town founded at the turn of the century in what had been Indian territory. It was incorporated in 1905. Many of the town's residents left when cotton prices dropped and the economy collapsed during the Great Depression. Some of the historic black businesses and buildings still stand.

Denver, Colorado: Black American West Museum and Heritage Center. Founded by Paul Stewart, this museum is dedicated to the black pioneers of the frontier west including cowboys, soldiers, barbers, and homesteaders. It has artifacts, photographs, recordings, and other memorabilia of nineteenth- and early twentieth-century African Americans. It is located in the former home of Dr. Justina Ford. As a black woman physician who delivered seven thousand babies of virtually every ethnic background, she was a pioneer as well.

REVIEW, RESEARCH & INTERACT

REVIEW QUESTIONS

1. How were black people prevented from voting in spite of the provisions of the Fifteenth Amendment?
2. What were the legal and ethical arguments used by white Americans to justify segregation?
3. What accounts for the epidemic of violence and lynching in the South in the late nineteenth century?
4. Why didn't more black people migrate from the South in this period?

Research Navigator.com **www.researchnavigator.com**

Chapter 14 explores the causes and consequences of the federal government's abandonment of its earlier commitment to protect the civil and legal rights of African Americans. For further research on this topic, use the tools available to you in Research Navigator.

As you investigate this topic, consider this question: "What forces fueled violence against blacks in the South?"

- **ContentSelect:** Search in the History database using the search term *Jim Crow.*
- **Links Library:** Access the History: U.S. History database and explore the links for *Jim Crow, Plessy v. Ferguson,* and *Lynchings.*
- **New York Times on the Web:** To find more information on African American life in the late nineteenth-century South, search the History database using the search term *sharecropper.*

DOCUMENTS AND ACTIVITIES IN AFRICAN-AMERICAN HISTORY

Documents

14-1 A Sharecrop Contract, 1882
14-2 John Hill, Testimony on Southern Textile Industry, 1883
14-3 Ida B. Wells, A Red Record, 1895
14-4 Anna Julia Cooper, From *A Voice from the South: By a Black Woman of the South,* 1892
14-5 Alex Manly and the 1898 Wilmington "Race Riot"
14-6 W. E. B. Du Bois, *A Negro Schoolmaster in the New South,* 1899

Interactive Figure

African-American Representation in Congress, 1867–1900, p. 311
http://www.prenhall.com/hine/figure14.1

15

Black Southerners Challenge White Supremacy

Henry Ossawa Tanner, the son of a bishop of the AME church, was raised in Philadelphia and studied there with artist Thomas Eakins. In *The Banjo Lesson* (1893) Tanner refuted the prevailing racism of the late nineteenth century with a painting that depicted humanity, decency, and the quiet dignity of black people, as well as the bonds that linked an older to a younger generation.

THE Anglo-Saxon said to the negro, in most haughty tones: "in this great 'battle for bread,' you must supply the brute force while I will supply the brain." . . . He will contribute the public funds to educate the negro and then exert every possible influence to keep the negro from earning a livelihood by means of that education.

They pay our teachers poorer salaries than they do their own; they give us fewer and inferior school buildings and they make us crawl in the dust before the very eyes of our children in order to secure the slightest concessions. . . .

In school, they are taught to bow down and worship at the shrine of men who died for the sake of liberty, and day by day they grow to disrespect us, their parents[,] who have made no blow for freedom. But it will not always be thus!—

Black novelist Sutton E. Griggs in *Imperium in Imperio*, 1899.

CHAPTER OUTLINE

Social Darwinism

Education and Schools
- Segregated Schools
- The Hampton Model
- Washington and the Tuskegee Model
- Critics of the Tuskegee Model

Church and Religion
- The Church as Solace and Escape
- The Holiness Movement and the Pentecostal Church
- Roman Catholics and Episcopalians

Red versus Black: The Buffalo Soldiers
- Discrimination in the Army
- The Buffalo Soldiers in Combat
- Civilian Hostility to Black Soldiers
- Brownsville

African Americans in the Navy

The Black Cowboys

The Spanish-American War
- Black Officers
- A Splendid Little War
- After the War

The Philippine Insurrection
- Would Black Men Fight Brown Men?

Black Businesspeople and Entrepreneurs

African Americans and Labor
- Unions
- Strikes

Black Professionals
- Medicine
- The Law

Music
- Ragtime
- Jazz
- The Blues

Sports
- Jack Johnson
- Baseball
- Basketball and Other Sports
- College Athletics

Conclusion

Industrialization and the rise of large, powerful corporations transformed the American economy in the late nineteenth century. As millions of European immigrants crowded into the cities of the North and Midwest to find jobs in the nation's new factories, agriculture production increased and prices declined, impoverishing many rural Southerners. Most black people—nearly eight million—remained in the Southern states, where they struggled to confront the malignant effects of white supremacy. Living in a society that largely sought to disregard their rights and to exclude them from its institutions and culture, black Americans increasingly relied on their own resources and depended on their own communities to adjust to the forces of white supremacy and to forge a path into the future.

Some African Americans turned to education to elevate themselves and their people, but they disagreed about the most appropriate approach to take to education. Some African-American men sought to advance themselves and prove their worth to American society through military service. By the late nineteenth century, however, black Americans mostly relied on each other and the people and institutions in their own communities to sustain themselves. As they had during Reconstruction, they continued to organize and support churches, schools, and colleges. They established businesses and sometimes formed labor unions and went on strike. They founded their own hospitals. They expressed themselves in music by creating ragtime, jazz, and blues. At times they were allowed to participate with white people in organized sports such as professional boxing, baseball, and college football. More often, they formed their own athletic teams. African Americans refused to allow white supremacy to prevent them from creating a meaningful place for themselves in American society.

Social Darwinism

Pseudoscientific evidence and academic scholarship bolstered the conviction of many Americans that white people, especially those of English and Germanic descent—Anglo-Saxons—were culturally and racially superior to nonwhites and even other Europeans. Sociologists Herbert Spencer and William Graham Sumner drew on Charles Darwin's theory of evolution and concluded that life in modern industrial societies mirrored life in the animal kingdom. This theory, called Social Darwinism, held that through a process of natural selection, the strong would thrive, prosper, and reproduce while the weak would falter, fail, and die. Life was a struggle; only the fittest survived.

Social Darwinism applied to both individuals and "races." It conveniently justified great disparities in wealth, suggesting that such men as John D. Rockefeller and Andrew Carnegie were rich because they were "fit," whereas many European immigrants and most African Americans were poor and unlikely to succeed because they were "unfit." The same logic explained the strength and prosperity of the United States, Great Britain, and Germany compared to countries such as Spain and Italy and conveniently explained why African, Asian, and Latin American societies seemed so backward and primitive. In absorbing this ideology of class and race, many Americans and Europeans came to believe that they had a responsibility—a duty—to introduce the political, economic, and religious benefits and values of Western cultures to the "less advanced" and usually darker peoples of the globe. This presumed responsibility was summed up in the words of the English poet Rudyard Kipling as "the white man's burden."

Social Darwinism increasingly influenced the way most Protestant white Americans perceived their society, leading them to believe that people could be ranked from superior to inferior based on their race, nationality, and ethnicity. Black people were invariably ranked at the bottom of this hierarchy, and the eastern and southern European immigrants who were flooding the country only slightly above them. Black people were capable, so the reasoning went, of no more than a subordinate role in a complex and advanced society as it rushed into the twentieth century. And if their position was biologically ordained, why should society devote substantial resources to their education?

Education and Schools

A black youngster who wanted an education in the late nineteenth century faced formidable obstacles. Most black people were poor farmers who had few opportunities for an education and even fewer prospects for a career in business or one of the professions. It is remarkable—and a testimony to black perseverance—that so many black people did manage to acquire some education and to free themselves from illiteracy (see Figure 15–1).

TRACK 18

Gaining even a rudimentary education was not easy. Rural schools for black children rarely operated for more than thirty weeks a year. Because of the demands of field work, most black youngsters could not attend school on a regular basis. Brothers and sisters sometimes alternated work and school with each other on a daily basis. Benjamin Mays was nineteen years old before he went to school for more than four months a year—and even then he had to defy his father's demand that he leave school in February to work on the farm.

Schools were often dilapidated shacks. They lacked plumbing, electricity, books, and teaching materials. Some schools were in churches and homes. Teachers were poorly paid and often poorly prepared. Septima Clark remembered her first teaching experience on Johns Island on the South Carolina coast in the early twentieth century.

Figure 15–1

Black and White Illiteracy in the United States and the Southern States, 1880–1900

Although more than half of adult black Southerners were still illiterate in 1900, black people had made substantial progress in education during the last two decades of the nineteenth century. This progress is especially remarkable considering the difficulties black youngsters and adults faced in acquiring even an elementary education.

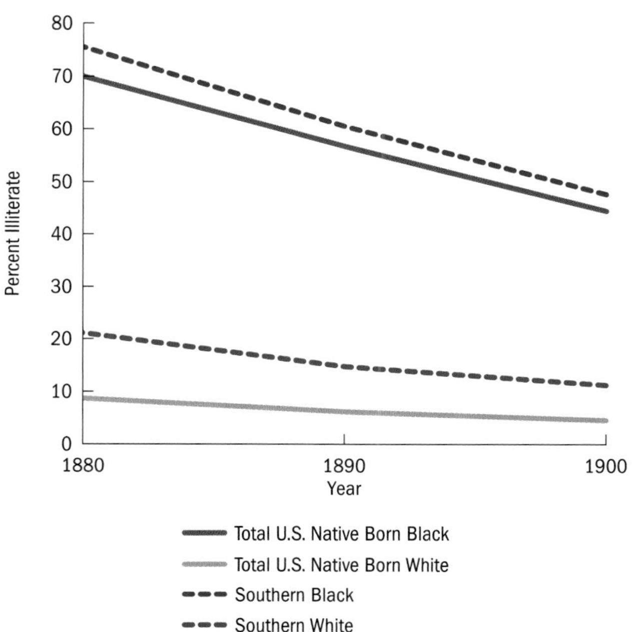

> Here I was, a high-school graduate, eighteen years old, principal in a two-teacher school with 132 pupils ranging from beginners to eighth graders, with no teaching experience, a schoolhouse constructed of boards running up and down, with no slats on the cracks, and a fireplace at one end of the room that cooked the pupils immediately in front of it but allowed those in the rear to shiver and freeze on their uncomfortable, hard, back-breaking benches.

Segregated Schools

Though southern states could not afford to support even one first-rate public school system, each of them operated separate schools for black and white children (see Table 15–1). The South had almost no public black high schools. In 1915 in twenty-three southern cities with populations of more than 20,000, including Tampa, New Orleans, Charleston, and Charlotte, there was not one black public high school. But these twenty-three cities had thirty-six high schools for white youngsters. In 1897 over the vehement protests of the black community, white school officials in Augusta, Georgia, closed Ware High School, the black secondary school, and transformed it into a black primary school. The U. S. Supreme Court in 1899 in *Cumming v. Richmond County [Georgia] Board of Education* unanimously refused to accept the contention of black parents that the elimination of the black high school violated the "separate but equal" doctrine announced in the *Plessy v. Ferguson* case three years earlier. Augusta was left with two white high schools—one for males and one for females, and none for black people.

Young black people who sought more than a primary education often had to travel to a black college or university that offered a high school program. For example, in 1911, at the age of 16, Benjamin Mays boarded a train and traveled one hundred miles to South Carolina State College and enrolled in the 7th grade. He graduated from high school there in 1916 at the age of 22 and then graduated from Maine's Bates College four years later.

In many communities, black people, with the assistance of churches and Northern philanthropists, operated private academies and high schools, such as

DATA EXPLORATION
To explore this data, go to **http://www.prenhall.com/hine/figure15.1**

TABLE 15–1
South Carolina's Black and White Public Schools, 1908–1909

Black Schools		White Schools
2,354	Public Schools	2,712
894	Men Teachers	933
1,802	Women Teachers	3,247
181,095	Total Pupils	153,807
123,481	Average Attendance	107,368
77	Pupils per School	55
63	Pupils per Teacher	35
14.7	Average Number of Weeks of School	25.2
$118.17	*Average Yearly Salary for Men Teachers*	*$479.79*
$91.45	*Average Yearly Salary for Women Teachers*	*$249.13*
$308,153.16	*Total Expenditures*	*$1,590,732.51*

School for most southern black students and teachers was a part-time activity. Because of the demands of agriculture, few rural students, black or white, attended school more than six months a year. Very few teachers were graduates of four-year college programs. The situation was better in urban communities and upper South schools, where the school year lasted longer and education was better financed. But all public schools were segregated in the South.

Source: Department of Education Annual Report, South Carolina, 1908–09, pp. 935, 961.

Georgia's Fort Valley High and Industrial School and Camden, South Carolina's, Mather Academy, to fill the void created by the lack of public schools. Typically students were charged a modest tuition, and those who attended came from the more prosperous families of the black community. In 1890, the number of black youngsters between the ages of fifteen and nineteen attending black public or private high schools in the South was 3,106. By 1910, that number had risen to 26,553.

The Hampton Model

Some black people and many white people regarded education for black youngsters a pointless exercise. Benjamin Mays's father put little value in education. "My greatest opposition to going away to school was my father. When I knew that I had learned everything that I could in the one-room Brickhouse School and realized how little that was, my father felt that this was sufficient—that it was all I needed. . . . He was convinced that education went to one's head and made him a fool and dishonest." In 1911, South Carolina's governor Coleman Blease was even more blunt: "Instead of making an educated negro, you are ruining a good plow hand and making a half-trained fool."

Many of those who did value schooling were convinced that the most appropriate education for a black child was industrial or domestic training. Black youngsters, these people maintained, should learn skills they could teach others and use to make themselves productive members of the community.

Hampton Normal and Agricultural Institute was founded in 1868 in Virginia and was dominated for decades by Samuel Chapman Armstrong, a white missionary with strong paternalistic inclinations. Hampton trained legions of African Americans and Native Americans to teach skills and to embrace the importance of hard work, diligence, and Christian morality. Armstrong stressed learning trades, such as shoemaking, carpentry, tailoring, and sewing. Hampton placed little emphasis on critical or independent thinking. Students were taught to conform to middle-class values. Armstrong cautioned against black involvement in politics, and he acquiesced in Jim Crow racial practices. The chapel walls at Hampton featured pictures of Robert E. Lee and Andrew Johnson.

Washington and the Tuskegee Model

Armstrong's prize student and Hampton's foremost graduate was Booker T. Washington, who became the nation's leading apostle of industrial training and one of the preeminent leaders and most remarkable men—black or white—in American history. Washington was born a slave in western Virginia in 1856. His father was a white man whose identity is unknown. He was raised by his mother, Jane, in an unimpressive, but tidy, cabin of split logs on a small farm. As a child, he was employed at a salt works and in coal mines. He was also a houseboy for a prominent white family. He attended a local school where he learned to read and write.

TRACK 19

Black and white land-grant colleges stressed training in agriculture and industry. Here Hampton Institute students learn milk production. Note that the men are in military uniforms, which was typical for males at both black and white agricultural and mechanical schools. Military training was a required part of the curriculum.

Booker T. Washington, looking regal in this portrait, was the most influential black leader in America by 1900. White business and political leaders were reassured by his message that black people themselves were responsible for their economic progress and that people of color should avoid a direct challenge to white supremacy. Although W. E. B. Du Bois appreciated Washington's commitment to the advancement of black people, he believed that more emphasis should be placed on developing an educated elite who would take the lead in solving the race problem. Washington was a Southerner who looked for practical solutions to the problems of everyday life, while Du Bois was a Northerner who stressed the need for intellectual advancement.

Intensely ambitious, Washington set off for Hampton Institute in 1872. While there, he was much affected by Armstrong and his curriculum and method of instruction. He worked his way through school and taught for two years at Hampton after graduating. In 1881 he accepted an invitation to found a black college in Alabama—Tuskegee Institute. The result was an institution, which he forged almost single-handedly, that reflected his experience at Hampton and the influence of Armstrong.

From the day he arrived at Tuskegee until his death in 1915, Washington worked tirelessly to persuade black and white people that the surest way for black people to advance was by learning skills and demonstrating a willingness to do manual labor. In a famous speech at the Cotton States Exposition in Atlanta in 1895 (the impact of which is discussed in Chapter 16), Washington told his segregated audience: "No race can prosper till it learns that there is as much dignity in tilling a field as in writing a poem. It is at the bottom of life we must begin, and not at the top." Washington believed that if black people acquired skills and became prosperous small farmers, artisans, and shopkeepers, they would in time earn the respect and acceptance of white Americans and eventually eradicate the race problem—all without unseemly protest and agitation.

Washington's message earned accolades from white political leaders and philanthropists, who were more inclined to support the promotion of trades and skills among black people than an academic and liberal education. Steel magnate Andrew Carnegie, impressed by Washington, financed the construction of twenty-nine buildings on the campuses of black schools and colleges. White railroad executive William H. Baldwin provided millions of dollars for black industrial education, and the John F. Slater Fund poured large sums of money into vocational education. Disciples of Washington and graduates of Tuskegee fanned out across the South as industrial and agricultural educational training for black youngsters proliferated.

The Morrill Act, which Congress passed in 1862, entitled each state to the proceeds from the sale of federal land (most of it in the West) for establishing land-grant colleges to provide agricultural and mechanical training. However, southern states did not admit black students to their A&M (Agricultural and Mechanical) schools. A second Morrill Act, however, passed in 1890 that permitted states to establish and fund separate black land-grant colleges. The 1890 act accelerated the development of practical education through the appropriation of federal money to such institutions as Alcorn A&M in Mississippi, Florida A&M, Southern University in Louisiana, Langston in Oklahoma, and Tuskegee Institute. By 1915, there were sixteen black land-grant colleges.

Most of the institutions were not actually colleges. Few of their students graduated with bachelor's degrees, and many of them were enrolled in primary and secondary programs. Virtually all the students at the black land-grant schools had to take courses in trades, agriculture, and domestic sciences. Most of the schools required students to do manual labor for which they were paid small sums. Students built and maintained the campuses, and they raised the food served in the school cafeteria. Some of the students

VOICES

Thomas E. Miller and the Mission of the Black Land-Grant College

In 1896 the South Carolina General Assembly established the Colored Normal, Industrial, Agricultural and Mechanical College of South Carolina. It derived funds from the Second Morrill Act of 1890 and from the state itself. Its first president was former black congressman and lawyer, Thomas E. Miller. In an address to the Bamberg County Colored Fair in 1897, Miller embraced the Hampton and Tuskegee models as he described the mission of his institution:

The work of our college is along the industrial line. We are making educated and worthy school teachers, educated and reliable mechanics, educated, reliable and frugal farmers. We teach your sons and daughters how to care for and milk the cows, how to make gilt-edged butter, how to make cheese, what kind of fertilizer each crop needs, the natural strength and productive qualities of the various soils, and last to make a compost heap and how to take care of it. We teach them how to make a wagon, plow and hoe, how to shoe a horse and nurse him when sick. We teach your children how to keep books and typewrite, we teach your girls how to make a dress or undergarment, how to cook, wash and iron. We teach your boys how to make and run an engine, how to make and control electricity, we teach them mechanical and artistic drawing, house and sign painting.

QUESTIONS

1. Given the racial climate of the 1890s, why was or wasn't agricultural and mechanical training the most suitable education for most black youngsters?
2. If a young black person did learn the skills mentioned by Miller, was he or she educated for an inferior place in society?

Source: I. A. Newby, *Black Carolinians, A History of Blacks in South Carolina from 1895 to 1968* (Columbia, 1973), p. 263.

were in the "normal" curriculum, which prepared them to teach at a time when most states did not require a college degree for a teaching certificate. Students enrolled in "normal" schools or programs earned a licentiate of instruction that certified them to teach.

Critics of the Tuskegee Model

Not everyone shared Washington's stress on industrial and agricultural training for young black men and women to the near exclusion of the liberal arts, including literature, history, philosophy, and languages. Washington's program, some critics charged, seemed to be designed to train black people for a subordinate role in American society. Black people, they worried, would continue to labor much as they had in slavery, and not far removed from it.

W. E. B. Du Bois, a Fisk- and Harvard-trained scholar, and AME Bishop Henry M. Turner believed that education went beyond mere training and the acquisition of skills. It involved intellectual growth and development. It would confront racial problems. It would create wise men. According to Du Bois, "The function of the Negro college, then, is clear, it must maintain standards of popular education, it must seek the social regeneration of the Negro, and it must help in the solution of problems of race contact and cooperation. And finally, beyond all this, it must develop men."

Many of the private black colleges resisted the emphasis on agricultural and mechanical training. American Missionary Association schools such as Fisk, Talladega, and Tougaloo; AME schools such as Allen, Paul Quinn, and Morris Brown; and Methodist institutions such as Claflin, Bennett, and Rust still promoted the liberal arts and taught Latin, Greek, mathematics, and natural sciences. Henry L. Morehouse of the American Baptist Home Missionary Society explained that the purpose of education was to develop strong minds. He believed that gifted intellectuals—a "talented tenth" as he characterized them in 1896—could lead people forward. Du Bois likewise stressed the need for the best educated 10 percent of the black population to promote progress and to advance the race.

In fairness to Washington, he did not deny the importance of a liberal arts education, but he also believed that industry was the foundation to progress:

> On such a foundation as this will grow habits of thrift, a love of work, economy, ownership of property, bank accounts. Out of it in the future will grow practical education, professional education, and positions of public responsibility. Out of it will grow moral and religious strength. Out of it will grow wealth from which alone can come leisure and the opportunity for the enjoyment of literature and the fine arts.

Ultimately, however, Washington was wrong to believe that education for black people that focused on economic progress would earn the respect of most white Americans. As Du Bois explained, most white people preferred ignorant and unsuccessful black people to educated and prosperous ones:

> If my own city of Atlanta had offered it to-day the choice between 500 Negro college graduates—forceful, busy, ambitious men of property and self-respect—and 500 black cringing vagrants and criminals, the popular vote in favor of the criminals would be simply overwhelming. Why? Because they want Negro crime? No, not that they fear Negro crime less, but that they fear Negro ambition and success more. They can deal with crime by chain-gang and lynch law, or at least they think they can, but the South can conceive neither machinery nor place for the educated, self-reliant, self-assertive black man.

As the next chapter will discuss, the conflict among black leaders over the most suitable form of education would expand by the early twentieth century into a larger controversy. What began as a disagreement over the value of practical education would become a passionate debate among Washington, Du Bois, and others over the most effective strategy—accommodation or confrontation—for overcoming Jim Crow and white supremacy.

Church and Religion

In a world in which white people otherwise so thoroughly dominated the lives and limited the possibilities of black people, the church had long been the most important institution—after the family—that African Americans controlled for themselves. After the Civil War, black people organized their own churches and religious denominations, which grew and thrived as sources of spiritual comfort and centers of social activity. Black clergymen were often the most influential members of the black community.

In 1890 the South had more black Baptists than all other denominations combined. Baptist congregations were more independent and under less supervision by church hierarchy than other denominations. Bishops, for example, in the African Methodist Episcopal Zion church and the African Methodist Episcopal (AME) church exercised considerable authority over congregations as did Methodist and Presbyterian leaders. Many black people (and many Southern white people as well) preferred the autonomy of the Baptist churches (Figure 15–2).

But whatever the denomination, the church was integral to the lives of most black people. It fulfilled spiritual needs through sermons and music. It gave black people the opportunity, free from white interference, to plan, organize, and lead. It was especially a sanctuary for black women, who immersed themselves in church activities. Though church members usually

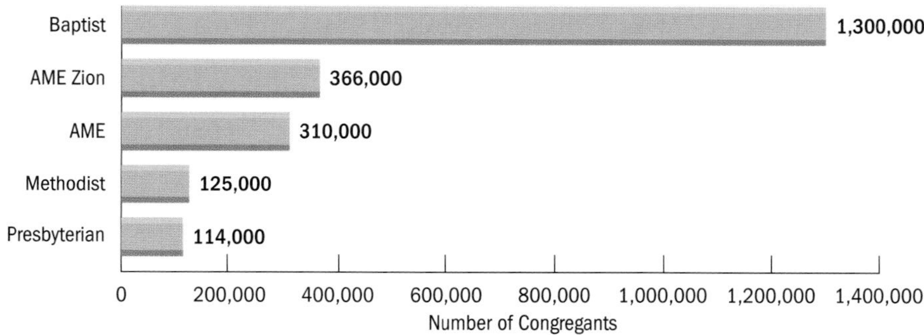

Figure 15–2
Church Affiliation among Southern Black People: 1890
The vast majority of black Southerners belonged to Baptist, Methodist, and Presbyterian congregations in the late nineteenth century, though there were about fifteen thousand black Episcopalians and perhaps two hundred thousand Roman Catholics.
Source: Edward L. Ayers, *The Promise of the New South*, pp. 160–161.

Harriet Powers was deeply inspired by religious faith which she expressed eloquently through quilts that she made. She was born a slave in 1837 and never learned to read or write. The eleven panels in *The Bible Quilt* (1886) illustrate stories from the Old and New Testaments that Powers absorbed from church sermons. Included are Adam and Eve, Cain and Abel, Jacob, the Birth of Christ, Betrayal of Judas, the Last Supper, and the Crucifixion.

had little money to spare, they helped the sick, the bereaved, and people displaced by fires and natural disasters. Black congregations also helped thousands of youngsters attend school and college.

The church service itself was the most important aspect of religious life for most black congregations. Parishioners were expected to participate in the service and not merely listen quietly to the minister's sermon. Black people had long considered white church services too sedate. One black school principal believed that black people gave added meaning to Christianity: While "the white man gives it system logic and abstraction, the Negro is necessary to impart feeling, sanctioned emotions, heart throes and ecstasy." In most black churches, members punctuated the minister's call with many an "Amen." They testified, shouted, laughed and cried, and sometimes fainted. Choirs provided joyful music and solemn songs.

Most congregations did not want scholarly sermons or theologically sound addresses. When Frederick Jones, a well-dressed new black minister in North Carolina, offered a deliberate message brimming with rationality, he was met with silence and rebuked by a senior member of the congregation. "Dese fellers comes out heah wid dere starched shirts, and dey' beaver hats, and dere kid gloves, but dey don't know nuffin b[o]ut 'ligion." The next time Jones preached, he had changed his clothes and delivered a passionate sermon.

Many black ministers had little or no education. Benjamin E. Mays's father told him that the clergy did not need an education. "God called men to preach; and when He called them, He would tell them what to say!" Poorly prepared and unqualified clergymen who relied on ungrammatical and rhetorical appeals disturbed some black leaders. In 1890 Booker T. Washington claimed that "three-fourths of the Baptist ministers and two-thirds of the Methodists are unfit, either mentally or morally, or both, to preach the Gospel to any one or to attempt to lead any one." W. E. B. Du Bois wanted black churches free of "the noisy and unclean leaders of the thoughtless mob" and the clergy replaced by thoughtful "apostles of service and sacrifice." But a black Alabama farmer observed that solemn and erudite preachers would not survive: "You let a man preach de true Gospel and he won't git many nickels in his pocket; but if he hollers and jumps he gits all the nickels he can hold and chickens besides."

Though infrequently, black women sometimes led congregations. Nannie Helen Burroughs established Women's Day in Baptist churches. Women delivered sermons and guided the parishioners. But Burroughs complained that Women's Day quickly became more an occasion to raise money than to raise women.

The Church as Solace and Escape

For many black people, the emotional involvement and enthusiastic participation in church services was an escape from their dreary and oppressive daily lives. Growing up in rural Greenwood County, South Carolina, Benjamin E. Mays admitted that his Baptist preacher, James F. Marshall, who barely had a fifth-grade education, "emphasized the joys of heaven and the damnation of hell" and that the "trials and tribulations of the world would all be over when one got to heaven." But Mays understood the need for such messages to assuage the impact of white supremacy. "Beaten down at every turn by the white man, as they were, Negroes could perhaps not have survived without this kind of religion."

Black clergymen like Marshall refused to challenge white supremacy. Even veiled comments might invite retaliation or even lynching. When a visiting minister began to criticize white people to Marshall's congregation, Marshall immediately stopped him. Despite the reluctance of many black clergymen to advocate improvement in race relations, many white people still viewed black religious gatherings as a threat. Black churches were burned and black ministers assaulted and killed with tragic regularity in the late-nineteenth-century South.

Black clergymen, like their white counterparts, often stressed middle-class values to their congregations while suggesting that many black people found themselves in shameful situations because of their sinful ways. They urged them to improve their behavior. The black clergyman at Mount Ever Rest Colored Church in rural Mississippi warned his congregation to quit their "cussin; lyin; stealin; crap shootin; whisky drinkin, and backbiting one another to de white folks." Black people who had acquired sinful reputations sometimes received funeral sermons that consigned them to eternal damnation in a fiery hell. As Benjamin Mays recalled, "The church was usually full at funerals, especially if the deceased had been well known; and when a man of bad reputation died the church was jammed."

Not all black religious leaders avoided discussing white supremacy. Some clergymen insisted that black people demand their rights. AME Bishop Henry M. Turner persistently spoke out on racial matters. In 1883 after the U.S. Supreme Court declared the 1875 Civil Rights Act unconstitutional, Turner called the Constitution "a dirty rag, a cheat, a libel and ought to be spit upon by every Negro in the land."

The Holiness Movement and the Pentecostal Church

Not all black people belonged to mainline denominations. The Holiness movement and the emergence of Pentecostal churches affected Methodist and Baptist congregations. Partly in reaction to the elite domination and stiff authority of white Methodism, the Holiness movement gained a foothold among white people and then spilled over among black Southerners. Holiness churches ordained women such as Neely Terry to lead them. Holiness clergy preached that sanctification allowed a Christian to receive a "second blessing" and to feel the "perfect love of Christ." Believers thus achieved an emotional reaffirmation and a new state of grace.

The Church of God in Christ (COGIC) became the leading black Holiness church. After a series of successful revivals in Mississippi and Memphis, two black former Baptists—Charles Harrison Mason and C. P. Jones—founded COGIC in 1907. However, Mason was expelled after reporting that "a flame touched [his] tongue," and his "language changed." He had spoken in tongues. Mason then organized the Pentecostal General Assembly of the Church of God in Christ, and he assigned several black men to serve as bishops in Mississippi, Arkansas, Texas, Missouri, and California. In 1911 Mason appointed Lizzee Woods Roberson to lead the Woman's Department, a post she held until 1945. She transformed that department into a financial powerhouse for COGIC.

In the meantime, Charles Fox Parham, a dynamic white minister, had founded the Pentecostal church in the early twentieth entury in the Houston-Galveston area of Texas. William J. Seymour, who was born a slave in Louisiana, played a key role in the development of the church. After hearing black people speak in tongues in Houston, he went to Los Angeles where he and others also began to speak in tongues. There he founded the highly evangelistic church that became the Pentecostal church. It attracted enormous interest and grew rapidly.

Charles Harrison Mason joined the Pentecostal movement, and under his leadership the Reorganized Church of God in Christ became the leading Pentecostal denomination. It soon spread across the South among black and white people. Thogh there were tensions between black and white believers, the Pentecostal church was the only movement of any significance that crossed the racial divide in the early twentieth-century America.

PROFILE

Henry McNeal Turner

Henry McNeal Turner began as a supporter of racial harmony and a U.S. patriot. As he aged, however, he became steadily more disenchanted with the way white Americans contradicted their professed dedication to the principles of fairness and justice by their treatment of black Americans.

Turner was born to free black parents in Newberry, South Carolina, in 1834. After his father's death, he worked in cotton fields and learned to be a blacksmith and a carriage maker. He also learned to read and write while working for a white lawyer. Drawn to religion, he was licensed to preach by the Methodist Episcopal church, a white denomination. In 1859 he moved to Baltimore and was ordained in the AME church. He then became pastor of Union Bethel Church, the largest black congregation in Washington, DC. During the Civil War, he served as a chaplain with the First Regiment of U.S. Colored Troops.

After the war, he briefly worked for the Freedmen's Bureau in Georgia. In an Emancipation Day address in Savannah in 1866 he praised the American flag and predicted that white people would soon accept black people.

Turner became active in Republican politics and was elected to the 1867–68 Georgia constitutional convention where he was the only black delegate to favor a literacy requirement for voting. He also supported a measure to help white planters who had not paid their taxes to keep their land. He conceded that "no man in Georgia has been more conservative than I. Anything to please white folks has been my motto."

In 1868 Turner was elected to the Georgia House of Representatives. When white legislators voted to remove the thirty-two black representatives, he objected: "I shall neither fawn nor cringe before any party, nor stoop to beg for my rights. . . . I am here to demand my rights, and to hurl thunderbolts at the men who dare to cross the threshold of my manhood." The black lawmakers were reinstated.

In 1880 he was elected one of the 12 bishops in the AME church and became president of Morris Brown College in Atlanta, where he served until 1900. He also became an advocate of emigration to Africa and supported the Liberian Exodus of 1877. Turner supported women's suffrage and ordained a woman as a deacon in the AME church in 1888, but the AME Council of Bishops withdrew the appointment.

Turner had little tolerance for those who considered Christianity a white man's religion. He asserted that "God is a Negro" and attacked those who "believe God is a white-skinned, blue-eyed, projecting-nosed, compressed-lipped, and finely-robed white gentleman."

He helped establish and edited a monthly AME newspaper, the *Voice of Missions.* In its pages he took a progressively black nationalist stance and criticized white supremacy and lynching. Growing older and angrier, he told black readers of the *Voice of Missions* to get guns and attack white predators. "Let every Negro in this country who has a spark of manhood in him supply his house with one, two, or three guns . . . and when your domicile is invaded . . . turn loose your missiles of death and blow the fiendish wretches into a thousand giblets."

He denounced black soldiers who fought to suppress the Philippine Insurrection. "I boil over with disgust when I remember that colored men from this country . . . are there fighting to subjugate a people of their own color. . . . I can scarcely keep from saying that I hope the Filipinos will wipe such soldiers from the face of the earth. . . . To go down there and shoot innocent men and take the country away from them, is too much for me to think about."

Embittered and tired, Turner lost faith in the intentions of white people and no longer praised the flag. "I used to love what I thought was the grand old flag, and sing with ecstasy about the Stars and Stripes, but to the Negro in this country the American flag is a dirty and contemptible rag. . . . Without multiplying words, I wish to say that hell is an improvement on the United States where the Negro is concerned."

Bishop Henry McNeal Turner died of a heart attack in 1915. He was married four times, outliving three wives and all but two of his children.

Roman Catholics and Episcopalians

Most African Americans belonged to one of the Baptist or Methodist churches. Booker T. Washington reportedly observed that "If a black man is anything but a Baptist or Methodist, someone has been tampering with his religion." Nevertheless, there were black people who belonged to other churches and denominations—or occasionally belonged to no organized religious group.

As many as 200,000 African Americans were Roman Catholic in 1890. They were rarely fully accepted by the church or white Catholics. They were segregated in separate churches with separate parish schools in the South. Augustus Tolton was the first African-American priest. Because no American seminary would accept him, he was educated and ordained in 1886 in Rome. For a time, he presided over a parish in Quincy, Illinois, made up mainly of Irish and German Catholics.

Mother Mathilda Beasley came from a prominent free black family in Savannah. Her efforts to establish a community of Franciscan sisters in rural Georgia ultimately failed. In New Orleans, where there were sizable numbers of black Catholics of French descent, the Sisters of Blessed Sacrament established a black high school in 1915 that became Xavier University in 1925.

Fairly or unfairly, most African Americans identified black Episcopalians with wealth and privilege. Many of those Episcopalians traced their heritage to free black families before the Civil War. By 1903 there were approximately 15,000 members of black Episcopal parishes in Richmond, Raleigh, Charleston, and other urban communities in the North and South.

Red versus Black: The Buffalo Soldiers

After the Civil War, the U.S. Army was reduced to fewer than 30,000 troops. Congressional Democrats tried to eliminate black soldiers and their regiments from this reduced force, but Radical Republicans, led by Massachusetts Senator Henry Wilson, prevailed to keep the military open to black men. The Army Reorganization Act of 1869 maintained four all-black regiments: the 9th and 10th Cavalry Regiments and the 24th and 25th Infantry Regiments. These four regiments spent most of the next three decades on the western frontier fighting the Plains Indians. Nearly 12,500 black men served during the late nineteenth century in these segregated units commanded—as black troops had been during the Civil War—by white officers. Unlike in the Civil War, however, many of these white officers were Southerners, and most of them did not hold black men in high regard.

Military service in the West was wretched for white troops and invariably worse for black soldiers. Too often officers considered black troops lazy, undisciplined, and cowardly. Black regiments were assigned mainly to the New Mexico and Arizona territories and to Texas because the Army thought that black people tolerated heat better than white people. The ancestors of the slaves were "from the tropics," claimed Army Quartermaster General Montgomery C. Meigs, and "not from the Northern or Southern extremities of Africa but from the Torrid Zone almost entirely." Most black soldiers were thus compelled to endure the hot, dry, and dusty Southwest desert. Still some black troops were sent to Kansas, Colorado, and the Dakotas, where they confronted instead howling blizzards, subzero temperatures, and frostbite.

Discrimination in the Army

Black troops faced more than adverse weather. The Army routinely provided them inferior food and inadequate housing. While white soldiers received dried apples and peaches, canned tomatoes, onions, and potatoes, black troops were given foul beef, bad bread, and canned peas unfit for human consumption. In 1867 white troops at Fort Leavenworth in Kansas lived in barracks while black troops were forced to sleep in tents on wet ground. Black regiments were allotted used weapons and equipment. The Army sent its worst horses—often old and lame—to the black cavalry.

TRACK 21

Long stretches of boredom, tedious duty, and loneliness marked army life for black and white men in the West. Weeks and months might pass without combat. Commanders constantly had to deal with desertion and alcoholism. Black soldiers were much less likely to desert or turn to drink than were white troops. For example, in 1877, eighteen men deserted from the all-black 10th Regiment, while 184 white soldiers deserted from the all-white 4th Regiment. Black troops realized that while army life could be harsh and dangerous, it compared favorably to the civilian world, which held few genuine opportunities for them. Army food was poor, but the private's pay of $13 per month was regular. Moreover, black troops developed immense pride in themselves as professional soldiers.

The Alert (1888). Famed western artist Frederic Remington spent part of a hot summer accompanying the 10th Cavalry Regiment on patrol in the desert and mountains of the Arizona Territory. Though Remington regarded black people as inferior to whites, he was impressed with the demeanor, endurance, and bravery of the buffalo soldiers.

The Plains Indians who fiercely resisted U.S. forces were so impressed with the performance of their black adversaries that they called them "buffalo soldiers." Indians associated the hair of black men with the shaggy coat of the buffalo—a sacred animal. Black troops considered it a term of respect and began to use it themselves. The 10th Cavalry displayed a buffalo in their unit emblem.

The Buffalo Soldiers in Combat

It was ironic that white military authorities would employ black men to subdue red people. Most black soldiers, however, had no qualms about fighting Indians, protecting white settlers, or apprehending bandits and cattle rustlers. From the late 1860s to the early 1890s, the four black regiments repeatedly engaged hostile Indians. In September 1867, 700 Cheyenne attacked fifty U.S. Army scouts along a dry riverbed in eastern Colorado. The scouts held out for over a week until the 10th Cavalry rescued them. For more than 12 months in 1879 and 1880, the 9th and 10th Cavalry fought the Apaches under Chief Victorio in New Mexico and Texas in a campaign of raid and counterraid. The Apaches slipped across the Mexican border and then returned to southwest Texas. In clashes at Rattlesnake Springs and near Fresno Spring, the 10th killed more than thirty Apaches before Victorio fled again to Mexico where he was killed by the Mexican Army. But the 9th and 10th Cavalry deserve most of the credit for Victorio's defeat with their dogged pursuit of the Apaches for months over hundreds of miles of rugged terrain.

In late 1890, military units including the 9th Cavalry were sent to the Pine Ridge Reservation in South Dakota where Sioux Indians were holding an intense religious ceremony known as the Ghost Dance. Confined to reservations, some Indians—out of desperation and yearning for the past—believed that their fervent participation in the Ghost Dance would bring both their ancestors and the almost extinct buffalo back to the Great Plains. Then white people would vanish, and Indian life would be restored to what it had been decades earlier. But white authorities considered the Ghost Dance a dangerous act of defiance.

On December 29, the 7th Cavalry attempted to disarm a band of Sioux at Wounded Knee on the Pine Ridge Reservation. Shooting erupted, and 146 Indian men, women, and children, and twenty-six soldiers were killed. The 9th Cavalry, 108 miles away in the Badlands, rode the next day through a blizzard and arrived tired and freezing to come to the aid of elements of the 7th Cavalry.

Civilian Hostility to Black Soldiers

Despite the gallant performance of the buffalo soldiers, civilians frequently treated them with hostility. In southern Texas in 1875, Mexicans ambushed five black soldiers, killed two of them, and mutilated their bodies. The next day the infuriated white commander of the 9th Cavalry, Colonel Edward Hatch, rode out with sixty soldiers and apprehended the Mexicans. A local grand jury indicted nine of them for murder, but the only one tried was acquitted, and the other eight were released without a trial. Hatch, another white officer, and three buffalo soldiers were then indicted for breaking into and burglarizing the shack where the Mexicans had sought refuge. The charges were eventually dropped, but the five men had to hire their own lawyers.

Brownsville

One of the worst examples of hostility to black troops, the so-called Brownsville Affair, also occurred in Texas. In 1906 the 1st Battalion of the 25th Infantry was transferred from Fort Niobrara, Nebraska, to Fort Brown in Brownsville, Texas, along the Rio Grande. The black soldiers immediately encountered discrimination from both white people and Mexicans in this border community. They were not permitted in public parks, and white businesses refused to serve them. Several times civilians provoked and attacked individual black soldiers.

Shortly after midnight on August 14, shooting erupted in Brownsville. About 150 shots were fired, and a policeman and a resident were injured. Black troops were blamed for the violence when clips and cartridges from the Army's Springfield rifles were found in the street. Two military investigations concluded that black soldiers did the shooting. The Army could not identify the specific soldiers responsible because no one would confess or name the alleged perpetrators.

With no hearing or trial, President Theodore Roosevelt dismissed three companies of black men—167 soldiers—from the Army. They were barred from rejoining the military and from government employment, and were denied veterans' pensions or benefits. The black community, which had supported Roosevelt, reacted angrily. Booker T. Washington, a Roosevelt supporter, privately wrote, "There is no law, human or divine, which justifies the punishment of an innocent man." Washington added, "I have the strongest faith in the President's honesty of intention, high mindedness of purpose, sincere unselfishness and courage, but I regret for all these reasons all the more that this thing has occurred."

Republican Senator James B. Foraker of Ohio later led a Senate investigation that upheld Roosevelt's dismissals. But Foraker, a strong opponent of Roosevelt, questioned the guilt of the black men. The clips and cartridges that served as evidence were apparently planted. After Roosevelt left office in 1909, the War Department reinstated fourteen of the soldiers. In 1972, the Justice Department determined that an injustice had occurred. The black soldiers were posthumously awarded honorable discharges. The only survivor of the Brownsville affair—Dorsie Willis—received $25,000 from Congress and the right to treatment at veteran's facilities.

African Americans in the Navy

Naval service was even more unappealing than life in the Army. In the late nineteenth century, as the Navy made the transition from timber and sail to steam and steel, approximately one sailor in ten was a black man. Although the Navy's ships were "integrated" in that black and white sailors served on them together, white sailors were hostile to black sailors. They would not eat or bunk with them or take orders from them. Increasingly, and to enforce a de facto shipboard segregation, black sailors were restricted to stoking boilers in the bowels of naval vessels and to cooking and serving food to white sailors.

Although several black men enrolled as midshipmen at the Naval Academy in the 1870s, they faced social ostracism and none of them graduated. Not until 1949 did a black man graduate from the academy.

The Black Cowboys

Black men before, during, and after the Civil War were familiar with horses and mules. As slaves, they tended and cared for animals. Some black men served with the 9th and 10th U. S. Cavalry Regiments and gained experience with horses. It is no wonder that perhaps 5,000 black men rode herd on cattle in the late nineteenth and early twentieth centuries. During the 1870s and 1880s black men joined several thousand Mexicans and white men on the long cattle drives from Texas to Kansas, Nebraska, and Missouri.

Managing cattle was monotonous, difficult, and dirty work. Yet it required considerable skill as a rider to manage hundreds of head of ornery and stinking animals. Cowboys had to tolerate weather that ranged from incredibly hot to bitter cold. They had to be willing to consume unappetizing food for weeks at a time. There was no bed to sleep in each night, and their closest companion most days and nights was the horse they rode.

The Spanish-American War

With the western frontier subdued by 1890, many Americans concluded that the United States should expand overseas. European nations had already carved out extensive colonies in Africa and Asia. Many, but by no means all, Americans favored the extension of U.S. political, economic, and military authority to Latin America and the Pacific. In 1893 the U.S. Navy and American businessmen toppled the monarchy in Hawaii, and the United States annexed that chain of islands in 1898.

The same year, the United States went to war to liberate Cuba from Spanish control. As in the Civil War, black men enlisted, fought, and died. Twenty-two black sailors were among the 266 men who died when the battleship U.S.S. Maine blew up in Havana harbor, the event that helped trigger the war. Many black Americans were convinced, as they had been in previous wars, that the willingness of black people to support the war against Spain would impress white Americans sufficiently to reduce or even eliminate white hostility. E. E. Cooper, editor of the Washington *Colored American*, declared that the war would bring black people and white people together in "an era of good feeling the country over and cement the races into a more compact brotherhood through perfect unity of purpose and patriotic affinity." The war, he asserted, would help white Americans "unloose themselves from the bondage of race prejudice."

Many black and white Americans, however, questioned the American cause. Some black people saw the war as an effort to extend American influence and racial practices, including Jim Crow, beyond U.S. borders. The Reverend George W. Prioleau, chaplain of the Ninth Cavalry, wondered why black Americans supported what he considered a hypocritical war:

> Talk about fighting and freeing poor Cuba and of Spain's brutality. . . . Is America any better than Spain? Has she not subjects in her very midst who are murdered daily without a trial of judge or jury? Has she not subjects in her own borders whose children are half-fed and half-clothed, because their father's skin is black. . . . Yet the Negro is loyal to his country's flag.

Whether or not they harbored doubts, black men by the thousands served in the Spanish-American War and in the Philippine Insurrection that followed it. Shortly before war was declared, the Army ordered its four black regiments of regular troops transferred from their western posts to Florida to prepare for combat in Cuba. President William McKinley also appealed for volunteers. The War Department designated four of the black volunteer units "immune regiments" because it believed that black men would tolerate the heat and humidity of Cuba better than white troops and that black people were immune or at least less susceptible to yellow fever, which was endemic to Cuba. (Yellow fever was carried by mosquitoes, but this was unknown in 1898. Most people believed that the disease was caused by the tropical Caribbean climate.)

State militia (national guard) units were also called into federal service, and several states, including Alabama, Ohio, Massachusetts, Illinois, Kansas, Virginia, Indiana, and North Carolina, sent all-black militias, as well as white units. But Georgia's governor refused to permit that state's black militia to serve, and New York would not permit black men to enlist in its militia. The states typically followed the federal example and kept black men confined to all-black units commanded by white officers, but there were exceptions.

Black Officers

The buffalo soldiers of the 9th and 10th Cavalry and the 24th and 25th Infantry remained under the leadership of white officers. But the men of several volunteer units insisted that they be led by black officers: "No officers, no fight." So for the first time in American military history, black men commanded all-black units: the 8th Illinois, the 23rd Kansas, and the 3rd North Carolina. Mindful that many people doubted the ability of black men to lead, the colonel of the 8th Illinois cautioned his men, "If we fail, the whole race will have to shoulder the burden." The War Department also permitted black men to serve as lieutenants with other black volunteer units, but all higher ranking officers were white men. Charles Young, a black graduate of West Point who was serving as a military science instructor at Wilberforce University in Ohio, was given command of Ohio's 9th Battalion, and he served with distinction and was promoted from captain to colonel.

As black and white troops assembled in Georgia and Florida before departing for Cuba, black men soon realized that a U.S. uniform did not lessen white racial prejudice. White civilians in Georgia killed four black men of the 3rd North Carolina. All-white juries acquitted those who were charged with the murders. After the white proprietor of a drug store in Lakeland, Florida, refused to serve a black soldier at the soda fountain, a mob of black troops gathered. The proprietor was pistol whipped, and another white man was killed by a stray bullet before the troops were disarmed. In Tampa, where the troops were embarking for Cuba, a bloody all-night riot broke out after drunken white soldiers from Ohio decided to shoot at a black child for target practice. Twenty-seven black soldiers and three white soldiers were seriously injured. It is not surprising that when the men of the all-black 3rd Alabama adopted an injured crow as the unit mascot, they named it Jim.

Most of the black units never saw combat. White military authorities considered black men unreliable and inadequately trained for combat. Black volunteer units stayed behind in Florida when white units embarked for Cuba. However, the four regiments of regular black troops, the buffalo soldiers, did go to Cuba, where they performed well despite the doubts and persistent criticism of some white men. The Spanish troops were impressed enough to give the black men the nickname "smoked yankees."

A Splendid Little War

In the summer of 1898, U.S. troops arrived in Cuba. Black men of the 10th Cavalry fought alongside Cuban rebels, many of whom were themselves black. Four black American privates earned the Congressional Medal of Honor for their part in an engagement in southwestern Cuba. Black and white troops were best remembered for their role in the assault on San Juan and Kettle Hills overlooking the key Cuban port of Santiago in eastern Cuba. Santiago was the main Spanish naval base in Cuba and its capture would break Spain's hold over the island.

In this assault, black soldiers from the 24th Infantry and the 9th and the 10th Cavalry Regiments fought alongside white troops including Theodore Roosevelt's volunteer unit, the Rough Riders. In the fiercest fighting of the war and amid considerable confusion, black and white men were thrown together as they encountered withering Spanish fire. Though for a time the outcome was in doubt, they took the high ground overlooking Santiago harbor. White soldiers praised the performance of the black troops. One commented: "I am not a negro lover. My father fought with Mosby's Rangers [in the Confederate Army] and I was born in the South, but the negroes saved that fight." In his campaign for vice president in 1900, Theodore Roosevelt stated that black men saved his life during the battle. Later, however, Roosevelt reversed himself and accused several black men of cowardice.

After the War

As hostilities concluded, men of the 24th Infantry agreed to work in yellow fever hospitals after white regiments refused the duty. About half the black soldiers—some 471 men—contracted yellow fever. Other black troops arrived in Cuba after the war to serve garrison duty. The 8th Illinois and the 23rd Kansas built roads, bridges, schools, and hospitals. The black men were especially pleased at the lack of

In 1898 during the Spanish–American War, the 9th and 10th Calvary regiments—the buffalo soldiers—were sent to fight in Cuba. At a battle near the village of Las Guasimos on June 24, black troops from the 10th fought against Spanish troops with white soldiers from the 1st Cavalry and the volunteer regiment known as the Rough Riders. John J. "Black Jack" Pershing was one of the 10th's white officers, and he praised their performance under intense Spanish fire. (Pershing acquired the nickname "Black Jack" because of his command of black troops.)

VOICES

Black Men in Battle in Cuba

On October 1, 1898, a letter appeared in the Illinois Record, *a black newspaper, from one of the men in the 10th Cavalry. The author was probably John E. Lewis, and he wrote the letter from Montauk Point on the eastern tip of Long Island in New York where black and white troops were sent after the war. Lewis described the enthusiastic reaction of the Rough Riders to the 9th and 10th Cavalry, but complained that the contributions of the black soldiers were too often overlooked and ignored:*

The Rough Riders were mustered out on the 12th and 13th [of September], and when Colonel Roosevelt bade the regiment good-bye he paid a glowing tribute to the 9th and 10th Cavalry, especially in saving them from ambush.

Mr. Editor, if your readers could have heard the Rough Riders yell when the 10th Cav. was mentioned as the 'Smoked Yankees' and that they were of a good breed, they would have been doubly proud of the members of their race who rendered such signal service on the battle field. . . .

When a troop of the 10th made their famous charge of 3,000 yards under the command of Capt. [William J.] Beck, the non-commissioned officers, all colored, distinguished themselves in a manner that will redound to the glory of the race. Among those who distinguished themselves are Carter Smith, acting 1st Sergeant, Sgts. Geo. Taylor, James F. Cole, James H. Williams, Smith Johnson and Corpl. Joseph G. Mitchell who was wounded at San Juan.

All are soldiers whose names should go down in history. They never faltered in the thickest of the battle; they encouraged on in a rain of shot and shell and showed by their actions that they were the leaders. They did not hesitate to take the lead, and when that charge was made it was "save your cartridges, don't waste a shot."

The half will never be told of their deeds upon the battlefield. All deserve praise from the private up, but the praise has been given those who should have been in the lead instead of laying in the rear under cover. And yet they say that the black is not fit to lead.

If our war reports would only give credit where credit is due there would be no need writing these poorly composed lines that your readers might know of the deeds and hardships their dear ones have passed through.

You will read that colored troops, or companies did so and so, but the white papers never mention a name and the world only knows one who has done an act of bravery as a Negro soldier, nameless and friendless. It was never mentioned how, at that famous charge of the 10th Cav. And the rescue of the Rough Riders at San Juan Hill, the yell was started by a single trooper of C Troop, 10th Cav. and was carried down the line.

Brave 1st Sgt. Adam Huston at the head of his troop commanded "forward" which seemed into almost certain death. In him the troop found an able leader; Lieut. [E.D.] Anderson who was in command and fell to the rear and when the command "Forward March," was given, the brave Major [Theodore J.] Wint only smiled, for he admired bravery and did not change the command although he knew that the troops was in a desperate position. The troops were carried safely through. . . .

Will it ever be known how Sgt. Thomas Griffith of Troop C cut the wire fence along the line so that the 10th Cav. and Rough Riders could go through?

Never once did these brave men give thought to danger. . . .

The Spaniard would have sent our army home in disgrace had it not been for the daring and almost reckless charge of the Negro regiments. God was with them in that charge and no man who has ever seen the place will say that it was possible to make the charge without being slaughtered. . . .

[Unsigned]

QUESTIONS

1. What is the source of the bitterness revealed in this letter?
2. What motivated black men to risk their lives in combat in the Spanish-American War?
3. Do any portions of this account seem strained, exaggerated, or unreliable? Why or why not?

Source: Willard B. Gatewood, Jr., *Smoked Yankees and the Struggle for Empire: Letters from Negro Soldiers*, 1898–1902, pp. 76–78 discrimination and absence of Jim Crow in Cuba. Some black soldiers discussed the possibility of organizing emigration to Cuba, but nothing came of it. Still other black troops from the 6th Massachusetts joined in the invasion of Puerto Rico as the United States took that island from Spain.

The Philippine Insurrection

With the resounding victory in the Spanish-American War, many Americans decided that their nation had an obligation to uplift those less fortunate peoples who had been part of the Spanish Empire. Thus, President William McKinley and American diplomats insisted that the United States acquire Guam, Puerto Rico, and the Philippines from Spain in the Treaty of Paris that ended the war in December 1898. The Filipinos, like the Cubans, had long opposed Spanish rule and fully expected the American government to support their independence. Instead, they were infuriated to learn that the United States intended to annex the Philippines. The Filipinos, under Emilio Aguinaldo, switched from fighting the Spanish to fighting the occupying U.S. forces.

Would Black Men Fight Brown Men?

Many black and white Americans denounced the U.S. effort to take the Philippines. They were unconvinced that the Filipinos would benefit from American benevolence. AME Bishop Henry Turner termed it an "unholy war of conquest," and Booker T. Washington believed that the Filipinos "should be given an opportunity to govern themselves." In a grim, but humorous, attempt to taunt those who proclaimed the superiority of white civilization, a group of black men formed the "Black Man's Burden Association."

Opposition to U.S. involvement in the Philippines notwithstanding, black men in the military served throughout the campaign in the Pacific islands. The black troops included the regular 25th Infantry and 24th Infantry, the 9th Cavalry, and the 48th and 49th Volunteer Regiments. Through propaganda, the Filipino rebels attempted to convince black troops to abandon the cause. Posters reminded "The Colored American Soldier" of injustice and lynching in the United States. White troops did not help by calling Filipinos "niggers." Though many black soldiers had reservations about the fighting, they remained loyal. By the time the conflict ended with an American victory in 1902, only five black men had deserted. David Fagen of the 24th Infantry joined Filipino forces and became an officer, fighting American troops for two years before he was killed. Two black men from the 9th Cavalry were executed for desertion, while fifteen white soldiers who deserted had their death sentences commuted.

Though black men had served with distinction as professional soldiers for forty years after the Civil War—on the frontier, in Cuba, and in the Philippines—the Army little valued their achievements and sacrifice, as the Brownsville Affair showed. White military and political leaders persistently relied on passions and prejudices over evidence of achievement. Time and again, these circumstances dashed the hopes of those black civilians and soldiers who believed that the performance of black troops would challenge white supremacy and demonstrate that black citizens had earned the same rights and opportunities as other Americans.

Black Businesspeople and Entrepreneurs

Well-educated black men and women stood no chance of gaining employment with any major business or industrial corporation at the turn of the century. White males not only monopolized management and supervisory positions, but also occupied nearly every job that did not involve manual labor. In 1899 black novelist Sutton E. Griggs described the frustrations that an educated black man encountered:

> He possessed a first class college education, but that was all. He knew no trade nor was he equipped to enter any of the professions. . . . He would have made an excellent drummer, salesman, clerk, cashier, government official (county, city, state, or national), telegraph operator, conductor, or anything of such a nature. But the color of his skin shut the doors so tight that he could not even peep in. . . . It is true that such positions as street laborer, hod carrier, cart driver, factory hand, railroad hand were open to him; but such menial tasks were uncongenial to a man of his education and polish.

While white supremacy and the proliferation of Jim Crow severely restricted opportunities for educated black people, those same limitations enabled enterprising black men and women to open and operate businesses that served black clientele. By the

PROFILE

Maggie Lena Walker

By the early 20th century, Maggie Lena Walker was a successful businesswoman, community leader, and one of the wealthiest black women in America. She was also an ardent advocate for her race and her gender. She was born Maggie Mitchell in Richmond, Virginia, on July 15, 1867, to Elizabeth Draper, a laundress. Her mother married William Mitchell in 1870. Young Maggie was much influenced by the determination, fortitude, and hard work of her mother. Throughout her childhood, she helped her mother wash, iron, and carry laundry.

Maggie Mitchell graduated from a normal school in 1883 and taught primary school. She was active in the First African Baptist Church and remained a committed member for life. In 1886 she married Armstead Walker. Her views on marriage were progressive. Explaining the responsibilities that she shared with her husband, she wrote, "Since marriage is an equal partnership, I believe that the woman and the man are equal in power and should by consultation and agreement, mutually decide as to the conduct of the home and the government of the children."

The Independent Order of St. Luke was one of many black mutual aid societies that flourished in the nineteenth century. Black people contributed small sums of money and, in the event of sickness or death, the society paid benefits to members or their survivors. But the Order was also a fraternal and social organization that stressed racial pride as well as compassion, generosity, and charity.

Maggie Lena Walker became active in the order at the age of fourteen in 1881. She was elected Grand Matron and became the Right Worthy Grand Secretary in 1899. When she assumed her duties, the Order had \$31.61 in funds and 1,080 members. She proved to be a dynamic leader and an inspirational speaker. She traveled extensively and spoke regularly to members. She stressed racial concerns and attacked discrimination and lynching. She appealed to audiences to patronize black enterprises. By the early twentieth century under Walker's guidance, the order operated in twenty-two states. Its membership had increased, and its financial standing had improved. In 1924 the Independent Order of St. Luke had funds totaling \$3,480,540.

The Order ran a newspaper, the *St. Luke Herald*, and a bank with Maggie Lena Walker as president. She was the first black woman to serve as the chief executive of a bank in the United States. The bank subsequently merged with two other banks and became the Consolidated Bank and Trust Company with Walker as president. She was especially pleased that the bank enabled black customers to purchase homes. By 1920, 645 black families had acquired their houses with the financial assistance of the bank.

Walker was deeply concerned with the plight of black women, and she made certain that the Order employed black women in significant positions. In 1909 she paid homage to women of color:

> And the great all absorbing interest, this thing which has driven sleep from my eyes and fatigue from my body, is the love I bear women, our Negro women, hemmed, circumscribed, with every imaginable obstacle in our way, blocked and held down by the fears and prejudices of the whites, ridiculed and sneered at by the intelligent blacks.

Maggie Lena Walker became a wealthy woman and lived in a twenty-two-room house. She was deeply involved in community affairs and organizations. She supported Virginia Union University, which later awarded her an honorary degree, and the Industrial School for Colored Girls. She worked with the Piedmont Tuberculosis Sanitarium for Negroes. She served on Richmond's Council for Colored Women and with the Virginia Federation of Colored Women's Clubs, and she was among the prominent women who helped organize the Council of Women of the Darker Races. She joined the National Association of Colored Women in 1912 and was active in the NAACP. She was also a committed Republican and ran unsuccessfully for state superintendent of public instruction. She died on December 15, 1934.

early twentieth century, black Americans not only had their own churches and schools, but they had also established banks, newspapers, insurance companies, retail businesses, barbershops, beauty salons, and funeral parlors. Virtually every black community had its own small businesses, markets, street vendors, and other entrepreneurs.

Some black men and women established thriving and substantial businesses. In Atlanta, Union Army veteran Alexander Hamilton was a successful building contractor. He supervised construction of the Good Samaritan Building, oversaw the erection of buildings on the Morris Brown College campus, and built many of the impressive houses on Peachtree Street. Hamilton employed both black and white workmen on his projects.

Alonzo Herndon was a former slave who also achieved financial success in Atlanta. He operated a fashionable barbershop on Peachtree Street that served well-to-do white men. The shop had crystal chandeliers and polished brass spittoons. Herndon expanded and opened two other shops, eventually employing seventy-five men. He also founded the Atlanta Life Insurance Company, the largest black stock company in the world.

In Montgomery, Alabama, H. A. Loveless, a former slave, became a butcher and then diversified his business operations by opening an undertaking establishment and operating a hack and dray company. By 1900, Loveless also ran a coal and wood yard and sold real estate.

In Richmond, Virginia, Maggie Lena Walker—the secretary–treasurer of the Independent Order of St. Luke, a mutual benefit society, and a founder of the St. Luke's Penny Savings Bank—became the wealthiest black woman in America. Also in Richmond, former slave John Dabney owned an exclusive catering business that served wealthy white Virginians. He catered two state dinners for President Grover Cleveland. He used his earnings to purchase several houses and to invest in real estate.

Madam C. J. Walker may have been the most successful black entrepreneur of them all. Born Sarah Breedlove in 1867 on a Louisiana cotton plantation, she married at age fourteen and was a widowed single parent by age twenty. She spent the next two decades struggling to make ends meet. In 1905 with $1.50, she developed a formula to nourish and enrich the hair of black women. She insisted that it was not a process to straighten hair.

She sold the product door-to-door in Denver but could not keep up with the demand. The business rapidly expanded and became a thriving enterprise that employed hundreds of black women. She established the company's headquarters in Indianapolis. In the meantime, she married Charles Joseph Walker and took his name and the title Madam. As she accumulated wealth, she shared it generously with Bethune Cookman College, Tuskegee Institute, and the NAACP. She was a major contributor to the NAACP's antilynching campaign. When she died of a stroke at age fifty-one in 1919, she was reportedly a millionaire.

Despite such successes, most black people who went into business had difficulty surviving, and many failed. Too often they depended on black customers who were themselves poor. White-owned banks were unlikely to provide credit to aspiring black businesspeople. And even the wealthiest black entrepreneurs did not come close to possessing the wealth the richest white Americans accumulated.

African Americans and Labor

Thousands of black Southerners worked in factories, mills, and mines. Though most textile mills refused to hire black people except for janitorial duties, many black laborers toiled in tobacco and cigarmaking facilities, flour mills, coal mines, sawmills, turpentine camps, and on railroads. Black women worked for white families as cooks, maids, and laundresses. Black workers usually were paid less than white men employed in the same capacity. Conversely, white working people frequently complained that they were not hired because employers retained black workers who worked for less pay. In 1904 in Georgia white railroad firemen went on strike in an unsuccessful attempt to compel railroad operators to dismiss black firemen. Invariably, there was persistent antagonism between black and white laborers.

Unions

When white workers formed labor unions in the late nineteenth century, they usually excluded black workers. The Knights of Labor, however, founded in 1869, was open to all workers (except whiskey salesmen, lawyers, and bankers), and by the mid-1880s counted 50,000 women and 70,000 black workers among its nearly 750,000 members. But by the 1890s, after unsuccessful strikes and a deadly riot in Chicago, the Knights had lost influence to a new organization, the American Federation of Labor (AFL). Founded in 1886, the AFL was ostensibly open to all skilled workers, but most of its local craft unions barred women and black tradesmen. In contrast, the United Mine Workers (UMW), formed in 1890, encouraged black coal miners to join the union rather than serve as strikebreakers. By 1900 approximately 20,000 of the 91,000 members of the UMW were black men. The Industrial Workers of the World (IWW), a revolutionary labor organization founded in 1905, brought black and white laborers together in, among other places, the Brotherhood of Timber Workers in the Piney Woods of east Texas.

In 1869 a Baltimore ship caulker, Isaac Myers, organized the National Colored Labor Union, which lasted for seven years. It discouraged strikes and encouraged its members to work hard and be thrifty. It lost whatever effectiveness it had when it was largely taken over by Republican leaders during Reconstruction.

Though most southern black people worked long hours in cotton fields, there were thousands who toiled in factories, mills, and mines. Here black women stem tobacco in a Virginia factory under the supervision of a white man.

Strikes

During the late nineteenth and early twentieth centuries, although some strikes by unions won concessions from business owners, most failed because owners could rely on strikebreakers and the police or national guard to intervene and bring the strikes to an often violent end. For a time, black shipyard workers in southern ports did achieve some success. Black stevedores who loaded and unloaded ships endured oppressive conditions and long hours for low pay. They periodically went on strike in Charleston, Savannah, and New Orleans. The Longshoremen's Protective Union in Charleston won several strikes in the 1870s. In Nashville in 1871 black dockyard workers went on strike, demanding twenty cents an hour. Steamboat owners broke the strike by hiring state convicts for fifteen cents an hour.

Black and white laborers who toiled in the Louisiana sugarcane fields earned an average of $13 a week in the 1880s. They were paid in scrip—not cash—that was redeemable only in stores the planters owned where prices were exorbitant. Workers lived in 12´ x 15´ cabins that they rented from the planters. In some ways, it was worse than slave labor.

Though the state militia had broken previous strikes, 9,000 black and 1,000 white workers responded to a call for a new strike in 1887 by organizers from the Knights of Labor. They quit the sugar fields in four parishes (as Louisiana counties are called) to demand more pay. The strike was peaceful, but planters convinced the governor to send in the militia. The troops fired into a crowd at Pattersonville and killed four people. The next day local officials killed several strikers who had been taken prisoner. In the town of Thibodaux, "prominent citizens" organized and armed themselves and had martial law declared. More than thirty-five unarmed black people, including women and children, were killed in their homes and churches. Two black strike leaders were lynched. The strike was broken.

Black washerwomen went on strike in Atlanta in 1881. The women, who did laundry for white families, refused to do any more until they were guaranteed $1 per twelve pounds of laundry. The strike was well organized through black churches, and it spread to cooks and domestics. A strike committee used persuasion and intimidation to ensure support. Some three thousand black people joined the strike. White families went two weeks without clean clothes. However, Atlanta's white community broke the strike. Police arrested strike leaders for disorderly conduct. Several black women were fined from $5 to $20. The city council threatened to require each member of the Washer Women's Association of Atlanta to purchase a city business license for $25. Though the strike gradually ended without having achieved its goal, it did demonstrate that poor black women could organize effectively.

Black Professionals

Like business and labor, the medical and legal professions were strictly segregated. Most black physicians, nurses, and lawyers attended all-black professional schools in the late nineteenth century. Black people in need of medical care were either excluded from white hospitals or confined to all-black wards. Black physicians were denied staff privileges at white hospitals. Thus black people in many communities formed their own hospitals. Most were small facilities with fifty or fewer beds.

Medicine

In 1891 Dr. Daniel Hale Williams established Provident Hospital and Training Institute in Chicago, the first black hospital operated solely by African Americans. In 1894 the Freedmen's Hospital was organized in Washington, D.C., and it later affiliated with Howard University. Frederick Douglass Memorial Hospital and Training School was founded in Philadelphia in 1895. Dr. Alonzo McClennan in cooperation with several other black physicians established the Hospital and Training School for Nurses in Charleston, South Carolina, in 1897.

In 1900 Williams, explaining why black medical institutions were necessary, wrote

> In view of this cruel ostracism, affecting so vitally the race, our duty seems plain. Institute Hospitals and Training Schools. Let us no longer sit idly and inanely deploring existing conditions. Let us not waste time trying to effect changes or modifications in the institutions unfriendly to us, but rather let us seek to promote the doctrine of helping and stimulating our race.

By 1890 there were 909 black (most of whom were male) physicians practicing in the United States. They served a black population of seven and a half million people. Barred from membership in the American Medical Association, black doctors organized the National Medical Association in Atlanta in 1895. Most black doctors had been educated at seven black medical schools that included Leonard Medical School at Shaw University in Raleigh, North Carolina; Flint-Goodridge Medical College in New Orleans; Meharry Medical School in Nashville; and the Howard University School of Medicine in Washington, D.C.

In 1910 in a report issued by the Carnegie Foundation for the Advancement of Teaching, Abraham Flexner recommended improving medical education in the United States by eliminating weaker medical schools. He suggested raising admission standards and expanding laboratory and clinical training in the stronger schools. As a result of the implementation of these recommendations, sixty of 155 white medical schools closed, and among black medical schools, only Howard and Meharry survived. By 1920 there were 3,885 black physicians. Many had completed medical school before the Flexner report was compiled.

The number of black women physicians was actually declining. In 1890 there were ninety black women practicing medicine, and by 1920 there were sixty-five. The number of medical schools had decreased, and most black and white men considered medicine an inappropriate profession for women. But black women also had to contend with the opposition of white women. Isabella Vandervall was a 1915 graduate of New York Medical College and Hospital who was accepted for an internship at the Hospital for Women and Children in Syracuse. When she appeared in person, however, the hospital's female administrator rejected Vandervall, ". . . we can't have you here! You are colored!"

Nursing was another matter. By 1920 there were thirty-six black nurse training schools and 2,150 white nursing schools. White nurses resented the competition from black nurses for positions as private duty nurses. And the black physicians who ran nurse training schools exploited their students by hiring them out, as part of their training, for private duty work but requiring them to relinquish their pay to the schools. Moreover, many people—black and white—regarded black nurses more as domestics than as trained professionals. Unlike white nurses, for example, black nurses were usually addressed by their first names. To confront such obstacles, fifty-two black nurses met in New York City in 1908 and formed the National Association of Colored Graduate Nurses (NACGN). By 1920, the NACGN had five hundred members.

Black physicians and nurses struggled to provide medical care to people who were often desperately ill and sought treatment only as a last resort. Disease and sickness flourished among people who were ill nourished, poorly clad, and inadequately housed. Tuberculosis, pneumonia, pellagra, hookworm, and syphilis afflicted many poor black people—as they also did poor white people. Bessie Hawes, a 1918 graduate of Tuskegee Institute's Nurse Training program, described the kind of situation she faced in rural Alabama:

> A colored family of ten were in bed and dying for the want of attention. No one would come near. I was glad of the opportunity. As I entered the little country cabin, I found the mother in bed. Three children were buried the week before. The father and the remainder of the family were running a temperature of 102-104. Some had influenza, others had pneumonia. No relatives or friends would come near. I saw at a glance I had work to do. I rolled up my sleeves and killed chickens and began to cook. . . . I milked the cow, gave medicine, and did everything I could to help conditions. I worked day and night trying to save them for seven days. I had no place to sleep. In the meantime the oldest daughter had a miscarriage and I delivered her without the aid of any physicians. . . . I only wished that I could have reached them earlier and been able to have done something for the poor mother.

The Law

Unlike black physicians and nurses, who were excluded from white hospitals, black lawyers were permitted to practice in what was essentially a white male court system. But white judges and attorneys did not welcome them. Rather than create additional problems for themselves, black defendants and plaintiffs often retained white lawyers in the hope that white legal counsel might improve their chances of receiving justice. As a result, many black attorneys had a hard time making a living from the practice of law.

The American Bar Association (ABA) would not admit black attorneys to membership. Attorney William H. Lewis, a graduate of Amherst College and the Harvard Law School who was appointed an assistant U.S. attorney general by President William Howard Taft in 1911, was expelled by the ABA in 1912 when its leaders discovered he was black. The leaders defended his expulsion by claiming that the association was mainly a social organization. In 1925, black lawyers—led by Howard Law School graduate George H. Woodson—organized the National Bar Association.

In 1910 the United States had about 800 black lawyers. Some, like Lewis, had attended white law schools, such as Harvard or the University of South Carolina during Reconstruction in the 1870s. Others attended black law schools such as Howard or Allen University's law school in South Carolina. Still other black men (and white men) learned the law by reading and working in the law offices of practicing attorneys.

Very few black women were lawyers. Charlotte Ray was the first (see p. 269). In 1900 there were ten black women practicing law. There were over 700 black men and 112,000 white men engaged in the legal profession. Lutie A. Lytle, who graduated from Central Tennessee Law School in 1879 later returned to that black institution and became the first black woman to be a law professor in the United States.

Music

In the half-century after the Civil War, music created and performed by black people evolved into the uniquely American art forms of ragtime, jazz, and blues. The roots of these extraordinary musical innovations are obscure and uncertain. Some late-nineteenth-century music can be traced to African musical forms and rhythms. One source is slave work songs; another is the spirituals of the slavery era.

TRACK 22

Traveling groups of black men, some of them ex-slaves, put on minstrel shows that featured "coon songs" after the Civil War. Many black Americans resented these popular shows as caricatures and exaggerations of black behavior. At least 600 "coon songs" that attracted a predominantly white audience were published by 1900 including "All Coons Look Alike to Me," "Mammy's Little Pickaninny," and "My Coal Black Lady."

Most black people did not perform in or enjoy the demeaning minstrel shows. They had other forms of musical entertainment. "The Civil Rights Juba" published in 1874, was a precursor to ragtime. In 1871 the Fisk University Jubilee Singers began the first of many fund-raising concert tours that entertained black and white audiences in the United States and Europe for years thereafter with slave songs and spirituals. Other black colleges and universities also sent choirs and singers on similar trips.

Ragtime

Ragtime, which emerged in the 1890s, was composed music, written down for performance on the piano. Ragtime pieces were not accompanied by lyrics and were not meant to be sung. The creative genius of the form, Scott Joplin, was born in Texarkana, Texas, in 1868. He learned to play on a piano his mother bought from her earnings as a maid, and he may have had some training in classical music. Joplin subsequently learned to transfer complex banjo syncopations to the piano as he fused European harmonies and African rhythms. He traveled to Chicago in 1893 and played at the Columbian Exposition. He soon began to write

Scott Joplin (1868–1917) was one of America's most prolific composers and his name is indelibly linked with ragtime. Though ragtime's popularity faded by the 1920s, Joplin's reputation and compositions were resurrected in 1974 when the Hollywood film, *The Sting*, relied on Joplin's 1902 rag, *The Entertainer* for its soundtrack. In 1976 Scott Joplin was posthumously awarded the Pulitzer Prize for music.

ragtime sheet music that sold well. In 1899 he composed his best-known tune, the "Maple Leaf Rag," named after a social club (brothel) in Sedalia, Missouri. It sold an astonishing one million copies.

Jazz

Jazz gradually replaced ragtime in popularity in the early twentieth century. Unlike ragtime, jazz was mostly improvised, not composed, and it was not confined to the piano. Jazz incorporated African and European musical elements drawn from such diverse sources as plantation bands, minstrel shows, river boat ensembles, and Irish and Scottish folk tunes. The first jazz bands emerged in and around New Orleans where they played at parades, funerals, clubs, and outdoor concerts. Instead of the banjos, pipes, fifes, and violins of earlier black musical groups, these bands relied more on brass, reeds, and drums.

Ferdinand J. La Menthe, regarded as the first prominent jazz musician, was born in 1890 and grew up in a French-speaking family in New Orleans. Young La Menthe played several musical instruments before settling on the piano. He was also a superb composer and arranger. Later he changed his name to Morton and came to be known as Jelly Roll Morton. He played in the "red light" district of New Orleans known as Storeyville where he was also a pool shark and gambler. He moved to Los Angeles in 1917 and to Chicago in 1922 where he subsequently led and recorded with "Morton's Red Hot Peppers." He died in 1941.

The Blues

In rural, isolated areas of the South, poor black people composed and sang songs about their lives and experiences. W. C. Handy, the father of the blues, later recalled: "Southern Negroes sang about everything. Trains, steamboats, steam whistles, sledge hammers, fast women, mean bosses, stubborn mules." They accompanied themselves on anything from a guitar, to a harmonica, to a washboard. They played in juke joints (rural nightclubs), at picnics, lumber camps, and urban night clubs.

Handy, who was born in Florence, Alabama, in 1873, took up music despite the opposition of his devoutly Christian parents. He learned to play the guitar, though his mother and father regarded it as the "devil's plaything." He later led his own nine-man band. In the Mississippi Delta in 1903, Handy encountered "primitive," or "boogie," music unlike anything he had heard before. Handy was not initially impressed by the mostly unskilled and itinerant musicians whose lives swirled around cheap whiskey, gambling, prostitution, and violence. "Then I saw the beauty of primitive music. They had the stuff people wanted. It touched the spot. Their music wanted polishing, but it contained the essence. People would pay money for it." Handy went on to compose many tunes including "Memphis Blues" and "St. Louis Blues."

Handy was not the only musician to "discover" the blues. Gertrude Pridget sang in Southern minstrel shows. In 1902 she heard a young black woman in a small Missouri town sing forlornly about a lover who had left her. Pridget took the song and included it in her shows. In 1904 she married William "Pa" Rainey, and became "Ma" Rainey. Rainey proceeded to create other "blues" songs based on ballads, hymns, and the experiences of black people. As "Mother of the Blues," she recorded extensively and continuously in the 1920s and 1930s.

An early jazz band arrives in a small Texas town in about 1915 for a performance at a black fair.

By 1920, two forms of American music were well along in their evolution—jazz and the blues. Both drew on African and American musical elements as well as on European styles. But most of all, jazz and the blues represented the experiences of African Americans and the creativity of the exceptional musicians who developed and performed the music.

Sports

While talented black men and women were making dramatic musical innovations, black athletes found that white athletes and sports entrepreneurs were increasingly opposed to the presence of black men in the boxing ring and on the playing field. In boxing, black men regularly fought white men through the end of the nineteenth century. But many white people, especially Southerners, were offended by the practice. In 1892, George Dixon, a black boxer, won the world featherweight title, and some white men cheered his victory, distressing a Chicago journalist. "It was not pleasant," he complained, "to see white men applaud a negro for knocking another white man out. It was not pleasant to see them crowding around 'Mr.' Dixon to congratulate him on his victory, to seek an introduction with 'the distinguished colored gentleman' while he puffed his cigar and lay back like a prince receiving his subjects." Despite such opinions, there was never any official prohibition of interracial bouts.

Jack Johnson

The success of another black boxer, heavyweight Jack Johnson, angered many white Americans. Johnson was born in Galveston, Texas, in 1878 and became a professional boxer in 1897. Between 1902 and 1907 he won fifty-seven bouts against black and white fighters. In 1908 he badly beat the white heavyweight champion, Tommy Burns, in Australia. Many white boxing fans were unwilling to accept Johnson as the champion and looked desperately for "a great white hope" who could defeat him. Jim Jeffries, a former champion, came out of retirement to take on Johnson. In a brutal fight under a scorching sun in Reno, Nevada, in 1910, Johnson knocked Jeffries out in the fifteenth round.

Johnson's personal life, as well as his prowess in the ring, provoked white animosity. Having divorced his black wife, he married a white woman in 1911. Several months later, overwhelmed by social ostracism, she committed suicide. After Johnson married a second white woman, he was convicted of violating the Mann Act, which made it illegal to transport a woman across state lines for immoral purposes. In Johnson's case the "immorality" was his marriage to white women. Sentenced to a year in prison and fined $1,000, Johnson fled to Canada and then to

France to avoid punishment. He lost his title to Jesse Willard in 1915 in Havana in the twenty-sixth round in a fight many people believe that Johnson threw. He returned to the United States in 1920 and served ten months in Leavenworth Prison.

Baseball

Baseball was a relatively new sport that became popular after the Civil War. As professional baseball developed in the 1870s and 1880s, both black and white men competed to earn money playing the game. It was not easy. They were the nation's first professional athletes, but professional baseball was unstable. Teams were formed and dissolved with depressing regularity. Players moved from team to team. Some thirty black men played professional baseball in the quarter century after the Civil War.

White players led by Adrian Constantine "Cap" Anson of the Chicago White Stockings tried to get baseball club owners to stop signing black men to contracts. Anson, who was from Iowa, bitterly resented having to play against black men. In 1887, International League officials rescinded a rule that had permitted them to sign black baseball players. One black player, Weldy Wilberforce Walker, protested the exclusion in a letter to *Sporting Life.* He insisted that black men be judged by their skills, not by their color. "There should be some broader cause—such as lack of ability, behavior, and intelligence—for barring a player, rather than his color. It is for these reasons and because I think ability and intelligence should be recognized first and last—at all times and by everyone—I ask the question again, 'Why was the law permitting colored men to sign repealed, etc.?' " There was no intelligent answer to Walker's question. But Jim Crow was now on the baseball diamond. Moses Fleetwood Walker—Weldy's brother—was the last black man to play major league baseball in the nineteenth century as a catcher with Toledo of the American Association. No black men would be allowed to play with white men in major league baseball until Jackie Robinson joined the Brooklyn Dodgers in 1947.

In reaction to their exclusion, black men formed their own teams. By 1900, there were five black professional teams including the Norfolk Red Stockings, the Chicago Unions, and the Cuban X Giants of New York. The Negro Leagues would be an integral (but not integrated) part of sports for the next half century.

Basketball and Other Sports

James Naismith invented basketball in 1891 in Springfield, Massachusetts. Black youngsters were playing organized basketball by 1906 in YMCAs and later YWCAs in New York City, Philadelphia, and Washington, D.C. By 1910–11, Howard University and Hampton Institute had basketball teams. In horse racing, black jockeys regularly won major races. Willie Simms won the Kentucky Derby in 1894, 1895, 1896, and 1898. Bicycling and bicycle racing were enormously popular by the 1890s, and in 1900 a black rider, Marshall W. "Major" Taylor, won the U.S. sprint championship.

College Athletics

Generally, white colleges and universities in the North that admitted black students would not let them participate in intercollegiate sports. (Southern colleges and universities did not admit black students.) There were, however, exceptions. In 1889, W. T. S. Jackson and William Henry Lewis played football for Amherst College. Lewis was the captain of the team in 1890. As a law school student, Lewis played for Harvard and was named to the Walter Camp All-American team in 1892. (Lewis became a distinguished attorney who was forced out of the American Bar Association because of his color. See the section "The Law" in this chapter.) White institutions with black players often encountered the racism so rampant during the era. In 1907, the University of Alabama baseball team canceled a game with the University of Vermont after learning that the Vermont squad had two black infielders. Moreover, black players were frequently subjected to abuse from opposing teams and their fans.

Intercollegiate athletics emerged at black colleges and universities in the late nineteenth century. White schools occasionally played black institutions. The Yale Law School baseball team, for example, played Howard in 1898. But black college teams were far more likely to play each other. The first football game between two black colleges took place on December 27, 1892, when Biddle University (today Johnson C. Smith University) defeated Livingston College in Salisbury, North Carolina.

Eventually black athletic conferences were formed. The Central Intercollegiate Athletic Association (CIAA) was organized in 1912 with Hampton, Howard, Virginia Union, and Shaw College in Raleigh, North Carolina, among its early members. The Southeastern Conference was established in 1913 and consisted of Morehouse, Fisk, Florida A&M, and Tuskegee among others. In Texas in 1920, five black colleges founded the Southwestern Athletic Conference: Prairie View A&M, Bishop College, Paul Quinn College, Wiley College, and Sam Houston College.

Timeline

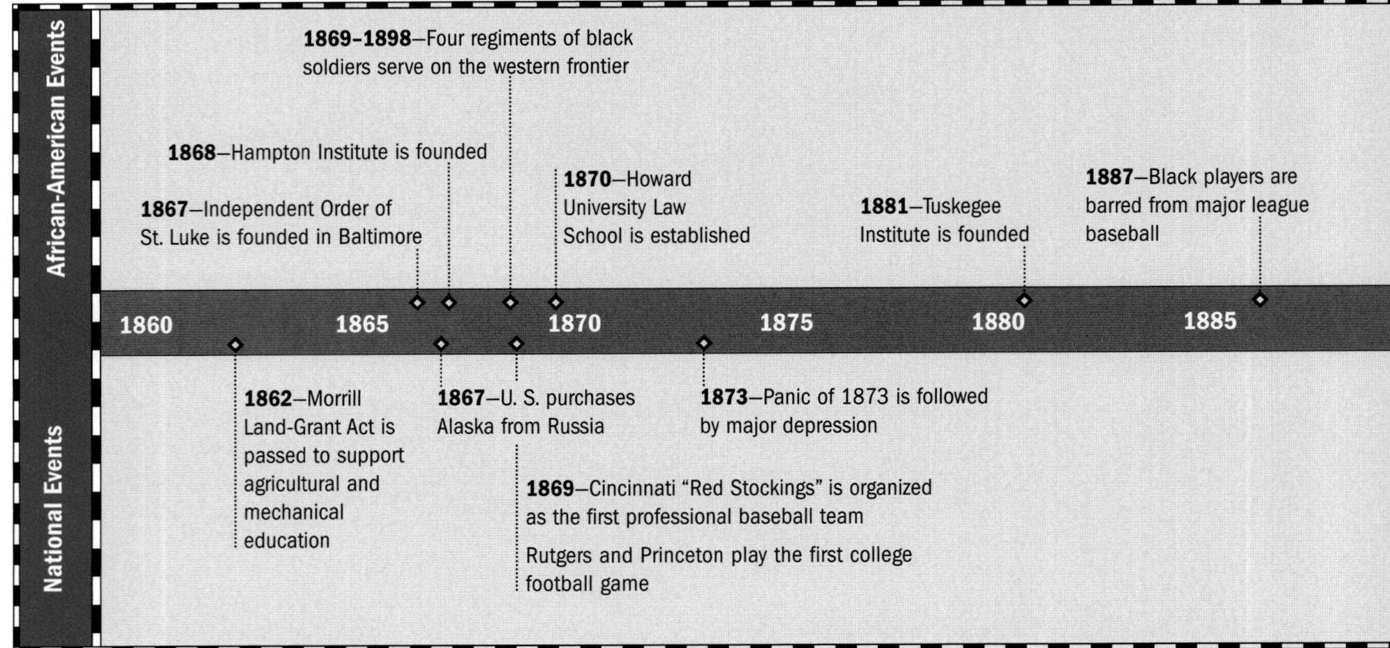

Conclusion

White supremacy was debilitating, discouraging, and dangerous, but black Americans were sometimes able to turn Jim Crow to their advantage. To lessen the effects of white racism and to improve the economic status of black people, educators like Samuel Chapman Armstrong and Booker T. Washington recommended agricultural and mechanical training for most black Americans. But critics such as W. E. B. Du Bois stressed the need to cultivate the minds as well as the hands of black people to develop leaders.

Black men served with distinction in all-black military units in the Indian wars, the Spanish-American War, and the Philippine Insurrection. But no matter how loyal or how committed black men in uniform were, the white majority never fully trusted nor displayed confidence in them. African Americans could only react with dismay and outrage when President Theodore Roosevelt dismissed 167 black soldiers in 1906 in the Brownsville Affair.

As they tried to shape their own destinies in the late nineteenth century, black Americans organized a variety of institutions. Mostly barred from white schools, churches, hospitals, labor unions, and places of entertainment, they developed businesses and facilities to serve their communities. Black businesses, organizations, and institutions functioned in an environment mostly free from white control and interference. Black people relied on their own experiences and imaginations to create new forms of music. They participated in sports with white athletes but more often played separately from them as segregation and white hostility spread.

While black people recognized that their churches, hospitals, schools, and businesses were often inadequately financed and usually less imposing than those of white people, they also knew that at a black school or church, in a black store, or in the care of a black physician or nurse, they would not be abused, mistreated, or ridiculed because of their color.

Recommended Reading

James D. Anderson. *The Education of Blacks in the South, 1860–1931.* Chapel Hill, NC: University of North Carolina Press, 1988. Anderson is highly critical of the education and philosophy promoted and provided by Hampton Institute and Tuskegee Institute.

Edward L. Ayers. *The Promise of the New South: Life after Reconstruction.* New York: Oxford University Press, 1992. This wide-ranging study encompasses almost every aspect of life in the late-nineteenth-century South, including religion, education, sports, and music.

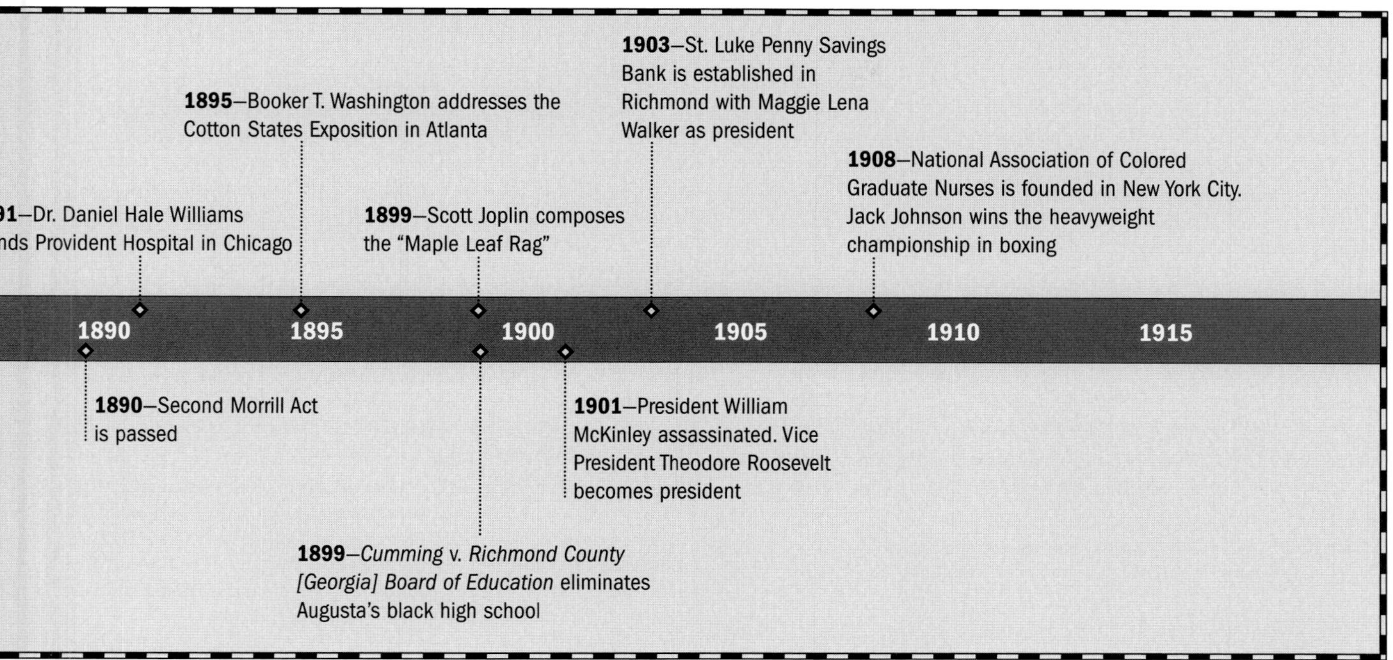

Sutton E. Griggs. *Imperium in Imperio.* New York: Arno Press reprint, 1899. This novel describes the formation of a separate black nation in Texas at the end of the nineteenth century.

Leon Litwack. *Trouble in Mind: Black Southerners in the Age of Jim Crow.* New York: Alfred A. Knopf, 1998. The author lets the words of black people of the time, including lawyers, physicians, and musicians, explain what life was like in an age of intense white supremacy.

Leon Litwack and August Meier, eds. *Black Leaders in the Nineteenth Century.* Urbana, IL: University of Illinois Press, 1988. This volume contains eighteen brief but valuable biographical essays.

Benjamin E. Mays. *Born to Rebel.* New York: Scribner, 1971. Mays's autobiography includes penetrating insights into religion and education among rural black Southerners.

Howard N. Rabinowitz. *Race Relations in the Urban South, 1865–1890.* New York: Oxford University Press, 1978. The author examines black life in Atlanta, Montgomery, Nashville, Raleigh, and Richmond.

Additional Bibliography

Education

Eric Anderson and Alfred A. Moss, Jr. *Dangerous Donations: Northern Philanthropy and Southern Black Education, 1902–1930.* Columbia, MO: University of Missouri Press, 1999.

James D. Anderson and V. P. Franklin, eds. *New Perspectives on Black Education.* Boston: G. K. Hall, 1978.

Henry A. Bullock. *A History of Negro Education in the South from 1619 to the Present.* Cambridge, MA: Harvard University Press, 1967.

Religion

Cyprian Davis. *The History of Black Catholics in the United States.* New York: Crossroad, 1990.

Harold T. Lewis. *Yet With a Steady Beat: The African American Struggle for Recognition in the Episcopal Church.* Valley Forge, PA: Trinity Press International, 1996.

Iain MacRobert. *The Black Roots and White Racism of Early Pentecostalism in the USA.* Basingstoke, United Kingdom: Macmillan, 1988.

Edwin S. Redkey, ed. *The Writings and Speeches of Henry McNeal Turner.* New York: Arno Press, 1971.

Clarence E. Walker. *A Rock in a Weary Land: The African Methodist Episcopal Church during the Civil War and Reconstruction.* Baton Rouge, LA: Louisiana State University Press, 1982.

The Military and the West

John M. Carroll, ed. *The Black Military Experience in the American West.* New York: Liveright, 1973.

Willard B. Gatewood, ed. *Smoked Yankees and the Struggle for Empire: Letters from Negro Soldiers, 1898–1902.* Urbana, IL: University of Illinois Press, 1971.

William Loren Katz. *The Black West.* New York: Touchstone Books, 1996.

William H. Leckie. *The Buffalo Soldiers: A Narrative of the Negro Cavalry in the West.* Norman, OK: University of Oklahoma Press, 1967.

John D. Weaver. *The Brownsville Raid.* New York: Norton, 1971.

Labor

Tera W. Hunter. *To 'Joy My Freedom: Southern Black Women's Lives and Labors after the Civil War.* Cambridge, MA: Harvard University Press, 1997.

Gerald D. Jaynes. *Branches without Roots: Genesis of the Black Working Class in the American South, 1862–1882.* New York: Oxford University Press, 1986.

The Professions

V. N. Gamble. *The Black Community Hospital: Contemporary Dilemmas in Historical Perspective.* New York: Garland, 1989.

Darlene Clark Hine. *Speak Truth to Power: Black Professional Class in United States History.* Brooklyn, NY: Carlson Publishing Co., 1996.

J. Clay Smith, Jr. *Emancipation: The Making of the Black Lawyer, 1844–1944.* Philadelphia: University of Pennsylvania Press, 1993.

J. Clay Smith, Jr., ed. *Rebels in Law: Voices in History of Black Women Lawyers.* Ann Arbor, MI: University of Michigan Press, 1998.

Music

W. C. Handy. *Father of the Blues: An Autobiography.* New York: Macmillan, 1941.

John Edward Hasse, ed. *Ragtime, Its History, Composers, and Music.* London: Macmillan, 1985.

Alan Lomax. *Mr. Jelly Roll: The Fortunes of Jelly Roll Morton, New Orleans Creole and "Inventor of Jazz."* New York: Grove Press, 1950.

Gunther Schuller. *Early Jazz: Its Roots and Musical Development.* New York: Oxford University Press, 1968.

Sports

Ocania Chalk. *Black College Sport.* New York: Dodd, Mead and Co., 1976.

Robert W. Peterson. *Only the Ball Was White: Negro Baseball: A History of Legendary Black Players and All-Black Professional Teams before Black Men Played in the Major Leagues.* New York: Prentice-Hall, 1970.

Andrew Ritchie. *Major Taylor: The Extraordinary Career of a Championship Bicycle Racer.* San Francisco: Bicycle Books, 1988.

Randy Roberts. *Papa Jack: Jack Johnson and the Era of White Hopes.* New York: The Free Press, 1983.

Retracing the Odyssey

Hampton, Virginia: Hampton University. Founded by Samuel Chapman Armstrong with the assistance of the American Missionary Association, Hampton Normal and Agricultural Institute opened in 1868 to train former slaves (and later Native Americans) in agricultural and mechanical skills. Virginia Hall (1874), Memorial Church (1886), the Hampton Museum, and the giant Emancipation Oak are all located on this picturesque campus overlooking Chesapeake Bay and Hampton Roads.

Tuskegee, Alabama: Tuskegee Institute National Historic Site. What is now Tuskegee University opened in 1881 and remained under the leadership of Booker T. Washington until his death in 1915. His home—The Oaks—was built by students and is now a museum. His grave and memorial are also on the campus as is the George Washington Carver Museum.

Atlanta, Georgia: Alonzo F. Herndon Home. Herndon was the founder of the Atlanta Life Insurance Company and was one of the wealthiest black men in America by the early 1900s. His fifteen-room mansion with immense white pillars was finished in 1910 and is open to the public. It is furnished with antiques, Roman and Venetian glass, as well as ornate artwork.

Richmond, Virginia: Maggie L. Walker National Historic Site. Built in 1883, this twenty-two-room Victorian mansion was home to the Walker family from 1904 to 1934 and is now open for tours. There is a visitor center that contains exhibits on the life of Maggie Lena Walker and the Jackson Ward community.

Indianapolis, Indiana: Madame C. J. Walker Center. In 1910 C. J. Walker (Sarah Breedlove) moved her thriving hair care and beauty products business from Denver to Indianapolis. The four-story triangular building was completed in 1919 shortly after Walker's death. It housed manufacturing facilities and was home to a beauty college that trained Walker's agents to care for the hair of African-American women and to sell Walker's products. It is currently a community center and theater.

Detroit, Michigan: Dunbar Hospital. This red brick structure was built in 1892 and served as a hospital for Detroit's black community from 1918 to 1928. It is currently operated by the Detroit Medical Society, and it has exhibits, medical devices, photographs, and papers documenting the medical care available to black Detroit.

REVIEW, RESEARCH & INTERACT

REVIEW QUESTIONS

1. How and why did the agricultural and mechanical training offered by Hampton Institute and Tuskegee Institute gain so much support among black people and white people? Why did black colleges and universities emphasize learning trades and acquiring skills?
2. How compatible was the educational philosophy of the late nineteenth century with the racial ideology of that era?
3. Of what value was an education for a black person in the 1890s or early 1900s? To what use could a black person put an education? What exactly was the benefit of an education?
4. What purpose did the black church serve? What were the strengths and weaknesses of the black church? How would you assess the role of black clergymen in late-nineteenth-century America?
5. How could a black man in the U.S. Army justify participating in wars against Native Americans, the Spanish, and the Filipinos? What motivated black soldiers to serve? How well did they serve?
6. What, if any, benefits did black people derive from the growth and expansion of segregation and Jim Crow?
7. How do you explain the emergence of ragtime, jazz, and the blues in American music? How do you account for their development and popularity?
8. How did segregation affect the development of amateur and professional athletics in the United States?

www.researchnavigator.com

Chapter 15 explores the efforts of late-nineteenth-century African Americans to improve their lives.

For further research on black resistance to white supremacy, use the tools available to you in Research Navigator.

As you investigate this topic, consider this question: "What place did religion have in late nineteenth-century African American life?"

- **ContentSelect:** Search in the History database using the search terms *social darwinism* and *Spanish American War.*
- **Links Library:** Access the History: U.S. History database and explore the links for *Tuskegee Institute.*
- **New York Times on the Web:** To find out more about black resistance to white supremacy, search in the History database using the search term *Booker T. Washington.*

DOCUMENTS AND ACTIVITIES IN AFRICAN-AMERICAN HISTORY

Documents

15-1 Booker T. Washington, The Atlanta Exposition Address
15-2 From *Plessy v. Ferguson,* 1896
15-3 *Plessy v. Ferguson:* Justice Harlan Dissents, 1896
15-4 Mary Church Terrell, The Progress Of Colored Women, 1898
15-5 W. E. B. DuBois The Talented Tenth, 1903

Interactive Figure

Black and White Illiteracy in the United States and the Southern States, 1880–1900, p. 337
http://www.prenhall.com/hine/figure15.1

16

Conciliation, Agitation, and Migration: African Americans in the Early Twentieth Century

Jacob Lawrence (1917–2000) never finished high school and had little formal training as an artist. But he had an abiding interest in the lives and history of African Americans. He painted sixty panels depicting the migration of black people from the South to the North. In Migration of the Negro, Panel 1 (1940–1941) he shows black Southerners bound for northern cities.

THE wisest among my race understand that the agitation of questions of social equality is the extremest folly, and that progress in the enjoyment of all privileges that will come to us must be the result of severe and constant struggle rather than of artificial forcing. No race that has anything to contribute to the markets of the world is long in any degree ostracized. It is important and right all privileges of the law be ours, but it is vastly more important that we be prepared for the exercises of these privileges.

Booker T. Washington, Atlanta Cotton States and International Exposition, September 18, 1895

Mr. Washington distinctly asks that black people give up, at least for the present three things,—
First, political power,
Second, insistence on civil rights,
Third, higher education of Negro youth,—
and concentrate all their energies on industrial education, the accumulation of wealth, and the conciliation of the South.

W. E. B. Du Bois, The Souls of Black Folk, 1903

As the twentieth century dawned, black and white Americans had profoundly different views on the future of black people in America. Most white people believed that black Americans were an inferior race capable of little more than manual labor and entitled to only the most basic legal rights. Black Americans rejected that assertion and worked for a more equitable place in society. Black scholar W. E. B. Du Bois announced in 1903 that race would be the century's most critical issue. "The problem of the twentieth century is

CHAPTER OUTLINE

Race and the Progressive Movement

Booker T. Washington's Approach
Washington's Influence
The Tuskegee Machine
Opposition to Washington

W. E. B. Du Bois

The Niagara Movement

The NAACP

Using the System

Du Bois and *The Crisis*
Washington versus the NAACP

The Urban League

Black Women and the Club Movement
The NACW: "Lifting as We Climb"
Phillis Wheatley Clubs
Anna Julia Cooper and Black Feminism
Women's Suffrage

The Black Elite
The American Negro Academy
The Upper Class
Fraternities and Sororities

Presidential Politics
Frustrated by the Republicans
Woodrow Wilson

Black Men and the Military in World War I
The Punitive Expedition to Mexico
World War I
Black Troops and Officers
Discrimination and Its Effects
Du Bois's Disappointment

Race Riots

The Great Migration
Why Migrate?
Destinations

Northern Communities

Families

the problem of the color-line—the relation of the darker to the lighter races of men in Asia and Africa, in America and the islands of the sea."

Black people refused to accept the inferiority to which they had been consigned. They devised strategies and organized institutions to enable them to prosper in a hostile society. However, African Americans and their leaders disagreed about how to secure the constitutional rights and the material comforts that so many white Americans took for granted. Some, following W. E. B. Du Bois, a founder of the Niagara Movement and the National Association for the Advancement of Colored People (NAACP), favored a frontal assault on discrimination, disfranchisement, and Jim Crow in the quest for racial progress. Others, following Booker T. Washington of the Tuskegee Institute, cautioned against the vigorous pursuit of civil rights and political power and insisted that agricultural and industrial training would generate prosperity and self-sufficiency among people of color.

The emergence of the club movement among black women and other self-help organizations (see Chapter 15) enabled more prosperous black people to aid those suffering acutely from poverty and prejudice. The black elite, often reviled for ostentatious social displays, came to be designated the Talented Tenth, and many of them took seriously their responsibilities to aid their brethren.

When the United States entered World War I in 1917, black men responded patriotically, as they had in previous conflicts. They joined a Jim Crow military that was fighting to make the world safe for democracy. But black people in America were not safe, and democracy did not prevail. Riots and racial violence erupted before, during, and after the war.

In the meantime one of the most important episodes in American history—a vast and prolonged migration of hundreds of thousands of rural black Southerners to northern cities—began in earnest after 1910. Drawn mainly by economic opportunities, black people moved to New York, Philadelphia, Cleveland, Chicago, and other urban centers.

Race and the Progressive Movement

By the first decade of the twentieth century, many Americans were concerned and even alarmed about the rapid economic and social changes that confronted the United States, including industrialization, the rise of powerful corporations, the explosive growth of cities, and the influx of millions of immigrants. Their apprehensions spawned a disparate collection of efforts at reform known as the progressive movement. In general, progressives believed that America needed a new social awareness to deal with the new social and economic problems. But most of the middle- and upper-class white people who formed the core of the movement showed little interest in white racism and its impact. Indeed, many were racists themselves. They were primarily concerned with the concentration of wealth in monopolies such as Standard Oil, with pervasive political corruption in state and local governments, and with the plight of working-class immigrants in American cities. They cared deeply about the debilitating effects of alcohol, tainted food, and prostitution, but little about the grim impact of white supremacy. When Upton Sinclair wrote his muckraking novel *The Jungle* to expose the exploitation of European immigrants in Chicago meatpacking houses, he depicted black people as brute laborers and strikebreakers.

The reforms of the progressive movement nonetheless offered at least a glimmer of hope that racial advancement was possible. If efforts were made to improve America, was it not possible that there be some advances achieved in policies and conditions affecting black Americans? But how much militancy or forbearance was necessary to achieve significant racial progress? Did it even make sense for black people to demand a meaningful role in a nation that despised them? Perhaps it was wiser to turn inward and rely on each other rather than plead for white recognition and respect.

Booker T. Washington's Approach

Booker T. Washington's commitment to agricultural and industrial education served as the basis for his approach to "the problem of the color line." By the beginning of the twentieth century, Washington was convinced that black men and women who had mastered skills acquired at institutions like Tuskegee and Hampton would be recognized, if not welcomed, as productive contributors to the southern economy. Washington believed that economic acceptance would lead in due course to political and social acceptance.

TRACK 23

The Tuskegee leader eloquently outlined his philosophy in the speech he delivered at the opening ceremonies of the Cotton States Exposition in Atlanta in 1895 (see Chapter 15). Black people, he told his segregated audience, would find genuine opportunities in the South. "[W]hen it comes to business, pure and simple, it is in the South that the Negro is given a man's chance in the commercial world." Washington added that black people should not expect too much but should welcome menial labor as a first step in the struggle for progress. Ever optimistic, he looked for opportunities while deprecating those who complained. "Nor should we permit our grievances to overshadow our opportunities." He told white listeners that the lives of black and white Southerners were historically linked and that black people were far more loyal and steadfast than newly arrived immigrants. "[I]n our humble way, we shall stand by you with a devotion that no foreigner can approach, ready to lay down our lives, if need be, in defence of yours, interlacing our industrial, commercial, civil, and religious life with yours in a way that shall make the interests of both races one."

Then in a striking metaphor, Washington reassured white people that cooperation between the races in the interest of prosperity did not endanger segregation. "In all things that are purely social we can be as separate as the fingers, yet one as the hand in all things essential to mutual progress." Finally, Washington implied that black people need not protest because they were denied rights white men possessed. Instead, he urged his black listeners to struggle steadily rather than make defiant demands. "The wisest among my race understand that the agitation of questions of social equality is the extremest folly, and that progress in the enjoyment of all the privileges that will come to us must be the result of severe and constant struggle rather than of artificial forcing." Washington was convinced that as African Americans became productive and made economic progress, white people would concede them their rights.

The speech was warmly received by both white and black listeners and by those who read it when it was widely reprinted. T. Thomas Fortune, the black editor of the New York *Age*, told Washington that he had replaced Frederick Douglass (who died in 1895) as a leader. "It looks as if you are our Douglass, the best equipped of the lot of us to be the single figure ahead of the procession."

But not everyone was complimentary. The black editor of the Washington *Bee*, W. Calvin Chase, complained: "He said something that was death to the Afro-American and elevating to white people." Bishop Henry M. Turner of the AME church added that Washington "will have to live a long time to undo the harm he has done our race."

White people regarded Washington's speech as moderate, sensible, and altogether praiseworthy. Almost overnight he was designated the spokesman for African Americans. Washington accepted the recognition and took full advantage of it.

Washington's Influence

Booker T. Washington was a complex man. Many people found him unassertive, dignified, and patient. Yet he was ambitious, aggressive, and opportunistic as well as shrewd, calculating, and devious. He had an uncanny ability to determine what he might say to other people that would elicit a positive response from them. He became extraordinarily powerful. In the words of his assistant, Emmett J. Scott, Washington was "the Wizard of Tuskegee."

After the Atlanta speech, Washington's influence soared. He received extensive and mostly positive coverage in black newspapers. Some of that popularity stemmed from admiration for his leadership and agreement with his ideas. But Washington also cultivated and flattered editors, paid for advertisements for Tuskegee, and subsidized struggling journalists.

He was especially effective in dealing with prominent white businessmen and philanthropists. William H. Baldwin, vice president of the Southern Railroad, was so impressed with Washington's management of Tuskegee that Baldwin agreed to serve as the chairman of Tuskegee's board. Washington developed support among the nation's industrial elite including steel magnate Andrew Carnegie and Julius Rosenwald, the head of Sears, Roebuck, and Company. They trusted Washington's judgment and invariably consulted him before contributing to black colleges and universities. Washington assured them of the wisdom of investing in the training of black men and women in agricultural and mechanical skills. These students, he repeatedly reminded donors, would be self-sufficient and productive members of southern society.

Booker T. Washington had access to and influence among the most powerful political and business leaders in the United States. Here he shares the podium with President Theodore Roosevelt. Washington persuaded Republican leaders like Roosevelt to appoint black men to an assortment of federal offices and convinced businessmen to contribute sizable sums to black colleges and universities. Nevertheless, some African Americans criticized the Tuskegee leader for not speaking out more candidly in opposition to white supremacy and Jim Crow.

The Tuskegee Machine

Washington advised black people to avoid politics, but he ignored his own advice. Though he never ran for office nor was appointed to a political position, Washington was a political figure to be reckoned with. His connections to white businesspeople and politicians gave him enormous influence. Critics and admirers alike referred to him as "the Wizard of Tuskegee," and the way he wielded his influence as "the Tuskegee Machine." In 1896 he supported winning Republican presidential candidate William McKinley over the Democratic and Populist William Jennings Bryan. Washington got along superbly with McKinley's successor, Theodore Roosevelt. Though Roosevelt subscribed to social Darwinism (see Chapter 15) and regarded black Americans as inferiors, he liked and respected Washington.

In 1901 Roosevelt invited Washington to dinner at the White House, where Roosevelt's wife, daughter, three sons, and a Colorado businessman joined them. Black people applauded, but the white South, alarmed by such a flagrant breach of racial etiquette (black people did not dine with white people), recoiled. "The most damnable outrage which has ever been perpetrated by any citizen of the United States," a Memphis newspaper fumed, "was committed yesterday by the President when he invited a nigger to dine with him at the White House." Roosevelt was unmoved, and a few days later the two men dined again together at Yale University. Still, Roosevelt never invited Washington for another meal at the Executive Mansion.

Washington and Roosevelt regularly consulted each other on political appointments. In the most notable case, Washington urged Roosevelt to appoint William D. Crum, a black medical doctor, as the collector of customs for the port of Charleston, South Carolina. White Southerners, led by Senator Benjamin R. Tillman, a South Carolina Democrat, opposed Crum's appointment and delayed final confirmation by the Senate for nearly three years. With Washington's assent, Roosevelt appointed black attorney and former all-American football player William Lewis to be U.S. District Attorney in Boston. Several years later, President William Howard Taft appointed Lewis Assistant Attorney General of the United States. (For more details on Lewis, see Chapter 15.)

Most of Washington's political activities were not public. He secretly helped finance an unsuccessful court case against the Louisiana grandfather clause. (The statute disfranchised those voters—black men—whose grandfathers had not possessed the right to vote; see Chapter 14.) Washington provided funds to carry two cases challenging Alabama's grandfather clause to the U.S. Supreme Court, which ultimately rejected both on a technicality. He tried to persuade railroad executives to improve the conditions on segregated coaches and in station waiting rooms. He worked covertly with white attorneys to free a black farm laborer imprisoned under Alabama's peonage law. In many of these secret activities, Washington used code names in correspondence to hide his involvement. In the Louisiana case he was identified only as X.Y.Z.

Washington was a conservative leader who did not directly or publicly challenge white supremacy. He was willing to accept literacy and property qualifications for voting if they were equitably enforced regardless of race. He also opposed women's suffrage. He attacked lynching only occasionally. But he did write an annual letter to white newspapers filled with data on lynchings that had been compiled at Tuskegee. Washington let the grim statistics speak for themselves rather than denounce the injustice himself.

Washington founded the National Negro Business League in 1900 and served as its president until he died in 1915. The League brought together merchants, retailers, bankers, funeral directors, and other owners and operators of small enterprises. It helped to promote black businesses in the black community and brought businessmen together to exchange information. Moreover, the League's annual meetings allowed Washington to develop support for the Tuskegee Machine from black businessmen who were community leaders from across the nation. Similarly, he worked closely with leaders in black fraternal orders such as the Odd Fellows and Pythians.

Opposition to Washington

Years before Washington rose to prominence, there were black leaders who favored a direct challenge to racial oppression. In 1889, delegates representing twenty-three states met to form the Afro-American League in Chicago. The League's main purpose was to press for civil and political rights guaranteed by the U.S. Constitution. "The objects of the League are to encourage State and local leagues in their efforts to break down color bars, and in obtaining for the Afro-American an equal chance with others in the avocations of life . . . in securing the full privileges of citizenship." But the League did not flourish, and it was eventually displaced by the Niagara Movement.

Opposition to Washington's conciliatory stance on racial matters steadily intensified. William Monroe Trotter became the most vociferous critic of Booker T. Washington and the Tuskegee Machine. Trotter was the Harvard-educated editor of the Boston *Guardian*, and he savagely attacked Washington as "the Great Traitor," "the Benedict Arnold of the Negro Race," and "Pope Washington." At a 1903 meeting of the National Negro Business League in Boston, Trotter stood on a chair and interrupted a speech by Washington, defiantly asking, "Are the rope and the torch all the race is to get under your leadership?" Washington ignored him, and the police arrested the editor for disorderly conduct. He spent thirty days in jail for what newspapers labeled "the Boston Riot."

W. E. B. Du Bois

William Edward Burghardt Du Bois, who was twelve years younger than Booker T. Washington, would eventually eclipse the influence and authority of the Wizard of Tuskegee. Du Bois emerged as the most significant black leader in America during the first half of the twentieth century. While Washington's life had been shaped by slavery, poverty, and the industrial work ethic fostered at Hampton Institute, Du Bois was born and raised in the largely white New England town of Great Barrington, Massachusetts. It was a small community where he encountered little overt racism and developed a passion for knowledge.

Du Bois possessed, as he put it, "a flood of Negro blood, a strain of French, a bit of Dutch, but, thank God! no Anglo-Saxon." He graduated from Great Barrington High School at a time when few white and still fewer black youngsters attended more than primary school. He went South to Fisk University in Nashville and graduated at age twenty. He was the first black man to earn a Ph.D. (in history) at Harvard in 1895, and he pursued additional graduate study in Germany.

Du Bois was perhaps the greatest scholar-activist in American history. He was an intellectual at ease with words and ideas. He wrote sixteen nonfiction books, five novels, and two autobiographies. He was a fearless activist determined to confront disfranchisement, Jim Crow, and lynching. While Washington solicited the goodwill of powerful white leaders and was comfortable with a gradual approach to the eradication of white supremacy, Du Bois was impatient with white people who accepted or ignored white domination. Moreover, he had little tolerance for black people who were unwilling to demand their civil and political rights.

Du Bois was well aware that he and Washington came from dissimilar backgrounds.

> I was born free. Washington was born a slave. He felt the lash of an overseer across his back. I was born in Massachusetts, he on a slave plantation in the South. My great-grandfather fought with the Colonial Army in New England in the American Revolution. I had a happy childhood and acceptance in the community. Washington's childhood was hard. I had many more advantages: Fisk University, Harvard, graduate years in Europe. Washington had little formal schooling.

Du Bois was not always critical of Washington. Following Washington's speech at the Cotton States Exposition in 1895, Du Bois, then a young Harvard Ph.D. teaching at Ohio's Wilberforce University, wrote to praise him. "Let me heartily congratulate you upon your phenomenal success at Atlanta—it was a word fitly spoken." But in 1903, the same year as the Boston Riot, Du Bois, by then an Atlanta University professor, published *The Souls of Black Folk.* One of the major literary works of the twentieth century, it contained the first formal attack on Washington and his leadership.

VOICES

W. E. B. Du Bois on Being Black in America

W. E. B. Du Bois's The Souls of Black Folk (1903) contained perhaps the most eloquent statement ever written on being black in white America. The difficulties of their circumstances, Du Bois believed, create a double consciousness among Americans of African descent.

After the Egyptian and Indian, the Greek and Roman, the Teuton and Mongolian, the Negro is a sort of seventh son, born with a veil, and gifted with second-sight in this American world,—a world which yields him no true self-consciousness, but only lets him see himself through the revelation of the other world. It is a peculiar sensation, this double-consciousness, this sense of always looking at one's self through the eyes of others, of measuring one's soul by the tape of a world that looks on in an amused contempt and pity. One ever feels his two-ness,—an American, a Negro; two souls, two thoughts, two unreconciled strivings; two warring ideals in one dark body, whose dogged strength alone keeps it from being torn asunder.

The history of the American Negro is the history of this strife,—this longing to attain self-conscious manhood, to merge his double self into a better and truer self. In this merging he wishes neither of the older selves to be lost. He would not Africanize America, for America has too much to teach the world and Africa. He would not bleach his Negro soul in a flood of white Americanism, for he knows that Negro blood has a message for the world. He simply wishes to make it possible for a man to be both a Negro and an American, without being cursed and spit upon by his fellows, without having the doors of Opportunity closed roughly in his face.

QUESTIONS

1. Why, in the judgment of W. E. B. Du Bois, is it impossible for a black person to be simply an American?
2. Would Du Bois agree, based on his concept of double consciousness, that African Americans have a separate identity and separate culture from other Americans?

Source: Du Bois, *The Souls of Black Folk*, pp. 8–9.

In *Of Booker T. Washington and Others*, Du Bois conceded that it was painful to challenge Washington, a man so highly praised and admired. "One hesitates, therefore, to criticise a life which, beginning with so little, has done so much. And yet the time is come when one may speak in all sincerity and utter courtesy of the mistakes and shortcomings of Mr. Washington's career, as well as the triumphs." Du Bois attacked Washington for failing to stand up for political and civil rights and higher education for black Americans. Du Bois found even more infuriating Washington's willingness to compromise with the white South and Washington's apparent agreement with white Southerners that black people were not their equals. "Mr. Washington represents in Negro thought the old attitude of adjustment and submission . . . and Mr. Washington's programme practically accepts the alleged inferiority of the Negro races."

In concluding, Du Bois stressed that he agreed with Washington on some issues, but disagreed even more about significant ones, and that on these issues it was vital to oppose Washington:

> So far as Mr. Washington preaches Thrift, Patience, and Industrial Training for the masses, we must hold up his hands and strive with him. . . . But so far as Mr. Washington apologizes for injustice, North or South, does not rightly value the privilege and duty of voting, belittles the emasculating effects of caste distinctions, and opposes higher training and ambition of our brighter minds,—so far as he, the South, or the Nation, does this,—we must unceasingly and firmly oppose them.

Washington worried that the opposition of Trotter, Du Bois, and others would jeopardize the flow of funds from white philanthropists to black colleges and universities. In an effort to reconcile with his opponents, he organized a meeting with them, funded by white philanthropists, at Carnegie Hall in New York City in 1904. But Du Bois and other opponents of Washington came to the gathering determined to adopt a radical agenda. When Washington loyalists monopolized the proceedings, Du Bois quit in disgust.

Du Bois, joined by a small cadre of black intellectuals, then set out to organize an aggressive effort to secure the rights of black citizens. He was convinced that the advancement of black people was the responsibility of the black elite, those he called the Talented Tenth, meaning the upper 10 percent of black Americans. Education, he believed, was the key.

> Work alone will not do it unless inspired by the right ideals and guided by intelligence. Education must not simply teach work—it must teach Life. The Talented Tenth of the Negro race must be made leaders of thought and missionaries of culture among people. No others can do this work, and Negro colleges must train men for it. The Negro race, like all other races, is going to be saved by its exceptional men.

The founders of the Niagara movement posed in front of a photograph of the falls when they met at Niagara Falls, Ontario, Canada, in 1905. W. E. B. Du Bois is second from the right in the middle row.

The Niagara Movement

In 1905 Du Bois carried the anti-Washington crusade a step further and invited a select group to meet at Niagara Falls, in Canada. The twenty-nine delegates to this meeting insisted that black people no longer quietly accept the loss of the right to vote. "We believe that [Negro] American citizens should protest emphatically and continually against the curtailment of their political rights." They also demanded an end to segregation, declaring, "All American citizens have the right to equal treatment in places of public entertainment." They appealed for better schools, health care, and housing; protested the discrimination endured by black soldiers; and criticized the racial prejudice of most churches as "wrong, unchristian and disgraceful to the twentieth century civilization." Perhaps most important, the Niagara gathering insisted that white people did not know what was best for black people. "We repudiate the monstrous doctrine that the oppressor should be the sole authority as to the rights of the oppressed."

The Niagara Movement that emerged from this meeting attracted four hundred members and remained active for several years. Du Bois composed annual addresses to the nation designed to arouse black and white support. But the Niagara Movement was no match for the powerful, efficient, and well-financed Tuskegee Machine. Washington used every means at his disposal to undermine the movement. Black newspaper editors like the *Washington Bee's* W. Calvin Chase, who had earlier attacked Washington's Atlanta Compromise address, were paid to attack Du Bois and to praise Washington. Washington dispatched spies to Niagara meetings to report on the organization's activities.

Washington sent a telegram requesting that black lawyer Clifford Plummer infiltrate the first Niagara meeting: "See Plummer at once. Give him fifty dollars. Tell him to go to Buffalo tonight or tomorrow morning ostensibly to attend Elks convention but to report fully what goes on at meeting. . . . Get into meeting, if possible but be sure [to get] name of all who attend and what they do." Washington let it be known that black federal workers might lose their positions if they joined in the Niagara Movement.

There were also internal problems among Niagara members. Du Bois was an inexperienced leader, and difficulties developed between Du Bois and Trotter. In

The Emergence of National African-American Organizations

1889	Afro-American League organized in Chicago
1892	Colored Women's League of Washington formed
1893	New Era Club founded in Boston
1895	National Federation of Afro-American Women organized in Boston
1896	National Association of Colored Women (NACW) formed in Washington
1897	American Negro Academy founded in Washington
1897	First Phillis Wheatley home established in Detroit
1900	National Negro Business League established in Boston
1905	Niagara Movement organized in Niagara Falls, Ontario, Canada
1909	National Association for the Advancement of Colored People (NAACP) founded in New York City
1910	National League on Urban Conditions among Negroes (Urban League) formed in New York City

1908, the Niagara Movement virtually collapsed. Most black and white Americans were not prepared to support an organization that seemed so uncompromising in its demands.

The NAACP

As the Niagara Movement expired, the National Association for the Advancement of Colored People (NAACP) came to life. There was no direct link between the demise of the Niagara Movement and the rise of the NAACP. But the relatively small numbers of people—black and white—who felt comfortable with the Niagara Movement's assertive stance on race were inclined to support the NAACP. In its early years the NAACP was a militant organization dedicated to racial justice. White leaders dominated it and white contributors largely financed it.

A few white progressives were deeply concerned about the rampant racial prejudice manifested so graphically in lynchings, Jim Crow, black disfranchisement, and a vicious riot in 1908 in Springfield, Illinois—Abraham Lincoln's hometown. After a gathering of leaders in January 1909 in New York City, Oswald Garrison Villard issued a call on February 12—Lincoln's Birthday—to "all believers in democracy to join a national conference to discuss present evils, the voicing of protests, and the renewal of the struggle for civil and political liberty."

Villard was the president and editor of the New York *Evening Post* and the grandson of abolitionist William Lloyd Garrison. Prominent progressives endorsed the call, including social workers Lillian Wald and Jane Addams, literary scholar Joel E. Spingarn, and respected attorneys Clarence Darrow and Moorfield Storey.

W. E. B. Du Bois, Ida Wells-Barnett, and Mary Church Terrell were the black leaders most involved in the formation of the NAACP.

Using the System

The NAACP was determined that black citizens should fully enjoy the civil and political rights the Constitution guaranteed to all citizens. It relied on the judicial and legislative systems in what would be a persistent and decades-long effort to secure those rights. The NAACP won its first major legal victory in 1915 when the Supreme Court overturned Oklahoma's grandfather clause in Guinn v. United States. But poll taxes and literacy tests continued to disfranchise black citizens.

In 1917 in a case brought by the Louisville NAACP branch and argued before the Supreme Court by Moorfield Storey, the court struck down a local law that enforced residential segregation by prohibiting black people and white people from selling real estate to people of the other race. The NAACP also tried in 1918 to secure a federal law prohibiting lynching. With the assistance of Congressman Leonidas Dyer, a white St. Louis Republican, the antilynching measure—the Dyer bill—passed in the House of Representatives in 1922 over vigorous Democratic opposition. But the Senate blocked it, and it never became law.

Du Bois and *The Crisis*

W. E. B. Du Bois was easily the most prominent black figure associated with the NAACP during its first quarter century. He became director of publicity and research and edited the NAACP publication, *The Crisis,* while largely leaving leadership and administrative tasks to others.

With *The Crisis,* Du Bois the scholar became Du Bois the propagandist. In the pages of *The Crisis,* he denounced white racism and atrocities and demanded that black people stand up for their rights. "Agitate, then, brother; protest, reveal the truth and refuse to be silenced. . . . A moment's let up, a moment's acquiescence, means a chance for the wolves of prejudice to get at our necks." He would not

TRACK 24

provoke violence, but he would not tolerate mistreatment either. "I am resolved to be quiet and law abiding, but to refuse to cringe in body or in soul, to resent deliberate insult, and to assert my just rights in the face of wanton aggression." These were not the even-tempered, cautious words of Booker T. Washington to which so many Americans had grown accustomed. *The Crisis* became required reading in many black homes. By 1913 it had thirty thousand subscribers when the membership of the NAACP was only three thousand.

This early twentieth-century illustration depicts a dapper young W. E. B. Du Bois (1868–1963). He was a key figure in opposing Booker T. Washington's Tuskegee machine. Du Bois helped found the NAACP and edited its publication, *The Crisis*, for two decades.

Washington versus the NAACP

In 1909 with the founding of the NAACP, Oswald Garrison Villard tried to reassure Washington that the organization posed no threat and to gain his support for the new association. "It is not to be a Washington movement, or a Du Bois movement. The idea is that there shall grow out of it, first, an annual conference . . . for the discussion by men of both races of the conditions of the colored people, politically, socially, industrially and educationally."

Many black leaders and members of the NAACP, however, despised Washington and his ideology, and Washington returned the sentiment. With the assistance of his followers, he worked to subvert the new organization. Washington looked on Du Bois as little more than the puppet of white people, who dominated the leadership of the NAACP, and the Tuskegee leader declined to debate Du Bois. One of Washington's aides commented that "it would be entirely out of place for Dr. Washington to enter into any discussion with a man occupying the place that Dr. Du Bois does, for the reason that Dr. Washington is at the head of a large institution. . . . Dr. Du Bois, on the other hand, is a mere hired man, as it were, in an institution completely controlled by white people."

Charles Anderson, a Tuskegee loyalist in New York City, wrote to Washington in 1909 that the NAACP was meeting secretly and that he would attempt to disrupt its efforts. "I will find out as much about them as possible and let you know the facts. I am doing all I can to discredit this affair." Washington relied again on allies who were editors of black newspapers to criticize the NAACP.

He also wrote Clark Howell, the white editor of the Atlanta *Constitution*, to attack Du Bois. "I think that it is too bad that an institution like Atlanta University has permitted Dr. Du Bois to go on from year to year stirring up racial strife in the South." Washington later told an alumnus of Tuskegee that the main aim of the NAACP was to destroy Washington and Tuskegee. "As a matter of straight fact, this organization is for the purpose of tearing down our work wherever possible and I think none of our friends should give it comfort."

Washington became so obsessed with the NAACP that he was not above manipulating white supremacists to damage those connected with the Association. When he learned that a group of black and white progressives associated with the NAACP were going to gather at the Café Boulevard in New York City in 1911, he allowed Charles Anderson to alert the hostile white press, which gleefully described the multiracial dinner in the most inflammatory terms. "Fashionable White Women Sit at Board with Negroes, Japs and Chinamen to Promote 'Cause' of Miscegenation" proclaimed one headline. The New York *Press* added: "White women, evidently of the cultured and wealthier classes, fashionably attired in low-cut gowns, leaned over the tables to chat confidentially with negro men of the true African type."

Ultimately, Washington's efforts to ruin the NAACP and to reduce the influence of its supporters failed. By the time of his death in 1915, the NAACP had grown steadily to over six thousand members and fifty local branches. Its aggressive campaign for civil and political rights replaced Washington's strategy of progress through conciliation and accommodation.

The Urban League

In 1910 the National League on Urban Conditions among Negroes was founded in New York City. The goal of this social welfare organization, soon known simply as the Urban League, was to alleviate conditions black people encountered as they moved into large cities in ever increasing numbers in the early twentieth century. Like the NAACP, the Urban League was created by black and white progressives. It worked to improve housing, medical care, and recreational facilities among black residents who lived in segregated neighborhoods in New York, Philadelphia, Atlanta, Nashville, Norfolk, and other cities. The league also assisted youngsters who ran afoul of the law, and it helped establish the Big Brother and Big Sister movements.

Black Women and the Club Movement

Years before the Urban League and the NAACP were founded, black women began creating clubs and organizations. The local groups that began forming in the 1870s and 1880s, such as the Bethel Literary and Historical Association in Washington, D.C., were mainly concerned with cultural, religious, and social matters. But many of the mostly middle-class women active in these clubs eventually became less interested in tea and gossip and more involved with community problems. In 1893 black women in Boston founded the New Era Club. They published a monthly magazine, *Woman's Era*, that featured articles on fashion, health, and family life.

In 1895 a New Era Club member, Josephine St. Pierre Ruffin, enraged by white journalist James W. Jack's vilification of black women as "prostitutes, thieves, and liars" who were "altogether without character," issued a call to "Let Us Confer Together" that drew 104 black women to a meeting in Boston. The result was the formation of the National Federation of Afro-American Women, which soon included thirty-six clubs in twelve states. In the meantime, the Colored Women's League of Washington, D.C., which had been founded in 1892, published an appeal in *Woman's Era* for black women to organize a national association at the 1895 meeting of the National Council of Women. At that gathering, representatives from several local black women's clubs organized the National Colored Woman's League.

The NACW: "Lifting as We Climb"

The two groups—The National Federation of Afro-American Women and the National Colored Woman's League—merged in 1896 to form the National Association of Colored Women (NACW) with Mary Church Terrell elected the first president. The NACW adopted the self-help motto "Lifting as We Climb," and in the reforming spirit of the progressive age, they stressed moral, mental, and material advancement. By 1914 there were fifty thousand members of the NACW in one thousand clubs nationwide.

There were sometimes unpleasant disagreements and conflicts among the club women. Margaret Murray Washington—Booker T. Washington's wife—served as NACW president from 1912 to 1916, and the organization's *National Notes* was published at Tuskegee until 1922. Not everyone was fond of this arrangement. Ida Wells Barnett was particularly incensed and claimed that the Tuskegee Machine censored the publication. Meanwhile Mary Church Terrell found Barnett abrasive and contentious. Terrell managed to exclude the Chicago leader from the initial NACW meeting in 1896. There were also regional rivalries and ideological disputes as well as sensitivity over the light complexion of leaders like Terrell.

More important than these internal struggles were the efforts of black women to confront the problems black people encountered in urban areas as rural Southerners migrated by the thousands in the second and third decades of the twentieth century. The NACW clubs worked to eradicate poverty, end racial discrimination, and promote education, including the formation of kindergartens and day nurseries. Members cared for older people, especially former slaves. They aided orphans; assisted working mothers by providing nurseries, health care, and information on child rearing; and established homes for delinquent and abandoned girls.

Phillis Wheatley Clubs

Black women also formed Phillis Wheatley clubs and homes across the nation (named in honor of the eighteenth-century African-American poet). The residences offered living accommodations for single, black working women in many cities where they were refused admittance to YWCA facilities. Some Phillis

PROFILE

Mary Church Terrell

Mary Church Terrell lived from the year of the Emancipation Proclamation (1863) to the year that the U.S. Supreme Court declared segregated schools unconstitutional (1954). During those nine decades, she exemplified the African-American leaders whom W. E. B. Du Bois called the Talented Tenth. The daughter of slaves, she acquired a superb education and became prominent in Washington's black elite. She was ever conscious of her social status, education, and fair complexion. She was also absolutely dedicated to the elimination of Jim Crow and the cause of African-American women.

Mary Church was born in Civil War Memphis and raised during Reconstruction. She led a sheltered life and went on to Oberlin College where she studied classics, became proficient in languages, and earned an M.A. In 1891 she married Robert H. Terrell, a Harvard graduate who had earned a law degree at Howard. He was an auditor in the U.S. Treasury Department and later became a District of Columbia municipal judge.

Mary Church Terrell immersed herself in literary, social, and political activities. She spearheaded the creation of the Colored Women's League and became the first president of the NACW in 1896. Terrell believed that well-to-do black women had a responsibility to assist struggling and poorer women of color.

Terrell was an inspirational speaker. She spoke in 1904 at the International Congress of Women in Berlin—in German, French, and English. Mamie Garvin Fields recalled a speech Terrell delivered in Charleston, South Carolina, in 1916:

> Oh, my, when I saw her walk onto that podium in her pink evening dress and long white gloves, with her beautifully done hair, she was the Modern Woman. . . . Regal, intelligent, powerful, reaching out from time to time with that long glove, she looked and sounded like the Modern Woman that she talked about.

Terrell was active in the NAACP, which was not easy in light of her close relationship with Booker T. Washington and his wife, Margaret Murray Washington. She could not afford to alienate Washington because he possessed enough influence to prevent her husband's reappointment as judge. Terrell managed to convince Washington that she supported him, but in fact, she was devoted to the NAACP and its program. She served on its board, and spoke forcefully on civil rights. She risked the wrath of President Theodore Roosevelt after she criticized his dismissal of three companies of black soldiers following the Brownsville incident (see Chapter 15). She presented President William Howard Taft with NAACP petitions against lynching. She wrote articles attacking chain gangs, peonage, disfranchisement, and lynching. She worked with progressive organizations, such as the Women's International League for Peace and Freedom, and supported women's suffrage and the Nineteenth Amendment.

The Terrells were active in Washington's black elite—the Four Hundred. They attended balls, concerts, and parties, traveled extensively, and belonged to Washington's most exclusive black congregation, the Lincoln Temple Congregational Church, and she was active in Delta Sigma Theta sorority.

Mary Church Terrell consistently opposed racial discrimination and protested to Oberlin College officials when her daughters encountered more prejudice as students than she had. A lifelong Republican, she opposed President Franklin Roosevelt's inaction on civil rights. At the age of eighty-seven she demonstrated against Thompson's Restaurant, an all-white establishment in Washington. Her death in 1954 ended her campaign against Jim Crow and for women's rights.

TRACK 25

Mary Church Terrell summed up her legacy in her 1940 autobiography, *A Colored Woman in a White World.* "This is the story of a colored woman living in a white world. It cannot possibly be like a story written by a white woman. A white woman has only one handicap to overcome—that of sex. I have two—both sex and race. I belong to the only group in this country which has two such huge obstacles to surmount. Colored men have only one—that of race."

Wheatley clubs also provided nurseries and classes in domestic skills. In Cleveland, nurse Jane Edna Hunter organized a residence for single, black working women who could not find comfortable and affordable housing. In 1911 she formed the Working Girls' Home Association for cleaning women, laundresses, and private duty nurses. With association members contributing five cents a week, Hunter opened a twenty-three-room residence in 1913 that expanded to a seventy-two-room building in 1917.

Anna Julia Cooper and Black Feminism

"Only the BLACK WOMAN can say 'when and where I enter, in the quiet, undisputed dignity of my womanhood, without violence and without suing or special patronage, then and there the whole Negro race enters with me.' " So wrote Anna Julia Cooper in the late nineteenth century. Not only was Cooper convinced that black women would play a decisive role in shaping the destiny of their people, she labored to dispel the stereotype that black women lacked refinement, grace, and morality.

Cooper was born a slave in Raleigh, North Carolina in 1858, and graduated from St. Augustine's school. She then earned a bachelor's degree from Oberlin College in 1884. Speaking and writing with increasing confidence and authority, she published *A Voice from the South By a Black Woman of the South* in 1892. In this collection of essays she stressed the pivotal role that black women would play in the future, and she chastised white women for their lack of support. In 1900 she addressed the Pan African Conference in London.

Cooper was principal of Washington's famed M Street Colored High School (later Paul Laurence Dunbar High School) from 1901 to 1906. She was forced out in 1906 amid allegations that supporters of the powerful Tuskegee Machine resented Cooper's emphasis on academic preparation over vocational training. She went on to teach for four years at Missouri's Lincoln University before returning to M Street High as a teacher. Fluent in French, she earned a Ph.D. at the Sorbonne in Paris.

She was active with the NACW, the NAACP, and YWCA. Married in 1877, her husband died only two years later. Cooper found time following his death to take in and raise five children. She died in 1964 at age 105.

Women's Suffrage

Historically, many black women had supported women's suffrage. Before the Civil War, many abolitionists, including Mary Ann Shadd Cary, Sojourner Truth, and Frederick Douglass, had also backed women's suffrage. Cary and Truth tried unsuccessfully to vote after the war. Black women, such as Caroline Remond Putnam of Massachusetts, Lottie Rollin of South Carolina, and Frances Ellen Watkins Harper of Pennsylvania attended conventions of the mostly white American Woman's Suffrage Association in the 1870s.

Black women were also involved in the long struggle for women's suffrage on the state level. Ida Wells-Barnett was a leader in the Illinois suffrage effort. By 1900 Wyoming, Utah, Colorado, and Idaho permitted women to vote, and by 1918 women in seventeen northern and western states had gained the vote. But as more women won voting rights, women's suffrage became more controversial. The proposed Nineteenth Amendment to the U.S. Constitution drove a wedge between black and white advocates of women's political rights. Many opponents of women's suffrage, especially white Southerners, warned that granting women the right to vote would increase the number of black voters. Some white women advocated strict literacy and educational requirements for voting in an effort to limit the number of black voters, both women and men.

As it turned out, only two southern states—Kentucky and Tennessee—ratified the Nineteenth Amendment before its adoption in 1920. Black suffragists understood that the right to vote meant political power, and political power could be exercised to acquire civil rights, improve education, and gain respect. White Southerners also grasped the importance of voting rights. Thus despite the Nineteenth Amendment, large numbers of black people in the South—both men and women—remained unable to vote.

The Black Elite

Many of the black leaders described by W. E. B. Du Bois as the Talented Tenth formed protest organizations, joined reform efforts, and organized self-help groups. The leaders were middle- and upper-class black people who were better educated than most Americans—black or white.

The American Negro Academy

In 1897 Episcopal Priest Alexander Crummel met with sixteen other black men in Washington, D.C., to form the American Negro Academy. This scholarly

PROFILE

Lewis Latimer, Black Inventor

Lewis H. Latimer (1848–1928) was a draftsman, inventor, and pioneer in the electrical industry. During his lifetime, Latimer was awarded eight patents for his inventions. He was born in Chelsea, Massachusetts, in 1848. His parents had fled from slavery and settled in Boston where abolitionists including William Lloyd Garrison and Frederick Douglass raised funds to purchase their freedom.

After a year in the Union Navy during the Civil War, Latimer worked as an office boy for the patent solicitor firm of Crosby and Gould. There he taught himself drafting. As a draftsman, Latimer worked closely with inventors and began to tinker with ideas for inventions. In 1874, he received his first patent for improving the toilet on passenger railroad cars. He developed a flushing mechanism that prevented the upflow of sewage and cinders. He also executed drawings for Alexander Graham Bell's patent application for the telephone. Latimer later worked on electric lights, and in 1882 he received a patent for producing carbon filaments that made electric lighting more practical.

Lewis H. Latimer published *Incandescent Lighting: A Practical Description of the Edison System*—one of the first books on electric lighting—in 1896.

Latimer became superintendent of the incandescent lamp department of the United States Electric Lighting Company and supervised the installation of lights for buildings in the United States and Canada. In 1883, Thomas A. Edison hired Latimer as an engineer, chief draftsman, and expert witness in patent infringement cases. In 1890, Latimer published a book entitled *Incandescent Lighting: A Practical Description of the Edison System.* He served as chief draftsman for General Electric/Westinghouse Board of Patent Control when it was established in 1896.

Men who had worked with Thomas A. Edison joined together in 1918 as the Edison Pioneers to preserve memories of their early days working together and to honor Edison's genius and achievements. Latimer was a founding member and the only African-American Edison Pioneer. He died in Flushing, New York, on December 11, 1928.

organization was made up of "men of African descent" who assembled periodically to discuss and publish works on history, literature, religion, and science. Among those who attended the initial gathering were W. E. B. Du Bois, Paul Laurence Dunbar, Kelly Miller, and Francis Grimke.

Crummel was an elderly, but a dynamic and distinguished, leader who did not hesitate to express his deeply felt convictions on race, religion, and Africa. He had been born in 1818 in New York and spent several years in Liberia in the 1850s and 1860s as an Episcopal missionary. Crummel died in 1898, but the Academy survived as a vibrant intellectual and elitist society.

Carter G. Woodson, Alain Locke, Arthur Schomburg, and James Weldon Johnson subsequently joined its ranks before it eventually disbanded in 1928. It afforded black intellectuals an opportunity to ponder what it meant to be black in America and to develop their racial consciousness, thus nurturing ideas and concepts that would mature during the Harlem Renaissance.

Most members of the Academy supported women's rights and women's suffrage. Consequently it was exceedingly ironic that black women were not invited to become members of the Academy, although several black women, including Anna Julia Cooper, Ida Wells Barnett, and Mary Church Terrell, were easily the intellectual equals of the male participants.

The Upper Class

By the early twentieth century, there were several hundred wealthy African Americans. These black aristocrats were as sophisticated, refined, and conscious of their status as any group in American society. They distanced themselves from less affluent black and white people, and lived in expensive houses. Many of them possessed fair complexions. They were medical doctors, lawyers, and businessmen. While they possessed vastly more wealth than most Americans, that wealth paled in comparison to the huge fortunes of the richest American families, such as the Rockefellers, Carnegies, and Vanderbilts.

The black elite formed exclusive organizations that jealously limited membership to the small black upper class. In the 1860s the Ugly Fishing Club was transformed into an organization made up of New York City's wealthiest black men. It soon came to be known simply as the Ugly Club, and its membership spread to Newport, Rhode Island, Baltimore, and Philadelphia. In 1904 two wealthy Philadelphia physicians, a dentist, and a pharmacist formed Sigma Pi Beta, better known as Boulé. It was restricted to male college graduates, and it aimed to provide "inspiration, relaxation, intellectual stimulation, and brotherhood." Boulé expanded to seven chapters in cities that included Chicago and Memphis, but its membership totaled a mere 177.

Organizations like the Diamondback Club and the Cosmos Club in Washington, the Loendi Club in Pittsburgh, and the Bachelor-Benedict Club in New York sponsored luxurious banquets, dances, and debutante balls. Several of these groups owned ornate clubhouses. These elite societies and cliques typically competed to demonstrate social exclusivity and preeminence.

Fraternities and Sororities

Among the black elite were also the African Americans who established the Greek letter black fraternities and sororities. In 1906, seven students at Cornell University formed Alpha Phi Alpha, the first college fraternity for black men. Within a few years, it had chapters at the University of Michigan, Yale, Columbia, and Ohio State. The first black sorority, Alpha Kappa Alpha, was founded in 1908 at Howard University.

Several other Greek letter organizations were subsequently launched at Howard: Omega Psi Phi fraternity in 1911, Delta Sigma Theta sorority in 1913, Phi Beta Sigma in 1914, and Zeta Phi Beta sorority in 1920. In addition, in 1911 Kappa Alpha Psi fraternity was founded at Indiana University, and Sigma Gamma Rho sorority was formed in Indianapolis in 1922.

Besides providing college students with an opportunity to enjoy each other's company, the black fraternities and sororities stressed scholarship, social graces, and community involvement. Alpha Phi Alpha created the "Go to High School, Go to College" campaign in 1919. Kappa Alpha Psi adopted the "Guide Right" program to assist black youngsters in 1922. In 1923 Alpha Kappa Alpha opened a mobile health clinic in Mississippi.

Presidential Politics

Since Reconstruction, black voters had loyally supported the Republican party and its presidential candidates. "The Party of Lincoln" welcomed that support and periodically rewarded black men with federal jobs. Republican presidents Theodore Roosevelt (1901–1909) and William Howard Taft (1909–1913) continued that policy.

Frustrated by the Republicans

But other presidential actions more than offset whatever goodwill these appointments generated. Roosevelt discharged three companies of black soldiers after the Brownsville incident in 1906, and Taft tolerated restrictions on black voters in the South and encouraged the development of a "lily white" Republican party, removing black people from federal jobs in the region.

In 1912 the Republican party split in a bitter feud between President Taft and Theodore Roosevelt, and a third political party—the Progressive party—emerged. The Progressives nominated Roosevelt to run against Taft and the Democratic candidate, Woodrow Wilson. But as the delegates at the Progressive convention in Chicago sang the "Battle Hymn of the Republic," southern black men who had come to the gathering stood outside the hall, denied admission by white Progressives.

Woodrow Wilson

It was not a complete shock that militant black leaders like William Monroe Trotter and W. E. B. Du Bois

PROFILE

George Washington Carver and Ernest Everett Just

George Washington Carver and Ernest Everett Just each rose from humble beginnings in the nineteenth century to become highly regarded biologists. Carver was born in 1864 or 1865 to slave parents in Diamond Grove, Missouri. Eager to learn, he spent much of his youth engaged in menial labor around Missouri, Iowa, and Kansas as he acquired an uneven education. He spent a year at Simpson College and then enrolled at Iowa State University in 1891 at age twenty-five as its sole black student. He compiled a superb academic record, participated in an array of student activities, and took charge of the campus greenhouse. He became fascinated with botany and focused on mycology (the study of fungi) and cross-fertilization.

Just was born in Charleston, South Carolina, in 1883 and grew up on nearby James Island where his mother toiled in phosphate mines following the death of his father. He attended local schools and earned a teacher training certificate in 1899 from what is now South Carolina State University. Just went on to Kimball Union Academy in New Hampshire, and he graduated with honors from Dartmouth College in 1907 with a major in biology and minors in Greek and history.

Just was hired by Howard University in Washington, D.C., and spent the rest of his teaching career there. In 1911 he helped establish Omega Psi Phi, which emerged as a major black fraternity. Although hired to teach English and rhetoric, he soon changed to zoology and biology, the subjects in which he had developed an abiding interest. He spent several summers at the Marine Biology Laboratory at Woods Hole, Massachusetts, and earned a Ph.D. in zoology from the University of Chicago in 1916.

While Just felt more at home engaged in research in a laboratory, Carver felt more comfortable experimenting with crops in a field. At the invitation of Booker T. Washington, Carver left a promising career at Iowa State in 1896 to take charge of the agriculture program at Tuskegee Institute. Having studied with two men at Iowa State—James Wilson and Henry C. Wallace—who became U.S. secretaries of agriculture, Carver established political ties to Washington, D.C., that greatly benefitted Tuskegee. He became the director of the nation's only black agricultural experiment station.

Carver was a superb teacher in and out of the classroom, but he was a less-than-efficient administrator who sometimes clashed with Booker T. Washington. Carver committed himself to working with impoverished black farmers, seeking to make them more productive and less dependent on cotton. He sponsored outreach programs and farmers' institutes. He discovered hundreds of uses for the protein-rich peanut. And he experimented extensively with sweet potatoes.

Carver became a folk hero by the 1930s with his gregarious personality and self-effacing demeanor. He never married and lived in a student dormitory at Tuskegee. He wore a tattered coat with a fresh flower in the lapel. Though he never earned more than $1,200 a year, he gave more than $60,000 to Tuskegee before he died in 1943.

Just, confronted with the lack of opportunities available to a dedicated black scientist at white universities, pursued his research in the fertilization of marine animals at Woods Hole. But even there some scientists shunned him and others patronized him. Nevertheless, by 1928 he had published thirty-five articles, mostly on fertilization. Awarded a sizable grant from the Julius Rosenwald Foundation, he spent much of the 1930s engaged in research in Italy, Germany, and France. In 1939 he published *Biology of the Cell Surface.*

Just married Ethel Highwarden, a Howard faculty member, in 1912. They had three children, but later divorced. In 1939 he married Maid Hedwig Schnetzler, a German scientist. Just died of cancer in 1941.

Both George Washington Carver and Ernest Everett Just were awarded the NAACP's Spingarn Medal—Just in 1915 and Carver in 1923.

In 1948 George Washington Carver became the second African American to be honored by the U.S. Post Office with a stamp. Booker T. Washington had been the first. As part of their Black Heritage series, the Postal Service recognized Ernest Everett Just in 1993.

urged black voters to support Woodrow Wilson, the Democrat, in the 1912 presidential election. Wilson was the reform governor of New Jersey, and he had been president of Princeton University. Trotter and Du Bois were impressed with Wilson's academic background and his promise to pursue a progressive policy toward black Americans. Du Bois wrote:

> Wilson is a cultivated scholar and he has brains. We have, therefore, a conviction that Mr. Wilson will treat black men and their interests with foresighted fairness. He will not advance the cause of an oligarchy in the South, he will not seek further means of 'jim crow' insult, he will not dismiss black men wholesale from office, and he will remember that the Negro has a right to be heard and considered.

But as president, Wilson proved to be no friend of black people. Born in Virginia and raised in South Carolina, Wilson had thoroughly absorbed white southern racial views. Federal agencies and buildings were fully segregated early during Wilson's tenure. In 1914 Trotter and a black delegation met with Wilson to protest segregation in the treasury department and the post office. Wilson defended separation of the races as a means to avoid friction. Trotter vehemently disagreed, and Wilson became visibly irritated. The president warned that he would no longer meet with the group if Trotter remained their spokesman.

Black Men and the Military in World War I

In 1915–1916, Wilson faced more than problems with dissatisfied black people. United States–Mexican relations had steadily deteriorated after a revolution and civil war in Mexico. War in Europe threatened to draw the United States into conflict with Germany.

The Punitive Expedition to Mexico

In 1914, war almost broke out between the United States and Mexico when U.S. marines landed at Vera Cruz after an attack on American sailors. Then in March 1916, Francisco "Pancho" Villa, one of the participants in Mexico's civil war, led a force of Mexican rebels across the border into New Mexico in an effort to provoke war between Mexico and the United States. Fifteen Americans were killed, including seven U.S. soldiers. In response, Wilson dispatched a "punitive expedition" that eventually numbered 15,000 U.S. troops under the command of General John J. "Black Jack" Pershing. Pershing acquired the nickname "Black Jack" after commanding black troops in Cuba during the Spanish–American War.

United States forces, including the black 10th Cavalry (see Chapter 15), spent ten months in Mexico in a futile effort to capture Villa. The 10th Cavalry was, as had been the case with black troops since the Civil War, commanded by white men. But Lieutenant Colonel Charles Young, an 1889 black graduate of the U.S. Military Academy at West Point, helped lead the regiment.

Young led the black troops against a contingent of Villa's rebels who had ambushed an element of the 13th Cavalry, a white unit, at Santa Cruz de Villegas.

Major Frank Tompkins of the 13th was so relieved to be rescued that he reportedly exclaimed to Young: "By God, Young, I could kiss every black face out there." Young supposedly replied, "If you want to, you may start with me." United States troops were withdrawn from Mexico in 1917 as the probability increased that the United States would enter World War I against Germany.

World War I

When World War I erupted in Europe in August 1914, Woodrow Wilson and most Americans had no intention and no desire to participate. Wilson promptly issued a proclamation of neutrality. Running for reelection in 1916 on the appealing slogan, "He Kept Us Out of War," Wilson narrowly defeated Republican candidate Charles Evans Hughes. Repeated German submarine attacks on civilian vessels and the loss of American lives infuriated Wilson and many Americans as a gross violation of U. S. neutral rights. On April 6, 1917, Congress declared war on Germany. Most African Americans supported the war effort. As in previous conflicts, black people sought to demonstrate their loyalty and devotion to the country through military service. "If this is our country," declared W. E. B. Du Bois, "then this is our war. We must fight it with every ounce of blood and treasure."

Some white leaders were less enthusiastic about the participation of black men. One southern governor wondered about the wisdom of having the military train and arm thousands of black men at southern camps and posts. General Pershing argued for the use of black troops, but insisted on white leadership. "Under capable white officers and with sufficient training, negro soldiers have always acquitted themselves creditably."

Black Troops and Officers

There were about 10,000 black regulars in the U.S. Army in 1917: The 9th and 10th Cavalry regiments and the 24th and 25th Infantry regiments. There were more than 5,000 black men in the Navy, but virtually all of them were waiters, kitchen attendants, and stokers for the ships' boilers. The Marine Corps did not admit black men. During World War I, the newly formed Selective Service system drafted more than 370,000 black men—13 percent of all draftees—though none of the local draft boards had black members. Several all-black state national guard units were also incorporated into federal service.

Though the military remained rigidly segregated, there was political pressure from black newspapers and the NAACP to commission black officers to lead black troops. The War Department created an officer training school at Fort Des Moines, Iowa. Nearly 1,250 black men enrolled—1,000 were civilians and 250 were enlisted men from the regular regiments—and over 1,000 received commissions. Black officers, however, were confined to the lower ranks. None of these new black officers were promoted above captain, and the overall command of black units remained in white hands.

Lieutenant Colonel Charles Young was eligible to lead black and white troops in World War I. He had already served in Cuba, the Philippines, Haiti, and Mexico. Several white soldiers complained, however, that they did not want to take orders from a black man, and over Young's protests, military authorities forced him to retire by claiming that he had high blood pressure. Young insisted that he was in good health, and he rode a horse from his home in Xenia, Ohio, to Washington, D.C., to prove it. But Young remained on the retired list until he was given command of a training unit in Illinois five days before the war ended.

Discrimination and Its Effects

Most white military leaders, politicians, and journalists embraced racial stereotypes and expected little from black soldiers. As in earlier American wars, black troops were discriminated against, abused, and neglected. Some were compelled to drill with picks and shovels rather than rifles. At Camp Hill, Virginia, black men lived in tents with no floors, no blankets, and no bathing facilities through a cold winter. White men failed to salute black officers, and black officers were denied admission to officers' clubs. Morale among black troops was low, and their performance sometimes reflected it.

Military authorities did not expect to use black troops in combat. The Army preferred to employ black troops in labor battalions, as stevedores, in road construction, and as cooks and bakers. Of more than 380,000 black men who served in World War I, only 42,000 went into combat. Black troops represented 3 percent of U.S. combat strength. The Army did not prepare black soldiers adequately for combat, but military leaders complained when black soldiers who did face combat performed poorly in battle.

The 368th Infantry Regiment of the 92nd Division came in for especially harsh criticism. Fighting

Lieutenant Colonel Charles D. Young, an 1889 graduate of the U.S. Military Academy at West Point who served in Cuba, the Philippines, Haiti, and Mexico, was not permitted to command troops during World War I. He returned to military service at the end of the war, and was sent to Liberia to help train that country's army. He died while on furlough in Nigeria in 1922.

alongside the French in September 1918, the second and third battalions fell back in disorder. Some black officers and enlisted men ran. The white regimental commander blamed black officers, and thirty of them were relieved of command. Five officers were court-martialed for cowardice; four were sentenced to death and one to life in prison. All were later freed. But black Lieutenant Howard H. Long agreed that the perceptions of white officers caused the poor performance. "Many of the [white] field officers seemed far more concerned with reminding their Negro subordinates that they were Negroes than they were in having an effective unit that would perform well in combat."

Even the white commander of the 92nd Division, General Charles C. Ballou, identified white officers as the main problem. "It was my misfortune to be handicapped by many white officers who were rabidly hostile to the idea of a colored officer, and who continually conveyed misinformation to the staff of the superior units, and generally created much trouble and discontent. Such men will never give the Negro the square deal that is his just due."

While white officials stressed the weaknesses of the 368th Infantry Regiment, they mostly ignored the commendable records of the 369th, 370th, 371st, and 372nd Regiments. The 369th compiled an exemplary combat record. Sent to the front for ninety-one consecutive days, these "Men of Bronze"—as they came to be known—consisted mainly of soldiers from the 15th New York National Guard. They fought alongside the French and were given French weapons, uniforms, helmets, and food (but not the wine that French soldiers received). They had an outstanding military band led by Jim Europe, one of the finest musical leaders of the early twentieth century. The 369th lived up to their motto, "Let's Go," as they took part in some of the war's heaviest fighting. They never lost a trench nor gave up a prisoner. By June 1918, French commanders were asking for all the black troops the Americans could send.

Most French civilians and troops, unfazed by racist warnings from white American officials about the presumed danger black men posed to white women, praised the conduct of black soldiers and accepted them as equals. Following the triumph of the Allies in World War I, French authorities awarded the *Croix de Guerre,* one of France's highest military medals, to the men of the 369th, the 371st, and the 372nd Regiments.

Black troops returned to America on segregated ships. The 15th New York National Guard Unit from the 369th Regiment and its famed band were not permitted to join the farewell parade in New York City. Even when white Americans offered praise, it was riddled with racist stereotypes. The Milwaukee *Sentinel* offered a typical compliment. "Those two colored regiments fought well, and it calls for special recognition. Is there no way of getting a cargo of watermelons over there?"

Du Bois's Disappointment

Black leaders who had supported American entry in the war were embittered at the treatment of black soldiers. During the war in 1918, Du Bois appealed to black people in *The Crisis* to "close ranks" and support the war.

> We of the colored race have no ordinary interest in the outcome. That which the German power represents today spells death to the aspirations of Negroes and all darker races for equality, freedom and democracy. Let us not hesitate. Let us, while this war lasts, forget our special grievances and close ranks with our own white fellow citizens and the allied nations that are fighting for democracy.

Du Bois's unequivocal support may well have been connected to his effort to secure an officer's commission in military intelligence through the intervention of Joel E. Spingarn, chairman of the NAACP Board of Directors. Du Bois did not get his commission. What he did get was criticism for his "close ranks" editorial. His former ally, William Monroe Trotter, said that Du Bois had "finally weakened, compromised, deserted the fight, [and] betrayed the cause of his race." To Trotter, Du Bois was "a rank quitter in the cause for equal rights."

In 1930 Du Bois confessed that he should not have supported U.S. intervention in the war:

> I was swept off my feet during the world war by the emotional response of America to what seemed to be a great call to duty. The thing that I did not understand is how easy and inevitable it is for an appeal to blood and force to smash to utter negation any ideal for which it is used. Instead of a war to end war, or a war to save democracy, we found ourselves during and after the war descending to the meanest and most sordid of selfish actions.

By the end of World War I, Du Bois—who had visited black troops in France—could see that black loyalty and sacrifice had not eroded white racism. He wrote defiantly in *The Crisis* that black people were determined to make America yield to its democratic ideals:

> But by the God of heaven, we are cowards and jackasses if now that the war is over, we do not marshal every ounce of our brain and brawn to fight a sterner, longer, more unbending battle against the forces of hell in our own land.
>
> We return.
>
> We return from fighting.
>
> We return fighting.
>
> Make way for Democracy! We saved it in France, and by the Great Jehovah, we will save it in the United States of America, or know the reason why.

Race Riots

Despite the reformist impulse of the progressive era and the democratic ideals trumpeted as the United States went to war against Germany, most white Americans clung to social Darwinism and white supremacy. White people reacted with contempt and violence to demands by black people for fairer treatment and equal opportunities in American society. The campaigns of the NAACP, the efforts of the black club women, and the services and sacrifices of black men in

MAP 16–1 Major Race Riots, 1900–1923 In the years between 1900 and 1923, race conflicts and riots occurred in dozens of American communities as black people migrated in increasing numbers to urban areas. The violence reached a peak in the immediate aftermath of World War I during the Red Summer of 1919. White Americans—in the North and South—were determined to keep black people confined to a subordinate role as menial laborers and restricted to well-defined all-black neighborhoods. African Americans who had made significant economic and military contributions to the war effort and who had congregated in large numbers in American cities insisted on participating on a more equitable basis in American society.

the war not only failed to alter white racial perceptions but were sometimes accompanied by a backlash against African Americans. Ten black men still in uniform were lynched in 1919.

Many white Americans concurred with Mississippi senator James K. Vardaman when he declared in 1914 that white people would not accept black claims for a meaningful political and legal role in America:

> God Almighty never intended that the negro should share with the white man in the government of this country. . . . Do not forget that. It matters not what I may say or others may think; it matters not what constitutions may contain or statutes provide, wherever the negro is in sufficient numbers to imperil the white man's civilization or question the white man's supremacy the white man is going to find some way around the difficulty. And that is just as true in the North as it is in the South. You need not deceive yourselves about that. The feeling against the negro in Illinois when he gets in the white man's way is quite as strong, more bitter, less regardful of the negro's feelings and conditions than it is in Mississippi.

The racial violence that had permeated southern life in the late nineteenth century expanded into northern communities as many white Americans responded with hostility to the arrival of black migrants from the South. Black people defended themselves, and casualties among both races escalated (see Map 16–1).

Atlanta 1906

In 1906—eleven years after Booker T. Washington delivered his Cotton States Exposition address there—white mobs attacked black residents in Atlanta. Several factors aggravated white racial apprehensions in the city. In 1902 four black and four white people had been killed in a riot there. Many rural black people, attracted by economic opportunities, had moved to Atlanta. But white residents considered the newcomers more lawless and immoral than the long-time black residents. The Atlanta newspapers—*The Constitution*, *The Journal*, and *The Georgian*—ran inflammatory accounts about black crime and black men who brutalized white women. Many of these stories were false or exaggerated. Two white Democrats—Hoke Smith and Clark Howell—were engaged in a divisive campaign for a U.S. Senate seat in 1906, and both candidates stirred up racial animosity. There were also determined and ultimately successful efforts underway to disfranchise black voters in Georgia.

On a warm Saturday night, September 22, 1906, a white man jumped on a box on Decatur Street, one of Atlanta's main thoroughfares, and waved an Atlanta newspaper emblazoned with the headline: "THIRD ASSAULT." He hollered, "Are white men going to stand for this?" The crowd roared, "No! Save our women!" "Kill the niggers." A five-day orgy of violence followed.

The mayor, police, and fire departments vainly tried to stop the mob. Thousands of white people roamed the streets in search of black victims. Black people were indiscriminately tortured, beaten, and killed. White men pulled black passengers off streetcars. They destroyed black businesses. As white men armed themselves, the police disarmed black men. Black men and women who surrendered to marauding white mobs in hopes of mercy were not spared. Black men who fought back only further infuriated the crazed white crowd. Twenty-five black people and one white person died, and hundreds were injured in the riot.

Du Bois hurried home to Atlanta from a trip to Alabama to defend his wife and child. He waited on his porch with a shotgun for a mob that never came. He later explained, "I would without hesitation have sprayed their guts over the grass." In New York, black editor T. Thomas Fortune called for a violent black response: "It makes my blood boil. I would like to be there with a good force of armed men to make Rome howl." Fortune demanded retribution. "I cannot believe that the policy of non-resistance in a situation like that of Atlanta can result in anything but contempt and massacre of the race."

Booker T. Washington looked for a silver lining in the awful affair by noting that "while there is disorder in one community there is peace and harmony in thousands of others." He said that black resistance would merely result in more black fatalities. Washington went to Atlanta and appealed for racial reconciliation.

A Committee of Safety of ten black and ten white leaders was formed. Charles T. Hopkins, an influential white Atlantan, warned in strong paternalist terms, "If we let this dependent race be butchered before our eyes, we cannot face God in the judgement day." But little real racial cooperation resulted. No members of the white mob were brought to justice. Black Georgia voters were disfranchised. Atlanta's streetcars were segregated. The city had no public high school for black youngsters. The Carnegie Library did not admit black people, and the Atlanta police force had no black officers.

Springfield 1908

Two years later in August 1908, white citizens of Springfield, Illinois, attacked black residents in an episode that led to the creation of the NAACP in 1909. George Richardson, a black man, was falsely accused of raping a white woman. The sheriff managed to save Richardson by getting him out of town. But an angry mob tore into Springfield's small black population. Six black people were shot and killed, two were lynched, dozens were injured, and damage in the thousands of dollars was inflicted on black homes and businesses. About 2,000 black people were driven out of the community.

There was even more violence in the second decade of the twentieth century as major racial conflicts occurred between 1917 and 1921 in East St. Louis, IL; Houston, TX; Chicago; Elaine, AR; and Tulsa, OK. Smaller violent confrontations occurred at Washington, D.C.; Charleston, SC; Knoxville, TN; Omaha, NE; and Waco and Longview, TX. While different incidents sparked each riot, the underlying causes tended to be similar. White residents were concerned that recently arrived black migrants would compete for jobs and housing.

East St. Louis 1917

East St. Louis, Illinois, was a gritty industrial town of nearly sixty thousand across the Mississippi River from St. Louis, Missouri. About 10 percent of the inhabitants were black. The town's schools, public facilities, and neighborhoods were segregated. Racial tensions increased in February 1917 after 470 black workers were hired to replace white members of the American Federation of Labor who had gone on strike against the Aluminum Ore Company. On July 1, several white people drove through a black neighborhood firing guns. Shortly after, two white plainclothes police officers drove into the same neighborhood and were shot and killed by residents who may have believed that the drive-by shooters had returned.

Angry white mobs then sought revenge. Black people were mutilated and killed, and their bodies were thrown into the river. Black homes, many of them little more than cabins and shacks, were burned. Hundreds of black people were left homeless. The

On July 28, 1917, the NAACP organized a silent march in New York City to protest the East St. Louis, Illinois, race riot in which thirty-five black people died as well as to denounce the on-going epidemic of lynchings. The marchers were accompanied by the beat of muffled drums.

police joined the rioters. Thirty-five black people and eight white people died in the violence.

The NAACP sent W. E. B. Du Bois and Martha Gruening to East St. Louis. They compiled a twenty-four-page report, "Massacre at East St. Louis," that documented instance after instance of brutality. "Negroes were 'flushed' from the burning houses, and ran for their lives, screaming and begging for mercy. A Negro crawled into a shed and fired on the white men. Guardsmen started after him, but when they saw he was armed, turned to the mob and said: 'He's armed boys. You can have him. A white man's life is worth the lives of a thousand Negroes."

To protest the riot, the NAACP organized a silent march in New York City and thousands of well-dressed black people marched to muffled drums down Fifth Avenue.

Houston 1917

A month after the East St. Louis riot, black soldiers in Houston attacked police officers and civilians. The Third Battalion of the 24th Infantry recently had been transferred from Wyoming and California to Camp Logan near Houston where the black troops came face-to-face with Jim Crow. Streetcars and public facilities were segregated. Local white and Hispanic people regularly called the black troops "niggers."

On August 23 a black soldier tried to prevent a police officer, Lee Sparks, from beating a black woman. Sparks clubbed the soldier and hauled him off to jail. Corporal Charles W. Baltimore later attempted to determine what had happened, and he was also beaten and incarcerated. Both soldiers were later released. But a rumor circulated that Baltimore had been slain.

About one hundred armed black soldiers mounted a two-hour assault on the police station. Sixteen white and Hispanic residents, including five policemen, and four black soldiers and two black civilians were killed. The Army charged the sixty-three black soldiers with mutiny. The NAACP retained the son of Texas legend Sam Houston to help defend them, but nineteen black troops were hanged (including Corporal Baltimore) and sixty-seven others sentenced to prison. Officer Lee Sparks remained on the force and killed two black people later that year.

Chicago 1919

Between 1916 and 1919, the black population of Chicago doubled as migrants from the South moved north in search of jobs, political rights, and humane treatment. Many encountered a violent reception. A severe housing shortage strained the boundaries between crowded, segregated black neighborhoods and white residential areas. In the months after World War I ended in November 1918, racial tensions increased as black men were hired to replace striking white workers in several industries in Chicago.

The Chicago riot began on Sunday, July 27, 1919—one day after black troops were welcomed home with a parade down the city's Michigan Avenue. Eugene Williams, a young black man, was swimming in Lake Michigan and inadvertently crossed the invisible boundary that separated the black and white beaches and bathing areas. He was stoned by white people and drowned. Instead of arresting the alleged perpetrators, the police arrested a black man who complained about police inaction.

Williams's death set off a week of violence that left twenty-three black people and fifteen white people dead. More than five hundred were injured, and nearly one thousand were left homeless after fire raged though a Lithuanian neighborhood. Not only did police fail to stem the violence; they often also joined roaming white mobs as they attacked black pedestrians and streetcar passengers. Black men formed a barrier along State Street to stop the advance of white gangs from the stockyard district. Three regiments of the Illinois National Guard were sent into the streets, but the violence ended only on Saturday, August 1, as heavy rains kept people indoors.

During the riot, the Chicago *Defender*, the city's black newspaper, reported many violent incidents. "In the early [Tuesday] morning a thirteen-year-old lad standing on his porch at 51st and Wabash Avenue was shot to death by a white man who, in an attempt to get away, encountered a mob and his existence became history. A mounted policeman, unknown, fatally wounded a small boy in the block of Dearborn Street and was shot to death by some unknown rioter."

Elaine 1919

In the fall of 1919, black sharecroppers in and around Elaine, Arkansas, attempted to organize a union and withhold their cotton from the market until they received a higher price. Deputy sheriffs tried to break up a union meeting in a black church, and one of the deputies was killed. In retaliation, white people killed dozens of black people. No white people were prosecuted, but twelve black men were convicted of the deputy's murder. They were sentenced to death, and sixty-seven other black men received prison terms of up to twenty years. Many were tortured and beaten while they were held in jail. Ida Wells-Barnett and the Equal Rights League generated enormous publicity about the case. The NAACP appealed the convictions and in 1923 the Supreme Court overturned them. The court agreed with NAACP attorney Moorfield Storey that the defendants had not received a fair trial.

Tulsa 1921

Violence erupted in Tulsa, Oklahoma, on May 31, 1921, after still another black man was accused of rape. Dick Rowland allegedly assaulted a white woman elevator operator, and rumors circulated that white men intended to lynch him. To protect Rowland, who was later found innocent, black men assembled at the courthouse jail where white men also gathered. Angry words were exchanged, and shooting erupted. Several black and white men died in the chaos that ensued.

Black men retreated to their neighborhood, known as Greenwood, to protect their families and homes. The governor dispatched the national guard, and the sheriff removed Rowland from the jail to an unknown location. By the morning of June 1, some five hundred white men confronted about one thousand black men across a set of railroad tracks. White men in sixty to seventy automobiles were also cruising around the black residential area. Approximately fifty armed black people defended themselves in a black church near the edge of their neighborhood as white men advanced on them. The attackers set fire to the church. As black people fled the burning building, they were shot. More fires were set. About two thousand black residents managed to escape to a convention hall. Forty square blocks and more than 1,000 of Greenwood's homes, churches, schools and businesses went up in flames. White men even utilized aircraft for reconnaissance and to drop incendiary devices on Greenwood. As many as three hundred black people and twenty white people may have perished in what was perhaps the worst episode of civilian violence in American history until September 11, 2001.

Following a three and a half year investigation, an eleven member commission made a series of recommendations in 2001 to the Oklahoma legislature to offer a measure of restitution. The legislators declined to set aside funds for survivors, but they did appropriate $750,000 to formulate plans for a museum and memorial. They also created a Greenwood Redevelopment Authority and instituted a scholarship program.

Rosewood 1923

During the first week of January 1923, the small town of Rosewood, Florida, was destroyed and its black residents driven out or killed. Rosewood was a mostly black community—it had a few white inhabitants—located in the pinewoods of west central Florida not far from the Gulf of Mexico. On New Year's Day, Fannie Taylor, a married white woman from a nearby town, claimed she had been raped and beaten by a black man. Many white people quickly assumed that Jessie Hunter was responsible. Other white people believed that Mrs. Taylor wanted to divert attention from herself because she had a white lover who was not her husband.

White men sought Hunter and vengeance. Unable to locate him, they brutally beat Aaron Carrier who may have helped Taylor's white lover escape. The mob shot and killed Samuel Carter after savagely mutilating him. Tensions dramatically escalated.

On January 4 a band of angry white men invaded Rosewood. Black people were prepared to defend themselves. Led by Sylvester Carrier and his mother, Sarah, many town's people had congregated in the Carrier home. The mob unleashed a hail of gunfire into the residence killing Sarah Carrier. Two white men who attempted to gain entry into the home were shot and killed. Shooting continued until the mob's supply of ammunition was depleted on January 5.

The following day a mob of two hundred fifty, including Ku Klux Klan members from Gainesville, invaded, burned, and destroyed Rosewood. The community's black residents fled to the nearby woods and swamps with little more than the clothes on their backs, never to return. Rosewood was no more.

The precise number of black people who died will never be known. It may have been well over one hundred. In 1994 the Florida legislature appropriated 2.1 million dollars to survivors of Rosewood and to families who lost property in the assault. Although seven decades had elapsed, ten survivors were still alive, and collected $150,000 each. But it proved impossible for many black people to verify that they had been in Rosewood in 1923 or that they were kin to people who had owned property in the town. Much of the money was not disbursed.

The Great Migration

The great migration of African Americans from the rural South to the urban North began as a trickle of people after the Civil War and became a flood of human beings by the second decade of the twentieth century (see Table 16–1). Between 1910 and 1940, 1,750,000 black people left the South. As a result, the black population outside the South doubled by 1940. Most of the initial wave of migrants were younger people born in the 1880s and 1890s who had no recollection of slavery, but who anticipated a better future for themselves and their families in the North.

Why Migrate?

People moved for many reasons. Often they were both pushed from their rural circumstances and pulled toward urban areas. The push resulted from disasters in southern agriculture in the 1910s. The boll weevil destroyed cotton crops across the South from Mexico to the Carolinas, and floods devastated Mississippi and Alabama in 1915. The pull resulted from labor shortages created by World War I in northern industry and manufacturing. The war all but ended European immigration to the United States, eliminating a main source of cheap labor. At the same time, European governments and the United States placed huge orders for war material with northern factories. Thousands of jobs became available in steel mills, railroads, meatpacking plants, and the automobile industry. Northern businessmen sent labor agents to recruit southern workers.

Many southern white people reacted ambivalently to the loss of black residents. They welcomed the departure of people whom they held in such low regard, but they also worried about the loss of tenants and sharecroppers. Southern states and municipalities required labor agents to obtain licenses to recruit workers. Angry white landowners and businessmen threatened some of these agents and forced them to leave southern towns.

Black newspapers, such as the Pittsburgh *Courier* and especially the Chicago *Defender*, encouraged black Southerners to move north. Black railroad porters and dining car employees distributed thousands of copies of the *Defender* throughout the South. One unnamed black man wrote in the *Defender* that sensible men would leave the poverty, injustice, and violence of the South for the cold weather of the North. "To die from the bite of frost is far more glorious than that of the mob. I beg of you, my brothers, to leave that benighted land. You are free men."

Table 16–1
Black Population Growth in Selected Northern Cities, 1910–1920

	1910		1920		
	Number	Percent*	Number	Percent*	Percent Increase
New York	91,709	1.9%	152,467	2.7%	66.3%
Chicago	44,103	2.0	109,458	4.1	148.2
Philadelphia	84,459	5.5	134,229	7.4	58.9
Detroit	5,741	1.2	40,838	4.1	611.3
St. Louis	43,960	6.4	69,854	9.0	58.9
Cleveland	8,448	1.5	34,451	4.3	307.8
Pittsburgh	25,623	4.8	37,725	6.4	47.2
Cincinnati	19,739	5.4	30,079	7.5	53.2
Indianapolis	21,816	9.3	34,678	11.0	59.0
Newark	9,475	2.7	16,977	4.1	79.2
Kansas City	23,566	9.5	30,719	9.5	30.4
Columbus	12,739	7.0	22,181	9.4	74.1
Gary	383	2.3	5,299	9.6	1,283.6
Youngstown	1,936	2.4	6,662	5.0	244.1
Buffalo	1,773	.4	4,511	.9	154.4
Toledo	1,877	1.1	5,691	2.3	203.2
Akron	657	1.0	5,580	2.7	749.3

*"Percent" refers to percent of city's population; "Percent Increase" refers to growth of black population.

Source: U.S. Department of Commerce.

A black resident of one of South Carolina's Sea Islands explained in 1917 that he left to earn more money. "I could work and dig all year on the Island and best I could do would be to make $100 and take a chance of making nothin'. Well, I figured I could make 'roun' thirty or thirty-five dollars every week and at that rate save possibly $100 every two months." Like many migrants, he moved more than once. He first went to Savannah, and then to Philadelphia, before finally settling in Brooklyn, New York.

Black people who departed the South escaped the most blatant forms of Jim Crow and the injustice in the judicial system. Black women fled the sexual exploitation of white and black men. Black people in the North could vote. The North offered better public schools. In the early twentieth century the South had almost no public high schools for black youngsters, and the longer school year in the urban North was not tied to the demands of planting and harvesting crops.

Some black people migrated to escape the dull, bleak, impoverished life and culture of the rural South. One young woman left South Carolina's St. Helena Island in 1919. "[I] got tired of the Island. Too lonesome. Go to bed at six o'clock. Everything dead. No dances, no moving picture show, no nothing. 'Coz every once in a while they would have a dance, but here you could go to 'em every Saturday night. That's why people move more than anything else."

The decision to migrate could take years of pondering and planning. To depart was to leave family, friends, and familiar surroundings behind for the uncertainty, confusion, and rapid pace of urban communities. Migrants often first moved to southern towns or cities, and then headed for a larger city. Poet and writer Langston Hughes was born in Joplin, Missouri, in 1902 and moved to Lincoln, Illinois. "I had no sooner graduated from grammar school in Lincoln than we moved from Illinois to Cleveland. My stepfather sent for us. He was working in a steel mill during the war, and making lots of money. But it was hard work, and he never looked the same afterwards."

Some people made the decision to move impulsively. After she was fired from her nursing position at Hampton Institute in Virginia in 1905, Jane Edna Hunter decided to go to Florida, but changed her mind:

> En route, I stopped at Richmond, Virginia, to visit with Mr. and Mrs. William Coleman, friends of Uncle Parris. They were at church when I arrived; so I sat on the doorstep to await their return. After these

VOICES

A Migrant to the North Writes Home

People who migrated to northern communities often wrote home to describe their new surroundings and experiences, and to confess that they missed their old homes. One unidentified black man who had moved to Philadelphia made his feelings known to a medical doctor.

Philadelphia, Pa., Oct. 7, 1919

Dear Sir:

I take this method of thanking you for yours early responding and the glorious effect of the treatment. Oh. I do feel so fine. Dr. the treatment reach me almost ready to move I am now housekeeping again I like it so much better than rooming. Well Dr. with the aid of God I am making very good I make $75 per month. I am carrying enough insurance to pay me $20 per week if I am not able to be on duty. I don't have to work hard. dont have to mister every little white boy comes along I havent heard a white man call a colored nigger you no now—since I been in the state of Pa. I can ride in the electric street and steam cars any where I get a seat. I dont care to mix with white what I mean I am not crazy about being with white folks, but if I have to pay the same fare I have learn to want the same accomidation. and if you are the first in a place here shoping you dont have to wait until the white folks get thro tradeing yet amid all this I shall ever love the good old South and I am praying that God may give every well wisher a chance to be a man regardless of his color, and if my going to the front [World War I] would bring about such conditions I am ready any day—well Dr. I dont want to worry you but read between the lines; and maybe you can see a little sense in my weak statement the kids are in school every day I have only two and I guess that all. Dr. when you find time I would be delighted to have word from the good old home state. Wife join me in sending love you and yours.

QUESTIONS

1. What is the letter writer's main reason for having migrated?
2. What was more important to this man, better living standards or the sense of liberation he enjoyed in Philadelphia?

Source: Emmett J. Scott, ed., "Letters of Negro Migrants of 1916–1918," *Journal of Negro History*, 4 (1 July 1919) in Fishel and Quarles, *The Negro American: A Documentary History*, pp. 398–99.

good friends had greeted me, Mrs. Coleman said, 'Our bags are packed to go to Cleveland, Jane. We are going to take you with us.' I was swept off my feet by the cheerful determination of the Colemans. My trunk, not yet removed from the station, was rechecked to Cleveland.

Most migrants maintained a genuine fondness for their southern homes and kinfolk. They returned regularly for holidays, weddings, and funerals. Kelly Miller, who had grown up in South Carolina, spent years as a scholar and teacher at Howard University in Washington, D.C., but he still had "an attachment for the old state that time and distance cannot destroy. After all, we love to be known as a South Carolinian." Thousands of black migrants routinely sent money home to the South. Over the years, several million dollars earned in the North flowed into southern communities.

Destinations

Though many black Southerners went to Florida, most migrants from the Carolinas and Virginia settled in Washington, Philadelphia, and New York (see Map 16–2). Black people who left Georgia, Alabama, and Mississippi tended to move to Pittsburgh, Cleveland, and Detroit. Migrants from Louisiana, Mississippi, and Arkansas often rode the Illinois Central Railroad to Chicago. Once they experienced a metropolis, many black people then resettled in smaller communities. Migrants to Philadelphia, for example, moved on to

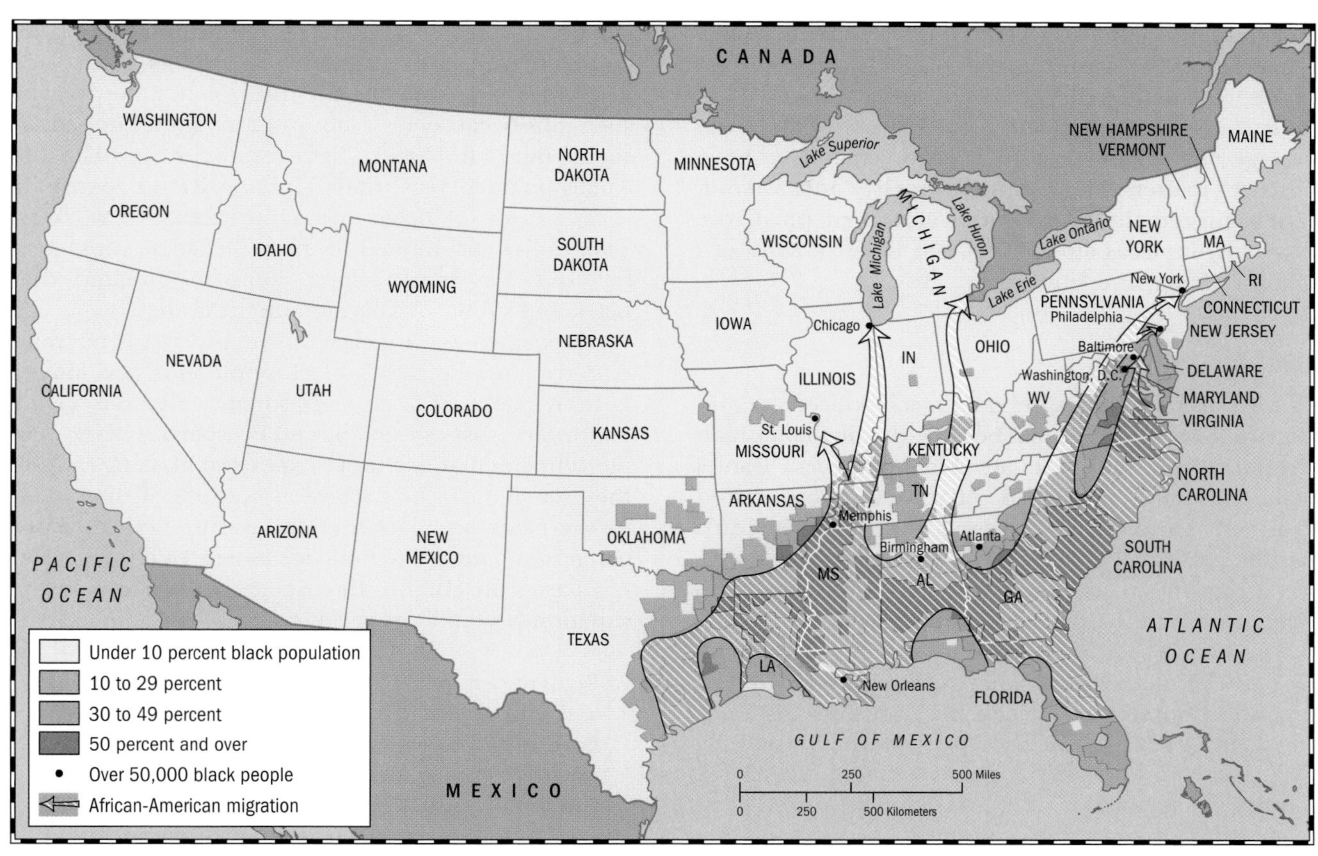

MAP 16–2 The Great Migration and the Distribution of the African-American Population in 1920 Though several hundred thousand black Southerners migrated north in the second and third decades of the twentieth century, most African Americans remained in the southern states.

Harrisburg or Altoona, Pennsylvania, or to Wilmington, Delaware.

Few black Southerners moved west to California, Oregon, or Washington. There were only twenty-two thousand black residents of California in 1910. Substantial black migration west did not occur until the 1930s and 1940s. But in 1920 Mallie Robinson made the long trek west. Deserted by her husband Jerry, she set out with her five children (including one-year-old Jackie who would become a baseball legend) and eight other relatives. They boarded a train in Cairo, Georgia, traveled to Los Angeles, and settled in nearby Pasadena. Mallie's half-brother, who had already moved west, assured her that she would be closer to heaven in California.

However, most black migrants found that their destination was neither near heaven nor the Promised Land. Black people congregated in all-black neighborhoods—Harlem in New York City, Chicago's South Side, Paradise Valley in Detroit, Cleveland's East Side, and the Hill District of Pittsburgh—that later would be called ghettoes. White property owners resisted selling or renting real estate to black people outside the confines of these neighborhoods. And many southern black migrants themselves, wary of white hostility, preferred to live among black people, often friends and family who had preceded them north.

Northern Communities

Even before the Civil War, most northern cities had small free black populations. By the late nineteenth century, southern migrants began to gravitate to these urban areas and make their presence felt. Black residents established churches, social organizations, businesses, and medical facilities. They gained representation in community and political affairs.

There was less overt segregation in the North. Most northern states, as well as California, had enacted laws in the late nineteenth century that prohibited racial discrimination in public transportation, hotels, restaurants, theaters, and barbershops. Most of these states also forbade segregated schools. However, passage of such laws and their enforcement were two different matters. Many white businesses and communities ignored the statutes and embraced Jim Crow, especially in areas along the Ohio River in southern Ohio, Indiana, and Illinois.

Chicago

As early as 1872, Chicago had a black policeman, and in 1876 John W. E. Thomas became the first black man elected to the Illinois Senate. Black physician Daniel Hale Williams established African-American-staffed Provident Hospital on Chicago's South Side in 1891. By 1900, black Chicagoans were the twelfth largest ethnic group in the city, behind such European immigrant groups as the Irish, Poles, and Germans.

Chicago's black population surged during the first three decades of the twentieth century as migrants poured into the city. Black institutions flourished. In 1912 an NAACP branch was established. By 1920 black Chicago had eighty Baptist and thirty-six Methodist churches. The Olivet Baptist Church grew from thirty-five hundred members in 1916 to nine thousand by 1922. Because the downtown YMCA barred black men, black people raised $50,000 and Julius Rosenwald of Sears, Roebuck, and Company contributed $25,000 to build the Wabash YMCA for the black community in 1913. However, many black Chicagoans considered this a surrender to segregation and insisted that black men should be admitted to the white YMCA.

The Chicago *Defender* was the city's leading black newspaper. Its founder, Robert S. Abbott, the son of slaves, began publishing the *Defender* in 1905, and by 1920 it had a nationwide circulation of 230,000. Chicago's first black bank, Jesse Binga's State Bank, was established in 1908, and in 1919 Frank L. Gillespie organized the Liberty Insurance Company.

In 1915 black Chicago's political influence expanded when Oscar DePriest was elected second ward alderman. Two other black men were elected to the city council by 1918. DePriest was then elected to the U.S. House of Representatives as a Republican in 1928, becoming the first black congressman since North Carolina's George White left the house in 1901.

As the number of black people in Chicago swelled, racial tensions increased and exploded in the 1919 race riot. Competition for jobs was a critical issue. White employers, such as the meatpacking companies, regularly replaced white strikers with black workers. Black men usually did not hesitate to take such jobs because most labor unions would not admit them. But a few weeks before the riot in 1919, the Amalgamated Meatcutters Union tried to sponsor a unity parade of black and white stockyard workers. The police prohibited it because, some observers believed, the meatpacking companies feared that black and white workingmen might unite.

Housing was an even more divisive issue than employment. Chicago's black population was almost entirely confined to an eight-square-mile area on the South Side east of State Street. Prosperous black people who could afford more expensive housing outside the area could not purchase it because of their race. As the black population grew, housing became more congested, and crime and vice increased.

Langston Hughes described the similar housing situation his family experienced in Cleveland:

> Rents were very high for colored people in Cleveland, and the Negro district was extremely crowded, because of the great migration. It was difficult to find a place to live. We always lived, during my high school years, either in an attic or a basement, and paid quite a lot for such inconvenient quarters. White people on the east side of the city were moving out of their frame houses and renting them to Negroes at double and triple the rents they could receive from others. An eight room house with one bath would be cut up into apartments and five or six families crowded into it, each two-room kitchenette apartment renting for what the whole house had rented for before.

Harlem

Harlem was a white community in upper Manhattan that had declined by the latter 1800s. It then enjoyed an incredible building boom that occurred in anticipation of the construction of the subway that would link upper Manhattan to downtown New York City by the early twentieth century. But real estate speculators overbuilt and were left with empty houses and apartments. Facing foreclosure, many white property owners sold or rented to black people in Harlem. In 1904 Philip A. Payton formed the Afro American Realty company that sold homes and rented apartments to black clients before it failed in 1908.

Harlem's white residents opposed the influx of black people. Some of them formed the Harlem Property Owners' Improvement Corporation in 1910 to block black settlement. Its founder, John G. Taylor, warned in 1913: "We are approaching a crisis, it is a question of whether the white man will rule Harlem or the Negro." However, many white property owners—eager for a profit—preferred to sell to black people than to maintain white unity.

As thousands of black people moved to Harlem, many left the "Tenderloin" and "San Juan Hill" areas of Manhattan's West Side where New York's black residents had lived in the nineteenth century. The construction of Pennsylvania Station forced many to vacate the "Tenderloin." Black churches took the lead in the "On to Harlem" movement as they occupied churches formerly used by white denominations. Some of the black churches were among the largest property owners in Harlem.

St. Philip's Protestant Episcopal Church, the wealthiest black church in the United States and noted for its solemn services and elite parishioners, moved from West 25th Street in the "Tenderloin" in 1910 to Harlem. In 1911, St. Philip's purchased ten apartment houses on West 135th Street between Lenox and Seventh Avenues for $640,000. The Reverend Adam Clayton Powell Sr. and the Abyssinian Baptist Church, St. Mark's Episcopal Church, and the African Methodist Episcopal Zion Church ("Mother Zion") also moved to Harlem and acquired extensive real estate holdings there. The black churches helped make Harlem a black community.

As the black population increased in Harlem, large houses and apartments were often subdivided among working families who could not rent or buy in other areas of New York. They paid higher prices for real estate than white people did. The average Harlem family paid $9.50 a room per month while white working families paid $6.50 for similar accommodations elsewhere in New York.

By 1920, seventy-five thousand black people lived in Harlem (see Map 16–3). Harlem became the "Negro Capital of the World." Black businesses and institutions, including the Odd Fellows, Masons, Elks, Pythians, the NAACP, the Urban League, and the YMCA and YWCA moved to Harlem. Black newspapers—the *New York News* and *Amsterdam News*—opened in Harlem to compete with the older *New York Age*. One resident observed, "If my race can make Harlem, good lord, what can't it do?"

Families

Migration placed black families under enormous strains. Relatives frequently moved north separately. Fathers or mothers would leave a spouse and children behind as they sought employment and housing. Children might be left with grandparents for extended periods. In other instances, extended family members— cousins, in-laws, brothers and sisters—crowded into limited living space.

Men generally found more opportunities for work in northern industries than did women. There was a huge demand for unskilled labor during and after World War I. In 1915, Henry Ford astounded industrial America when he began to pay employees of the Ford Motor Company in Detroit the unprecedented sum of $5 per day, and that included black men and occasionally black women. Rarely, however, would a black man be promoted beyond menial labor. Except for some opportunities in manufacturing during the war, black women were confined to domestic and janitorial work. Mary Ellen Washington recalled the experience in her family. "In the 1920s my mother and five aunts migrated to Cleveland, Ohio from Indianapolis and, in spite of their many talents, they found every door except the kitchen door closed to them."

Black women employed as domestics lived with white families, worked long hours, and saw more of their white employer's children than they did their own. One maid explained her dreary and unhappy situation:

> I am now past forty years of age and am the mother of three children. My husband died nearly fifteen years ago. . . . For more than thirty years—or since I was ten years old—I have been a servant in one capacity or another in white families.
>
> I frequently work from fourteen to sixteen hours a day. I am compelled . . . to sleep in the house. I am allowed to go home to my own children, the oldest of whom is a girl of 18 years, only once in two weeks, every other Sunday afternoon—even then I'm not permitted to stay all night. . . . I don't know what it is to go to church; I don't know what it is to go to a lecture or entertainment of any kind; I live a treadmill life. . . . You might as well say that I'm on duty all the time—from sunrise to sunrise, every day in the week. I am the slave, body and soul, of this family.

Some vulnerable younger women were lured into prostitution in the intimidating urban environment. Black women's organizations worked to prevent newly arrived migrants from falling prey to sexual exploitation. They did not always succeed. Some women made a calculated decision to turn sex to their economic advantage. Sara Brooks caustically commented, "Some women woulda had a man to come and live in the house and had an outside boyfriend too, in order to get the house paid for and the bills. They meet a man

MAP EXPLORATION
To explore this map, go to http://www.prenhall.com/hine/map16.3

MAP 16–3 The Expansion of Black Harlem, 1911–1930 Before the American Revolution, Harlem was a small Dutch village located at the northern end of Manhattan Island. In the early twentieth century, African Americans transformed it into a thriving black metropolis. Migrants who arrived either after a short trip of just a few miles from the "Tenderloin" or "San Juan Hill" sections of midtown Manhattan or after much longer journeys from the Carolinas or Georgia took over block after block of Harlem homes and apartments.

Adapted from: Steven Watson, *The Harlem Renaissance*, New York: Pantheon Books. 1996.

and if he promises 'em four or five dollars to go to bed, they's grab it. That's called sellin' your own body, and I wasn't raised like that."

Despite the stresses and pressures, most black families survived intact. Most northern black families, though hardly well-to-do, were two-parent households. Women headed comparatively few families. Fathers were present in seven of ten black families in New York City in 1925. But the great migration transformed southern peasants into an urban proletariat.

Conclusion

In 1900, Booker T. Washington was the nation's most influential black leader. He soothed white people and reassured black Americans as he counseled conciliation, patience, and agricultural and mechanical training as the most effective means to bridge the racial divide. His 1895 speech at the Cotton States Exposition in Atlanta elicited support and praise from both white and black listeners.

The Wizard of Tuskegee, as Washington was known, had little appreciation for criticism and did not hesitate to attack his opponents, including William Monroe Trotter and W. E. B. Du Bois. He worked to subvert the Niagara Movement and the NAACP. But support for Washington and his conservative strategy gradually diminished as the NAACP openly confronted racial discrimination. Washington died in 1915. By 1920 the NAACP assumed the lead in the struggle for civil rights as it fought in the courts and legislatures.

The Talented Tenth of black Americans, distinguished by their educational and economic resources, promoted "self-help" through a variety of organizations—from women's groups to fraternities and sororities—to enhance their own status and to help less affluent black people.

As black men served in World War I and as thousands of black Southerners migrated north, many white Americans became alarmed that African Americans were not as content with their subordinate and isolated status as Booker T. Washington had suggested they were. Some white Americans responded with violence in race riots as they attempted to prevent black Americans from assuming a more equitable role in American society. By 1920, despite white opposition, black Americans had demonstrated that they would not accept economic subservience and the denial of their rights.

Recommended Reading

W. E. B. Du Bois. *The Souls of Black Folk.* New York: Library of America, 1903. An essential collection of superb essays.

John Hope Franklin and August Meier. *Black Leaders of the Twentieth Century.* Urbana, IL: University of Illinois Press, 1982. A series of "mini biographies" of fifteen people including Washington, Du Bois, T. Thomas Fortune, and Ida Wells-Barnett.

Willard Gatewood. *Aristocrats of Color: The Black Elite, 1880–1920.* Bloomington, IN: Indiana University Press, 1990. An examination of the lives and activities of well-to-do black people.

Lawrence Otis Graham. *One Kind of People: Inside America's Black Upper Class.* New York: HarperCollins, 1999. An informative history and analysis of black America's wealthiest families and organizations.

Louis R. Harlan. *Booker T. Washington: The Making of a Black Leader, 1856–1901.* New York: Oxford University Press, 1972 and *Booker T. Washington: The Wizard of Tuskegee, 1901–1915.* New York: Oxford University Press, 1983. The definitive two-volume biography of Washington.

David Levering Lewis. *W. E. B. Du Bois: Biography of a Race, 1868–1919.* New York: Henry Holt and Co., 1993; *W. E. B. Du Bois: The Fight for Equality and the American Century, 1919–1963.* New York: Henry Holt and Co., 2001. A magisterial and exhaustive account of the 95-year life and times of Du Bois.

Deborah Gray White. *Too Heavy a Load: Black Women in Defense of Themselves.* New York: Norton, 1999. An exploration of the contours of black women's history in the twentieth century.

Additional Bibliography

Leadership Conflicts and the Emergence of African-American Organizations

Charles F. Kellogg. *NAACP: A History of the National Association for the Advancement of Colored People.* Baltimore: Johns Hopkins University Press, 1967.

August Meier. *Negro Thought in America, 1880–1915.* Ann Arbor, MI: University of Michigan Press, 1967.

Alfred A. Moss, Jr. *American Negro Academy: Voice of the Talented Tenth.* Baton Rouge, LA: Louisiana State University Press, 1981.

B. Joyce Ross. *J. E. Spingarn and the Rise of the N.A.A.C.P.* New York: Atheneum, 1972.

Lawrence C. Ross, Jr. *The Divine Nine: The History of African-American Fraternities and Sororities.* New York: Kensington Books, 2000.

Elliott Rudwick. *W. E. B. Du Bois.* New York: Atheneum, 1968.

Nancy Weiss. *The National Urban League, 1910–1940.* New York: Oxford University Press, 1974.

Shamoon Zamir. *Dark Voices: W. E. B. Du Bois and American Thought, 1888–1903.* Chicago: University of Chicago Press, 1995.

African-American Women in the Early Twentieth Century

Anna Julia Cooper. *A Voice from the South.* New York: Oxford University Press, 1988.

Elizabeth Clark-Lewis. *Living In, Living Out: African American Domestics in Washington, D.C., 1910–1940.* Washington: Smithsonian Institution Press, 1994.

Cynthia Neverdon-Morton. *Afro-American Women of the South and the Advancement of the Race, 1895– 1925.* Knoxville. TN: University of Tennessee Press, 1998.

Jacqueline A. Rouse. *Lugina Burns Hope: A Black Southern Reformer.* Athens, GA: University of Georgia Press, 1989.

Stephanie J. Shaw. *What a Woman Ought to Be and to Do: Black Professional Women Workers during the Jim Crow Era.* Chicago: University of Chicago Press, 1996.

Rosalyn Terborg-Penn. *African American Women in the Struggle for the Vote, 1850–1920.* Bloomington, IN: Indiana University Press, 1998.

African Americans in the Military in the World War I Era

Arthur E. Barbeau and Florette Henri. *Black American Troops in World War I.* Philadelphia: Temple University Press, 1974.

Edward M. Coffman. *The War to End All Wars: The American Military Experience in World War I.* Madison, WI: University of Wisconsin Press, 1986.

Arthur W. Little. *From Harlem to the Rhine: The Story of New York's Colored Volunteers.* New York: Covici, Friede, 1936.

Bernard C. Nalty. *Strength for the Fight: A History of Black Americans in the Military.* New York: The Free Press, 1986.

Timeline

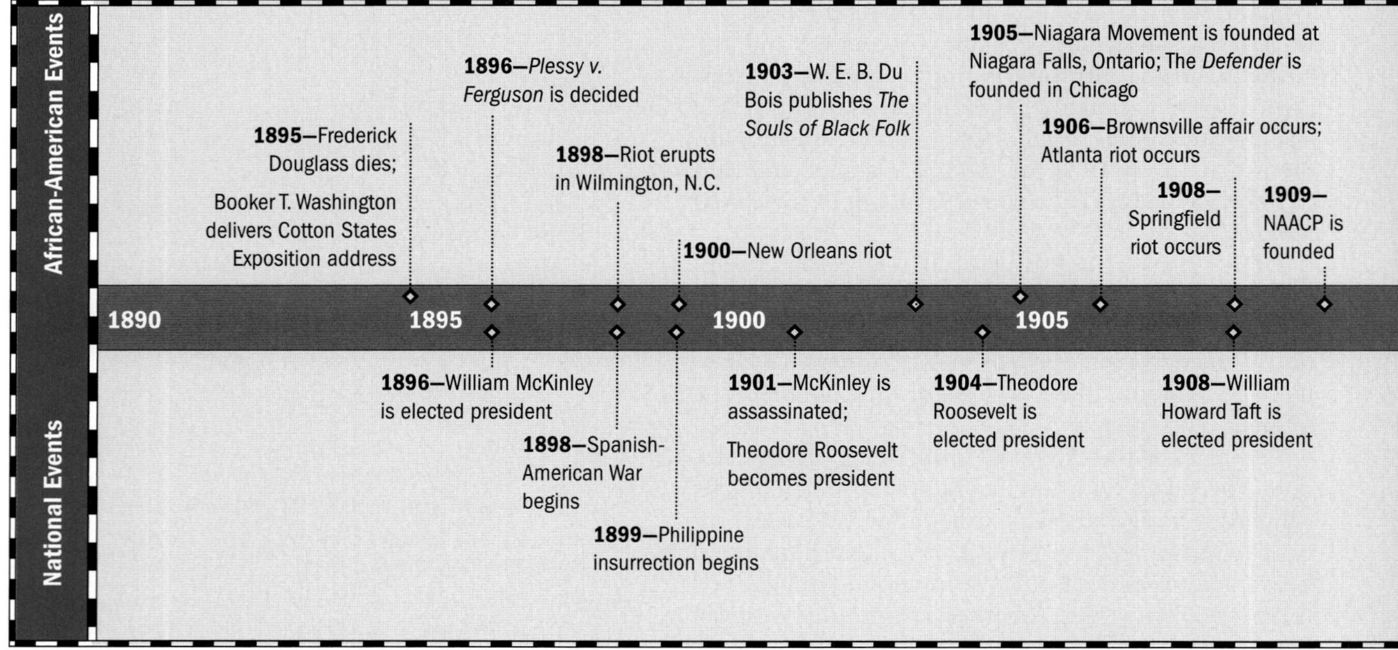

Cities and Racial Conflict

St. Clair Drake and Horace R. Clayton. *Black Metropolis: A Study of Negro Life in a Northern City.* 2 vols. Chicago: Harcourt, Brace and Co., 1945.

Michael D'Orso. *Rosewood.* New York: Boulevard Press, 1996.

Sherry Sherrod Dupree. *The Rosewood Massacre at a Glance.* Gainesville, FL: Rosewood Forum, 1998.

Scott Ellsworth. *Death in a Promised Land: The Tulsa Race Riot of 1921.* Baton Rouge, LA: Louisiana State University Press, 1982.

Robert V. Haynes. *A Night of Violence: The Houston Riot of 1917.* Baton Rouge, LA: Louisiana State University Press, 1976.

Hannibal Johnson. *Black Wall Street, From Riot to Renaissance in Tulsa's Historic Greenwood District.* Austin, TX: Eakin Press, 1998.

David M. Katzman. *Before the Ghetto: Black Detroit in the Nineteenth Century.* Urbana, IL: University of Illinois Press, 1973.

Kenneth L. Kusmer. *A Ghetto Takes Shape: Black Cleveland, 1870–1930.* Urbana, IL: University of Illinois Press, 1976.

Gilbert Osofsky. *Harlem: The Making of a Ghetto, 1890–1930.* New York: Harper & Row, 1966.

Christopher Reed. *The Chicago NAACP and the Rise of Black Professional Leadership, 1910–1966.* Bloomington, IN: Indiana University Press, 1997.

Elliott M. Rudwick. *Race Riot at East St. Louis, July 2, 1917.* Cleveland: World Publishing, 1966.

Roberta Senechal. *The Sociogenesis of a Race Riot: Springfield, Illinois, in 1908.* Urbana, IL: University of Illinois Press, 1990.

Allan H. Spear. *Black Chicago: The Making of a Negro Ghetto, 1890–1920.* Chicago: University of Chicago Press, 1967.

Joe William Trotter, Jr. *Black Milwaukee: The Making of an Industrial Proletariat, 1915–1945.* Urbana, IL: University of Illinois Press, 1985.

William Tuttle. *Chicago in the Red Summer of 1919.* New York: Atheneum, 1970.

Lee E. Williams. *Anatomy of Four Race Riots: Racial Conflict in Knoxville, Elaine (Arkansas), Tulsa, and Chicago, 1919–1921.* Hattiesburg, MS: University and College Press of Mississippi, 1972.

The Great Migration

Peter Gottlieb. *Making Their Own Way: Southern Blacks' Migration to Pittsburgh, 1916–1930.* Urbana, IL: University of Illinois Press, 1987.

James R. Grossman. *Land of Hope: Chicago, Black Southerners, and the Great Migration.* Chicago: University of Chicago Press, 1989.

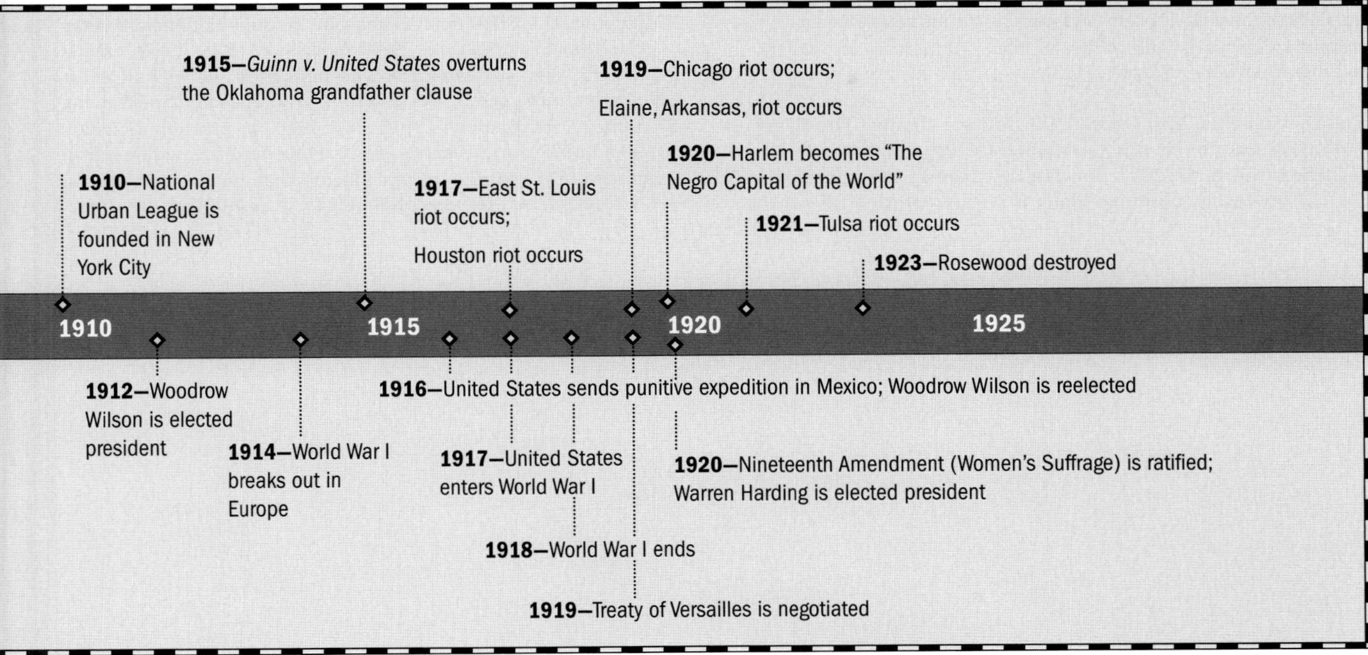

Florette Henri. *Black Migration, 1900–1920.* Garden City, NY: Anchor Press, 1975.

Carole Marks. *Farewell—We're Good and Gone: The Great Black Migration.* Bloomington, IN: Indiana University Press, 1989.

Milton C. Sernett. *Bound for the Promised Land: African American Religion and the Great Migration.* Durham, NC: Duke University Press, 1997.

Joe William Trotter, Jr., ed. *The Great Migration in Historical Perspective.* Bloomington, IN: Indiana University Press, 1991.

Autobiography and Biography

W. E. B. Du Bois. *Dusk of Dawn.* New York: Harcourt, Brace & Co., 1940.

———. *The Autobiography: A Soliloquy on Viewing My Life from the Last Decade of Its First Century.* New York: International Publishers, 1968.

Stephen R. Fox. *The Guardian of Boston: William Monroe Trotter.* New York: Atheneum, 1970.

Kenneth R. Manning. *Black Apollo of Science: The Life of Ernest Everett Just.* New York: Oxford University Press, 1983.

Linda O. McMurry. *George Washington Carver: Scientist and Symbol.* New York: Oxford University Press, 1981.

Arnold Rampersad. *The Art and Imagination of W. E. B. Du Bois.* Cambridge, MA: Harvard University Press, 1976.

Mary Church Terrell. *A Colored Woman in a White World.* New York: Arno Press reprint, 1940.

Emma Lou Thornbrough. *T. Thomas Fortune.* Chicago: University of Chicago Press, 1970.

Booker T. Washington. *Up from Slavery.* New York: Doubleday, 1901.

Retracing the Odyssey

Hardy, Virginia: The Booker T. Washington National Monument. Booker T. Washington lived his first nine years on this farm. There are tours available, as well as a museum and restored school house that depict rural life in nineteenth-century America, especially for slaves.

Diamond, Missouri: The George Washington Carver National Monument. George Washington Carver was born a slave here in 1864 or 1865 in a cabin that no longer exists. The 210-acre park has a visitor center that has exhibits on Carver's life as well as a short film about his boyhood. There are also nature trails and the Carver Science Discovery Center.

New York, New York: The 369th Historical Society. The 369th all-black regiment distinguished itself during World War I in combat with French units. Previously it had been the 15th Infantry Regiment of the New York National Guard. The 369th armory is located on Fifth Avenue in Harlem and contains a museum that features weapons, equipment and photos of black troops from World War I to Operation Desert Storm of 1991.

Tulsa, Oklahoma: The Greenwood Cultural Center. The Greenwood Cultural Center has a permanent exhibit of forty-five photos taken during the 1921 riot that devastated a large portion of the Greenwood community. There is also a replica of one of the houses that was destroyed. The center maintains exhibits on other aspects of local black history as well, and is home to a Jazz Hall of Fame.

Washington, D.C.: The Smithsonian Institution: National Museum of American History: From Field to Factory. This major exhibit depicts the lives and experiences as well as the hopes and disappointments of the people who migrated from the rural South to the industrial North between 1915 and 1940. It includes a tenant farmer's house, a train station, and a Philadelphia row house as it examines the economic and racial factors that motivated thousands of black people to leave their homes and surroundings.

REVIEW, RESEARCH & INTERACT

REVIEW QUESTIONS

1. Compare and evaluate the strategies promoted by Booker T. Washington with those of W. E. B. Du Bois and the NAACP.
2. On which specific issues did Booker T. Washington and W. E. B. Du Bois agree? On which did they disagree?
3. Assess Booker T. Washington's contributions to the advancement of black people.
4. To what extent did middle-class and prosperous black people contribute to progress for their race? Were their efforts effective?
5. Why did most African Americans support U.S. participation in World War I? Was that support justified?
6. What factors contributed to race riots and violence in the World War I era?
7. Why did many black people leave the South in the 1920s? Why didn't this migration begin earlier or later?
8. What factors affected the decision to migrate or stay?

Research Navigator.com RESOURCES FOR COLLEGE RESEARCH ASSIGNMENTS **www.researchnavigator.com**

Chapter 16 examines the various strategies African Americans used to resist the inferior status they had been assigned by white society. For further research on this topic, use the tools available to you in Research Navigator.

> *As you investigate this topic, consider this question: "Compare and contrast W. E. B. Du Bois' and Booker T. Washington's approach to the position of black Americans in early twentieth-century society. What were the key differences in the two men's positions?"*

- **ContentSelect:** Search in the History database using the search terms *Du Bois* and *NAACP.*
- **Links Library:** Access the History: U.S. History database and explore the links for *Du Bois, W. E. B.* and *Woodrow Wilson.*
- **New York Times on the Web:** To find out more, search the History database using the terms *Du Bois* and *NAACP.*

DOCUMENTS AND ACTIVITIES IN AFRICAN-AMERICAN HISTORY

Documents

16-1 W. E. B. Du Bois, from *The Souls of Black Folks,* 1903
16-2 The Niagara Movement, Declaration of Principles, 1905
16-3 Platform Adopted by the National Negro Committee, 1909
16-4 An NAACP Official Calls for Censorship of *The Birth of a Nation,* 1915
16-5 Letters from the Great Migration, 1916–1917
16-6 "Our Reason for Being": A. Philip Randolph Embraces Socialism, 1919

Interactive Map

The Expansion of Black Harlem, 1911–1930, p 394
http://www.prenhall.com/hine/map16.3

Learning Activity

The Struggle for Woman Suffrage
From the time of the American Revolution through World War I, American women fought to gain the right to vote (called *suffrage*).

17

African Americans and the 1920s

Aaron Douglas (1899–1979) was one of America's finest artists, and a major contributor to the Harlem Renaissance. In *Aspects of Negro Life from Slavery through Reconstruction* (1934), Douglas captured the creative energy of African Americans as he depicted their struggles to contribute to American society and culture.

I, TOO

I, too, sing America.
I am the darker brother.
They send me to eat in the kitchen
When company comes.
But I laugh,
And eat well,
And grow strong.
To-morrow
I'll sit at the table
When company comes
Nobody'll dare
Say to me,
"Eat in the kitchen"
Then.
Besides, they'll see how beautiful I am
And be ashamed,—
I, too, am America.

—Langston Hughes, 1926

TRACK 26

CHAPTER OUTLINE

Strikes and the Red Scare

Varieties of Racism
- Scientific Racism
- *The Birth of a Nation*
- The Ku Klux Klan

Protest, Pride, and Pan-Africanism: Black Organizations in the Twenties
- The NAACP
- "Up You Mighty Race": Marcus Garvey and the UNIA
- Pan-Africanism

Labor
- The Brotherhood of Sleeping Car Porters
- A. Philip Randolph

The Harlem Renaissance
- Before Harlem
- Writers and Artists
- White People and the Harlem Renaissance

Harlem and the Jazz Age
- Song, Dance, and Stage

Sports
- Rube Foster
- College Sports

Conclusion

Many Americans had difficulty adjusting to life following World War I. The Allied victory brought little long-term satisfaction or security, and the U.S. Senate's rejection of the Treaty of Versailles and membership in the League of Nations in 1920 left many Americans disillusioned. The Bolshevik Revolution in Russia in 1917 and labor agitation at home heightened fears and increased anxiety. Racial and ethnic intolerance escalated as thousands of rural black Southerners continued to stream into northern cities, and more than 800,000 immigrants arrived in America in 1920 and 1921.

Americans shunned Europe and its problems and closed their eyes to the imperfections of American society. Enthusiasm for progressive reforms faded as many Americans concluded that governmental efforts to mitigate poverty, control vice, improve working conditions, and regulate big business had been excessive. Middle-class Americans became preoccupied with making money and with acquiring—usually on credit and for the first time—automobiles, radios, and home appliances.

Many native white Americans, convinced that black people and immigrants—especially Jewish and Catholic immigrants—posed a threat to their Anglo-Saxon ethnic purity, ever more fervently embraced social Darwinism. Many sought reassurance in organizations that stressed religious, racial, and national pride. Millions of white Americans joined the revived Ku Klux Klan in the 1920s as it promoted white supremacy, American patriotism, and Protestant values.

Led by the NAACP, African Americans denounced injustice and pressed for inclusion in society, for the enforcement of civil rights, and for economic opportunities. Black workers—notably the members of Brotherhood of Sleeping Car Porters—organized and demanded recognition and improved working conditions, hours, and wages. But the 1920s also saw hundreds of thousands of African Americans enthusiastically support Marcus Garvey and the Universal Negro Improvement Association. Garvey celebrated black nationalism and urged his followers to forsake white America, take pride in themselves, and look to Africa. And the 1920s also saw black culture blossom and flourish as the artists, writers, musicians, and entertainers of the Harlem Renaissance celebrated black life and society.

Strikes and the Red Scare

In 1919 and 1920, Americans were bewildered and angered by labor unrest and afraid that the communists (or "Reds") in the new Soviet Union would try to incite a revolution in America. There were 3,600 strikes in 1919 as workers who had deferred demands during the war for pay raises and improved working conditions walked off their jobs. More than 300,000 steel workers in Pittsburgh and Gary, Indiana, struck, including 7,000 unskilled black steel workers in Pittsburgh. In a demonstration of solidarity with striking shipyard workers, most of Seattle's working people shut the city down in a general strike. Americans were even more alarmed when police officers in Boston went on strike. Many worried that labor agitation was a prelude to revolution.

Political leaders exacerbated these feelings by warning that communists and foreign agents were plotting to overthrow the government. Woodrow Wilson's Attorney General A. Mitchell Palmer grimly warned Americans of the Red menace and the threat aliens posed. He ordered 249 aliens deported and some six thousand arrested and imprisoned in gross violation of their rights, but it was an action that many Americans warmly approved. Palmer went too far, however, when he predicted that the Red revolution would begin in the United States on May 1, 1920. There was no revolution, and confidence in Palmer waned. There were, however, several terrorist bombings, including one on Wall Street in September 1920 that killed thirty-three people. There is, moreover, some evidence that some business leaders supported the raids as a means of discouraging workers from forming and joining labor unions and participating in strikes.

Prompted in part by the Red Scare, xenophobia (fear of foreigners) swept the nation in the 1920s. Two Sicilian immigrants, Nicola Sacco and Bartolomeo Vanzetti, who were anarchists, were charged in 1920 with a murder that had occurred during a payroll robbery near Boston. They were found guilty, and after a prolonged controversy they were executed in 1927. But their supporters believed that the guilty verdict was due more to their foreign origins and radical beliefs than to conclusive proof that they had committed the murder.

Varieties of Racism

The entrenched racism of American society found continued expression in more than one form in the twenties. There was the sophisticated racism associated with supposedly scholarly studies that reflected the ideology of Social Darwinism. There was also the raw bigotry that manifested itself in various aspects of popular culture and in the ideology of the increasingly popular Ku Klux Klan.

Scientific Racism

Many white Americans believed that the United States was under siege as European immigrants and black migrants flooded American cities. Pseudoscholars gravely warned about the peril these "inferior" peoples posed. In 1916 Madison Grant published *The Passing of the Great Race.* Grant warned that America was committing "race suicide," because northern Europeans and their descendants—the Great Race—were being diluted by inferior people from eastern and southern Europe. Lothrop Stoddard's *The Rising Tide of Color* in 1920 argued that people of color would never be equal to white Americans. Stoddard stated his case unequivocally in 1927.

> Even a general knowledge of historical and scientific facts suffices to show the need for a racial basis to our national life,—as it has been, and as we intend that it shall be. We know that our America is a White America. "America," in the traditional sense of the word, was founded by White men, who evolved institutions, ideals, and cultural manifestations which were spontaneous expressions of their racial temperament and tendencies. And the overwhelming weight of both historical and scientific evidence shows that only so long as the American people remains White will its institutions, ideals, and culture continue to fit the temperament of its inhabitants,—and hence continue to endure.

These racist claims were cloaked in the trappings of legitimate scholarship, and they strengthened the cause of white supremacy in the 1920s and helped "protect" America from the "threat" of immigration. In 1921 and in 1924, Congress imposed quotas that severely restricted immigration from southern and eastern Europe and prohibited it entirely from Asia.

The glorification of the Ku Klux Klan in D. W. Griffith's *The Birth of a Nation,* reflected in this publicity poster, outraged African Americans. The NAACP protested when the silent film was first distributed in 1915 and again when a sound version was released in 1930. The demonstrations attracted publicity to both the film and the NAACP.

The Birth of a Nation

In 1915 D. W. Griffith released *The Birth of a Nation,* a cinematic masterpiece and historical travesty based on Thomas Dixon's 1905 novel, *The Clansman.* Both the book and the film purported to depict Reconstruction in South Carolina authentically. In this account, immoral and ignorant Negroes joined by shady mulattoes and greedy white Republicans ruthlessly seize control of state government until the heroic and honorable Ku Klux Klan save the state and rescue its white womanhood. The film was enormously popular. President Woodrow Wilson had it screened in the White House. It grossed 18 million dollars (254 million in 2000 dollars) and helped to assure a future for Metro Goldwyn Mayer (MGM), which produced it. It also distorted public perceptions about Reconstruction and black Americans.

The NAACP was enraged by *The Birth of a Nation* and fought to halt its presentation. W. E. B. Du Bois complained in *The Crisis* that in the film "the Negro [was] represented either as an ignorant fool, a vicious rapist, a venal or unscrupulous politician or a faithful but doddering idiot." The motion picture unleashed racist violence. After seeing the film in Lafayette, Indiana, an infuriated white man killed a young black man. In Houston, white theatergoers shouted, "Lynch him!" during a scene in which a white actor in blackface pursued the film's star, Lillian Gish. In front of a St. Louis theater, white real-estate agents passed out circulars calling for residential segregation.

Thanks largely to NAACP opposition, the film was banned in Pasadena, California; Wilmington, Delaware; and Boston. With an election looming in Chicago, Republican Mayor "Big Bill" Thompson appointed AME bishop Archibald Carey to the board of censors, which temporarily banned the film there. When the sound version of *The Birth of a Nation* was released in 1930, the NAACP renewed its opposition. Ironically, the NAACP campaign may have provided publicity that attracted more viewers to the film. By the same token, however, the campaign also helped increase NAACP membership.

The Ku Klux Klan

The Ku Klux Klan, which disappeared after Reconstruction, was resurrected a few months after *The Birth of a Nation* was released. On Thanksgiving night in 1915, William J. Simmons and thirty-four other men gathered at Stone Mountain near Atlanta, and in the flickering shadows of a fiery cross, they brought the Klan back to life.

The Ku Klux Klan that rose to prominence and power in the 1920s stood for white supremacy—and more. Klansmen styled themselves as "100 percent Americans" who opposed perceived threats from immigrants, as well as black Americans. The Klan claimed to represent white, Anglo-Saxon, Protestant America. With European immigrants flocking to America, William Simmons announced that the United States was no melting pot. "It is a garbage can! . . . When the hordes of aliens walk to the ballot box and their votes outnumber yours, then that alien horde has got you by the throat."

The Klan found enormous support among apprehensive white middle-class Americans in the North and West. Many of these people believed that the liberal, immoral, and loose lifestyles that they associated with urban life, immigrants, and African Americans threatened their religious beliefs and conservative cultural values. The Klan attacked the theory of evolution, fought for the prohibition of alcoholic beverages, and claimed to uphold the "sanctity" of white womanhood. The KKK opposed Jews, Roman Catholics, and black people. Klansmen often used violent intimidation to convey their patriotic, religious, and racial convictions. They burned synagogues and Catholic churches. They beat, branded, and lynched their opponents.

By 1925 the Klan had an estimated five million members, and 40,000 of them marched in Washington, D.C., that year. The Klan attracted small businessmen, shopkeepers, clerks, Protestant clergymen, farmers, and professional people. It was open only to native-born white men, but it also had a Women's Order, a Junior Order for boys, and a Tri K Klub for girls. The Klan was active in Oregon, Colorado, Illinois, and Maine, and it became a potent political force in Indiana, Oklahoma, and Texas. In those three states in particular, candidates for public office who refused to support or join the Klan stood little chance of election.

The Klan was also a highly effective money-making machine. Its leaders collected millions of dollars in initiation fees, membership dues, and income from selling Klan paraphernalia. But the Klan declined rapidly in the late 1920s when its leaders fought among themselves. Its claim to uphold the purity of white womanhood was damaged when one of its leaders, D. C. Stephenson, was arrested in Indiana and charged with raping a young woman who subsequently committed suicide. Stephenson was sentenced to life in prison, and the Klan never fully recovered.

Protest, Pride, and Pan-Africanism: Black Organizations in the Twenties

African Americans responded to racism and to larger cultural and economic developments in the 1920s in several ways. The NAACP forged ahead with its efforts to secure constitutional rights and guarantees by advocacy in the political and judicial systems. Many working-class black people who had migrated to northern cities were attracted to the racial pride promoted by Marcus Garvey and the Universal Negro Improvement Association. There were also ongoing attempts to foster racial cooperation among peoples of African descent and to exert diplomatic influence through the work of several Pan-African congresses that were held during the first three decades of the twentieth century.

The NAACP

During its second decade, the NAACP expanded its influence and increased its membership. In 1916 James Weldon Johnson (who wrote "Lift Every Voice and Sing") joined the NAACP as field secretary. He played a pivotal role in the organization's development and in its growth from 9,000 members in 1916 to 90,000 in 1920. Johnson traveled tirelessly, recruiting members and establishing branches. He jour-

VOICES

The Negro National Anthem: Lift Every Voice and Sing

In 1900 to celebrate Abraham Lincoln's birthday, James Weldon Johnson wrote "Lift Every Voice and Sing." His younger brother John Rosamond Johnson composed music to accompany the words. It was published in 1921 and soon thereafter—with the encouragement of the NAACP—the song was embraced as the Negro National Anthem. (In 1998, the New Yorker *magazine suggested that it replace the "Star Spangled Banner" as the U.S. National Anthem):*

–1–

Lift every voice and sing, 'til earth and heaven
ring,
Ring with the harmonies of liberty
Let our rejoicing rise, high as the list'ning skies,
Let it resound loud as the rolling sea.
Sing a song full of the faith that the dark past has
taught us,
Sing a song full of the hope that the present has
brought us;
Facing the rising sun of our new day begun
Let us march on till victory is won.

–2–

Stony the road we trod, bitter the chast'ning rod
Felt in the days when hope unborn had died
Yet with a steady beat, have not our weary feet
Come to the place for which our fathers sighed?
We have come over a way that with tears has been
watered,
We have come, treading our path thro' the blood of
the slaughtered
Out from the gloomy past, 'til now we stand at last
Where the white gleam of our bright star is cast.

–3–

God of our weary years, God of our silent tears
Thou who has brought us thus far on the way
Thou who hast by Thy might, led us into the light
Keep us forever in the path, we pray.
Lest our feet stray from the places, our God, where
We met Thee
Lest our hearts, drunk with the wine of the world,
we forget Thee
Shadowed beneath Thy hand, may we forever stand
True to our God, true to our native land.

QUESTIONS

1. What does James Weldon Johnson mean in the last line: "True to our God, true to our native land"? To what native land does he refer?
2. Do the words of the song apply to all Americans or only to African Americans? Would the song be appropriate as the American national anthem?

neyed to rural southern communities, to northern cities, and to the West coast.

Johnson impressed both black and white people. He got along well with W. E. B. Du Bois—not always an easy task considering Du Bois's sometimes haughty and acerbic demeanor. Johnson was an excellent diplomat who could negotiate and compromise, but he could also be blunt when necessary. He methodically reported the gruesome details of lynchings, and when some NAACP directors complained in 1921 that these graphic descriptions offended people, Johnson stood his ground. "What we need to do is to root out the thing which makes possible these horrible details. I am of the opinion that this can be done only through the fullest publicity."

In 1918 Johnson hired Walter White to assist him. White was from Atlanta and, like Johnson, a graduate of Atlanta University. White's fair complexion permitted him to move easily among white people to investigate racial discrimination and violence. Though his domineering personality offended some NAACP officials and supporters, White devoted his life to the organization and to racial justice.

Johnson and the NAACP fought hard in Congress to secure passage of the Dyer Anti-Lynching bill in 1921 and 1922 (see Chapter 16). The legislation ultimately failed, but the NAACP succeeded in publicizing the persistence of barbaric behavior by mobs in a nation supposedly devoted to fairness and the rule of law. It was the first campaign by a civil rights organization to

PROFILE

James Weldon Johnson

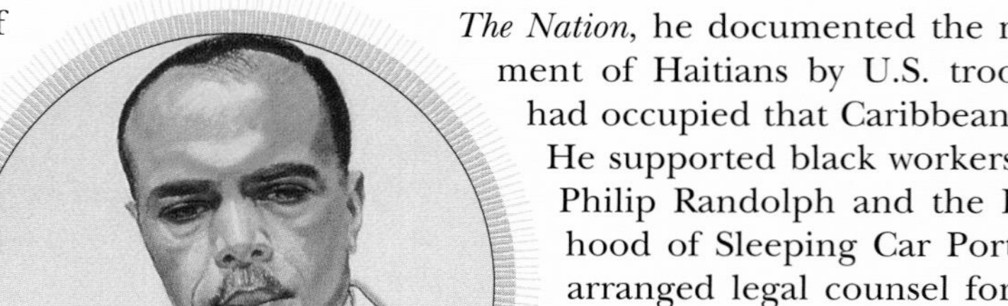

James Weldon Johnson in a portrait by Winold Reiss.

James Weldon Johnson was a man of immense talents. At various times he was a lawyer, diplomat, journalist, teacher, and gifted writer of prose and poetry. Most important, he was an effective and dynamic civil rights leader.

Johnson was born in 1871 in Jacksonville, Florida, to parents who had not been slaves. His father was a waiter in a fashionable hotel, and his mother was a schoolteacher. He received his secondary and collegiate education at Atlanta University where he also earned a master's degree. He read law in the office of a white Jacksonville attorney and was admitted to the Florida bar. In 1902 he moved to New York City.

With his brother John Rosamond and black entertainer Robert Cole, he became part of a successful song-writing team. They contributed two musical numbers to Theodore Roosevelt's 1904 presidential campaign: "You're All Right Teddy" and "The Old Flag Never Touched the Ground." Johnson's connection to the Republican party and his support for Booker T. Washington helped secure diplomatic appointments for him. Johnson spent seven years as a consul in Venezuela and Nicaragua. In 1910 he married Grace Neal, the sister of a prominent New York real estate broker.

TRACK 27

With the election in 1912 of Woodrow Wilson, a Democrat, Johnson's diplomatic career ended. He became an editorial writer for the *New York Age*. He also published anonymously *The Autobiography of an Ex-Colored Man*. In 1916 Joel Spingarn, the president of the NAACP, asked Johnson to take a leadership role with that organization, and Johnson—who had not openly supported the NAACP before Booker T. Washington's death in 1915—became its field secretary.

Johnson spent the next fourteen years with the NAACP. In 1920 he became chief executive, responsible for the association's day-to-day operations. He had organized the silent march on Fifth Avenue on July 28, 1917, to protest the East St. Louis riot (see Chapter 16). He publicized lynchings. He recruited members and established new branches. In 1920 in *The Nation*, he documented the mistreatment of Haitians by U.S. troops who had occupied that Caribbean nation. He supported black workers and A. Philip Randolph and the Brotherhood of Sleeping Car Porters. He arranged legal counsel for Ossian Sweet in Detroit in 1925 after Sweet and several of his supporters were charged with murder.

Johnson also managed to write prolifically and imaginatively. In 1920, he wrote "The Creation: A Negro Sermon." He wrote "God's Trombones: Seven Negro Sermons in Verse" in 1927 and many other works of prose and poetry. In 1930 he finished *Black Manhattan*, which traced the cultural contributions of black people in music, poetry, and theater to New York City from the seventeenth to the twentieth centuries.

Like so many civil rights leaders, Johnson could be inconsistent in his stands on racial issues. Though dedicated to the proposition that black and white people should enjoy equal access to public facilities, he supported an all-black YMCA in Harlem and the separate training of black military officers during World War I. He opposed moving NAACP headquarters from Fifth Avenue to Harlem. He supported building an all-black veteran's hospital at Tuskegee, Alabama, as long as it would be staffed by black physicians and nurses. He appreciated Marcus Garvey's emphasis on black pride, but he considered the back-to-Africa movement as an attempt to escape from America's racial problems rather than a solution to them.

In 1930 Johnson left the NAACP to become a professor of creative writing at Fisk University in Nashville. He left the NAACP a far more visible and stronger organization than he had found it in 1916. At Fisk, he worked with some of the twentieth century's leading black scholars, including Horace Mann Bond, Alrutheus A. Taylor, and E. Franklin Frazier. Historian John Hope Franklin was one of his students. Johnson's autobiography, *Along the Way*, was published in 1933. He died in an automobile accident in 1938.

lobby Congress, and—like the attempt to block *The Birth of a Nation*—it won favorable publicity and goodwill for the NAACP.

Johnson blamed the Dyer bill's failure on Republican senators. He charged that the Republican party took black support for granted because southern Democrats remained openly committed to white supremacy and, therefore, black people had little choice but to vote Republican: "The Republican Party will hold the Negro and do as little for him as possible, and the Democratic Party will have none of him at all." He warned, however, that black voters in the North would abandon the Republicans:

> The Negro can serve notice that he is no longer a part of the agreement by voting in the coming elections in each State against Republicans who have betrayed him, who are in league with the Ku Klux Klan, who are found to be hypocrites and liars on the question of the Negro's essential rights, and by letting them know he has done it. I am in favor of doing the job at once.

Johnson pointed out that black voters in Harlem had elected a black Democrat to the state legislature.

The NAACP continued to rely on the judicial system to protect black Americans and enforce their civil rights. By the 1920s, the Democratic party in virtually every southern state barred black people from membership, which excluded them from voting in Democratic primary elections. The result was what were known as "white primaries." Because the Republican party had almost ceased to exist in most of the South, victory in the Democratic primary elections led invariably to victory in the general election. In 1924 the NAACP, in cooperation with its branch in El Paso, filed suit over the exclusion of black voters from the Democratic primary in Texas. In 1927 the Supreme Court ruled in *Nixon v. Herndon* that the Democratic primary was unconstitutional—the first victory in what would become a twenty-year legal struggle to permit black men and women to vote in primary elections across the South.

In Detroit in 1925, black physician Ossian Sweet and his family moved into an all-white neighborhood. For several nights a mob threatened the Sweet family and other people who joined in their defense. One evening, shots were fired from the Sweet home that killed a white man. Twelve occupants of the house were charged with murder. The NAACP retained Clarence Darrow and Arthur Garfield Hayes, two of the nation's finest criminal attorneys, to defend the Sweets. The Sweets pleaded self-defense, and after two trials, they were acquitted.

"Up You Mighty Race": Marcus Garvey and the UNIA

With several million loyal and enthusiastic followers, Marcus Garvey's Universal Negro Improvement Association (UNIA) became the largest mass movement of black people in American history. The UNIA enabled people—often dismissed by the white majority for having no genuine history or culture—to celebrate one another and their heritage and to anticipate a glorious future. Garvey was an energetic, charismatic, and flamboyant leader who wove racial pride, Christian faith, and economic cooperation into a black nationalist organization that had spread throughout the United States by the early 1920s.

Garvey was born in 1887 in the British colony of Jamaica, the eleventh child in a rural family. He quit school at age fourteen and became a printer in Kingston, the island's capital; he was promoted to foreman before he was fired in 1907 for prolabor activities during a strike. He traveled to Costa Rica, Panama, Ecuador, and Nicaragua and became increasingly disturbed over the conditions black workers endured in fields, factories, and mines. He returned to Jamaica and with a growing appreciation of the power of the written and spoken word, he set out to educate himself. He spent two years in London where he sharpened his oratorical and debating skills discussing the plight of black people with Africans and people from the Caribbean.

He returned to Jamaica and founded the UNIA in 1914. With the slogan: "One God! One Aim! One Destiny!" he stressed the need for black people to organize for their own advancement. Garvey had read Booker T. Washington's *Up from Slavery* and was much impressed with Washington's emphasis on self-help and on progress through education and the acquisition of skills. Garvey also—like Washington—could criticize black people for their lack of progress: "The bulk of our people are in darkness and are really unfit for good society." They had no right to aspire to equality because they had "done nothing to establish the right to equality."

Garvey came to the United States in 1916 just as thousands of African Americans were migrating to cities. A dynamic speaker whose message resonated among the disaffected urban working class, Garvey quickly built the UNIA into a major movement. He urged his listeners to take pride in themselves as they restored their race to its previous greatness. "We must canonize our own saints, create our own martyrs, and elevate to positions of fame and honor black men and women who have made their distinct contributions to our racial history." He reminded people that Africa had

VOICES

Marcus Garvey Appeals for a New African Nation

Marcus Garvey and the UNIA offered hope to African Americans in the 1920s. In the following words, Garvey passionately calls for African Americans and West Indians to support the creation of a new African nation.

For five years the Universal Negro Improvement Association has been advocating the cause of Africa for the Africans—that is, that the Negro peoples of the world should concentrate upon the object of building up for themselves a great nation in Africa. . . .

It is only a question of a few more years when Africa will be completely colonized by Negroes, as Europe is by the white race. What we want is an independent African nationality, and if America is to help the Negro peoples of the world establish such a nationality, then we welcome the assistance.

It is hoped that when the time comes for American and West Indian Negroes to settle in Africa, they will realize their responsibilities and duty. It will not be to go to Africa for the purpose of exercising an over-lordship over the natives, . . .

It will be useless, as stated before, for bombastic Negroes to leave America and the West Indies to go to Africa, thinking that they will have privileged positions to inflict upon the race that bastard aristocracy that they have tried to maintain in this Western world at the expense of the masses. Africa shall develop an aristocracy of its own, but it shall be based upon service and loyalty to race. Let all Negroes work toward that end. . . .

The time has really come for the Asiatics to govern themselves in Asia, as the Europeans are in Europe and the Western world, so also is it wise for the Africans to govern themselves at home, and thereby bring peace and satisfaction to the entire human family.

So Negroes, I say, through the Universal Negro Improvement Association, that there is much to live for. I have a vision of the future, and I see before me a picture of redeemed Africa, with her dotted cities, with her beautiful civilization, with her millions of happy children going to and fro. Why should I lose hope, why should I give up and take a back place in this age of progress? . . .

Africa shall reflect a splendid demonstration of the worth of the Negro, of the determination of the Negro, to set himself free and to establish a government of his own.

QUESTIONS

1. On what logical basis does Garvey rest his call for a black homeland in Africa? How realistic was this call in the 1920s for nationhood in Africa?
2. Who does Garvey believe should lead (or should not lead) the new African nation? What are the qualifications for such leadership?
3. What vision does Garvey offer for what the globe will look like in the future? Does he suggest how peoples of various colors will coexist?

Source: David Levering Lewis, ed., *The Portable Harlem Renaissance Reader* (Viking Penguin, 1994), pp. 17, 19, 20, 21, 25.

a remarkable past. "Africa was peopled with a race of cultured black men, who were masters in art, science and literature; men who were cultured and refined; men, who, it was said, were like the gods. . . Black men, you were once great; you shall be great again." He insisted that his followers change their thinking. "We have outgrown slavery, but our minds are still enslaved to the thinking of the Master Race. Now take these kinks out of your mind, instead of out of your hair."

With the formation of the New York division of the UNIA in Harlem in 1917, Garvey exhorted, "Up you mighty race!" as he commanded black people to take control of their destiny. Still, he blamed them for their predicament. "That the Negro race became a race of slaves was not the fault of God Almighty . . . it was the fault of the race." Their salvation would result from their own exertion and not from concessions by white people.

Garvey's message and the UNIA spread to black communities large and small. He regularly couched his rhetoric in religious terms, and he came to be known as the Black Moses, a messiah. Garvey dwelled on Christ's betrayal as he identified himself with Jesus. "If Garvey dies, Garvey lives." "Christ died to make men free, I shall die to give courage and inspiration to my race."

Garvey's followers enjoyed the pageantry, ceremonies, and titles that were a part of the UNIA. The African Legionnaires and the Black Cross Nurses, resplendent in their uniforms, assembled in New York's Liberty Hall, and they paraded through Harlem. They prayed from The Universal Negro Catechism and reflected on their connection to Africa: "O Blessed Lord Jesus, redeem Africa from the hands of those who exploit and ravish her."

Garvey and the UNIA also established businesses that employed nearly one thousand black people. The weekly newspaper, *Negro World*, promoted Garvey's ideology. In New York City, the Negro Factories Corporation operated three grocery stores, two restaurants, a printing plant, a steam laundry, and a factory that turned out uniforms, hats, and shirts for UNIA members. The association also owned buildings, vehicles, and facilities in other cities. Garvey proudly declared to white Americans that the UNIA "employs thousands of black girls and black boys. Girls who could only be washer women in your homes, we made clerks, stenographers. . . . You will see from the start we tried to dignify our race."

Garvey may be best remembered for his proposal to return black people to Africa by way of the Black Star Line, a steamship company he founded in 1919. Garvey sold stock in the company for five dollars a share, and he hoped to establish a fleet with black officers and crew members. In 1920 the company purchased the *Yarmouth*, a dilapidated vessel that became the first ship in the fleet. Garvey raised enough capital to buy two additional ships, the *Kanawha* and the *Booker T. Washington*, but lacked the financial resources to maintain them or to transport anyone to Africa.

Moreover, he knew that it was unrealistic to expect several million black residents of the Western Hemisphere to join the back-to-Africa enterprise, but he genuinely believed that the UNIA could liberate Africa from European colonial rule. "Wake up Ethiopia! Wake up Africa! Let us work towards the one glorious end of a free, redeemed and mighty nation." The UNIA adopted a red, green, and black flag for the proposed African republic that represented the blood, land, and race of the people of the continent.

Jamaican-born Marcus Garvey arrived in the United States in 1916 and quickly rose to prominence as the head of the Universal Negro Improvement Association. Garvey appears here in a 1924 parade in Harlem attired in a uniform similar to those worn by British colonial governors in Jamaica, Trinidad, and elsewhere.

The UNIA attempted to establish a settlement on the Cavalla River in southern Liberia. Garvey also petitioned the League of Nations to permit the UNIA to take possession of the former German colony of Tangaruyka (today's Tanzania) in East Africa. But the major colonial powers in Africa—Britain and France—and the United States thwarted Garvey's plans, and the UNIA never gained a foothold on the continent.

The United States government and several black American leaders also undermined the UNIA and Garvey. J. Edgar Hoover and the Bureau of Investigation (the predecessor of the FBI) considered Garvey a serious threat to the racial status quo. Hoover employed black agents to infiltrate the UNIA and compile information that could be used to deport Garvey, who had never become an American citizen.

Garvey had few friends or admirers among African-American leaders because he and they differed fundamentally on strategy and goals. Garvey deplored efforts to gain legal and political rights within the American system. By appealing to the black masses, he rejected Du Bois's notion that the Talented Tenth would lead the race to liberation. He mocked the NAACP as the National Association for the Advancement of Certain People. Not long after he arrived in the United States, Garvey visited the NAACP office in New York, and he commented sourly that it was essentially a white organization. "There was no representation of the race there that any one could recognize. . . . you had to be as near white as possible, otherwise there was no place for you as stenographer, clerk or attendant in the office of the National Association for the Advancement of 'Colored' People."

Garvey called W. E. B. Du Bois a "lazy, dependent mulatto." In return, Du Bois described Garvey as "a little, fat black man, ugly but with intelligent eyes and big head," who was "the most dangerous enemy of the Negro race in America and the world . . . either a lunatic or a traitor." A. Philip Randolph, the black labor leader, was no less critical, calling Garvey "the supreme Negro Jamaican Jackass," an "unquestioned fool and ignoramus."

Unlike African-American leaders, Garvey believed that black and white people had separate destinies, and he regarded interracial cooperation as absurd. Thus Garvey considered a meeting he had with Ku Klux Klan leaders in Atlanta in 1922 consistent with his racial views. He praised the white supremacist organization. "They are better friends to my race, for telling us what they are, and what they mean, thereby giving us a chance to stir for ourselves." He added that "every whiteman is a Klansman . . . and there is no use lying about it."

In 1922 Garvey and three other UNIA leaders were arrested and indicted on twelve counts of fraudulent use of the U.S. mail to sell stock in the Black Star Line. Eight African-American leaders wrote to the U.S. Attorney General to condemn Garvey and insist on his prosecution. Though Garvey was guilty of no more than mismanagement and incompetence, he was eventually found guilty and sent to the federal penitentiary in Atlanta in 1925. President Calvin Coolidge commuted his sentence in 1927, and he was deported.

The UNIA barely survived the loss of its inspirational leader, and it declined steadily in the late 1920s and the 1930s. The various UNIA businesses closed, and its property—including the *Yarmouth*—was sold. Garvey was never permitted to return to the United States, and he died in London in 1940. However, his legacy persisted. The Reverend Earl Little, a Baptist minister and the father of Malcolm X, belonged to the UNIA and much admired Garvey. Malcolm X recalled his father's association with Garvey. "I remember hearing that he had black followers not only in the United States but all around the world, and I remember how the meetings always closed with my father saying, several times, and the people chanting after him, 'Up, you mighty race, you can accomplish what you will!' "

Pan-Africanism

As diametrically opposed as Garvey and Du Bois were on most matters, they shared an abiding interest in Africa. Garvey, Du Bois, and other black leaders believed that people of African descent from around the world should come together to share their heritage, discuss their ties to the continent, and to explore ways to moderate—if not eliminate—colonial rule in Africa.

By 1914, Britain, France, Germany, Portugal, Belgium, Spain, and Italy had established colonies across almost all of Africa. Only Liberia and Ethiopia (then called Abyssinia) remained independent. The Europeans assumed the "white man's burden" in their imperialist "scramble" for Africa. Christian missionaries sought to convert Africans, and European companies exploited Africa's human and natural resources. As they gained control over the continent, the European powers confirmed their conviction that they represented a superior race and culture.

The first Pan-African Congress had convened in London in 1900 and was organized principally by Henry Sylvester Williams, a lawyer from Trinidad who had resided in Canada and then London. Du Bois attended and chaired the Committee on the Address to the Nations of the World. He called for the creation of "a great central Negro state of the world." But Du Bois did not insist on the immediate withdrawal of the European powers from Africa. Instead he offered a modest recommendation that would provide "as soon as practicable the rights of responsible self-government to the black colonies of Africa and the West Indies."

The second Pan-African Congress met in Paris for three days in February 1919, near Versailles, where the peace conference ending World War I was assembled. There were fifty-eight delegates from sixteen nations. Du Bois was among the sixteen African Americans in attendance. (None of them had been to Africa.) Marcus Garvey did not attend. The delegates took seriously the Fourteen Points that U.S. President Woodrow Wilson had proposed to fashion the postwar world. They were especially interested in the fifth point, which called for the interests of colonial peoples to be given "equal weight" in the adjustment of colonial claims after the war. The congress recommended that the League of Nations assume authority over the former German colonies in East Africa. The League later established mandates over those colonies, but delegated authority to administer those mandates to Britain, France, and Belgium. Two more Pan-African Congresses in the 1920s met in Brussels and London, but also failed to influence the policies of the colonial powers.

Labor

The arrival of thousands of black migrants in American cities during and after World War I changed the composition of the industrial workforce and intensified pressure on labor unions to admit black members. By 1916, twelve thousand of the nearly fifty thousand workers in the Chicago stockyards were black people. In Detroit, black laborers made up nearly 14 percent of the workforce in the automobile industry. The Ford Motor Company employed fifty black people in 1916 and 2,500 by 1920.

Yet even with the industrial revolution and the great migration, more than two-thirds of black workers in 1920 were employed in agriculture and domestic service (see Figure 17–1). Less than 20 percent were engaged in manufacturing. Those who were part of industrial America disproportionately worked in the dreary, dirty, and sometimes dangerous unskilled jobs that paid the least. Still work in the factories, mills, and mines paid more than agricultural labor.

Most of the major labor unions would not admit black workers. Since its founding in 1886, the American Federation of Labor (AFL) officially prohibited racial discrimination, but most of its local unions were all white and all male. The AFL was made up of skilled laborers, and less than 20 percent of black workers were skilled (see Figure 17–2). But even those with skills were usually not admitted to the local craft unions that made up the AFL. More than fifty trade unions within the AFL had no black members. Unions that did admit black workers included those representing cigarmakers, coal miners, garment workers, and longshoremen.

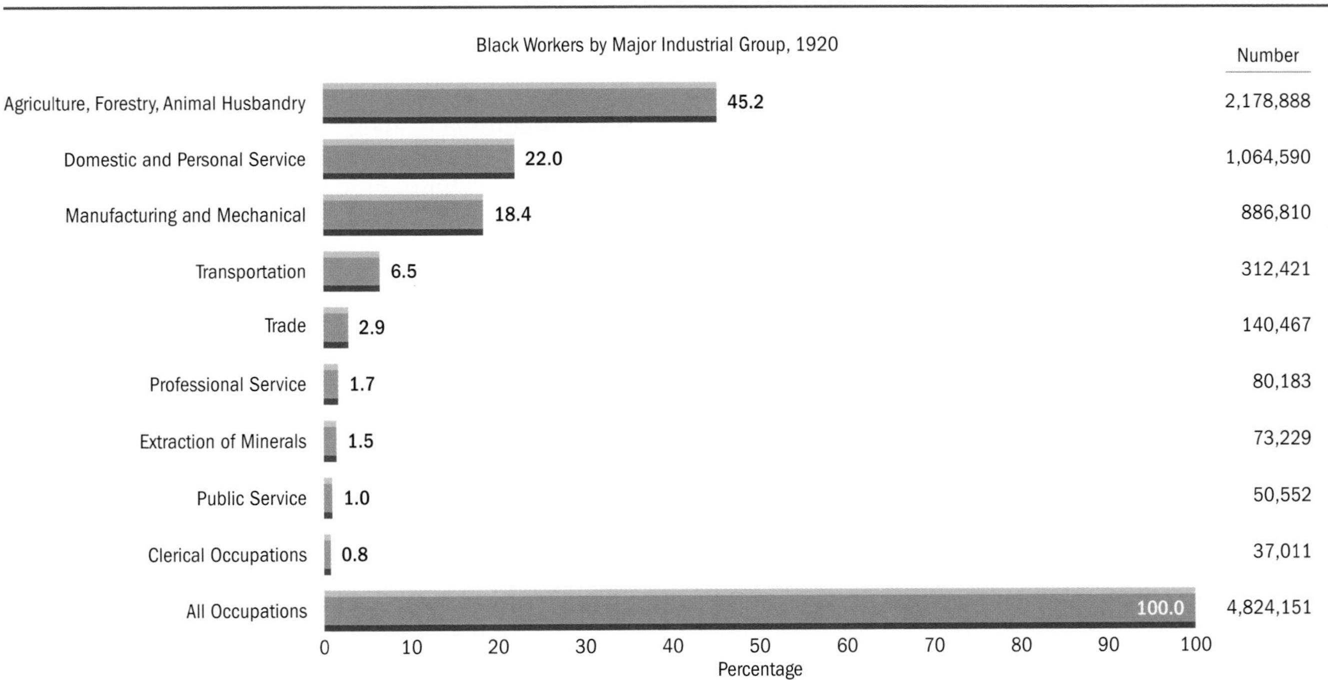

FIGURE 17–1 Black Workers by Major Industrial Group, 1920 By 1920 thousands of African Americans had moved to northern cities and were employed in a variety of mostly unskilled and low-paying industrial jobs that nonetheless paid more than farm labor. Still, agriculture remained the largest single source of employment among black people, and agriculture and domestic service together employed more than two-thirds of African-American men and women. About 5 percent were employed in "white collar" jobs.

Source: Sterling D. Spero and Abram L. Harris, *The Black Worker: The Negro and the Labor Movement* (1928), 81.

DATA EXPLORATION
To explore this data, go to **http://www.prenhall.com/hine/figure17.1**

FIGURE 17–2 Black and White Workers by Skill Level, 1920 Only one-third of black workers, compared to slightly more than one-half of white workers, found employment in skilled or semiskilled jobs in 1920.

Source: Sterling D. Spero and Abram L. Harris, *The Black Worker: The Negro and the Labor Movement* (1928), 85.

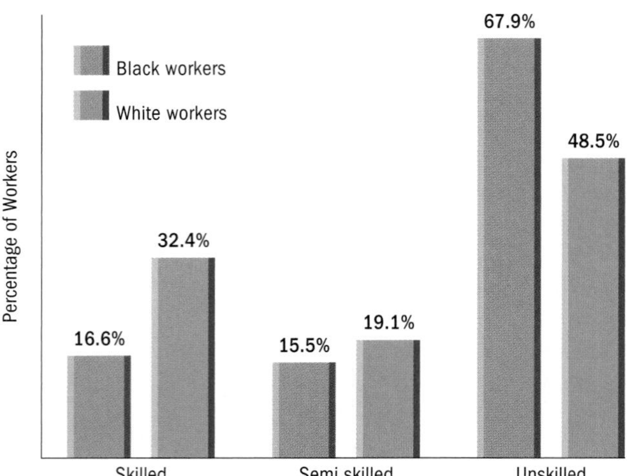

By the World War I years, the NAACP and the Urban League regularly appealed to employers and unions to accept black laborers. The Urban League attempted to convince business owners that black employees would be efficient and reliable. But many employers preferred to divide black and white workers by hiring black men and women as strikebreakers, thereby enraging striking white workers. In 1918 Urban League officials met with Samuel Gompers, the long-time president of the AFL, and he agreed to bring more black people into the federation, but there were few tangible results. The Urban League did succeed in persuading the U.S. Department of Labor to establish a Division of Negro Economics to advise the secretary of labor on issues involving black workers.

The Brotherhood of Sleeping Car Porters

By the 1920s, the Pullman company, which owned and operated passenger railroad coaches, was the single largest employer of black people in the United States. More than twelve thousand black men worked as porters on Pullman railroad cars. After founding the Pullman Palace Car Company in 1867, George Pullman decided to employ only black men as porters—on the assumption that prosperous white people were accustomed to being waited on by black servants. Furthermore, black employees could be and were paid less than white workers.

Pullman porters toiled for upwards of four hundred hours each month to maintain the coaches and serve the passengers. Porters had to prepare the cars before the train's departure and service them after the train arrived at its destination, though they were paid only for the duration of the trip. They assisted passengers, shined shoes (they had to purchase the polish themselves), and arranged sleeping compartments. Considered mere servants by most passengers, porters had little time for rest. To add to the indignity, white travelers invariably referred to these black men as "George," no matter what their actual name was. Porters were paid an average of $67.50 per month—about $810 per year. But with tips, they earned more, occasionally as much as $300 a month, but usually far less. They were required to buy their own uniforms during their first ten years of employment.

Though strenuous and time-consuming, Pullman employment was the most satisfactory work many black men could hope to achieve. Barred from business and industry, black men with college degrees worked as sleeping car porters. As poorly paid as they were compared with many white workers, they still earned more than most black schoolteachers. Most of these Pullman employees regarded themselves as solid, respectable members of the middle class.

It seemed unlikely that men as subservient and unobtrusive as the Pullman porters would form a labor union to challenge one of America's most powerful corporations. But they did. The key figure in this effort was A. Philip Randolph. In 1925 a gathering of Pullman porters in Harlem invited Randolph to become their "general organizer" as they formed the Brotherhood of Sleeping Car Porters (BSCP). Randolph accepted the invitation.

A. Philip Randolph

Randolph was a socialist with superb oratorical skills who had earned a reputation as a radical on the streets of Harlem. He was born in 1889 in Crescent City, Florida. He attended high school at Cookman Institute (later Bethune Cookman College) and migrated to New York City in 1911 where he attended City College and joined the Socialist party. With Chandler Owen, he founded *The Messenger*, a monthly socialist journal that drew the attention of federal agents. Randolph vigorously opposed American involvement in World War I. In 1919 Department of Justice officials arrested Randolph and Owen for their radical activities and held them briefly.

Randolph was an improbable militant. He was handsome, dignified, impeccably dressed, and aloof.

In this painting by Betsy G. Reyneau, A. Philip Randolph hardly resembles the militant, agitator, activist, and labor leader that he was. He became the head of the Brotherhood of Sleeping Car Porters, and he eventually rose to power in the American Federation of Labor. He planned the first March on Washington in 1941 and was responsible for organizing the 1963 March on Washington.

Save for his color, he could have been mistaken for the sort of Wall Street broker or powerful corporate attorney he detested. But blessed with a rich baritone voice, he "damned the claasses and exalted the maasses" and maintained an unwavering commitment to economic and racial change. He became one of the nation's foremost protest leaders and remained so for more than five decades.

Randolph faced the daunting task of recruiting support for the brotherhood, winning recognition from the Pullman company, and gaining the union's acceptance by the AFL. There was considerable opposition, much of it from within the black community. Many porters were too frightened to join the brotherhood. Black clergymen counseled against union activities. Black newspapers, including the Chicago *Defender*, editorially opposed the BSCP.

But Randolph persevered with the assistance of Milton Webster, who became vice president of the Brotherhood after Randolph assumed the presidency. With the slogan "Service not servitude," the two men recruited members, organized the brotherhood, and attempted to negotiate with the Pullman company. Pullman executives ignored Randolph's overtures. They fired porters who joined the union, infiltrated union meetings with company agents, and organized the Employees' Representation Plan, an alternative company union that they claimed actually represented the black employees.

Though the NAACP and the Urban League strongly supported the BSCP, progress was painfully slow. In 1928 Randolph threatened to call a strike against the Pullman company, but called it off after AFL President William Green promised modest assistance to the as-yet unrecognized union. Green's offer simply saved face for Randolph. It is unlikely that a strike would have succeeded or that most porters would have followed Randolph's leadership and left the trains. The Great Depression of the 1930s brought layoffs and mass resignations from the brotherhood. The AFL barely responded to repeated charges of discrimination by Randolph, the NAACP, and Urban League. The BSCP nearly collapsed. Not until the passage of legislation during President Franklin D. Roosevelt's New Deal in the mid-1930s did the BSCP make substantial gains.

The Harlem Renaissance

For most of American history, most black and white Americans have shown little interest in serious literature or intellectual developments. The 1920s were no exception. People were far more fascinated by sports, automobiles, the radio, and popular music than they were by poetry, plays, museums, or novels. Still the twenties witnessed a proliferation of creative works by a remarkable group of gifted writers and artists. Among white writers T. S. Eliot, Ezra Pound, Edith Wharton, Ernest Hemingway, Sinclair Lewis, Eugene O'Neill, Willa Cather, and F. Scott Fitzgerald produced literary works that explored a range of themes but were mostly critical of American life and society. Eliot, Pound, Wharton, Fitzgerald, and Hemingway found American culture so unappealing that they exiled themselves in Europe.

The Harlem Renaissance

1919	Claude McKay publishes "If We Must Die"
1920	Eugene O'Neill's *The Emperor Jones* opens featuring Charles Gilpin Langston Hughes publishes *The Negro Speaks of Rivers*
1922	*Shuffle Along,* by Noble Sissle and Eubie Blake, opens on Broadway with Florence Mills and Josephine Baker Claude McKay publishes *Harlem Shadows*
1923	Jean Toomer publishes *Cane* The Cotton Club opens *Opportunity: A Journal of Negro Life,* edited by Charles S. Johnson and supported by the National Urban League begins publication
1924	Jessie R. Fauset publishes *There Is Confusion* Walter White publishes *The Fire in the Flint* Paul Robeson stars in Eugene O'Neill's drama *All God's Chillun Got Wings*
1925	Countee Cullen publishes his book of poetry, *Color* James Weldon Johnson publishes *The Book of American Negro Spirituals* *The New Negro,* edited by Alain Locke, is published
1926	Langston Hughes publishes *The Weary Blues* George Schuyler's "The Negro Art Hokum" appears in *The Nation* The Savoy Ballroom opens Wallace Thurman publishes one issue of *Fire* Florence Mills dies
1927	Langston Hughes publishes *Fine Clothes to the Jew* James Weldon Johnson publishes *God's Trombones: Seven Negro Sermons in Verse*
1928	Claude McKay publishes *Home to Harlem* Duke Ellington's band appears at the Cotton Club
1929	Jessie R. Fauset publishes *Plum Bun* Wallace Thurman publishes *The Blacker the Berry . . .* Claude McKay publishes *Banjo* Countee Cullen publishes *The Black Christ* Fats Waller's *Ain't Misbehavin'* opens on Broadway
1930	James Weldon Johnson publishes *Black Manhattan*
1931	Jessie R. Fauset publishes *The Chinaberry Tree*
1933	Jessie R. Fauset publishes her last novel, *Comedy American Style* James Weldon Johnson publishes his autobiography, *Along the Way*
1934	Wallace Thurman dies
1935	Zora Neale Hurston publishes *Mules and Men*
1937	Zora Neale Hurston publishes *Their Eyes Were Watching God*

Black intellectuals congregated in Manhattan and gave rise to the creative movement known as the Harlem Renaissance. Alain Locke promoted *The New Negro.* Poets, novelists, and painters probed racial themes and grappled with what it meant to be black in America. There was no precise beginning to this renaissance. As early as 1920, W. E. B. Du Bois wrote in *The Crisis* that the nation was on the verge of a "renaissance of American Negro literature." In 1925 the New York *Herald Tribune* declared that America was "on the edge, if not already in the midst of, what might not improperly be called a Negro renaissance." No matter when it began, the Harlem Renaissance produced a stunning collection of artistic works, especially in creative writing, that continued into the 1930s.

Before Harlem

There had certainly been serious cultural developments among African Americans before the 1920s. From 1897 to 1928 the American Negro Academy functioned as a forum for "the Talented Tenth" as men such as Alain Locke, Kelly Miller and Du Bois reflected on race and color.

TRACK 28

At the turn of the century, novelist Charles W. Chestnutt depicted a young black woman's attempt to pass for white in *The House behind the Cedars,* and he wrote about racist violence in the post-Reconstruction South in *The Marrow of Tradition.* Ohio poet Paul Lawrence Dunbar wrote evocatively of black life, frequently relying on black dialect, before he died at age thirty-four in 1906. Henry Ossawa Tanner attended the Pennsylvania Academy of Fine Arts and had an illustrious career as a painter. Shortly after he produced "The Banjo Lesson" in 1893, Tanner left for Paris and spent most of the rest of his life in Europe. He died there in 1937.

TRACK 29

Carter G. Woodson, the son of Virginia slaves, earned a Ph.D. at Harvard in history and founded the Association for the Study of Negro Life and History in 1915. He stressed the need for the scholarly examination of Negro history and established the *Journal of Negro History* and the *Negro History Bulletin.* He also founded Associated Publishers to publish books on black history. Woodson wrote several major works, including *The Negro in Our History.* In 1926 he established Negro History Week during February. Not surprisingly, Woodson became known as the "father of Negro history."

During the bloody Red Summer of 1919 when racial violence erupted in Chicago and elsewhere, Claude McKay, a Jamaican who settled—like Marcus

Garvey—in New York City wrote a powerful poem, "If We Must Die," in response to the brutal attacks by white people in Chicago on black residents:

If we must die, let it not be like hogs
Hunted and penned in an inglorious spot,
While round us bark the mad and hungry dogs,
Making their mock at our accurséd lot.
If we must die, O let us nobly die,
So that our precious blood may not be shed
In vain; then even the monsters we defy
Shall be constrained to honor us though dead!
O kinsmen! We must meet the common foe!
Though far outnumbered let us show us brave,
And for their thousand blows deal one deathblow!
What though before us lies the open grave?
Like men we'll face the murderous, cowardly pack,
Pressed to the wall, dying, but fighting back!

McKay left the United States for the Soviet Union in 1922, and spent the next twelve years in Europe. In 1928 while in France, he wrote *Home to Harlem*, a novel that depicted life among pimps, prostitutes, loan sharks, and petty criminals. McKay was not on cordial terms with the African-American intellectuals who formed the core of the Harlem Renaissance, and he did not consider himself part of the Talented Tenth. He later commented, "I was an older man and not regarded as a member of the renaissance, but more as a forerunner."

During the summer of 1927, three of the major figures associated with the Harlem Renaissance visited the Booker T. Washington Memorial on the Tuskegee Institute campus in Alabama. One can only wonder what pointed comments about the "Wizard of Tuskegee" were exchanged as (from left to right) Jessie Fauset, Langston Hughes, and Zora Neale Hurston posed to have their photograph taken.

Writers and Artists

Few white Americans and still fewer black Americans had access to a college education in the early twentieth century. Only slightly more than two thousand African Americans were pursuing college degrees by 1920. Yet the writers and artists who came to be associated with the Harlem Renaissance were the products of some of the nation's finest schools, and with the exception of Zora Neale Hurston, they did not come from isolated, rural southern communities. Hurston was born in Notasulga, Alabama, and raised in the all-black town of Eatonville, Florida, near Orlando. She attended Morgan State University and Howard University, and graduated from Barnard College. Alain Locke was a native of Philadelphia and Phi Beta Kappa graduate of Harvard. He was the first African American to win a Rhodes scholarship to Oxford University, and he also earned a Ph.D. in philosophy from Harvard. Aaron Douglas (one of whose works graces the cover of this book) was born in Kansas and was an art major at the University of Nebraska.

Langston Hughes was born in Joplin, Missouri, graduated from high school in Cleveland, and attended Columbia University before he graduated from Pennsylvania's Lincoln University. Jessie Fauset came from a prominent Philadelphia family of color. She was a graduate of Cornell University and a member of Phi Beta Kappa; she earned an M.A. from the University of Pennsylvania in romance languages. Jean Toomer was born in Washington, D.C., and was raised largely by his grandparents in a fashionable white neighborhood. Toomer went to the University of Wisconsin and then the Massachusetts College of Agriculture. Wallace Thurman was born in Salt Lake City and attended both the University of Utah and the University of Southern California. Countee Cullen was a native of Lexington, Kentucky, and a Phi Beta Kappa graduate of New York University.

The Renaissance gradually emerged in the early 1920s and then expanded dramatically later in the decade as more creative figures were drawn to Harlem. In 1923 Jean Toomer published *Cane*, a collection of stories and poetry about southern black life. It sold a mere five hundred copies, but it had a major impact on Jessie Fauset and Walter White. Fauset was the literary editor of *The Crisis*, and in 1924 she finished *There Is Confusion*, the first novel published during the Renaissance. Her novels explored the manners and color consciousness among well-to-do Negroes. Walter White, who was James Weldon Johnson's assistant at the NAACP, published *The Fire in the Flint* in 1924, a novel that dealt with a black physician who confronted white brutality in Georgia.

In the meantime, *The Crisis*, as well as *Opportunity*, a new publication of the Urban League, published the poetry and short stories of black authors, including Langston Hughes, Countee Cullen, and Zora Neale Hurston. White publishers were also attracted to black literary efforts. In 1925 *Survey Graphic* published a special edition devoted to black life and culture called "Harlem: Mecca of the New Negro." Howard University Professor Alain Locke then edited *The New Negro*, which drew much of its material from *Survey Graphic* as well as *Opportunity* and included silhouette drawings with Egyptian motifs by Aaron Douglas. In his opening essay, Locke explained Harlem's literary significance: "Harlem has the same role to play for the new Negro as Dublin has had for the New Ireland or Prague for the New Czechoslovakia."

Sharp disagreements erupted during the Harlem Renaissance over the definition and purpose of black literature. Some, such as Alain Locke, W. E. B. Du Bois, Jessie Fauset, and Benjamin Brawley, wanted black writers to promote positive images of black people in their works. They hoped that inspirational literature could help resolve racial conflict in America, and they believed that black writers should be included in the larger (and mostly white) American literary tradition. Claude McKay, Langston Hughes, and Zora Neale Hurston disagreed. They portrayed the streets and shadows of Harlem and the lives of poor black people in their poetry and stories. In *The Ways of White Folks*, Hughes ridiculed the notion that writers could promote racial reconciliation. One of his characters derisively declares, "Art would break down color lines, art would save the race and prevent lynchings! Bunk!"

W. E. B. Du Bois commented caustically after he read Claude McKay's bawdy *Home to Harlem:* "I feel distinctly like taking a bath." Du Bois was less than impressed with Jake, the novel's protagonist, who is intimately involved with the reality of life in Harlem that included opium, alcohol, and sex. Alain Locke dismissed McKay as a mere propagandist, and McKay in turn called Locke "a dyed-in-the-wool pussy-footing professor." Black critic George Schuyler's "The Negro Art Hokum" in *The Nation* ridiculed black writers who contended that black people even had their own expressive culture that was separate from that of white people. "As for the literature, painting, and sculpture of Afroamericans—such as there is—it is identical in kind with the literature, painting, and sculpture of white Americans."

Langston Hughes meanwhile defended the authenticity of black art and literature but insisted that the approval or disapproval of white people and black people was of little consequence:

> We younger Negro artists who create now intend to express our individual dark-skinned selves without fear or shame. If white people are pleased, we are glad. If they are not, it doesn't matter. We know we are beautiful. And ugly too. The tom-tom cries and the tom-tom laughs. If colored people are pleased we are glad. If they are not, their displeasure doesn't matter either. We build our temples for tomorrow, strong as we know how, and we stand on top of the mountain, free within ourselves.

Hughes pursued racial themes in *Fine Clothes to the Jew* (1927), which contained "Red Silk Stockings," a poem that depicted young black women who were tempted by liaisons with white men, a subject that offended some readers:

> **Red Silk Stockings**
>
> Put on yo' red silk stockings,
> Black gal.
> Go out an' let de white boys
> Look at yo' legs.
> Ain't nothin' to do for you, nohow.
> Round this town.—
> You's too pretty.
> Put on yo' red silk stockings, gal,
> An' tomorrow's chile'll
> Be a high yaller.
> Go out an' let de white boys
> Look at yo' legs.

Even more upsetting to those who wanted to safeguard the reputation of black people was Wallace Thurman, who arrived in New York in 1925. Thurman worked briefly at *The Messenger*, the socialist publication that had been absorbed by A. Philip Randolph's Brotherhood of Sleeping Car Porters. He was a voracious reader with a brilliant mind and an eccentric personality who attracted many loyal admirers. He once wrote, "I cannot bear to associate with the ordinary run of people. I have to surround myself with individuals who for the most part are more than a trifle insane."

In 1926 Thurman published *Fire,* a journal that lasted only one issue, but managed to incite enormous controversy and leave Thurman deeply in debt. *Fire* included Thurman's short story, "Cordelia the Crude," about a prostitute, and a one-act play by Zora Neale Hurston, "Color Struck." Hurston effectively replicated the speech of rural black Southerners while depicting the jealousy a darker woman feels when a light-skinned rival tries to take her man. Black critic Benjamin Brawley complained that with *Fire* "vulgarity had been mistaken for art."

Thurman, who was a dark black man, antagonized still more people when *The Blacker the Berry . . .* was published in 1929. In it he described the tribulations and sorrows of Emma Lou, a young woman who did not mind being black, "but she did mind being too black." The book made it plain that many black people had absorbed a color prejudice that they did not hesitate to inflict on darker members of their own race.

White People and the Harlem Renaissance

Like many of the writers associated with the Harlem Renaissance, Zora Neale Hurston had a pen that sliced like a scalpel. She called the white people who took an interest in Harlem "Negrotarians," and she labeled her black literary colleagues the "Niggerati." But no matter how they were described, black and white people developed pleasant but often uneasy relationships during the Renaissance.

No white man was more attracted to the cultural developments in Harlem than photographer and writer Carl Van Vechten. In 1926 he caused a furor with his novel, *Nigger Heaven.* Many people were offended by the title, which referred to the balcony where black patrons had to sit in segregated theaters and auditoriums. The novel dealt with the coarser aspects of life in Harlem, which irritated Du Bois, Fauset, and Countee Cullen. But Van Vechten's purpose was in part a call for a more honest depiction of the black experience, and James Weldon Johnson, Walter White, and Langston Hughes approved of the novel.

Most black writers and artists welcomed the encouragement, support, and financial backing they received from white authors, critics, and publishers. White writers, including Eugene O'Neill, Sherwood Anderson, Sinclair Lewis, and Van Wyck Brooks, were fascinated by black people and interested in the works of black authors. Major publishers, such as Alfred A. Knopf, brought out the works of Harlem writers. Black and white literary figures sometimes gathered for cocktails, small talk, and music at Carl Van Vechten's spacious apartment on West 55th Street.

The attention and support of white people were sometimes accompanied by condescension and disdain. Too many "Negrotarians" considered Harlem and its inhabitants exotic, curious, and uncivilized. They found life in Harlem—its clubs, music, and entertainers, as well as its poetry, prose, and painting—energetic, lively, and sensual compared to white life and culture. Black culture was also—many white people believed—unsophisticated and primitive, which is what made it so fascinating. Black writers like Langston Hughes, Claude McKay, and Countee Cullen wanted to depict black life realistically—from its gangsters to its gamblers. But they and other black artists resented the notion that black culture was inherently crude and unrefined.

White patrons like Amy Spingarn, whose husband Joel was president of the NAACP Board of Directors, and Charlotte Osgood Mason "Godmother" supported black writers and artists. Spingarn helped finance Langston Hughes's education at Lincoln University. "Godmother" Mason was a wealthy widow who offered substantial amounts of money to black artists. She worked closely with Alain Locke who helped identify Langston Hughes, Zora Neale Hurston, and Aaron Douglas among others who became her "godchildren."

Mason wanted no publicity for herself, but the acceptance of her money had its costs. Mason gave Hughes $150 a month and Hurston $200 a month, as well as an automobile. She also gave Hughes expensive clothing and writing supplies. In return, Mason demanded that the black writers keep her fully informed about their activities, and she did not hesitate to tell them when they were not productive enough. She also tried to influence what they wrote. She preferred that black writers confine themselves to exotic themes. As helpful as Mason's financial assistance and personal encouragement were, she created a system of dependency, and Hughes and Hurston finally broke free from the arrangement. Hughes later fondly recalled, "I can only say that those months when I lived by and through her were the most fascinating and fantastic I have ever known."

Harlem's cultural icons sometimes congregated away from the curiosity and paternalism of white admirers. The plush twin town houses of A'Lelia

Walker at 108–110 West 136th Street also attracted Harlem's literary figures as well as entertainers. Walker was the daughter of black cosmetics millionairess Madam C. J. Walker. Though she read little herself, A'Lelia Walker enjoyed hosting musicians, writers, and artists at "The Dark Tower," as she called it. Her home was named for Countee Cullen's column, "The Dark Tower," that appeared regularly in *Opportunity*. But Harlem artists also gathered in the much less luxurious surroundings of "Niggerati Manor" on 267 West 136th Street. This was a rooming house where Thurman, Hurston, and Hughes resided in the late 1920s.

The profusion of literary works associated with the Harlem Renaissance did not so much end as fade away. Black writers remained active into the 1930s. Zora Neale Hurston wrote her two most important works then—*Mules and Men* in 1935 and *Their Eyes Were Watching God* in 1937. Claude McKay and Langston Hughes continued to write and have their work published. But the Great Depression that began in 1929 devastated book and magazine sales. Subscriptions to *The Crisis* and *Opportunity* declined, and both journals published fewer works by creative writers. Many black intellectuals left Harlem. James Weldon Johnson and Aaron Douglas went to Fisk University in Nashville.

W. E. B. Du Bois had a falling out with the NAACP and returned to Atlanta University. Alain Locke remained on the faculty at Howard University. Jessie Fauset married an insurance executive and took up housekeeping after her last novel was published in 1931. Wallace Thurman died an alcoholic in 1934. Countee Cullen taught French at DeWitt Clinton High School in New York City where James Baldwin was one of his students in the late 1930s.

Harlem and the Jazz Age

As powerful and important as these black literary voices were, they were less popular than the entertainers, musicians, singers, and dancers who were also part of the Harlem Renaissance. Without Harlem, the twenties would not have been the Jazz Age. From wailing trumpets, beating drums, dancing feet, plaintive and mournful songs, Harlem's clubs, cabarets, theaters, and ballrooms echoed with the vibrant and soulful sounds of African Americans. By comparison, white American music seemed sedate and bland.

Black and white people flocked to Harlem to enjoy themselves—and to break the law. In 1919–1920, the Eighteenth Amendment and the Volstead Act prohibited the manufacture, distribution, and sale of alcoholic beverages. But liquor flowed freely in Harlem's fancy establishments and smoky dives. Musicians and entertainers, such as Harlem's working-class residents, had migrated there from elsewhere. The blues and their sorrowful tales of troubled and broken relationships arrived from the Mississippi Delta and rural South. Jazz had its origins in New Orleans, but it drew on ragtime and spirituals as it moved up the Mississippi River to Kansas City and Chicago on its way to Harlem.

The Cotton Club was Harlem's most exclusive and fashionable nightspot. Opened in 1923 by white gangster Owney Madden to peddle illegal beer, it catered to well-to-do white people who regarded a trip to Harlem as a foreign excursion. The Cotton Club's entertainers and waiters were black, but the customers were white. Black patrons were not admitted. The club featured well-choreographed and fast paced two-hour revues that included a chorus line of attractive young women—all brown skinned, all under twenty-one years old, and all over 5'6" tall. No dark women appeared. Music was provided by assorted ensembles. Cab Calloway might sing "She's Tall, She's Tan and She's Terrific," or "Cotton Colored Gal of Mine."

In 1928, Edward K. "Duke" Ellington and his orchestra began a twelve-year association with the Cotton Club. Although Ellington had not yet begun to compose his own music in earnest, his band already had an elegant, sophisticated, and recognizable African-American sound. Another club, Connie's Inn, also served a mostly white clientele. Thomas "Fats"

Edward Kennedy "Duke" Ellington directed one of the finest musical ensembles in American history from 1927 until his death in 1974. He wa also a superb composer. In this 1926 photograph Ellington is at the piano. Accompanying him are: "Tricky Sam" Nanton, trombone; Sonny Greer, drums; Bubber Miley, trumpet; Harry Carney, alto and baritone saxophone; Wellman Bravo, bass; Rudy Jackson, tenor sax; Fred Evy, banjo; Nelson Kincaid, alto sax; and Ellsworth Reynolds, violin.

PROFILE

Bessie Smith

No one personified the blues more than Bessie Smith. She knew the blues. She sang the blues. She lived the blues. She was the "Empress of the Blues." During the 1920s, no singer in America was more popular than she was.

Bessie Smith was born in poverty on April 15, 1894, in Chattanooga, Tennessee. She was one of seven children of a Baptist preacher, William Smith, and his wife, Laura. Bessie's parents and two brothers died while she was still a child and the surviving children were raised by an older sister, Viola.

With her brother Andrew accompanying her on the guitar, Bessie began to sing on Chattanooga street corners to earn money for the family, an apprenticeship that helped shape her career. In 1912 she toured briefly with a musical group that featured Gertrude "Ma" Rainey. In 1913 she worked in Atlanta for ten dollars a week plus tips. Her fame spread and soon she was touring the South. By the 1920s she was singing in Philadelphia and Atlantic City.

No one has ever sung the blues better than Bessie Smith. "The Empress of the Blues" appeared in theaters and clubs across the country before mostly all-black audiences, but thousands of white people bought her recordings in the 1920s and 1930s. Her contract with Columbia Records, which earned her only $28,575 for eight years of recordings, profited the company at her expense.

Initially her voice was considered too rough for the infant recording industry. But in 1923 Frank Walker signed her to a contract with Columbia Records. She recorded what were known in the 1920s as "race" records, produced for black audiences by white recording companies. Her first recordings included "Downhearted Blues" and "Gulf Coast Blues." Her second session brought "Tain't Nobody's Business If I Do." She sold an astonishing 780,000 records within months.

In 1925 she recorded "St. Louis Blues" and "Careless Love" with Louis Armstrong—their only recordings together. She toured major cities, including Pittsburgh, Cleveland, and Chicago, in a private railroad coach and huge crowds lined up at clubs and theaters to hear her. Though it could sound coarse, she had a striking and appealing voice that conveyed the depths of her emotions and experiences.

She knew of what she sang. When she sang "Money Blues," "Pickpocket Blues," or "Empty Bed Blues," she revealed the pathos, but also the humor, that so many black people had experienced. Smith's blues tore at the raw feelings that sociologists and academics missed when they discussed poverty, unemployment, alcoholism, or sexual relationships. Her blues were firmly grounded in African-American oral and musical traditions.

Bessie Smith was not a delicate woman. She was married twice. Her first husband, Earl Love, died shortly after they married. Her second marriage, to Jack Gee, was marked by jealousy, drinking, and physical conflict and ended in separation in 1930. She had a profusion of lovers—male and female. Her warmest and most enduring relationship was with Richard Morgan, a Chicago bootlegger.

People did not trifle with Bessie Smith. A large lady, over two hundred pounds, she ate, drank, and fought to excess. She could be mean, contentious, and violent. She physically attacked others and was herself attacked. But she also had a sweet and loyal side and could be helpful, generous, and compassionate. However, she seemed fond of some of the sleaziest, most dangerous nightclubs in America. She could not resist Detroit's Koppin Theater, a den of debauchery. She admitted wanting to go where "the funk was flying."

She continued to record even after record sales declined during the Depression. Her last recording session included "Nobody Knows When You're Down and Out." Bessie Smith died at age forty-three in 1937 in a car accident near Clarksdale, Mississippi. Perhaps Louis Armstrong summed up her musical legacy best. "She used to thrill me at all times, the way she could phrase a note with a certain something in her voice no other blues singer could get. She had music in her soul and felt everything she did."

Waller played a rambunctious piano at Connie's. Waller's father was the deacon at the Abyssinian Baptist Church in Harlem, and his mother was the organist. The songs and music their son wrote, including "Honeysuckle Rose" and "Ain't Misbehavin," were hardly sacred, but they were popular. Connie's also put on stunning musical revues, perhaps the best known of which was *Hot Chocolates.* Dancers who performed at Connie's included the legendary Bill "Bojangles" Robinson and Earl "Snakehips" Tucker. A young cornetist from New Orleans, Louis Armstrong, played briefly at Connie's. Armstrong amazed listeners with his virtuoso trumpet and his gravelly singing voice.

Harlem's black residents avoided the Cotton Club or Connie's Inn. They were more likely to step into one of Harlem's less pretentious and less expensive establishments, such as the Sugar Cane. The beer and liquor were cheap. The food was plentiful. The music was good, and there were no elaborate production numbers. Even less impressive clubs and bars remained open after the legal closing hour of 3 A.M. "Arrangements" were made with the police who looked the other way as the music and alcohol continued through the night. Musicians from "legal" clubs drifted into the after-hours joints and played until dawn.

Another popular—and sometimes necessary—form of entertainment among Harlemites was the rent party. Housing costs in Harlem were extravagant, and white people and real-estate agents refused to rent or sell to black people in most other areas of New York City. To make the steep monthly rent payments, apartment dwellers would push the furniture aside, begin cooking chicken, chitterlings, rice, okra, and sweet potatoes. They would distribute a few flyers and hire a musician or two. The party was usually on a Saturday or a Thursday night. (Most domestic servants had Thursdays off.) Party-goers paid ten cents to fifty cents admission. Food and liquor were sold. With a decent crowd, the month's rent was paid.

Song, Dance, and Stage

Black women became popular as singers and dancers in Harlem and then often appeared in Broadway shows and revues. Florence Mills entranced audiences with her diminutive singing voice in several Broadway productions including *Plantation Review, Dixie to Broadway,* and *Blackbirds* before she died of appendicitis in 1927. Adelaide Hall also appeared in *Blackbirds* and later opened her own nightclubs in London and Paris. Ethel Waters worked her way up from smoky gin joints in Harlem basements where she sang risqué and comic songs to Broadway shows, and then to films. Many years later she toured with the Billy Graham crusade.

TRACK 30

White men wrote many of the popular Broadway productions that starred black entertainers. In 1921, however, Eubie Blake and Noble Sissle put on *Shuffle Along,* which became a major hit. Its most memorable tune was "I'm Just Wild about Harry." Sissle and Blake wrote several more shows, including *Chocolate Dandies* in 1924. It was created especially for a thin, lanky, dark, and funny young lady named Josephine Baker. But in 1925 Baker left New York and moved to Paris where she starred in the *Revue Nègre,* which created a sensation in the French capital. She remained in France for the rest of her life.

White playwright Eugene O'Neill wrote serious drama involving black people. Charles Gilpin and then Paul Robeson appeared in O'Neill's *Emperor Jones.* Robeson—who went on to an illustrious performing career—was a graduate of Rutgers University where he was an All-American football player. He earned a law degree at Columbia University, but abandoned the law for the stage. He appeared in numerous productions, including O'Neill's *All God's Chillun Got Wings,* Shakespeare's *Othello,* Gershwin's *Porgy and Bess,* and Kern and Hammerstein's *Showboat.* He often sang spirituals in his magnificent, rich voice, and later recorded many of them.

Sports

Sports flourished in America in the 1920s. Americans worshiped their athletic heroes. Babe Ruth and Jack Dempsey were as well known as President Calvin Coolidge. Professional athletics, especially baseball and boxing, expanded dramatically. Professional football and basketball emerged later. Black men had been banned from major league baseball in 1887 (see Chapter 15). Nevertheless, in 1901 New York Giants' manager John J. McGraw signed a black man, Charlie Grant, to play second base. McGraw claimed that Grant was "Chief Tokohoma," a full-blooded Cherokee Indian. Chicago White Sox owner Charles Comiskey knew otherwise, and Grant did not play in the major leagues.

Playing among themselves, black baseball players barely made a living as they moved from team to team in an ever-fluctuating and disorganized system that saw teams come and go with monotonous regularity. No leagues functioned effectively for the black teams and players. Black teams crisscrossed the country on trains and in automobiles as they played each other in small towns and large cities for meager amounts of money shared from gate receipts. It was an insecure and nomadic life.

Rube Foster

Andrew "Rube" Foster was the father of black baseball in twentieth-century America. He was a crafty pitcher from Texas who combined athletic skills with mental dexterity. In 1911 he founded the Chicago American Giants, and he pitched with them regularly until 1915 and then mainly managed after that. As fine an athlete as Foster was, he was an even more talented organizer and administrator.

In 1919 in the Chicago *Defender*, he argued for the establishment of a Negro baseball league. In 1920 he was the catalyst in the formation of the eight-team Negro National League and became its president and secretary. It was the first stable black league, with franchises in Kansas City, St. Louis, Indianapolis, Detroit, Dayton, and two teams in Chicago. The eighth team was the Cuban Stars.

Foster and the new league took advantage of the migration of black people to northern cities. The black ball clubs usually played late in the afternoon or in the early evening so that fans could attend after a day's work. (This was before night baseball.) Sunday doubleheaders in Chicago or Kansas City might draw eight thousand to ten thousand people. Players were paid regularly, and athletes on Foster's Giants earned at least $175 a month. The biggest obstacle black teams faced was the lack of their own fields or stadiums. They were forced to rent, often at exorbitant rates, from major league clubs, which frequently kept the profits from concessions.

Black baseball thrived in the 1920s thanks mostly to Foster's force of personality and dedication. He was a tireless worker and strict disciplinarian, but the pressure may have been too much. In 1926 he suffered a mental breakdown and died in 1930. Foster's loss—combined with the impact of the Depression—severely disrupted the league system.

College Sports

Football, baseball, basketball, and track and field were popular at the collegiate level. Amateur sports were not as rigidly segregated as professional baseball. Black men continued to play for white northern universities, although few teams had more than one black player. Paul Robeson was on the Rutgers football team in 1916 that played against Frederick Douglass "Fritz" Pollard and Brown University. Pollard was the first black man to play in the Rose Bowl where his Brown team lost to Washington State in 1916.

Black players on white teams encountered discrimination when the teams traveled. Spectators taunted and threatened them. The Big Ten had an unwritten agreement that basketball coaches would not accept black players. All-white college teams sometimes refused to play against schools with black players. In 1920, Virginia's Washington and Lee University canceled a football game against Washington and Jefferson College of Pennsylvania because Charles West, a black man, played in the Washington and Jefferson backfield.

Sports in black colleges and universities thrived in the 1920s. Baseball and football were the most popular spectator events. Traditional rivalries attracted large crowds. Several schools played baseball religiously each Easter Monday. In 1926 Livingston College defeated Biddle University (now Johnson C. Smith University) before a crowd of six thousand in Charlotte, North Carolina. With the migration of black people to the North, black colleges began to play football in northern cities. Howard and Lincoln played to a scoreless tie before eighteen thousand people in Philadelphia on Thanksgiving in 1925. Hampton and Lincoln played at New York's Polo Grounds on the edge of Harlem in 1929 in a game won by Lincoln 13–7 before ten thousand spectators.

Conclusion

For African Americans who lived through it, the 1920s must have seemed little more than a depressing continuation of earlier decades. Little appeared to have changed. Racial violence and lynching persisted. *The Birth of a Nation* mocked black people and inflamed racial animosity. "Experts" offered "proof" that people of color were inferior and threatened America's ethnic purity. The Ku Klux Klan became a formidable organization again. Millions of white men joined the Klan, and millions of other Americans supported it.

Nevertheless, some genuinely positive developments in the twenties gave hope for a more promising future. The NAACP became an organization to be reckoned with as it fought for antilynching legislation in Congress and for civil and political rights in the courts. Its membership exceeded one hundred thousand during the twenties. Though many black and white Americans ridiculed Marcus Garvey for his

Timeline

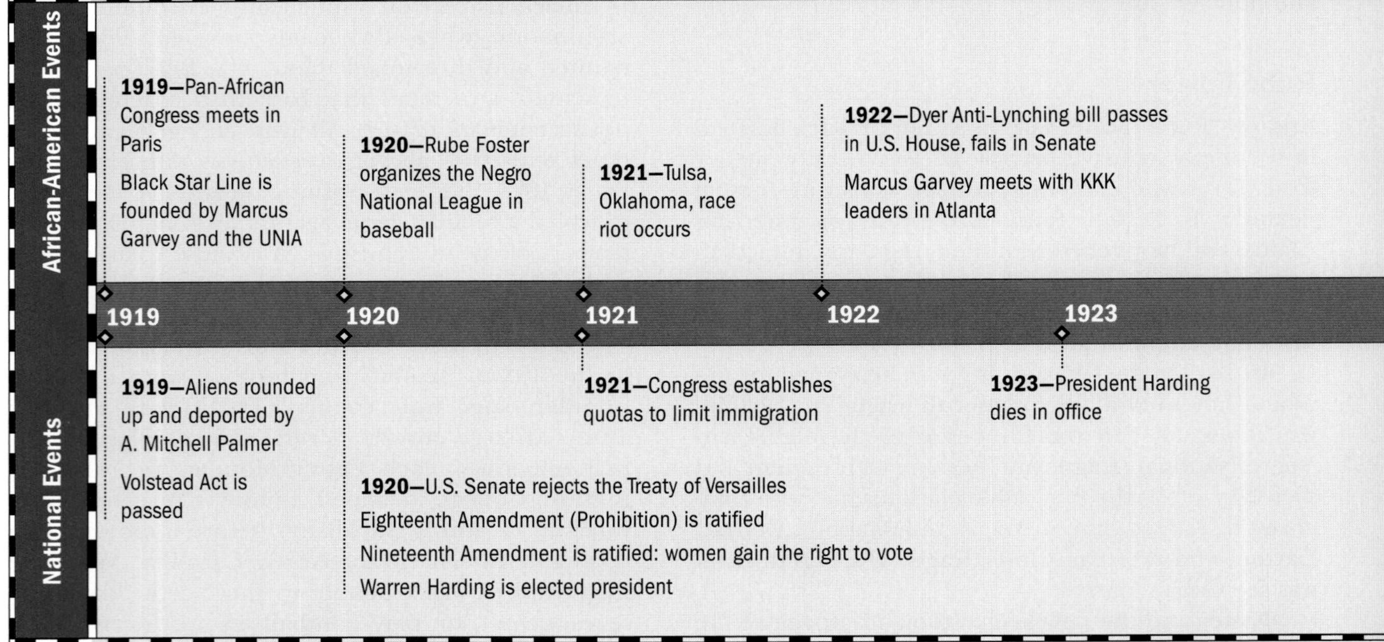

flamboyant style and excessive rhetoric, he offered racial pride and self-respect as he enrolled hundreds of thousands of black people in the UNIA.

Black workers made very little progress as they sought concessions from big business and representation within the ranks of organized labor. A. Philip Randolph founded the Brotherhood of Sleeping Car Porters and began a struggle with the Pullman company and the American Federation of Labor that would begin to pay off in the 1930s.

The Harlem Renaissance was a cultural awakening in literature and the arts that was unprecedented in African-American history. A torrent of words poured forth from novelists, essayists, and poets. Though they disagreed—sometimes vehemently—on the purposes of black art, the writers and artists who were a part of the Renaissance had an enduring impact. The Renaissance allowed thoughtful and creative men and women to grapple with what it meant to be black in a society in which the white majority had defined the black minority as inferior, incapable, and culturally backward. Hereafter African Americans were less likely to let other people characterize them in demeaning ways.

Black musicians, dancers, singers, entertainers, and athletes made names for themselves and contributed to popular culture in a mostly urban environment. As the nation moved into the 1930s, it remained to be seen whether the modest but real progress of the 1920s would be sustained.

Recommended Reading

William H. Harris. *Keeping the Faith: A. Philip Randolph, Milton P. Webster and the Brotherhood of Sleeping Car Porters, 1925–1937.* Urbana, IL: University of Illinois Press, 1977. This is an excellent account of the struggle of Randolph and the BSCP for recognition.

David Levering Lewis. *When Harlem Was in Vogue.* New York: Alfred A. Knopf, 1981. Lewis captures the life and vitality of Harlem in the twenties.

David Levering Lewis, ed. *The Portable Harlem Renaissance Reader.* New York: Penguin Books, 1994. Essays, poems, and excerpts from the works of virtually every writer associated with the Renaissance are contained in this volume.

Nancy MacLean. *Behind the Mask of Chivalry: The Making of the Second Ku Klux Klan.* New York: Oxford University Press, 1994. This is the most recent study of the revived KKK.

Arnold Rampersad. *The Life of Langston Hughes,* Vol. 1, 1902–1941, *I, Too, Sing America.* New York: Oxford University Press, 1986. Here is a rich study of a complex and extraordinary man and writer.

Judith Stein. *The World of Marcus Garvey: Race and Class in Modern Society.* Baton Rouge, LA: Louisiana State University Press, 1991. This is an effective examination of Garvey and the Universal Negro Improvement Association.

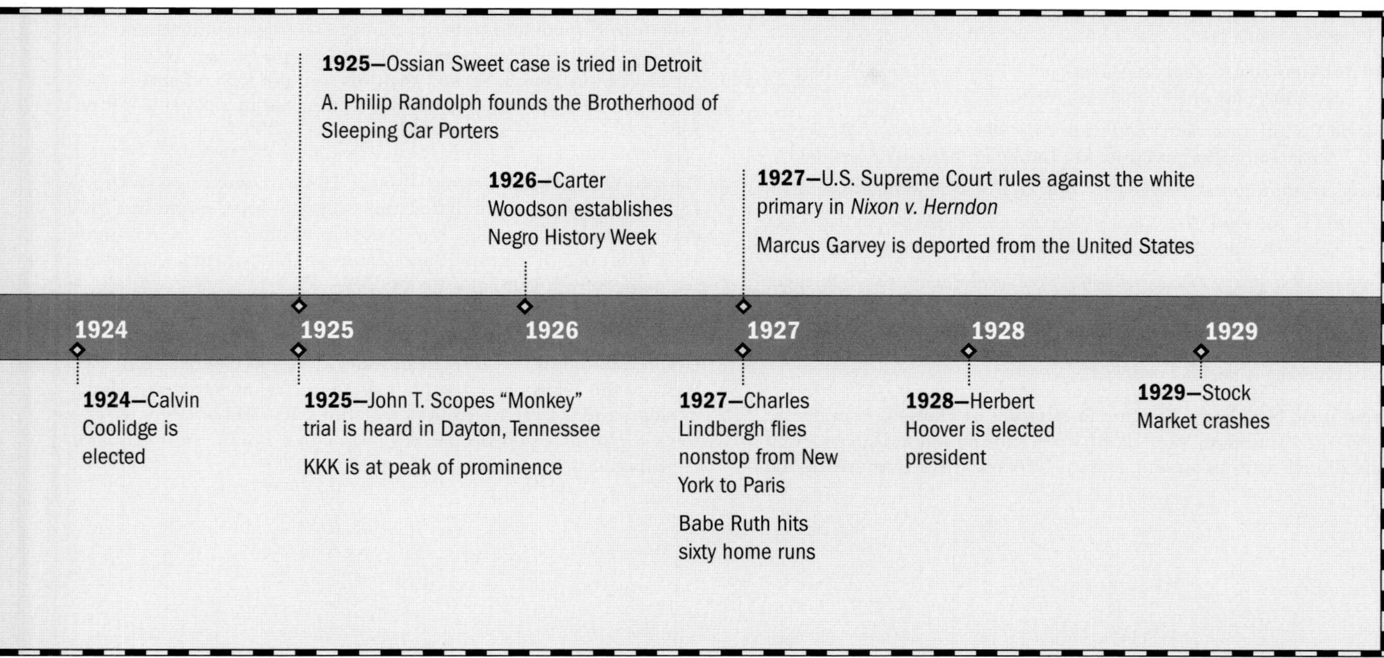

Additional Bibliography

The Ku Klux Klan

David M. Chalmers. *Hooded Americanism: A History of the Ku Klux Klan.* New York: Franklin Watts, 1965.

Kenneth T. Jackson. *The Ku Klux Klan in the City.* New York: Oxford University Press, 1967.

The NAACP

Charles F. Kellogg. *NAACP: A History of the National Association for the Advancement of Colored People.* Baltimore: Johns Hopkins University Press, 1967.

Robert L. Zangrando. *The NAACP Campaign against Lynching, 1909–1950.* Philadelphia: Temple University Press, 1980.

Black Workers, A. Philip Randolph, and the Brotherhood of Sleeping Car Porters

Jervis B. Anderson. *A. Philip Randolph: A Biographical Portrait.* New York: Harcourt, Brace, Jovanovich, 1973.

David E. Bernstein. *Only One Place of Redress: African Americans, Labor Regulations and the Courts from Reconstruction to the New Deal.* Durham, NC: Duke University Press, 2001.

Jack Santino. *Miles of Smiles, Years of Struggle: Stories of Black Pullman Porters.* Urbana, IL: University of Illinois Press, 1989.

Marcus Garvey and the Universal Negro Improvement Association

Randall K. Burkett. *Garveyism as a Religious Movement: The Institutionalization of a Black Civil Religion.* Metuchen, NJ: Scarecrow Press, 1978.

E. David Cronon. *Black Moses: The Story of Marcus Garvey and the Universal Negro Improvement Association.* Madison, WI: University of Wisconsin Press, 1955.

Marcus Garvey. *Philosophy and Opinions of Marcus Garvey.* New York: Atheneum, 1969.

Theodore Kornweibel, Jr. *Seeing Red: Federal Campaigns against Black Militancy, 1919–1925.* Bloomington, IN: Indiana University Press, 1998.

The Harlem Renaissance

Arna W. Bontemps, ed. *The Harlem Renaissance Remembered.* New York: Dodd, Mead, 1972.

Nathan Huggins. *Harlem Renaissance.* New York: Oxford University Press, 1971.

Bruce Kellner, ed. *The Harlem Renaissance: A Historical Dictionary of the Era.* Westport, CT: Greenwood Press, 1984.

Steven Watson. *The Harlem Renaissance: Hub of African American Culture, 1920–1930.* New York: Pantheon, 1995.

Biographies and Autobiographies

Pamela Bordelon, ed. *Go Gator and Muddy the Water: Writings by Zora Neale Hurston from the Federal Writers Project.* New York: Norton, 1999.

Thadious M. Davis. *Nella Larsen: Novelist of the Harlem Renaissance.* Baton Rouge, LA: Louisiana State University Press, 1994.

Wayne F. Cooper. *Claude McKay, Rebel Sojourner in the Harlem Renaissance: A Biography.* Baton Rouge, LA: Louisiana State University Press, 1987.

Robert Hemenway. *Zora Neale Hurston: A Literary Biography.* Urbana, IL: University of Illinois Press, 1977.

Gloria T. Hull. *Color, Sex, and Poetry: Three Women Writers of the Harlem Renaissance.* Bloomington, IN: Indiana University Press, 1987.

James Weldon Johnson. *Along the Way.* New York: Viking Press, 1933.

Cynthia E. Kerman. *The Lives of Jean Toomer: A Hunger for Wholeness.* Baton Rouge, LA: Louisiana State University Press, 1987.

Eugene Levy. *James Weldon Johnson: Black Leader, Black Voice.* Chicago: University of Chicago Press, 1973.

Retracing the Odyssey

New York, New York: The Studio Museum of Harlem. Founded in 1967 and located on West 125th Street, this museum displays a rich and diverse array of art and artifacts by black artists from Africa, the Caribbean, and America and thus maintains the legacy of the Harlem Renaissance.

New York, New York: Abyssinian Baptist Church. The best known church in Harlem and home to a huge congregation, it was led for most of the first three-quarters of the twentieth century by the Rev. Adam Clayton Powell, Sr. and then his son, the Rev. Adam Clayton Powell, Jr. The present structure was completed in 1923 at a cost of $330,000. It contains a small museum.

Dayton, Ohio: Paul Lawrence Dunbar Home. Dunbar was born in 1872 in Dayton. He purchased this two-story brick home in 1903 and lived in it until his death in 1906. His mother resided in it until 1936. It is open to the public and features exhibits, artifacts, photos, and papers from Dunbar's life and era.

Kansas City, Missouri: The Negro Leagues Baseball Museum. Devoted to the history of African Americans and baseball from the 1860s to the 1950s, the museum opened in 1991 and contains films, exhibits, and interactive computer stations. Its Field of Legends features twelve life-sized bronze sculptures that honor the men who contributed the most to black baseball.

REVIEW, RESEARCH & INTERACT

REVIEW QUESTIONS

1. To what extent, if any, had the intensity of white supremacy changed by the 1920s from what it had been two to three decades earlier?
2. What specific examples of progress could leaders like W. E. B. Du Bois, James Weldon Johnson, A. Philip Randolph, and Marcus Garvey point to in the twenties?
3. How do you account for Marcus Garvey's lack of acceptance among African-American leaders?
4. Explain how the black nationalism of the Universal Negro Improvement Association differed from the white nationalism of the Ku Klux Klan.
5. What specific economic opportunities existed for African Americans who had migrated to northern cities?
6. How do you explain the emergence of the literary and artistic movement known as the Harlem Renaissance?
7. How distinctive and unique were black writers, artists, and musicians? Were their creative works essentially a part of American culture or separate from it?
8. Were there any genuine reasons for optimism among African Americans by the late 1920s?

Research Navigator.com RESOURCES FOR COLLEGE RESEARCH ASSIGNMENTS **www.researchnavigator.com**

Chapter 17 describes the social, cultural, and political development of African American communities in the 1920s. For further research on African American life during this time in history, use the tools available to you in Research Navigator.

As you investigate this topic, consider this question: "What factors explain the resurgence of white racism in the 1920s? How did blacks respond?"

- **ContentSelect:** Search in the History database using the search term *Marcus Garvey*.
- **Links Library:** Access the History: U.S. History database and explore the links for *Harlem*.
- **New York Times on the Web:** To find out more, search in the African American Studies database using the search terms *Harlem* and *jazz*.

DOCUMENTS AND ACTIVITIES IN AFRICAN-AMERICAN HISTORY

Documents

17-1 "The Eruption of Tulsa": An NAACP Official Investigates the Tulsa Race Riot of 1921
17-2 "If You Believe the Negro Has a Soul": "Back to Africa" with Marcus Garvey, 1921
17-3 Elsie Johnson McDougald on "The Double Task: The Struggle of Negro Women for Sex and Race Emancipation," 1925
17-4 Charles S. Johnson, *The City Negro,* 1925
17-5 Alain Locke, from *The New Negro,* 1925
17-6 Claude McKay, "White Houses" 1925
17-7 The Harlem Renaissance: George Schuyler Argues against "Black Art," 1926
17-8 Hiram Evans, The Klan's Fight for Americanism, 1926

Interactive Figure

Black Workers by Major Industrial Group, 1920, p. 411
http://www.prenhall.com/hine/figure17.1

Learning Activity

Harlem Renaissansce
The Harlem Renaissance is not simply a story of individual and group achievement. What was the significance of so many writers, painters, musicians, photographers, poets, and other artists all gathering in the same place?

PART

V

The Great Depression and World War II

RELIGION

1919 Father Divine begins what comes to be known as the Peace Mission Movement

1929 Nation of Islam emerges

1933 Father Divine establishes his Peace Mission in Harlem

1934 Elijah Muhammed becomes leader of the Detroit Temple of Islam

CULTURE

1930s–1940s Heyday of Chicago's Black Renaissance

1930 Duke Ellington's "Mood Indigo"

Langston Hughes publishes *Not Without Laughter*

1931 Katherine Dunham forms the Negro Dance Group

1933 Paul Robeson stars in *The Emperor Jones*

1935 Marvel Cooke and Ella Baker publish "The Bronx Slave Market" in the *Crisis*

1936 Jesse Owens wins four gold medals at the Berlin Olympics

1937 Joe Louis wins heavyweight championship

1939 Billie Holiday premiers "Strange Fruit"

Marian Anderson sings at the Lincoln Memorial

"Bojangles" Robinson organizes Black Actors Guild

1940s Black musicians introduce bebop

1940–1948 Oscar Micheaux's films

1940 Richard Wright publishes *Native Son*

1941 Mary Dawson founds the National Negro *Opera* Company

1942 Margaret Walker publishes *For My People*

1945 Nat King Cole becomes the first black star to have his own radio variety show

1947 Jackie Robinson becomes first black major leagues baseball player

1948 Alice Coachman becomes the first African-American woman to win an Olympic gold medal

1952 Ralph Ellison publishes *Invisible Man*

POLITICS & GOVERNMENT

1925 U.S. War College concludes that African Americans are not fit for combat

1930 NAACP helps block John J. Parker's appointment to the Supreme Couirt

1932 "Scottsboro Boys" arrested

1933 FDR's "Black Cabinet" formed

1936 African-American voters switch to the Democratic Party

1937 William Hastie named first black federal judge

1938 Oscar DePriest elected, first African-American congressman from the North

1941 U.S. Army forms Tuskegee Air Squadron

1942 Marine Corps accepts first African Americans

1943 Navy officer schools accept African Americans

1944 Adam Clayton Powell elected to Congress

Port of Chicago "mutiny"

U.S. Supreme Court declares "white primaries" unconstitutional

1945 U.S. Army desegregates its Nurse Corps

1946 President Truman creates the Committee on Civil Rights

1948 Executive Order 9981 desegregates the U.S. military

1950 State Department revokes Paul Robeson's passport

1951 House Un-American Activities Committee indicts W.E.B. DuBois

1954 *Brown v. Board of Education* declares "separate but equal" unconstitutional

SOCIETY & ECONOMY

1899 North Carolina Mutual Life Insurance Company becomes the largest black-owned business in the United States

1908 Binga Bank opens in Chicago

1930 Fannie Peck founds Detroit Housedwives League

1932 Tuskegee Experiment begins

1935 Mary M. Bethune founds the National Council of Negro Women

National Negro Congress founded

NAACP sues to integrate University of Maryland School of Law

1936 First National Negro Congress held

1937 Mary M. Bethune organizes conference on the Negro and Negro Youth

1940s Many African Americans move from agriculture to jobs in industry

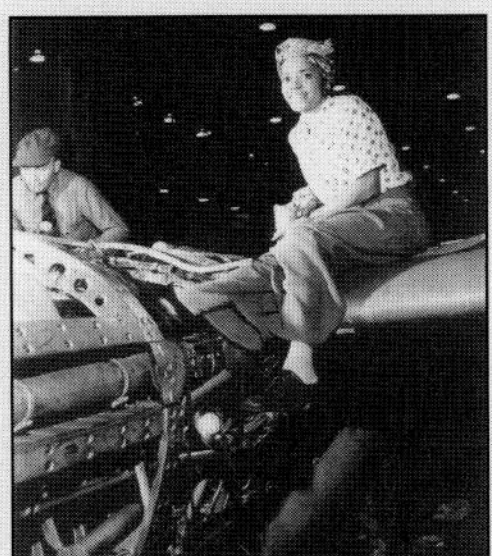

1941 A. Philip Randolph organizes The March on Washington Movement

1942 CORE founded

1943 Detroit race riots

1944 *An American Dilemma* published

Southern Regional Council established

1946 Journey of Reconciliation begins

1950 Ralph Bunche becomes the first African-American recipient of the Nobel Peace Prize

NOTEWORTHY INDIVIDUALS

George H. White (1852–1918)
Charles C. Spaulding (1874–1952)
Mary M. Bethune (1875–1955)
Thurgood Marshall (1908–1993)
Daisey A. Lampkins (1884–1965)
Juanita Mitchell (1913–1992)
Ella Baker (1903–1986)
Ralph Ellison (1914–1994)
Charlie "Bird" Parker (1920–1955)
Dizzy Gillespie (1917–1993)
Hattie McDaniel (1898–1952)
Oscar Micheaux (1884–1951)
Margaret Walker (1915–1998)
Anna Bontemps (1902–1973)
Richard Wright (1908–1960)
Thomas Dorsey (1899–1993)
Mahalia Jackson (1912–1972)
Katherine Dunham (1910–)
Billie Holiday (1915–1959)
Dox Thrash (1892–1965)
Aaron Douglas (1899–1988)
James Baldwin (1924–1987)
Jesse Owens (1913–1980)
Joe Louis Barrow (1914–1981)
Jackie Robinson (1919–1972)
Elijah Muhammed (1897–1975)
Father Major J. Divine (1879–1965)
Mabel K. Staupers (1890–1989)
William H. Hastie (1904–1976)
Bayard Rustin (1910–1987)

Ralph Bunche (1904–1971)
Constance B. Motley (1931–)
Imamu Amari Baraka, aka LeRoi Jones (1934–)
Selma Burke (1900–1995)
"Bojangles" Robinson (1878–1949)

The Great Depression and the New Deal

Isaac Sayer (1907–1981). *Employment Agency*, 1937, Oil on Canvas, 34¼ × 45 in. (87 × 114.3 cm). Collection of the Whitney Museum of American Art, NY.

Issac Sayer's *Employment Agency*, a 1937 oil painting captures the quiet desperation and the interminable waiting for nonexistent jobs that many Americans experienced during the Great Depression.

THE Depression brought everyone down a peg or two. And the Negro had but a few pegs to fall.

Langston Hughes

The only thing that we not only can, but must do, is voluntarily and insistently to organize our economic and social power, no matter how much ségregation it involves. Learn to associate with ourselves and to train ourselves in methods of democratic control within our own group. Run and support our own institutions.

W. E. B. Du Bois

For African Americans the Great Depression was both an era of suffering made worse by the horrors and burdens of American racism and a time of profound political change that would lay the foundation for the progress of ensuing decades. At the beginning of the economic collapse most African Americans were either trapped in the already failing southern agricultural system or eking out a bare existence at the margins of the booming urban economy. The fall of the economy pushed many black Americans to the edge of starvation throwing them off the land and out of the small niches they had carved out in other occupations. Coming out of the southern dominated Democratic party, President Franklin Roosevelt's New Deal program for fighting the Depression might have simply reinforced existing racism, as in fact it did to some extent. From another perspective, the emerging political power of African-American voters in the north, the continuing development of civil rights organizations, and the growth of an antiracist agenda among radicals and labor unions created the preconditions for a profound change in American politics. Amid economic despair, peonage, lynchings, and labor conflict, black men, women, and their children saw glimmers of hope in protests against racial segregation and radical critiques of capitalist exploitation. The 1930s were thus the dark dawn of a new era.

CHAPTER OUTLINE

The Cataclysm, 1929–1933
- Harder Times for Black America
- Black Business in the Depression: Collapse and Survival
- The Failure of Relief

African Americans and the New Deal
- Roosevelt and the First New Deal, 1933–1935
- Black Officials in the New Deal
- Black Social Scientists and the New Deal
- African Americans and the Second New Deal

Black Protest during the Great Depression
- The NAACP and Civil Rights Struggles
- Du Bois Ignites a Controversy
- Challenging Racial Discrimination in the Courts
- Black Women and Community Organizing

Organized Labor and Black America

The Communist Party and African Americans
- The International Labor Defense and the "Scottsboro Boys"
- Debating Communist Leadership
- The National Negro Congress

The Tuskegee Experiment

Conclusion

DATA EXPLORATION
To explore this data, go to http://www.prenhall.com/hine/figure18.1

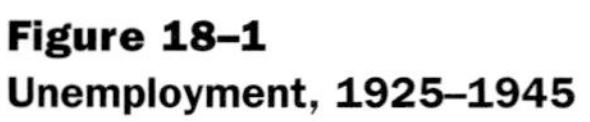

Figure 18–1
Unemployment, 1925–1945
With the collapse of the American economy, unemployment soared in the 1930s. New Deal programs alleviated some of the suffering, but full recovery did not come until the defense industries swung into action with the U.S. entry into World War II.

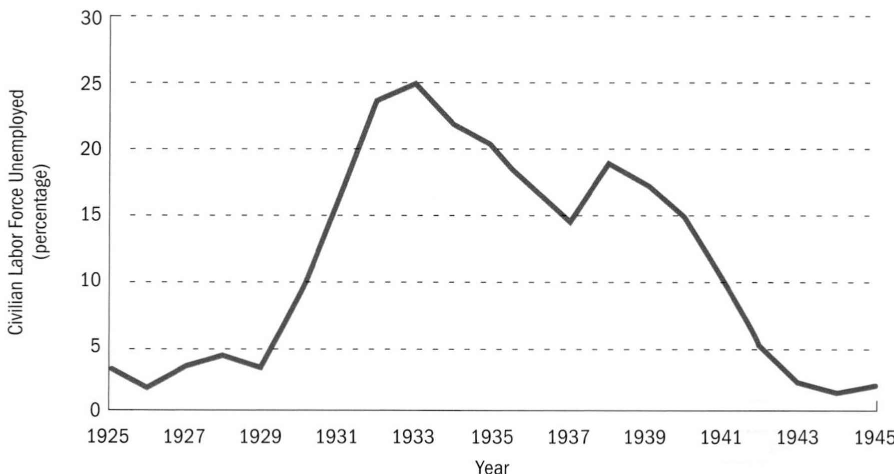

The Cataclysm, 1929–1933

The Great Depression was a cataclysm. National income fell from $81 billion in 1929 to $40 billion in 1932. Americans lost faith in banks, and the resulting panic deepened the despair. Overnight millions of Americans lost their life savings in bank closings and foreclosures. Individual Americans responded by buying fewer consumer goods and, in turn businesses cut back production, investment, and payrolls. The result was a downward spiral of economic activity made worse by increasing numbers unemployed. According to the American Federation of Labor (AFL), the number of unemployed people increased from 3,216,000 in January 1930 to 13,689,000 in March 1933 (see Figure 18–1). The standard of living of nearly everyone from farmers to small businessmen and entrepreneurs to wage laborers dropped to a fraction of what it had been before 1929.

Most people blamed the stock market crash and Republican president Herbert Hoover for the hard times, but the explanation is more complicated. Although still a hotly debated issue, the Great Depression was probably caused by a combination of factors, including rampant speculation, corporate capitalism's drive for markets and profits unchecked by federal regulation, the failure of those in the government or private sector to understand the workings of the economy, a weak international trading system, and most important, the great inequality of wealth and income that limited the purchasing power of millions of Americans.

Harder Times for Black America

The collapse of the American economy hit African Americans particularly hard. Most black people remained in the rural South mired in an increasingly exploitive agricultural system. Indeed, the Depression exacerbated the key problems besetting cash-crop production in the 1920s. Consumer demand for cotton and sugar fell with the economy, but as farmers grew more of these crops to make ends meet, the supply of these staples increased. The result was a catastrophe, with prices for cotton, still the mainstay of the southern economy, plunging from eighteen cents a pound in 1929 to six cents in 1933. Families of black sharecroppers and tenant farmers, nearly powerless in the rural South, found themselves reduced to starvation or thrown off the land.

The hard times also struck those one and a half million African Americans who had escaped the South for northern urban communities. Even during the height of the prosperous 1920s black Americans suffered layoffs and witnessed a steady deterioration in their living standards. After 1929 the same forces that impoverished those in the countryside swept those in urban areas further toward the economic margins as waves of refugees from the farms crowded into the cities (see Table 18–1). By 1934, when the federal government noted that 17 percent of white citizens could not support themselves, the figure for black Americans had increased to 38 percent overall. In Chicago, the jobless rate for African-American men was 40 percent, in Pittsburgh 48 percent, in Harlem 50 percent, in Philadelphia 56 percent, and in Detroit 60 percent. The figures were even more

Table 18–1
Median Income of Black Families Compared to the Median Income of White Families for Selected Cities, 1935–1936

City and Type of Family	Black	White	Black Income as a Percentage of White Income
Husband–Wife Families			
New York	$980	$1,930	51%
Chicago	$726	$1,687	43%
Columbus	$831	$1,622	51%
Atlanta	$632	$1,876	34%
Columbia	$576	$1,876	31%
Mobile	$481	$1,419	34%
Other Families			
Atlanta	$332	$940	35%
Columbia	$254	$1,403	18%
Mobile	$301	$784	38%

Source: Gunnar Myrdal, et al., *An American Dilemma*, New York: Harper and Brothers, 1944.

dire for black workers in southern cities. In Atlanta, Georgia, 65 percent of black workers needed public assistance, and in Norfolk, Virginia, a stunning 80 percent had to apply for welfare.

African Americans lost jobs in those parts of the economy where they had gained a tenuous foothold. Before 1929, jobs in low-status or demeaning occupations such as garbage collection, foundries, or domestic service had been regarded as "Negro work" and, hence, were generally immune from white competition. As desperation set in, white Southerners not only competed for these jobs, but also used the old tactics of terror and intimidation to compel employers to fire black people. Unions, north and south, continued to exclude African Americans from membership and pressured manufacturers to hire white people.

Black women workers, overwhelmingly concentrated in domestic service and laundry work, were affected even more than black men. There were fewer jobs because many families could no longer afford domestic help. With many impoverished women coming into the cities, those white people with the money to hire help found that they could pay almost nothing and still employ these desperate women. In 1935 two black women, Marvel Cooke and Ella Baker, published an exposé of the exploitation of these women laborers in *The Crisis.* They entitled the article "The Bronx Slave Market" because the buying and selling of labor reminded them of the old slave marts in the antebellum South. Cooke and Baker described how the street corner market worked: "The Simpson avenue block exudes the stench of the slave market at its worst. Not only is human labor bartered and sold for a slave wage, but human love also is a marketable commodity." The black women gathered on particular street corners and waited as well-to-do white women selected them for a day's labor. They received "wages as low as 15 to 25 cents an hour, some working only two or three hours a day." Some black people were hired but never paid.

African Americans were no strangers to adversity and many used the survival strategies developed through centuries of hardship to eke out an existence during the first years of the Great Depression. Survival demanded that black women pool their resources and adhere to a collective spirit that found such fertile ground in segregated northern neighborhoods. In Chicago, for example, women and their families lived in crowded tenements in which they shared bathrooms and other facilities including hot plates, stoves, and sinks. They bartered and exchanged goods and services because money was so scarce. One woman might dress the hair of a neighbor in return for permission to borrow her dress or use her pots and pans. Another woman might trade bread and sugar or some other household staple for milk, beans, or soap. Grandmothers watched over children as their mothers went to look with rising futility for a domestic job. They helped each other as best they could.

Rural black women, like their urban sisters, had to rely on their individual and collective ingenuity to survive. As one observer of black women household heads in rural Georgia noted, "In their effort to maintain existence, these people are catching and selling fish, reselling vegetables, sewing in exchange for old clothes, letting out sleeping space, and doing odd jobs. They understand how to help each other. Stoves are used in common, wash boilers go their rounds, and garden crops are exchanged and shared." Nonetheless, the depth and duration of this downturn pressed these mutual aid strategies to the breaking point. By 1933 the clock seemed to have been turned back to 1865 when many African Americans could claim to own little more than their bodies.

Black Businesses in the Depression: Collapse and Survival

Members of the black elite also experienced economic losses. African Americans who had built successful businesses faced the same depression-borne problems as other businesses, but suffered even more because the communities on which they depended were poorer. A description of two kinds of business,

This photograph by Margaret Bourke White captures the contrast between the American dream of prosperity—for white families—and the harsh realities of life for black Americans during the Depression.

banking and insurance, illustrates how black enterprises stood or fell during the economic crisis.

The Binga Bank, Chicago's first black-owned-and-operated financial institution had been founded in 1908 by its president Jesse Binga (1865–1950), a Detroit-born real-estate broker who had worked as a barber and a Pullman porter. Binga had managed the bank so effectively that by 1930 its deposits had grown to more than $1.5 million. Binga once boasted that he could lay claim to more footage on State Street, Chicago's principal thoroughfare, than any other man in the city. The Binga Bank was, during its early years, an important symbol of successful black capitalism and as such it represented the hopes and aspirations of Chicago's black people. But the bank's assets were too heavily invested in mortgage loans to black churches and fraternal societies, many of which could not meet their payments after their members lost their jobs. Binga refused to seize the properties of these community institutions, but his restraint, coupled with financial improprieties, led to the bank's failure. On July 31, 1930, Illinois state bank auditors padlocked the institution and filed a federal misuse-of-funds charge against the once proud financier. Sentenced to prison in 1932, Binga was pardoned by President Franklin Delano Roosevelt a year later. However, he never rebuilt his bank or his fortune.

Some black businesses did survive the economic cataclysm, although often in a much weakened state. Among the fortunate businesses still standing when prosperity finally returned in the 1940s were the leading insurance companies, such as Atlanta Life, Supreme Life, Golden State, and the North Carolina Mutual Life Insurance Company. Atlanta Life Insurance Company, for example—founded by a former Georgia slave, Alonzo Franklin Herndon in 1905—not only survived the Depression but recorded substantial profit. Between 1931 and 1936, the company's assets increased by more than $1 million. This was in part because insurance companies such as Atlanta Life provided an essential service for African Americans, particularly in an era before government provided social security, and could thus depend on a continued flow of premiums. And unlike Binga Bank the officers of the Atlanta Life Insurance Company drastically reduced the percentage of their investment capital that secured mortgage loans in the black community.

The North Carolina Mutual Life Insurance Company, in Durham, North Carolina, weathered the Great Depression under the astute leadership of Charles Clinton Spaulding (1874-1952), a former manager of a black cooperative grocery store. In 1899 Spaulding joined with two other African Americans to transform the insurance company into the nation's largest black business. His partners were John Merrick, a former slave and leading realtor and barber (he owned six barbershops, three for whites and three for blacks), and his uncle, Dr. Aaron McDuffie Moore,

Durham's only black physician. Following on the heels of the great migration to the North, Spaulding expanded the company's territory into Virginia, Maryland, and the District of Columbia. The company adhered to the thrift, hard work, and self-help philosophy so ardently expressed by Booker T. Washington. It remains today, one of the three largest, black-owned insurance companies in the United States.

The Failure of Relief

Before Franklin Roosevelt's New Deal, private charities or, as a last resort, state and local governments were responsible for providing relief from economic hardships. Even in good times these institutions provided too little for all those in need. Moreover, African Americans had a much harder time getting aid than white people and were given less when they did get it. The Depression made it impossible for the nation's charitable organizations to meet the needs of more than a small portion of the hungry, homeless, and unemployed millions. In turn, state and local governments could not or would not provide unemployment insurance or increased welfare benefits to ease the pain and suffering of those most vulnerable to the economic disaster. Even when these governments wanted to help the magnitude of the economic collapse so lowered tax receipts as to make it nearly impossible for relief agencies to act.

A market woman in the 1930s with burdens on her head and in her arms. Black women drew upon proven strategies of self-help, hard work, and communal sharing to survive the Great Depression.

Despite the great need to alleviate the economic disaster, President Herbert Hoover hesitated to act. Steeped in the free market orthodoxy of his time, he believed that government should do little to interfere with the workings of the economy. Nevertheless, he did more to counteract a depression than any previous president had done. Hoover tried to convince businesses to retain employees and not to cut wages, believing that companies would understand that by doing so they would contribute to the health of the general economy and promote their own long-term interests. The president also approved loans to banks, railroads, and insurance companies by the Reconstruction Finance Corporation, a federal agency set up to rescue large corporations. He hoped that these businesses would reinvigorate production, create new jobs, and restore consumer spending. His faith was misplaced; businesses, seeking to save themselves, took the government loans and still laid off workers.

Hoover's reluctance to use the federal government to intervene in the economy extended to the provision of relief. He suggested that local governments and charities should address the needs of the unemployed, the homeless, and the starving masses. Hoover was not a callous person, but he was trapped in a rigid ideology. He watched with dismay the wandering groups of men, women, and children who began settling into what they called, with grim humor, "Hoovervilles," sordid clusters of shacks made of tin, cardboard, and burlap adjacent to railroad tracks and dumps. Still, he refused to allow the federal government to directly provide relief.

Hoover's inactivity was bad enough, but his politics were as racist as that of the Democratic party. He wanted to create a white Republican party in the South and cultivated white Southerners by attempting to appoint John Parker, a racist judge, to the U.S. Supreme Court and by displacing black Republican party leaders. Hoover's policy was not new; for decades the national Republican party had treated black voters with contempt and often declined to reward them with patronage appointments. This policy took on a different meaning during the early 1930s against the backdrop of black suffering. As NAACP director Walter White put it, Hoover:

> ...sat stolidly in the White House, refusing bluntly to receive Negro citizens who wished to lay before him the facts of their steadily worsening plight or to consider any remedial legislation or governmental action. His attitude toward Negroes caused me to coin a phrase which gained considerable currency, particularly in the Negro world, in which I described Hoover as "the man in the lily-White House."

African Americans and the New Deal

In 1932, the third year of the Great Depression, voters elected New York governor Franklin Delano Roosevelt to the presidency with a total of nearly twenty-three million votes. Roosevelt's lopsided victory over Hoover, who received fewer than sixteen million votes, demonstrated the country's loss of faith in the Republican party and its economic philosophy and heralded the emergence of a new electoral coalition. The new president appealed to the Democratic party's base of support in the white South, but to this group he added a coalition of western farmers, industrial workers, urban voters from the white ethnic groups in northern cities, and reform-minded intellectuals. For the time being, however, black Americans still clung to the Republican banner. In Chicago, for example, less than 25 percent of black voters cast their ballots for Roosevelt. But this was the last election in which the party of Lincoln could take them for granted. In his first term Roosevelt inaugurated a multitude of programs to counter the Depression—collectively known as the New Deal—which would shift the allegiance of African Americans. Initially his programs continued past patterns of discrimination against African Americans, but by 1935 the New Deal was providing more equal benefits and prompting profound social changes. The result was a new political order that ultimately undermined key portions of the edifice of American racism.

Roosevelt and the First New Deal, 1933–1935

During his first 100 days in office Franklin Roosevelt pressed through Congress a profusion of bold new economic initiatives that came to be known as the first New Deal. To combat the Depression, Roosevelt, unlike Hoover, followed no predetermined plan. Instead he favored experimentation—tempered by political expediency—over ideology as the guide to federal action. With little resistance Congress passed the president's sprawling and complex laws aimed at overhauling the nation's financial, agricultural, and industrial systems. Most hoped, vainly as it turned out, that these changes would eventually bring a return to prosperity. In the meantime Roosevelt moved forcefully to counter the immediate suffering of the unemployed with a massive emergency federal relief effort. Many of the first New Deal's programs benefited both white and black people, but the strength of white Southerners in the Democratic party and the nearly complete lack of African-American political power in the South caused much of this early program to be unfairly administered.

The Agricultural Adjustment Act (AAA), designed to protect farmers by giving them subsidies to limit production and thereby stabilize prices, illustrates the key benefits and problems African Americans experienced during the first New Deal. The theory underlying the AAA was that creating scarcity would increase agricultural prices. So farmers would be paid to grow less. The program provided for sharecroppers and tenant farmers to get part of the subsidies and allowed new rural relief agencies to dispense supplementary income to off-season wage workers.

This program helped many African Americans, mainly because it pumped billions of dollars into an economic sector on which over 4,500,000 black people relied for their livelihood. Also, the AAA was designed to remedy the problems of those farmers—disproportionately African American—who were overreliant on such cash crops as cotton. By 1929 three out of four black farmers, compared with two out of five white farmers, received at least 40 percent of their gross income from cotton. The flow of money from the AAA did, for a time, slow the exodus of black people from farming. Fewer left the farms in the first two years of the program than in the two years before it began. Indeed, from a broader perspective the New Deal appears to have slowed the rate at which black people left the land. During the 1930s, only 4.5 percent of African Americans abandoned farming, compared with 8.6 percent who did so during the 1920s.

But if the AAA brought real benefits to black farmers, it was often, contrary to protections written into the law, administered unfairly and corruptly. Local control of the AAA resided in the hands of the Extension Service and County Agricultural Conservation Committees, which were supposed to represent all farmers. The county agents, however, were often the planters themselves and the committees mirrored southern politics as a whole by excluding black people. African Americans were further disadvantaged by the system of unilateral bookkeeping and oppressive credit relations between landlords and tenants. During the first two years of the AAA, black

When unscrupulous white landowners pocketed AAA payments intended to aid all farmers, thousands of evicted sharecroppers congregated in refugee-like camps along the roads to protest the injustice. This is a scene from the sharecropper's strike that occurred in the bootheel of Missouri in 1935.

farmers complained bitterly that white landlords simply grabbed and pocketed the millions of dollars of benefit checks they were supposed to forward to tenants. To compound the injury, some planters then evicted the sharecroppers and tenants from the land.

The experience of African Americans with the National Industrial Recovery Act (NIRA) mimicked that with the AAA. The NIRA was intended to promote the revival of manufacturing by allowing various industries to cooperate in establishing codes of conduct governing prices, wage levels, and employment practices, all of which were to be overseen by a National Recovery Administration (NRA). The NRA oversaw the drafting of the codes, but faced tremendous resistance from employers and unions in eliminating racial disparities in wage rates and working conditions. Even when African-American advocates did win wage increases for occupations in which black people predominated, the result was often a shift to white labor. These policies prompted some African-American newspapers and protest organizations to claim that "NRA" really stood for the "Negro Removal Agency" or "Negroes Robbed Again." To the relief of many African-American advocates and workers, the United States Supreme Court declared the NIRA unconstitutional in spring 1935.

The New Deal's national welfare programs included the Federal Emergency Relief Administration (FERA), the Civilian Conservation Corps (CCC), Public Works Administration (PWA), and Civil Works Administration (CWA). Although inadequate and unfairly administered on local levels, these programs were often the only thing standing between black people and starvation. FERA provided funds for local and state relief operations to restart and expand their programs. The program pulled millions of people back from the brink of starvation. Because African Americans suffered greater economic devastation, they received benefits at a higher rate than whites. In most cities north and south, 25 to 40 percent of African Americans were on relief rolls that FERA funded wholly or in part. Direct welfare, however, was deemed by many in the Roosevelt administration to be debilitating, so it emphasized hiring the unemployed for public works projects. The CWA was a temporary agency created to help people through the winter of 1933–1934. The Civilian Conservation Corps (CCC) built segregated camps to employ young men and to take them away from the poverty and hopelessness of urban areas. By the time it was abolished in 1945, more than two hundred thousand African-American youth had taken part in the program.

All these relief programs included substantial numbers of African Americans and helped many through the worst parts of the Depression. But the programs also tended to be less helpful to black people than they were to whites. In its early days, the CCC, for example, was a tightly segregated institution, with only about 5 percent of its slots going to black youths during its first year. Likewise, although FERA tended to be administered fairly in northern cities, in the South it reached few of those in need.

Black Officials in the New Deal

The first New Deal was not completely bleak for African Americans. In addition to the benefits, however grudgingly disbursed, that they derived from New Deal relief programs, African Americans also gained new influence and allies within the Roosevelt administration. Their experience reflected both the growing availability of highly trained African Americans for government service and the emerging consciousness among white liberals about the problems—and potential electoral power—of black people.

Black people found a staunch ally in First Lady Eleanor Roosevelt. She was revered for her relentless commitment to racial justice. She arranged meetings at the White House for some black leaders. She cajoled her husband to consider legislation on behalf of black rights. She personally defied Jim Crow laws by refusing to sit in a "white only" section while attending a meeting in the South. Moreover, she wrote newspaper columns calling for "fair play and equal opportunity for Negro citizens." Roosevelt further endeared herself to black Americans when she resigned her membership in

VOICES

A Black Sharecropper Details Abuse in the Administration of Agricultural Relief

This is one of many letters black sharecroppers sent to the NAACP in search of assistance to halt the mass evictions and abuse of New Deal relief efforts.

Alabama
June 21, 1934

Dear Sir:—I am writing you these few lines ask you if it is any possible chance of you fining out just why F.E.R.A. office here in . . . refuse to gave me work when I have six in family to care for and also my wife's mother who is over 65 years old and been under the Doctor care for the past seven years of course my wife has a little job but its not with the relief work which some weeks she makes five dollars and some weeks less with four children to take care off which range in age 8–6–4–3 years old and we have $5 per month rent and also $1.74 per week Insurance which that don't enclude Food and Clothing and Fuel to burn. Now Mr. White in the past two and half months I am being going to the relief office trying to get on the relief work and it seem like it is empossible and also just before the first of April I went up to the relief office and explain my case to Mr. . . , the man that gave out the work cards and he gave me a food order for the amount of $2—two dollars and also I got some work to do. But as soon as I got paid for the 24 hours work he came to me to collect $2 for the food order that he gave me and I refuse to gave him $2 and I havent been able to get any more work to do and I have been going up to the office each day sence. But they tell me at the office that they cant gave me work because my wife is working. Of course if that maybe the case I can gave you the name and the address of at least a hundred families where there is two and three in one family who are working on the relief project and I know of at least twenty single men with no one but theirself to take care of and are working twenty-four hours every week and they got to gave their foreman one dollar each every week if they want to stay on the job.

Now Mr. White the white man who my wife work for and my wife told him that they refuse to gave me work because she was working for me and he went up to relief office to see about it But they told him that they didnt cut me out of work because my wife were working but they cut me off because I were unable to do the work. and of course I know that to be very much untrue. The trouble is I refuse to be a fool like so many of my race here and else where around here to pay for a food order that is supose to be giving to the needy free of charge but lots are paying for them and also paying for their job. Of course Mr. White I am colored and when you go up to the relief office The Colored people is treated just as if they were dogs and not human beings. I have been up in the office and I have seen with my own eyes my color kicked and beaten down a whole flight of stairs. I have seen everything done except been murder. Understand Mr. White the little job that my wife has isn't on the relief is a private and everybody that is head of any thing here in the relief office is kin to one another. Now Mr. White the lady that is head of the relief is Mrs. . . . which I saw here once since I was cut off from work and I explained my case to her and she told that she would send a investigator around to my home the next morning whose name is Miss. . . . and she told me that when I gave Mr. . . . the $2 for the food order she would O.K. my work card. Mr. White if possible will you please fine out for me just what is the reason they refuse to gave me work when I have six in family and rent to pay. Insurance, Doctor bill, milk bill, buy food and clothing and with only my wife at work it is impossible Mr. White.

QUESTIONS

1. What conditions led the writer to seek help from Walter White and the NAACP?
2. What were some of the factors and reasons implied and noted that prevented even more black people from protesting economic inequality?

Source: Herbert Aptheker, ed., *A Documentary History of the Negro People in the United States, 1933–1945* (New York: Citadel Press Book, 1990), pp. 58–60.

the Daughters of the American Revolution after that organization refused to allow a young black opera singer, Marian Anderson, to perform at its Constitution Hall in Washington in 1939. (Administration officials subsequently arranged for Anderson to perform in front of the Lincoln Memorial on Easter Sunday before a crowd of 75,000. The first song she sang was "My Country, 'Tis of Thee.")

Eleanor Roosevelt was joined by other liberals to press the cause of racial justice and to seek the appointment of African Americans throughout the government. Early in 1933 President Roosevelt acceded to their request that he appoint someone in his administration to assume responsibility for ensuring that African Americans received fair treatment. He asked Harold Ickes, a former president of the Chicago chapter of the NAACP, and a white man whom most black Americans recognized as a tried and true friend, to make this happen. Ickes invited Clark Foreman, a young white Georgian who had rejected his region's racism, to handle the assignment. Foreman recognized the irony of a white man representing black people in the government and immediately began to recruit highly trained African Americans. Similar efforts to bring African Americans into government positions were made by Eleanor Roosevelt, Ickes, and other administration officials such as Daniel Roper, Secretary of Commerce, and Harry Hopkins, FDR's relief administrator. The result was that doors to the government began opening in an unprecedented way. For the first time, the government employed professional black architects, lawyers, engineers, economists, statisticians, interviewers, office managers, social workers, and librarians. The Department of Commerce hired Eugene K. Jones, on leave from the National Urban League. The National Youth Administration brought in Mary McLeod Bethune and the Department of Interior employed William H. Hastie and Robert Weaver. Ira De A. Reid joined the Social Security Administration, and Lawrence W. Oxley worked for the Department of Labor, with Ambrose Caliver serving in the Office of Education.

A core of highly placed African Americans became linked in a network called the Federal Council on Negro Affairs, more loosely known as Roosevelt's "Black Cabinet." Mary McLeod Bethune was the undisputed leader of this body, which consisted primarily of "New Deal race specialists." It numbered twenty-seven men and three women working mostly in temporary emergency agencies such as the Works Progress Administration (WPA) and included such stalwarts as housing administrator Robert Weaver. This group met every Friday in Bethune's Washington home, while a smaller and younger group met occasionally in Robert Weaver's apartment. This cadre of advisers pressured the president and the heads of federal agencies to adopt and support color-blind policies and lobbied to advance the status of black Americans.

Black Social Scientists and the New Deal

Many black intellectuals, scholars, and writers believed that the social sciences could be used to adjudicate race relations in the country and during the New Deal they found greater receptiveness to their work than ever before. Nearly 200 African Americans received Ph.D.s during the 1930s, more than four times the combined total from the first three decades of the century. Several of these young scholars reached the top ranks of the social sciences studying the economic, political, and sociological problems of black people with a depth of experience and theoretical sophistication lacking in earlier generations of scholars. In sociology E. Franklin Frazier and Charles S. Johnson took the lead. Frazier's pioneering studies of black families, although now dated, placed him at the forefront of debates on social policy. As the editor of *Opportunity*, the journal of the Urban League, throughout the 1930s, Johnson published insightful critiques of American racial practices and policies, as well as the work of emerging black novelists, poets, and playwrights. Meanwhile Ralph Bunche became well known within the field of political science, while Abram Harris and Robert Weaver gained renown in economics.

Historians such as Carter G. Woodson, Lorenzo Greene, Benjamin Quarles, and John Hope Franklin advanced the idea that black people had been active agents in the past and not simply the passive objects of white people's actions. Through the Association for the Study of Negro Life and History as well as the Negro History Week, Woodson and his coworkers Greene, Alrutheus Taylor, and Monroe Work deployed their scholarship to dismiss claims of black inferiority. Their scholarly emphasis on racial pride, achievement, and autonomy helped to raise black morale.

The increasing importance of black scholars became apparent late in the 1930s when the Carnegie Corporation, a philanthropic foundation, sponsored a major study of black life. Although the study was led by Gunnar Myrdal, a Swedish social scientist, nearly half the large staff of scholars were African Americans, and several, particularly Bunche, had a major impact on the work. Published in 1944 as *An American Dilemma*, this massive study profoundly affected public understanding of how racism undermined the progress of African Americans and it helped to set the agenda for the civil rights movement.

PROFILE

Mary McLeod Bethune

Mary McLeod Bethune played a powerful role in Roosevelt's black cabinet, but this was only one of the many forums in which she exercised consummate leadership and diplomatic skill. Bethune's life and work are major links connecting the social reform efforts of post-Reconstruction black women to the civil rights protest activities of the generation emerging after World War II. All the various strands of black women's struggle for education, political rights, racial pride, and sexual autonomy are united in Bethune's writings, speeches, and organizational work.

Mary McLeod Bethune forged a mutually sustaining friendship with First Lady Eleanor Roosevelt that gave her considerable access to the president.

Bethune, born on July 10, 1875, near Mayesville, South Carolina, graduated from Scotia Seminary in 1894 and entered Dwight Moody's Institute for Home and Foreign Missions in Chicago. After teaching in mission schools, she settled in Daytona, Florida, where she founded the Daytona Educational and Industrial Institute for Training Negro Girls. Reflecting on her work years later Bethune recalled, "The school expanded fast. In less than two years I had two hundred fifty pupils. . . . I concentrated more and more on girls, as I felt that they especially were hampered by lack of educational opportunities." Eventually, however, she agreed to merge with Cookman Institute, an educational facility for black boys under the auspices of the Methodist Church. Thus, in 1923 the now coeducational institution was renamed Bethune-Cookman College.

During the 1920s Bethune became the leader of the National Association of Colored Women, a federation of women's clubs. As the NACW's president she attempted to turn the organization away from its previous focus on self-help and moral uplift and toward broader goals. Although she made progress, by 1935 she had become frustrated by the NACW's caution and founded the National Council of Negro Women (NCNW), an "organization of organizations." The women present at the creation of the NCNW were the who's who of black women's activism. They included educators Charlotte Hawkins Brown and Mary Church Terrell; executive director of the National Association of Colored Graduate Nurses Mabel K. Staupers; NAACP national field director Daisy Lampkin; and Addie W. Hunton, former president of the Empire State Federation of Women's Clubs and of the International Council of Women of the Darker Race. Eventually, the NCNW included twenty national affiliates and ninety local councils located in cities, towns, and rural communities across the country. Club engagement strengthened their resolve to struggle for black rights and provided safe space for them to develop the skills and networks that proved critical in the post-World War II civil rights movement.

With the New Deal Bethune became a Democratic party activist and a government official. She had a close personal relationship with First Lady Eleanor Roosevelt that gave her access to the president that few others enjoyed. She and Eleanor Roosevelt had persuaded the president that the National Youth Administration (NYA) needed a Negro division to assure that benefits would be distributed fairly. When the organization started, Bethune was named the NYA's Director of Negro Affairs. She was the first African-American woman to hold a high position in the government. Bethune supported the administration during the 1936 campaign by helping to convince African Americans that their best interests lay with the Democratic rather than Republican party.

One of Bethune's many noteworthy accomplishments was the 1937 conference held by the Department of Labor on the Problems of the Negro and Negro Youth, at which Eleanor Roosevelt delivered a key speech. During the session entitled "Security of Life and Equal Protection under the Law" the conference called for a federal antilynching law, equal access to the ballot in federal elections, and elimination of segregation and discrimination on interstate carriers. This was a virtual blueprint of the agenda of the civil rights movement. No other general meeting on civil rights during the Roosevelt administration generated the interest, support, and publicity of this 1937 conference. With this Negro Youth Conference, Bethune assumed the middle ground of black politics.

African Americans and the Second New Deal

By late 1935, after two years marked by a slow recovery, much of the first New Deal lay in shambles. The U. S. Supreme Court had invalidated major parts of it and a conservative backlash was emerging against the Roosevelt administration. In response Roosevelt pressed for a second burst of legislation marked by the passage of the Social Security Act (SSA), the National Labor Relations Act (NLRA), the creation of the Works Progress Administration (WPA), and other measures considerably more radical than those that had come in 1933. The NLRA, for example, helped unions get established and grow. The SSA provided the rudiments of a social welfare system as well as unemployment and retirement insurance. This new set of laws, known as the second New Deal, survived legal challenges and changed the United States, particularly by strengthening the role of the federal government.

Roosevelt's leftward political shift helped him to win the 1936 presidential election in a landslide. This election cemented a new electoral coalition that yoked the southern wing of the Democratic party with more liberal farmers and working-class voters who were labor union members in the North and West. The Democratic party began to win the votes of the large African-American populations in the great cities of the North. The great migration had effectively relocated tens of thousands of prospective black voters in northern urban centers, traditional strongholds of Democratic party machines, such as in Chicago. Institutionalized housing segregation combined with the often conscious choice to live in their own neighborhoods concentrated the black electorate and increased its political power. This power had already appeared in the 1928 election of Republican Oscar De Priest to the United States House of Representatives, the first African-American congressman from the North. In 1934, reflecting a shift in partisan allegiance, Chicago's black voters elected Democrat Arthur W. Mitchell to Congress to replace De Priest. Mitchell, a registered Republican at the outset of the Great Depression, switched to the Democratic party and thus became the first black Democrat ever to win a seat in the House of Representatives.

Mitchell's election was only the beginning of the change in black people's political party identification. The powerful black press fanned the shifting winds and many more black urban dwellers developed an intense interest in politics. They began to connect political power with the prospect of improving their economic conditions. By the end of the decade, black urban voters garnered noteworthy influence in key states such as Illinois, Ohio, Pennsylvania, and New York. This political consciousness led to the election of black state legislators in California, Illinois, Indiana, Kansas, Kentucky, New Jersey, New York, Ohio, Pennsylvania, and West Virginia.

In another indication of change, some Democrats began supporting antilynching legislation. Congressman Mitchell gave a strong speech printed in the *Congressional Record* in 1935 supporting President Roosevelt as an antilynching advocate. "No President," he declared, "has been more outspoken against the horrible crime of lynching than has Mr. Roosevelt. In speaking of lynching some time ago he characterized it as 'collective murder' and spoke of it as a crime which blackens the record of America." Mitchell told black audiences, "Let me say again, the attitude of the administration at the White House is absolutely fair and without prejudice, insofar as the Negro citizenry is concerned."

So the 1936 election results revealed that Roosevelt had captured the allegiance of most African Americans. Robert Vann, editor of the Pittsburgh *Courier* had urged black people, after casting their ballots, to go home to "turn Lincoln's picture to the wall." There are many complex reasons for this revolutionary transformation in black political allegiance. The shift to the Democratic party did not occur without anxiety. At least some black people feared that by joining the party they would open the door for even more white southern Democrats to assume national political power and thwart black advancement. But by 1936 most African-American voters were willing to take the risk.

Roosevelt's "Black Cabinet" in a 1938 photograph. Mary McLeod Bethune is in the center of the front row. The advisors included Robert Weaver, Eugene Kinckle Jones, Ambrose Caliver, and William H. Hastie among many others.

The increased participation of African Americans in the Democratic party sent chills down the spines of the white southern elite. The tension between black Democrats and white conservative Democrats erupted at the party's 1936 convention in Philadelphia. The seating of thirty-two black Democratic party delegates provoked the wrath of southern politicians. The selection of a black Baptist minister to open one session with a prayer especially outraged South Carolina Senator Ellison D. "Cotton Ed" Smith, who, accompanied by Mayor Burnet Maybank of Charleston, South Carolina, and one or two other delegates, marched ostentatiously off the floor proclaiming that they refused to support "any political organization that looks upon the Negro and caters to him as a political and social equal." Smith declared that he was "sick of the whole damn thing." Undaunted, the black minister simply observed that "Brother Smith needs more prayer." The next day when Congressman Mitchell of Illinois took to the floor, Ed Smith repeated his walkout. The South Carolina delegation subsequently adopted a protest resolution denouncing the appearance of black men on the convention's program. The protests of southern white politicians, however, had no effect on the political decisions of black men and women. Heeding the advice of the NAACP, they voted their personal interests.

Despite the rise of black people in the Democratic party, southern congressmen succeeded in excluding many African Americans from key government programs. For example, they insisted on denying the benefits of the National Labor Relations Act and Social Security Act to agricultural laborers and domestic servants. These white Southerners could not, however, stop the tilt toward fairer administration of programs or the revival of the push for equal rights, which had lain all but dormant since the end of the Reconstruction Era.

An examination of the Works Progress Administration (WPA) illustrates the changes that the second New Deal and the increasing shift of African Americans to the Democratic party wrought. The WPA, with Harry Hopkins (1890–1946) as its head, was created to employ the unemployed. Under Hopkins's direction, and sustained with $1.39 billion in federal funds, the WPA put thousands of men and women to work building new roads, hospitals, city halls, courthouses, and schools. Under the aegis of the WPA, American citizens built bridges, ports, and local water-supply systems. Larger scale projects included the Lincoln Tunnel under the Hudson River connecting New York and New Jersey, the Triborough Bridge system linking Manhattan to Long Island, and the Bonneville and Boulder Dams. (Boulder Dam was later renamed the Hoover Dam by a Republican-controlled Congress in 1946.)

The WPA was administered far more fairly than were the first New Deal programs. The national government explicitly rejected racial discrimination and worked to make sure local officials complied. Although far from perfect by 1939 it provided assistance to one million black families on a far more equitable basis than ever before.

The same pattern prevailed in the WPA's four arts programs—the Federal Art Project, the Federal Music Project, the Federal Theater Project, and the Federal Writers Project—which employed thousands of musicians, intellectuals, writers, and artists. A fifth program, the Historical Records Survey, created in 1937, sent teams of writers, including Zora Neale Hurston, to collect folklore and study various ethnic groups. One team collected the life histories and reminiscences of some two thousand former slaves.

Between 1935 and 1943 the WPA helped artists display their talents and made their work widely available. Among the black artists hired to adorn government buildings, post offices, and public parks were Aaron

In the 1930s black theater benefited greatly from the support of the WPA's Federal Theater Project. One of the most provocative and theatrically creative results was this production of Shakespeare's *Macbeth* with a cast composed entirely of black performers.

Douglas, Charles Alston, Richmond Barthe, Sargent Johnson, Archibald Motley, Jr., and Augusta Savage. Savage was a sculptor who worked in clay, marble, and bronze; she established arts schools in the 1930s—the Savage School of Arts and Crafts, Savage Studios, and the Uptown Art Laboratory. She became the first director of the Harlem Community Art Center in 1937. Her students included Jacob Lawrence, William Artis, Norman Lewis, and Elton Fax.

The Federal Theater Project established sixteen black theater units. Among their most notable productions was a version of *Macbeth* set in Haiti with an all-black cast. White actor John Houseman and black actress Rose McClendon directed the Harlem Federal Theater Project. This project—more than the others—proved controversial due to the fear of communist influence and the leftist political views of some African American writers and performers.

Black Protest during the Great Depression

During the 1930s African-American men and women initiated their own agenda and determined to use every resource at their disposal to destroy the obstacles to racial justice and barriers to equal opportunity. The NAACP sponsored a legal campaign against educational discrimination and political disfranchisement led by Charles Houston and Thurgood Marshall, mobilized black communities, and sustained hope in struggle. Black people benefitted from the New Deal, but less than white people did. The disparity between black and white lives was a spur to action. The juxtaposition of black subordination and misery alongside the new forms of federal aid so willingly distributed to white citizens convinced black Americans to intensify their own struggle for their American rights. Many embraced radical critiques of American capitalism, but few ever considered communism a viable alternative to American democracy. Black people would emerge from the Depression more determined than ever to make democracy work for them.

The NAACP and Civil Rights Struggles

During the 1930s the NAACP developed a new effectiveness as an advocate for African-American civil rights. The biracial organization took the lead in pressing the government to protect African-American rights and to eliminate the blatant racism in government programs. Part of the reason for this new dynamism was the astute leadership of Walter White, a man whose physical characteristics could have easily permitted him to pass for white—he had blonde hair and blue eyes—and turn away from the problems of black people. Instead he became an insistent voice of protest, personally investigating forty-two lynchings and eight race riots, and he was an ardent lobbyist for civil rights legislation and racial justice. Throughout the thirties African Americans of all hues moved into leadership positions in the NAACP and added their names to the membership roles of its many branches.

The new dynamism of the NAACP became apparent in 1930 when Walter White took a prominent role in the successful campaign to defeat Hoover's nomination of Circuit Court Judge John J. Parker of North Carolina to a seat on the United States Supreme Court. Parker had infuriated the organization because he openly embraced white supremacy, stating, for example, that the "participation of the Negro in politics is a source of evil and danger to both races." The NAACP formed a coalition with the American Federation of Labor to derail the Parker nomination. Although the NAACP could take only part of the credit, White trumpeted the victory and let it be known that African Americans would not be silent while "the Hoover administration proposed to conciliate southern white sentiment by sacrificing the Negro and his rights."

Du Bois Ignites a Controversy

The NAACP had critics, even within its own ranks. Many younger black people criticized its focus on civil liberties and deplored it for ignoring the economic misery of most African Americans. In 1934 W. E. B. Du Bois, editor of the NAACP's journal *The Crisis*, joined the chorus. Criticizing what he considered the group's overemphasis on integration, Du Bois advocated a program of self-determination he hoped would permit black people to develop "an economic nation within a nation." Du Bois acknowledged that this internal economy could only meet part of the needs of the African-American community. But he insisted it could be developed and expanded in many ways: "This smaller part could be so important and wield so much power that its influence upon the total economy of Negroes and the total industrial organization of the United States would be decisive for the great ends towards which the Negro moves."

The black intellectual community quickly attacked Du Bois for advocating "voluntary segregation." Sociologist E. Franklin Frazier, for example, called the idea of black businesses succeeding within a segregated economy a black upper-class fantasy and social myth. Nevertheless, Du Bois held fast to his position that the

NAACP should continue to oppose legal segregation yet combine that opposition with vigorous support to improve segregated institutions as long as discrimination persisted. He was eventually forced from the editorship of *The Crisis*, but his resignation did not end the controversy. By the late 1930s the NAACP had developed, alongside its older activities, a much greater emphasis on economic policy and worked to develop stronger ties to the burgeoning labor movement.

Challenging Racial Discrimination in the Courts

A dramatic expansion of its legal campaign against racial discrimination enhanced the NAACP's effectiveness. Central to this project was the hiring of Charles Hamilton Houston, a Harvard-trained African-American lawyer and scholar, to lead it. Houston had been vice-dean of Howard University Law School, which he had transformed into a powerful institution for training black attorneys in the intricacies of civil rights law. At the NAACP, Houston laid out a plan for a legal program to challenge inequality in education and the exclusion of black people from voting in the South. Houston used lawsuits both to force state and local governments to live up to the Constitution and to inspire community organization. "This is no star performance," he said of his strategy. "My ideal of administration is to make the movement self-perpetuating. . . . Our idea should be to press upon the opposition and public that what we have is a real program, sweeping up . . . [from] popular demand."

Houston did not focus directly on eliminating segregation, but rather sought to force southern states to equalize their facilities. Studies by the NAACP had revealed great disparities in per capita expenditures for white and black students, and huge differences in salaries paid to white and black teachers. In Georgia, for example, the average annual per pupil expenditure for white students was $36.29, compared with $4.59 for black students. White teachers' salaries averaged $97.88 per month, while black teachers received only $49.41. Houston was no supporter of segregation. He hoped to use litigation to secure judgments that would so increase the cost of separate institutions that states would be forced to abandon them.

To execute his agenda, Houston convinced Walter White to hire his former student at the Howard University Law School, Thurgood Marshall, in 1936. Marshall was born in Baltimore in 1908. His father was a dining-car waiter and club steward; his mother had been a teacher before her marriage. During the 1930s Marshall and Houston focused on bringing greater parity between black and white teachers, a project that they hoped would increase NAACP membership among teachers, their students, and parents. The two men, working with a remarkable network of African-American attorneys, also attempted to end discrimination against black men and women in professional and graduate schools. Inequalities were obvious here because many southern states offered no graduate facilities of any kind to black students. Like other campaigns, this focus on graduate education was intended to establish precedents that might be used to gain equality in other areas and as an organizing tool for developing strong local NAACP branches. The first significant accomplishment in the NAACP's legal campaign against segregation in graduate and professional education was the United States Supreme Court's 1938 decision in *Gaines v. Canada.* The Supreme Court ordered the state of Missouri to provide black citizens an opportunity to study law in a state-supported institution. Failure to do so, the Court held, would violate the equal protection of the law clause of the Fourteenth Amendment to the United States Constitution. Although Lloyd Gaines, the prospective student for whom the case was brought, disappeared before the final resolution of this challenge, Missouri hastily established a law school for African Americans at the historically black Lincoln University. In the 1940s several southern states, including North Carolina, Texas, Oklahoma, and South Carolina, followed Missouri's lead and established law schools for their black citizens.

Thrugood Marshall and the NAACP were encouraged by the Gaines decision to persist in challenging the constitutionality of the "separate but equal" doctrine. The case of *Sipuel v. Board of Regents of the University of Oklahoma* (1947) was another such effort. In this case Ada Lois Sipuel sought admission to the law school of the University of Oklahoma at Norman. In accordance with state statutes she was refused admission, but granted an out-of-state tuition award. Thurgood Marshall argued that this arrangement failed to meet the needs of the state's black citizens. The United States Supreme Court declared that Oklahoma was obliged under the equal protection clause of the Fourteenth Amendment to provide a legal education for Sipuel. The case established the principle that the state had to provide a separate law school for African-American students in their home states.

Heman Sweatt, a black mail carrier, tested this principle in a suit against the University of Texas Law School. In *Sweatt v. Painter* (1950), the U. S. Supreme Court again sided with the NAACP lawyers. In response to Sweatt's initial challenge Texas had created a separate law school that had inadequate library facilities, faculty, and support staff. It was separate but hardly equal. Marshall and local Texas black lawyers argued that the legal education offered Sweatt at the black law school was so inferior that it violated the equal protection clause of the Fourteenth Amendment. Marshall declared, "whether the University of Texas Law School is compared with the original or new law school for Negroes, we cannot find substantial equality in the educational opportunities offered white and Negro law students by the state. In terms of number of the faculty, variety of courses and opportunity for specialization, size of the student body, scope of the library, availability of law review and similar activities, the University of Texas Law School is superior." The victories registered in these early cases laid the legal foundation for the 1954 *Brown v. Topeka Board of Education* decision.

The fight against political disfranchisement also helped to mobilize local and state communities and branches. Nowhere was this more apparent than in Texas. In 1923 the Texas legislature enacted the Terrell Law, which expressly declared: "In no event shall a Negro be eligible to participate in a Democratic primary election . . . in . . . Texas." In the one-party South, the primary elections were more important than the general elections, which often merely rubber-stamped the choice made in the primary. Thus to be denied the right to vote in Democratic party primary elections was to be disfranchised. The NAACP developed a case to test the constitutionality of the Terrell Law and commenced a twenty-year battle through the courts. The Texas branches of the NAACP raised money and coordinated local involvement in the campaign to overthrow the Democratic white primary that disfranchised so many black Texans.

The Texas white primary fight was the most sustained and intense effort that any NAACP chapter undertook during the interwar period. It began in the 1920s and won its first victory when the Supreme Court ruled in 1927 in *Nixon v. Herndon* that the Texas Democratic primary was unconstitutional (see Chapter 17). At the national headquarters, Charles H. Houston and Thurgood Marshall orchestrated the assault. Their efforts were rewarded in subsequent decisions that further chipped away at the legal basis for the white primary. Finally, in 1944 the U. S. Supreme Court issued a ruling in *Smith v. Allwright* that ended the white primary altogether. It was the NAACP's greatest legal victory to that time. Many more would soon follow.

Black Women and Community Organizing

Black women made exceptional contributions to the NAACP during the 1930s through their successful fund-raising efforts and membership drives. Three agitators for racial justice were Daisy Adams Lampkin (c. 1884–1965), Juanita Mitchell (1913–1992), and Ella Baker (1903–1986). These women worked closely with White and the NAACP throughout the Depression and World War II. Lampkin, a native of Washington, DC, became in 1915 the president of the Negro Women's Franchise League, a group dedicated to fighting for the vote. During World War I she directed Liberty Bond sales in the black community of Pennsylvania's Allegheny County and in Pittsburgh, selling some $2 million worth of government securities. In 1930, Walter White enlisted her as regional field secretary of the NAACP, a post she held until she was made national field secretary in 1935. She continued raising funds for the NAACP and played leading roles within organized black womanhood.

Juanita E. Jackson was born in Hot Springs, Arkansas, and raised in Baltimore, Maryland. She earned a degree in education from the University of Pennsylvania in 1931, then returned to Baltimore, where she helped to found the City-Wide Young People's Forum. This organization encouraged young people to discuss and plan attacks on such scourges as unemployment, segregation, and lynching. The success of the group, which she headed from 1931 to 1934, attracted Walter White's attention and he subsequently offered her the leadership of the NAACP's new youth program. From 1935 to 1938 she served as NAACP national youth director. In 1938 Jackson married fellow civil rights activist Clarence Mitchell, had four sons, and directed the NAACP's voter registration campaigns. In 1950 she received a law degree from the University of Maryland. As the first black woman admitted to practice law in Maryland she embarked upon a series of cases that helped to destroy racial segregation on the state's public beaches and in its public schools.

Ella Baker, who became one of the most important women in the civil rights movement of the 1950s and 1960s, began her life's work during the Depression. Born in Norfolk, Virginia, Baker moved to New York City in 1927 and worked as a waitress and as an organizer involved in radical politics. She was also on the staff of two local newspapers, *The American West Indian News*, and *Negro National News*. Within two years after her arrival she had cofounded with George Schuyler the Young Negroes' Cooperative League in Harlem. The group practiced collective decision making and attempted to involve all segments of the community in the cooperatives. As she worked with the young men and women, Baker developed a strong belief in grass-roots mobilization. Meanwhile, she also worked with women's and labor groups, such as the Harlem Housewives Cooperative, the Women's Day Workers and Industrial League, and the YWCA. In 1935 she served as publicity director of the Sponsoring Committee of the National Negro Congress. In 1936 she worked as a teacher with the WPA and eventually became an assistant project supervisor of the WPA. Walter White was impressed with her relentless organizing and manage-

The NAACP in the 1930s and 1940s depended on the formidable fund-raising talents of black women like Daisy Lampkin (shown here in a Black Baptist church), Ella Baker, and Juanita Mitchell. These women played a major role in building NAACP membership.

ment skills. After much persuasion Baker accepted, in 1941, White's offer to become an assistant field secretary of the NAACP. This position enabled her to travel across the country and throughout the South, making friendships that would serve her well in the coming decades. From 1943 to 1946 Baker worked as director of NAACP branches and measurably enhanced the membership of the organization. After resigning from the NAACP she joined the staff of the New York Urban League.

Other black women organized outside the NAACP. Black women in Detroit provide a potent illustration of this kind of activity. On June 10, 1930, fifty black women responded to a call issued by Fannie B. Peck, wife of Reverend William H. Peck, pastor of the two-thousand-member Bethel African Methodist Episcopal Church and the president of the Booker T. Washington Trade Association. Out of this initial meeting emerged the Detroit Housewives' League, an organization that combined economic nationalism and black women's self-determination to help black families and businesses survive the Depression. Peck had been inspired by M. A. L. Holsey, secretary of the National Negro Business League. Holsey described the directed spending campaigns that enabled housewives in Harlem to consolidate their economic power to persuade businesses to hire black women and children. Peck became convinced that such an organization would be equally as successful in Detroit. An admirer recalled that Peck effectively "focused the attention of women on the most essential, yet most unfamiliar factor in the building of homes, communities, and nations, namely, 'The Spending Power of Women.' "

The Detroit organization grew rapidly. By 1934 ten thousand black women belonged to it. According to Peck, the black woman had finally realized "that she has been traveling through a blind alley, making sacrifices to educate her children with no thought as to their obtaining employment after leaving school." The only requirement for membership was a pledge to support black businesses, buy black products, and patronize black professionals, thereby keeping money in the community. The League quickly spread to other cities. Housewives' leagues in Chicago, Baltimore, Washington, Durham, North Carolina, Harlem, and Cleveland used boycotts of merchants who refused to sell black products and employ black children as clerks or stock persons to secure an estimated seventy-five thousand new jobs for black people.

Organized Labor and Black America

The relationship of African Americans to labor unions changed profoundly during the 1930s. Before this time most local unions affiliated with the national American Federation of Labor barred black people or restricted them to segregated locals. The railroad unions, which called themselves "brotherhoods," excluded black workers entirely. The New Deal, especially after 1935, did much to transform the labor movement. The National Labor Relations Act and the militancy of workers provided the opportunity to organize the nation's great mass production industries. Still, leaders of the AFL dragged their feet, unwilling to incorporate into their unions the masses of unskilled workers, many of whom were African American or recent European immigrants. Frustrated by this situation, in 1935 John L. Lewis (1880–1969), head of the United Mine Workers, and his followers formed the Committee for Industrial Organization (CIO) to take on the task.

Unlike the AFL, the CIO was committed to interracial and multiethnic organizing and so enabled more African Americans to participate in the labor movement. Its leaders knew that it was in organized labor's best interest to admit black men and women to membership. As one black union organizer said, "We colored folks can't organize without you and you white folks can't organize without us." But it took a massive change in outlook to achieve this unity. By 1940, the CIO had enlisted approximately 210,000 black members. Unions that valued and sustained interracial cooperation included the International Mine, Mill, and Smelter Workers; the Food, Tobacco, and Agricultural Workers Union; and the United Farm Equipment and Metal Workers.

A. Philip Randolph's Brotherhood of Sleeping Car Porters (BSCP) remained with the AFL, but it also benefited from New Deal legislation. In 1934 Congress had amended the Railway Labor Act in a way that helped the BSCP to overcome the opposition of the Pullman company. The law required that corporations bargain in good faith with unions if the unions could demonstrate through elections monitored by the National Mediation Board that they genuinely represented the corporations' employees. The Pullman company resisted, but in 1937, long after an election certified the BSCP as the workers' representative, the company finally recognized the brotherhood. Then—and only then—did the AFL grant the BSCP full membership as an international union. After more than twelve years, A. Philip Randolph and thousands of black men won their struggles against a giant corporation and a powerful labor organization. These were no small victories.

Although most black people in unions were men, some unions also represented and helped improve the lives of black working women. For example, there had been a rigid hierarchy among workers in the tobacco industry since the early nineteeth century, one of the few areas of the economy outside agriculture or domestic service that employed many black women. Jobs were assigned on the basis of race and gender, with black women receiving the most difficult and tedious job, that of "stemmer." In 1939, stemmer Louise "Mama" Harris instigated a series of walkouts at the I. N. Vaughn Company in Richmond. The strikes, which were supported by CIO affiliates, including the white women of the International Ladies Garment Workers Union, led to the formation of the Tobacco Workers Organizing Committee, another CIO affiliate. In 1943, black women union leaders and activists, including Theodosia Simpson and Miranda Smith, were involved in a strike against the R. J. Reynolds tobacco company to force it to the negotiating table. Smith later became southern regional director of the Food, Tobacco, Agricultural, and Allied Workers of America. It was the highest position held by a black woman in the labor movement up to that time.

The Communist Party and African Americans

Throughout the 1930s the Communist party intensified its support of African Americans' efforts to address unemployment and job discrimination and to seek social justice. Some African Americans were attracted to the party because of its militant antiracism and its determination to be interracial. The party expelled members who exhibited racial prejudice and gave black men key leadership positions. James Ford, an African American, ran as the party's vice-presidential candidate in the election of 1932. While few black men and women actually joined the Communist party, some became increasingly sympathetic to left-wing ideas and prescriptions as the Depression wore on.

Many black workers were drawn to the Communist party because it criticized the refusal of organized white labor to include them. The communists maintained that "the low standard of living of Negro workers is made use of by the capitalists to reduce the wages of the white workers." They chided "the mis-leaders of labor, the heads of the reformist and reactionary trade union organizations" for refusing to organize black workers. They insisted "this anti-Negro attitude of the reactionary labor leaders helps to split the ranks of labor, allows the employers to carry out their policy of 'divide and rule,' frustrates the efforts of the working class to emancipate itself from the yoke of capitalism, and dims the class-consciousness of the white workers as well as of the Negro workers." Indeed, much of the push for racial equality within the CIO emanated from those connected with the party.

The International Labor Defense and the "Scottsboro Boys"

The Scottsboro case brought the Communist party to the attention of many African Americans. The case began when nine black youths who had caught a ride on a freight train in Alabama were tried, convicted, and sentenced to death for allegedly raping two white women. Their ordeal began on the night of March 25, 1931, when they were accosted by a group of young white hobos. A fight broke out. The black youths threw the white youths off the train. The losers filed a complaint with the Scottsboro, Alabama, sheriff, charging that black hoodlums had viciously assaulted them. The sheriff ordered his deputies to round up every black person on the train. The sweep netted the nine young black men: Ozie Powell, Clarence Norris, Charlie Weems, Olen Montgomery, Willie Robertson, Haywood Patterson, Eugene

PROFILE

Angelo Herndon

In the South, the Communist party gravitated toward those areas where black and white laborers were grossly exploited. The party's efforts in Georgia, Alabama, and Mississippi produced black organizers such as Hosea Hudson, Nate Shaw, and Angelo Herndon, who by virtue of their activism became targets of white supremacists.

In 1932, a young organizer, Angelo Herndon was arrested, tried, and convicted in Atlanta for inciting insurrection. One of thirteen children, Herndon was born May 6, 1913, in Ohio. Seeking better opportunities, Herndon, at age thirteen escaped the poverty of his home region to work in the coal mines in Alabama. At eighteen he was already a seasoned miner but deeply disillusioned and angry at the exploitation of coal miners. He attended a meeting called by the Communist party and was impressed by its commitment to equality, both racially and socially. He joined the party and poured enormous energy into organizing and recruiting members from among the mine workers and the unemployed. In 1934, Angelo Herndon explained why he joined the party:

Following his release from prison in Georgia, Angelo Herndon was met at New York City's Penn Station by a group of supporters that included Ruby Bates and Communist leader Robert Minor in 1937.

> All my life I'd been sweated and stepped on and Jim-Crowed. I lay on my belly in the mines for a few dollars a week, and saw my pay stolen and slashed, and my buddies killed. I lived in the worst section of town, and rode behind the "Colored" signs of streetcars, as though there was something disgusting about me? I heard myself called "nigger" and "darky" and I had to say "Yes, sir" to every white man. . . . I had always detested it, but I had never known that anything could be done about it. And here, all of a sudden, I had found organizations . . . that weren't scared to come out for equality for the Negro people, and for the rights of workers. The Jim-Crow system, the wage–slave system, weren't everlasting after all! It was like all of a sudden turning a corner on a dirty, old street and finding yourself facing a broad, shining highway. . . . I felt then, and I know now, that the Communist program is the only program that the Southern workers—whites and Negroes both—can possibly accept in the long run. It's the only program that does justice to the southern worker's ideas that everybody ought to have an equal chance, and that every man has rights that must be respected.

The party sent Herndon to Atlanta, Georgia, where he organized an interracial relief group and staged peaceful demonstrations against hunger. This was to prove his undoing. One week later, while picking up his mail at the post office, he was arrested on the charge that he had violated an old ordinance forbidding black and white people from mingling together. Herndon's trial and conviction made him the best-known African-American communist in the nation. The case underscored the fear that white Southerners had concerning the specter of social equality across racial lines. The Communist party assigned a young black attorney, Benjamin Davis, Jr. of Atlanta, to represent Herndon. Davis challenged the constitutionality of the ordinance as well as Atlanta's jury system, which excluded African Americans from service. Davis's defense was unsuccessful and the judge sentenced Herndon to twenty years on a chain gang. The severity of the sentence and the judge's racist sentiments sparked a nationwide movement to free Herndon as black organizations, labor unions, and religious groups joined with the Communist party to fight for Herndon's immediate release. After four years of appeals, in 1937 the United States Supreme Court, in a five-to-four decision, declared Georgia's slave insurrection law unconstitutional and ordered the state to let him go.

Williams, Andy Wright, and Roy Wright. The police also discovered two young white women: nineteen-year-old Victoria Price and seventeen-year-old Ruby Bates.

Afraid of being arrested, and perhaps ashamed of being hobos, Price and Bates falsely claimed that the nine black youths had sexually assaulted them. On the basis of that accusation, the "Scottsboro Boys" (ranging in ages from thirteen to twenty), were given a hasty trial. They never had a chance. Their white, court-appointed attorney came to court drunk each day. Three days after the trial started, and fifteen days after their arrest, the jurors found all of them guilty. Eight received the death sentence and the youngest, a thirteen-year-old, was sentenced to life imprisonment, even though medical examinations of Price and Bates proved that neither had been raped.

While other organizations either dawdled or refused to intervene, the Communist party's International Labor Defense (ILD) rushed to the aid of the "boys" by appealing the conviction and death sentence to the United States Supreme Court. The case produced two important decisions that reaffirmed black people's right to the basic protections that all other American citizens enjoyed. In *Powell v. Alabama* (1932), the Court ruled that the nine Scottsboro defendants had not been given adequate legal counsel and that the trial had taken place in a hostile and volatile atmosphere. Asserting that the youths' right to due process as set forth in the Fourteenth Amendment had been violated, the Court ordered a new trial. Alabama did as instructed, but the new trial resulted in another guilty verdict and sentences of death or life imprisonment. The ILD promptly appealed and in *Norris v. Alabama* (1935), the Supreme Court decided that all Americans have the right to a trial by a jury of their peers. The systematic exclusion of African Americans from the Scottsboro juries, the Court held, denied the defendants equal protection under the law, which the Fourteenth Amendment guaranteed. Chief Justice Charles Evans Hughes pointed out that no black citizens had served on juries in the Alabama counties for decades, even though there were many qualified to serve. The Court noted that the exclusion was blatant racial discrimination and called for yet another trial.

Despite these stunning defeats and increasing evidence that the "boys" had been falsely convicted, Alabama still pursued the case. Even when Ruby Bates publicly admitted that the rape charge had been a hoax, white Alabamians ignored her. Finally, in 1937, Alabama dropped its charges against five of the nine men, and in the 1940s the state released those still in jail. Altogether, nine innocent black men had collectively served some three-quarters of a century in prison. Clarence Willie Norris, however, escaped and fled to Michigan, returning decades later to receive a ceremonious pardon from Governor George Wallace. When a reporter asked Norris how he felt, he declared, "I'm just glad to be free." The experience had taught him "to stand up for your rights, even if it kills you. That's all life consists of."

Debating Communist Leadership

Throughout the Scottsboro case, the NAACP tried unsuccessfully to wrest control from the Communist party. Indeed, as the case evolved, tensions and competition between the Communist party and the NAACP for leadership of black America flared into open hostility. At first, the NAACP had hesitated to defend accused rapists, but it moved more decisively after the Communist party had taken the lead.

The contest between the NAACP and the communists reveals the differences between the two groups. The party organized protest marches and demonstrations and used its press to denounce more cautious middle-class organizations. In Harlem, for example, the communists staged a 1931 protest march that attracted over three thousand black men and women and ended with an address by Ada Wright, the mother of two of the defendants, who praised the ILD for its help. The NAACP countered with a carefully orchestrated campaign that questioned the sincerity and effectiveness of the communists and sought to repair its own reputation as a respectable and effective advocate for African Americans.

Black public opinion divided in its evaluation of the party. Some black men and women applauded the communists. Journalist Eugene Gordon wrote:

> Negro workers think of the countless times Communists have been beaten insensible for defending . . . Negro workers. . . . They see the ILD . . . supported by the Communist Party, rushing to the defense of the nine Negro youths at Scottsboro before other Negro organizations in the country condescended to glance superciliously in their direction. . . . Seeing and hearing all these things, the Negro worker in the United States would be a fool not to recognize the leadership that he has been waiting for since his freedom.

Historian Carter G. Woodson praised the Communist party in the *New York Age:*

> I have talked with any number of Negroes who call themselves Communists, and I have never heard one express a desire to destroy anyone or anything but oppression. . . . Negroes who are charged with being Communists advocate the stoppage of peonage, equality in employment of labor. . . . If this makes a man 'Red,' the world's greatest reformers belong to this class, and we shall have to condemn our greatest statesmen, some of whom have attained the presidency of the United States.

But other African Americans ridiculed the party. George Schuyler, a columnist for the Pittsburgh *Courier*, used his razor-sharp wit to castigate the party and persuade black people that its claim to champion African Americans was a lie. Shuyler objected to the communists' "campaign of vilification . . . against the NAACP:"

> No Ku Kluxer ever denounced the latter organization more vigorously and unfairly. The Communists know they are lying when they assert time and time again that the NAACP wants to see the boys convicted and is betraying the race. They have quite the same sort of grooved mentality as Ku Kluxers, Garveyites and other race fanatics, black and white. The course they tentatively pursue is held the only true one and whoever takes exception is denounced as an enemy of humanity, even though they may have to change that course in a few months.

Although most African Americans applauded the antiracist work that the Communist party supported and performed, there was no chance that they would defect from the traditional American political system as W. E. B. Du Bois wrote in 1931:

> American Negroes do not propose to be the shock troops of the Communist Revolution, driven out in the front to death, cruelty and humiliation in order to win victories for white workers. . . . Negroes know perfectly well that whenever they try to lead revolution in America, the nation will unite as one fist to crush them and them alone.

The National Negro Congress

The infighting between the Communist party and other groups doomed a major attempt to unite all the disparate African-American protest groups into the National Negro Congress (NNC). John P. Davis, a Washington-based economist, organized the NNC, modeling it on his experience as the executive secretary of the Joint Committee on National Recovery (JCNR), a coalition of black groups that pressed for fairness in the early New Deal. The NNC was to be a federation of organizations on a national scale supported by regional councils. Over 800 delegates representing 585 organizations attended its first meeting, held in Chicago in 1936. However, prominent black activists, leaders, and intellectuals were conspicuously absent, notably those associated with the NAACP. A. Philip Randolph was elected president, and Davis became the executive secretary. The group resolved not to be dominated by any one political faction and to build on the strength of all parts of the black community. Although handicapped by lack of funds, the NNC initially worked effectively at the local or community level. With branches in approximately seventy cities, the organization gained for its members increased employment opportunities, better housing, and adequate relief work.The NNC also prodded labor unions, in particular the CIO, to fight for better conditions and higher wages for black workers.

At the NNC's second meeting in Philadelphia in 1937, a skeptical Davis maintained that the Democratic party would never allow black people to benefit justly and fairly from the New Deal. Eventually the increasing importance of communists in the NNC alienated most other groups and reduced the organization's ability to speak for the majority of black people. By 1940 it was greatly weakened. Randolph was voted out of office, and the once-promising NNC became little more than a front group for the Communist party.

The Tuskegee Study

The 1930s marked the rising prominence of black scholars and intellectuals, but paradoxically, the decade also witnessed the worst manifestation of racism in American science. This most shocking episode of virulent bigotry and racial mistreatment occurred in Macon County, Alabama. There, in 1932, United States Public Health Service (USPHS) officials initiated a major study of syphilis, a sexually transmitted disease that can cause paralysis, insanity, and heart failure. For the subjects of its program—entitled the Tuskegee Study of Untreated Syphilis in the Male Negro—the USPHS recruited 622 black men, all of them poor sharecroppers and the majority illiterate. Of these men, 431 had advanced cases of syphilis; the rest were free of the disease and served as controls for comparison.

The Tuskegee Study was called a treatment program, but it turned out to be an experiment, designed to chart the progression and development of a potentially fatal disease. To gain the trust of the men, the government doctors centered their work at Tuskegee Institute and hired a black nurse, Eunice Rivers, who convinced the men that they had "bad blood" and needed special treatment. Although the drug penicillin, which could cure the disease, became available in the 1940s, the sharecroppers never received it. Instead, they were given ineffective placebos, which they were told would cure them.

Initially the Tuskegee Study was to last only six to twelve months, but it was repeatedly extended. The men received regular physical examinations, which included a painful lumbar puncture. This insertion of a needle into the spinal cord to obtain fluid for diagnosis often caused the men severe headaches, and in a few isolated cases, resulted in paralysis and even death. For almost forty years, Tuskegee Study doctors

VOICES

Hoboing in Alabama

Ralph Ellison, the noted author of the great novel Invisible Man *(1952), here vividly recalls his harrowing experience as a young black "hobo" in the aftermath of the arrest of the "Scottsboro Boys":*

During June of 1933, I found myself traveling by freight train in an effort to reach Tuskegee Institute in time to take advantage of a scholarship granted me. Having little money and no time left in which to earn the fare for a ticket, I grabbed an armful of freight car, a form of illegal travel quite common during the Great Depression. In fact, so many young men, young women, prostitutes, gamblers, and even some quite respectable but impoverished elderly and middle-aged couples were hoboing that it was quite difficult for the railroad to control such passengers. I justify this out of sheer desperation, college being my one hope of improving my condition.

But I was young and adventurous and regarded hoboing as the next best thing to floating down the Mississippi on a raft. My head was full of readings of the Rover Boys and Huckleberry Finn. I converted hoboing into a lark until I found myself in the freight yards of Decatur, Alabama, where two white railroad detectives laying about them with the barrels of long nickel-plated .45 revolvers forced some forty or fifty of us, black and white alike, off the train and ordered us to line up along the tracks. For me, this was a most frightening moment. Not only was I guilty of stealing passage on a freight train, but I realized that I had been caught in the act in the town where, at that very moment, the Scottsboro case was being tried. The case and the incident leading to it were widely reported in the black press, and what I had read of the atmosphere of the trial led me to believe that the young men in the case had absolutely no possibility of receiving a just decision. As I saw it, the trial was a macabre circus, a kangaroo proceeding that would be soon followed by an enactment of the gory rite of lynching, that ultimate form of racial victimage.

I had no idea of what the detectives intended to do with me, but given the atmosphere of the town, I feared that it would be most unpleasant and brutal. I, too might well be a sacrificial scapegoat, simply because I was the same race as the accused young men then being prepared for death. Therefore, when a group of white boys broke and ran, I plunged into their midst, and running far closer to the ground than I had ever managed to do as a high school football running back, I kept running and moving until I came to a shed with a railroad loading dock, under which I scooted; and there I remained until dawn, when I grabbed the first thing that was smoking and headed south.

A few days later I reached Tuskegee, but that scrape with the law—the fear, the horror and sense of helplessness before legal injustice—was most vivid in my mind, and it has so remained.

QUESTIONS

1. How does Ralph Ellison's experience as a hobo illuminate the nature of race relations in the South?
2. How did the "Scottsboro Boys" case increase Ellison's sense of vulnerability? Why were so many people engaged in "hoboing"? How did the black experience of "hoboing" differ from that of white Americans?

Source: Ralph Ellison, "Perspective of Literature," in *Going to the Territory* (New York: Vintage Books, 1995), pp. 324–25.

observed the men, keeping careful records of their health and performing autopsies on those who died; but they never treated them for syphilis. So little understood was the Tuskegee Study that men not only remained in the program, but believed that they were fortunate to have the physical examination, the hot lunches provided on examination days, and the burial allowance the government guaranteed their families. The medical community knew of the Tuskegee experiment, but the general public learned of it only in 1972 when a reporter broke the story. Black attorney Fred D. Gray of Alabama sued the U.S. government on behalf of the participants and their families, but before the case went to trial, the government made a $9 million settlement to the Tuskegee survivors and the descendants of those who had died.

Timeline

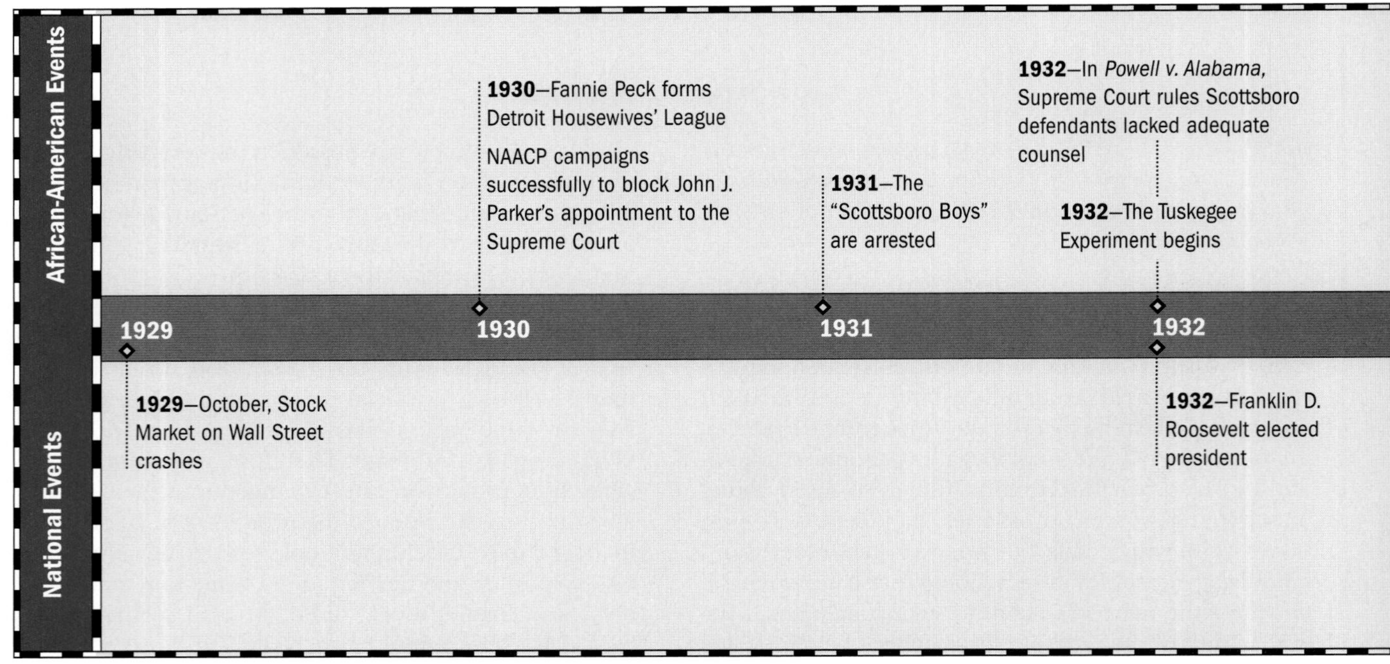

Conclusion

Notable political changes occurred during the early 1930s: the NAACP came of age, black women found their voice, white left-wing leaders joined with black men and women in interracial alliances, organized labor bridged the race chasm, and black men and women switched from the Republican party to the Democratic party. The New Deal had stimulated some economic recovery, and more important, laid the basis for a strong national state and a political coalition that, beginning with World War II, would sharply challenge the nation's racial system.

Recommended Reading

John Egerton. *Speak Now against the Day: The Generation before the Civil Rights Movement in the South.* New York: Knopf, 1994. An excellent survey of the period before the southern civil rights era, with chapters on the Depression in the South and black and white Southerners' reactions to it.

James H. Jones. *Bad Blood: The Tuskegee Syphilis Experiment.* New York: Free Press, 1981. The best and most comprehensive study of the Tuskegee experiment.

Robin D. G. Kelley. *Hammer and Hoe: Alabama Communists during the Great Depression.* Chapel Hill, NC: University of North Carolina Press, 1990. A splendid study of the radicalizing activism of working people in the steel industry and on the farm during the thirties. Kelley does an excellent job of showing why the Communists appealed to black workers.

Mark Naison. *Communists in Harlem during the Depression.* Urbana, IL: University of Illinois Press, 1983. A well-researched and clear-sighted study of the Communist party in Harlem and the history of the National Negro Congress.

Susan Reverby. *Tuskegee Truths: Rethinking the Tuskegee Syphillis Study.* Chapel Hill, NC: University of North Carolina Press, 2000.

Harvard Sitkoff. *A New Deal for Blacks: The Emergence of Civil Rights as a National Issue, Vol. I: Depression Decade.* New York: Oxford University Press, 1978. An important work that covers the New Deal era and presents it as a period when the groundwork for the civil rights movement was laid.

Patricia Sullivan. *Days of Hope: Race and Democracy in the New Deal Era.* Chapel Hill, NC: University of North Carolina Press, 1996. An invaluable study showing how the ideas of civil rights and democracy were forged in the New Deal South.

Raymond Wolters. *Negroes and the Great Depression: The Problem of Economic Recovery.* Westport, CT: Greenwood Publisher Group Incorporated, 1974. A solid survey of African Americans in the Depression that covers the impact of the Depression on African Americans, the workings of the Black Cabinet, and the effects of the New Deal agencies on the lives of black Americans.

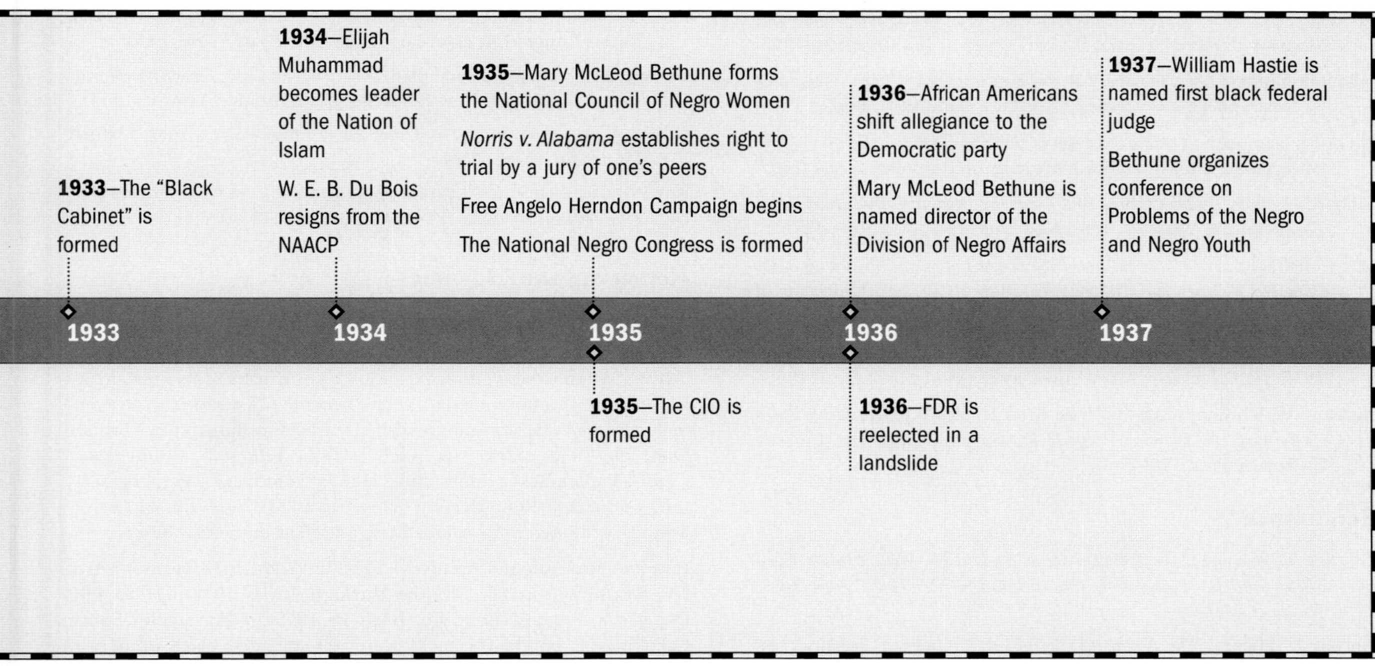

Additional Bibliography

Politics

Adam Fairclough. *Better Day Coming: Blacks and Equality, 1890–2000.* New York: Viking, 2001.

Kenneth W. Goings. *"The NAACP Comes of Age": The Defeat of Judge John J. Parker.* Bloomington, IN: Indiana University Press, 1990.

Charles V. Hamilton. *Adam Clayton Powell, Jr., the Political Biography of an American Dilemma.* New York: Atheneum, 1991.

Darlene Clark Hine. *Black Victory: The Rise and Fall of the White Primary in Texas.* Millwood, NY: KTO Press, 1979.

Charles F. Kellogg. *NAACP: A History of the National Association for the Advancement of Colored People.* Baltimore: Johns Hopkins University Press, 1967.

John B. Kirby. *Black Americans in the Roosevelt Era: Liberalism and Race.* Knoxville, TN: University of Tennessee Press, 1980.

Christopher R. Reed. *The Chicago NAACP and the Rise of Black Professional Leadership, 1910–1966.* Bloomington, IN: Indiana University Press, 1997.

Bernard Sternsher, ed. *The Negro in Depression and War: Prelude to Revolution, 1930–1945.* Chicago: Quadrangle Books, 1969.

Mark V. Tushnet. *The NAACP's Legal Strategy against Segregated Education, 1925–1950.* Chapel Hill, NC: University of North Carolina Press, 1987.

Nancy J. Weiss. *Farewell to the Party of Lincoln: Black Politics in the Age of Lincoln.* Princeton, NJ: Princeton University Press, 1983.

Labor

Lizabeth Cohen. *Making a New Deal: Industrial Workers in Chicago, 1919–1939.* New York: Cambridge University Press, 1990.

Dennis C. Dickerson. *Out of the Crucible: Black Steelworkers in Western Pennsylvania, 1875–1980.* Albany, NY: SUNY Press, 1986.

William H. Harris. *The Harder We Run: Black Workers since the Civil War.* New York: Oxford University Press, 1982.

August Meier and Elliott Rudwick. *Black Detroit and the Rise of the UAW.* New York: Oxford University Press, 1979.

Education

James D. Anderson. *The Education of Blacks in the South, 1860–1935.* Chapel Hill, NC: University of North Carolina Press, 1988.

Horace M. Bond. *The Education of the Negro in the American Social Order.* New York: Octagon Books, 1934, rev. 1966.

Richard Kluger. *Simple Justice: The History of Brown v. Board of Education and Black America's Struggle for Equality*, 1976.

Mark V. Tushnet. *Making Civil Rights Law: Thurgood Marshall and the Supreme Court, 1935–1961*, 1994.

Doxey Wilkerson. *Special Problems in Negro Education.* Washington, DC: U.S. Government Printing Office, 1939.

Black Radicalism

Dan Carter. *Scottsboro: A Tragedy of the American South.* Baton Rouge, LA: Louisiana State University Press, 1969.

Kenneth W. Goings. *Mammy and Uncle Mose: Black Collectibles and American Stereotyping.* Bloomington, IN: Indiana University Press, 1994.

Michael K. Honey. *Southern Labor and Black Civil Rights: Organizing Memphis Workers.* Urbana, IL: University of Illinois Press, 1993.

Jacqueline Jones. *Labor of Love, Labor of Sorrow: Black Women, Work, and the Family from Slavery to the Present.* New York: Basic Books, 1985.

Nicholas Natanson. *The Black Image in the New Deal: The Politics of FSA Photography.* Knoxville, TN: University of Tennessee Press, 1992.

Richard H. Pells. *Radical Visions and American Dreams: Culture and Social Thought in the Depression Years.* New York: Harper & Row, 1973.

Daryl Michael Scott. *Contempt and Pity: Social Policy and the Image of the Damaged Black Psyche, 1880–1996.* Chapel Hill, NC: University of North Carolina Press, 1997.

Mark Solomon. *The Cry Was Unity: Communists and African Americans, 1917–1936.* Jackson, MS: University Press of Mississippi, 1998.

Richard W. Thomas. *Life for Us Is What We Make It: Building Black Community in Detroit, 1915–1945.* Bloomington, IN: Indiana University Press, 1992.

Economics

Charles T. Banner-Haley. *To Do Good and to Do Well: Middle Class Blacks and the Depression, Philadelphia, 1929–1941.* New York: Garland, 1993.

Abram L. Harris. *The Negro as Capitalist: A Study of Banking and Business among American Negroes.* Originally published by the American Academy of Political and Social Sciences, 1936; Reprint, Chicago: Urban Research Press, 1992.

Alexa Benson Henderson. *Atlanta Life Insurance Company: Guardian of Black Economic Dignity.* Tuscaloosa, AL: University of Alabama Press, 1990.

Robert E. Weems, Jr. *Black Business in the Black Metropolis: The Chicago Metropolitan Assurance Company, 1924–1985.* Bloomington, IN: Indiana University Press, 1996.

Biography and Autobiography

Andrew Buni. *Robert L. Vann of the Pittsburgh Courier.* Pittsburgh: University of Pittsburgh Press, 1974.

Joanne Grant. *Ella Baker: Freedom Bound.* New York: John Wiley, 1998.

Wil Haywood. *King of the Cats: The Life and Times of Adam Clayton Powell, Jr.* Boston: Houghton Mifflin, 1993.

Spencie Love. *One Blood: The Death and Resurrection of Charles R. Drew.* Chapel Hill, NC: University of North Carolina Press, 1996.

Genna Rae McNeil. *Groundwork: Charles Hamilton Houston and the Struggle for Civil Rights.* Philadelphia: University of Pennsylvania Press, 1983.

Nell Irvin Painter. *The Narrative of Hosea Hudson: His Life as a Negro Communist in the South.* Cambridge, MA: Harvard University Press, 1979.

Paula F. Pfeffer. *A. Philip Randolph, Pioneer of the Civil Rights Movement.* Baton Rouge, LA: Louisiana State University Press, 1990.

George S. Schuyler. *Black and Conservative: The Autobiography of George S. Schuyler.* New Rochelle, NY: Arlington House, 1966.

Gilbert Ware. *William Hastie: Grace under Pressure.* New York: Oxford University Press, 1984.

Roy Wilkins with Tom Mathews. *Standing Fast: The Autobiography of Roy Wilkins.* New York: Da Capo Press, 1994.

Retracing the Odyssey

Apollo Theatre (212-749-5838), 253 West 125th St., Manhattan, New York. Monday through Saturday tours, appointment only. Admission charge. When other venues were closed to African Americans, many talented men and women destined to become top performers in twentieth-century America launched their careers at the Apollo Theatre. Since the 1930s, performers such as Duke Ellington, Count Basie, Charlie Parker, Bessie Smith, Billie Holiday, and Ella Fitzgerald graced the Apollo stage. Renown comedians such as Bill Cosby, Richard Pryor, Redd Foxx honed their talents here, as well as numerous others.

Bethune Museum and Archives (202-332-1233), 1318 Vermont Ave. NW, Washington, D.C. Monday through Friday 10:00 A.M. to 4:00 P.M. Mary McLeod Bethune, born in 1875 in Mayesville, South Carolina was one of the most politically engaged black women in the first half of the twentieth century. She was the president of Bethune-Cookman College in Daytona Beach, Florida, when President Franklin Delano Roosevelt appointed her the Director of Negro Affairs of the National Youth Council. An ardent Black club woman, Bethune is celebrated as the founder, in 1935, and first president of the National Council of Negro Women (NCNW). It remains a significant umbrella group for organizations of black women. The Bethune Museum and Archive Center was her home and headquarters of the NCNW from 1943 to 1966. It contains exhibits and sponsors programs that emphasize the contributions of African-American women to American society. The Archive contains important manuscript collections and other research materials pertaining to the NCNW and to black women's history.

Wright Museum of African-American History (313-494-5800). East Warren Avenue and Brush Street, Detroit, Michigan. Tuesday through Sunday, 9:30 A.M. to 5:00 P.M. Voluntary donation. The largest African-American history museum in America. The exhibits vary, but two permanent exhibits depict the middle passage of Africans to the Americas. It includes a full-scale model of slaves chained in an eighteenth-century ship. The Field to Factory exhibit documents the Great Migration of African Americans from the rural South to the industrial North during the twentieth century. It sponsors a variety of educational programs throughout the year.

REVIEW, RESEARCH & INTERACT

REVIEW QUESTIONS

1. Why did most black Americans switch to the Democratic party? How did President Roosevelt entice black people to identify with the Democratic party and abandon their long association with the Republican party?
2. How did black people respond to and survive the Great Depression? How did the experiences of black women during the Depression reflect their race, class, and gender status in American society?
3. How did the New Deal agencies and programs affect the lives of African Americans and their communities? How did the New Deal adversely affect black sharecroppers, tenants, and farmers?
4. Discuss the political, social, and economic repercussions of the large-scale migration of African Americans out of the South during the 1930s.
5. Compare and contrast the Tuskegee Experiment with the "Scottsboro Boys" case.
6. Why were W. E. B. Du Bois's Crisis editorials "on segregation" so divisive and explosive? Discuss the various responses of black activists and scholars to the idea of voluntary self-segregation.

Research Navigator.com RESOURCES FOR COLLEGE RESEARCH ASSIGNMENTS **www.researchnavigator.com**

Chapter 18 examines the effect of the Depression and the New Deal on race relations in the United States. For further research on African American life in the 1930s, use the tools available to you in Research Navigator.

As you investigate this topic, consider this question: "What role did the federal government play in combating racism in the 1930s? What role did the courts play?"

- **ContentSelect:** Search in the History database using the search terms *Franklin Roosevelt* and *New Deal.*
- **Links Library:** Access the History: U.S. History database and explore the links for *New Deal* and *Great Depression.*
- **New York Times on the Web:** To find out more, search in the History database using the search term *New Deal.*

DOCUMENTS AND ACTIVITIES IN AFRICAN-AMERICAN HISTORY

Documents

18-1 Lester B. Granger, Negro Workers and Recovery, 1934
18-2 National Labor Relations Act, 1935
18-3 The Victims of the Ku Klux Klan, 1935
18-4 Luther C. Wandall, A Negro in the CCC, 1935
18-5 E. E. Lewis, Black Cotton Farmers and the AAA, 1935

Interactive Figure

Unemployment, 1925–1945, p. 430
http://www.prenhall.com/hine/figure18.1

Learning Activity

Dealing with Hard Times

This activity looks at ways in which people coped with the Great Depression and at some of the alternatives that were proposed to change the political and economic system that had led to it.

19

Black Culture and Society in the 1930s and 1940s

Archibald Motley, Jr., *Barbecue*, 1934. Oil on canvas, 36¼ × 40⅛ in. The Howard University Gallery of Art, Washington, D.C.

Archibald Motley (1891–1981) captures in *Barbecue* (1934) the exuberance and vitality of nightlife in Chicago's Bronzeville. Motley was a major artistic talent during Chicago's Black Renaissance during the 1930s and 1940s.

HE would not Africanize America, for America has too much to teach the world and Africa. He would not bleach his Negro soul in a flood of white Americanism, for he knows that Negro blood has a message for the world. He simply wished to make it possible for a man to be both a Negro and an American, without being cursed and spit upon by his fellows, without having the doors of opportunity closed roughly in his face. This, then, is the end of his striving: to be a co-worker in the kingdom of culture, to escape both death and isolation, to husband and use his best powers and his latent genius.

W. E. B. Du Bois, *The Souls of Black Folk: Essay and Sketches*

W. E. B. Du Bois commented often on the gifts black people had made to America. Even before he wrote the passage that opens this chapter, Du Bois had proclaimed, "We are the first fruits of this new nation. . . . We are the people whose subtle sense of song has given America its only American music, its only American fairy tales, its only touch of pathos and humor amid its money-getting plutocracy." African-American "destiny is not a servile imitation of Anglo-Saxon culture, but a stalwart originality which shall unswervingly follow Negro ideals."

A key theme in black life during the 1930s and 1940s was the many strategies African Americans devised to protest segregation, discrimination, and disfranchisement, and to resist the negative racial stereotypes and the appropriation of black culture by white entrepreneurs. At heart this was a quest to shape the representation of black people in American society and create a viable black culture for a rapidly urbanizing people. A central issue in this chapter is the extent to which black culture during the 1930s and 1940s became a source of strength—cultural power—that helped African Americans define and assert themselves within American society.

CHAPTER OUTLINE

Black Culture in a Midwestern City

The Black Culture Industry and American Racism

Music Culture from Swing to Bebop

Popular Culture for the Masses: Comic Strips, Radio, and Movies
- The Comics
- Radio and Race
- Race, Representation, and the Movies

The Black Chicago Renaissance
- Jazz in Chicago
- Gospel in Chicago
- Chicago in Dance and Song: Katherine Dunham and Billie Holiday

Black Graphic Art

Black Literature
- Richard Wright's *Native Son*
- James Baldwin Challenges Wright
- Ralph Ellison and *Invisible Man*

African Americans in Sports
- Jesse Owens and Joe Louis
- Breaking the Color Barrier in Baseball

Black Religious Culture
- The Nation of Islam
- Father Divine and the Peace Mission Movement

Conclusion

Cultural power allowed African Americans to define and create new images that replaced the distortion of the true appearance, intellect, religious practice, and family values of black people in American society. The new black cultural power had to fight the well-worn stereotypes of the dumb, lazy black man; the selfless mammy; and the promiscuous dark Venus. As we have seen throughout this book, black people were disfranchised and socially and economically marginalized. But in the arts, black people drove a small wedge into the wall of racism through which they could explode onto America's center stage. In the performing arts, talented African Americans compelled the attention of white Americans. The 1930s and 1940s—ironically also a time when most black people were suffering from the combined effects of the Depression and the entrenched Jim Crow regime—were a fertile period in the history of black expressive culture.

Black Culture in a Midwestern City

During the 1930s and 1940s black migrants flocked to St. Louis, swelling its population to make it the fifth largest city in the United States. Yet because of segregation and discrimination, the black community in St. Louis developed institutions to address their own educational and cultural needs. While attention has usually focused on St. Louis's contributions to popular culture, there was also considerable interest in the city in classical music. Black community residents had to struggle to secure training in this genre of music and for opportunities to perform it:

> St. Louis! The town where Scott Joplin and Tom Turpin used to play ragtime. The town that W. C. Handy made famous in his great song, "The St. Louis Blues." The town where Josephine Baker started out as a $15.00 a week waitress, and end[ed] up in Paris as one of the most glamorous stars of the international theater. St. Louis, the town that gave a laugh-hungry world the joy of E. Simms Campbell and his rib-tickling cartoons of Esquire and King Features fame. The town where the river boats used to run from New Orleans with Louis Armstrong's horn blasting the night away.

Langston Hughes' words recall the possibilities and excitement that life in a midwestern city held for black people. St. Louis is in the heart of a region often considered remote from the nation's cultural centers. Yet it has produced outstanding jazz musicians, and Chuck Berry virtually invented rock and roll there. A closer look at black support for classical music in St. Louis during the 1930s and 1940s reveals the interior diversity of black community life; even though white St. Louisians marginalized or ignored the contributions of black artists in the city. But not all black musicians wanted to play ragtime and jazz, and many resented being relegated to these forms.

Schools, churches, labor, and media within the St. Louis black community had to create opportunities for black children to study, appreciate, and perform classical music. The two largest black newspapers, the St. Louis Argus and the St. Louis American, publicized recitals and concerts. Two all-black institutions supported classical music education: Lincoln University in Jefferson City (founded in 1866 as a school created by and for black Civil War veterans and their families) and Sumner High School (founded in 1875 as the first secondary school for black people west of the Mississippi).

By the 1940s Lincoln University had become the institution for training St. Louis musicians, and its music instructors were active in the black community's cultural affairs. Sumner High School had orchestras, bands, choirs, and glee clubs. Many of its music teachers had advanced degrees from prestigious music departments. The most influential teacher was Kenneth Billups, an arranger, composer, and founding director of the Legend Singers, a black professional chorus.

The Legend Singers appeared with the St. Louis Symphony and with the Municipal Opera Company (MUNY) in productions of Showboat, where they dressed in demeaning slave costumes. Billups's response to criticism of these appearances indirectly addressed the dilemma of black artists in a racially restrictive environment:

> I've seen situations where I felt inwardly . . . I might have had to do some things; for example, let's take this Showboat thing at MUNY Opera. There is the need of a black chorus to go there, and I had the privilege of doing that with my Legend Singers, simply because one of the first requirements was to have a black chorus.

Black churches, including Antioch Baptist, Central Baptist, and Berea Presbyterian, sponsored religious programs highlighting the works of both black and white composers. Local 197 of the American Federation of Musicians and the St. Louis Music Association, which was the local branch of the National Association of Negro Musicians, promoted black performing organizations and training. These groups sponsored choirs, orchestras, and other musical organizations and devoted part of their members' dues to scholarships and summer choirs for boys and girls.

The Black Culture Industry and American Racism

Black American artists had to confront institutional racism in the culture industry. Individual black creative artists could rarely afford to produce and disseminate their work. This power often resided in the hands of record companies, publishers, and the owners of radio stations and film studios. Yet black artists in the 1930s and 1940s were shaping a new black consciousness that would erupt in the 1950s as the modern civil rights movement.

The political content of black art provoked heated debates among black artists. Many black Americans insisted that music, the visual and performing arts, literature, and oratory serve both a functional and an aesthetic purpose. They expected black artists not only to create beauty, but also to use their art to further black freedom from white oppression. The involvement of white people also created tension among black artists during these decades. While many white Americans had long appreciated black culture, some had also appropriated it for their own profit.

During the late 1930s and 1940s, corporate America recognized the money that could be made in producing and marketing black culture. But there was a problem: Black artists had to be made "acceptable" if they were to be successfully marketed to affluent white consumers. These artists had to compromise, mask, and subordinate their true feelings and expressiveness if they wanted to earn income from their work. Artists who exhibited the right combination of showmanship, charm, and talent could reap some of the financial rewards their creativity generated. The paradox of the black performer—using your art to entertain your oppressor—was nowhere more apparent than in music.

The Music Culture from Swing to Bebop

Ironically, the very creativity that white Americans valued and often appropriated depended on the artists' ability to preserve some intellectual and emotional autonomy. Black artists had to juxtapose the requirements of earning a living with the need to remain true to their art. Black musicians continuously had to refine, expand, and perfect their art not only for themselves and each other but for a white-dominated marketplace. In many respects black music is virtually synonymous with black culture, and segregation or self-imposed separation often made possible the creation of new cultural expressions. Music encapsulates and reflects the core values and underlying tensions and anxieties in black communities. In black music we witness cultural producers developing strategies of resistance against white domination.

Trumpeter Cootie Williams entertains a rapt audience at the popular Harlem night club, the Savoy. His music provided temporary escape from the ravages of the Great Depression.

The Great Depression wrought havoc on the vibrant black culture industry of the 1920s. Record sales in 1932 were only a sixth of those in 1927. Black musicians like Louis Armstrong had enjoyed a golden age of creativity during the 1920s. The record companies had their separate black music labels and sold thousands of records to southern migrants to the big cities. New bands sprouted up from Kansas City to Chicago; Memphis to Detroit; Washington, D.C., to New York. Los Angeles, San Francisco, and Seattle had their own black music enthusiasts and performers. The territorial (traveling) bands took the music to the outposts of black America, while the big bands under Fletcher Henderson, Duke Ellington, Count Basie, and Cab Calloway played in white urban dance halls and ballrooms that admitted black people only as staff or entertainers.

New York was where black musicians felt they had to go to prove themselves. After entertaining affluent white people, or providing backup music for the Apollo Theater in Harlem, black musicians discarded their masks of docility and deference and

PROFILE

Charlie Parker, 1920–1955

Charlie Parker was one of the most innovative and influential of all American musicians. With his inspired saxophone playing; his technical mastery of his instrument; his melodic, rhythmic, and harmonic innovations, he was one of the architects of modern jazz, or "bebop." His playing challenged his contemporaries, profoundly influenced subsequent generations of jazz musicians, and helped transform jazz from entertainment to one of America's most respected art forms. But Parker was also troubled by drug addiction, mental instability, and tumultuous personal relationships.

Charlie Parker (1920–1955), playing the alto sax, with Miles Davis on trumpet.

Charles Parker, Jr. was born on August 29, 1920, in Kansas City, Kansas. In 1927, his family moved across the state line to Kansas City, Missouri. He had little formal musical instruction. But Kansas City had a rich, dynamic jazz scene. Pianist and composer Mary Lou Williams remembered the freewheeling atmosphere this way: "Now, at this time, which was still Prohibition . . . [m]ost of the night spots were run by politicians and hoodlums, and the town was wide open for drinking, gambling, and pretty much every form of vice. Naturally, work was plentiful for musicians though some of the employers were tough people." Young Parker became a fixture at many of the local clubs where he also acquired a heroin habit that plagued him the rest of his life.

In 1939, searching for a wider audience and hoping to learn from the great instrumentalists of the time, Parker left Kansas City for New York, then the jazz capital of the country. In New York, Parker began to sit in, or "jam," at Harlem nightclubs such as Monroe's and Minton's. In 1942 he was back in Kansas City playing as a member of Jay McShann's band, a popular "territory band" that traveled as far north as Lincoln, Nebraska, and as far south as New Orleans, Louisiana. During this time he acquired the nickname "Bird."

Parker left the McShann Band in 1942 to join pianist Earl Hines's band in New York. In March and April 1943, all the following musicians were in the band with Parker: "Little" Benny Harris, Bennie Green, Wardell Gray, and vocalists Billy Eckstine and Sarah Vaughan. This collection of talent reflected a musical environment that fostered innovation. New ideas spread by word of mouth from musician to musician and in late night jam sessions. It was from the close collaboration between Parker and Dizzy Gillespie in this period that bebop emerged.

Charlie Parker joined the first bebop big band, formed by Billy Eckstine in 1944. Eckstine's friend and valet, Bob Redcross, remembers a particular night when the band was at its best.

> Everybody was on. [Art] Blakey was on; John [Gillespie] was on; Bird was on; Bidd [Johnson] was on; everybody. Man, they upset this place. They had people screaming and hollering.

In the same year a recording of Parker's composition, "Red Cross," the first to be copyrighted in his name, was released on the Savoy label.

Parker and Gillespie first recorded together commercially in 1945. Gillespie formed his first bebop big band and took it on a tour of the South as part of the "Hepations 1945" package tour. Also in 1945, Parker led an expanded group at the Spotlite club that included trumpeter Miles Davis, tenor saxophonist Dexter Gordon, bassist Leonard Gaskin and drummer Stan Levey. During a disastrous trip to California, Parker had a nervous breakdown and spent several months at Camarillo State Hospital.

In 1947, when Parker returned to New York, he formed his "classic" quintet, with trumpeter Miles Davis, drummer Max Roach, pianist Duke Jordan, and Tommy Potter on bass. The recordings produced by this quintet, four sides on the Savoy label, are the foundation on which much of Parker's reputation rests.

In 1949, in a fitting tribute to his genius by his contemporaries, a New York nightclub, "Birdland," was named for him. Charlie Parker died in New York on March 12, 1955.

made a different sound in their own space and on their own time in late-night jam sessions. The small clubs, such as Monroe's Uptown House and Minton's Playhouse in Harlem a few blocks from the Apollo Theater, became the most fertile sites for innovation in melody, tempo, and dexterity. In them a new kind of jazz was born.

The big band swing style that became popular in the 1930s transformed white American culture. Swing emerged as white bands reduced the music of the more innovative black bandleaders to a broadly appealing formula based on a swinging 4/4 beat, well-blended saxophone sections, and pleasant-sounding vocals. The big swing bands of the 1930s played written-out, completely arranged music. The popularity of swing helped to boost the careers of black and white bandleaders, but it also led to a creative slump that disheartened many of the younger black musicians. Tired of swing's predictability, they began improvising in the jazz clubs, sharpening their reflexes, ears, and minds.

In the 1940s at least seven musicians were among the men most responsible for making a revolution in jazz, ushering in a new sound and dimension that became known, scornfully at first, as bebop. These musicians were Charlie Parker, Dizzy Gillespie, Thelonious Monk, Bud Powell, Kenny Clarke, Max Roach, and Ray Brown. Bebop featured complex rhythms and harmonies and highlighted improvisation. Gillespie (1917–1993) said that Kansas City-born Charlie "Yardbird" and then just "Bird" Parker (1920–1955) was "the architect of the style." "Yard and I," Gillespie reminisced, "were so close, so wrapped up in one another, that he would think 'three,' and I would say 'four,' and I would say 'seven,' and he'd say 'eight'. . . . It wasn't difficult for us, really together, sometimes it sounded like one horn playing, and sometimes it was one horn, but sometimes it was both of us sounding like one horn."

Bebop met resistance from white America. The nation was about to enter World War II and was too preoccupied to switch from the big band swing ballroom dancing music to bebop. Moreover, because jazzmen played in small, intimate clubs, not big bands, they had more freedom from the expectations of white society. Bebop music was of such enduring quality, however, that it shaped the contours of American popular culture and style for two generations. Before long, bebop became the principal musical language of jazz musicians around the world.

Bebop was a way of life and had its own attendant styles whose nuances depended on class status and, perhaps, age. Gillespie helped to create one side of bebop style in dress, language, and demeanor. He began to wear dark glasses on stage to reduce the glare from lights after he had cataract surgery. He grew a goatee because shaving every day irritated his bottom lip. He wore pegged pants, jackets with wide lapels, and a beret when men were still wearing hats with brims. Other bebop musicians emulated and modified this attire. For example, they wore cashmere jackets without lapels. Beboppers also created their own slang, or hip black English that mingled colorful and obscene language. They challenged convention in other ways too, engaging in a freewheeling lifestyle that often included love across the color line. There was also a down side to bebop. Some musicians became drug addicts, engaged in parasitical relationships with women, and spent their money recklessly.

Black working-class young men adopted their own style of talking and of hip dressing, reflected in their zoot suits and conked hair. Zoot suits featured high-waisted, baggy, pegged pants and long draped coats. A sixteen-year-old Malcolm Little (later to take the name Malcolm X) purchased a zoot suit when he moved to Boston and plunged into hipster culture. His first zoot suit was sky blue with a matching hat, gold watch chain, and a monogrammed belt. To savor this new identity, he recalled, "I took three of those twenty-five cent sepia-toned, while-you-wait pictures of myself, posed the way 'hipsters' wearing their zoots would 'cool it'—hat dangled, knees drawn close together, feet wide apart, both index fingers jabbed toward the floor." He then mastered the lindy hop dance style and took to the floor of the Roseland Ballroom where he shed his life as an unskilled wage worker and became someone freer and more empowered. He recalled the Ballroom's patrons' escape from their dreary urban lives: "They'd jampack that ballroom, the black girls in wayout silk and satin dresses and shoes, their hair done in all kinds of styles, the men sharp in their zoot suits and crazy conks, and everybody grinning and greased and gassed."

Bebop was the dominant black music of the war decade, but after 1945, returning veterans preferred a slower-paced music, simple love songs, and melodies. This contributed to bebop's waning and led to more transformations. All artistic innovation extracts a high price. Bebop was no exception. Many of the most talented musicians, like Billie Holiday, whom we discuss later in this chapter, paid that price in lives decimated by drugs, poverty, sickness, and broken relationships. Few black musicians received the respect, recognition, and financial rewards from white America that their creativity warranted. Ultimately, white Americans wanted the art, but not the artists.

Popular Culture for the Masses: Comic Strips, Radio, and Movies

The masses of African Americans participated in more accessible black popular culture outlets. Everyone needed relief from the bleakness and despair of the Depression years. Comic strips, radio programs, and movies were affordable forms of artistic creativity that allowed momentary escape. Newspapers were widely shared, passing from hand to hand, and whole families gathered around the radio for nightly programs of comedy and music. For black city dwellers, the movies offered momentary escape from poverty and want.

The Comics

African Americans quickly noted the difference between the fun that black people made of each other, and the mockery white people made of them. These differences were reflected in tone, intent, and sympathetic versus derisive laughter. During the Depression, comic strips in newspapers and comic books featuring superheroes diverted millions of Americans. Comic strips in black newspapers entertained, but also affirmed, the values and ideals of black people. They portrayed humorous situations and elaborated tales of intrigue and action.

The Philadelphia *Independent*, a black paper, ran a serial in the thirties called "The Jones Family." This strip, drawn by an editorial cartoonist named Branford, was a good example of the dual function of entertaining and affirming. The strip emphasized black people's desire for achievement and respectability. The plot centered around the young Jones boy's search for the "good life" of money, success, love and a happy marriage. But at every turn he confronts a harsh environment. Unable to get a job because of the Depression, he becomes an outlaw and narrowly escapes jail. He is constantly "on the run" from oppression. His only consolations are his family and his beautiful, ever-faithful girlfriend.

"The Jones Family" illuminates the gray areas that most African Americans, regardless of their class, faced when attempting to live rational and coherent lives in the northern cities. While they espoused and cherished middle-class values, they often had to live among poverty, crime, and racial oppression. The black comic strips sought to provide entertaining, nonjudgmental prescriptions and blueprints for middle-class life, but to more cynical and alienated black people they seemed to be promoting unattainable values and lifestyles.

Radio and Race

Although there were individual exceptions, during the Depression black performers in radio and film were marginalized, exploited, or excluded. Commercial radio operated to deliver an audience of white consumers to white advertisers, and it denied black people jobs as announcers, broadcast journalists, or technicians. White entertainers schooled in blackface minstrelsy portrayed black radio characters. The major labor unions involved in the entertainment side of the radio industry restricted membership to white people. Still—with its offerings of vaudeville, big bands, drama, and comedy—radio provided relief from the miseries of the Depression to all Americans, black as well as white.

The most popular comedy radio program in the early thirties—a precursor to the soap operas and sitcoms that were to become staples of radio and television programming—was *The Amos 'n' Andy Show.* The inauguration of this program was a significant moment in radio history. The title roles were played by two white performers, Charles Correll and Freeman Gosden, who wrote and performed scripts laced with oxymorons and malapropisms. Skillful showmen, Correll and Gosden ingratiated themselves in Chicago's black community, appearing at parades and posing with black children. The Chicago *Defender* endorsed them and they received standing ovations at the Regal Theater in Chicago's black south side. Part of the amusement they generated derived from their mispronounced words, garbled grammar, and their show's minstrel ambience. Each episode highlighted an improbable situation involving the black cab driver (Amos) and his gullible overweight friend (Andy). Other characters included the scheming con artist Kingfish, his overbearing wife Sapphire, and his domineering mother-in-law, Mama. On radio, Gosden and Correll furnished voices for the members of Amos and Andy's fraternal lodge and for a whole array of other characters. The characters and their humor reinforced unflattering racial and gender stereotypes, but the show was not mean spirited. Some of the characters conducted themselves with dignity, modeling such positive values as marital fidelity, strong families, hard work, and economic independence. An *Amos 'n' Andy* movie, *Check and Double Check*—released in 1930 when hard times made black entertainers grateful for any employment they could get—featured music by Duke Ellington's orchestra. The movie introduced Ellington to a wider audience of affluent white people and enhanced his reputation.

Black audiences recognized the minstrel stereotyping in *Amos 'n' Andy*, yet many among them still enjoyed the show. A vocal component of the ever more sophisticated and urbanized black population, however, complained that this show, and other radio programs, reinforced negative images—of black women as bossy Sapphires or Mammies and black men as childish clowns—in the nation's consciousness. Educator and activist Nannie Helen Burroughs considered the show demeaning. Robert L. Vann, editor of the Pittsburgh *Courier*, argued that it exploited African Americans for white commercial gain. Vann sponsored a petition to the Federal Communications Commission to ban the show, but his efforts were futile.

By the 1940s *The Amos 'n' Andy Show* was less popular. In the early 1950s it had a brief life as a television series, this time with black actors. Alvin Childress, an experienced stage actor and director, became Amos, and Spencer Williams Jr. who had written, directed, and starred in several independent all-black movies played Andy. Tim Moore assumed the role of the Kingfish of the Mystic Knights of the Sea Lodge, while Johnny Lee portrayed the shyster lawyer, Algonquin J. Calhoun.

For almost two decades, *Amos 'n' Andy* was the only depiction of black people on the nation's airwaves. Its negative stereotypes of African Americans buttressed white people's notions of their own superiority. The show never demonstrated how the characters' race affected their lives or the psychological or economic costs of racism. It taught white America that it was permissible to laugh at striving black men and women.

The best-known and most successful African American on network radio in the late 1930s was Eddie Anderson, who played Jack Benny's sidekick Rochester in NBC's *The Jack Benny Show*. Like the characters in *Amos 'n' Andy*, Anderson's character reinforced negative racial stereotypes. Anderson rationalized his role in a way that suggests discomfort with it:

> I don't see why certain characters are called stereotypes. The Negro characters being presented are not labeling the Negro race any more than "Luigi" is labeling the Italian people as a whole. The same goes for "Beulah," who is not playing the part of thousands of Negroes, but only the part of one person, "Beulah." They're not saying here is the portrait of the Negro, but here is "Beulah."

Race, Representation, and the Movies

In the 1930s and 1940s—after the introduction of sound in motion pictures—black and white producers began to make what were known as race films for African-American audiences. Except for these race films, white film executives, since the beginning of the film industry, had cast black men and women in roles designed to comfort, reassure, and entertain white audiences. Continuing this trend, African Americans in Hollywood movies of the 1930s, were usually cast in servile roles and often portrayed as buffoons. For example, the first black actor to receive major billing in American films, Stepin Fetchit (1902–1985, born Lincoln Theodore Monroe Perry), purportedly earned two million dollars in ten years playing a cringingly servile, dim-witted, slow-moving character.

Black performers appeared as servants in many other box office successes during the Depression era. Among them were Gertrude Howard and Libby Taylor, who played servants to Mae West's characters in *I'm No Angel* (1933) and *Belle of the Nineties* (1934). In *Imitation of Life* (1934), Louise Beavers played a black servant whose light-skinned daughter, played by Fredi Washington, tries to pass for white. The black tap dancer and stage performer Bill "Bojangles" Robinson was featured in four popular films—*The Little Colonel* (1935), *The Littlest Rebel* (1935), *Just around the Corner* (1938), and *Rebecca of Sunnybrook Farm* (1938)—as a servant to white child star Shirley Temple.

The film that most firmly cemented the role of black Americans as servants in the American consciousness was *Gone with the Wind* (1939). Hattie McDaniel and Butterfly McQueen were the black "stars" in this epic adaptation of Margaret Mitchell's romanticized literary salute to the Old South. McDaniel had played servant or "Mammy" roles throughout the 1930s. The image of Mammy, the headscarf-wearing, obese, dutiful black woman who preferred nurturing white families to caring for her own children appealed to white America. But in *Gone with the Wind*, McDaniel gave the performance of a lifetime and in 1940 became the first African American to win an Oscar. Many in the black community criticized her for playing "female Tom" roles. Defensively, McDaniel retorted that she would rather play a maid and earn $700 a week than be one and earn only $7 a week. Some black actors such as McDaniel, dismayed by their relegation to demeaning roles, formed the Fair Play Committee (FPC) to lobby the

Louise Beavers (1908–1962) was a splendid actress whose talent was largely restricted to "mammy" roles. Here she appears with Claudette Colbert in a scene from the melodramatic film *Imitation of Life* (1934) , which deals with the theme of black people passing for white.

white-dominated movie industry for more substantial roles, to get rid of dialect speech, and to ban the term nigger from the screen. But in the *Beulah* radio show, which premiered in 1947, McDaniel again played a wise but subservient maid who provides the family that employs her with advice, guidance, and direction.

Eventually, during and after World War II, Hollywood developed more sophisticated race-directed movies. Of particular significance was the positive, even romanticized, portrayal of black Americans in a movie financed by the War Department to gain support among African Americans for the U.S. role in WWII. *The Negro Soldier,* directed by Frank Capra in 1944, played to vast audiences of enthusiastic black people. But even before the *The Negro Soldier,* some motion pictures had displayed African Americans positively. Paul Robeson made two movies, *The Emperor Jones* (1933) and *Showboat* (1936), in which he attempted to change how black men and women were represented on screen. He proclaimed in 1934, "In my music, my plays, my films I want to carry always this central idea: to be African. Multitudes of men have died for less worthy ideals; it is even more eminently worth living for." Robeson's films, however, were not box office successes, and he left the United States to pursue his career in Europe. There his commitment to communism and leftist politics made him a target of the anticommunist hysteria that gripped the United States as the Cold War took hold in the late 1940s (see Chapter 20).

To succeed commercially, African-American filmmakers had to disguise their dissent or create art purely for other black people. One of the most enterprising black filmmakers, Oscar Micheaux (1884–1951), made films aimed primarily at the black public, a group that Hollywood directors and producers of race movies ignored or insulted with stereotypical representations. Unlike the dominant Hollywood stereotypes, the black men and women in Micheaux's films were often educated, cultured, and prosperous. Micheaux endowed black Americans with cinematic voice and subjectivity. His films, featured middle-class or identity issues such as "passing for white."

Micheaux produced more than thirty feature films between 1919 and 1948. In 1932, he released *The Exile,* the first sound motion picture to be made by, with, and for black Americans. The following year he produced *Veiled Aristocrats,* about passing for white among Chicago's black professional class. The characters in the film are considered "aristocrats" because they are descended from the white gentry of the Old South and Europe; they are "veiled" because of their color. The plot turns on the revelation that the wealthy "white" heroine is actually "colored," which enables her to marry the talented mulatto hero.

Micheaux tried to transform Hollywood without changing it, much as members of the black bourgeoisie struggled to be included in American society. His films capture the dilemma of black double consciousness. As W. E. B. Du Bois put it, black people always experienced that "peculiar sensation," that "sense of always looking at one's self through the eyes of others, of measuring one's soul by the tape of a world that looks on in amused contempt and pity." Black culture existed within and was shaped by, while simultaneously transforming, American culture. To the degree that black Americans had been assimilated, white American culture was their culture as well.

The white ethnic immigrants who created Hollywood were determined to help marginal and excluded groups like Jews and Italians assimilate into the American mainstream. Hollywood sought to create the illusion that these groups belonged to the power elite. However, these Hollywood entrepreneurs did not do the same for African Americans. Their films during the Depression represented black people as unassimilable. A small cadre of black filmmakers and actors created independent films and showed them in cinema houses exclusively for black patrons. Following the lead of pioneers like Micheaux, they created an alternative cinema in which they introduced nuanced and fully human characters.

The Black Chicago Renaissance

Like Harlem in the 1920s, Chicago during the 1930s and 1940s was an important center of black culture. In contrast to some of the artists of the "Harlem Renaissance," the leading writers in Chicago harbored no illusions that art would solve the problems caused by white supremacy and black subordination. The Chicago writers of the 1930s and 1940s emphasized the idea that black art had to combine aesthetics and function. It had to serve the cause of black freedom.

Arna Bontemps (1902–1973) was to the Chicago Renaissance what Alain Locke had been to the Harlem Renaissance. "The Depression," Bontemps asserted,

> put an end to the dream world of renaissance Harlem and scattered the band of poets and painters, sculptors, scholars and singers who had in six exciting years made a generation of Americans aware of unnoticed and hitherto unregarded creative talents among Negroes. . . . What they did not dream was that a second awakening, less gaudy but closer to realities, was already in prospect. . . . One way or the other, Harlem got its renaissance in the middle twenties, centering around the *Opportunity* contests and the Fifth Avenue Awards Dinners. . . . Ten years later Chicago reenacted it on WPA [Works Progress Administration] without finger bowls but with increased power.

Born in Louisiana, Bontemps migrated in 1935 from California to Chicago where he met Richard Wright and joined the South Side Writers Group, which Wright founded in 1936. The Group included poet Margaret Walker and playwright Theodore Ward. It offered criticism and moral support to black writers. Bontemps's own writing was influenced by his association with the group. After 1935 his novels and short stories reflected a militant restlessness and revolutionary spirit. In 1936, he published *Black Thunder* about the nineteenth-century slave conspiracy led by Gabriel and in 1939 *Drums at Dusk* about the Haitian Revolution and Toussaint L'Ouverture (1746–1803). Richard Wright's writings also celebrated resistance, but with more nuance. He published *Uncle Tom's Children* in 1938 and, his masterpiece, *Native Son*, in 1940.

Among the artists who launched their careers on WPA funds were Margaret Walker and Willard Motley. Walker attracted widespread attention when her collected poems appeared as the book *For My People* in the Yale Series of Younger Poets. Willard Motley worked with a radio group while writing his powerful novel *Knock on Any Door* (1947), which depicted the transformation of an Italian-American altar boy into a criminal headed for the electric chair. The novel invited comparisons with Wright's *Native Son.*

Before the 1930s, several black intellectuals misjudged the potential of Chicago to become a vibrant center of black culture. In the late 1920s, black social scientists Charles S. Johnson and E. Franklin Frazier expressed disdain for black Chicago's artistic and intellectual prospects. Frazier proclaimed that "Chicago has no intelligentsia," and in 1923, Johnson asked rhetorically,

> Who can write of lilies and sunsets in the pungent shadows of the stockyards? . . . It is no dark secret why literary societies fail, where there are no Art exhibits or libraries about, why periodicals presuming upon an I.Q. above the age of 12 are not read, why so little literature comes out of the city. No, the kingdom of the second ward [the black neighborhood] has no self-sustaining intelligentsia, and a miserably poor acquaintance with that of the world surrounding it.

Johnson did, however, admit one saving grace in Chicago's cultural wasteland. "[I]t leads these colored United States in its musical aspirations with, perhaps, the best musical school in the race, as these go."

Johnson and Frazier were too harsh. Just as Chicago's industrial economy attracted working-class black people, it also nurtured artists who drew inspiration from and reflected this stratum of moving and striving, strolling and styling black people who wanted

PROFILE

Langston Hughes

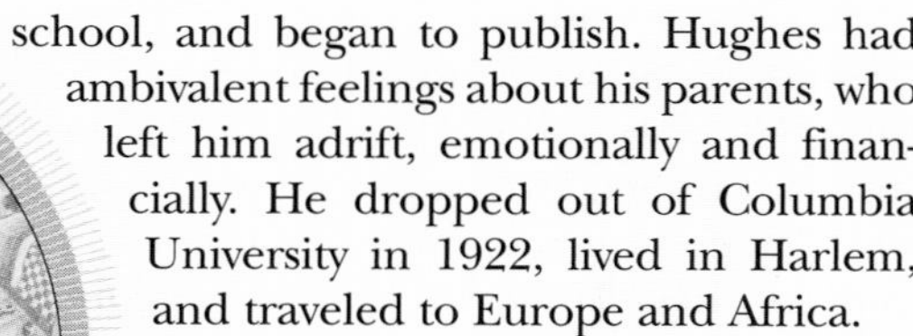

Langston Hughes, in a painting by Winold Reiss.

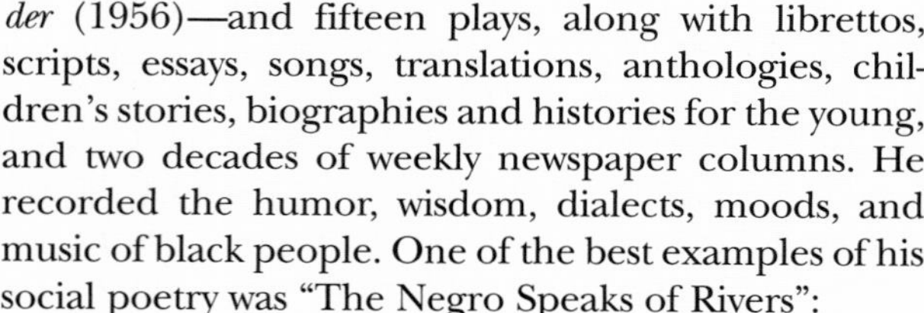

Langston Hughes identified with poor and working-class black people. He used his poetry, prose, and playwriting skills to make the dignity and beauty of black people visible and known.

Hughes once referred to himself as "a literary sharecropper." Admirers called him a range of names—"Poet Laureate of the Negro People," for starters. During his career he produced fifteen volumes of poetry, two collections of short stories, one novel, two volumes of autobiography—*The Big Sea* (1940), and *I Wonder as I Wander* (1956)—and fifteen plays, along with librettos, scripts, essays, songs, translations, anthologies, children's stories, biographies and histories for the young, and two decades of weekly newspaper columns. He recorded the humor, wisdom, dialects, moods, and music of black people. One of the best examples of his social poetry was "The Negro Speaks of Rivers":

I've known rivers:
I've known rivers ancient as the world and older than
the flow of human blood in human veins.
My soul has grown deep like the rivers.
I bathed in the Euphrates when dawns were young.
I built my hut near the Congo and it lulled me to sleep.
I looked upon the Nile and raised the pyramids above it.
I heard the singing of the Mississippi when Abe
Lincoln went down to New Orleans, and I've seen
its muddy
bosom turn all golden in the sunset.
I've known rivers:
Ancient, dusky rivers.
My soul has grown deep like the rivers.

Hughes was born in Joplin, Missouri, in 1902 and was raised by his maternal grandmother, Mary Langston. His father, James Hughes emigrated to Mexico, and his mother Carrie Langston remarried. Hughes became fascinated by black urban folk culture, which had been transplanted from the rural South by the great migration. He joined his mother in Cleveland in 1916, attended an integrated high school, and began to publish. Hughes had ambivalent feelings about his parents, who left him adrift, emotionally and financially. He dropped out of Columbia University in 1922, lived in Harlem, and traveled to Europe and Africa.

With the publication of *The Weary Blues* in 1926, his career took off. Hughes was enraptured by the language of the blues—its warmth, stoicism, incongruous humor, ironic laughter mixed with tears, and the "pain that was swallowed in a smile." In 1943 he introduced in his Chicago *Defender* column the character Jesse B. Semple, a racially conscious barfly philosopher—unlettered, but wise. The college-educated, somewhat uptight narrator of the series interrogates Semple about black life, from love of women and watermelon to the fortunes of rich gospel singers and the whereabouts of leaders who hide from the black people they lead. At one point Semple observed:

> Not only am I half dead right now from pneumonia, but everything else has happened to me! I've been cut, shot, stabbed, run over, hit by a car, and tromped by a horse. I have also been robbed, fooled, deceived, two-timed, double-crossed, dealt seconds, and mightily near blackmailed—but I'm still here! . . . I have been fired, laid off, and last week given an indefinite vacation, also Jim Crowed, segregated, barred out, insulted, eliminated, called black, yellow, and red, locked in, locked out, locked up, and also left holding the bag.

In 1932 Hughes visited Moscow, where he felt comfortable and appreciated. He was impressed by the absence of Jim Crow segregation and discrimination and ignored Stalin's oppression and murders. But Hughes was never a member of the Communist party and eventually become disillusioned with the Soviet Union. Hughes remains an enduring symbol of the artist who championed black folk culture as authentic American culture.

to transgress class and geographical lines. These working-class people aspired to enjoy the middle-class life of accomplishment and consumption. A critical pulse point on Chicago's South Side came to be known as Bronzeville. It measured and reflected the reality of the lives of ordinary working-class people. As Harlem had its 125th Street, Chicago had 35th and State Street and 47th and South Park (now Martin Luther King Jr. Drive).

Chicago was heir to the Harlem Renaissance. In 1930, Langston Hughes published *Not without Laughter*, the first major novel about the black experience in Chicago. Hughes moved to the city himself in 1941 and wrote often for the widely read Chicago *Defender*. The city epitomized urban industrial America. As the northern terminus of the Illinois Central Railroad and the home of the *Defender*, it had long attracted displaced agricultural workers from the southern cotton fields, and by 1930 it had a black population of 233,903. The migrants arrived eager to absorb Chicago's hard-driving blues and jazz culture.

During the 1920s a discernible class structure among African Americans emerged in Chicago, fueled in part by the new migrants. These men and women expanded the consumer base and gave rise to a cadre of educated professionals and entrepreneurs who developed an appreciation for the arts. The Black Metropolis, as social scientists St. Clair Drake and Horace R. Cayton designated Chicago's South Side, became a black city within a city. Black businesses, such as banks and insurance companies, formed the financial foundation. Entrepreneur Walter L. Lee started Your Cab Company and each day put on the streets a half dozen chauffeur-uniformed drivers of vehicles. In the late 1940s, John Johnson would launch a publishing empire with such magazines as *Negro Digest*, *Jet*, and *Ebony*. These businesses depended less on white patronage than on black support. It was in their best interest to support the arts and provide venues for performances.

Revolutionary work in music also occurred in Chicago. It was a pioneering center both for recording and performing music. As black music became a commodity, influential black disk jockeys, like Al Benson, appeared on radio in Chicago. Benson proved to be as skilled a businessman as he was a cultural impresario. Music was the primary inspiration for the creativity that characterized black cultural movements in America. Avant-garde developments in black music preceded black cultural activity in the visual arts, poetry, drama, dance, literature, film, and sports. Cultural creativity was a potent force for black liberation and occurred simultaneously in different locations in America.

Jazz in Chicago

Within the confines of the South Side of Chicago, black musical giants, such as trumpeter Louis Armstrong (1898–1971) and his wife, Lillian Hardin Armstrong (1898–1971), a well-known and respected jazz pianist, performed and nurtured a distinct jazz culture. "Lil" Armstrong was born in Memphis, Tennessee, and received formal music training at Fisk University, the Chicago College of Music (earning a teaching certificate in 1924) and the New York College of Music (graduated in 1929). "Lil" Hardin Armstrong led her own band and was talented at arranging, composing and singing. She played with great performers of the day and befriended Louis Armstrong when he arrived in Chicago. They were married in 1924. Lil Armstrong eventually encouraged her husband to leave King Oliver's Creole Jazz Band and to join Fletcher Henderson in New York. The Armstrongs were divorced in 1938. She continued her recording career with Decca records under the name Lil Hardin.

Duke Ellington in his autobiography, *Music Is My Mistress*, remarked,

> Chicago always sounded like the most glamorous place in the world to me when I heard the guys in Frank Holliday's poolroom talking about their travels. . . . They told very romantic tales about nightlife on the South Side. By the time I got there in 1930, it glittered even more . . . the Loop, the cabarets . . . city life, suburban life, luxurious neighborhoods—and the apparently broken-down neighborhoods where there were more good times than any place in the city.

At this point Ellington was recording some of his best jazz, such as *Mood Indigo* (1930) and *Ko-Ko* (1940). Ellington's stay in Chicago left a powerful impression on vocalist Joe Williams. Williams recalled,

> I used to arrange my classes so that I could get home in time to hear a program they [Ellington's band] had in Chicago called "Red Hot and Low Down." . . . The program's theme was Ellington's East St. Louis Toodle-oo. Later on, they changed the theme to "Sepia Panorama." Then they changed it again, to "Take the 'A' Train." But I used to come home early from high school so that I could hear Duke Ellington on the radio.

The seeds that blossomed into full-bodied jazz culture were planted across America at the turn of the century. The most famous musicians, however, all went to or passed through Chicago. As the Chicago Jazz Age came into its own, the beguiling tune *Pretty Baby* became the city's theme song. It was written by Tony Jackson, whom Jelly Roll Morton (the self-proclaimed "inventor of jazz") called "maybe the best entertainer the world has ever seen." The South Side, specifically along State Street between 31st and 35th, was the beating heart of the city's Jazz Age. Although Chicago did not replace New York as the major location for the aspiring jazz musician, it was the place you went to prove you had what it took to make a name for yourself.

Gospel in Chicago: Thomas Dorsey

The term gospel designates the traditional religious music of the black church. It was nurtured and flourished in Chicago's Holiness, Sanctified, Pentecostal, Baptist, and Methodist churches, in storefronts or large edifices. Gospel music became the backbone of urban and contemporary black religion and is deeply entrenched in worship. The use of instruments—tambourines, drums, pianos, horns, guitars, and Hammond organs—characterizes gospel and distinguishes it from the earlier spiritual and black folk music. During the 1930s and 1940s, it developed its own idioms and performance techniques.

TRACK 32

The doctrines of black "folk churches" encourage free expression, group participation, spontaneous testimonies, prayers, witnessing, and music. Singers and choirs rarely perform the same songs in the same way more than once. The performer must pay attention to the quality of the sound and to the careful manipulation of timbre, range, and shading. The style of the delivery uses the whole body in synchronized movement. The mechanics of the delivery are designed to intensify the performance, giving it added textual variation and melodic improvisation. Performers expand a melody by a variety of technical devices, including repetition, shouts, slides, slurs, moans, and grunts. The supporting piano and organ frequently engage in call-and-response interplay.

Gospel singer Pearl Williams-Jones makes clear the distinction between black church music and music of the other churches: "The traditional liturgical forms of plain chant, chorales, and anthems do not fulfill the needs of traditional black folk religious worship and rituals."

In Chicago, Thomas Dorsey (1899–1993)—one of Chicago's leading composers of the blues since the mid-twenties—was most responsible for developing black urban gospel. Dorsey's genius lay in his ability to synthesize elements of the blues with religious hymns to create a gospel blues. His gospel pieces, performed with a ragtime-derived, boogie-woogie piano accompaniment, radiated an urban religious spirit. In 1930 Dorsey gained widespread attention when gospel singer Willie Mae Ford Smith (1904–1994) performed his "If You See My Savior, Tell Him That You Saw Me" at the National Baptist Convention meeting in Chicago. Two years later, in 1932, Dorsey's place in musical history was assured when Theodore Frye, with Dorsey at the piano, performed in the Ebenezer Baptist Church in Chicago his now classic gospel song, "Take My Hand, Precious Lord." The song had a profound impact on gospel performers and their audiences. Dorsey's abundant works provided a foundation for shout worship in the urban Protestant churches formed by transplanted black Southerners in the 1930s and succeeding decades.

One of the greatest gospel singers, Chicago-based Mahalia Jackson (1911–1972), sang and promoted Dorsey's songs all over the country on the church circuit and at religious conventions between 1939 and 1944. Jackson once said of the music, "Gospel songs are the songs of hope. When you sing them you are delivered of your burden." During the Depression and World War II, gospel became big business.

Chicago in Dance and Song: Katherine Dunham and Billie Holiday

The influence of the WPA in Chicago was especially reflected in dance. Dance has always been an integral part of African-American life, and the dances of black people have always been important in the American theater. The first performances by black dancers given within and taken seriously by the concert dance world occurred in the 1930s. The first "Negro Dance Recital in America" was performed in 1931 by the New Negro Art Theater Dance Company, co-founded by Edna Buy and Hemsley Winfield. In that same year, Katherine Dunham (1909–) founded the Negro Dance Group in Chicago, which survived thanks to WPA support. As Dunham later recalled, "Black dancers were not allowed to take classes in studios in the '30s. I started a school because there was no place for blacks to study dance. I was the first to open the way for black dancers and I was the first to form a black dance company."

Dunham was unique. Trained in anthropology, she studied African-based ritual dance in the Caribbean. In 1938 her troupe stunned an audience with the sexual vitality of its performance of one of her works. When the company, now renamed the Katherine Dunham Dance Company, performed in February 1940, audiences and critics were awed. *The New York Times* declared, "With the arrival of Katherine Dunham on

VOICES

Margaret Walker on Black Culture

In 1942, poet Margaret Walker (1915–1998) published For My People, *the most important collection of poetry written by a participant in the Black Chicago Renaissance before Gwendolyn Brooks's* A Street in Bronzeville *(1945). In a 1992 collection of her essays, Walker reflected on the meaning and significance of black culture:*

Black culture has two main streams: a sociological stream . . . and an artistic stream. . . . In this artistic stream black culture has five branches. These are language, religion, art, music, and literature. . . .

Black music is perhaps the most acceptable of our black culture. The modern world is willing to accept the unique character of African rhythms and the language of the drum. White America, in general, reluctantly admits that black American music is the American music and most indigenous to our culture. In every category or classification of music, moreover, Black America has achieved monumentally. With a broad base of folk music—spirituals and gospel music, seculars (blues, work songs, prison hollers)—individuals have risen in notable achievement in classical, popular, and various forms of jazz. From Black Patti to Marian Anderson and Leontyne Price, the great black American singer has gained worldwide eminence. Roland Hayes, William Warfield, Todd Duncan, the late Ellabelle Davis, Dorothy Maynor, and Mattiwilda Dodds are notable black artists known the world over. Our blues singers like Bessie Smith, Ma Rainey, and B.B. King; folk singers like Leadbelly, and the greats like Louis Armstrong, Jimmie Lunceford, and Count Basie; great composers like Scott Joplin, Eubie Blake, Charlie Parker, and the incomparable Duke Ellington are significant contributors to the modern world and all represent the undeniable genius of the black American musician.

TRACK 33

Individual achievement, while part of our general cultural picture is not all. It is in language and religion that Black Americans as a group have made a significant contribution to the national fiber of American life and to the modern world. As spiritual creatures we have shown through unmerited suffering that we have a sense of humanity that can enrich the moral fiber and contribute to a new world ethos. Our black culture is aware of human needs and human values. Handicapped as we have been by a racist system of dehumanizing slavery and segregation, our American history of nearly five hundred years reveals that our cultural and spiritual gifts brought from our African past are still intact. It is not only that we are singers and dancers, poets and prophets, great athletes and perceptive politicians—but we are also a body of charismatic and numinous people yet capable of cultic fire as seen in our black churches and still creative enough in intellect to signal the leap forward into a new and humanistic age. We are the authors of the new paradigm. . . .

How then has black culture been disseminated and kept alive? Black culture has survived in the black institutions of Black America. In the black family, the Black Church, the black school, the black press, the black nation, and the black world. This is where our black culture has survived and thrived. This is where it must continue to grow. The ground of common humanity is not yet a reality in the modern world but when it comes as it must in the twenty-first century, Black Africa, and black humanity must be as always the foundation on which it stands and from which it logically proceeds. One world of international brotherhood does not negate the nationalism of black people. It only enforces and re-enforces our common humanity.

QUESTIONS

1. According to Walker, what significant external factors influenced and sustained black culture? What are some of the central themes found in black culture?
2. What political and symbolic use have African Americans made of black culture?

Source: *On Being Female, Black, and Free:* Essays by Margaret Walker, 1932–1992, edited by Maryemma Graham, 1997. Reprinted by permission of Maryemma Graham.

One of America's premier dance artists, the internationally acclaimed Katherine Dunham (1909–) performed in the Bobli Gardens in Florence, Italy in 1950. A talented choreographer, anthropologist, and writer, Dunham founded one of the first black dance companies. She was an outspoken critic of Jim Crow segregation.

the scene the development of a substantial Negro dance Art begins to look decidedly bright." The reviewer continued,

> Her performance with her group at the Windsor Theater may very well become a historic occasion, for certainly never before in all efforts of recent years to establish the Negro dance as a serious medium has there been so convincing and authoritative approach. . . . The potential greatness of the Negro dance lies in its discovery of its own roots and the crucial nursing of them into growth and flower. . . . It is because she has showed herself to have both the objective quality of the student and the natural instinct of the artist that she has done such a truly important job.

What kept audiences returning to Dunham dance performances, however, was the dancer's bold sensuality. A reviewer of *Tropical Revue*, for example, wrote that it was "likely to send thermometers soaring to the bursting point. . . . Tempestuous and torrid, raffish and revealing." *The New York Sun* marveled, "Shoulders, midsections and posteriors went round and round. Particularly when the cynosure was Miss Dunham, the vista was full of pulchritude."

Dunham explained her motivation:

> I felt a new dance form was needed for black people to be able to appear in any theater in the world and be accepted and exciting. One of the prerequisites of art is uniqueness. Rather than taking years to build a classical ballet company for blacks, I decided to create a dance with an authentic base for black people. Through my anthropological work, I studied primitive and folk dances and created the Dunham dance from them.

The success in New York led to film offers. The producers of the all-black musical extravaganza *Cabin in the Sky* hired the dance troupe and gave the feature role of Georgia Brown to Dunham. The role gave Dunham, as the *Times* dance critic wrote, the chance "to sizzle." But it also undermined her seriousness, allowing white audiences to view her as the stereotypical sultry black sexpot.

Nevertheless, the profits from the film funded the dancers' stage performances and Dunham's research. In 1943 Dunham moved to New York and opened the Katherine Dunham School of Arts and Research, which trained artists not only in dance, but in theater, literature, and world cultures.

Dunham was not afraid to protest racial segregation, even though it hurt her popularity. In the early 1940s, she denounced discrimination. In 1944 in Louisville, Kentucky, after a performance, Dunham announced, "We are glad we have made you happy. We hope you have enjoyed us. This is the last time I shall play Louisville because the management refuses to let people like us sit by people like you. Maybe after the war we shall have democracy and I can return." Dunham is important for two reasons. First, she was a gifted and talented pioneer in dance whose choreography inspired future generations. Second, she underscored the responsibility that a black artist had to the black community to fight racism.

Billie Holiday (1915–1959), another great performer whose career took shape during the Depression, also used her art to challenge the oppression of black people. Holiday, popularly known as "Lady Day," began singing at age fifteen and was discovered three years later by John Hammond, a Chicago jazz producer and promoter. In 1933, Hammond arranged for Holiday's first recording session, and in 1934 she made her debut at the Apollo Theater in Harlem. An

PROFILE

Billie Holiday, 1915–1959, and "Strange Fruit"

"Strange Fruit," which Billie Holiday first performed in 1929, became her signature piece. It was written by a white schoolteacher who went by the name of Lewis Allan (his real name was Abel Meerpol). While the lyrics capture the brutality of lynching, it was Holiday's incomparable vocal style and delivery that gave the song its political, emotional, and cultural power and made it the antilynching anthem:

Southern trees bear a strange fruit,
Blood on the leaves and blood at the root,
Black body swinging in the Southern breeze,
Strange fruit hanging from the poplar trees.

Pastoral scene of the gallant South,
The bulging eyes and the twisted mouth,
Scent of magnolia sweet and fresh,
And the sudden smell of burning flesh!

Here is a fruit for the crows to pluck
For the rain to gather, for the wind to suck,
For the sun to rot, for a tree to drop.
Here is a strange and bitter crop.

Billie Holiday (1915–1959) was one of the greatest jazz singers of all time. Between 1935 and 1938, she released some eighty titles on the Brunswick label for marketing to the black jukebox audience.

"Every time she sang that song," recalled Barney Josephson, a New York nightclub owner,

> it was unforgettable. . . . I made her do it as her last number. . . . When she sang "Strange Fruit" she never moved. Her hands were down. She didn't even touch the mike. With the little light on her face. The tears never interfered with her voice, but the tears would come and just knock everybody in that house out.

Billie Holiday was born Eleanora Fagan in Philadelphia, Pennsylvania, on April 7, 1915 to teenagers Sadie Fagan and Clarence Holiday. She grew up in Baltimore, Maryland, and became perhaps the greatest jazz singer ever recorded, a unique improviser and soloist. She set the standards to which future vocalists such as Sarah Vaughan, Carmen McRae, and Lena Horne would aspire. Much attention has focused on the tragic and destructive dimensions of her private life, but it is her musical talent that compels interest and admiration. Holiday used her talent to do more than to entertain; she challenged and often disturbed her listeners, especially with her soul-shattering rendition of "Strange Fruit." While frequently factually inaccurate, Holiday's autobiography, *Lady Sings the Blues* (1956), and the equally distorted 1972 movie staring Diana Ross emphasize her struggle against sexism and racism within the music world and society. Holiday appeared in two movies. In 1935 she performed in Duke Ellington's short film, *Symphony in Black*, singing "Big City Blues." In 1946 she performed three songs in a movie, *New Orleans*, opposite her musical mentor Louis Armstrong. Saxophonist Lester Young, who began recording with Holiday in 1937, gave her the nickname, Lady Day. By the late 1940s, Holiday's addiction to drugs was hurting her career. In 1947 she entered a private clinic, but was unable to stay clean. Following her discharge, the police arrested her for possession, and she served nine and one-half months at the Federal Reformatory for Women at Alderson, West Virginia. New York officials revoked her cabaret card and prohibited her from performing in night clubs in the city. Still, she gave concerts in other cities and went on international tours. A year before her death, Holiday recorded her most popular album, "Lady in Satin" (1958). She died in New York City on July 17, 1959. Thousands of friends and fans attended the funeral, a formal requiem high mass held at Saint Paul the Apostle Cathedral. She was buried in Saint Raymond's Catholic Cemetery in the Bronx.

incomparable singer known for subtle and artful improvisation, she left a wealth of recordings.

Black Graphic Art

Chicago artists, such as Charles White, Elizabeth Catlett, and Eldzier Cortor, and Harlem's Jacob Lawrence, celebrated both rural and urban working-class black people while implicitly criticizing the racial hierarchy of power and privilege. Their art belonged to the social realism school that flourished in the United States in the 1930s. Social realist art was intensely ideological. It strove to fuse propaganda—both left wing and right wing—to art to make it socially and politically relevant.

As the Depression worsened, black artists became even more determined to use their art to portray the crisis in capitalism. This involved depicting social and racial inequality. Chicago's Charles White wrote that "paint is the only weapon I have with which to fight what I resent. If I could write I would write about it. If I could talk I would talk about it. Since I paint, I must paint about it."

Defense Worker, a painting by Dox Thrash, reflects these concerns. Completed in 1942, just after the United States had entered World War II, it shows an isolated black worker looming over the horizon. The heroic proletarian imagery alludes to the dream of a racially integrated labor force, equal opportunity, and social reform in the wake of the New Deal and the sudden demand for labor triggered by the war.

The Harmon Foundation sponsored five juried exhibitions (1926–31, 1933) of the work of black artists. The William E. Harmon Awards for Distinguished Achievement among Negroes celebrated black artists in the hope that they would serve as role models for others. William E. Harmon, a real-estate investor from Iowa, established the New York-based foundation in 1925. In the 1930s the WPA established art workshops and community art centers in black urban communities, such as Chicago (Southside Community Art Center), Cleveland (Karamu House Artist Association), Detroit (Heritage House), and Harlem (Harlem Art Workshop and the Harlem Community Art Center) to teach art to neighborhood young people and provide work for artists. Sculptor Augusta Savage, as the first director of the Harlem Community Art Center, presided over more than 1,500 students enrolled in day and evening classes in drawing, painting, sculpture, printmaking, and design. Among the teachers was Selma Burke (1900–1995) who sculpted the relief of Franklin D. Roosevelt that appears on the dime.

One of the initiatives of the Federal Arts Project, another New Deal agency, was to sponsor the creation of murals in public buildings, such as post offices and schools, that celebrated American ideals. Murals by black artists celebrated the heritage, contributions to society, and struggles of African Americans. Aaron Douglas, a leading painter of such public art, spoke about his work and that of his colleagues in a 1936 essay, "The Negro in American Culture":

> One of our chief concerns has been to establish and maintain recognition of our essential humanity, in other words, complete social and political equality. This has been a difficult fight as we have been the constant object of attack by all manner of propaganda from nursery rhymes to false scientific racial theories. . . . In this struggle the rest of the proletariat almost invariably has been arrayed against us. . . . But the Negro artist, unlike the white artist, has never known the big house. He is essentially a product of the masses and can never take a position above or beyond their level.

Douglas and other black artists pressed the WPA to appoint more African Americans to its local boards and to hire them for more projects. The Harlem Artists Guild and the Arts and Crafts Guild in Chicago provided forums where black artists could meet and plan strategies to foster the visual arts and support the social and political issues that affected black people's lives.

Black Literature

Black literature, like black art, has been assessed in terms of what it reveals about the social, cultural, and political landscape at a given historical moment. The most distinguishing feature of black literature may be the way that black writers have attempted to create spaces of freedom in their work, to liberate place, a trait that also marks black religious culture and folk cultural practices, such as storytelling. Black literature, like all black cultural production, is valued both for aesthetic reasons on its own and for the way it represents the struggles of black people to attain freedom. In their work black writers in the 1930s and 1940s felt obliged to address questions of identity and to define and describe urban life to the dispossessed and impoverished black migrants to the cities. They tried to delineate the dimensions of a shared American heritage by portraying the specific contributions that African Americans had made to American society. Finally, and perhaps most ambitiously, black writers explored the issue of the rights African Americans were entitled to as Americans and the demands they could and should make on the state and society.

Richard Wright's *Native Son*

In 1940, Richard Wright (1908–1960) published *Native Son*, the first of many important novels by Depression-generation black authors. Reviewers hailed it as "the new American tragedy." Its tale of the downfall of the young Bigger Thomas could be read as a warning about how economic hardship combined with segregation and discrimination could lead young black men to lash out in violence and rage. Setting out for an interview for a job as a chauffeur, Bigger meets with his neighborhood friends who want him to help them rob a grocery store. Bigger's fear of whites prevents him from going along. Instead, he picks a fight to camouflage his fear and avoid committing the crime. Bigger gets the chauffeur's job, which requires him to drive the wealthy Dalton family. On his first assignment, he is supposed to drive young Mary Dalton to a university lecture. But she talks him into picking up her boyfriend, Jan—a communist—and taking them to a restaurant in the black neighborhood. Jan and Mary are oblivious to the offensively patronizing way they treat Bigger. After dinner Bigger drives them around the city while they drink and make love in the back seat.

When Jan leaves, Bigger takes an intoxicated Mary home. Because Mary is too drunk to walk, Bigger carries her to her room and is putting her to bed when blind Mrs. Dalton comes to check on her daughter. Bigger panics. He covers Mary's head with a pillow to keep her quiet. When Mrs. Dalton leaves, Bigger discovers that he has inadvertently smothered Mary. He then burns her body in the basement furnace. Not fully grasping what he has done, Bigger writes a ransom note signed with a phony name to make it seem that Mary has been kidnapped. When Mary's remains are discovered, Bigger flees. Fearing that she might betray him, Bigger then murders his girlfriend, Bessie. Bigger is captured, tried, and condemned. The remainder of the novel explores the hysteria and bigotry that envelops the case, the harsh criminal justice system, the insensitivity of the Communist party, which seeks to exploit Bigger's plight, and the poverty and social ills that plagued Chicago's African-American communities during the Depression.

At the center of the drama is Wright's exploration of how Bigger comes to terms with his murder of Mary and Bessie. In conversations with Max, his communist lawyer, he realizes that his irrational fear of white people had caused him to kill the two women. Bigger realizes that he was in fact a product of his experiences in the ghetto. At the end of the novel he says, "What I killed for I am."

Wright's novel poignantly and chillingly thrust the impact of urbanization and racism on black men and women into the collective consciousness of the American people. One white critic declared, "Speaking from the black wrath of retribution, Wright insisted that history can be punishment. He told us the one thing even the most liberal whites preferred not to hear: that Negroes were far from patient or forgiving, that they were scarred by fear, that they hated every moment of their suppression even when seeming most acquiescent, and that often enough they hated us the decent and cultivated white men who from complicity or neglect shared in the responsibility of their plight."

In his closing arguments, the lawyer, Max, describes the psychological conditions that led Bigger to kill and warns of the destructive potential of suppressed black rage:

> The hate and fear which we have inspired in him, woven by our civilization into the very structure of his consciousness and into his blood and bones, into the hourly functioning of his personality, have become the justification of his existence. . . . Kill him and swell the tide of pent up lava that will some day break loose, not in a single, blundering crime, but in a wild cataract of emotion that will brook no control.

Native Son was an immediate success. It became a Book-of-the-Month Club selection, and has sold millions of copies.

James Baldwin Challenges Wright

Wright's influence on American literature has been immense. He was the first African-American writer to enjoy an international reputation and showed that success and militancy were not mutually exclusive. A younger generation of black writers, however, especially James Baldwin (1924–1987), took issue with Wright. African Americans, they argued, need not all be portrayed as hapless victims of American racism. In a famous short essay, "Everybody's Protest Novel" in 1949, Baldwin argued that Bigger's tragedy was not that he was black, poor, and scared, but that he had accepted "a theology that denies him life, that he admits the possibility of his being sub-human and feels constrained, therefore, to battle for his humanity according to those brutal criteria bequeathed him at his birth." Baldwin concluded, "The failure of the protest novel lies in its rejection of life, the human being, the denial of his beauty, dread, power, in its insistence that it is his categorization alone which is real and which cannot be transcended." In turn, Wright accused Baldwin of trying to destroy his reputation and of betraying all African-American writers who wrote protest literature. "What do you mean, protest!" Wright demanded. "All literature is protest. You can't name a single novel that isn't protest."

Baldwin answered Wright in a second essay in 1951 entitled, "Many Thousand Gone." "Wright's work," Baldwin declared, "is most clearly committed to the social struggle. . . . [T]hat artist is strangled who is forced to deal with human beings solely in social terms; and who has, moreover, as Wright had, the necessity thrust on him of being the representative of some thirteen million people. It is a false responsibility (since writers are not congressmen) and impossible, by its nature, of fulfillment."

The controversy ended the budding friendship between Wright and Baldwin, and Baldwin, whose work would soon include many powerful and revealing novels and insightful essays, inherited the mantle of "best-known black American male writer" (see Chapter 22).

Ralph Ellison and *Invisible Man*

The most intricate novel about the black experience in America written during this era was Ralph Ellison's (1914–1994) *Invisible Man*, which won the National Book Award for fiction in 1952. Partially autobiographical, it traces the life of a young black man from his early years in a southern school (a thinly disguised Tuskegee Institute) through his migration to New York City. The novel explores class tensions within American society and within the black community. It illuminates the interaction between white and black Americans with a balanced incisive perspective.

Although he wrote many essays, *Invisible Man* was Ellison's only completed novel. He argued that the black tradition teaches one "to deflect racial provocation and to master and control pain. . . . It is a tradition which abhors as obscene any trading on one's own anguish for gain or sympathy. . . . It takes fortitude to be a man and no less to be an artist. Perhaps it takes even more if the black man would be an artist." He concluded, "It would seem to me, therefore, that the question of how the 'sociology of his existence' presses upon the Negro writer's work depends upon how much of his life the individual writer is able to transform into art."

Echoing Du Bois's now classic characterization of the "twoness" of the African-American character, Ellison observed, "[Black people] are an American people who are geared to what is and who yet are driven by a sense of what it is possible for human life to be in this society."

African Americans in Sports

It is in the arena of professional sports that black Americans have demonstrated of what human life can achieve when unconstrained by racism. The experiences of black men and women in American sports are a microcosm of their lives in American society. The privileges whites enjoyed in sports in this era paralleled the disadvantages and exclusions that were a constant part of black life. In the 1930s two black athletes, Jesse Owens and Joe Louis, captured the world's attention and inspired African Americans with pride, hope, and pleasure.

Jesse Owens and Joe Louis

Jesse Owens (1913–1980) was born on an Alabama sharecropping farm but grew up in Cleveland, Ohio. A talented runner, he studied at Ohio State University and prepared for the 1936 Olympics, which were to be held in Berlin, the capital of Nazi Germany. Many African-American leaders objected to participating in the games because they believed this would help legitimate the

African-American Milestones in Sports

1934	The Negro National League is revived.
1936	Jesse Owens wins four gold medals at Berlin Olympics.
1937	Joe Louis defeats James J. Braddock to win world heavyweight title. The Negro American League is formed.
1938	Joe Louis defeats the German Max Schmeling.
1947	Jackie Robinson signs with the Brooklyn Dodgers to become the first black major league baseball player. Dodgers win the National League Pennant.
1948	Alice Coachman wins a gold medal in the high jump to become the first black woman Olympic champion.
	Larry Doby joins the Cleveland Indians, becoming the first black player in the American League.
	Brooklyn Dodgers hire their second black player, Roy Campanella.
1949	Jackie Robinson wins the National League's Most Valuable Player Award.

Nazi myth of the superiority of the so-called Aryan race. Owens participated to debunk that myth and he succeeded, becoming the first Olympian ever to win four gold medals. Though Hitler left the stadium to avoid congratulating Owens, his snub meant little to African Americans who relished Owens's victory over racism.

Joe Louis Barrow (1914–1981), like Owens, was the son of Alabama sharecroppers. His family migrated to Detroit, Michigan, when he was twelve. Although his mother wanted him to be a violinist, Joe Louis—he dropped the name Barrow—had other interests. As a youth, Louis displayed impressive boxing ability and won a string of local victories. In 1935 he faced former heavyweight champion, Primo Carnera. A record crowd of 62,000 attended the fight in New York. The fight had political overtones. Louis was fighting an Italian-American at a time when Benito Mussolini, the Fascist dictator of Italy, was about to invade Ethiopia; this was the oldest black independent nation in Africa, whose ruler, Emperor Haile Selassie, many black Americans admired. Sports writers and police were amazed to observe everybody cheering when Louis beat Carnera in the sixth round.

Louis won the world heavyweight title against James J. Braddock in 1937 and beat the German Max Schmeling in a symbolic victory over Nazism in 1938. Louis retained the world heavyweight title until 1949.

Jackie Robinson (1919–1972) broke baseball's color barrier when he joined the Brooklyn Dodgers in 1947. He silently endured considerable hostility and threats from angry white citizens.

Breaking the Color Barrier in Baseball

While African Americans were integrated in track and in boxing, professional baseball remained strictly segregated until after World War II. Despite the hardships of the Depression, however, virtually every major black community tried to field its own baseball team. The Negro National League, which had folded in 1932, was revived in 1934, and a second league, the Negro American League, formed in 1937. Many of the players in the Negro leagues, including such legends as Josh Gibson, Satchel Paige, Leon Day, and Cool Papa Bell, would have equaled or excelled their white counterparts in the major leagues, but, except for Paige, they never had the chance.

In 1947, however, major league baseball, which had been a white man's game since the departure of Fleetwood Walker in 1887, became integrated again when Jackie Robinson (1919–1972) signed to play with the Brooklyn Dodgers. In 1945 Branch Rickey, the General Manager of the Dodgers, decided to sign a black ball player to improve the Dodgers' chances of winning the National League pennant and the World Series. After scouting the Negro Leagues, he signed twenty-six-year-old Jackie Robinson.

Robinson was the ideal choice. He was a superb athlete and a man of fortitude and immense determination. Born in Georgia and raised in southern California, he had been an All-American running back in football at UCLA and then had played baseball for the legendary Kansas City Monarchs of the Negro leagues. Robinson was also committed to black people and racial progress. Robinson played the 1946 season for the Brooklyn Dodgers minor league team in Montreal where he and his wife Rachel were warmly received by the Canadians. But spring training in segregated Florida was difficult to endure.

Robinson broke the color barrier when he opened at first base for the Dodgers in April 1947. Taunted, ridiculed, and threatened by some spectators and players, he responded by playing spectacular baseball. He won the Rookie of the Year honors in 1947, and the Dodgers won the National League pennant. Robinson retired in 1957, but remained outspoken on racial issues until his death from diabetes in 1972.

In July 1947 Larry Doby became the first black player in the American League when he joined the Cleveland Indians. As other major league teams also signed black players, the once-popular Negro Leagues withered.

Black Religious Culture

Just as black religion was the "invisible institution" that helped African Americans to survive slavery, the black church was the visible institution that helped hundreds of thousands of migrants adjust to urban life while affirming an enduring set of core values consisting of freedom, justice, equality, and an African heritage. There was of course, no single "black church." The term is a shorthand way of referring to a pluralistic collection of institutions, including most prominently seven independent, historic, and black-controlled denominations: the African Methodist Episcopal Church, the African Methodist Episcopal Zion Church; the Christian Methodist Episcopal Church; The National Baptist Convention, Incorporated; the National Baptist Convention of America, Unincorporated; the Progressive National Baptist Convention; and the Church of God in Christ. Together, these denominations account for more than 80 percent of all black Christians.

The black church helped black workers make the transition from being southern peasants to being part of a northern urban proletariat. Yet the relationship between black religious tradition and the secular lives of black people was always changing. The blues and jazz performed in nightclubs were transformed into urban gospel music. Many of the nightclub musicians and singers received their training and first public performances in their churches. During the Depression, the black church helped black people survive by enabling them to pool their resources and by offering inspiration and spiritual consolation. Here we focus on alternative religious groups that became prominent during the 1930s and 1940s and addressed specific needs growing out of the Depression and the traumatic experience of relocating to alien and often hostile northern cities. Elijah Muhammad's Nation of Islam and Father Divine's Peace Mission Movement combined secular concerns with sacred beliefs. Both strengthened a sense of identity, affirmation, and community among their members.

The Nation of Islam

The Nation of Islam emerged in 1929, the year Timothy Drew died. Drew, who took the name Nobel Drew Ali, was founder of the Moorish Science Temple of America, which flourished in Chicago, Detroit, and other cities in the 1920s. After his death, a modified version of the Moorish Science Temple emerged in 1930 in Detroit. It was led by a mysterious door-to-door peddler of silks and other items that supposedly originated in Africa, known variously as Wallace D. Fard, Master Farad Muhammad, or Wali Farad. He wrote two manuals of instruction, *The Secret Ritual of the Nation of Islam* and *Teaching for the Lost-Found Nation of Islam in a Mathematical Way*. His teachings that black people were the true Muslims attracted many poor residents in Depression-era Detroit. In addition to the beliefs of Nobel Drew Ali, Fard's Nation of Islam also taught a mixture of Koranic principles, the Christian Bible, his own beliefs, and those of nationalist Marcus Garvey.

In 1934, after establishing a Temple of Islam, Fard disappeared, and one of his disciples, Elijah Poole (1897–1975), renamed Elijah Muhammad by Fard, became leader of the Detroit temple and then of a second temple in Chicago. The Nation attracted the attention of federal authorities during World War II when its members refused to serve in the military. Muhammad was arrested in May 1942 on charges of inciting his followers to resist the draft and was imprisoned in Milan, Michigan, until 1946. After his release he settled in Chicago and began to expand his movement.

The Nation of Islam taught that black people were the Earth's original human inhabitants who had lived, according to Elijah Muhammad, in the Nile Valley. Approximately six thousand years ago, a magician named Yakub produced white people. These white people proved so troublesome that they were banished to Europe where they began to spread evil. Their worst crime was their enslavement of black people. Elijah Muhammad taught that white supremacy was ending and that black people would rediscover their authentic history and culture. To prepare for the coming millennium, he instructed members to adhere to a code of behavior that included abstaining from many traditionally southern black foods, especially pork. Members subscribed to a family-centered culture in which women's role was to produce and rear the next generation. The Nation also demanded part of the South for a black national state.

Father Divine and the Peace Mission Movement

Father Major Jealous Divine (ca. 1877–1965) was born George Baker in Savannah. Like Elijah Muhammad, little is known about his early life. He captured attention in 1919 when he settled with twenty followers in Sayville, New York, and began what became known in the 1930s as the Peace Mission Movement. Divine secured domestic jobs for many of his followers on the surrounding estates and preached a gospel of hard work, honesty, sobriety, equality, and sexual abstinence. He provided free, or nearly free, meals and shelter for anyone who asked. In 1930, he changed his name to Father Divine. His Peace Movement espoused a racially neutral and economically empowering dogma that appealed to poor and needy black and white urbanites by offering them spiritual guidance and mental and physical healing. The movement embodied ideas from the New Thought, Holiness, Perfectionist, and Adventist religions. Hundreds of people traveled to see Father Divine on weekends, feast at his communal banquet table, and listen to his promises of heaven on earth. The feasts were symbolic of the early Christian Eucharist and became the defining practices of Divine's religion.

In 1931, the police arrested Divine and eighty followers on charges of being a "public nuisance." Three days after a judge sentenced Divine to a year in jail and a $500 fine, the judge died of a heart attack. Divine was quoted as saying, "I hated to do it." The conviction was reversed, and Divine's reputation as a master of cosmic forces soared. Some of his followers now believed that he was God. Aside from the belief in the divinity of Father Divine, members of the Peace Movement were drawn to the mission's strong emphasis on ending racial prejudice and economic inequalities.

In 1933, Divine moved his headquarters to Harlem, where his Peace Mission Movement prospered, eventually purchasing key real estate and housing projects called "heavens." These acquisitions and other businesses in the Midwest enhanced Divine's ability to provide shelter, jobs, and incomes for his followers. He launched a journal entitled *New Day* in 1937 and used it to disseminate his teachings. Divine also protested social injustice and encouraged his followers to become politically engaged. Between 1936 and 1940, he lobbied strenuously for a federal antilynching law. At the time of Divine's death in 1965, the holdings of the Peace Mission were estimated to be worth $10 million. Father Divine's movement echoed the Protestant ethic: work hard, keep both your mind and body healthy; eat right; dress properly; keep good company; and avoid all manner of evil and vice.

Conclusion

The Depression ushered in a period of intense hardship, but as this chapter indicates, it was also a period in which black Americans had an unprecedented impact on American culture. Black people excelled in sports, arts, drama, and music. The Works Progress Administration (WPA) funded a wide spectrum of artists whose cultural productions were accessible, inclusive, and populist.

The Chicago Black Renaissance reflected the impact of the WPA on the lives and fortunes of hundreds of artists. A new generation of black jazz musicians transformed black music into an art form that won worldwide admiration and emulation. Black musicians weaned Americans from swing to bebop, while gospel music became a dynamic genre that satisfied the needs of the black urban migrants to express their spiritual and communal feelings.

These positive changes were made against a backdrop of entrenched racism. While some African Americans found satisfying jobs in film and radio, many others were excluded or relegated to demeaning, stereotypical roles. This bias and negative typecasting motivated innovative filmmakers to develop alternative films and artistic institutions that allowed a more balanced and accurate representation of black life and culture to develop. Such creative ventures seldom produced the profits that white entrepreneurs reaped from marketing black cultural productions to white consumers. The mass appeal and unparalleled success of entertainers such as Louis Armstrong and Duke Ellington should not obscure the fate of those artists who refused to entertain white America and instead sought to oppose racism and social and economic injustice. They remained poor and unnoticed by the dominant culture.

Still, black counterculture artists had a tremendous impact on America and reflected a growing pride and a determination to resist complete assimilation into white culture. The comic strips, the Semple stories of Langston Hughes, the black press, and the black church preserved black people's dignity. Black culture prepared black people for the next level of struggle against the American Jim Crow regime and against all ideologies of white supremacy, both in the United States and abroad.

Recommended Reading

William Barlow. *Voice Over: The Making of Black Radio.* Philadelphia: Temple University Press, 1999. A lucidly written, informative cultural history of the evolution of black radio and the personalities who made it a powerful instrument for disseminating black music, culture, language, and politics, and for constructing an African-American public sphere.

Scott DeVeaux. *BeBop: A Social and Musical History.* Berkeley, CA: University of California Press, 1997. A perceptive study of the creative artistry and lives of the pivotal black professional musicians in the jazz world during the 1930s and 1940s and how they made bebop into a commercially successful art movement.

TIMELINE

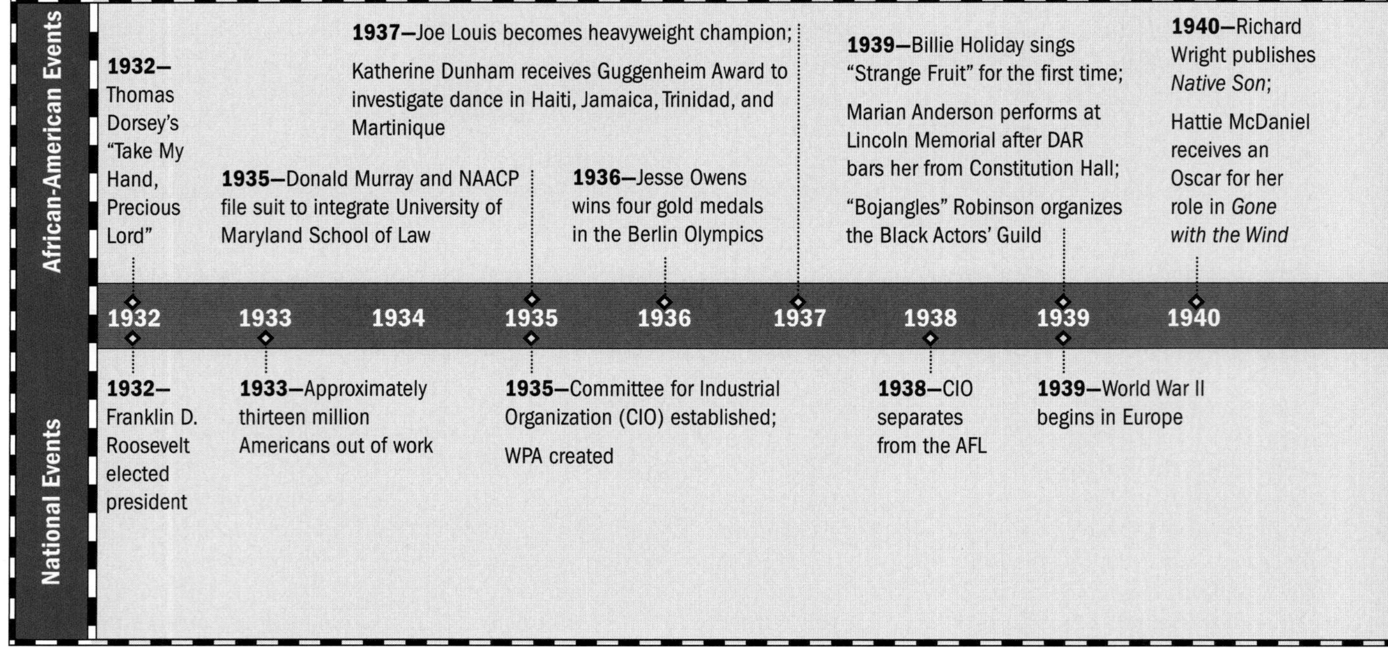

Manthia Diawara, ed. *Black American Cinema.* New York: Routledge, 1993. A collection of provocative essays. Three examine the work of filmmaker Oscar Micheaux. Others provide fresh interpretations of the recent independent cinema movement.

Melvin Patrick Ely. *The Adventures of Amos 'N' Andy: A Social History of an American Phenomenon.* New York: Free Press, 1991. A subtle and penetrating examination of the complexities of racial stereotyping in one of the most influential and controversial radio and television programs in the history of media race relations.

Samuel A. Floyd Jr. *The Power of Black Music: Interpreting Its History from Africa to the United States.* New York: Oxford University Press, 1995. An excellent overview of the history of black music with an insightful comparison of the Harlem and Chicago flowerings.

Additional Bibliography

Art

Sharon F. Patton. *African-American Art.* New York: Oxford University Press, 1998.

Richard J. Powell. *Black Art and Culture in the 20th Century.* New York: Thames and Judson, 1997.

William E. Taylor and Harriet G. Warkel. *A Shared Heritage: Art by Four African Americans.* Bloomington, IN: Indiana University Press, 1996.

Black Chicago Renaissance

Robert Bone. "Richard Wright and the Chicago Renaissance." *Callaloo* 9, no. 3 (1986):446–468.

Craig Werner. "Leon Forrest, the AACM and the Legacy of the Chicago Renaissance." *The Black Scholar* 23, no. 3/4 (1993): 10–23.

Culture

St. Clair Drake and Horace R. Cayton. *Black Metropolis: A Study of Negro Life in a Northern City.* New York: Harper & Row, 1962.

Gerald Early, ed. *"Ain't But a Place": An Anthology of African American Writing about St. Louis.* St. Louis: Missouri Historical Society Press, 1998.

Geneviève Fabre and Robert O'Meally, eds. *History and Memory in African-American Culture.* New York: Oxford University Press, 1994.

Kenneth W. Goings. *Mammy and Uncle Mose: Black Collectibles and American Stereotyping.* Bloomington, IN: Indiana University Press, 1994.

Robin D. G. Kelley. *Race Rebels: Culture, Politics, and the Black Working Class.* New York: Free Press, 1994.

Lawrence Levine. *Black Culture and Black Consciousness: Afro-American Folk Thought from Slavery to Freedom.* New York: Oxford University Press, 1977.

Tommy L. Lott. *The Invention of Race: Black Culture and the Politics of Representation.* Malden, MA: Blackwell Publishers, 1999.

Daryl Scott. *Contempt and Pity: Social Policy and Image of the Damaged Black Psyche, 1880–1996.* Chapel Hill, NC: University of North Carolina Press, 1997.

Mel Watkins. *On the Real Side: Laughing, Lying, and Signifying.* New York: Simon & Schuster, 1994.

Robert E. Weems Jr. *Desegregating the Dollar: African American Consumerism in the Twentieth Century.* New York: New York University Press, 1998.

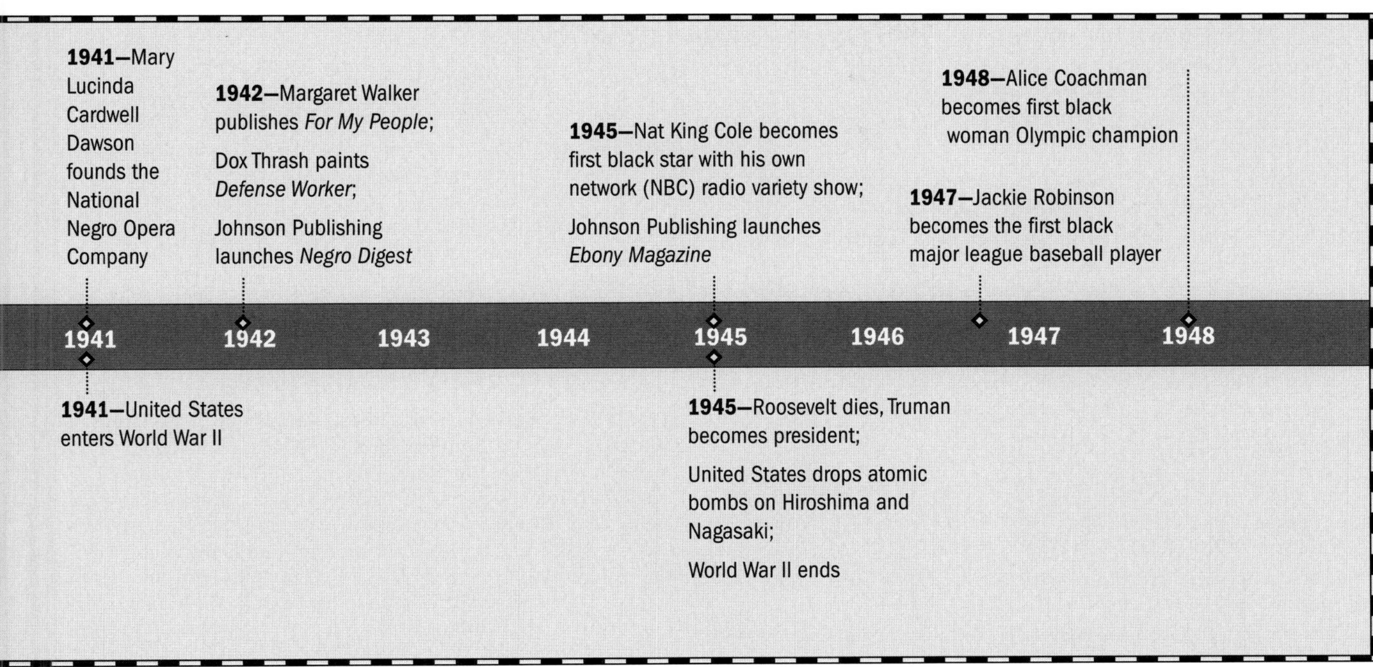

Dance

Katherine Dunham. *A Touch of Innocence.* London: Cassell, 1959.

Terry Harnan. *African Rhythm–American Dance.* New York: Knopf, 1974.

Films

Donald Bogle. *Brown Sugar: Eighty Years of America's Black Female Superstars.* New York: Crown Publishers, 1980.

Thomas Cripps. *Making Movies Black: The Hollywood Message Movie from World War II to the Civil Rights Era.* New York: Oxford University Press, 1993.

Literature

Ralph Ellison. "The World and the Jug." In Joseph F. Trimmer, ed. *A Casebook on Ralph Ellison's Invisible Man* (pp. 172–200). New York: T. Y. Crowell, 1972.

Michael Fabre. *The Unfinished Quest of Richard Wright.* Iowa City: University of Iowa Press, 1973.

Henry Louis Gates and Nellie Y. McKay, eds. *Norton Anthology of African American Literature.* New York: W. W. Norton, 1997.

Joyce Ann Joyce. *Richard Wright's Art of Tragedy.* New York: Warner Books, 1986.

Robert G. O'Meally. *The Craft of Ralph Ellison.* Cambridge, MA: Harvard University Press, 1980.

Arnold Rampersad. *The Life of Langston Hughes.* New York: Oxford University Press, 1986.

Margaret Walker. *Richard Wright, Daemonic Genius: A Portrait of the Man, a Critical Look at His Work.* New York: Morrow, 1988.

Music and Radio

William Barlow. *Looking Up at Down: The Emergence of Blues Culture.* Philadelphia: Temple University Press, 1989.

Thomas Brothers, ed. *Louis Armstrong: In His Own Words.* New York: Oxford University Press, 1999.

Jack Chalmers. *Milestones I: The Music and Times of Miles Davis to 1960.* Toronto, Canada: University of Toronto Press, 1983.

John Chilton. *The Song of the Hawk: The Life and Recordings of Coleman Hawkins.* Ann Arbor, MI: University of Michigan Press, 1990.

Donald Clarke. *Wishing on the Moon: The Life and Times of Billie Holiday.* New York: Viking Penguin, 1994.

Linda Dahl. *Morning Glory: A Biography of Mary Lou Williams.* New York: Pantheon Books, 2000.

Miles Davis and Quincy Troupe. *Miles: The Autobiography.* New York: Simon & Schuster, 1989.

Duke Ellington. *Music Is My Mistress.* New York: Da Capo Press, 1973.

John Birks Gillespie and Wilmot Alfred Fraser. *To Be or Not . . . to Bop: Memoirs/Dizzy Gillespie with Al Fraser.* New York: Doubleday, 1979.

Michael Harris. *The Rise of Gospel Blues: The Music of Thomas Andrew Dorsey in the Urban Church.* New York: Oxford University Press, 1992.

Allan Keiler. *Marian Anderson: A Singer's Journey.* New York: Scribner, 2000.

Robert G. O'Meally. *Lady Day: The Many Faces of Billie Holiday.* New York: Arcade Publishers, 1991.

Thomas Owens. *Bebop: The Music and Its Players.* New York: Oxford University Press, 1955.

Barbara Dianne Savage. *Broadcasting Freedom: Radio, War, and the Politics of Race, 1938–1948.* Chapel Hill, NC: University of North Carolina Press, 1999.

Jules Schwerin. *Got to Tell It: Mahalia Jackson, Queen of Gospel.* New York: Oxford University Press, 1992.

Alyn Shipton. *Groovin' High: The Life of Dizzy Gillespie.* New York: Oxford University Press, 1999.

Eileen Southern. *The Music of Black Americans: A History*, 2d ed. New York: W. W. Norton, 1983.

J. C. Thomas. *Chasin' the Trane: The Music and Mystique of John Coltrane.* Garden City, NY: Doubleday, 1975.

Dempsey J. Travis. *Autobiography of Black Jazz.* Chicago: Urban Research Press, 1983.

Sports

Arthur Ashe, with the assistance of Kip Branch, Ocania Chalk, and Francis Harris. *A Hard Road to Glory: A History of the African-American Athlete.* New York: Warner Books, Inc., 1988.

Richard Bak. *Joe Louis: The Great Black Hope.* New York: Da Capo Press, 1998.

Robert Peterson. *Only the Ball Was White: A History of Legendary Black Players and All-Black Professional Teams.* New York: McGraw Hill, 1984.

Arnold Rampersad. *Jackie Robinson: A Biography.* New York: Knopf, 1997.

Jackie Robinson. *I Never Had It Made.* New York: G. P. Putnam's Son, 1972.

Jeffrey T. Sammons. *Beyond the Ring: The Role of Boxing in American Society.* Urbana, IL: University of Illinois Press, 1988.

Religion

Claude Andrew Clegg III. *An Original Man: The Life and Times of Elijah Muhammad.* New York: St. Martin's Griffin, 1997.

C. Eric Lincoln and Lawrence H. Mamiya. *The Black Church in the African American Experience.* Durham, NC: Duke University Press, 1990.

Elijah Muhammad. *The True History of Elijah Muhammad: Autobiographically Authoritative.* Atlanta: Secretrius Publications, 1997.

Jill Watts. *God, Harlem USA: The Father Divine Story.* Berkeley, CA: University of California Press, 1992.

Robert Weisbrot. *Father Divine and the Struggle for Racial Equality.* Urbana, IL: University of Illinois Press, 1983.

Retracing the Odyssey

Harold Washington Library Center (312-747-4300), 400 S. State Street, Chicago, Illinois. Tuesday and Thursday, 11:00 A.M. to 7:00 P.M. Wednesday, Friday and Saturday, 9:00 A.M. to 5:00 P.M. Sunday, 1:00 P.M. to 5:00 P.M. Named in honor of Chicago's first African American Mayor, Harold Washington, the ten-story library, art, and computer reference center features the Harold Washington Archives and Collections (on the 9th floor), and the Chicago Blues Archive, and the work of several African-American artists. Jacob Lawrence contributed a mural-sized mosaic entitled "Events in the Life of Harold Washington," on the north wall of the Library.

DuSable Museum of African-American History (773-947-0600), 740 East 56th Place, Chicago, Illinois. Monday through Saturday, 10:00 A.M. to 4:00 P.M. Sunday, Noon to 4:00 P.M. Admission charge. Artist Margaret Goss Burroughs opened the Ebony Museum in 1961 in her home. She moved it in 1973 to its present location at Washington Park and renamed it the DuSable Museum of African-American History. The DuSable Museum honors the accomplishment of Jean Baptiste Pointe DuSable, a Haitian-born immigrant who arrived in Chicago in 1779 and was the first non-Indian to settle in the area. The Museum houses an extensive collection of artifacts, art, books, civil rights documents and sponsors a diverse array of cultural and educational programs and exhibits.

Carter G. Woodson Regional Library (312-747-6910) 9525 S. Halsted Street, Chicago, Illinois. Monday through Thursday, 10:00 A.M. to 8:00 P.M. Friday and Saturday, 9:00 A.M. to 5:00 P.M. Free admission. This branch of the Chicago Public Library, named in honor of the "Father of Black History," Carter G. Woodson, contains a wealth of photographs, books, documents, and manuscript collections concerning the artists and authors, women's clubs, and social institutions that detail the Black Chicago Renaissance. The Vivian Harsah Collection of Afro-American History and Literature contains over 70,000 volumes by Langston Hughes, Richard Wright, Gwendolyn Brooks, and Arna Bontemps among others.

REVIEW, RESEARCH & INTERACT

REVIEW QUESTIONS

1. How did the Great Depression affect black culture? What role did the New Deal's Works Progress Administration (WPA) play in democratizing of black expressive culture? How did black religious culture change during this era?
2. How did black artists, musicians, filmmakers, and writers negotiate the dilemma of dual consciousness as articulated by W. E. B. Du Bois? Which parts of black art did white corporate executives find easiest to appropriate and shape for white consumption?
3. How did swing era big band music lead to bebop? What problems did the bebop musicians encounter? How did black music affect American culture?
4. How did Hollywood films portray black Americans during the 1930s and 1940s? How did these images affect white Americans' attitudes and behavior toward black Americans? How did these representations contribute to the emergence of an alternative or independent black cinema?
5. How did the cultural production of the Chicago Renaissance compare with that of the Harlem Renaissance? Why did black athletes become prominent during the 1930s and 1940s? What was their impact on American culture? To what extent did the experiences of black sports figures reflect the status of race relations in the United States?

Research Navigator.com
RESOURCES FOR COLLEGE RESEARCH ASSIGNMENTS
www.researchnavigator.com

Chapter 19 investigates the role of African American culture in strengthening black communities and presenting a positive picture of African Americans to the rest of society. For further research on black culture and society in the 1930s and 1940s, use the tools available to you in Research Navigator.

As you investigate this topic, consider this question: "What were the major themes of black literature? Who read black writers?"

- **ContentSelect:** Search in the History database using the search term *Langston Hughes.*
- **Links Library:** Access the Literature: English database and explore the links for *Ellison, Ralph* and *Wright, Richard.*
- **New York Times on the Web:** To find out more, search the Music database using the search term *Charlie Parker.*

DOCUMENTS AND ACTIVITIES IN AFRICAN-AMERICAN HISTORY

Documents

19-1 Paul Robeson "Welcome Home Rally," June 19, 1949
19-2 W. C. Handy: How the Blues Came to Be, 1941
19-3 Marian Anderson, "Easter Sunday"
19-4 Ethel Waters, On Black Movies
19-5 Richard Wright, "Are We Solving America's Race Problem?" 1945

20

The World War II Era and the Seeds of a Revolution

Courtesy of the Library of Congress.

This World War II War Department recruitment poster recognizes the heroism of Dorie Miller (1919–1943) at Pearl Harbor. HIs bravery, however, did not alter the Navy's policy of restricting black sailors to the kitchens and boiler rooms of navy vessels.

THE treatment that the Negro soldier has received has been resented not only by the Negro soldier but by the Negro civilian population as well. In fact, any straight-thinking person with a sense of justice and right, without any respect to color or race, must realize the dangers inherent in the evil practices that have been permitted to exist in the Army. It is not a pleasant thought for Negroes to ponder that their tax money is being spent to help maintain an army that has little regard for the real principles of democracy.

David H. Bradford, *The Louisville Courier Journal*, September 2, 1941

Between 1939 and 1954 the role of the United States in the world was transformed. The victory in World War II of the Allies—the Soviet Union, Great Britain, the United States, and dozens of other countries—over the Axis powers of Germany, Italy, and Japan marked the emergence of America as the dominant global power. This international role placed new constraints on the nation's domestic policies, particularly when, after the Axis surrender in 1945, mutual suspicions between the United States and the Soviet Union quickly developed into a "Cold War." This long conflict, which lasted until 1989, led to a vast expansion in the size and power of the federal government, particularly its military, and cast a long shadow over domestic politics.

International events replaced the Great Depression as the defining force in the lives of African Americans. In preparing for and in fighting World War II, America finally emerged from the Depression and laid the basis for an era of unprecedented prosperity. Industrial and military mobilization resulted in the movement of millions of people, many of them African American, from agriculture into the cities. This population shift substantially increased black voting strength in the North and West, which, combined with a moral recoil from the savage racial policies of the Nazis, drove the issue of black equality to the forefront of national

CHAPTER OUTLINE

On the Eve of War, 1936–1941

- African Americans and the Emerging World Crisis
- A. Philip Randolph and the March on Washington Movement
- Executive Order #8802

Race and the U.S. Armed Forces

- Institutional Racism in the American Military
- The Costs of Military Discrimination
- Soldiers and Civilians Protest Military Discrimination
- Black Women in the Struggle to Desegregate the Military
- The Beginning of Military Desegregation
- The Tuskegee Airmen
- The Transformation of Black Soldiers

Black People on the Home Front

- Black Workers: From Farm to Factory
- The FEPC during the War
- Anatomy of a Race Riot: Detroit, 1943
- Old and New Protest Groups on the Home Front

The Transition to Peace

The Cold War and International Politics

- African Americans in World Affairs:
- W. E. B. Du Bois and Ralph Bunche
- Anticommunism at Home
- Paul Robeson
- Henry Wallace and the 1948 Presidential Election
- Desegregating the Armed Forces

The Road to *Brown*

- Constance Baker Motley and Black Lawyers in the South
- *Brown* and the Coming Revolution

Conclusion

politics. Moreover, hundreds of thousands of black men and women learned new skills and ideas while serving in the armed forces and many resolved to come home and claim their rights.

The Cold War also had a tremendous impact on African Americans and their struggle for freedom. The two sides of this conflict avoided direct confrontation with each other; instead, to a great degree, they enlisted the peoples of Africa, Asia, and Latin America as proxies. U.S. leaders, seeking to convince these peoples of America's virtues as a democracy, were pressed to address the segregation and racial discrimination that remained firmly imbedded in the basic fabric of American life. The advocacy groups and black press that had come of age during the 1930s and 1940s focused attention on fighting racism and demanded the full rights and responsibilities of citizens for all people. The result was a powerful movement for civil rights that many liberal white Americans and, increasingly, key institutions in the national government supported.

These favorable developments, however, provoked strong resistance. Egged on by their politicians, white Southerners used all the power at their command to defend segregation. The emerging hostilities with the Soviet Union prompted many white conservatives to charge that all those seeking to fight racial injustice were in fact agents of the communist enemy. These contrary currents—the push for a new democracy, on one hand, and the Cold War mentality, on the other—would indelibly place their stamp on the emerging civil rights movement.

On the Eve of War, 1936–1941

As the world economy wallowed in the Great Depression, the international order collapsed in Europe and Asia. Germany under the dictatorship of Adolf Hitler (1889–1945) and Italy under the dictatorship of Benito Mussolini (1883–1945) created an alliance, known as the Axis, aimed to take economic and political control of Europe. These fascist dictators advocated a political program based on extreme nationalism that brutally suppressed internal opposition, and used violence to gain their will abroad. Germany was the dominant partner in the Axis. Its Nazi or National Socialist party in part blamed communists and foreign powers for the nation's economic depression and loss of power. But more than by anticommunism, however, Hitler was driven by a virulent form of racism. Unlike racists in the United States, he focused his hatred on Jews, blaming them for all Germany's social and economic problems. But the Nazis also despised black people, discriminating against Germans with African ancestors and banning jazz as "nigger" music. Through the late 1930s the Germans and Italians embarked on a series of military campaigns that placed much of Central Europe under their power. In August 1939 Germany signed a nonaggression pact with the Soviet Union, a prelude to a September 1 attack on Poland by Germany, which the Soviets joined a few weeks later. Britain and France reacted to the invasion by declaring war on Germany, thus beginning World War II.

As Germany and Italy pursued their plans in Europe during the 1930s, the Empire of Japan sought to extend its power and territory in Asia. The Japanese considered themselves the foremost power in the Far East and wanted to drive out or supplant the European states, mainly Britain, France, and the Netherlands, and the United States, which had extensive economic interests and colonial possessions in Asia. (The U.S. controlled the Philippines, Hawaii, Guam, and other Pacific islands.) Japan's aggressive and expansionist policies also led to conflict with the Soviet Union in Manchuria and with the Nationalist regime in China, against which the Japanese became involved in a long and bloody struggle in the 1930s. The U.S. supported China and encouraged the European powers to resist Japanese demands for economic and territorial concessions in their Asian colonies. Japan's alliance with Nazi Germany and Fascist Italy further aggravated United States–Japanese relations, which deteriorated rapidly after the outbreak of World War II in Europe in September 1939. These tensions led to war on December 7, 1941, when the Japanese bombed American warships at Pearl Harbor, Hawaii, and launched a massive offensive against British, Dutch, and American holdings throughout the Pacific.

President Franklin D. Roosevelt watched the events in Europe and Asia with growing concern, but had only a limited ability to react. Despite its large economy, America was not a preeminent military power at the time. FDR had trouble convincing Congress to enlarge the Army and Navy, because a significant segment of the American population, the Isolationists, believed that the United States had been hoodwinked into fighting World War I and should avoid again becoming entangled in a foreign war. During the late 1930s the president had managed to overcome some of this opposition and had won the authority to increase the size of the nation's armed forces. By early 1940 the United States had instituted its first peacetime draft to provide men for the U.S. Army and Navy.

African Americans and the Emerging World Crisis

Many African Americans responded to the emerging world crisis with growing activism. When Ethiopia was invaded by Italy in 1935, it was, along with Liberia and Haiti, one of three black-ruled nations in the world, and black communities throughout the United States organized to send it aid. Mass meetings in support of the embattled Ethiopians were held in New York and other large cities while reporters from black newspapers, such as J. A. Rogers of the Pittsburgh *Courier*, brought the horror of this war home to their readers. Despite fierce resistance, the Italians won the war, in part, by using poison gas. The conflict alerted many African Americans to the dangers of fascism and reawakened an interest in Africa.

A war in Spain had a similar effect on leftist African Americans. In 1936 the left-leaning Spanish Republic became embroiled in a civil war against a fascist movement led by General Francisco Franco (1892–1975) whom Germany and Italy supported. About 100 African Americans traveled to Spain in 1936–1937 to serve with the Abraham Lincoln Battalion, an integrated fighting force of 3,000 American volunteers. Among the 100 were two women: Salaria Kee, who nursed on the battlefield, and Chicagoan Thyra Edwards, who participated in the Medical Bureau and North American Committee to Aid Spanish Democracy. Support of the Abraham Lincoln Battalion reflected a commitment by a few African Americans to the communists' vision of internationalism. Mobilization for war, however, would soon bring most black people and their organizations into the fight against fascism abroad and for equality and justice in the United States.

A. Philip Randolph and the March on Washington Movement

In 1939 and 1940 the American government, along with the governments of France and Britain, spent so much on arms that the U.S. economy was finally lifted out of the Depression. But the United States mobilized its economy for war and rebuilt its military in keeping with past practices of discrimination and exclusion. As unemployed white workers streamed into aircraft factories, shipyards, and other centers of war production, most jobless African Americans were left waiting at the gate. Most aircraft manufacturers, for example, would hire black people only in janitorial positions no matter what their skills. Many all-white AFL unions enforced closed-shop agreements that prevented their employers from hiring black workers who were not members of the labor organization. Government-funded training programs regularly rejected black applicants, often reasoning that training them would be pointless given their poor prospects of finding skilled work. The United States Employment Service (USES) filled "whites only" requests for defense workers. The military itself made it clear that although it would accept black men in their proportion to the population, about 11 percent at the time, it would put them in segregated units and assign them to service duties. The Navy limited black servicemen to menial positions while the Marine Corps and the Army Air Corps refused to accept them altogether.

When a young African-American man wrote the Pittsburgh *Courier* and suggested a "Double V" campaign—victory over fascism abroad and over racism at home— the newspaper adopted his words as the battle cry for the entire race. Fighting this struggle in a nation at war would be difficult, but the effort led to the further development of black organizations and transformed the world view of many African American solders and civilians.

Embodying the spirit of the "Double V" campaign, African-American protest groups and newspapers criticized discrimination in the defense program. Two months before the 1940 presidential election, the NAACP, Urban League, and other groups pressed President Roosevelt to take action. The president listened to their protests, but aside from a few token gestures—appointing Howard University Law School dean William Hastie as a "civilian aide on Negro affairs" in the Department of War and promoting Benjamin O. Davis, the senior black officer in the army, to brigadier general—he responded with little of substance. As a result, during late 1940 the NAACP and other groups staged mass protest rallies around the nation. With the election safely won, the president, anxious not to offend white southern politicians he needed to back his war program, refused even to meet with black leaders.

In January 1941, A. Philip Randolph, who was president of the Brotherhood of Sleeping Car Porters and who had been working with other groups to get Roosevelt's attention, called on black people to unify their protests and direct them at the national government. He suggested that ten thousand African Americans march on Washington under the slogan "We loyal Negro-American citizens demand the right

Posters like this sought both to attract black support for A. Philip Randolph's March on Washington Movement and to convince political leaders of the strength of the movement.

to work and fight for our country." In the coming months Randolph helped to create the March on Washington Movement (MOWM), which soon became the largest mass movement of black Americans since the activities of Marcus Garvey's Universal Negro Improvement Association of the 1920s. The MOWM's demands included a presidential order forbidding companies with government contracts from engaging in racial discrimination, eliminating race-based exclusion from defense training courses, and requiring the USES to supply workers on a nonracial basis. Randolph also wanted an order to abolish segregation in the armed forces and the president's support for a law withdrawing the benefits of the National Labor Relations Act from unions that refused to grant membership to black Americans. Departing from the leadership tactics of most other African-American protest groups of the time, Randolph prohibited white participation and encouraged the participation of the black working class.

Randolph's powerful appeal captured the support of many African Americans who had not before taken part in the activities of middle-class dominated groups like the NAACP. Soon he alarmed the president by raising the number expected to march to fifty thousand. Roosevelt, fearing that the protest would undermine America's democratic rhetoric and provide grist for the German propaganda mills, dispatched First Lady Eleanor Roosevelt and New York City Mayor Fiorello La Guardia to dissuade Randolph from marching. Their pleas for patience fell on deaf ears, compelling Roosevelt and his top military officials to meet with Randolph and other black leaders. The president offered a set of superficial changes but the African Americans stood firm in their demands and raised the stakes by increasing their estimate of the number of black marchers coming to Washington to one hundred thousand. By the end of June 1941, the president capitulated and had his aides draft Executive Order #8802, prompting Randolph to call off the march. It was a grand moment. "To this day," NAACP leader Roy Wilkins wrote in his autobiography, "I don't know if he would have been able to turn out enough marchers to make his point stick . . . but, what a bluff it was. A tall, courtly black man with Shakespearean diction and the stare of an eagle had looked the patrician Roosevelt in the eye—and made him back down."

Executive Order #8802

On the surface at least, the president's order marked a significant change in the government's stance. It stated in part:

> I do hereby affirm the policy of the United States that there shall be no discrimination in the employment of workers in the defense industry or government because of race, creed, color, or national origin.

The order instructed all agencies that trained workers to administer such programs without discrimination. To ensure full cooperation with these guidelines, Roosevelt created the Fair Employment Practices Committee (FEPC) with the power to investigate complaints of discrimination. The order said nothing about desegregation of the military, but private assurances were made that the barriers to entry in key services would be lowered.

Executive Order #8802, although the first major presidential action countering discrimination since Reconstruction, was no new Emancipation Proclamation. Black excitement with the order soon soured as many industries, particularly in the South, evaded its clear intent and engaged in only token hirings. What the black community learned in this instance and would witness repeatedly in the decades to come were that mere articulation of antidiscrimination principles and the establishment of commissions and committees did not lead to eradication of inequalities. Moreover, the order did not mention union discrimination. Nonetheless, the threat of the march, the issuance of the executive order, and creation of the FEPC marked the formal acknowledgment by the federal government that it bore some responsibility for protecting black and minority rights in employment. Black activists and their allies would have to continue their fight if the order was to have any meaning. Randolph sought to lead them but would find it difficult to do so because of the opposition of key government agencies—notably the military—the political power of southern congressmen, and a belief among white people that winning the war took precedent over racial issues.

Race and the U.S. Armed Forces

The demands of A. Philip Randolph and other black leaders to end segregation in the armed forces initially met stiffer resistance than their pleas for change in the civilian sector. Black men were expected to serve their country, but at the beginning of the war, most were assigned to segregated service battalions, relegated to noncombat positions, kept out of the more prestigious branches of the service, and faced tremendous obstacles to appointment as commissioned officers. This situation was particularly galling because military segregation was a symbol of the rampant discrimination black men and women encountered in their daily lives.

Institutional Racism in the American Military

Much of the armed forces' policy derived from negative attitudes and discriminatory practices common in American society. Reflecting this ingrained racism, a 1925 study by the American War College concluded that African Americans were physically unqualified for combat duty, were by nature subservient and mentally inferior, believed themselves to be inferior to white people, were susceptible to the influence of crowd psychology, could not control themselves in the face of danger, and did not have the initiative and resourcefulness of white people.

Based on this and later studies the War Department laid out two key policies in 1941 for the use of black soldiers. Although they would be taken into the military at the same rate as white inductees, African Americans would be segregated and would serve primarily in noncombat units. Responding with characteristic disdain for those who criticized these policies, Under Secretary of War Robert Patterson wrote the following:

> The Army is not a sociological laboratory; to be effective it must be organized and trained according to principles which will insure success. Experiments to meet the wishes and demands of the champions of every race and creed for the solution of their problems are a danger to efficiency, discipline and morale and would result in ultimate defeat. Out of these fundamental thoughts have been evolved broad principles relating to the employment of all persons in the military service.

In creating these policies the Army and Navy ignored evidence of the fighting ability that African Americans had shown in previous wars, and that the heroism of Dorie Miller confirmed during the attack on Pearl Harbor. Miller was the son of Texas sharecroppers who had enlisted in the Navy in 1938 and, like all black

Horace Pippin (1888–1946), *Mr. Prejudice*, 1943. Oil on canvas, 18 × 14 inches. Philadelphia Museum of Art, Gift of Dr. and Mrs. Matthew T. Moore. Photo by Graydon Wood.

Horace Pippins' (1888–1946) *Mr. Prejudice* (1943) hammers a wedge of racism through a giant V (the sign of victory). It is a powerful expression of black Americans' ongoing struggle against racial discrimination, segregation, and violence even within a nation at war against facism and Nazism, and the spread of Communism. It is located at the Philadelphia Museum of Art.

sailors in the Navy at the time, had been assigned to mess attendant duty. In other words, he was a cook and a waiter. When the Japanese air force attacked the naval base on December 7, 1941, the twenty-two-year-old Miller was below decks on the battleship *Arizona.* When his captain was seriously wounded, Miller braved bullets to help move him to a more protected area of the deck. He then took charge of a machine gun, shooting down at least two and perhaps six enemy aircraft before running out of ammunition. Miller had never before fired the gun. On May 27, 1942, the Navy cited him for "distinguished devotion to duty, extraordinary courage and disregard for his own personal safety" and awarded him a Navy Cross. The Navy then sent Miller back to mess duty without a promotion.

The Costs of Military Discrimination

Although the War and Navy Departments held to the fiction of "separate but equal" in their segregation program, their policies gave black Americans inferior resources or excluded them entirely. Segregation at Army camps most often meant that black soldiers were placed in the least desirable spots and denied the use of officers' clubs, base stores, and recreational areas. Four-fifths of all training camps were located in the South, where black soldiers were harassed and discriminated against off base as well as on. Even on leave black soldiers were not offered space in the many hotels the government leased, but had to make do with the limited accommodations that had been available to black people before the war. For southern African Americans, even going home in uniform could be dangerous. For example, when Rieves Bell of Starkville, Mississippi, was visiting his family in 1943, three young white men cornered him on a street and attempted to strip off his uniform. Bell fought back and injured one of them with a knife. The Army could not save him from the wrath of local civilian authorities who tried and sentenced Bell to three and a half years in the notorious Parchman state penitentiary for the crime of self-defense.

Perhaps most galling was to see German prisoners of war accorded better treatment than African-American soldiers. Dempsey Travis of Chicago recalled his experiences at Camp Shenango, Pennsylvania: "I saw German prisoners free to move around the camp, unlike black soldiers who were restricted. The Germans walked right into the dog-gone places like any white American. We were wearin' the same uniform, but we were excluded."

Due to the military's policies, most of the nearly one million African Americans who served during World War II did so in auxiliary units, notably in the transportation and engineering corps. Soldiers in the transportation corps, almost half of whom were black, loaded supplies and drove them in trucks to the front lines. Operating in the Redball or Whiteball express, the names for the trucking operations used to supply the American forces as they drove toward Germany in 1944 and 1945, African Americans braved enemy fire and delivered the fuel, ammunition, and other goods that made the fight possible. Black engineers built camps and ports, constructed and repaved roads, and performed many other tasks to support frontline troops.

Black soldiers performed well in these tasks but were often subject to unfair military discipline. In Europe, black soldiers were executed in vastly greater numbers than whites even though African Americans made up only 10 percent of the total number of soldiers. One of the most glaring examples of unfair treatment was the Navy's handling of a "mutiny" at its Port Chicago base north of San Francisco. On July 17, 1944, in the worst home-front disaster of the War, an explosion at the base killed 320 American sailors, of whom 202 were black ammunition loaders. In the following month 328 of the surviving ammunition loaders were sent to fill another ship. When 258 of them refused to do so, they were arrested. Eventually the Navy charged fifty men with mutiny, convicted them, and sentenced them to terms of imprisonment ranging from eight to fifteen years at Terminal Island in Southern California. The NAACP's Thurgood Marshall filed a brief on behalf of the fifty men arguing that they had been railroaded into prison because of their race, but to no avail.

Soldiers and Civilians Protest Military Discrimination

In military segregation, black American leaders, including A. Philip Randolph; Walter White of the National Association for the Advancement of Colored People (NAACP); both T. Arnold Hill and Lester Granger of the National Urban League; New York Congressman Adam Clayton Powell Jr.; Robert Vann, editor of the Pittsburgh *Courier*; and Mabel K. Staupers of the National Association of Colored Graduate Nurses, among others, identified a potent but vulnerable target. Employing a variety of strategies they mobilized the black civilian workforce, black women's groups, college students, and an interracial coalition to participate in resistance to this blatant inequality. They provoked a public dialogue with government and military officials at a pivotal moment when America's leaders most desired to present a united democratic front to the world.

Examples of black protest abound. In 1942 the NAACP's *Crisis*, and *Opportunity*, the organ of the National Urban League, published numerous editorials denouncing the Army's segregation policy. Walter White traveled across the country and throughout the world visiting camps and making contacts with black soldiers and their white officers. He inundated the War Department and the president with letters citing examples of improper, hostile, and humiliating treatment of black servicemen by military personnel and in the white communities in which bases were located. Frustration with continued military intransigence, however, forced William Hastie into a dramatic protest. He tendered his resignation as an advisor on negro affairs on January 5, 1943.

Black Women in the Struggle to Desegregate the Military

The role of black women in the struggle to desegregate the military has often been overlooked, but their militance contributed to the effort. A 1942 editorial in the *Crisis* suggested why:

> [T]he colored woman has been a more potent factor in shaping Negro society than the white woman has been in shaping white society because the sexual caste system has been much more fluid and ill-defined than among whites. Colored women have worked with their men and helped build and maintain every institution we have. Without their economic aid and counsel we would have made little if any progress.

The most prominent example of black women's struggle is found in the history of the National Association of Colored Graduate Nurses (NACGN). Mabel K. Staupers, its executive director, led an aggressive fight to eliminate quotas established by the U.S. Army Nurse Corps. Although many black nurses volunteered their services during World War II, they were refused admittance into the Navy, and the Army allowed only a few to serve. To draw attention to the unfairness of quotas, Staupers requested a meeting with Eleanor Roosevelt. In November 1944, the First Lady and Staupers met, and Staupers described black nurses' troubled relationship with the armed forces. She informed the First Lady that eighty-two black nurses were serving 150 patients at the station hospital at Fort Huachuca, Arizona, at a time when the Army was complaining of a dire nursing shortage and debating the need to draft nurses. Staupers expounded on the practice of using black women to care for German prisoners of war. She asked, rhetorically, if this was to be the special role of the black nurse in the war? Staupers elaborated, "When our women hear of the great need for nurses in the Army and when they enter the service it is with the high hopes that they will be used to nurse sick and wounded soldiers who are fighting our country's enemies and not primarily to take care of these enemies."

Soldiers and sailors also resisted segregation and discrimination while in the service. Their action included well-organized attempts to desegregate officers' clubs. At Freeman Field, Indiana, for example, one hundred black officers refused to back down when their commanders threatened to arrest them for seeking to use the officers' club. In other bases African-American soldiers responded with violence to violence, intimidation, and threats. Their actions, although put down with dispatch, prompted the Army brass to reevaluate their belief in the military efficiency of discrimination.

VOICES

William H. Hastie Resigns in Protest

In January 1943, William H. Hastie, who had been on leave from his post as dean of the Howard University Law School, resigned as civilian aide to Secretary of War Henry L. Stimson to protest official failure to outlaw discrimination in the military. Hastie had taken the position in 1940, and throughout his tenure he had experienced frustration and hostility in attempting to secure equal treatment for black men and women in uniform. In his letter of resignation, which he published in the Chicago Defender, *he explains that the Army Air Forces' reactionary policies and discriminatory practices were the immediate catalyst to his resignation:*

The Army Air Forces are growing in importance and independence. In the post war period they may become the greatest single component of the armed services. Biased policies and harmful practices established in this branch of the army can all too easily infect other branches as well. The situation had become critical. Yet, the whole course of my dealings with the Army Air Forces convinced me that further expression of my views in the form of recommendations within the department would be futile. I, therefore, took the only course which can, I believe, bring results. Public opinion is still the strongest force in American life.

To the Negro soldier and those who influence his thinking, I say with all the force and sincerity at my command that the man in uniform must grit his teeth, square his shoulders and do his best as a soldier, confident that there are millions of Americans outside of the armed services, and more persons than he knows in high places within the military establishment, who will never cease fighting to remove every racial barrier and every humiliating practice which now confront him. But only by being, at all times a first class soldier can the man in uniform help in this battle which shall be fought and won.

When I took office, the Secretary of War directed that all questions of policy and important proposals relating to Negroes should be referred to my office for comment or approval before final action. In December, 1940, the Air Forces referred to me a plan for a segregated training center for Negro pursuit pilots at Tuskegee. I expressed my entire disagreement with the plan, giving my reasons in detail. My views were disregarded. Since then, the Air Command has never on its own initiative submitted any plan or project to me for comment or recommendation. What information I obtained, I had to seek out. Where I made proposals or recommendations, I volunteered them.

This situation reached its climax in late December, 1942, when I learned through army press releases sent out from St. Louis and from the War Department in Washington that the Air Command was about to establish a segregated officer candidate school at Jefferson Barracks, Mo., to train Negro officers for ground duty with the Army Air Forces. Here was a proposal for a radical departure from present army practice, since the officer candidate training program is the one large field where the army is eliminating racial segregation.

Moreover, I had actually written to the Air Command several weeks earlier in an attempt to find out what was brewing at Jefferson Barracks. The Air Command replied as late as December 17, 1942, giving not even the slightest hint of any plan for a segregated officer candidate school. It is inconceivable to me that consideration of such a project had not then advanced far enough for my office to have been consulted, even if I had not made specific inquiry. The conclusion is inescapable that the Air Command does not propose to inform, much less counsel with, this office about its plans for Negroes.

QUESTIONS

1. Why did African Americans fight so relentlessly to end segregation in the U.S. military? What did the military represent or symbolize to the nation?
2. Under what circumstances did African Americans appear to accept segregation and the establishment of separate programs such as the Tuskegee Airmen? Why then did African Americans object strenuously to the military's efforts to provide equal but separate facilities and educational programs?

Source: William H. Hastie, "Why I Resigned," *Chicago Defender*, February 6, 1943. Reprinted courtesy of the *Chicago Defender*.

Black women army nurses, like black male servicemen, served in all-black units in the U.S. military during World War II. The War Department assigned them to care for German prisoners of war, but initially prohibited them from caring for sick and wounded white Americans. Under the leadership of Mabel Staupers, black nurses successfully fought against enlistment quotas and other discriminatory treatment.

The Beginning of Military Desegregation

In response to the militancy of black officers, civil rights leaders, and the press, the War Department made changes and began to take on the challenge of reeducating soldiers, albeit in a limited fashion. The Advisory Committee on Negro Troop Policies was charged with coordinating the use of black troops and developing policy on social questions and personnel training. In 1943 the War Department also produced its own propaganda film—*The Negro Soldier*, directed by Frank Capra—to alleviate racial tensions. This patronizing film emphasized the contributions black soldiers had made in the nation's wars since the American Revolution and was designed to appeal to both black and white audiences.

The War Department also attempted to use propaganda to counter black protest groups and the claims of discrimination found in the black press. The key to this effort was fighter Joe Louis, whom the Army believed was "almost a god" to most black Americans. "The possibilities for using him," a secret internal report stated, "are almost unlimited, such as touring the army camps as special instructor on physical training; exhibition bouts, for use in radio or in movies; in a movie appearance a flashback could be shown of Louis knocking out Max Schmeling, the champion of the Germans." The same report also mentioned other prominent black men and women who had "great value in any propaganda programs. Other athletes like Ray Robinson, also track athletes, etc.; name bands like Cab Calloway, [Jimmy] Lunceford; stage, screen and concert stars like Ethel Waters, Bill Robinson, Eddie Anderson, Paul Robeson, etc." The effect of this propaganda barrage is impossible to gauge, but it did little to counter the real incidents of prejudice and discrimination that most black people experienced in their daily lives.

Racism remained strong throughout the war, but the persistent push of protest groups and the military's need for manpower gradually loosened its grip. After the attack on Pearl Harbor, nearly all the services had to relax their restrictions on African Americans. The Navy, previously the most resistant service, began to accept black men as sailors and noncommissioned officers. By 1943 it allowed African Americans into officer training schools. The Marine Corps, exclusively white throughout its history, began taking African Americans in 1942. Black officers were trained in integrated settings in all services except the Army's Air Corps. The War Department even acted to compel recalcitrant commanding officers to recommend black servicemen for admission to the officer training schools, and soon, over two thousand a year were graduated.

Many African Americans also saw combat, although under white officers. Several African-American artillery, tank destroyer, antiaircraft, and

VOICES

Separate but Equal Training for Black Army Nurses?

In August 1944, Maple Staupers received this reply from Under Secretary of War Robert Patterson in response to her query about a segregated training center the Army had established at Fort Huachuca, Arizona, for black nurses:

August 7, 1944
Mrs. Mabel K. Staupers R.N.,
Executive Secretary,
National Association
of Colored Graduate Nurses, Inc.,
1790 Broadway,
New York 19, N.Y.

Dear Mrs. Staupers:

Thank you for your letter of July 19 with reference to the establishment of the first basic training center for Army Negro nurses at Fort Huachuca.

In establishing the first basic training center for Army Negro nurses at Fort Huachuca, the War Department desired that these nurses receive the best possible training and the most valuable experience for the type of service they would be required to render as Army nurses. It is the policy of the War Department to assign Negro nurses to those hospitals where there is a substantial number of Negro troops in relation to the personnel of the entire installation. The trainee at Fort Huachuca will therefore have the advantage of serving in a facility and under conditions parallel to those under which she will serve as an Army nurse.

You may be assured that the facilities for training afforded Negro nurses at Fort Huachuca will in no way be inferior to those of other similar establishments, and in their subsequent assignments these nurses will have full opportunity to render valuable service to the Army.

Sincerely yours,
(Signed) ROBERT P. PATTERSON
ROBERT P. PATTERSON,
Under Secretary of War

QUESTIONS

1. How does Patterson's letter reflect the U.S. military's position that "separate but equal" did not constitute discrimination against African Americans?
2. Why did Mabel Staupers and the National Association of Colored Graduate Nurses object to the establishment of separate training facilities for black women?

Source: War Department Files, File #2912, National Archives, Washington, DC.

combat engineer battalions fought with distinction in Europe and Asia. Military prejudice seemed to be borne out by the poor showing of the all-black 92nd Combat Division, but investigation revealed that its failure was the result of poor training and leadership by a white officer with no confidence in his men. After the Battle of the Bulge, a massive late-1944 German counterattack, 2,500 black volunteers fought in integrated units. Although the experiment would not be repeated during the war, its success laid the groundwork for later changes. Although subject to many of the same kinds of discrimination as African-American men, African-American women also found expanded opportunities in the military. Approximately 4,000 black women served in the Women's Army Auxiliary Corps (WAACs).

Mabel Staupers's efforts also bore fruit in early 1945. When the War Department claimed that there was a shortage of nurses, Staupers mobilized nursing groups of all races to write letters and send telegrams protesting the discrimination against black nurses in the Army and Navy Nurse Corps. There was an immediate groundswell of public support to remove quotas. Buried beneath an avalanche of telegrams from an inflamed public, the War Department declared an end to quotas and exclusion. On January 10, 1945, the Army opened its Nurse Corps to all applicants without regard to race, and five days later the Navy followed suit. Within a few weeks, Phyllis Daley became the first black woman inducted into the Navy's Nurse Corps. Over three hundred black nurses were eventually accepted into the Army Nurse Corps.

PROFILE

Mabel K. Staupers (1890–1989)

Mabel K. Staupers was born in Barbados, in the British West Indies, on February 27, 1890 to Thomas Clarence and Pauline (Lobo) Doyle. The family emigrated to New York in 1903 and in 1917 Mabel became a naturalized citizen of the United States. In short order, Mabel married James Max Keaton, from whom she was later divorced, and received her RN diploma from Freedmen's Hospital School of Nursing in Washington, DC. She worked as a private duty nurse in Washington, DC, and in New York City where she helped to organize, and served as the superintendent of from 1920 to 1922, the Booker T. Washington Sanatorium, an inpatient clinic for African Americans with tuberculosis.This was one of the few facilities in New York City that permitted black physicians to treat their patients when they were hospitalized. Most other hospitals denied black medical professionals attending or staff privileges and positions. Staupers further honed her organizing and leadership skills when she became executive secretary of the Harlem Committee of the New York Tuberculosis and Health Association, serving from 1922 to 1934. In 1935, Staupers joined with Mary McLeod Bethune to found the National Council of Negro Women. Staupers also accepted the challenge of revitalizing the National Association of Colored Graduate Nurses (NACGN), becoming its first executive director in 1934 and served until 1949, when she was named the organizations's president. Under her stewardship the NACGN, in 1951, officially dissolved, and black nurses gained membership in the American Nursing Association.

Staupers's organizing and leadership talent was put to its greatest test during World War II. With verve and perfect timing she mobilized wide-ranging support to end quotas that the United States military had established to limit the numbers of black nurses accepted into the Armed Forces Nurse Corps. While the Army initially indicated that it would accept fifty-six black nurses to work in the hospital units at Camp Livingston in Louisiana and Fort Bragg in North Carolina, the Navy refused to accept any black women nurses. The matter came to a head when, in January 1945, President Franklin D. Roosevelt announced his support of legislation to draft nurses. Staupers was appalled that the government would entertain such a notion when hundreds of black women nurses were available and eager to serve. She led the struggle to end quotas and discrimination against black women nurses in the armed forces. In 1961 Staupers published her account of this struggle in a book entitled, *No Time for Prejudice: A Story of the Integration of Negroes in Nursing in the United States* (New York: Macmillan, 1961). In recognition of her courageous and relentless struggle against racial discrimination, the NAACP awarded Staupers the Spingarn Medal in 1951. An array of honors followed. In 1967, New York Mayor John V. Lindsay gave her a citation of appreciation, which read, "To an immigrant who came to the United States and by Individual Effort through Education and Personal Achievement has become an Outstanding American Leader and Distinguished Citizen of America." She died of pneumonia at her home in Washington, DC, in 1989.

The Tuskegee Airmen

The most visible group of black soldiers served in the Army Air Force. In January 1941, the War Department announced the formation of an all-black Pursuit Squadron and the creation of a training program at Tuskegee Army Air Field, Alabama, for black pilots.

Unlike all other units in the Army, the 99th Squadron and the 332nd Group, made up of the 100th, 301st, and 302nd Squadrons, had black officers. The 99th went to North Africa in April 1943 and flew its first combat mission against the island of Pantelleria on June 2. Later the squadron participated in the air battle over Sicily, operating from its base in North Africa, and supported the invasion of Italy. The squadron regularly engaged German pilots in aerial combat. General Benjamin O. Davis, Jr. commanded the 332nd Group when it

The distinguished World War II record of the "Tuskegee Airmen," pilots who trained and fought in all-black fighter squadrons, confounded the expectations of white officers who doubted that black men had the ability or nerve to pilot fighter aircraft.

was deployed to Italy in January 1944. In July, the 99th was added to the 332nd and the Group participated in campaigns in Italy, France, Germany, and the Balkans.

The Tuskegee Airmen amassed an impressive record. They flew over 15,500 sorties and completed 1,578 missions. During the two hundred missions in which they escorted heavy bombers deep into Germany's Rhineland, not one of the "heavies" was lost to enemy fighter opposition. They destroyed 409 enemy aircraft, sank an enemy destroyer, and knocked out numerous ground installations. They were well regarded and recognized for their heroism. They accumulated 150 Distinguished Flying Crosses, one Legion of Merit, one Silver Star, fourteen Bronze Stars, and 744 Air Medals. Tuskegee pilot Coleman Young (1919–1997, mayor of Detroit 1973–1993) recalled, "once our reputation got out as to our fighting ability, we started getting special requests for our group to escort their group, the bombers. They all wanted us because we were the only fighter group in the entire air force that did not lose a bomber to enemy action. Oh, we were much in demand."

The Transformation of Black Soldiers

A new generation of African Americans became soldiers during World War II and many would emerge from the experience with an enhanced sense of themselves and a commitment to the fight for black equality. Unlike the black soldiers in World War I, a greater percentage of those drafted at the outset of World War II had attended high school and more were either high school or college graduates. Some black soldiers brought "radical" ideas with them as they were drafted and sent to segregated installations. The urban and northern black servicemen and women and many of the southern rural recruits had a strong sense of their own self-worth and dignity. In their study of Chicago, sociologists St. Clair Drake and Horace Cayton noted the following:

> At least half of the Negro soldiers—and Bronzeville's men fall into this class—were city people who had lived through a Depression in America's Black Ghettoes, and who had been exposed to unions, the Communist movement, and to the moods of racial radicalism that occasionally swept American cities. Even the rural southern Negroes were different this time—for the thirty years between the First and Second World War has seen a great expansion of school facilities in the South and distribution of newspapers and radios.

Serving in the armed forces first exposed many African Americans to a world outside the segregated South. Haywood Stephney of Clarksdale, Mississippi, recalled that when he first encountered segregation in the military he simply thought it was supposed to be that way. He explained, "Because you grow up in this situation you don't see but one side of the coin. Having not tasted the freedom or the liberty of being and doing like other folks then you didn't know what it was like over across the street. So we accepted it." Like many others, his experiences during the war quickly removed him from "total darkness" and raised fundamental questions about the racial system of the nation.

Douglas Conner, another Mississippi veteran, captured the collective understanding of the social and political meaning of the war shared by the men in his unit, the 31st Quartermaster Battalion stationed in Okinawa: "The air people in Tuskegee, Dorie Miller, and the others gave the blacks a sense that they could succeed and compete in a world that had been saying that 'you're nothing.' " Conner insisted that "because of the world war, I think many people, especially blacks, got the idea that we're going back, but we're not going back to business as usual. Somehow we're going to change this nation so that there's more equality than there is now." The personal transformation that Conner and others experienced combined with a number of international, national, and regional forces to lay the foundation for a Second Reconstruction in the American South.

Black People on the Home Front

TRACK 34

Just as they did in the military, African Americans on the home front fought a dual war against the Axis and discrimination. Black workers and volunteers helped staff the factories and farms that produced goods for the fight while also purchasing war bonds and participating in other defense activities. The changes brought on by the war also created new points of conflict while exacerbating preexisting problems and occasionally igniting full-scale riots. Throughout the war, protest groups and the black press continued to fight employment discrimination and political exclusion.

TRACK 35

Black Workers: From Farm to Factory

The war accelerated the migration of African Americans from rural areas to the cities. Even though the farm economy recovered during the war, the lure of high-paying defense jobs and other urban occupations tempted many black farmers to abandon the land. By the 1940s the bitter experiences of the previous decades had made it clear that there was little future in the cotton fields. Boll weevils, competition from other parts of the world, and mechanization reduced the need for black labor. Indeed, by the end of the war, only 28 percent of black men worked on farms, a decline of 13 percent since 1940. More than three hundred thousand black men left agricultural labor between 1940 and 1944 alone.

The wartime need for workers, backed by pressure from the government, helped break down some of the barriers to employing African Americans in industry. During the war the total number of black workers in nonfarm employment rose from 2,900,000 to 3,800,000. Nearly all industries relaxed their resistance to hiring African-American workers, and thousands moved into previously whites-only jobs. African Americans found employment in the aircraft industry, and likewise tens of thousands were employed in the nation's shipyards.

With so many of their men away at war, black women increasingly found work outside the laundry and domestic service that had previously been their

Before World War II, few white women, and still fewer black women, worked in heavy industries, but with so many men in the armed forces, women were recruited for jobs in shipyards and airplane factories like this aircraft worker. Between 1940 and 1944, the percentage of black women in the industrial workforce increased from 6.8 percent to 18 percent.

lot. Nationally 600,000 black women—400,000 of them former domestic servants—shifted into industrial jobs. As one aircraft worker wryly put it, "Hitler was the one that got us out of the white folks' kitchen." Even those women who stayed in domestic work often saw their wages improve as the supply of competing workers dwindled.

The abundance of industrial jobs helped spur and direct the migration of African Americans during and after World War II. Some 1,500,000 migrants, nearly 15 percent of the population, left the South, swelling the black communities in northern and western cities that had significant war industries. By 1950 the proportion of the nation's black population living in the South had fallen from 77 percent to 68 percent. The most dramatic rise in black population was in southern California. Because of its burgeoning aircraft industry and the success of civil rights groups and the federal government in limiting discrimination, Los Angeles saw its relatively small African-American community increase by more than 340,000 during the war.

During the war many unions became more open to African-American workers. As black men and women took jobs in industries, many joined unions. Between 1940 and 1945, black union membership rose from two hundred thousand to 1.25 million. Those unions connected to the CIO, particularly the United Automobile Workers, were the most open to black membership, whereas AFL affiliates were the most likely to treat African Americans as second-class members or to continue to exclude them altogether. Some white unionized workers continued to oppose hiring black workers, even going on strike to prevent it, but their resistance was often deflected by the union leadership, the government, or employers. The growth in black membership did not end racism in unions, even in the CIO, but it did provide African Americans a stronger foundation upon which to protest continuing discrimination in employment.

The FEPC during the War

Responding to the ineffectiveness of the Fair Employment Practices Committee during the first years of the war, in May 1943 President Roosevelt issued Executive Order #9346. The order established a new Committee on Fair Employment Practice, increased its budget, and placed its operation directly under the Executive Office of the President. Roosevelt appointed Malcolm Ross, a combative white liberal, to head the committee. Ross proved to be more effective than the committee's previous leadership. He initiated nationwide hearings of cases concerning discrimination in the shipbuilding and railroad industries. These proceedings caused embarrassment for companies and brought some compliance with the FEPC's orders. Resistance, however was more common. In Mobile, Alabama, for example, the white employees of the Alabama Dry Dock and Shipbuilding Company opposed the FEPC's efforts to pressure the company to promote twelve of the 7,000 African Americans it employed in menial positions to racially mixed welding crews. The white workers went on a rampage, assaulting fifty African Americans. The FEPC thereupon withdrew its plan and acquiesced in the traditional Jim Crow arrangements for all work assignments. White workers retained their more lucrative positions. As a result of this kind of intransigence, the committee failed to redress most of the grievances of black workers. A concerted effort to continue the committee after the war was defeated.

Anatomy of a Race Riot: Detroit, 1943

One of the bloodiest race riots in the nation's history took place in 1943 in Detroit, Michigan, where black and white workers were competing fiercely for jobs and housing. Relations between the two communities in the city had been smoldering for months, with open fighting in the plants and on the streets. White racism, housing segregation, and economic discrimination were part of the problem. The brutality of white police officials was an especially potent factor. Tensions were so palpable that weeks before the riot NAACP leader Walter White had warned that the city could explode in violence at any moment.

The immediate trigger for the riot was a squabble on June 20 between groups of white and black bathers at the segregated city beaches on Belle Isle in the Detroit River. Within hours, two hundred white sailors from a nearby base joined the white mob that pursued and attacked individual black men and women. A rumor that white citizens had killed a black woman and thrown her baby over the bridge spread across the city. The riot was in full swing, spreading quickly along Woodward Avenue, the city's major thoroughfare, into Paradise Valley where some thirty-five thousand southern black migrants had, in the spring of 1943, joined the city's already crowded black population. By Monday morning downtown Detroit was overrun with white men roaming in search of more victims. At first the mayor refused to acknowledge that the situation had gotten out of hand, but by Tuesday evening he could no longer deny the crisis.

Six thousand federal troops had to be dispatched to Detroit to restore order. When the violence ended, thirty-four people had been killed (twenty-five black and nine white people) and more than 700 injured. Of the twenty-five black people who died, the Detroit police killed seventeen. The police did not kill any of the white men who assaulted African Americans or committed arson. Property damage exceeded two million dollars and one million man hours were lost in war production.

In the aftermath, the city created the Mayor's Interracial Committee, the first permanent municipal body designed to promote civic harmony and fairness. Despite the efforts of labor and black leaders, many white people in Detroit, including the Wayne County prosecutor William E. Dowling, blamed the black press and the NAACP for instigating the riot. Dowling and others accused the city's black citizens of pushing too hard for economic and political equality and insisted that they operated under communist influence. One of many commissioned reports concluded that black leaders provoked the riot because they had compared "victory over the axis . . . [with] a corresponding overthrow in the country of those forces which . . . prevent true racial equality." In contrast, black leaders, radical trade unionists, and members of other ethnic organizations, especially Jewish groups, blamed, "the KKK, the Christian Front, the Black Dragon Society, the National Workers League, the Knights of the White Camelia, the Southern Voters League, and similar organizations based on a policy of terror and . . . white supremacy."

Old and New Protest Groups on the Home Front

The NAACP grew tremendously during the war, and by its end stood poised for even greater achievements. Under the editorial direction of Roy Wilkins, the circulation of the NAACP's *Crisis* grew from 7,000 to 45,000. During the war, the *Crisis* was one of the most important sources for information on the status of black men and women. The NAACP's membership increased from 50,000 in 1940 to 450,000 at the end of the war. Even more important, much of this growth occurred in the South, which had more than 150,000 members by 1945. Supreme Court victories and especially close monitoring of the "Double V" campaign help explain these huge increases.

With success, however, came conflict and ambivalence. Leaders split over the value of integration versus self-segregation and questioned the benefit of relying so heavily on legal cases rather than paying more attention to the concerns and needs of working-class black men and women. Wilkins acknowledged the organization's uncertainty and indecisiveness:

> The war was a great watershed for the NAACP. We had become far more powerful, and now the challenge was to keep our momentum. Everyone knew the NAACP stood against discrimination and segregation, but what was our postwar program to be? Beyond discrimination and segregation, where would we stand on veterans, housing, labor-management relations, strikes, the Fair Employment Practices Commission, organizations at state levels, education? What would we do to advance the fight for the vote in the South? . . . We had a big membership . . . but we didn't know how to use them.

In 1944, southern white liberals joined with African Americans to establish the Southern Regional Council (SRC). This interracial coalition, an important example of the local initiative of private citizens, was devoted to expanding democracy in a region better known for the political and economic oppression and exploitation of its black citizens. The SRC conducted research and focused attention on the political, social, and educational inequalities endemic to black life in the South. Although its patient, gradualist program would soon be overtaken by the events of the 1950s and 1960s, the SRC challenged the facade of southern white supremacy.

In 1942 a far more strident group called the Congress of Racial Equality (CORE) had been formed. It pursued different tactics from those of the NAACP, Urban League, and other existing civil rights groups. CORE began in Chicago when an interracial group of Christian pacifists gathered to find ways to make America live up to the ideals of equality and justice on which it based its war program. Activists James Farmer and Bayard Rustin were key in getting the group off the ground. Unlike the NAACP, CORE was a decentralized, intensely democratic organization. CORE dedicated itself to the principles of nonviolent direct action as expounded by Indian leader Mohandas Gandhi. Over the course of the war this pacifist organization expanded to other cities and challenged segregation in the North with sit-ins and other protest tactics that the civil rights movement would later adopt.

African Americans found many ways to fight discrimination. Women were central to these efforts. Throughout the 1940s, in countless communities across the South and the Middle West, black women organized women's political councils and other groups to press for integration of public facilities—hospitals, swimming pools, theaters, and restaurants—and for the right to pursue collegiate and professional studies. Others were galvanized by the war and took advantage of the limited social and political spaces afforded them to create lasting works in the arts, literature, and popular culture. Women whose names would become virtually synonymous with the modern civil rights movement in the 1950s and 1960s helped to lay its foundation in the World War II era. Ella Baker was accumulating contacts and sharpening her organizing skills as she served as the NAACP field secretary. Rosa Parks began resisting segregation laws on Montgomery, Alabama, buses in the 1940s.

Black college students also began protesting segregation in public accommodations. The spark that ignited the Howard University campus civil rights movement came in January 1943. Three sophomore women, Ruth Powell from Massachusetts and Marianne Musgrave and Juanita Morrow from Ohio, sat at a lunch counter near the campus and were refused service. They demanded to see the manager and vowed to wait until he came. Instead of the manager, two policemen

PROFILE

Bayard Rustin

Bayard Rustin, the preeminent strategist of nonviolent resistance, was born on March 17, 1910, in West Chester, Pennsylvania. Rustin worked behind the scenes to give shape and coherence to the modern civil rights movement. During his youth he belonged to the Young Communist League. But in the 1940s he, along with Pauli Murray and James Farmer, became staff members of the pacifist organization Fellowship of Reconciliation (FOR) and experimented with Gandhian techniques of nonviolent resistance to racial injustice. In 1942, Rustin and Farmer were active in founding the Congress of Racial Equality (CORE). A year later, Rustin refused to be drafted, rejecting even the traditional Quaker compromise of alternative service in an army hospital. Convicted of violating the Selective Service Act, he served three years in a federal penitentiary in Ashland, Kentucky.

Bayard Rustin (1910–1987) spent his life actively engaged in Civil Rights causes. He struggled against discrimination during the 1940s, was special assistant to Martin Luther King, Jr. in the 1940s, a behind-the-scenes architect of the March on Washington in 1963, and executive director of the A. Philip Randolph Institute. Robert Maass captures his quite dignity in this 1982 photograph.

While in prison, Rustin honed the philosophy that would guide his life, which he summed up this way:

> There are three ways in which one can deal with an injustice. (a) One can accept it without protest. (b) One can seek to avoid it. (c) One can resist the injustice nonviolently. To accept it is to perpetuate it. To avoid it is impossible. To resist by intelligent means, and with an attitude of mutual responsibility and respect, is much the better course.

Upon release from prison, Rustin became race relations secretary for FOR and participated in countless protest organizations. He organized a Free India Committee and directed A. Philip Randolph's Committee against Discrimination in the Armed Forces. He orchestrated CORE's 1947 Journey of Reconciliation, a precursor to the Freedom Rides of 1961, in which sixteen black and white men traveled by bus through the upper South to test new federal laws prohibiting segregated services in interstate transportation. Outside Chapel Hill, North Carolina, the group was assaulted and arrested. Rustin and three of his colleagues were sentenced to thirty days on a road gang, of which he served twenty-two days. In the late 1950s Rustin served as an important adviser to Martin Luther King, Jr. and was one of the key figures in nearly all phases of the civil rights movement of the 1950s and 1960s.

Rustin, who was gay, fought oppression all his life. After the ebbtide of the civil rights movement he shifted his attention to combating homophobia. He declared shortly before his death on August 24, 1987, that "the barometer of where one is on human rights questions is no longer the black community, it's the gay community. Because it is the community which is most easily mistreated."

arrived who instructed the waitress to serve them. When the check arrived the trio learned that they had been charged 25 cents each instead of the customary 10 cents. They placed 35 cents on the counter, turned to leave, and were arrested. Ruth Power later reported that "the policemen who arrested us told us we were being taken in for investigation because he had no proof that we weren't 'subversive agents.'" In fact, no charges were lodged against the women. The purpose of their arrest had been to intimidate them, but the incident instead fanned the smoldering embers of resentment in the Howard University student body.

The Transition to Peace

After the German surrender in May 1945 and the Japanese surrender in August 1945, the United States began the transition to peace. Many of the gains of black men and women were wiped away as the armed forces demobilized and the factories began reinstituting the discriminatory hiring systems in place before the conflict. Nonetheless, in 1945 it was clear that segregation would face a huge challenge in the coming years and that the African-American community was ready, willing, and able to fight in ways undreamed of in earlier eras.

America's Cold War propaganda targeted all citizens, black and white. This anticommunism poster was one of many designed to remind Americans of threats to their freedom and to fan the flames of patriotism.

The Cold War and International Politics

As the defeat of the Axis powers neared in early 1945, the United Nations began planning for the peace. Within a short time, however, the opposing interests of the Soviet Union and the United States led to a long period of intense hostility that became known as the Cold War. This conflict soon led to a division of Europe into two spheres, with the Soviets dominating part of Germany and the nations to its east and a coalition of democratic capitalist regimes allied with the United States in the west. Thereafter the overriding goal of the United States and its allies was the "containment" of communism. To this end, the North Atlantic Treaty Organization (NATO) was formed in 1949 to provide a military counterforce to Soviet power in Europe while American dollars helped rebuild Western Europe's war shattered economy. The United States forged a similarly close relationship with Japan. Much of the rest of the world, however, became contested terrain during the Cold War.

As the nations of Asia and Africa gained independence from colonial domination over the ensuing decades, the United States struggled to keep them out of the Soviet orbit. It did so through foreign aid, direct military force, and, occasionally through clandestine operations run by the Central Intelligence Agency (CIA). These military interventions were matched by a rising diplomatic and propaganda effort to convince the emerging nations of the world that the United States was a model to be emulated and an ally to be trusted.

The Cold War had an enormous influence on American society precisely when the powerful movement for African-American rights was beginning to emerge. The long conflict resulted in the rise of a permanent military establishment in the United States. Small in scope before World War II, the reorganized American military enlisted millions of men and women by the early 1950s and claimed most of the national budget. The federal government also grew in power during the war and provided a check on the control that white Southerners had so long exercised over race relations in their region. American policy makers also became concerned about the nation's ability to win the allegiance of Africans and other nonwhite people who formed the population of the emerging nations. The Soviet Union possessed a powerful propaganda advantage because it could discredit American sincerity by pointing to the deplorable state of race relations within the United States. Hence, during the Cold War, external pressures reinforced efforts to change American racial policy.

African Americans in World Affairs: W. E. B. Du Bois and Ralph Bunche

The Cold War gave new importance to the voices of African Americans in world affairs. Two men, W. E. B. Du Bois and Ralph Bunche, represent alternative strategies for responding to this opportunity. Du Bois took a highly critical approach to American policy. For half a century he had linked the fate of African Americans with that of Africans and by 1945 was widely hailed as the Father of Pan-Africanism. In that year he directed the Fifth Pan-African Congress, which met in Manchester, England. The Africans who had been radicalized by World War II dominated the conference and encouraged it to denounce western imperialism. Du Bois considered the United States a protector of the colonial system and opposed its stance in the Cold War. On returning from the Manchester congress, he declared,

> We American Negroes should know . . . until Africa is free, the descendants of Africa the world over cannot escape their chains. . . . The NAACP should therefore put in the forefront of its program the freedom of Africa in work and wage, education and health, and the complete abolition of the colonial system.

In contrast to Du Bois, scholar diplomat Ralph Bunche opted to work within the American system. Bunche held a Harvard doctorate in government and international relations and had spent much of the 1930s studying the problems of African Americans. During World War II the American government found his expertise on Africa of tremendous value and Bunche became one of the key policy makers for the region. Bunche's analysis of events and changes in Africa and the Far East after World War II led to his appointment as adviser to the United States delegation at the San Francisco conference that drafted the United Nations (UN) Charter. In 1948 he served as Acting Mediator of the U.N. Special Committee on Palestine, and in 1949 he negotiated an armistice between Egypt and Israel. He received the Spingarn Medal of the NAACP in 1949 and in 1950 he became the first African American to receive the Nobel Peace Prize. Although Bunche worked in concert with national policy makers, he was committed to winning independence for African nations and freedom for his own people. As he wrote,

> Today, for all thinking people, the Negro is the shining symbol of the true significance of democracy. He has demonstrated what can be achieved with democratic liberties even when grudgingly and incompletely bestowed. But the most vital significance of the Negro . . . to American society . . . is the fact that democracy which is not extended to all of the nation's citizens is a democracy that is mortally wounded.

Anticommunism at Home

The rising tensions with the Soviet Union affected all aspects of domestic life in the United States. Conservatives used fears of communist subversion to attack anyone who advocated change in America. This included people who were, or had been, members of the Communist party, union members, liberals, and people who had fought for African-American rights. The Truman administration (1945–1952) responded to fears of subversion by instituting government loyalty programs. Government employees were dismissed for the merest suspicion of disloyalty. Militant American anticommunism reached a feverish peak in the immediate postwar years and gave rise to an explosion of red-baiting hysteria that led to the rise of Wisconsin Republican Senator Joseph McCarthy (1909–1957) and the House Un-American Activities Committee (HUAC). The relentless pursuit of "communist sympathizers" by McCarthy and HUAC ruined many lives. HUAC in particular hounded people in the media and in the entertainment industry. Even so prominent a figure as W. E. B. Du Bois was ripe for attack. On February 8, 1951, HUAC indicted him for allegedly serving as an "agent of a foreign principal" in his work with the Peace Information Center. In November a federal judge dismissed all charges against Du Bois. The government had been unable to prove that he was an agent of communism. Despite Du Bois's past contributions, fear and personal malice prevented most African-American leaders from defending him.

Paul Robeson

Paul Robeson was one of the most tragic victims of these anticommunist witch hunts. This fine scholar and star collegiate athlete, Columbia Law School graduate, consummate performer, and star of stage and screen had always been an advocate for the rights of African Americans and workers. During the 1930s he worked closely with the Communist party (although he was never a member), becoming one of the most famous defenders of the Soviet Union. Many leftists of the time became disaffected with the USSR after its 1939 pact with Hitler and after its brutal repressiveness became clear. Robeson, however, doggedly stuck to his belief in Soviet communism through the 1940s and beyond.

In the late 1940s, Robeson's pro-Soviet views and inflammatory statements aroused the ire of the U.S. government and its red hunters. A statement he made at the communist-dominated World Congress of the Defenders of Peace in Paris in 1949 provoked particular outrage. "It is unthinkable," Robeson said, "that American Negroes would go to war on behalf of those [the United States] who have oppressed us for generations against a country [the Soviet Union] which in one generation has raised our people to full human dignity of mankind." Later in 1949 crowds of rock-throwing locals twice disrupted a Robeson concert in Peekskill, New York, the first time preventing the concert from being held, the second time terrorizing performers and audience members at the concert's conclusion.

Throughout the 1940s Robeson consistently linked the struggles of black America with the struggles of black Africa, brown India, yellow Asia, the black men and women of Brazil and Haiti, and oppressed workers throughout Latin America. Robeson also refused to sign an affidavit concerning past membership in the Communist party. In response, the U.S. State Department revoked his passport in 1950, explaining that "the action was taken because the Department considers that Paul Robeson's travel abroad at this time would be contrary to the best interest of the United States." The travel ban remained in effect until ruled unconstitutional by the Supreme Court in 1958.

Robeson had combined his art and his politics to launch a sustained attack against racial discrimination, segregation, and the ideology of white supremacy and black inferiority as practiced in American society. During the Cold War the state would tolerate no such dissent by even a world-acclaimed black artist.

Henry Wallace and the 1948 Presidential Election

Robeson's struggles illustrate how conservative attacks choked off left-wing involvement in the struggle for black equality. The attacks destroyed Robeson's brilliant singing career. The increasing importance of black votes to Democrats, however, meant that key elements of the African-American liberation struggle remained at the center of national politics. Nowhere was this more apparent than in the 1948 presidential election.

President Harry S Truman was not expected to win this election because he faced a strong challenge from Thomas Dewey, the popular and well-financed Republican governor of New York. Truman's problems were compounded by a challenge from his former Secretary of Commerce Henry Wallace, who had been Roosevelt's vice president from 1941 to 1945. Wallace ran on the ticket of the communist-backed Progressive Party, which sought to take the votes of liberals, leftists, and civil rights advocates disappointed by Truman's moderation. Wallace also supported a peaceful accommodation with the Soviet Union. To undercut Wallace's challenge, Truman began to press Congress to pass liberal programs.

Black votes in key northern states were central to Truman's strategy for victory. African Americans in these tightly contested areas could make the difference between victory and defeat, so Truman, to retain their allegiance, sought to demonstrate his administration's support of civil rights. In January 1948 he embraced the findings of his biracial Committee on Civil Rights and called for their enactment into law. The committee's report, "To Secure These Rights," was a blueprint for changing the racial caste system in the United States. It recommended passage of federal antilynching legislation, ending discrimination at the ballot box, abolishing the poll tax, desegregating the military, and a whole range of other measures.

The reaction of white southern politicians was swift and threatening, causing Truman to pause; but as the election neared, fear of black abandonment at the polls became so great that the Democratic convention passed a strong pro-civil rights plank. Many white Southerners, led by South Carolina's Governor Strom Thurmond, bolted the convention and formed their own States' Rights, or "Dixiecrat," party. The Dixiecrats carried South Carolina, Alabama, Mississippi, and Louisiana in the election; Wallace carried no state. The failure of the bulwark of white supremacy to prevent the Democratic party from advocating African-American rights, and Truman's ultimate victory despite the defection of hard-line racists, represented a profound turning point in American politics.

Desegregating the Armed Forces

The importance of the black vote, the fight for the allegiance of the emerging nations, and the emerging civil rights movement hastened the desegregation of the military. In February 1948, a communist coup in

Czechoslovakia raised the possibility of war between the United States and the Soviet Union and heightened concerns among military leaders about the willingness of African Americans to serve yet again in a Jim Crow army. When President Truman reinstated the draft in March 1948, A. Philip Randolph, who, in a replay of the March on Washington scenario, had formed the League for Non-Violent Civil Disobedience against Military Segregation in 1947, warned the nation that black men and women were fed up with segregation and Jim Crow and would not take a Jim Crow draft lying down. New York Congressman Adam Clayton Powell Jr. also supported this stance. He declared that there weren't enough jails in America to hold the black men who would refuse to bear arms in a Jim Crow army. On June 24, 1948, the Soviet Union heightened tensions even further when it imposed a blockade on West Berlin. On July 26, Truman, anticipating war between the superpowers and hoping to shore up his support among black voters for the approaching November elections, issued Executive Order #9981, officially desegregating the armed forces.

Executive Order #9981, which mandated "equality of treatment and opportunity for all persons in the armed services without regard to race, color, religion, or national origin," signaled the victorious culmination of a decades-long struggle by black civilians and soldiers to win full integration into the nation's military. After Truman signed the order, Randolph and Grant Reynolds, a former minister and co-chair of the League for Nonviolent Civil Disobedience against Military Segregation, disbanded the organization and called off marches planned for Chicago and New York.

Not until 1950 and the outbreak of the Korean War, however, was Truman's order fully implemented. The war reflected the American Cold-War policy of containment, which was intended to stop what American leaders believed to be a worldwide conspiracy orchestrated by Moscow to spread communism. In 1950, North Koreans, allied to the Soviets, attacked the American-supported government in South Korea and launched the "hot war" in the midst of the Cold War. After the North Koreans invaded South Korea, the United States under UN auspices intervened. Heavy casualties early in the war depleted many white combat units. Thus, early in 1951 the Army acted on Truman's executive order and authorized the formal integration of its units in Korea. By 1954 the Army had disbanded its last all-black units and the armed forces became one of the first sectors of American society to abandon segregation.

The Road to *Brown*

In 1954, with the United States Supreme Court's decision in *Brown v. Board of Education of Topeka, Kansas*, progress in the desegregation of American society moved from the military into the civilian realm. Ultimately, the Brown decision would undermine state-sanctioned segregation in all aspects of American life. The NAACP's legal program of the 1920s and 1930s was largely responsible for this turn of events. In 1940 the NAACP set up the Legal Defense and Educational Fund (NAACP-LDEF) to pursue its assault on the legal foundations of race inequality in American education. Thereafter, NAACP-LDEF fought segregation and discrimination in education, housing, employment, and politics. In the first years of its existence, attorneys for the Fund won stunning victories including a 1944 U.S. Supreme Court decision, *Smith v. Allwright*, declaring white primaries unconstitutional. The life and career of one of the NAACP-LDEF lawyers, Constance Baker Motley, symbolizes the struggle to overcome exclusion in American life and the coalescence of disparate forces that carried the seeds of the coming revolution. Motley is our guide on the road to *Brown*.

Constance Baker Motley and Black Lawyers in the South

Constance Baker Motley was born in 1921 to immigrant parents, Rachel Huggins and Willoughby Alva Baker, from Nevis, in the British West Indies. She grew up in a tightly knit West Indian community in New Haven, Connecticut. The members of New Haven's black community, including Baker's parents, worked as domestics or in service jobs for Yale University. Baker attended integrated schools and experienced episodic racism, including being refused admission to a local beach or to a roller-skating rink. During her high school years, Baker developed a strong racial

The Road to *Brown*

1938	*Missouri ex rel. Gaines* v. *Canada*
1948	*Sipuel* v. *Oklahoma State Board of Regents*
1950	*McLaurin* v. *Oklahoma*
	Sweatt v. *Painter*
1954	*Brown* v. *Board of Education of Topeka*

Constance Baker Motley endured many hardships and even assaults as she tried school desegregation cases in the South. Here she leaves the Federal Court in Birmingham after an unsuccessful attempt to force the University of Alabama to accept a black student.

consciousness. She recalled: "[M]y interest in civil rights [was] a very early interest which developed when I was in high school. The fact that I was a Black, a woman, and a member of a large, relatively poor family was also the base of this great ambition [to enter the legal profession]."

The most important event in her early life was the lecture that George Crawford, a 1903 Yale Law School graduate, who worked as an NAACP lawyer in New Haven, gave at the local Dixwell Community Center. The talk concerned the Supreme Court decision in *State of Missouri ex rel. Gaines v. Canada.* Crawford explained that the University of Missouri's law school had denied Gaines admission, but had offered to pay his tuition expenses to an out-of-state school. The NAACP Legal Committee under Charles H. Houston's leadership won a victory before the U.S. Supreme Court when it ruled that the state had violated the clause in the Fourteenth Amendment mandating that state laws provide equal protection regardless of race. After Gaines, states were required to furnish within their borders facilities for legal education for black people equal to those offered white citizens.

Baker desperately wanted to go to law school, but her family could not even afford to send her to college. For a year and a half after graduation from high school in 1939, Baker earned $50 a month varnishing chairs for a building restoration project under the auspices of the National Youth Administration. In 1940, however, Baker came to the attention of Clarence Blakeslee, a local white businessman and philanthropist who, after hearing her speak at a meeting of black and white community residents, offered to finance her education. She attended Fisk University until 1942 and then transferred to New York University, where she earned a bachelor's degree in economics in 1943. She then became the second black woman ever to attend Columbia University Law School. In 1946, shortly after she finished her legal training she married a former New York University law student Joel Motley and went to work with the NAACP's LDEF.

Constance Baker Motley first met Thurgood Marshall in October 1945 when he hired her as a law clerk during her second year in law school. Marshall assigned her to work on the hundreds of Army court martial cases filed after World War II. Motley recalled, "From the first day I knew that this was where I wanted to be. I never bothered interviewing anywhere else." She added, "But for this fortuitous event, I do not think that I would have gotten very far as a lawyer. Women were simply not hired in those days."

In the late 1940s the NAACP-LDEF's attack on inequality in graduate education provided the basis for a full-scale assault on segregation. No longer would the organization be satisfied only to push for fulfillment of the promise of "separate but equal" facilities. In 1948 Ada Lois Sipuel was denied admission to the University of Oklahoma Law School because she was black. The U.S. Supreme Court, signaling that it was willing to take a more activist stance, quickly heard the case and ordered Oklahoma, in *Sipuel v. Board of Regents of the University of Oklahoma*, to "provide [a legal education] for [Sipuel] in conformity with the equal protection clause of the Fourteenth Amendment and provide it as soon as it does for applicants of any other group." Another case, *Sweatt v. Painter*, which the Supreme Court decided in 1950, began when the University of Texas at Austin attempted to circumvent court orders to admit Heman Sweatt into its law school by creating a separate facility consisting of three basement rooms, a small library, and a few instructors who would lecture to him alone. The court ruled that the University of Texas had deprived Sweatt of intangibles such as "the essential ingredient of a legal education . . . the opportunity for students to discuss the law with their peers and others with whom they would be associated professionally in later life." On the same day the Justices ruled in *Sweatt*, they also declared illegal the University of Oklahoma's segregation of George W. McLaurin from white students attending the Graduate School of Education. The University of Oklahoma had admitted McLaurin, but made him sit in the hallway at the classroom door, study in a private part of the balcony of the library, and eat in a sequestered part of the lunch room. When he finally gained a seat in the classroom, it was marked "reserved for colored." In these precedent-setting cases, the U.S. Supreme Court signaled a readiness to reconsider the "separate but equal" doctrine and to redefine the meaning of the "equal protection of the laws" clause. These cases were important stepping-stones on the road to *Brown*.

A year after the *Sweatt* and *McLaurin* decisions, black parents and their lawyers filed suits in Kansas, South Carolina, Virginia, Delaware, and the District of Columbia asking the courts to apply the qualitative test of the *Sweatt* case to elementary and secondary schools and to declare the "separate-but-equal" doctrine invalid in public education.

Brown and the Coming Revolution

Black lawyers in the South handling civil rights cases were frequently assaulted. On February 27, 1942, for example, NAACP attorney Leon A. Ransom was attacked by a former deputy sheriff in the hall of the Davidson County Courthouse in Nashville, Tennessee. The *Crisis* reported:

> The attack came when Ransom walked out into the hall from the courtroom where he was sitting with Z. Alexander Looby, local NAACP attorney, on a case involving the exclusion of Negroes from a jury. . . .

This black student at the University of Oklahoma was not allowed to sit in a classroom with white students. It took two Supreme Court decisions to end such segregation at the University of Oklahoma.

> When the scuffle began, Negroes who would have aided Ransom were held back by a former constable (white) named Hill, who drew his gun and shouted: "We are going to teach these northern Negroes not to come down here raising fancy court questions."

At Ransom's death in 1954, Thurgood Marshall eulogized:

> Negro Americans, whether they know it or not, owe a great debt of gratitude to Andy Ransom and men like him who battled in the courts down a span of years to bring us to the place we now occupy in the enjoyment of our constitutional rights as citizens, in helping to build up the NAACP legal program step by step, in the skill which he gave to individual cases and to the planning of strategy, Dr. Ransom left a legacy to the whole population.

It was no less difficult for a black woman lawyer to venture into the South in search of justice. Black attorney Derrick Bell, who also worked for the LDEF, said of Motley's work,

> Nothing in the Southern lawyers' background could have prepared them for Connie. To them Negro women were either mammies, maids, or mistresses. None of them had ever dealt with a Negro woman on a peer basis, much less on a level of intellectual equality, which in this case quickly became superiority.

Motley was keenly aware of her precarious situation. "Often a southern judge would refer to men attorneys as Mister, but would make a point of calling me 'Connie,' since traditionally Black women in the South were only called by their first name." Housing was another problem. Motley recalled that when in a southern town for a long trial, "I knew that it was going to be impossible to stay in a decent hotel." These lawyers had to depend upon the good graces and courage of local people. Motley explained, "Usually in these situations a Black family would agree to put you up. But there was so much publicity involved with civil rights cases that no Black family dared have us—they were too afraid." While in Mississippi arguing a teachers' equalization of salaries case, Motley, declared, "A Black doctor invited us to dinner, but that was about it." She privately mused, "I wonder how many lawyers have had the experience of preparing for trial in a flophouse. That was the only room I could get."

The black parents of Scott's Branch School in Clarendon County, South Carolina, had approached R.W. Elliott, the chairman of the school board, with a modest request. There were 6,531 black students and only 2,375 whites students enrolled in the county's schools. Although the county had thirty buses to convey the white students to their schools, not one bus was available to black school children. Some of the black students had to walk eighteen miles round trip each day. Once they arrived they entered buildings heated by wood stoves and lit by kerosene lamps. For a drink of water or to go to the toilet they had to go outdoors.

A jubilant George E. Hayes (left), Thurgood Marshall (center), and James Nabrit (right) share a triumphant moment following the 1954 Supreme Court decision in *Brown* v. *Board of Education of Topeka.*

With the encouragement of AME pastor and schoolteacher, the Reverend Joseph A. DeLaine, the parents mustered the courage and resolve to petition the school board for buses. Elliott's reply was short: "We ain't got no money to buy a bus for your nigger children." In 1949 DeLaine went to the NAACP officials in Columbia, and Thurgood Marshall was there. On December 20, 1950, Harry Briggs, a navy veteran, and twenty-four other Clarendon County residents sued the Summerton School District (Clarendon District 22). The case, *Briggs v. Elliott*, was the first legal challenge to elementary school segregation to originate in the South. Meanwhile, however, four other cases in different parts of the country were inexorably advancing through the federal courts. These would be combined into one case that would decide the fate of the *Plessy* doctrine of "separate but equal."

TIMELINE

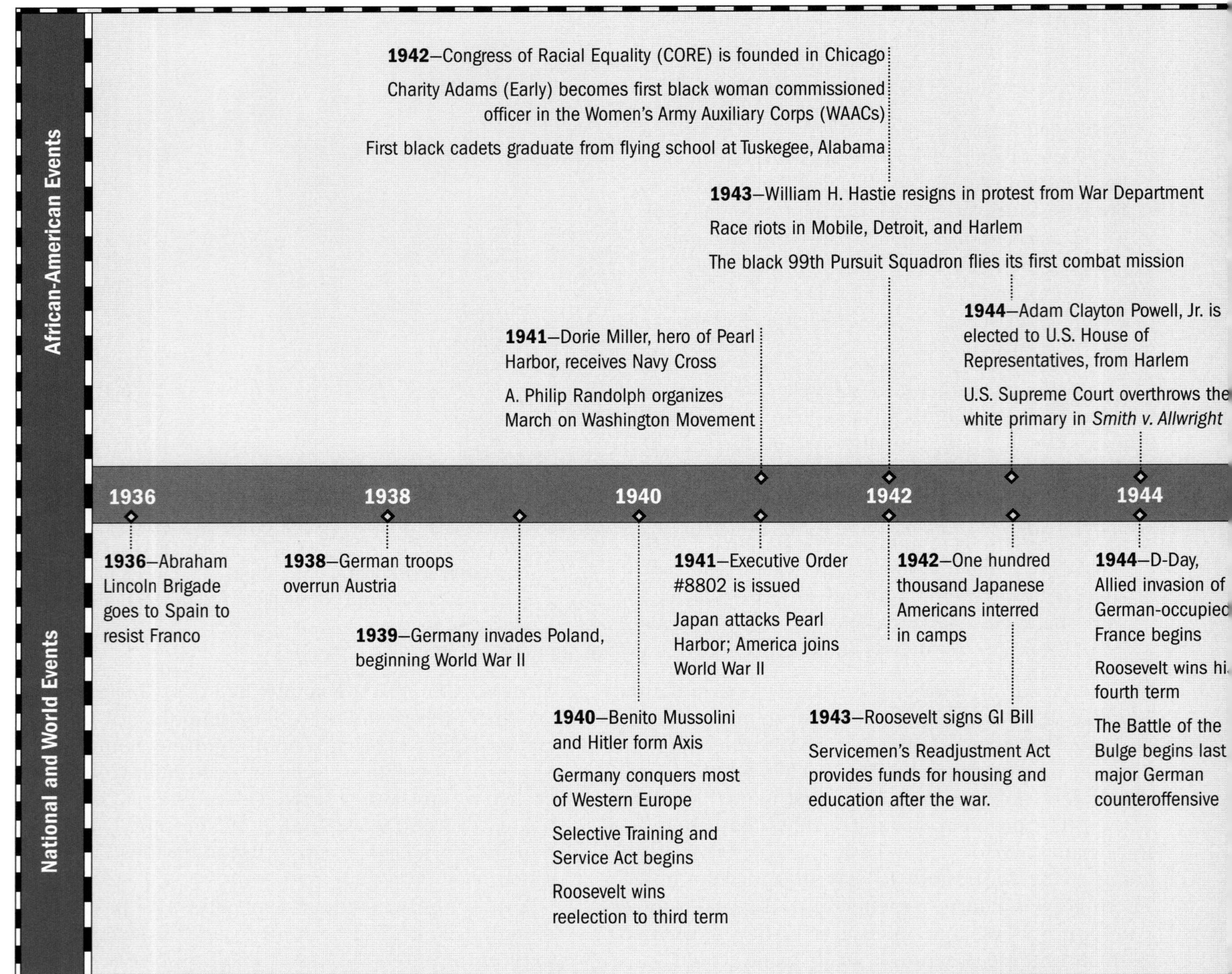

The years of preparation and hardship paid off. Motley worked with the dream team of black lawyers and academics, an inner circle of advisers that included Louis Redding from Wilmington, Delaware; James Nabrit from Washington, D.C.; Robert Ming from Chicago; psychologist Kenneth Clark from New York; and historian John Hope Franklin to prepare the case, *Brown v. Board of Education of Topeka*, and argue it before the U. S. Supreme Court. Motley, Robert Carter, Jack Greenberg, and Marshall also sought assistance from Spottswood Robinson of Richmond, Virginia, and read papers prepared by historians C. Vann Woodward and Alfred Kelly about the original equalitarian intentions of the post-Civil War amendments and other legislation.

> In his argument, Marshall appealed to the Court to meet the *Plessy* doctrine head on and declare that it is erroneous. It stands mirrored today as a legal aberration, the faulty conception of an era dominated by provincialism, by intense emotionalism in race rela-

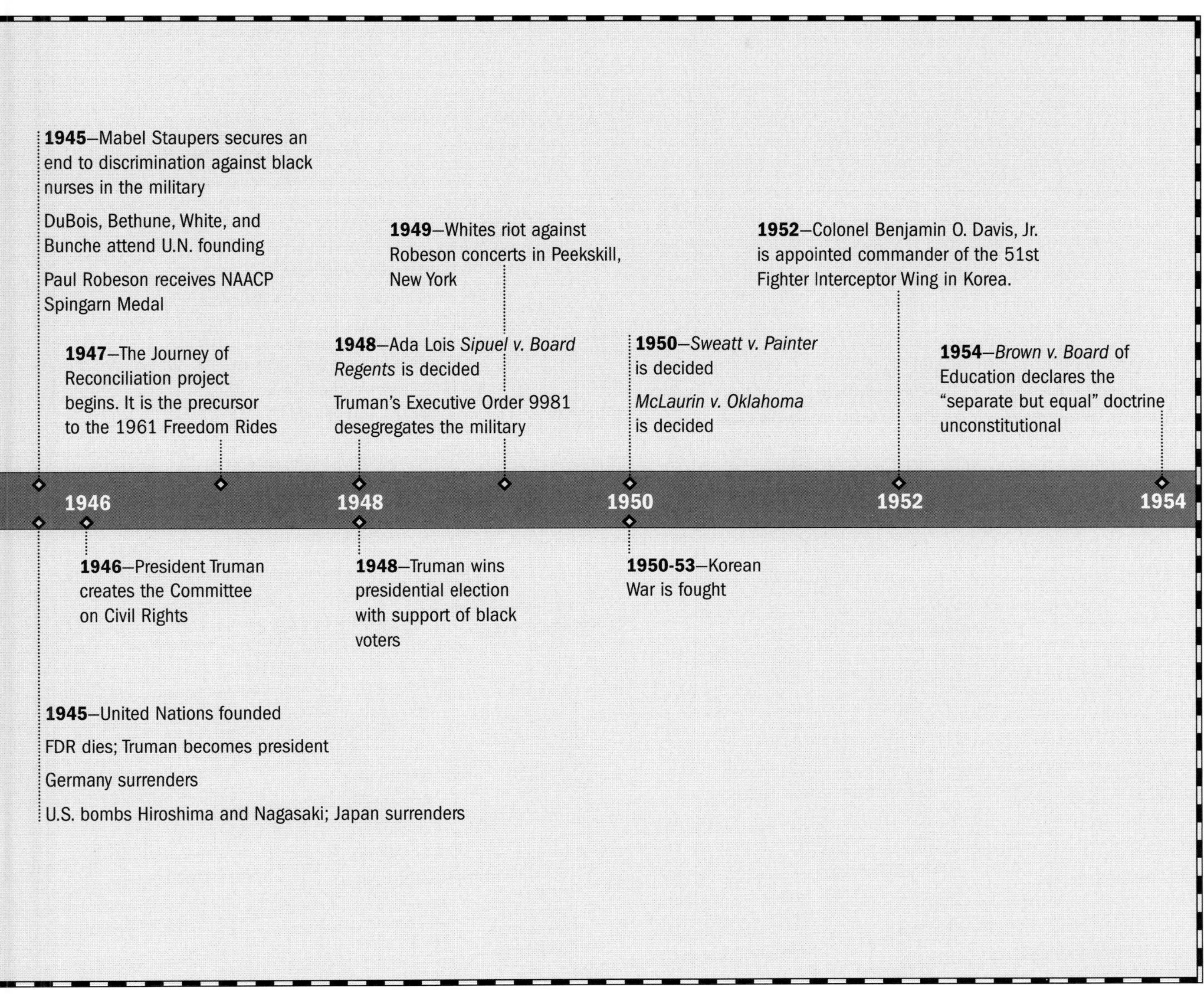

> tions . . . and by the preaching of a doctrine of racial superiority that contradicted the basic concept upon which our society was founded. Twentieth century America, fighting racism at home and abroad, has rejected the race views of *Plessy v. Ferguson* because we have come to the realization that such views obviously tend to preserve not the strength but the weakness of our heritage.

By the time Marshall made this argument, black intellectuals, scholars, and activists and their progressive white allies had closed ranks in support of integration. To suggest alternatives as the goal for African Americans was to find oneself swimming against the current.

During late 1953 and early 1954, Chief Justice Earl Warren brought the court in support of Marshall's position. On May 17, 1954, the court ruled unanimously in favor of the NAACP lawyers and their clients that a classification based solely on race violated the Fourteenth Amendment to the U.S. Constitution. In a stirring passage Warren declared,

> We come then to the question presented: Does segregation of children in public schools solely on the basis of race, even though the physical facilities and other 'tangible' factors may be equal, deprive the children of the minority group of equal educational opportunities? We believe that it does. . . . To separate them from others of similar age and qualifications solely because of their race generates a feeling of inferiority as to the status in the community that may affect their hearts and minds in a way unlikely ever to be undone. . . . We conclude that in the field of public education the doctrine of "separate but equal" has no place. Separate educational facilities are inherently unequal.

The *Brown* decision would eventually lead to the dismantling of the entire structure of Jim Crow laws that regulated important aspects of black life in America: movement, work, marriage, education, housing, even death and burial. The *Brown* decision, more than any other case, signaled the emerging primacy of equality as a guide to constitutional decisions. This and subsequent decisions helped to advance the rights of other minorities and women. As Motley reflected, "In the *Brown* case and in the decisions that followed, we blazed a trail for others by showing the competence of Black lawyers."

Conclusion

The years between 1940 and 1954 were a dynamic period of black activism and witnessed a rising international consciousness among African Americans. The quest for racial justice in the military and on the home front became an integral part of the ongoing struggle for economic, political, and social progress. President Roosevelt's Executive Order #8802 was a significant victory for A. Philip Randolph's March on Washington Movement and for black workers who were able to appeal racial discrimination in defense industries to the Fair Employment Practices Commission. The rise of fascism in Europe alarmed black and white Americans who correctly perceived ideologies based on racial tyranny and state dominance to be inimical to individual freedom and democracy. World War II also had far-reaching consequences. It profoundly transformed black servicemen and servicewomen.

Following the victory in World War II, the Cold War created a climate in America that was at once hospitable and hostile to the emerging African-American freedom movement. Radicals such as Paul Robeson and W.E.B. Du Bois found no place in the movement or American society in general. Moderate organizations, such as the NAACP-LDEF, pursuing their goals within the ideological and legal constraints of the nation, would meet with some success. The coming civil rights movement would, however, soon expand this narrow field of action and pave the way for a more varied, vibrant, and successful challenge to racism.

Recommended Reading

Richard Kluger. *Simple Justice: The History of "Brown v. Board of Education" and Black America's Struggle for Equality.* New York: Knopf, 1976. An excellent treatment of the historical events leading up to the *Brown* decision and the local individuals and national leaders who played instrumental roles in the legal challenge to Jim Crow segregation in the South.

Genna Rae McNeil. *Groundwork: Charles Hamilton Houston and the Struggle for Civil Rights.* Philadelphia: University of Pennsylvania Press, 1983. An excellent biography of the brilliant Howard University Law School Dean who, as head of the NAACP Legal Council, planned the legal strategy that resulted in the *Brown* decision and transformed American civil rights jurisprudence.

Paula F. Pfeffer. *A. Philip Randolph, Pioneer of the Civil Rights Movement.* Baton Rouge, LA: Louisiana State University Press, 1990. A richly insightful biography of a pioneering labor leader and activist whose March on Washington Movement in 1941 was essential to the formation of the first Fair Employment Practices Committee and the integration of the armed services.

Mark V. Tushnet. *Making Civil Rights Law: Thurgood Marshall and the Supreme Court, 1936–1961.* New York: Oxford University Press, 1994. A fine overview of Charles Houston's protege and his impressive legal campaign against Jim Crow in numerous cases argued before the United States Supreme Court.

Additional Bibliography

African Americans and the Military

Robert Allen. *Port Chicago Mutiny: The Story of the Largest Mass Mutiny in U.S. Naval History.* New York: Warner Books-Amistad Books, 1989.

Richard Dalfiume. *Desegregation of the U.S. Armed Forces: Fighting on Two Fronts 1939–1953.* Columbia, MO: University of Missouri Press, 1969.

Charles W. Dryden. *A-Train: Memoirs of a Tuskegee Airman.* Tuscaloosa, AL: University of Alabama Press, 1997.

Charity Adams Earley. *One Woman's Army: A Black Officer Remembers the WAC.* College Station, TX: Texas A & M University Press, 1989.

Darlene Clark Hine. *Black Women in White: Racial Conflict and Cooperation in the Nursing Profession, 1890–1950.* Bloomington, IN: Indiana University Press, 1989.

Ulysses Lee. *The Employment of Negro Troops.* Washington, DC: Center of Military History, 1990.

Neil McMillen, ed. *Remaking Dixie: The Impact of World War II on the American South.* Jackson, MS: University Press of Mississippi, 1997.

Mary Penick Motley. *The Invisible Soldier: The Experience of the Black Soldier, World War Two.* Detroit: Wayne State University Press, 1975.

Alan M. Osur. *Blacks in the Army Air Forces during World War II: The Problem of Race Relations.* Washington, DC: Office of Air Force History, 1977.

Lou Potter. *Liberators: Fighting on Two Fronts in World War II.* New York: Harcourt Brace Jovanovich, 1992.

Stanley Sandler. *Segregated Skies: All-Black Combat Squadrons of WWII.* Washington, DC: Smithsonian Institution Press, 1992.

Howard Sitkoff. "Racial Militancy and Interracial Violence in the Second World War," *Journal of American History* 58, no. 3 (1971): 663–83.

Paul Stillwell, ed. *The Golden Thirteen: Recollections of the First Black Naval Officers.* Annapolis, MD: Naval Institute Press, 1993.

Black Urban Studies

Albert Broussard. *Black San Francisco: The Struggle for Racial Equality in the West, 1900–1954.* Lawrence, KS: University of Kansas Press, 1993.

Dominic Capeci. *The Harlem Riot of 1943.* Philadephia: Temple University Press, 1977.

Dominic Capeci. *Race Relations in Wartime Detroit: The Sojourner Truth Housing Controversy of 1942.* Philadelphia: Temple University Press, 1984.

Dominic Capeci and Martha Wilkerson. *Layered Violence: The Detroit Rioters of 1943.* Jackson, MS: University Press of Mississippi, 1991.

St. Clair Drake and Horace R. Cayton. *Black Metropolis: A Study of Negro Life in a Northern City.* New York: Harcourt Brace, 1945.

August Meier and Elliott Rudwick. *Black Detroit and the Rise of the UAW.* New York: Oxford University Press, 1979.

Robert Shogan and Tom Craig. *The Detroit Race Riot: A Study in Violence.* New York: Chilton Books, 1964.

Richard W. Thomas. *Life for Us Is What We Make It: Building Black Community in Detroit, 1915–1945.* Bloomington, IN: Indiana University Press, 1992.

Black Americans, Domestic Radicalism, and International Affairs

William C. Berman. *The Politics of Civil Rights in the Truman Administration.* Columbus, OH: Ohio State University Press, 1970.

John Morton Blum. *V Was for Victory: Politics and American Culture during World War II.* New York: Harcourt Brace Jovanovich, 1996.

Mary L. Dudziak. *Cold War Civil Rights: Race and the Image of American Democracy.* Princeton, NJ: Princeton University Press, 2000.

Richard M. Freeland. *The Truman Doctrine and the Origins of McCarthyism.* New York: New York University Press, 1985.

Herbert Garfinkel. *When Negroes March: The March on Washington Movement in the Organizational Politics for FEPC.* New York: Atheneum, 1973.

Joseph Harris. *African American Reactions to War in Ethiopia, 1936–1941.* Baton Rouge, LA: Louisiana State University Press, 1994.

Gerald Horne. *Black and Red: W. E. B. Du Bois and the Afro-American Response to the Cold War.* Albany, NY: State University of New York Press, 1986.

Sudarshan Kapur. *Raising Up a Prophet: The Afro-American Encounter with Gandhi.* Boston: Orbis, 1992.

Andrew Edmund Kersten. *Race and War: The FEPC in the Midwest, 1941–46.* Urbana, IL: University of Illinois Press, 2000.

George Lipsitz. *Rainbow at Midnight: Labor and Culture in the 1940s.* Urbana, IL: University of Illinois Press, 1994.

August Meier and Elliott Rudwick. *CORE: A Study in the Civil Rights Movement, 1942–1968.* Urbana, IL: University of Illinois Press, 1975.

Gail Williams O'Brien. *The Color of the Law: Race, Violence and Justice in the Post-World War II South.* Chapel Hill, NC: University of North Carolina Press, 1999.

James T. Patterson. *Brown v. Board of Education: A Civil Rights Milestone and Its Troubled Legacy.* New York: Oxford University Press, 2000.

Brenda Gayle Plummer. *Rising Wind: Black Americans and U.S. Foreign Affairs, 1935–1960.* Chapel Hill, NC: University of North Carolina Press, 1996.

Linda Reed. *Simple Decency and Common Sense: The Southern Conference Movement, 1938–1963.* Bloomington, IN: Indiana University Press, 1991.

William R. Scott. *The Sons of Sheba's Race: African-Americans and the Italo-Ethiopian War, 1935–1941.* Bloomington, IN: Indiana University Press, 1993.

Patricia Scott Washburn. *A Question of Sedition: The Federal Government's Investigation of the Black Press during World War II.* New York: Oxford University Press, 1986.

Autobiography and Biography

Andrew Buni. *Robert Vann of the Pittsburgh Courier.* Pittsburgh: University of Pittsburgh Press, 1974.

Martin Bauml Duberman. *Paul Robeson: A Biography.* New York: Ballantine Press, 1989.

Shirley Graham DuBois. *His Day Is Marching On: A Memoir of W. E. B. DuBois.* New York: Lippincott, 1971.

Kenneth R. Janken. *Rayford W. Logan and the Dilemma of the African-American Intellectual.* Amherst, MA: University of Massachusetts Press, 1993.

Spencie Love. *One Blood: The Death and Resurrection of Charles Drew.* Chapel Hill, NC: University of North Carolina Press, 1996.

Manning Marable. *W. E. B. DuBois: Black Radical Democrat.* Boston: Twayne, 1986.

Constance Baker Motley. *Equal Justice under Law: An Autobiography.* New York: Farrar, Straus and Giroux, 1998.

Pauli Murray. *Song in a Weary Throat: An American Pilgrimage.* New York: Harper and Row, 1987.

Bayard Rustin. *Troubles I've Seen.* New York: HarperCollins, 1996.

Studs Terkel, ed. *The Good War.* New York: Pantheon, 1984.

Brian Urquhart. *Ralph Bunche: An American Life.* New York: W. W. Norton, 1993.

Gilbert Ware. *William Hastie: Grace under Pressure.* New York: Oxford University Press, 1984.

Roy Wilkins with Tom Mathews. *Standing Fast: The Autobiography of Roy Wilkins.* New York: Da Capo Press, 1994.

Juan Williams. *Thurgood Marshall: American Revolutionary.* New York: Times Books, 1998.

Retracing the Odyssey

National Museum of the Tuskegee Airmen at Historic Fort Wayne (303-843-8849). 6325 West Jefferson Avenue, Detroit, Michigan. Donation requested. Former Detroit Mayor Coleman Young was a Tuskegee Airman. This museum documents the achievements of the combat aviators who served as a segregated unit of the U.S. Armed Forces in World War II. They received their training at the Army Air Corps base in Tuskegee, Alabama. During World War II these black aviators shot down enemy aircraft, bombed barges and enemy power stations, and successfully escorted other fighter pilots to their missions across Europe.

Port Chicago Naval Magazine National Memorial. Concord Naval Weapons Station, California. Write to: National Park Service, P.O. Box 280, Danville, CA 94526. Annual memorial ceremony is held in July. Guided tours are available. The memorial contains artifacts and exhibits. (By car, the memorial at Concord is easily accessible from the Oakland and San Francisco Bay Area. Divers will need a valid license, registration and insurance verification to get a base visitor pass.) A large portion of the base is designated as a wildlife preserve.

REVIEW, RESEARCH & INTERACT

REVIEW QUESTIONS

1. How did World War II alter the status of African Americans? What were some of the consequences of so many black servicemen fighting in Europe against fascism and Nazism?
2. How did black women participate in the campaign to desegregate the United States military and in the Abraham Lincoln Brigade? How did Mabel Staupers win acceptance of black women into the military nurses corps?
3. What were the consequences of the "Double V" campaign? How did African-American civilians indicate their support of black servicemen? What institutional resources were African Americans able to marshall in their campaign for victory against racism at home?
4. How did World War II affect the status of black workers in America? What was the significance of A. Philip Randolph's March on Washington Movement, and how did President Roosevelt respond to it?
5. Why did the Cold War originate, and what is its significance for black activism? How did the World War II era promote the rising internationalization of African-American consciousness? How did the State Department attempt to downplay black dissent in America and why?
6. Why was 1954 a watershed year in the history of African Americans in the twentieth century? Why did President Harry S Truman decide to desegregate the U.S. military? Discuss the decades of preparation by black lawyers that resulted in the victorious Brown decision. What conditions did black men and women lawyers face during the long years of fighting antisegregation cases in the South?

Research Navigator.com RESOURCES FOR COLLEGE RESEARCH ASSIGNMENTS **www.researchnavigator.com**

Chapter 20 examines the impact of World War II on the struggle for full and equal rights for African Americans. For further research on this era, use the tools available to you in Research Navigator.

As you investigate this topic, consider this question: "How did the military experience of African Americans effect their expectations when they returned home to the United States?"

- **ContentSelect:** Search in the History database using the search term *Tuskegee Airmen.*
- **Links Library:** Access the History: U.S. History database and explore the links for *Harry Truman.*
- **New York Times on the Web:** To find out more, search the Music database using the search term *Robeson, Paul.*

DOCUMENTS AND ACTIVITIES IN AFRICAN-AMERICAN HISTORY

Documents

20-1 Executive Order 8802, 1941
20-2 *Brown v. Board of Education,* 1954
20-3 Thurgood Marshall, "The Legal Attack to Secure Civil Rights," 1942
20-4 *Jim Crow in The Army Camps,* 1940 and *Jim Crow Army,* 1941
20-5 Henry Wallace, Radio Address, 1948
20-6 Executive Order 9981: Desegregation of the Armed Forces, 1948
20-7 *McLaurin v. Oklahoma State Regents,* 1950
20-8 "Get on the Ground and We Will Kick Your Head In": A Reporter Tells of Terrorism in Alabama

PART VI

The Black Revolution

RELIGION

1954 Malcolm X Becomes minister of Harlem's Temple 7

1963 Malcolm X founds the Muslim Mosque

1978 Lewis Farrakhan becomes leader of the Nation of Islam

1989 Barbara Harris first African-American woman elected bishop of the Episcopal Church

1990 Black Baptists constitute the fourth largest U.S. religious group with 8.7 million members

1991 George A. Stallings consecrated a Roman Catholic bishop

1993 Pope John Paul II aplogizes for the Catholic Church's support of slavery

2000 Vashti M. McKenzie first woman elected bishop of AME church

2001 Bishop Wilton D. Gregory elected President of the United States Conference of Catholic Bishops

CULTURE

1959 Miles Davis records "Kind of Blue"

1963 James Baldwin publishes *The Fire Next Time*

1965 Alex Haley publishes *The Autobiography of Malcolm X*

LeRoi Jones founds the Black Arts Repertory Theater

1966 San Francisco State University sets up nation's first black studies program

1968 Eldridge Cleaver publishes *Soul on Ice*

1969 Harvard University's African-American Studies program established

Robert Chrisman and Nathan Hare start "The Black Scholar"

1970 Imamu Amiri Baraka organizes the Congress of African Peoples

1974 National Council for Black Studies formed

1979 Sugar Hill Gang records "Rapper's Delight"

1980 Toni C. Bambara's *Salt Eaters* wins American Book Award

Molete Kete Asante publishes *Afrocentricity*

1982 Alice Walker's *The Color Purple* wins Pulitzer Prize

1984 Prince films "Purple Rain"

1986 "The Oprah Winfrey Show" becomes nationally syndicated

1987 Rita Dove wins Pulitzer Prize for poetry

1988 Temple University becomes first college to offer a Ph.D. in African-American studies

1989 N.W.A. records "Straight Outta Compton"

1990 August Wilson's *The Piano Lesson* wins Pulitzer Prize

1993 Rita Dove becomes Poet Laureate

Toni Morrison becomes the first African American to win Noble Prize for Literature

1999 Hip-Hop perfomer Lauryn Hill wins five Grammy Awards

POLITICS & GOVERNMENT

1946 Women's Political Council founded

1955 Brown II decision calls for schools to desegregate

1957 Federal troops enforce school desegregation in Little Rock, AR

1963 Federal government forces Governor George Wallace to desegregate University of Alabama

1964 Equal Employment Opportunity Commission established

Mississippi Freedom Democratic party denied seating at the Democratic National Convention

1965 President Lyndon Johnson first uses the term "affirmative action"

Voting Rights Act of 1965 enacted by Congress

1966 Edward Brooke of Massachusetts elected the first black U.S. senator since Reconstruction

Black Panther party founded

1967 Thurgood Marshall becomes first black Supreme Court Justice

1968 Kerner Report released

1977 Randall Robinson founds TransAfrica

Patricia Harris becomes the first black woman to serve in the Cabinet

1983–1984 Jesse Jackson runs for president

1989 L. Douglas Wilder of Virginia becomes first African-American governor since Reconstruction

1991 Clarence Thomas nominated to the Supreme Court

1996 California approves Proposition 209

2001 Colin Powell becomes first African-American secretary of state

SOCIETY & ECONOMY

1955 Rosa Parks arrested for refusing to give up her seat on a bus in Montgomery, Ala.

1958 Southern Christian Leadership Conference organized

1960 Black students launch the sit-in movement

SNCC founded

1961 Freedom Riders attacked in Alabama

1962 James Meredith admitted to the University of Mississippi

1963 Medgar Evers assassinated

Martin Luther King, Jr. delivers "I Have a Dream" speech

Baptist church bombed in Birmingham, Ala.

1964 Mississippi Freedom Summer Project

Civil rights workers murdered in Mississippi

Martin Luther King, Jr. awarded Nobel Peace Prize

1965 Watts Riot

Selma March

1967 Riots in Detroit, Newark, and other cities

1968 Poor People's Campaign

Martin Luther King assassinated

1969 Chicago police kill Black Panther leaders Fred Hampton and Mark Clarke

1970 Jackson State killings

1971 Jesse Jackson founds PUSH

1973 National Black Feminist Organization founded

1991 Los Angeles Riot after police officers who beat Rodney King are acquitted

1995 Million Man March

1997 Million Woman March

2000 Census records large gains in income and education by African Americans

NOTEWORTHY INDIVIDUALS

Clarence Thomas (1948–)
Anita Hill (1956–)
Oprah Winfrey (1954–)
Randall Robinson (1942–)
Jesse Jackson (1941–)
Marian W. Edelman (1939–)
Colin Powell (1937–)
Condeleezza Rice (1954–)
Spike Lee (1957–)
August Wilson (1945–)
Alice Walker (1944–)
Toni Morrison (1931–)
Henry L. Gates (1950–)
Molefe Kete Asante (1942–)
Cornell West (1953–)
James Farmer (1920–1999)
Maxine Waters (1938–)
Martin Luther King, Jr. (1929–1968)
Rosa Parks (1918–)
Ralph Abernathy (1926–1990)
Ella Baker (1903–1986)
John Lewis (1940–)
Medgar Evers (1925–1963)
Coretta Scott King (1927–)
Fannie Lou Hamer (1917–1977)
Malcolm X (1925–1965)
Barbara Jordan (1936–1996)
James Meredith (1933–)
Huey Newton (1942–1989)
Bobby Seale (1936–)
Eldridge Cleaver (1935–1998)
Stokely Carmichael (1941–1998)
Angela Davis (1944–)
Muhammed Ali (1942–)
Vernon Jordan (1935–)
Carl Stokes (1927–1996)
Nikki Giovanni (1943–)
Aretha Franklin (1942–)
Miles Davis (1926–1991)
James Brown (1933–)
Maya Angelou (1928–)
Jamaica Kincaid (1949–)
Terri McMillan (1943–)
Alex Haley (1921–1992)

21

The Freedom Movement, 1954–1965

Romare Bearden, *Watching the Trains Go By*, 1964. Photograph by Sharon Goodman. © Romare Bearden Foundation/Licensed by VAGA, New York, NY.

Romare Bearden's (1911–1988) photomontages, often evocative of jazz and blues, poignantly captured in *Watching the Trains Go By* (1964) the resilience of rural life and the determination of black Americans to persevere in their struggle against white domination and for equality of opportunity.

WHEN the history books are written in the future, somebody will have to say, "There lived a race of people, black people, fleecy locks and black complexion, people who had the moral courage to stand up for their rights. And thereby they injected a new meaning into the veins of history and of civilization." And we're gonna do that. God grant that we will do it before it's too late.

—Martin Luther King Jr., December 5, 1955

CHAPTER OUTLINE

The 1950s: Prosperity and Prejudice
- *Brown II*
- Massive White Resistance
- The Lynching of Emmett Till

New Forms of Protest: The Montgomery Bus Boycott
- The Roots of Revolution
- Rosa Parks
- Montgomery Improvement Association
- Martin Luther King, Jr.
- Walking for Freedom
- Friends in the North
- Victory

No Easy Road to Freedom: 1957–1960
- Martin Luther King and the SCLC
- Civil Rights Act of 1957
- Little Rock, Arkansas

Black Youth Stand Up by Sitting Down
- Sit-Ins: Greensboro, Nashville, Atlanta
- The Student Nonviolent Coordinating Committee
- Freedom Rides

A Sight to Be Seen: The Movement at High Tide
- The Election of 1960
- The Kennedy Administration and the Civil Rights Movement
- Voter Registration Projects

The Albany Movement

The Birmingham Confrontation

A Hard Victory
- The March on Washington
- The Civil Rights Act of 1964
- Mississippi Freedom Summer
- The Mississippi Freedom Democratic Party
- Selma and the Voting Rights Act of 1965

Conclusion

Between 1955 and 1965 the civil right's movement reached its peak of effectiveness and achieved so many of its goals that the era has been dubbed the "Second Reconstruction." Bold movements, beginning with the Montgomery bus boycott of 1955–1956 and culminating in massive protests throughout the South in 1963 and 1964, changed the face of race relations in the United States. Despite fierce resistance, legally sanctioned segregation, racial discrimination, and disfranchisement fell before a mighty coalition of civil rights groups and their allies. Demonstrations and the pressures of the Cold War compelled high government officials to abandon their early caution. Although racism remained powerful in American life after 1965 and African Americans continued to suffer from economic disadvantages, the changes of this Second Reconstruction far outstripped those of the first.

The heart of the story of the modern civil rights movement is the remarkable courage and tenacity people in their own communities showed in their determination to attack segregation and exclusion from the political process. Behind the charismatic leaders and the powerful spectacle of marches and demonstrations captured so dramatically on television were the ordinary citizens who initiated protests, formulated strategies and tactics, and garnered other essential resources that made collective action work. The people's actions were made effective through their families, churches, voluntary associations, political organizations, women's clubs, and college organizations and facilities. The sacrifices and experience gained in the previous one hundred years of struggle had, by the mid-1950s, accumulated sufficiently to permit an all-out attack on white supremacy. The civil rights movement would be long and bloody and it would not lead to the promised land, but it would profoundly change America.

The 1950s: Prosperity and Prejudice

For most white Americans, the 1950s ushered in an era of unparalleled prosperity. The more affluent fled to the suburbs and by 1960, 52 percent of Americans owned their own homes. The decade is remembered nostalgically as a time of large stable nuclear families untroubled by drugs and juvenile delinquency. It was a time of backyard barbecues and hula hoops, when nightly television shows like *Ozzie and Harriet* and *I Love Lucy* projected a vision of domestic tranquillity.

For most black Americans, however, the 1950s were less blissful. American society remained rigidly segregated. Despite the gains African Americans made during the World War II era, Jim Crow still reigned. Although the *Smith v. Allwright* Supreme Court decision in 1944, which declared the "white primary" unconstitutional, helped reenfranchise black voters in Florida, Tennessee, and Texas, Jim Crow restrictions and the ever-present threat of white violence kept millions of African Americans from voting in the deep South.

Nor did most African Americans benefit from the economic boom of the 1950s that allowed so many white Americans to purchase homes in the suburbs. Moving into urban centers just as the number of factories and jobs there began to decline, they suffered a higher unemployment rate than any other segment of the population. White workers, fearing for their jobs, felt threatened by competition from unemployed black workers. As urban neighborhoods deteriorated, conditions ripened for a massive explosion.

Brown II

A year after the 1954 *Brown* decision, in May 1955, the Supreme Court issued a second ruling, commonly known as *Brown II*, which addressed the practical process of desegregation. The Court underscored that the states in the suits should begin prompt compliance with the 1954 ruling, but that this should be done with "all deliberate speed." Many black Americans interpreted this to mean "immediately." White Southerners hoped it meant a long time, or never. Ominously, President Eisenhower seemed displeased with the Court's rulings and refused to put the moral authority of his office behind their enforcement.

Nevertheless, in 1955 and early 1956, desegregation proceeded without hindrance in Maryland, Kentucky, Delaware, Oklahoma, and Missouri. Alabama governor Jim Folsom declared that his state would obey the courts and, initially, many other moderate white southern politicians counseled calm and worked to head off a full-scale conflict between their region and the federal government.

Massive White Resistance

White moderates, however, soon found themselves a shrinking minority, as extremists, determined to maintain white supremacy at any cost, prepared for mass resistance to the Court's decisions. The rhetoric of these extremists bordered on hysteria, but found a receptive audience among many white people. A young minister from Virginia named Jerry Falwell, for example, explained that black people were the descendants of Noah's son Ham and destined to be servants because of a curse God had put on him. Falwell also claimed the Supreme Court's decisions were inspired by Moscow. In 1955, leading businessmen, white-collar professionals, and clergy began organizing White Citizens' Councils in virtually every southern city; these were groups dedicated to preserving the southern way of life and the South's "sacred heritage of freedom." The councils used their economic and political power to intimidate black people who challenged segregation. They fired people from their jobs, evicted them from their homes, and refused them credit.

Many white politicians took up the banner of massive resistance. Senator James O. Eastland, from Mississippi, called the Brown decision a "monstrous crime." The Virginia legislature closed all public schools in Prince Edward County to thwart integration. Most dramatically, on March 12, 1956, ninety-six southern congressmen led by North Carolina's Senator Sam Ervin Jr. issued "The Southern Manifesto" vowing to fight to preserve segregation and the southern way of life. The Manifesto called the *Brown* decisions an "unwarranted exercise of power by the court, contrary to the Constitution."

The NAACP came under siege after the *Brown* decision as southern states tried to wipe it out of existence. By 1957 nine southern states had filed suit to eradicate the organization. Some states, alleging that the NAACP was linked to a worldwide communist

After Emmett Till was lynched on August 28, 1955, in Money, Mississippi, his mother, Mamie Bradley, had his body returned to Chicago for a public burial. The Till lynching had a profound impact on young African-American civil rights activists.

conspiracy, made membership illegal. Membership plummeted from 128,716 to 79,677, and the association lost 246 branches in the South.

Under these pressures, desegregation ground to a halt. By 1958, thirteen school systems had been desegregated. By 1960, two years later, the total had risen to only seventeen. Massive resistance was challenging the possibility of achieving change through court action alone.

The Lynching of Emmett Till

The violent reaction of white Southerners to the growing assertiveness of black people found expression in the summer of 1955 in the lynching of fourteen-year-old Emmett Till of Chicago, an event that helped galvanize the emerging civil rights movement. Till was visiting relatives in the small town of Money, Mississippi. On a dare from his friends, he entered Bryant's grocery store, bought candy, and said "Bye, baby" to Carolyn Bryant, the wife of the owner, as he left. Till was unaware how far white people in the town would go to avenge this small breach of white supremacy's racial etiquette. In the middle of the night a few days after the incident, Bryant's husband and brother-in-law arrived at the small home where Till was staying and kidnaped him at gunpoint. His body was subsequently found in the Tallahatchie River tied to a heavy cotton gin fan. Till had a bullet in his head and had been tortured before his murder. Despite overwhelming evidence and the brave testimony of Mose Wright, Till's uncle, and other local black people, an all-white jury acquitted the two men who lynched Till. In early 1956, the murderers sold their confession to *Look* magazine and gloated over their escape from justice.

The Till lynching shaped the consciousness of an entire generation of young African-American activists. Partly this was due to the efforts of Till's mother, Mamie Bradley. Unwilling to let America turn away from this crime, Till's mother had her son's mangled body displayed in an open casket in Chicago. Thousands of mourners paid their respects, and many committed themselves to fighting the system that made this crime possible. Bradley also traveled around the nation speaking to groups on whom her grief had a profound impact. Myrlie Evers, who would later have a role in the movement, remembered how she felt. "I bled for Emmett Till's mother. I know when she came to Mississippi and appeared at the mass meetings how everyone poured out their hearts to her, went into their pockets when people had only two or three pennies, and gave."

New Forms of Protest: The Montgomery Bus Boycott

Strong local communities formed the core of the civil rights movement and they were often sparked to action by the deeds of brave and committed

MAP EXPLORATION To explore this map, go to **http://www.prenhall.com/hine/map21.1**

MAP 21–1 Major Events of the Civil Rights Movement This map shows the location of key events in the struggle for civil rights between 1954 and 1965.

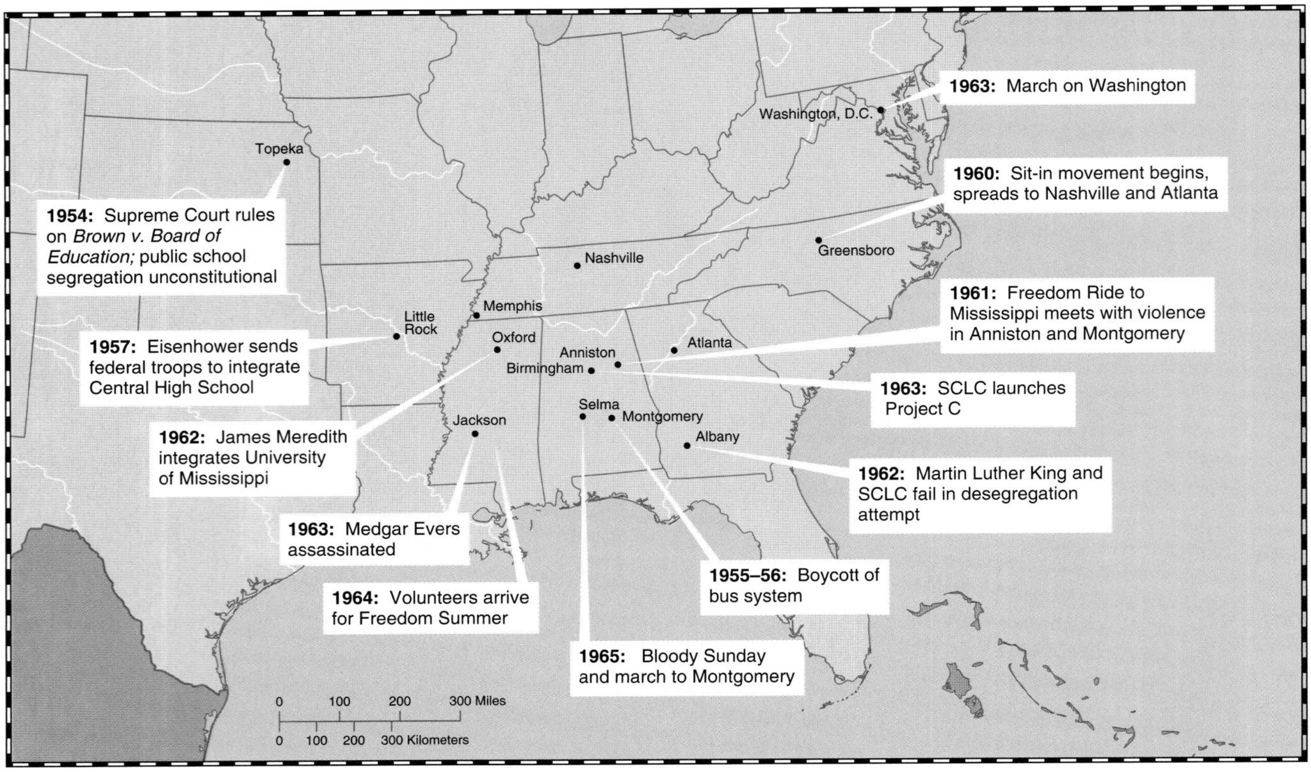

individuals. The first and one of the most important expressions of this process occurred in Alabama's small capital city of Montgomery (see Map 21–1). Blessed with well-organized educational, religious, and other institutions, this city's African-American community of forty-five thousand was poised to make history.

The Roots of Revolution

The movement in Montgomery did not emerge out of the blue, although it must have seemed that way to many white residents in the city; it was the result of years of organization and planning by protest groups. In addition to its numerous churches, two black colleges, and other social organizations, the Alabama capital had a strong core of protest groups. One, the Women's Political Council (WPC), had been founded in 1946 by Mary Frances Fair Burks, chair of Alabama State College English Department, after the all-white League of Women Voters had refused to allow black women to participate in its activities. Although the WPC had only forty members, all middle-class women, its courageous and competent leaders were willing to stand up to powerful white people. The WPC was joined by a chapter of the NAACP led by E. D. Nixon, a Pullman train porter and head of the Alabama chapter of the Brotherhood of Sleeping Car Porters. In 1943, Nixon had founded the Montgomery Voters League, an organization dedicated to helping African Americans navigate Alabama's tortuous voter registration process. In the decade after 1945 these groups searched for a way to mobilize the black community to challenge white power.

The 1954 *Brown* decision seemed to provide a means to destroy segregation and discrimination in the city. Four days after it was announced, Jo Ann Robinson, a professor at Alabama State College, wrote a letter to Montgomery's mayor on behalf of the WPC. In it she reiterated the complaints of the black community concerning conditions on the city's buses and ended, "Please consider this plea, for even now plans are being made to ride less, or not at all, on our buses." The mayor ignored the warning and the buses remained as segregated as before. All seemed quiet on the surface, but Montgomery's black lawyers and NAACP chapter began laying the groundwork for a test case challenging segregation of the city's bus lines.

VOICES

Letter of the Montgomery Women's Political Council to Mayor W. A. Gayle

In this letter threatening a boycott of Montgomery's buses, the Women's Political Council politely asks not for the desegregation of the buses but only for new regulations that would prevent black riders from being forced to move to accommodate white riders:

May 21, 1954
Honorable Mayor W. A. Gayle
City Hall
Montgomery, Alabama

Dear Sir:
The Women's Political Council is very grateful to you and the City Commissioners for the hearing you allowed our representative during the month of March, 1954, when the "city-bus-fare-increase case" was being reviewed. There were several things the Council asked for:

1. A city law that would make it possible for Negroes to sit from back toward front, and whites from front toward back until all the seats were taken.
2. That Negroes would not be asked or forced to pay fare at front and go to the rear of the bus to enter.
3. That buses stop at every corner in residential sections occupied by Negroes as they do in communities where whites reside.

We are happy to report that buses have begun stopping at more corners now in some sections where Negroes live than previously. However, the same practices in seating and boarding the bus continue.

Mayor Gayle, three-fourths of the riders of these public conveyances are Negroes. If Negroes did not patronize them, they could not possibly operate.

More and more of our people are already arranging with neighbors and friends to ride to keep from being insulted and humiliated by bus drivers.

There has been talk from twenty-five or more local organizations of planning a city-wide boycott of buses. We, sir, do not feel that forceful measures are necessary in bargaining for a convenience which is right for all bus passengers. We, the Council, believe that when this matter has been put before you and the Commissioners, that agreeable terms can be met in a quiet and in a sensible manner to the satisfaction of all concerned.

Many of our Southern cities in neighboring states have practiced the policies we seek without incident whatsoever. Atlanta, Macon and Savannah in Georgia have done this for years. Even Mobile, in our own state, does this and all the passengers are satisfied.

Please consider this plea, and if possible, act favorably upon it, for even now plans are being made to ride less, or not at all, on our buses. We do not want this.

Respectfully yours,
The Women's Political Council
Jo Ann Robinson, President

QUESTIONS

1. When the Women's Political Council made their initial requests to the Mayor of Montgomery, what were these designed to accomplish?
2. What does this letter suggest about the importance of black women's political organization in the early years of the civil rights movement?

Source: Stewart Burns, *Daybreak of Freedom: The Montgomery Bus Boycott*. Chapel Hill, NC: University of North Carolina Press, 1997, 58.

On March 2, 1955, a fifteen-year-old girl, Claudette Colvin, was arrested for refusing to give up her seat on a bus to a white person. The WPC was ready to use this incident to initiate the threatened bus boycott, but Nixon dissuaded them. He felt that Colvin, who was unmarried and pregnant, would not be an appropriate symbol around which to organize. He and other activists resolved to wait for another chance.

Rosa Parks

On Thursday, December 1, 1955, Rosa Parks, a forty-three-year-old department store seamstress and civil

PROFILE

Rosa Louise McCauley Parks (1913–)

Rosa McCauley Parks was born on February 4, 1913 to James and Leona (Edwards) McCauley, a carpenter and school teacher, of Tuskegee, Alabama. Her father migrated north when his daughter was two years old. When she was eleven, Rosa attended the Montgomery Industrial School for Girls while living with a widowed aunt. In 1932 Rosa married Raymond Parks, a socially aware young man who worked in the Atlas Barber Shop in Montgomery. They were both active in the efforts to secure the release of the Scottsboro Boys, nine black youths accused of raping two white girls. Rosa Parks enjoyed a full and busy life, working as a self-employed seamstress and serving as the secretary of the Montgomery branch of the NAACP (1943–1956), and as a member of the African Methodist Episcopal Church. In the 1950s she worked as a seamstress at Montgomery Fair, a department store in downtown Montgomery.

Rosa Parks (1913–), in this 1999 photograph by Paul Richards, is venerated as the Mother of the Civil Rights Movement and remains an important symbol of hope and courage ever since her historic act of resistance on December 1, 1955 in Montgomery, Alabama.

On December 1, 1955, Rosa Parks had had enough. When she refused to give up her seat on that fateful day in Montgomery little could she have anticipated that she would become a living symbol of the African-American quest for freedom, justice, and equality of opportunity. With great dignity and little fanfare, Parks chose to be arrested rather than to comply with the white bus driver's order to move to the back-of-the-bus section reserved for black people. Parks's behavior was thoughtful. Her defiance on this occasion was part of a larger pattern of personal and public resistance. In the 1940s Parks had participated in voter registration campaigns. In 1954, she attended the Highlander Folk School, a training center for social change in Monteagle, Tennessee.

As soon as word of Parks's arrest reverberated through the Montgomery community. JoAnn Robinson and members of the Women's Political Council (WPC), swung into action. On December 2, 1955, Robinson wrote and circulated, with assistance from students and club women, thirty thousand copies of a flyer, declaring that "Another Negro woman has been arrested and thrown in jail because she refused to get up out of her seat on the bus for a white person to sit down. It is the second time since the Claudette Colvin (a pregnant fifteen-year old who had also been arrested for violating the segregation ordinance) case that a Negro woman has been arrested for the same thing. This has to be stopped. Negroes have rights too, for if Negroes did not ride the buses, they could not operate. . . ." Robinson and the WPC asked the community to stay off the buses for a day to show their opposition to bus segregation and their solidarity with Rosa Parks.

The success of the one-day boycott aroused the community and motivated thousands to attend the first mass meeting at the Holt Street Baptist Church and to found, under the leadership of Reverend Martin Luther King, Jr., the Montgomery Improvement Association. A year later, December 20, 1956, the U.S. Supreme Court ruled Alabama's state and local segregation laws unconstitutional. In retaliation, the department store fired Parks from her seamstress job. The response was, perhaps, irrelevant.

Parks's resistance ignited the civil rights movement of the 1950s and 1960s. In 1957, Parks, her husband, and mother moved to Detroit, Michigan where her brother resided. For a quarter of a century, Rosa Parks worked as a special assistant to Michigan U.S. Congressman John Conyers. In 1979 the NAACP awarded Parks its Spingarn Medal. Detroit has named a street, Rosa Parks Boulevard, in her honor. In keeping with a lifetime commitment to social justice and the pursuit of freedom, at the celebration of her seventy-seventh birthday in 1990 at the Kennedy Center in Washington, D.C., Parks implored the three thousand revelers to "Pray and work for the freedom of Nelson Mandela and all of our sisters and brothers in South Africa." Rosa Parks continues to write, lecture, and inspire countless Americans.

rights activist boarded a city bus and moved to the back where African Americans were required to sit. All seats were taken so she sat in one toward the middle of the bus. When a white man boarded the bus, the driver ordered Parks to vacate her seat for him. There was nothing unusual in this, but on this fateful day, Rosa Parks refused to move. She had not planned to resist on that day, but, as she later said, she had "decided that I would have to know once and for all what rights I had as a human being and a citizen. . . . I was so involved with the attempt to bring about freedom from this kind of thing . . . I felt just resigned to give what I could to protest against the way I was being treated, and felt that all of our meetings, trying to negotiate, bring about petitions before the authorities . . . really hadn't done any good at all." At the time Parks was portrayed as someone who was simply tired, but she had been training for just this kind of challenge for years. When her moment came, she seized it and with this act of resistance launched the Montgomery bus boycott movement and inspired the modern civil rights struggle for freedom and equality.

The plans of the WPC and NAACP came into play after Parks's arrest for violating Montgomery's transportation laws. She was ordered to appear in court on the following Monday. Meanwhile, E. D. Nixon bailed her out of the city jail and began mobilizing the leadership of the black community behind her. Working in tandem with Nixon, Robinson wrote and circulated a flyer calling for a one-day boycott of the buses followed by a mass meeting of the community to discuss the matter. Robinson took the flyer to the Alabama State College campus, stayed up all night and, with the help of a colleague, mimeographed thirty thousand copies of it. The WPC had planned distribution routes months earlier, and the next day, Robinson and nearly two hundred volunteers distributed bundles of flyers to beauty parlors and schools, to factories and grocery stores, to taverns and barber shops throughout the black neighborhoods.

Montgomery Improvement Association

On December 5, 1955, the black community did not ride the buses, and the movement had begun. Nixon and other community leaders decided to form a new organization, the Montgomery Improvement Association (MIA) to coordinate the protest; they also selected a twenty-six-year-old minister, Martin Luther King, Jr., to act as its president. That evening there was an overflowing mass meeting of the black community at the large Holt Street Baptist church to decide whether to continue the boycott. King, with barely an hour to prepare, spoke to the crowd and delivered a message that would define the goals of the boycott and the civil rights movement that followed. In his dramatic voice he connected the core values of America and of the Judeo-Christian tradition to the goals of African Americans nationwide as well as in Montgomery. "We are here this evening," he began,

> for serious business. We are here in a general sense because first and foremost we are American citizens, and we are determined to apply our citizenship to the fullness of its means. . . . You know, my friends, there comes a time when people get tired of being trampled over by the iron feet of oppression. There comes a time, my friends, when people get tired of being flung across the abyss of humiliation, when they experience the bleakness of nagging despair. . . . We are not wrong in what we are doing. If we are wrong, the Supreme Court of this nation is wrong. If we are wrong, the Constitution of the United States is wrong. If we are wrong, God Almighty is wrong. If we are wrong, Jesus of Nazareth was merely a utopian dreamer that never came down to earth. If we are wrong, justice is a lie. Love has no meaning. And we are determined here in Montgomery to work and fight until justice runs down like water, and righteousness like a mighty stream.

Martin Luther King, Jr.

King's speech electrified the meeting, which unanimously decided to stay off the city's buses until the MIA's demands were met. The speech also marked the beginning of King's role as a leader of the civil rights movement. King had been raised in a prominent ministerial family with a long history of standing up for African-American rights. King's grandfather had led a protest to force Atlanta to build its first high school for African Americans. King's father spoke out for African-American rights as pastor of Ebenezer Baptist Church. At age fifteen, King had entered Morehouse College but did not embrace the ministry as his profession until he came under the influence of its president, Dr. Benjamin E. Mays. By age twenty-five, King had been awarded a Ph.D. in theology from Boston College. He moved to Alabama with his wife, Coretta Scott King, to become pastor of Dexter Avenue Baptist Church in Montgomery.

TRACK 36

In addition to his verbal artistry, King had the ability to inspire moral courage and to teach people how to maintain themselves under excruciating pressure. King merged Gandhian nonviolence with black Christian faith and church culture to create a unique ideology well suited for the civil rights struggle. King declared that the boycott would continue with or without its leaders because the conflict was not "between the white and the Negro" but "between justice and injustice." He explained to the boycotting community, "If we are arrested every day, if we are exploited every day, if we are trampled over every day, don't ever let anyone pull you so low as to hate them. . . . We must realize so many people are taught to hate us that they are not totally responsible for their hate." King's faith was severely tested. As the boycott proceeded, his home was bombed. Segregationists also bombed Nixon's home and those of two other black clergymen and MIA leaders, Ralph Abernathy and Fred Shuttlesworth, and inflicted violence on many other boycott participants.

Walking for Freedom

Although men occupied the top leadership positions in the boycott, women were the key to its effectiveness. The boycott lasted more than a year—381 days—and over its course nearly all the black women previously dependent on the buses to get to work refused to ride them. Some walked twelve miles a day. Others had the support of their white women employers, who provided transportation. And many helped to organize an efficient car pool of two hundred vehicles that proved critical to sustaining the boycott. The community at large participated in mass meetings held nightly in local churches. Robinson edited the MIA newsletter. Other women supported the boycott in dozens of ways. Some organized bake sales, and others made door-to-door solicitations to raise the $2,000 per week needed to keep the car pools going.

The boycott took 65 percent of the bus company's business, forcing it to cut schedules, lay off drivers, and raise fares. White merchants also suffered. The bus company, however, could scarcely afford to break the laws of the city that chartered it, and despite the company's losses, the city government refused to capitulate. Officials would not even accede to such a modest demand as a "first come, first served" seating arrangement—like that proposed by the Montgomery Women's Political Council before the boycott began—in which black riders would sit from back to front and white riders from front to back.

Impressive as it was, the boycott by itself could not end segregation on the buses. Black Montgomery needed a two-pronged strategy of mass local pressure and legal recourse through the courts. The legal backing of the federal government was necessary to end Jim Crow. Thus NAACP lawyers and MIA's lawyer Fred Gray filed a suit in the names of Claudette Colvin, Mary Louise Smith, and three other women.

Friends in the North

The Montgomery movement was not without allies outside the South. Money poured into the MIA's coffers from concerned Americans. Many northern activists who had long been hoping that black Southerners would begin just this kind of resistance also swung into action to help. Two people were particularly important at this juncture: Bayard Rustin, and liberal Jewish lawyer Stanley Levinson. Two and a half months into the boycott, Montgomery officials indicted King and one hundred other leaders on charges of conspiracy to disrupt the bus system. At this juncture Bayard Rustin arrived in Montgomery and immediately encouraged the leaders to follow Gandhian practice and submit freely to arrest. In a diary entry, Rustin wrote,

> Many of them did not wait for the police to come but walked to the police station and surrendered. Nixon was the first. He walked into the station and said, "You are looking for me? Here I am." This procedure had a startling effect on both the Negro and the white communities. White community leaders, politicians, and police were dumbfounded. Negroes were thrilled to see their leaders surrender without being hunted down. Soon hundreds of Negroes gathered outside the police station and applauded the leaders as they entered, one by one.

Rustin continued working behind the scenes as one of King's most trusted advisers on nonviolent principles and tactics. Levinson and Ella Baker created a group called In Friendship, which raised money for the boycott.

Levinson was a wealthy attorney committed to social justice. He had worked with the Communist party, and Rustin had a long history of association with radical groups. Their influence soon attracted the attention of the Federal Bureau of Investigation, which had long been obsessed with black leaders and organizations. King was not a communist, but FBI director J. Edgar Hoover developed an intense hatred of him and other black leaders. At one point Hoover called King, "the most dangerous man in America," and he pressed his subordinates to prove King was a communist and that the civil rights movement was a Moscow-inspired conspiracy. Hoover and his men began tapping King's telephone and hotel rooms and even threatened to expose his extramarital affairs if he did not commit suicide. By the early 1960s the FBI had stopped warning King when it uncovered threats to his life.

Victory

As the bus boycott reached the one-year mark, it was obvious that the all-white city government would not budge, no matter how long the boycott lasted. Any white politician who hoped to remain in office had to defend segregation. King and all the others who suffered through the ordeal grew discouraged and their hopes seemed to fade in November 1956 when it became clear that the state courts would soon move to declare the car pools illegal.

Salvation for the movement came from the cases local women and the NAACP had taken to the federal courts. In keeping with the *Brown* precedent, on November 13, 1956, the Supreme Court ordered an end to Montgomery's bus segregation. The *Gayle v. Browder* decision, unlike the *Brown* decision, expressly overturned the 1896 *Plessy v. Ferguson* decision, because like *Plessy* it applied to transportation. Ironically, the ruling was handed down on the same day that the city of Montgomery finally secured a state court injunction to end the MIA car pool. The bus company agreed not only to end segregation but to hire African-American drivers and to treat all passengers with equal respect.

The city's black community rejoiced. On the morning of December 21, 1956, black citizens of Montgomery boarded the buses and sat wherever they pleased.

No Easy Road to Freedom: 1957–1960

The victory at Montgomery set an example for future protests. It was the result of a highly organized black community led by committed and capable black leaders. These local efforts were bolstered by the advice and involvement of activists outside the South, the attention of a sympathetic national press, and, crucially, intervention from the federal courts. But local victories could only go so far, particularly as white resistance intensified. In the three years following the boycott, black Southerners and their allies across the nation prepared for a broader movement. At the same time, federal officials outside the judiciary found that they could not ignore the white South's incipient rebellion without grave consequences for the nation and their own power.

Martin Luther King and the SCLC

By the end of the campaign in Montgomery, Martin Luther King, Jr. had emerged as a moral leader of national stature. On the advice of Levinson, Rustin, and Ella Baker, he helped create a new organization, the Southern Christian Leadership Council (SCLC) to provide an institutional base for continuing the struggle. The SCLC was a federation of civil rights groups, community organizations, and churches that sought to coordinate all the burgeoning local movements. King assumed leadership of the SCLC, crisscrossing the nation in the ensuing years to build support for the organization and to raise money to fund its activities. Members of the organization also began training black activists, particularly on college campuses, in the tactics of nonviolent protest. Because the ballot was deemed the critical weapon needed to complete school desegregation and secure equal employment opportunity, adequate housing, and equal access to public accommodations, the SCLC focused on securing voting rights for black people. In the three years after the Montgomery bus boycott, the SCLC also aided black communities in applying the lessons of that struggle to challenge bus segregation in Tallahassee, Florida, and in Atlanta.

The SCLC shared many of the NAACP's goals, but tensions arose between the two organizations. The NAACP's leadership doubted the effectiveness of the protest tactics favored by the SCLC. They resented having to divert resources away from work on important court cases to defend people arrested in protests and were troubled by the left-wing connections of King's advisers. The fortunes of the NAACP in the South, however, plummeted in the late 1950s as southern states persecuted its members; this left the field to the SCLC. Despite their differences, the SCLC and the NAACP worked together, but the tensions over tactics were never far from the surface.

Civil Rights Act of 1957

Despite President Eisenhower's tepid response to *Brown*, Congress proved willing to take a modest step toward ending racial discrimination. Buttressing the Supreme Court's desegregation initiatives, it enacted the Civil Rights Act of 1957, the first such legislation since the end of Reconstruction. In a departure from the past, liberals in the Senate were able to end a filibuster by Southerners, but the bill they passed was, for

Elizabeth Eckerd, one of nine black students who sought to enroll at Little Rock Central High School in September 1957, endures the taunts of an angry white crowd as she tries to make her way to the school.

all its symbolic import, weak. It created a commission to monitor violations of black civil rights and to propose remedies for infringements on black voting. It upgraded the Civil Rights Section into a division within the Justice Department and gave it the power to initiate civil proceedings against those states and municipalities that discriminated on the basis of race. Although an important step on the long road toward black enfranchisement, this act disappointed black activists because it was not strong enough to counter white reaction and because they felt the Eisenhower administration would not enforce it.

Little Rock, Arkansas

Eisenhower may have had little inclination to support the fight for black rights, but the defiance of Arkansas governor Orville Faubus would soon force him to. At the beginning of the school year in 1957, Faubus posted 270 soldiers from the Arkansas National Guard outside Little Rock Central High School to prevent nine black youths from entering. Faubus was determined to flout the *Brown* ruling and to maintain school segregation. When a federal district court order forced the governor to allow the children into the school, he simply withdrew the state guard and left the children alone to face a hate-filled mob.

To defend the sovereignty of the federal court and the Constitution, Eisenhower had to act. He sent in 1,100 paratroopers from the 101st Airborne to Little Rock and put the state national guard under federal authority. It was the first time since Reconstruction that troops had been sent to the South to protect the rights of African-American citizens. The troops remained in Little Rock Central High School for the rest of the school year. Governor Faubus closed the Little Rock public schools in 1958–1959. Eight of the nine black students valiantly withstood the abuse, harassment, and curses of segregationists both inside and outside the facility and eventually desegregated the High School. Other young African Americans throughout the South would show similar courage.

Black Youth Stand Up by Sitting Down

Beginning in 1960, motivated black college students adapted a strategy that CORE had used in the 1940s—the sit-in—and emerged as the dynamic vanguard of the civil rights movement. Their distinctive and independent contributions to the black protest movement accelerated the pace of social change. Before long the movement would inspire an even larger number of northern black and white students.

Sit-Ins: Greensboro, Nashville, Atlanta

Early on the morning of February 1, 1960, Ezell Blair, Jr., Joseph McNeil, Francis McCain, and David Richmond, all freshmen at North Carolina Agricultural and Technical College (A & T), decided to desegregate local restaurants by sitting at the lunch counter of Greensboro, North Carolina's Woolworth five-and-dime store. Although black people were welcome to spend their money in the store, they were not permitted to dine at the lunch counter, making it a painful symbol of white supremacy. At 4:30 in the afternoon the students sat at the counter. They received no service that day, but sat quietly doing their school work until the store closed. The action of these four young men electrified their fellow students, and the next day many others joined them. Soon, black women students from Bennett College and a few white students from the University of North Carolina Women's College joined the protest, and by the fifth day hundreds of young, studious, neatly dressed African Americans crowded the downtown store demanding their rights.

Like the black people of Montgomery, the students in Greensboro acted with forethought and with the support of their community. They had long debated how they could best participate in the desegregation movement. All four of the black students had been members of NAACP college or youth groups and were aware of the currents of change flowing through the South. Although they began the sit-in on their own, it quickly gained the support of the black community. Many people in the North and West—both black and white—also joined the campaign by picketing local stores of the national chains that approved of segregation in the South. After facing the collective

Four students—from the left they are Joseph McNeil, Franklin McCain, Billy Smith, and Clarence Henderson—sit patiently at Woolworth's lunch counter on February 2, 1960, the second day of the sit-in in Greensboro, North Carolina. Although not the first sit-in protest against segregated facilities, the Greensboro action triggered a wave of sit-ins by black high school and college students across the South.

power of the black community and their allies for many months, white businessmen and politicians finally gave in to the black community's demands.

The students at Greensboro were not alone in their desire to strike out at discrimination. Indeed, at Fisk University in Nashville, Tennessee, Diane Nash, John Lewis, Marion Barry, James Bevel, Curtis Murphy, Gloria Johnson, Bernard Lafayette, and Rodney Powell had begun organizing nonviolent workshops before the Greensboro sit-in. Imbued with youthful exuberance and idealism, they determined to follow the Reverend James Lawson's courageous leadership and his teaching on nonviolence and Christian brotherhood. Even better organized than their comrades in North Carolina, they had been undergoing intensive training for a sit-in campaign. Twelve days after the first sit-ins began, the Nashville group swung into action. Hundreds were arrested, and those who sat suffered insults, mob violence, beatings, arrest, and torture while in jail. Nonetheless, they compelled major restaurants to desegregate by May 1960.

Atlanta, Martin Luther King, Jr.'s home base and the site of a large African-American community, spawned an even more dramatic movement. It began after Spelman College freshman Ruby Doris Smith persuaded her friends and classmates to launch sit-ins in the city. On March 15, 1960, at Atlanta University, two students, Julian Bond and Lonnie King, executing a carefully orchestrated plan, deployed two hundred sit-in students to ten different eating places. They targeted government-owned property and public places, including bus and train stations and the state capitol, that should have been willing to serve all customers. At the Federal Building, Bond and his classmates attempted to eat in the municipal cafeteria and were arrested. After hours of incarceration they were released. In earlier years, a jail stint had been a mark of shame, but these students returned as heroes to the campus. The Atlanta sit-in students broadened their campaign demands to include desegregation of all public facilities, black voting rights, and equal access to educational and employment opportunities. On September 27, 1961, the Atlanta business and political elite gave in.

Just as in Greensboro, the students in Nashville, Atlanta, and numerous other southern cities won the support of local people who had not been involved in organized resistance before. By April 1960 more than two thousand students from black high schools and colleges had been arrested in seventy-eight southern towns and cities. Local people demonstrated their allegiance to them in numerous ways, but their most effective tactic was the economic boycott. When business began to suffer as a result of the protests, white leaders proved willing to negotiate the racial status quo. By the summer, more than thirty southern cities had set up community organizations to respond to the complaints of local black citizens.

The Student Nonviolent Coordinating Committee

Recognizing the significance of the regionwide student action and fearing that it would soon melt away, the SCLC's Ella Baker organized a conference for 150 students at her alma mater, Shaw University, in Raleigh, North Carolina. Baker, who managed operations in the SCLC's Atlanta headquarters, chafed under the rigid male leadership of the organization. In contrast, she advocated decentralized leadership and celebrated participatory democracy. Her skepticism about the SCLC struck a chord with the students.

On April 15–17, 1960, delegates representing over fifty colleges and high schools from thirty-seven communities in thirteen states arrived and began discussing how to keep the movement going. Baker addressed the group in a speech entitled "More Than a Hamburger" and became the midwife of a new organization named the Student Nonviolent Coordinating Committee (SNCC). The newest addition to the roster of civil rights associations adhered to the ideology of nonviolence, but it also acknowledged the possible need for increased militancy and confrontation. More accommodating black leaders, even some of those in the SCLC, objected to the students' use of direct confrontational tactics that disrupted race relations and community peace.

Freedom Rides

The sit-in movement paved the way for the "Freedom Rides" of 1961. CORE's James Farmer and Bayard Rustin resolved that it was time for a reprise of their 1947 mission to ride interstate buses and trains in the upper South. That early effort—a planned bus trip from Washington, D.C., to Kentucky—reached only as far as Chapel Hill, North Carolina. There the group of interracial riders met violent resistance, were arrested, and were sentenced to thirty days on a road gang. This new journey tested the Justice Department's willingness to protect the rights of African Americans to use bus terminal facilities on a nonsegregated basis.

The Freedom Rides showed the world how far some white Southerners would go to preserve segregation. The first ride ran into trouble on May 4, 1961, when John Lewis, one of the seven black riders, tried to

On May 14, in Anniston, Alabama, a white mob firebombed this Freedom Riders' bus and attacked passengers as they escaped the flames.

enter the white waiting room of the Greyhound bus terminal in Rock Hill, South Carolina, and was brutally beaten by local white people in full view of the police. The interracial group continued through Alabama toward Jackson, Mississippi, but repeated acts of white violence made escape from Alabama difficult. At Anniston, Alabama, a mob firebombed the bus and beat the escaping riders. A group of local African Americans led by the Reverend Fred Shuttlesworth took many of the shocked and injured riders to Birmingham.

With the police offering no protection, CORE abandoned the Freedom Rides, and all but a few of the original riders left Alabama. But SNCC activists and students in Nashville refused to let the idea die. At least twenty civil rights workers went to Birmingham where they vowed on May 20 to ride on to Montgomery. John Lewis remained with the group that arrived in Montgomery. Awaiting them was another angry mob of more than 1,000 white people, and not a policeman in sight. This time Lewis was knocked unconscious, and all the riders had to be hospitalized. Even a presidential aide assigned to monitor the crisis was injured.

News services flashed graphic images of the violence around the world, and the federal government resolved to end the bloodletting. Attorney General Robert Kennedy sent four hundred federal marshals to restore law and order. Martin Luther King, Jr. and Ralph Abernathy joined the conflict on May 21, as 1,200 men, women, and children met at Abernathy's church. The federal marshals averted further bloodshed by surrounding the building. Only then did Governor John Patterson order the National Guard and state troopers to protect the protesters. When the group arrived in Jackson, Mississippi, white authorities promptly arrested them. By summer's end, more than three hundred Freedom Riders had served time in Mississippi's notorious prisons.

A Sight to Be Seen: The Movement at High Tide

Between 1960 and 1963 the civil rights movement developed the techniques and organization that would finally bring America face to face with the conflict between its democratic ideals and the racism of its politics. Day after day the movement squared off against the die-hard resistance of the white South and created a situation that demanded that the president and Congress take action.

The Election of 1960

One of the persistent fears of white Southerners was that black Americans, if armed with the ballot, would possess the balance of political power. The presidential election of 1960 proved this to be the case. Initially,

PROFILE

Robert Parris Moses

Bob Moses, one of the most dedicated and revered young civil rights activists, was a soft-spoken man possessed of a powerful intellect, iron courage, and a rare purity of moral conviction. Born in 1935 in Harlem, Moses was an excellent student. He attended Hamilton College in New York State and from his reading in philosophy there, including works on Buddhism and Existentialism, he developed a sophisticated understanding of nonviolent protest, a topic he continued to explore during his graduate studies in philosophy at Harvard University.

Robert "Bob" Moses instructs volunteers for the Freedom Summer campaign of 1964.

When Moses learned of the sit-ins in 1960, he immediately went south to participate. It was a fateful trip during which he met Amzie Moore, one of the World War II veterans who had returned home to make Mississippi safe for democracy. Moore was the vice president of the state conferences of the NAACP branches. The two men developed a deep-seated appreciation for each other's strengths, and Moore soon convinced Moses to center his work in Mississippi. By August 1961 Moses was a SNCC organizer in the small town of McComb, Mississippi. There his group registered black voters. In early 1962 the SNCC activist became the program director of the Council of Federated Organizations (COFO) and remained in the center of the struggle in Mississippi for the next three years.

The violence of white people and the courage of local black people had a profound effect on Moses. In McComb he was arrested, jailed, beaten, and threatened with death. One of the local black people who helped his group was murdered in cold blood by a state senator who was subsequently acquitted of the crime by an all-white jury. Moses respected anyone who had the courage to take a stand after suffering a lifetime of such abuse. He sought to give local people the tools to continue to control their lives long after movement organizers had left.

Although Moses refused to become a formal leader of the SNCC forces in Mississippi, he profoundly affected the movement. The young civil rights worker set an example of nonviolent resistance for other members of SNCC and encouraged the entire organization to avoid developing a hierarchical leadership structure. In late 1963 Moses became the driving force behind the Freedom Summer project and played a central role in persuading SNCC to accept white volunteers from the North. He also stood for principle rather than expediency when he rejected the meager deal offered the Mississippi Freedom Democratic party (discussed later in the chapter) at the 1964 Democratic Convention. Moses spoke for many young activists when he said in disgust, "You can't trust the political system. I will have nothing to do with the political system any longer."

In 1965 Moses began to drift away from the civil rights movement and toward active opposition to the war in Vietnam. Exhausted from his ordeal in the South and seeking to avoid the draft, he emigrated first to Canada and then to the African nation of Tanzania. Moses returned soon after President Jimmy Carter offered amnesty to draft resisters in 1977 and began teaching math and science to inner-city black children. After receiving a MacArthur Foundation "genius grant," he developed the Algebra Project, which uses many of the empowerment strategies pioneered during the civil rights era to help children and their families gain the education they need in the emerging computer-oriented economy.

many African Americans favored the Republican party's nominee, Richard Nixon, who had advocated strong civil rights legislation. Baseball star Jackie Robinson was a Nixon supporter as were many other well-known African Americans. It seemed as if the New Deal coalition had weakened and that black citizens would reverse their move into the Democratic party. The Democratic nominee, Massachusetts Senator John F. Kennedy, in contrast, had done little to distinguish himself to black Americans in the struggles of the 1950s. As the campaign progressed, however, Kennedy made more sympathetic statements in support of black protests. Meanwhile, Nixon attempted to strengthen his position with white southern voters and remained silent about civil rights issues, even though the Republican party had a strong pro-civil rights record.

Shortly before the election, Martin Luther King was sentenced to four months in prison for leading a nonviolent protest march in Atlanta. Kennedy seized the opportunity to telephone King's wife, Coretta Scott King, to offer his support while his brother Robert F. Kennedy used his influence to obtain King's release. These acts impressed African Americans and won their support. African-American voters in key northern cities provided the crucial margin that elected John F. Kennedy. In Illinois, for example, with black voters casting 250,000 ballots for Kennedy, the Democrats carried the state by merely 9,000 votes.

The Kennedy Administration and the Civil Rights Movement

Early in his administration John F. Kennedy grew concerned about the mounting violence occasioned by the civil rights movement. As the Freedom Rides continued across the deep South, the activists provoked crises and confrontations and forced the federal government to intervene in their behalf. Kennedy's primary interest at this point was to prevent disorder from getting out of hand and to avoid compromising America's position with the developing nations. But Kennedy had little room to maneuver given the continued power of white Southerners in his party and in Congress.

Despite these limitations, Kennedy did aid the cause of civil rights. He issued Executive Order 11063, which required government agencies to discontinue discriminatory policies and practices in federally supported housing, and he named Vice President Lyndon B. Johnson to chair the newly established Committee on Equal Employment Opportunity. Kennedy also pleased black Americans when he nominated Thurgood Marshall to the Second Circuit Court of Appeals on September 23, 1961 (although determined opposition in the Senate blocked Marshall's confirmation until September 11, 1963). He named journalist Carl Rowan deputy assistant secretary of state. More than forty African Americans took positions in the new administration, including Robert Weaver, director of the Housing and Home Finance Agency; Mercer Cook, ambassador to Norway; and George L. P. Weaver, assistant secretary of labor. Moreover, Kennedy's brother Robert put muscle into the Civil Rights Division of the Justice Department by hiring an impressive team of lawyers headed by Washington attorney Burke Marshall.

Like Eisenhower, when President Kennedy felt that intractable southern governors were challenging his authority, he acted decisively. On June 25, 1962, one year after James Meredith had filed a complaint of racial discrimination against the University of Mississippi, the U.S. Circuit Court of Appeals for the Fifth Circuit ruled that the university had to admit him. Mississippi governor Ross Barnett vowed to resist the order but Kennedy sent three hundred federal marshals to uphold it. Thousands of students rioted at the campus; two people died, two hundred were arrested, and nearly half the marshals were injured. Kennedy did not back down. He federalized the Mississippi National Guard to ensure Meredith's admission. Although isolated and harassed throughout his time at Ole Miss, Meredith was eventually graduated. Likewise, in June of 1963, the Kennedy administration compelled Governor George Wallace of Alabama to allow the desegregation of the University of Alabama.

Voter Registration Projects

On June 16, 1961, Robert Kennedy met with student leaders and urged them to redirect their energies to voter registration projects and to lessen their concentration on direct-action activities. He and the Justice Department aides persuaded the students that the free exercise of the ballot would result in profound and significant social change. James Foreman, SNCC's executive director, followed Kennedy's lead. By October 1961, SNCC had joined forces with the NAACP, SCLC, and CORE in the voter education project funded by major philanthropic foundations and administered by the Southern Regional Council. SNCC was responsible for Alabama and Mississippi. Drawing heavily on the expertise of Robert Moses and working closely with a cadre of local leaders like Amzie Moore, head of the NAACP in Mississippi's Cleveland county, and Fannie Lou Hamer of Ruleville,

VOICES

Bernice Johnson Reagon on How to Raise a Freedom Song

Civil rights activists created a special culture in which black music helped communicate a sense of common purpose, strengthen the resolve to endure hardship and pain, and overcome despair and fear. One of the great singers to emerge out of the Albany Movement was Bernice Johnson Reagon, who today is known internationally as the founder of the a capella group, Sweet Honey in the Rock. During the 1960s, she and Cordell Reagon and others formed the SNCC Freedom Singers and traveled the country performing freedom songs. In this statement Reagon describes the significance of song to the civil rights participants.

If you cannot sing a congregational song at full power, you cannot fight in any struggle. . . . It is something you learn.

In congregational singing you don't sing a song—you raise it. By offering the first line, the song leader just offers the possibility, and it is up to you, individually, whether you pick it up or not. . . . It is a big personal risk because you will put everything into the song. It is like stepping off into space. A mini-revolution takes place inside you. Your body gets flushed, you tremble, you're tempted to turn off the circuits. But that's when you have to turn up the burner and commit yourself to follow that song wherever it leads. This transformation in yourself that you create is exactly what happens when you join a movement. You are taking a risk—you are committing yourself and there is no turning back. . . .

Organizing is not gentle. When you organize somebody, you create great anxiety in that person because you are telling them to risk everything. Put yourself in the place of a woman getting by as a hairdresser. You spend your day curling and frying hair, curling and frying. Somebody asks you to put up some civil rights workers in your home. You have to imagine what is going to happen: there may be people shooting up your home; you have to picture the check you get, the car you drive; everything you own, going on the block. You decide to take that risk because this is important enough. . . .

When you get together at a mass meeting you sing the songs which symbolize transformation, which make that revolution of courage inside you. . . . You raise a freedom song.

QUESTIONS

1. How does Reagon compare singing a freedom song to deciding to become involved in civil rights protest activity?
2. What different personal, social, and economic risks did people run when they became part of the black freedom movement? Given the dangers, why did so many ordinary people become involved?

Source: Bernice Johnson Reagon, "We'll Never Turn Back," in *Everybody Says Freedom: A History of the Civil Rights Movement in Songs and Pictures,* edited by Pete Seeger and Bob Reiser, New York: W. W. Norton, 1989, p. 82.

SNCC opened a series of voter registration schools. The "graduates" thereupon attempted to register to vote. These attempts unleashed a wave of white violence and murder across Mississippi.

The Albany Movement

In Albany, Georgia, the burgeoning civil rights movement met sophisticated resistance and experienced its most profound defeat up to that time. The movement in Albany began in the summer of 1961 when SNCC members moved into the city to conduct a voter registration project. Soon representatives of various local groups decided to form a coalition called the Albany Movement and elected osteopath William G. Anderson as its president. The movement's goal quickly expanded from securing the vote to the total desegregation of the town.

In Laurie Pritchett, Albany's police chief, the movement faced an uncommonly sophisticated opponent. Pritchett studied the past tactics of SNCC and King and resolved not to confront the federal government directly and to avoid the kind of violence that brought negative media attention. When students from a black college decided to begin demonstrations by desegregating the bus terminal, Pritchett immediately arrested them after they entered the white waiting room and attempted to eat in the bus terminal dining room. Shrewdly, he charged the students with violating a city ordinance for failing to obey a law enforcement officer. They were not arrested on a federal charge.

The Albany Movement decided to invite King and the SCLC to aid them and to overwhelm the police department by filling the jails with protesters. King answered the call. On December 16, 1961, he and more than 250 demonstrators were arrested, joining the 507 people already in jail. The plan was to stay in jail in order to, as Charles Sherrod explained, "break the system down from within. Our ability to suffer was somehow going to overcome their ability to hurt us." King vowed to remain in jail until the city desegregated. Sheriff Pritchett, however, made arrangements to house almost two thousand people in surrounding jail facilities and trained his deputies in the use of nonviolent techniques. Thus Pritchett avoided confrontation, violence, and federal intervention.

On December 18, 1961, two days after King's arrest, the city and the Albany Movement announced a truce. King returned to Atlanta, and the city refused to implement the terms of the agreement. When King and Ralph Abernathy returned to Albany in July 1962 for sentencing on their December arrests, they chose forty-five days in jail rather than admit guilt by paying a fine. The mass marches resumed, but again Pritchett thwarted King by having him released from jail to avoid negative publicity. The city's attorney then secured a federal injunction to prevent King and the other leaders from demonstrating. Given his dependence on the federal government, King felt he could not violate the injunction and abandoned the protest. For King, the Albany Movement was a failure, his most glaring defeat, and one that called into question the future of the movement.

The Birmingham Confrontation

By early 1963 the movement appeared to be stalled. Black communities in many parts of the South were strong and well organized, but their enormous efforts had achieved only modest changes. It was impossible to overcome the power of southern state and local governments without the intervention of the federal government, but national politicians, including President Kennedy, remained reluctant to act unless faced with open defiance by white people or televised violence against peaceful protesters. King and other black leaders knew that if city governments throughout the South followed the model of Sheriff Pritchett in Albany, the civil rights movement might lose momentum. To rejuvenate the movement, the SCLC decided to launch a massive new campaign during 1963, the year of the one hundredth anniversary of the Emancipation Proclamation.

Birmingham, Alabama, a large, tightly segregated industrial city, was chosen as the site for the action. The city was ripe for such a protest, in part because its black community suffered from severe police brutality as well as economic, educational, and social discrimination. The Ku Klux Klan terrorized people with impunity. The black community had, however, developed a strong phalanx of protest organizations called the Alabama Christian Movement for Human Rights (ACMHR) led by the Reverend Fred Shuttlesworth. The ACMHR and SCLC planned a campaign of boycotts, pickets, and demonstrations code-named Project C for Confrontation. Their program would be far more extensive than any before, with demands to integrate public facilities, for guarantees of employment opportunities for black workers in downtown businesses, to desegregate the schools, to improve services in black neighborhoods, and to provide low-income housing. Organizers hoped to provoke the city's public safety commissioner Eugene T. "Bull" Connor, who, unlike Sheriff Pritchett, had a reputation for viciousness. Civil rights leaders believed that Conner's conduct would horrify the nation and compel Kennedy to act.

Project C began on the third of April with college students conducting sit-ins. Days later, marches began, and Connor, following the lead of Pritchett, arrested all who participated but avoided overt violence. When the state courts prohibited further protests, King and Abernathy among others violated the ruling. They were arrested and jailed on Good Friday, April 12, 1963.

While in jail, King received a letter from eight local Christian and Jewish clergymen who objected to what they considered the "unwise and untimely" protest activities of black citizens. King had smuggled a pen into jail and on scraps of paper, including toilet paper and the margins of the Birmingham News, he wrote an eloquent treatise on the use of direct action. His "Letter from Birmingham Jail" was widely published in newspapers and magazines. In it, King dismissed those who called for black people to wait: "I guess it is easy for those who have never felt the stinging darts of segregation to say, 'Wait.' " But, he declared, "freedom is never voluntarily given by the oppressor; it must be demanded by the oppressed." In the letter King also explained, "Nonviolent direct action seeks to create such a crisis and foster such a tension that a community which has constantly refused to negotiate is forced to confront the issue. It seeks so to dramatize the issue that it can no longer be ignored. . . . Any law that degrades human personality is unjust. All segregation statutes are unjust because segregation distorts the soul and damages the personality. It gives the segregator a false sense of superiority and the segregated a false sense of inferiority."

King's letter had a powerful national impact, but the Birmingham movement was beginning to lose momentum because many of the protesters were either in jail or could not risk new arrests. At this juncture James Bevel of the SCLC proposed using schoolchildren to continue the protests. Many observers criticized this idea, as did some of those in the movement. But King and other leaders believed that it was necessary to risk harm to children in order to ensure their freedom. Thus, on May 2 and 3, 1963, a "children's crusade" involving thousands of youths, some as young as six, marched. This tactic enraged "Bull" Connor and his officers. The police not only arrested the children, but flailed away with nightsticks and set vicious dogs on them. On Connor's order, firefighters aimed their powerful hoses at the youngsters, ripping the clothes from backs, cutting flesh, and tumbling children down the street. In the ensuing days many of the children and their parents began to fight back, hurling bottles and rocks at their uniformed tormentors. As the violence escalated, white businessmen became concerned, and the city soon came to the bargaining table.

President Kennedy deployed Assistant Attorney General for Civil Rights Burke Marshall to negotiate a settlement. On May 10, 1963, white businessmen agreed to integrate downtown facilities and to hire black men and women. The following night the KKK bombed the A. G. Gaston Motel, where the SCLC had its headquarters, and the house that belonged to King's brother, the Reverend A. D. King. Black citizens in turn burned cars and buildings and attacked the police. Only intervention by King and other movement leaders prevented a riot. White moderates delivered on the promises and the agreement stuck.

Although the SCLC did not win on every demand, Birmingham was a major triumph and a turning point in the movement. The summer of 1963 saw a massive upsurge in protests across the South with nearly eight hundred marches, demonstrations, and sit-ins. Ten civil rights protesters were killed and twenty thousand arrested as the white South desperately sought to stem the tide. In one of the most tragic losses for the movement, white extremist Byron de la Beckwith gunned down Medgar Evers in the driveway of his home on June 12, 1963, in Jackson, Mississippi. Evers had been the executive secretary of the NAACP's Mississippi organization and the center of a powerful movement in that city. His cold-blooded murder dramatized the depth of hatred among some white southerners and the lengths to which they would go to prevent change.

A Hard Victory

The sacrifices in Birmingham and the intensification of the movement throughout the South set the stage for Congress to pass legislation for a Second Reconstruction that would at last fulfill the promise of the first.

The March on Washington

The lingering image of Birmingham and the growing number of demonstrations throughout the South compelled action from President Kennedy. On June 11, 1963, he addressed the nation with his strongest statement about civil rights. He declared, "We face . . . a moral crisis as a country and a people. It cannot be met by repressive police action. It cannot be left to increased demonstrations in the streets. It cannot be quieted by token moves or talk. It is a time to act in the Congress, in your state and local legislative body, and above all, in all our daily lives. A great change is at hand, and our task, our obligation, is to make that revolution . . . peaceful and constructive for all." Kennedy subsequently proposed the strongest civil rights bill the country had yet seen, but despite the public's heightened awareness of discrimination, he still could not muster sufficient support in Congress to counter the powerful southern bloc within his own party.

TRACK 37

TRACK 38

To demonstrate their support for Kennedy's civil rights legislation, a coalition of civil rights organizations—SCLC, NAACP, CORE, SNCC, and the National Urban League—and their leaders resurrected the idea of organizing a march on Washington that A. Philip Randolph had first proposed in 1941. In 1962 Randolph and Bayard Rustin had proposed a march to protest black unemployment. Their call received a tepid response, but after Birmingham many of the major civil rights organizations reconsidered. Reflecting renewed hope, Randolph christened it a march for "Jobs and Freedom."

In August 1963, nearly 250,000 marchers gathered before the Lincoln Memorial to show their support for the civil rights bill and the movement at large. Throughout the day they sang freedom songs and listened to speeches from civil rights leaders. Finally, late in the afternoon, Martin Luther King, Jr. arose, and casting aside his prepared remarks, delivered an impassioned speech. Most powerfully, King spoke of this vision of the future:

> I say to you today, my friends, that in spite of the difficulties and frustrations of the moment I still have a dream. It is a dream deeply rooted in the American dream. I have a dream that one day this nation will rise up and live out the true meaning of its creed: "We hold these truths to be self-evident; that all men are created equal." I have a dream that one day on the red hills of Georgia the sons of former slaves and the sons of former slaveowners will be able to sit down together at the table of brotherhood. I have a dream that one day even the state of Mississippi, a desert state sweltering with the heat of injustice and oppression, will be transformed into an oasis of freedom and justice. I have a dream that my four children will one day live in a nation where they will not be judged by the color of their skin but by the content of their character. I have a dream today. I have a dream that one day the state of Alabama, whose governor's lips are presently dripping with the words of interposition and nullification, will be transformed into a situation where little black boys and black girls will be able to join hands with little white boys and white girls and walk together as sisters and brothers. I have a dream today . . .

At the height of his moral authority, Martin Luther King, Jr. (1929–1968) delivers the memorable "I Have A Dream" speech at the 1963 March on Washington. He conveyed a vision of a future America free of the evil of racism where all God's children would be judged by the content of their character, not the color of their skin. King received the Nobel Peace Prize in 1964, and since 1986 the nation honors him with a holiday in his name.

King's words did not still the angry opposition of some white Southerners. On September 15, 1963, only days after the march on Washington, white racists bombed the 16th St. Baptist Church in Birmingham and killed four little girls attending Sunday school: Addie Mae Collins, Denise McNair, Carole Robertson, and Cynthia Wesley. Chris McNair, the father of the youngest victim, pleaded for calm out of the depth of his own pain, "We must not let this change us into something different than who we are. We must be human." In a similar vein, Martin Luther King sadly intoned, "The innocent blood of these little girls may well serve as the redemptive force that will bring new light to this dark city. . . . Indeed, this tragic event may cause the white South to come to terms with its conscience." The event shook the nation, and combined with the reaction to the assassination of John F. Kennedy in November 1963, set the stage for real change.

The Civil Rights Act of 1964

Kennedy's successor Lyndon B. Johnson lobbied hard to secure passage of the landmark Civil Rights Act. Many in the civil rights movement feared that Johnson, a Southerner, would back his region's defiance. Nonetheless, only four days after taking the oath of office, Johnson told the nation that he planned to support the civil rights bill as a memorial for the slain president. A master politician, Johnson pushed the bill through Congress despite a marathon filibuster by its opponents.

The Civil Rights Act of 1964 was the culmination of the civil rights movement to that time. The act banned discrimination in places of public accommodation, including restaurants, hotels, gas stations, and entertainment facilities, as well as schools, parks, playgrounds, libraries, and swimming pools. The desegregation of public accommodations irrevocably changed the face of American society. The issue of legally mandated racial separation was now settled. The act also banned discrimination by employers, of labor unions

Violence and the Civil Rights Movement

May 7, 1955	The Reverend George Lee killed for leading voter registration drive, Belzoni, MS
August 13, 1955	Lamar Smith murdered for organizing black voters, Brookhaven, MS
August 28, 1955	Emmett Louis Till murdered for speaking to white woman, Money, MS
October 22, 1955	John Earl Reese slain by nightriders opposed to black school improvements, Mayflower, TX
January 23, 1957	Willie Edwards, Jr. killed by Klan, Montgomery, AL
September 24, 1957	President Eisenhower orders federal troops to enforce school desegregation, Little Rock, AR
April 27, 1959	Mack Charles Parker taken from jail and lynched, Popularville, MS
May 14, 1961	Freedom Riders attacked in Alabama while testing compliance with bus desegregation laws
September 25, 1961	Voter registration worker Herbert Lee killed by a white legislator, Liberty, MS
April 1, 1962	Civil rights groups join forces to launch voter registration drive
April 9, 1962	Roman Ducksworth, Jr. taken from bus and killed by police, Taylorsville, MS
September 30, 1962	Riots erupt when James Meredith, a black student, enrolls at the University of Mississippi. Paul Guihard, European reporter, killed
April 23, 1963	William Lewis Moore slain during one-man march against segregation, Attalla, AL
May 3, 1963	Birmingham police attack marching children with dogs and fire hoses
June 12, 1963	Medgar Evers, civil rights leader, assassinated, Jackson, MS
September 15, 1963	Schoolgirls Addie Mae Collins, Denise McNair, Carole Robertson, and Cynthia Wesley die in the bombing of the 16th St. Baptist Church, Birmingham, AL
September 15, 1963	Virgin Lamar Ware killed during racist violence, Birmingham, AL
January 31, 1964	Louis Allen, witness to the murder of a civil rights worker, assassinated, Liberty, MS
April 7, 1964	The Reverend Bruce Klunder killed protesting construction of segregated school, Cleveland, OH
May 2, 1964	Henry Hezekiah Dee and Charles Eddie Moore killed by Klan, Meadville, MS
June 21, 1964	Civil rights workers James Chaney, Andrew Goodman, and Michael Schwerner abducted and slain by Klan, Philadelphia, MS
July 11, 1964	Lt. Col. Lemuel Penn killed by Klan while driving north, Colbert, GA
February 26, 1965	Jimmie Lee Jackson, civil rights marcher killed by state trooper, Marion, AL
March 11, 1965	Selma to Montgomery march volunteer, the Reverend James Reeb, beaten to death, Selma, AL
March 25, 1965	Viola Gregg Liuzzo killed by Klan while transporting marchers, Selma Highway, AL
June 2, 1965	Oneal Moore, black deputy, killed by nightriders, Varnado, LA
July 18, 1965	Willie Wallace Brewster killed by nightriders, Anniston, AL
August 20, 1965	Jonathan Daniels, seminary student, killed by deputy, Hayneville, AL
January 3, 1966	Samuel Younge Jr., student civil rights activist, killed in dispute over whites-only restroom, Tuskegee, AL
January 10, 1966	Vernon Dahmer, black community leader killed in Klan bombing, Hattiesburg, MS
June 10, 1966	Ben Chester White killed by Klan, Natchez, MS
July 30, 1966	Clarence Triggs slain by nightriders, Bogalusa, LA
February 2, 1967	Wharlest Jackson, civil rights leader, killed when police fired on protesters, Jackson, MS
February 8, 1968	Students Samuel Hammond Jr., Delano Middleton, and Henry Smith killed when highway patrolmen fire on protesters, Orangeburg, SC
April 4, 1968	Dr. Martin Luther King, Jr. assassinated, Memphis, TN

on the basis of race, color, religion, national origin, and sex in regard to hiring, promoting, dismissing, or making job referrals. The act had strong provisions for enforcement. Most important, it allowed government agencies to withhold federal money from any program permitting or practicing discrimination. This provision had particular import for the desegregation of schools and colleges across the country. The act also gave the U.S. attorney general the power to initiate proceedings against segregated facilities and schools on behalf of people who could not do so on their own. Finally it created the Equal Employment Opportunity Commission to monitor discrimination in employment.

Mississippi Freedom Summer

While Congress considered the Civil Rights Act, movement activists renewed their focus on voter registration in the deep South. In the fall of 1963, many CORE and SNCC workers saw segregation crumbling, but they knew that without the ballot, African Americans could never drive racist politicians from office, gain a fair hearing in court, reduce police and mob violence, or get equal services from state and local governments. CORE took responsibility for running registration campaigns in Louisiana, South Carolina, and Florida while SNCC took on the two most repressive states, Alabama and Mississippi. Mississippi was widely known in the movement as the "toughest nut to crack"—the symbolic center of American racism and white violence. By the summer of 1964 national attention had shifted from Alabama to Mississippi, the site of a massive project known as "Freedom Summer."

The voter registration campaign in Mississippi began in late 1963 when Robert "Bob" Moses mobilized the Council of Federated Organizations (COFO), which had been established in 1961 to aid imprisoned freedom riders. Moses convinced the members of COFO (CORE, SNCC, SCLC, and the NAACP) to sponsor a mock Freedom Election in Mississippi. On election day 80,000 disfranchised black people cast ballots for COFO candidates. Impressed with the turn-out, Moses and other COFO members believed that a massive effort to register voters during the summer of 1964 might break the white monopoly on the ballot box.

After much debate, COFO decided to invite northern white students to participate in the Mississippi project. These students, about one thousand in all, were to be drawn primarily from the nation's most prestigious universities. This move contradicted the movement's emphasis on black empowerment, but COFO leaders calculated that the presence of elite white students in the Magnolia State would attract increased media attention and pressure the federal government to provide protection.

Shortly after the project began, three volunteers, two white New Yorkers—twenty-four-year-old Michael Schwerner and twenty-one-year-old Andrew Goodman—and a black Mississippian, twenty-one-year-old James Chaney disappeared. Unknown at the time, Cecil Price, deputy sheriff of Philadelphia, Mississippi, had arrested the three on a trumped-up speeding charge. That evening the young men were delivered to a deserted road where three carloads of Klansmen waited. Schwerner and Goodman were shot to death. Chaney was beaten with chains and then shot.

These events were not publicly known until Klan informers, enticed by a $30,000 reward, led investigators to the earthen dam in which Goodman, Schwerner, and Chaney had been buried. The disappearance of the three nonetheless focused national attention on white terrorism. During the summer, approximately thirty homes and thirty-seven churches were bombed, thirty-five civil rights workers were shot at, eighty people were beaten, six were murdered, and more than one thousand were arrested. In the face of this violence, uncertainty, and fear, many SNCC activists rejected Martin Luther King's commitment to nonviolence, the inclusion of white activists in the movement, and the wisdom of integration. Divisions over these issues greatly increased tensions among the groups that made up the movement.

Despite the problems it encountered, the Freedom Summer organized dozens of Freedom Schools and community centers throughout Mississippi. Its efforts mobilized the state's black people to an extent not seen since the first Reconstruction. Many communities began to develop the rudiments of a political movement, one that would grow in coming years.

The Mississippi Freedom Democratic Party

Freedom Summer intersected with national politics at the Democratic Party's national convention in August 1964 in Atlantic City, New Jersey. White Mississippians routinely excluded African Americans from the political process, and Robert Moses encouraged COFO to set up the Mississippi Freedom Democratic Party (MFDP) to challenge the state's regular Democratic delegation at the convention. Under the leadership of veteran activists Fannie Lou Hamer, Victoria Gray, Annie Divine, and Aaron Henry, the MFDP held its first state convention on August 6. Approximately 80,000 citizens put their names on the rolls. The convention elected

PROFILE

Fannie Lou Hamer

Fannie Lou Hamer (1917–1977) emerged from the ranks of "local people" in Mississippi to become one of the most powerful leaders and orators of the civil rights movement. Unlike many major leaders, Hamer, the youngest of twenty children, had grown up in extreme poverty and had only a few years of education. She worked and lived as a timekeeper on a plantation in Ruleville, Mississippi. When SNCC workers came to the community for a voting rights campaign, Hamer was one of the first to participate. Despite the great danger of doing so, Hamer supported the civil rights workers because, as she said,

Fannie Lou Hamer and other delegates from the Mississippi Freedom Democratic Party protest outside the convention hall in Atlantic City after being denied seats in the 1964 Democratic National Convention.

> Nobody ever came out into the country and talked to real farmers and things because this is the next thing this country has done: it divided us into classes, and if you hadn't arrived at a certain level, you wasn't treated no better by blacks than you was by the whites. And it was these kids who broke a lot of that down. They treated us like we were special and we loved 'em. . . . We didn't feel uneasy about our language might not be right or something. We just felt we could talk to 'em. We trusted 'em.

On August 1, 1962, Hamer attempted to register to vote in Indianola, Mississippi. In response, she was fired from her plantation job and evicted from her land. Still, she refused to capitulate and accepted full-time employment as a field secretary for SNCC where she worked on the Voter Education Project. This aroused even more police hostility. On June 9, 1963, she and eight other women on their way back from a workshop in South Carolina were arrested by the police in Winona, Mississippi. Hamer was beaten and never fully recovered from the injuries she suffered.

Despite her lack of education, Hamer was a spellbinding orator who had the ability to move not only her friends and neighbors, but the nation as well. Her televised testimony before the 1964 Democratic convention won national support for the MFDP's challenge to the party regulars from Mississippi. The next year Hamer, who had run for the House of Representatives, challenged the seating of the Mississippi congressional delegation. Although unsuccessful, her action helped to reduce tolerance for disfranchisement and paved the way for the Voting Rights Act of 1965.

After 1965, Hamer continued to fight for her people. Although basic civil and voting rights had been won by then, most black people in the Mississippi Delta still lived in deep poverty. In 1968 Hamer sought to address this problem by setting up the nonprofit Freedom Farms Corporation as an agricultural cooperative. With help from northern supporters, the enterprise had some success, but the problems it confronted proved overwhelming. The mixed results of this last campaign, however, cannot diminish the profound changes that Fannie Lou Hamer was so instrumental in bringing about. She died in 1977.

sixty-four delegates who traveled to the national convention to present their credentials.

The MFDP challenge caused considerable difficulty for the Democratic party. Many liberals wanted to seat the civil rights delegation, but President Lyndon Johnson, who was running for reelection, did not want to alienate white Southerners, fearing that they would vote for Barry Goldwater, his Republican opponent. Liberal Democratic senator Hubert H. Humphrey, from Minnesota worked out a compromise calling for Mississippi regulars to be seated if they swore loyalty to the national party and agreed to cast their forty-four votes accordingly. The compromise also provided for the creation of two "at large" seats to be filled by MFDP members, Aaron Henry and Ed King. The rest of the Freedom Democrats could attend the convention as nonvoting guests.

Martin Luther King, Jr., Bayard Rustin, and other black leaders counseled acceptance of this compromise. Johnson and the Democrats, they argued, had achieved much of the legislative program favored by the movement, and if the party were returned to power they could do much more. But most of the MFDP delegation, fed up with the violence of Mississippi and unwilling to settle for token representation, rejected the compromise. Many members of SNCC, bitter and angry, turned their backs on liberalism and cooperation with white people of any political persuasion.

Selma and the Voting Rights Act of 1965

The Civil Rights Act of 1964 contained provisions for helping black voters to register, but white resistance in the deep South had rendered them ineffective. In Alabama, for example, at least 77 percent of black citizens were unable to vote. Their cause was taken up by businesswoman Amelia P. Boynton, owner of an employment and insurance agency in Selma, along with her husband and a high school teacher, the Reverend Frederick Reese, who also led the Dallas County Voters League. These three, with others, fought for black enfranchisement and an end to discriminatory treatment. Their struggle would help to pass the Voting Rights Act of 1965, which finally ended the systematic exclusion of African Americans from southern politics.

Selma's sheriff James G. Clark worked to block the voter registration activity sponsored by the Boyntons, Reese, and SNCC suffrage workers. By 1964 fewer than four hundred of the fifteen thousand eligible African Americans had registered to vote in Dallas County. President Lyndon Johnson refused requests to deploy federal marshals to the county to protect voter registration workers. Seeking reinforcements, the workers sent a call to Martin Luther King, Jr. and the SCLC. King came and was promptly arrested. In mid-February 1965, during a night march in neighboring Perry County, twenty-six-year-old Jimmie Lee Jackson was shot in the stomach as he tried to shield his mother from a beating by a state trooper. His death and the thrashing of several reporters attracted the national media.

The SCLC announced plans for a mass march from Selma to Montgomery, the state capital, to begin on Sunday, March 7, 1965. At the forefront of six hundred protesters were King; one of his aides, Hosea Williams; and the chairman of SNCC, John Lewis. As the marchers approached the Edmund Pettus Bridge, state troopers and Sheriff Clark's county police, in a shocking display of aggression, teargassed and beat the retreating marchers while their horses trampled the fallen. Captured in graphic detail by television cameras, this battle became known as "Bloody Sunday." Seizing the moment, King and the activists rescheduled a pilgrimage for March 9. The SCLC leader soon found himself in a dilemma. A federal judge, who was normally supportive of civil rights, had issued an injunction against the march. Moreover, President Johnson and many other key figures in the government urged King not to go through with it. King was reluctant to violate a federal injunction, and he knew that he needed Johnson's support to win strong voting rights legislation. But the people of Selma and the hundreds of young SNCC workers would probably march even if King did not.

When the day of the march came, 1,500 protesters marched to the bridge singing "Ain't Gonna Let Nobody Turn Me 'Round" and other freedom songs. To their surprise, King crossed the Pettus Bridge, prayed briefly, and turned around. He had privately made a face-saving compromise with the federal authorities. SNCC workers felt betrayed, and King's leadership suffered. That evening a white Unitarian minister from Boston, James Reeb, was clubbed to death by local white people. His martyrdom created a national outcry and prompted Johnson to act. On March 15, the president in a televised address to Congress, announced that he would submit voter registration legislation. In his address he praised civil rights activists electrifying them when he invoked the movement's slogan to declare, in his Texas drawl, "We shall overcome."

The protests at Selma and the massive white resistance spurred Congress to pass the Voting Rights Act of 1965, which President Johnson signed on August 6. The act outlawed educational requirements for voting in states or counties where less than half the voting age population had been registered on November 1, 1964, or had voted in the 1964 presidential election. It also empowered the attorney general to have the Civil Rights Commission assign federal registrars to enroll voters. The attorney general, Nicholas Katzenbach, immediately deployed federal registrars in nine southern counties. Within months, they had registered approximately 80,000 new voters. In Mississippi, black

On March 25, 1965, more than two weeks after "Bloody Sunday," when police brutalized civil rights marchers trying to cross Selma's Edmund Pettus Bridge, a second march finally completed the 53-mile trek to Montgomery. Among the leaders are Martin Luther King, Jr., Coretta Scott King, Hosea Williams, Bayard Rustin, and Ralph Bunche. The violence preceding this successful march convinced President Johnson, proclaiming "We shall overcome," to submit voting rights legislation to Congress.

registrants soared from 28,500 in 1964 to 251,000 in 1968 (see Map 21–2).

Gaining voting rights made a tremendous difference. Before passage of the act, Fannie Lou Hamer had unsuccessfully challenged the seating of the regular Mississippi representatives before the U.S. House of Representatives. In 1968 she was selected a delegate to the Democratic party convention. To be sure, southern state legislators resisted the act. They instituted a dazzling array of disfranchisement devices such as gerrymandering, at-large elections, more appointive offices, and higher qualifications for candidates. But the era when white supremacy lay at the core of southern politics was over.

Conclusion

The success of the civil rights movement depended on many factors. The federal government intervened at crucial moments to enact historic civil rights legislation, issue judgments on behalf of the civil rights protesters, and protect the rule of law with federal marshals and soldiers. Black leaders deliberately pursued strategies to provoke confrontations that would ensure intervention by the federal government and garner widespread media coverage. For more than a decade, the victorious freedom fighters of the civil rights movement stormed the legal barricades of segregation. The uncompromising struggle of African Americans, their organizations, and their white allies pressured federal officials in the legislative, executive, and judicial branches of government to enact major civil rights legislation, issue executive orders, and deliver judicial decisions that dismantled segregation in the South.

The victories of this era were far reaching, but as they were achieved, new issues arose that would fracture the movement. The civil rights movement had largely been focused on the South. Black Northerners already had many of the rights granted by the federal legislation of the era; nonetheless, they still suffered from many forms of discrimination. Addressing their problems required different techniques and new ways of thinking that would emerge over the coming decade.

Recommended Reading

Taylor Branch. *Parting the Waters: America in the King Years, 1954–63.* New York: Simon & Schuster, 1988. Richly researched, lively study that places King at the center of American politics during a critically transformative decade.

Clayborne Carson. *In Struggle: SNCC and the Black Awakening of the 1960s.* Cambridge, MA: Harvard University Press, 1981. One of the best historical studies of SNCC and the contributions students made to galvanize the civil rights movement.

Vickie Crawford, Jacqueline Rouse, and Barbara Woods, eds. *Women in the Civil Rights Movement: Trailblazers and Torchbearers.* Brooklyn, NY: Carlson Publishing, 1990. An anthology of essays presented at a symposium. The meeting was designed to draw attention to the women whose contributions to the freedom struggle of the 1950s and 1960s are often overlooked or neglected.

Henry Hampton and Steve Fayer, eds. *The Voices of Freedom: An Oral History of the Civil Rights Movement from the 1950s through the 1980s.* New York: Bantam Books, 1990. A remarkable and indispensable oral history of all the participants in the civil rights movement, from the least well known to the internationally celebrated.

Steven F. Lawson. *Running for Freedom: Civil Rights and Black Politics in America since 1941.* Philadelphia: Temple University Press,

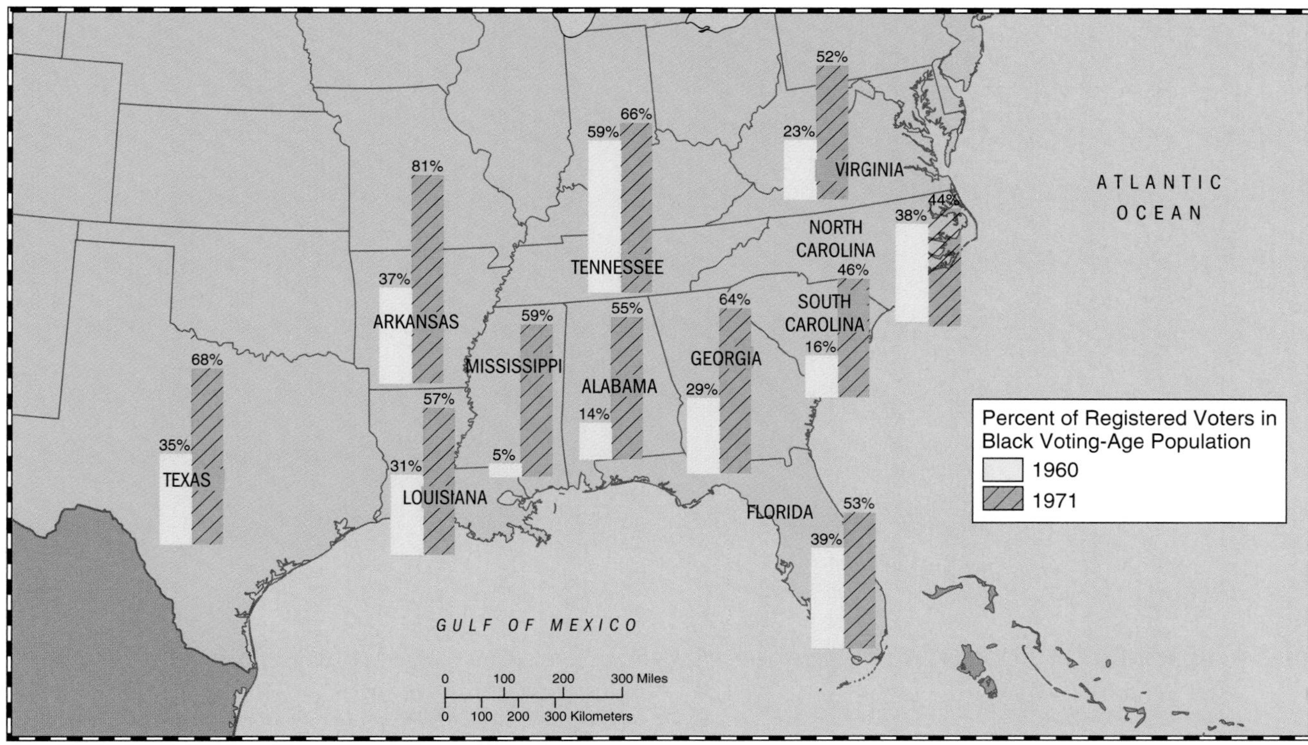

MAP 21–2 The Effect of the Voting Rights Act of 1965 The Voting Rights Act enabled millions of previously disfranchised African Americans in the South to vote.

1991. A succinct analysis of the politics, legislative measures, and individuals that figured in the successes and failures of the civil rights movement.

Aldon D. Morris. *The Origins of the Modern Civil Rights Movement: Black Communities Organizing for Change.* New York: Free Press; London: Collier Macmillan, 1984. An important and insightful analysis of the mobilization and organizing strategies pursued by diverse communities for social change that paved the way for the modern civil rights movement.

Additional Bibliography

General Overviews of Civil Rights Movement and Organizations

Robert Fredrick Burk. *The Eisenhower Administration and Black Civil Rights.* Knoxville, TN: University of Tennessee Press, 1984.

Stewart Burns. *Daybreak of Freedom: The Montgomery Bus Boycott.* Chapel Hill, NC: University of North Carolina Press, 1997.

John Dittmer. *Local People: The Struggle for Civil Rights in Mississippi.* Urbana, IL: University of Illinois Press, 1994.

Adam Fairclough. *To Redeem the Soul of America: The Southern Christian Leadership Conference and Martin Luther King, Jr.* Athens, GA: University of Georgia Press, 1987.

David R. Goldfield. *Black, White and Southern: Race Relations and the Southern Culture, 1940 to the Present.* Baton Rouge, LA: Louisiana State University Press, 1991.

Martin Luther King, Jr. *Stride Towards Freedom: The Montgomery Story.* New York: Harper, 1958.

Steven F. Lawson. *Black Ballots: Voting Rights in the South, 1944–1969.* New York: Columbia University Press, 1976.

Manning Marable. *Race, Reform, and Rebellion: The Second Reconstruction in Black America, 1945–1982.* Jackson, MS: University Press of Mississippi, 1984.

August Meier and Elliot Rudwick. *CORE: A Study of the Civil Rights Movement, 1942–1968.* New York: Oxford University Press, 1973.

Anne Moody. *Coming of Age in Mississippi.* New York: Dial Press, 1968.

Donald G. Nieman. *Promises to Keep: African-Americans and the Constitutional Order, 1776 to the Present.* New York: Oxford University Press, 1991.

Robert J. Norrell. *Reaping the Whirlwind: The Civil Rights Movement in Tuskegee.* New York: Knopf, 1985.

Charles M. Payne. *I've Got the Light of Freedom: The Organizing Tradition and the Mississippi Freedom Struggle.* Berkeley, CA: University of California Press, 1995.

Fred Powledge. *Free at Last? The Civil Rights Movement and the People Who Made It.* Boston: Little, Brown, 1991.

Howell Raines. *My Soul Is Rested: Movement Days in the Deep South Remembered.* New York: Putnam, 1977.

Belinda Robnett. *How Long? How Long? African-American Women in the Struggle for Civil Rights.* New York: Oxford University Press, 1997.

Juan Williams. *Eyes on the Prize: America's Civil Rights Years, 1954–1965.* New York: Viking, 1987.

Timeline

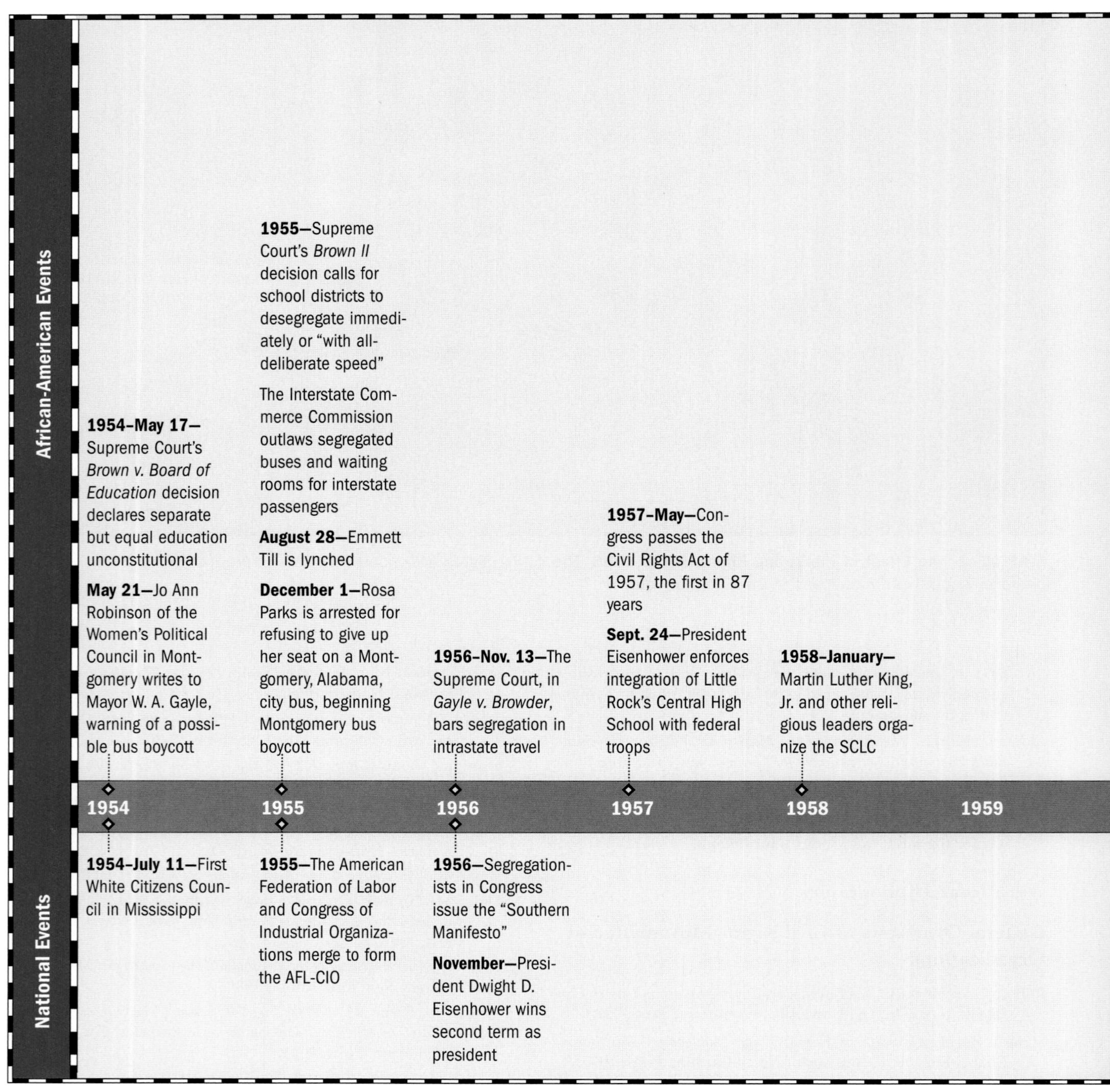

African-American Events

1954–May 17—Supreme Court's *Brown v. Board of Education* decision declares separate but equal education unconstitutional

May 21—Jo Ann Robinson of the Women's Political Council in Montgomery writes to Mayor W. A. Gayle, warning of a possible bus boycott

1955—Supreme Court's *Brown II* decision calls for school districts to desegregate immediately or "with all-deliberate speed"

The Interstate Commerce Commission outlaws segregated buses and waiting rooms for interstate passengers

August 28—Emmett Till is lynched

December 1—Rosa Parks is arrested for refusing to give up her seat on a Montgomery, Alabama, city bus, beginning Montgomery bus boycott

1956–Nov. 13—The Supreme Court, in *Gayle v. Browder*, bars segregation in intrastate travel

1957–May—Congress passes the Civil Rights Act of 1957, the first in 87 years

Sept. 24—President Eisenhower enforces integration of Little Rock's Central High School with federal troops

1958–January—Martin Luther King, Jr. and other religious leaders organize the SCLC

1954 | 1955 | 1956 | 1957 | 1958 | 1959

National Events

1954–July 11—First White Citizens Council in Mississippi

1955—The American Federation of Labor and Congress of Industrial Organizations merge to form the AFL-CIO

1956—Segregationists in Congress issue the "Southern Manifesto"

November—President Dwight D. Eisenhower wins second term as president

1960–Feb. 1—Black students sit in at Woolworth lunch counter in Greensboro, North Carolina launching the sit-in movement

April—SNCC founded

November—Black vote critical to Kennedy's election

1960–November—John F. Kennedy elected president

1961–May—Freedom Riders attacked in Alabama and Mississippi

Sept. 23—Kennedy names Thurgood Marshall to the Second Circuit Court of Appeals

Sept. 25—Herbert Lee, a local activist, is killed in Amite County, Mississippi

1962–February—The Council of Federated Organizations (COFO) is formed.

June 25—James Meredith desegregates the University of Mississippi with federal support

July—The Albany Movement fails

August—Voter Education Project launched

1963–April–May—Project C highlights racial injustices in Birmingham

King writes his celebrated "Letter from Birmingham Jail"

June—Federal government compels Alabama Governor George C. Wallace to desegregate the University of Alabama

June 12—Medgar Evers is murdered

Aug. 17—W. E. B. Du Bois dies in Ghana, Africa, at 95

Aug. 28—The March on Washington; Martin Luther King, Jr. delivers his "I Have A Dream" speech

Sept. 15—Ku Klux Klan bombs the 16th Street Baptist Church in Birmingham, Alabama, killing four girls

December—Malcolm X breaks with Elijah Muhammad and the Nation of Islam and founds his own movement, Muslim Mosque

1963–Nov. 22—President Kennedy is assassinated

Lyndon Johnson succeeds to the presidency

1964—SNCC launches the Mississippi Freedom Summer Project to promote voter registration

January—Twenty-fourth Amendment to the United States Constitution is ratified, outlawing the poll tax

June 21—James E. Chaney, Michael Schwerner, and Andrew Goodman murdered in Mississippi

July 2—Civil Rights Act of 1964 enacted

August—The Mississippi Freedom Democratic Party denied seating at the Democratic National Convention

December—Martin Luther King, Jr. wins the Nobel Peace Prize

1964—Equal Employment Opportunity Commission established

1965–March 21—Civil rights marchers walk from Selma to Montgomery after violent confrontation in Selma

Aug. 6—Voting Rights Act of 1965 enacted

1965—Lyndon Johnson outlines the Great Society Program to attack poverty

Black Politics/White Resistance

Numan V. Bartley. *The Rise of Massive Resistance: Race and Politics in the South during the 1950's.* Baton Rouge, LA: Louisiana State University Press, 1969.

Elizabeth Jacoway and David R. Colburn. *Southern Businessmen and Desegregation.* Baton Rouge, LA: Louisiana State University Press, 1982.

Doug McAdam. *Freedom Summer.* New York: Oxford University Press, 1988.

Neil R. McMillen. *The Citizen's Council: A History of Organized Resistance to the Second Reconstruction.* Urbana, IL: University of Illinois Press, 1971.

Frank R. Parker. *Black Votes Count: Political Empowerment in Mississippi after 1965.* Chapel Hill, NC: University of North Carolina Press, 1990.

Autobiography and Biography

Daisy Bates. *The Long Shadow of Little Rock: Memoir.* New York: David McKay Co., 1962.

Taylor Branch. *Pillar of Fire: America in the King Years, 1963–65.* New York: Simon & Schuster, 1998.

Eric R. Burner. *And Gently He Shall Lead Them: Robert Parris Moses and Civil Rights in Mississippi.* New York: New York University Press, 1994.

Septima Clark. *Ready from Within: Septima Clark and the Civil Rights Movement.* Navarro, CA: Wild Tree Press, 1986.

Robert S. Dallek. *Flawed Giant: Lyndon Johnson and His Times, 1961–1973.* New York: Oxford University Press, 1998.

Dennis C. Dickerson. *Militant Mediator: Whitney M. Young, Jr., 1921–1971.* Lexington, KY: University Press of Kentucky, 1998.

James Farmer. *Lay Bare the Heart: An Autobiography of the Civil Rights Movement.* New York: Arbor House, 1985.

Cynthia Griggs Fleming. *Soon We Will Not Cry: The Liberation of Ruby Doris Smith Robinson.* Lanham, MD: Rowman & Littlefield, 1998.

David J. Garrow. *Bearing the Cross: Martin Luther King, Jr., and the Southern Christian Leadership Conference.* New York: William Morrow & Company, 1986.

_____. *The FBI and Martin Luther King, Jr.* New York: Penguin Books, 1981.

Chana Kai Lee. *For Freedom's Sake: The Life of Fannie Lou Hamer.* Urbana, IL: University of Illinois Press, 1999.

David Levering Lewis. *King: A Critical Biography.* New York: Praeger, 1970.

Timothy B. Tyson. *Radio Free Dixie: Robert F. Williams and the Roots of Black Power.* Chapel Hill, NC: University of North Carolina Press, 1999.

Jo Ann Gibson Robinson, with David Garrow. *The Montgomery Bus Boycott and the Women Who Started It.* Knoxville, TN: University of Tennessee Press, 1987.

Reference Works

Charles Eagles, ed., *The Civil Rights Movement in America.* Jackson, MS: University Press of Mississippi, 1986.

Charles S. Lowery and John F. Marszalek, eds. *Encyclopedia of African-American Civil Rights: From Emancipation to the Present.* New York: Greenwood Press, 1992.

Retracing the Odyssey

Civil Rights Movement Museums

Brown v. Board of Education National Historic Landmark. 330 Western Avenue (Sumner School) and 1515 Monroe Street (Monroe School), Topeka, Kansas. The Sumner and Monroe Elementary Schools composed the *Brown v. Board of Education* National Historic Landmark. The 1954 *Brown v. Topeka Board of Education* decision written by U.S. Supreme Court Chief Justice Earl Warren removed the legal foundation upon which the entire system of racial segregation and discrimination in the South was based and reaffirmed the ideal of the equal protection under the law clause in the Fourteenth Amendment to the U.S. Constitution. The *Brown* decision struck down the 1896 *Plessy v. Ferguson* doctrine of "separate but equal." *Brown* was the culmination of a long struggle waged by the NAACP's team of lawyers headed by Thurgood Marshall and dozens of ordinary citizens in local communities.

Birmingham Civil Rights Institute. 560 16th St., Birmingham, Alabama. (205) 328-9696. Tues–Sat. 10:00 A.M.–5:00 P.M. Sunday 1:00–5:00 P.M. Suggested donation. Exhibits depict the history of the black freedom struggle. The museum chronicles the dramatic and often violent activities that occurred in Birmingham during the 1960s as black protest confronted massive white resistance.

The Lincoln Memorial. National Mall, Washington, D.C. 2004. Daily (except Christmas), 8:00 A.M. until 11:45 P.M. (202) 485-9889. The Lincoln Memorial was built to celebrate President Abraham Lincoln and the Civil War (1861–1865) to preserve the union. It possesses a particular relevance and meaning to African Americans. The Lincoln Memorial was the site of the August 1963 March on Washington during which Martin Luther King delivered his powerful "I Have a Dream" speech.

The Vietnam Veterans Memorial. National Mall, Washington, D.C. The Memorial contains all of the names of Americans who lost their lives in the Vietnam War.

The Martin Luther King, Jr. Center for Nonviolent Social Change. 449 Auburn Avenue, N.E. Atlanta, Georgia 30312. (404) 526-8900. Founded by Mrs Coretta Scott King in 1968 as a living memorial dedicated to the preservation and advancement of the work of her husband, The Martin Luther King, Jr. Center for Nonviolent Social Change features exhibits that detail the life and legacy of Martin Luther King, Jr. It contains a unique exhibit of his personal memorabilia. The King Library and Archives contain the world's largest existing collection of civil rights materials.

REVIEW, RESEARCH & INTERACT

REVIEW QUESTIONS

1. What role did "ordinary" or local people play in the civil rights movement? What were some of the specific contributions of children to the overall struggle for social change?
2. What key issues and events provoked intervention by the federal government into the civil rights movement? What were the major pieces of legislation enacted and how did they dismantle legalized segregation?
3. What were the ideologies, objectives, and tactics of the major civil rights organizations and their leaders?
4. What were the human costs of the civil rights movement? Who were some of the people who lost their lives in the struggle?
5. What were the major successes and failures of the freedom movement? What were some of the intergenerational tensions that plagued the movement? In what way did the movement transform American politics and society?

Research Navigator.com RESOURCES FOR COLLEGE RESEARCH ASSIGNMENTS **www.researchnavigator.com**

Chapter 21 examines the causes, course, and consequences of the civil right's movement. For further research on this pivotal era in African American history, use the tools available to you in Research Navigator.

As you investigate this topic, consider this question: "Compare and contrast nineteenth-century Reconstruction with the "Second Reconstruction" of the mid-twentieth century. Why did the Second Reconstruction have more lasting effects?"

- **ContentSelect:** Search in the History database using the search term *Martin Luther King.*
- **Links Library:** Access the History: U.S. History database and explore the links for *King, Martin Luther* and *Voting Rights Act of 1965.*
- **New York Times on the Web:** To find more about the early years of the antislavery movements, search in the History database using the search term *Parks, Rosa.*

DOCUMENTS AND ACTIVITIES IN AFRICAN-AMERICAN HISTORY

Documents

21-1 "Digest Of Jim-Crow Laws Affecting Passengers in Interstate Travel"
21-2 Jo Ann Gibson Robinson, Bus Boycott
21-3 Southern Manifesto, 1956
21-4 Executive Order 10730: Desegregation of Central High School,1957
21-5 Julian Bond, Sit-ins and the Origins of SNCC, 1960
21-6 Martin Luther King, Jr.: Letter from Birmingham City Jail, 1963
21-7 Fannie Lou Hamer, Voting Rights in Mississippi, 1962–1964

Interactive Map

Major Events of the Civil Rights Movement, p. 516
http://www.prenhall.com/hine/map21.1

Learning Activity

The Civil Rights Movement
A close look at the ideas, events, and people involved in the struggle to end discrimination based on race.

22

The Struggle Continues, 1965–1980

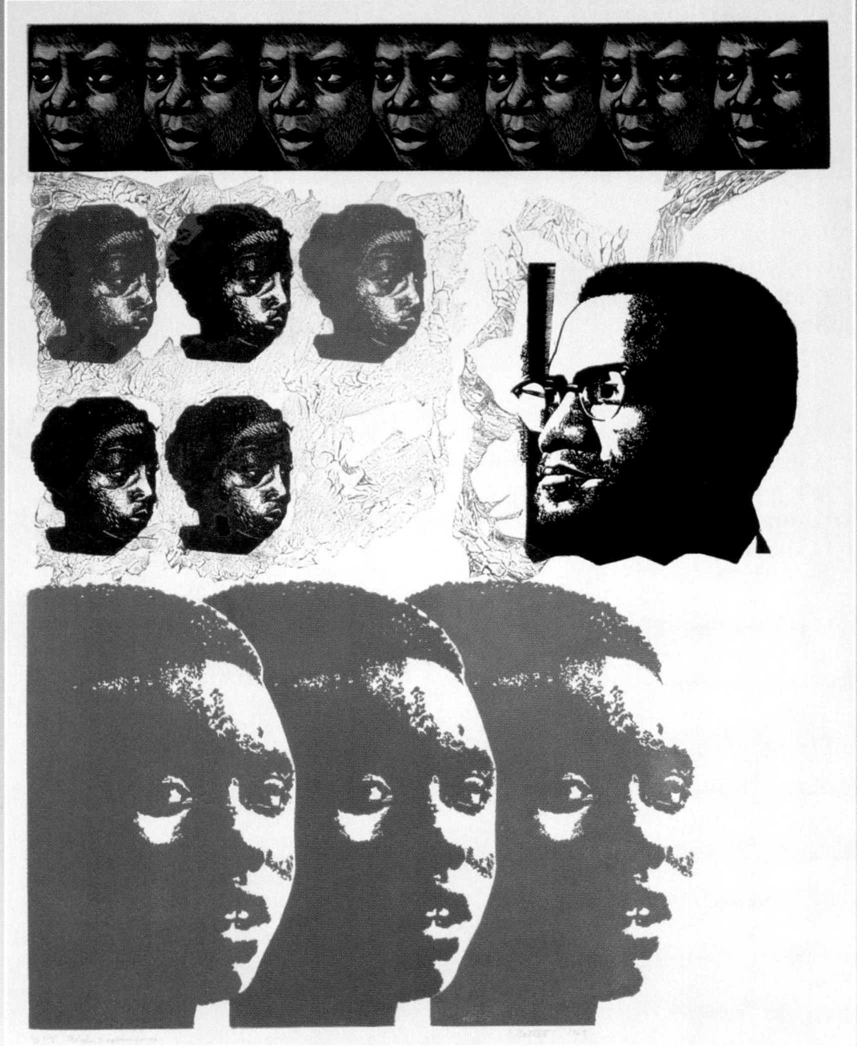

Elizabeth Catlett (1919–   ) created *Malcolm X Speaks for Us* (1969), a linoleum block print as part of her series on African-American heroes. Since his assassination, the eloquently outspoken champion of black people and critic of American racism, Malcolm X (1925–1965) has become the subject of poems, song, films, operas, plays, and books. The memorialization of Malcolm X continues today.

WE must work on two levels. In every city we have a dual society. . . . In every city, we have two economies. In every city, we have two housing markets. In every city, we have two school systems. This duality has brought about a great deal of injustice. . . . Black Power in the positive sense is a psychological call to manhood . . . and a sense of dignity. . . . Black Power is pooling black political resources in order to achieve our legitimate goals. . . . Black Power in its positive sense is a pooling of black economic resources in order to achieve legitimate power. . . . What is necessary now is to see integration in political terms. . . . [T]here are times when we must see segregation as a temporary way-station to the ultimate goal which we seek . . . a truly integrated society where there is shared power.

—Martin Luther King Jr.

Black Power . . . a call for black people in this country to unite, to recognize their heritage, to build a sense of community . . . to define their own goals, to lead their own organizations . . . to reject the racist institutions and values of this society. The concept of Black Power rests on a fundamental premise: *Before a group can enter the open society, it must first close ranks.* [emphasis in the original]

—Stokely Carmichael and Charles V. Hamilton

When Lyndon Johnson became president in 1963 after John F. Kennedy's assassination, he brought to the office impressive political skills and a determination to reconcile the racial, social, and economic disparities dividing black from white Americans. Johnson's escalation of America's involvement in

CHAPTER OUTLINE

The Fading Dream of Racial Integration: White Backlash and Black Nationalism
- Malcolm X
- Malcolm X's New Departure
- Stokely Carmichael and Black Power
- The National Council of Churches

The Black Panther Party
- Police Repression and the FBI's COINTELPRO
- Prisoners' Rights

The Inner-City Rebellions
- Watts
- Newark
- Detroit
- The Kerner Commission

Difficulties in Creating the Great Society

Johnson and the War in Vietnam
- Black Americans and the Vietnam War
- Project 100,000

Johnson: Vietnam Destroys the Great Society

King: Searching for a New Strategy
- King on the Vietnam War
- King's Murder

The Black Arts Movement and Black Consciousness
- Poetry and Theater
- Music

The Second Phase of the Black Student Movement
- The Orangeburg Massacre
- Black Studies

The Election of 1968

The Nixon Presidency
- The "Moynihan Report" and FAP
- Busing
- Nixon and the War
- Nixon's Downfall

The Rise of Black Elected Officials
- The Gary Convention and the Black Political Agenda
- Black People Gain Local Offices

Economic Downturn

Black Americans and the Carter Presidency
- Black Appointees
- Carter's Domestic Policies

Conclusion

Vietnam, however, undermined his domestic social policies. Meanwhile, some African Americans lost faith in and patience with American society. In the face of a white backlash against the gains of the civil rights movement, many leaders and scholars—like Stokely Carmichael and Charles Hamilton—argued for black power and black separatism. Black power, which challenged both the interracialism of the civil rights movement and Johnson's democratic liberalism, became the dominant ideology for many younger activists. King remained ambivalent about black power, preferring to define it as a temporary strategy for black solidarity in the struggle for an integrated society. A. Philip Randolph called black power a "menace to peace and prosperity" and added, "No Negro who is fighting for civil rights can support black power, which is opposed to civil rights and integration." These opposing ideologies represent a generational shift, and the tensions between them frame many of the key events of the post-civil rights movement years.

The Fading Dream of Racial Integration: White Backlash and Black Nationalism

Even though President Johnson easily defeated Republican senator Barry Goldwater, the 1964 election was hardly a mandate for civil rights. In California, for example, voters gave Johnson a decisive victory, but also approved an amendment to the state constitution that not only repealed all existing legislation prohibiting discrimination in the sale or rental of housing, but prevented such legislation from ever being enacted in the future. Although the amendment was later struck down by the Supreme Court, its passage suggested that white opposition to racial integration was not confined to the South. When, in 1966, Johnson asked Congress for federal legislation to ban discrimination in housing, a weakened version of his bill died in the Senate. In elections that year, white opposition to civil rights helped elect Republicans, including former movie actor Ronald Reagan as governor of California.

Meanwhile, Alabama governor George Wallace, an outspoken opponent of racial integration and civil rights legislation, was emerging as a national political figure. With limited resources, he had run surprisingly well against Johnson in the 1964 Wisconsin, Indiana, and Maryland Democratic primaries. Heartened by the favorable response he received from northern white voters, Wallace was planning a full-scale presidential race in 1968.

With many white Americans increasingly reluctant to support the goals of the civil rights movement, many black Americans began searching for new approaches to their problems. The reign of terror experienced by COFO (Council of Federated Organizations) workers in Mississippi had undermined the commitment to integration and nonviolence of the civil rights movement and would help radicalize a new, younger generation of activists. Men like Floyd McKissick of the Congress of Racial Equality (CORE) and Stokely Carmichael of the Student Nonviolent Coordinating Committee (SNCC) became disillusioned, rejecting King's moderation, nonviolence, and universalism. The differences between King's SCLC (Southern Christian Leadership Conference) and Carmichael's SNCC grew with each confrontation. Carmichael had argued after the 1964 failure of the Mississippi Freedom Democratic party that it was time to form an independent black political party. In 1965, after the Selma-to-Montgomery march, he helped found the Lowndes County (Mississippi) Freedom Organization (LCFO). It became the first political organization in the civil rights movement to adopt the symbol of the black panther.

Black residents of northern and western cities also lost patience with the slow pace of change. Increasing numbers of young black churchmen castigated mainstream white religious groups for their complicity with racism, demanded reparations, and agitated for substantive power or leadership roles within the governing structures of the National Council of Churches. Out of the interracial conflict and tension emerged a Black Theology that critiques racism within white religious groups, and it was followed by a Black Feminist Theology that offered searing critiques of sexism within the black church. Leaders in the development of Black Theology and the expression of a black nationalist Christianity were theologians James H. Cone, author of *Black Theology and Black Power* (1969) and the Reverend Albert Cleage Jr. of Detroit who was pastor of the Shrine of the Black Madonna and a passionate advocate of black liberation theology as defined in his books, *Black Christian Nationalism* and *The Black Messiah.* In ways reminiscent of Marcus Garvey, black Christian nationalism argued for black symbols of religious faith. Jesus Christ was, as Rev. Cleage expounded, a black Messiah. Black liberation theology asserted the importance of conjoining religious practice and faith with political activism and social change. Growing numbers of young African Americans, along with diverse black religious leaders, dismayed by the great political and economic disparities between themselves and white Americans, became catalysts for an increasingly radical turn in the civil rights movement.

Malcolm X

After 1965, the year in which he died, no one had more influence on young black activists and the residents of America's ghettoized inner cities than Malcolm X. The son of a Baptist preacher, he was born Malcolm Little in Omaha, Nebraska, and grew up in Lansing, Michigan. His family's home was burned by Klan terrorists, and his father was murdered two years later. His mother was subsequently committed to a mental institution, and welfare agencies separated the children. Malcolm was sent to a juvenile detention home, quit school after the eighth grade, and moved to Boston to live with his sister. There he became involved in the street life of gambling, drugs, and burglary. He was arrested and sentenced to a ten-year prison term in 1942. During the six and a half years he spent in prison, he embraced the teachings of Elijah Muhammad of the Nation of Islam and renounced what he considered his "slave name" to become Malcolm X. In 1954 he became minister of Harlem's Temple Number 7. Articulate, charismatic, and forceful, Malcolm did not believe in nonviolence or advocate integration. His was the voice of the northern urban "second ghettoes." In 1961 he began publishing *Muhammad Speaks*, the official newspaper of the Nation. In *The Autobiography of Malcolm X*, published in 1965 by the writer Alex Haley of *Roots* fame, Malcolm declared.

> Few white people realize that many black people today dislike and avoid spending any more time than they must around white people. This "integration" image, as it is popularly interpreted, has millions of vain, self-exalted white people convinced that black people want to sleep in bed with them—and that's a lie! Oh you can't tell the average white man that the Negro man's prime desire isn't to have a white woman—another lie! Like a black brother recently observed to me, "Look, you ever smell one of them wet?"

Malcolm X attracted black people's attention. His dismissal of the goal of racial integration and King's message of redemption through brotherly love resonated with many younger civil rights workers disillusioned by white violence. "The day of nonviolent resistance is over," Malcolm insisted. And in 1964, he declared, "Revolutions are never based upon love-your-enemy, and pray-for-those-who-despitefully-use-you. And revolutions are never waged by singing 'We Shall Overcome.' Revolutions are based on bloodshed."

Malcolm X's New Departure

Malcolm X's popularity created tensions between himself and the leadership of the Nation of Islam. He grew disillusioned with Elijah Muhammad's aversion to political activism, and Elijah Muhammad grew jealous of Malcolm's success. When Malcolm described the Kennedy assassination as a case of "the chickens coming home to roost" (meaning Kennedy was a victim of the same kind of violence that afflicted black people), Elijah Muhammad suspended him. In 1964, Malcolm broke with the Nation of Islam and founded his own organization, the Muslim Mosque, Inc. That same year he went on a pilgrimage to Mecca that profoundly influenced him. He changed his name to El-Hajj Malik El-Shabazz, founded the Organization for Afro-American Unity (after the Organization of African Unity), repudiated the Nation of Islam doctrine that all white people are evil, and began lecturing on the connection between the civil rights struggle in the South and the struggle against colonialism in Africa. On February 14, 1965, assassins associated with the Nation of Islam killed Malcolm X as he addressed an audience in Harlem.

Malcolm's militant advocacy of self-defense, of "overturning systems" that deprive African Americans of basic human rights, helped to radicalize other black leaders of the civil rights movement.

Stokely Carmichael and Black Power

In 1966 Stokely Carmichael, a native of Trinidad who had been raised in New York City and educated at Howard University, became chairman of SNCC. By then he had given up on the ideal of interracial collaboration and was determined to move SNCC toward black nationalism. He dismissed SNCC's few white staffers, including Bob Zellner, who had been with the organization since its inception.

About this time, James Meredith began a one-man "march against fear" from Tennessee to Jackson, Mississippi, to encourage black Southerners to register and vote. On this march, he was shot and wounded by white gunmen. In June 1966, after this incident, SNCC and Carmichael joined with other organizations to complete the march. It was at this time that Carmichael popularized the slogan "Black Power" that was to become SNCC's rallying cry. "The only way we gonna stop them white men from whippin' us," he announced to a cheering crowd, "is to take over. We been saying freedom for six years and we ain't got nothin'. What we gonna start saying is Black Power." Carmichael was specific about what black power meant to black Southerners:

> In Lowndes County [Mississippi], for example, black power will mean that if a Negro is elected sheriff, he

> can end police brutality. If a black man is elected tax assessor, he can collect and channel funds for the building of better roads and schools serving black people—thus advancing the move from political power into the economic arena. . . . Politically, black power means what it has always meant to SNCC: the coming-together of black people to elect representatives and to force those representatives to speak to their needs. It does not mean merely putting black faces into office.

Critics accused advocates of black power of reverse racism, but Carmichael argued on the contrary that they were promoting positive self-identity, racial pride, and the development of independent political and economic power. There was another more disruptive side of the black freedom movement. All of the organizations suffered internal problems concerning gender roles, relations between white women and black men, and separatism versus integration. As the leaders became more disillusioned about the slow pace of social change some questioned whether white people belonged in their organizations. In 1968, CORE followed SNCC's example and ejected its white members with a resulting loss of financial resources. For various reasons both organizations began to decline, and by the end of the 1960s, SNCC had virtually disappeared.

Martin Luther King had mixed feelings about the ideology of black power. He welcomed its promotion of black political and economic strength, psychological assertiveness, and cultural pride. But when black power degenerated into a mantra of taunts against white people, King denounced it as "a nihilistic philosophy born out of the conviction that the Negro can't win." King also objected to black power's "implicit and often explicit belief in black separatism" and the assertion of its proponents that "there can be a separate Black road to power and fulfillment."

In May 1967 Hubert G. Brown followed Carmichael as head of SNCC. "H. Rap" Brown, as he became known, raised the militancy of the black power movement's rhetoric to a new level, calling white people "honkies," and the police "pigs." "Violence," he said, was "as American as apple pie." In August 1967 Brown told enthusiastic listeners in the black neighborhood of Cambridge, Maryland, that "black folks built America, and if America don't come around, we're going to burn America down." When a few hours later, a fire erupted in a dilapidated school in the heart of the city's black community, white firemen refused to fight it. Police charged Brown with inciting a riot and committing arson, but he posted bail and fled. Later he was arrested on other charges.

The National Council of Churches

Black and white leaders of mainstream religious organizations were transformed by black power. In 1946, the Federal Council of Churches, composed of Protestants, Catholics, and Jews, pledged to work for "a non-segregated church and a non-segregated society." Between 1963 and 1965, the National Council of Churches (NCC), contributed financial and moral support to the Civil Rights Movement. In 1963 the NCC founded its Commission on Religion and Race to support the black freedom movement. Although a white controlled and managed operation, three of the eight staff members of the commission were African American: Anna Hedgeman, J. Oscar Lee, and James Breeden. The NCC supported events such as the March on Washington and lobbied for passage of the Civil Rights Act of 1964 and the Voting Rights Act of 1965.

In 1965, the NCC appointed Benjamin Payton as director of the Commission on Religion and Race. Payton, a native of Orangeburg, South Carolina had been educated at Harvard Divinity School and had earned a Ph.D. at Yale. Payton had taught at Howard University and he was a member of the National Baptist Convention, U.S.A., the largest African-American denomination. Under his stewardship the Commission on Religion and Race was incorporated into the Division of Christian Life and Mission, and later became part of the NCC's Department of Social Justice that included five other special task forces.

Payton had his own views about how organized religion could help to address racial problems. He viewed the economic development of black people and their communities as the critical prerequisite to improving national racial relations. In his first address to the National Council, Payton emphasized the need for "a program of economic development to make civil rights real, in housing, employment, education and health care." In July 1966 he convened a small cadre of men that included Gayraud S. Wilmore who served as the director of the United Presbyterian's Commission on Religion and Race. Out of this gathering emerged the National Commission of Black Churchmen (NCBC), which became a key mainstream ecumenical church group advocating black power concepts and strategies throughout the rest of the 1960s. In May 1967, however, the NCC's Department of Social Justice lost some of its momentum and direction when Payton left to become president of Benedict College, a black Baptist affiliated college in Columbia, South Carolina.

The black power movement spurred the creation of black caucuses within the predominantly white churches. In February 1968 James Lawson headed the Black Methodists for Church Renewal, a caucus that crystallized within the United Methodist Church. In the same year, the United Presbyterian Church witnessed the formation of the Black Presbyterian United that replaced the Presbyterian Interracial Council. The Episcopal Society for Racial and Cultural Unity, an interracial group, was replaced by an Episcopal Union of Black Clergy and Laity. By the early 1970s there were nine such caucuses. Within the Roman Catholic Church, black Catholics insisted that the Church demonstrate more respect for African-American patterns of worship. All these black religious groups pressed for more black leadership within the denominations. Thus the stage was set for James Forman's Black Manifesto.

In April 1969, James Forman, former Chicago school teacher renowned for his work with SNCC, addressed the National Black Economic Development Conference in Detroit, sponsored by the Interreligious Foundation for Community Organizations (which was supported by predominantly white churches). Forman demanded that white churches pay $500 million in reparations for their participation in and benefit from American slavery and racial exploitation. His sharply secular critique of American religion precipitated the withdrawal of mainstream white religion groups from active participation in the civil rights movement. These white groups were offended by Forman's black power rhetoric and revolutionary Marxist ideology. Black and other minority groups wanted to share real power within the white dominated churches. Relations between Blacks and Jews also deteriorated as countercharges circulated of "Jewish racism" and "Black anti-Semitism."

The Black Panther Party

The most institutionalized expression of the new black militancy was the Black Panther Party for Self-Defense created by Huey P. Newton and Bobby Seale in Oakland, California, in October 1966. Newton and Seale took the name of the party from the black panther symbol of the Lowndes County Freedom Organization (LCFO). The Black Panthers combined black nationalist ideology with Marxist-Leninist doctrines. Working with white radicals, they hoped to fashion the party into a revolutionary vanguard dedicated to overthrowing capitalist society and ending police brutality. For a few months Stokely Carmichael, who had become estranged from SNCC, aligned himself with the Panthers and was named the party's prime minister. (However, Carmichael soon shifted his interest to pan-Africanism. He moved to Africa and changed his name to Kwame Turé.) Eldridge

Some members of the Black Panther party raised funds to pay for the legal fees of those arrested and charged with various offenses, such as Bobby Seale and Ericka Huggins. The Panthers advocated a radical economic, social, and educational agenda that made it the target of a determined campaign of suppression by the police and the FBI.

Cleaver, the Panther's minister of education, helped formulate the party's ideology. Cleaver was a convicted rapist who had spent most of his youth in prison, where he became a follower of Malcolm X and began writing the autobiographical essays that would be published as *Soul on Ice* in 1968, the year the party dropped "Self-Defense" from its name. Black people, Cleaver maintained, were victims of colonization, not just disfranchised American citizens. Thus integrationism could not meet their needs. They needed, instead, like other colonized peoples, to be liberated. "To achieve these ends," he wrote, "we believe that political and military machinery that does not exist now and has never existed must be created. We need functional machinery that is able to deal with these two interrelated sets of political dynamics which, strictly speaking, make up the total political situation on the North American continent." Cleaver and other top Panther leaders were arrested after a shootout with Oakland police in 1968. Cleaver escaped and fled into exile. While abroad, he abandoned his radicalism, and became involved with the Republican party and fundamentalist Christianity after his return to the United States in 1975.

Police Repression and the FBI's COINTELPRO

The Panthers, imposing in black leather jackets, berets, and "Afro" haircuts, alarmed white Americans when they took up arms for self-defense and patrolled their neighborhoods to monitor the police. A series of bloody confrontations and shoot-outs in Oakland distracted

VOICES

The Black Panther Party Platform

Huey Newton and Bobby Seale's Ten-Point Program reflects their determination to move from the pursuit of civil rights to a radical restructuring of American society along socialist lines, with work and rewards equally shared.

ctober 1966

BLACK PANTHER PARTY, PLATFORM AND PROGRAM
WHAT WE WANT, WHAT WE BELIEVE

1. We want freedom. We want power to determine the destiny of our Black Community . . .
2. We want full employment for our people . . .
3. We want an end to the robbery of the capitalists of our Black Community . . .
4. We want decent housing fit for shelter of human beings . . .
5. We want education for our people that exposes the true nature of this decadent American society. We want education that teaches us our true history and our role in present-day society . . .
6. We want all Black men to be exempt from military service . . .
7. We want an immediate end to POLICE BRUTALITY and MURDER of Black people . . .
8. We want freedom for all Black men held in federal, state, county and city prisons and jails . . .
9. We want all Black people when brought to trial to be tried in court by a jury of their peer group or people from their Black communities, as defined by the Constitution of the United States . . .
10. We want land, bread, housing, education, clothing, justice, and peace. And as our major political objective, a United Nations supervised plebiscite to be held throughout the Black colony in which only Black colonial subjects will be allowed to participate, for the purpose of determining the will of Black people as to their national destiny.

QUESTIONS

1. In what ways is the Panthers' Ten Point Program similar to the Bill of Rights in the United States Constitution? How do they differ?
2. How did the Panthers propose to achieve black liberation? What significance did they place on the study of history? How did the Panthers' program conflict with that of the older civil rights organizations?

Source: Clayborne Carson, et al., eds., *The Eyes on the Prize Civil Rights Reader: Documents, Speeches, and Firsthand Accounts from the Black Freedom Struggle, 1954–1990.* New York: Viking Penguin, 1991 346–347.

attention from the Panthers' broader political objectives and community service projects. In Oakland and Chicago, the Panthers arranged free breakfast and health care programs, worked to instill racial pride, lectured and wrote about black history, and launched some of the earliest drug education programs. These activities were captured in the slogan, "Power to the People."

FBI director J. Edgar Hoover was determined to infiltrate, harass, destabilize, and destroy all nationalist groups and their leaders. The FBI cooperated with local law enforcement officials to ridicule and discredit leaders and to undermine and weaken the Black Panther party. In August 1967 Hoover distributed an explanatory memorandum that detailed the FBI's Counterintelligence Program directed toward black nationalist groups. The purpose, according to the memo, of this new "counterintelligence (COINTELPRO) endeavor is to expose, disrupt, misdirect, discredit, or otherwise neutralize the activities of black nationalist, hate-type organizations and groupings, their leadership, spokesmen, membership, and supporters, and to counter their propensity for violence and civil disorder." Undercover agents infiltrated the Panthers and provoked violence and criminal acts. Not that the Panthers were saints. Huey P. Newton, for example, had a long criminal record. He was imprisoned for murder in 1968, but was acquitted and released only to be charged with murder and assault again in 1974. After fleeing to Cuba to avoid trial, he returned in 1977 and was again acquitted. He was eventually killed at age forty-two in a drug dispute in Oakland in 1989. Still, the FBI and its counter-intelligence agents may have provoked much of the mayhem and violence that became associated with the Black Panther party. Certainly, COINTELPRO helped to shape negative public opinion of black nationalist ideology.

In their effort to destroy the party, law enforcement officials killed an estimated twenty-eight Panthers and imprisoned 750 others. In perhaps the most egregious incident, police in Chicago killed Fred Hampton and Mark Clark in their sleep in a predawn raid on the Illinois Black Panther Headquarters on December 4, 1969. While the police fired hundreds of rounds, only two shots were fired from within the apartment.

Prisoners' Rights

Despite such repression, black militancy survived in many forms, including the prisoners' rights movement. One of the Black Panthers' social programs had focused on the conditions of black prisoners. By 1970, more than half the inmates in United States prisons were African American. In New York State, black Americans were around 70 percent of the prison population. Black activists argued that many African Americans were in jail for political reasons and suffered from unfair sentences and deplorable conditions because of racism and class exploitation.

TRACK 39

Angela Davis, an assistant professor of philosophy at the University of California at Los Angeles, became the first black woman to be listed on the FBI's Ten Most Wanted list because of her involvement in prisoners' rights. In 1969 UCLA's board of regents refused to renew her contract citing her lack of a Ph.D., but in fact they objected to her membership in the Communist party. During the late 1960s, she had worked on behalf of the Soledad Brothers, three prisoners—George Jackson, John Clutchette, and Fleeta Drumgo—accused of murdering a white guard at Soledad Prison. On August 7, 1970, George Jackson's younger brother, seventeen-year-old Jonathan Jackson, staged a one-man raid on the San Rafael courthouse in Marin County, California, to try to seize hostages to trade for the Soledad Brothers. In the ensuing shoot-out, Jonathan Jackson, two prisoners, and a judge were killed. Angela Davis, accused of supplying the weapons for the raid, was charged with murder, kidnaping, and conspiracy. She escaped and lived as a fugitive, but she was eventually captured and spent over a year in jail. After a long ordeal and a national "Free Angela" campaign, a jury acquitted Davis. On August 21, 1971, George Jackson was shot and killed at San Quentin Prison by guards who claimed he was trying to escape.

Across the country, prisoners at Attica, a maximum security prison in northern New York State, began a fast in memory of George Jackson that within days erupted into a full-scale rebellion. On September 9, 1971, 1,200 inmates seized control of half of Attica and took hostages. Four days later, state police and prison guards suppressed the uprising. Tom Wicker, a columnist for *The New York Times*, filed this report:

> A task force consisting of 211 state troopers and corrections officers retook Attica using tear gas, rifles, and shotguns. After the shooting was over, ten hostages and twenty-nine inmates lay dead or dying. At least 450 rounds of ammunition had been discharged. Four hostages and eighty-five inmates suffered gunshot wounds that they survived. After initial reports that several hostages had died at the hands of knife-wielding inmates, pathologists' reports revealed that hostages and inmates all died from gunshot wounds. No guns were found in the possession of inmates.

A state commission that, assembled in October 1971 to reconstruct the events at Attica concluded: "With the exception of Indian massacres in the late nineteenth-century, the State Police assault which ended the four-day prison uprising was the bloodiest one-day encounter between Americans since the Civil War."

The Inner-City Rebellions

The militant nationalism of Malcolm X and Stokely Carmichael and the radicalism of the Panthers reflected growing alienation and anger in America's impoverished inner cities. In 1965, 29.1 percent of black households, compared with only 7.8 percent of white households, lived below the poverty line. Almost 50 percent of nonwhite families lived in substandard housing compared with 18 percent of white families. Despite a drop in the number of Americans living in poverty from 38.0 million in 1959 to 32.7 million in 1965, the percentage of poor black people increased from 27.5 percent to 31 percent. In 1965 the black unemployment rate was 8.5 percent, almost twice the white unemployment rate of 4.3. For black teenagers the unemployment rate was 23 percent compared with 10.8 percent for white teenagers. As psychologist Kenneth Clark declared in 1967, "The masses of Negroes are now starkly aware of the fact that recent civil rights victories benefitted a very small percentage of middle-class Negroes while their predicament remained the same or worsened."

The passage of civil rights legislation did not resolve these disparities or diminish inner-city alienation. As jobs moved increasingly to suburbs to which inner-city residents could neither travel nor relocate, inner-city neighborhoods sank deeper into poverty. School dropout rates reached epidemic proportions, crime and drug use increased, and fragile family structures weakened. It was these conditions that led militants like the Panthers to liken their neighborhoods to exploited colonies kept in poverty by repressive white political and economic institutions. Few white Americans understood the depths of the black despair that flared into violence each summer between 1965 and 1969, beginning with the Watts rebellion of 1965.

Watts

In the summer of 1965, a section of Los Angeles called Watts exploded. Watts was 98 percent black. Its residents suffered from overcrowding, unemployment, inaccessible health care facilities, inadequate public transportation, and increasing crime and drug addiction. Almost 30 percent of the black male population was unemployed. The poverty, combined with anger at the often brutal behavior of Los Angeles's police force in Watts, proved to be an incendiary combination. On August 11, 1965, a policeman pulled over a young black man to check him for drunk driving. The man was arrested, but not before a crowd gathered. The policeman called for reinforcements, and when they arrived, the crowd pelted them with stones, bottles, and other objects. Within a few hours, Watts was in a total riot.

Governor Pat Brown, a Democrat, sent in the National Guard to restore order, but by the sixth day of the conflagration, Watts had been reduced to rubble and ashes. One reporter commented that Watts looked like Germany at the end of World War II. Thirty-four people had been killed; more than 900 injured; and 4,000 arrested. Total property damage was more than $35 million, equivalent to hundreds of millions of dollars today. The Watts rebellion was the beginning of four summers of uprisings that would engulf cities in the North and Midwest. There were riots in the summer of 1966, but even worse ones erupted in Newark and Detroit in 1967.

The first major urban uprising of the 1960s was in the Watts neighborhood of East Los Angeles in August 1965. It lasted nearly a week and left thirty-four people dead.

Newark

Newark, New Jersey, had more than four hundred thousand inhabitants in 1967. As was true in many other urban areas, white flight to the suburbs in the 1950s and 1960s made Newark a majority black city, but one that operated on an inadequate tax base and under white political control. The city lacked the means to meet its inhabitants' social needs. The school system deteriorated as unemployment had increased. In 1967, Newark had the highest unemployment rate among black men in the entire nation. As tensions flared and police brutality escalated, white officials paid little attention to black people's complaints. On July 12, after a black cab driver in police custody was beaten, protesters gathered at the police station near the Hayes Homes housing project. When a firebomb hit the wall of the station house, the police charged, clubbing the crowd. This triggered one of the most destructive civic rebellions of the period. During four days of rioting, the police and National Guard killed twenty-five black people—most of them innocent bystanders, including two children; a white policeman and fireman were also killed. Widespread looting and arson caused millions of dollars in property damage.

Detroit

When Detroit erupted a few days after Newark, it caught everyone by surprise except the residents of its inner-city neighborhoods. On the surface Detroit seemed like a model of prosperity and interracial accord. Some of the country's most dynamic popular music flowed from Detroit's Motown recording company. Owned by the astute Berry Gordy, Motown was a classic up-by-the-bootstraps success story. Gordy and his wife Raynoma and their extended family had, by 1967, produced such stars as Diana Ross and Mary Wells. "Before Motown," said Wells, "there were three careers available to a black girl in Detroit—babies, the factories or daywork."

But success like Gordy's was rare among the black migrants and their children, who poured into Detroit during and after World War II. The parents held their disappointment in check, but the children, particularly young men aged between seventeen and thirty-five, sought an outlet for their anger and alienation. Some joined the Nation of Islam; others embraced the Panthers or formed even more radical organizations calling for an all-black nation.

On the night of Saturday, July 23, police raided an after-hours drinking establishment in the center of the black community where more than eighty people were celebrating the return of two veterans from Vietnam. Police efforts to clear the club triggered five days of rioting. Congressman John Conyers, the black U.S. representative for Michigan's First District, knew many of the people in the area and tried to get them to disperse, but they refused. Later, Conyers said, "People were letting feelings out that had never been let out before, that had been bottled up. It really wasn't that they were that mad about an after-hours place being raided and some people being beat up as a result of the closing down of that place. It was the whole desperate situation of being black in Detroit."

Of the fifty-nine urban rebellions that occurred in 1967, Detroit's was the deadliest. Forty-three black people died, most of them shot by members of the National Guard, which had been sent in by Republican governor George Romney. But even the National Guard, combined with 200 state police and 600 Detroit police, could not restore order. A reluctant President Johnson had to order 4,700 troops of the elite 82nd and 101st Airborne units to Detroit. Republicans criticized Johnson's move as designed to embarrass Romney, who was a contender for the Republican presidential nomination in 1968. Johnson vehemently denied the charge. Others argued that Johnson's social welfare policies had raised expectations beyond the country's ability or desire to fulfill them and had subsidized the rioters.

The Kerner Commission

On July 29, 1967, in the wake of the Newark and Detroit riots, Johnson established the National Advisory Commission on Civil Disorders, headed by Illinois governor Otto Kerner. The commission included two black members, Republican senator Edward W. Brooke of Massachusetts (elected in 1966 the first black senator since Reconstruction) and Roy Wilkins, executive director of the NAACP. In a speech explaining why he had set up the commission, Johnson declared:

> The only genuine, long-range solution for what has happened lies in an attack—mounted at every level—upon the conditions that breed despair and violence. All of us know what those conditions are: ignorance, discrimination, slums, poverty, disease, not enough jobs. We should attack these conditions—not because we are frightened by conflict, but because we are fired by conscience. We should attack them because there is simply no other way to achieve a decent and orderly society in America.

In its final report, released in 1968, the Kerner Commission indicted white racism as the underlying cause of the riots and warned that America was "moving towards two societies, one white, one black—separate and unequal." The commission emphasized that "Negroes firmly believe that police brutality and harassment occur repeatedly in Negro neighborhoods. This belief is unquestionably one of the major reasons for intense Negro resentment against the police." The report added, "Physical abuse is only one source of aggravation in the ghetto. In nearly every city surveyed, the Commission heard complaints of harassment of interracial couples, dispersal of social street gatherings and the stopping of Negroes on foot or in cars without objective basis." The report called for massive government aid to the cities, including funds for public housing, better and more integrated schools, two million new jobs, and funding for a "national system of income supplementation." None of its major proposals was enacted.

Difficulties in Creating the Great Society

The urban riots of the late 1960s undercut support for the broadest attack the federal government had yet waged on the problems of poor Americans, what President Johnson in his election campaign in 1964 had called "the Great Society." Much of the legislation Johnson pushed through Congress in 1964 and 1965—the Medicare program, for example, which provided medical care for the elderly and disabled under the Social Security system, or federal aid to education from elementary through graduate schools—remained popular. But the most ambitious Great Society programs—what Johnson called "an unconditional war on poverty"—were controversial and tested the limits of American reform.

Lyndon Johnson was a savvy politician. He had to be to rise from Stonewall, Texas, to the pinnacle of power. But he never lost a deep sympathy for the disadvantaged and the powerless. Entering the House of Representatives in 1937, he had been an enthusiastic New Dealer. Elected to the Senate in 1948, he had refused to sign the Southern Manifesto (see Chapter 21) and, as majority leader, had overcome southern filibusters to win passage of the 1957 and 1960 Civil Rights

Acts. As president, he pushed the 1964 Civil Rights Act and the 1965 Voting Rights Act through Congress.

Johnson's concern for the disadvantaged showed itself in the cornerstone of his War on Poverty, the Economic Opportunity Act of 1964. This act created an Office of Economic Opportunity that administered several programs: Head Start to help disadvantaged preschoolers, Upward Bound to prepare impoverished teenagers for college, and Volunteers in Service to America (or VISTA) to serve as a domestic peace corps to help the poor and undereducated across the country. These programs included community governing boards on which black men and women gained representation, learning such essential political skills as bargaining and organizing.

The War on Poverty was the first government-sponsored effort to involve poor African Americans directly in designing and implementing programs to serve low-income communities. For example, in the New Careers program, residents of poor neighborhoods found jobs as community organizers, day care workers, and teacher aides. The program provided meaningful work, access to education, and critical material resources to poor people, so that they would become leaders in their own communities and run for office. The Community Action Programs (CAPs) insisted on "maximum feasible participation" by the poor. On another level, the Education Act increased federal funding to colleges and universities and provided low-interest student loans. This initiative increased college enrollments and put higher education within the reach of many more Americans than before.

One of the most prominent programs of President Johnson's War on Poverty was the Job Corps, which provided occupational training for poor Americans. In this photo, Johnson speaks with James Truesville at a Job Corps center in Camp Catoctin, Maryland.

Johnson faced considerable opposition to CAPs and other Great Society programs. Local politicians, fearing that the federal government was subsidizing their opponents and undercutting their power, were especially threatened by programs that empowered the previously disfranchised and dispossessed. Others, reflecting persistent white stereotypes of African Americans, complained that Johnson was rewarding lawlessness and laziness with handouts to the undeserving poor. The black residents of America's inner cities, for their part, had their expectations raised by the promises of the Great Society only to be frustrated by white backlash and minimal gains. They felt as betrayed by its programs as Johnson's white critics felt robbed by them.

No one will ever know whether Lyndon Johnson could have won his War on Poverty had he been given the resources to do so. As it turned out, the nation's resources were increasingly going into his other war, the war in Vietnam. Statistics tell the story. Government spending, including spending for domestic programs, increased dramatically under Johnson. But most of the money spent on domestic programs during Johnson's presidency, $44.3 billion, went to Social Security benefits, which now included Medicare. Appropriations for the War on Poverty came to only $10 billion. The war in Vietnam, in contrast, consumed $140 billion.

Johnson and the War in Vietnam

Vietnam was a French colony from the 1860s until the Japanese seized it during World War II. After the war the Vietnamese communists, led by Ho Chi Minh, declared independence, but the French, with massive U.S. financial aid, fought to reassert their control from 1945 until they were finally defeated in 1954. In retrospect it is easy to argue that American policy makers should have been more impressed by the failure of the French to defeat the communists in Vietnam. But in 1954, with the French pulling out, the Americans arranged a temporary division of the country into a communist-controlled North Vietnam and a U.S. supported South Vietnam (which, however, contained many communist guerrillas, called by the Americans "Viet Cong"). The United States ignored the possibility that as guarantor of South Vietnam, it would replace the French as targets for those Vietnamese who were determined to end white colonial domination and unify their country.

For nine years, under Presidents Eisenhower and Kennedy, American aid and advisers propped up the corrupt and incompetent South Vietnamese government in Saigon. By the time Johnson became president, only the dramatic escalation of American involvement—the bombing of North Vietnam and the introduction of large numbers of American troops into combat in South Vietnam—could keep the South Vietnamese government in power. Johnson himself doubted the advisability of a wholesale American commitment and did not want a foreign war to distract the public's attention or take away resources from the Great Society programs about which he cared so much. "I knew from the start," Johnson claimed later,

> that I was bound to be crucified either way I moved. If I left the woman I really loved—the Great Society—in order to get involved with that bitch of a war on the other side of the world, then I would lose everything at home. All my programs. All my hopes to feed the hungry and shelter the homeless. All my dreams to provide education and medical care to the browns and the blacks and the lame and the poor. But if I left that war and let the Communists take over South Vietnam, then I would be seen as a coward and my nation would be seen as an appeaser and we would both find it impossible to accomplish anything for anybody anywhere on the entire globe.

And so, half-aware that he was entering a quagmire but determined to slug through it, Johnson intervened in Vietnam—gradually, massively, and inexorably.

After an incident involving an alleged North Vietnamese attack on U.S. Navy destroyers in the Gulf of Tonkin in August 1964, Johnson pushed a resolution through Congress that gave him authority to escalate American involvement in Vietnam. In the spring of 1965 he authorized the bombing of selected North Vietnamese targets, but the bombing failed to stop the North Vietnamese from resupplying and reinforcing their forces in the south. The American military presence in South Vietnam then grew rapidly. By the end of 1966 there were more than 385,000 U.S. troops there, and by 1968 more than 500,000.

Black Americans and the Vietnam War

In the mid-1960s, black Americans made up 10 percent of the armed forces. This percentage increased during America's involvement in the Vietnam War. (In the Persian Gulf War in 1991, African Americans were 25 percent of the troops deployed.) Black overrepresentation among the U.S. troops in Vietnam resulted, in large part, from draft deferments for college and graduate students who were predominantly white and middle class (such as Dan Quayle and George W. Bush.) Black men and women entered the military for many compelling reasons, in addition to the draft. One was patriotism. Another was that the military offered educational and vocational opportunities that the children of the working black poor could not otherwise obtain. Still another was Project 100,000.

Project 100,000

In 1966 the United States Defense Department launched Project 100,000 to reduce the high rejection rate of African Americans by the military. The project enabled recruitment officers to accept applicants whom

Black men served in disproportionately high numbers in Vietnam. Black and white troops fought together but tended mostly to keep to themselves behind the lines.

they otherwise would have rejected because of criminal records or lack of skills. The project supplied more than 340,000 new recruits for Vietnam, 136,000 of whom were African Americans. As some have argued, this made the Vietnam War a white man's war but a black man's fight. Although the recruits were promised training and "rehabilitation," they saw more combat duty than regular recruits.

Johnson: Vietnam Destroys the Great Society

By the end of 1967, the nation seemed to be heading toward total racial polarization. In their rage against economic exploitation and police brutality, some inner-city black people had destroyed many of their own neighborhoods. Frightened white people, unable to comprehend black anger, rallied behind those who promised to restore order by any means. The two men who, only a few years before, had seemed the most effective advocates of racial reconciliation—Lyndon Johnson and Martin Luther King, Jr.—were both trying to regain the initiative. Each, tragically, ended by alienating himself from the other.

By 1967 Johnson's situation was untenable. He had escalated the war in Vietnam without convincing many Americans that it was worth fighting. With misleadingly optimistic claims about the progress of the war, his administration had forfeited public trust and opened what journalists called "the credibility gap." Johnson hoped that, with more bombing and more troops, the Vietnamese communists would give up, but he knew that if Congress had to choose between spending on the war and spending on domestic programs, it would choose the war. After Johnson asked for a tax increase, his Great Society programs met increasing resistance. When, for example, he proposed a special program to exterminate the rats that infested inner-city neighborhoods, congressional opponents turned it into a joke, calling it a "civil rats bill," and proposing to enlist an army of cats.

An even more dramatic example of the ugly mood on Capitol Hill was the House of Representatives expulsion in 1967 of the most prominent African-American politician in the United States, Adam Clayton Powell, Jr. (1908–1972). Pastor of the Abyssinian Baptist Church in Harlem and a long-time civic activist, Powell had first been elected to represent his Harlem district in 1944 and became the foremost champion of civil rights in the House. Because of his seniority he became chairman of the Education and Labor Committee in 1961 and had been instrumental in passing Johnson's education and antipoverty legislation.

Powell gave ammunition to his enemies. He mismanaged the committee's budget, took numerous trips abroad at government expense, and was exiled from his district when threatened with arrest there because of his refusal to pay a slander judgment against him. Yet the sentiment behind his ouster owed much to the dislike he inspired as a champion of minorities and the poor and as a flamboyant black man. The Supreme Court, overruling the House action, upheld his right to his seat, and his Harlem constituents kept him in office until his death.

Despite opposition in Congress, Johnson did not give up on the Great Society. He knew he could initiate no major programs while the Vietnam war lasted, but he continued to push a variety of measures, including a law to prohibit discrimination in housing. He also named the architect of the NAACP's attack on segregation, Thurgood Marshall, to the Supreme Court in 1967.

Vietnam trapped Johnson. As the hundreds of thousands of people who demonstrated against the war reminded him, Vietnam was incontestably "Lyndon Johnson's war." It was not, he would have replied, the war he had wanted to fight—that was the war against poverty and discrimination—but he was committed to seeing it through. He believed that his and the nation's honor were at stake. Even though objective commentators considered the conflict a stalemate, optimistic reports in 1967, from military commanders and intelligence agents, convinced the president that he might yet prevail.

Then, on January 30, 1968, at the start of the Vietnamese new year (called Tet), communist insurgents attacked thirty-six of the forty-four provincial capitals in South Vietnam as well as its national capital, Saigon, where they penetrated the grounds of the American embassy. Although American and South Vietnamese forces quickly recaptured all the territory that was lost and inflicted massive casualties on the enemy, the Tet Offensive was a major psychological blow for the American public, deepening the suspicion that the administration had not been telling the truth about the war. Washington was forced to reconsider its strategy.

On March 31, 1968, President Johnson told the nation that he would halt the bombing of North Vietnam to encourage the start of peace negotiations, which began in Paris in May. Then, as if an afterthought, he added that he would not seek renomination as president. Worn out by Vietnam, frustrated in his efforts to achieve the Great Society, the target of bitter criticism, and dispirited by a poor showing in the New Hampshire primary, Lyndon Johnson ended his public career rather than engage in a potentially bruising renomination battle.

VOICES

They Called Each Other "Bloods"

Captain Joseph B. Anderson Jr. of Topeka, Kansas, served as a platoon leader at An Khe, June 1966-June 1967, and as company commander in Cambodia, Phouc Vinh, May 1970–April 1971, 1st Cavalry Division, U.S. Army. His unit was the subject of The Anderson Platoon, *a 1967 French documentary film:*

Shortly after I got to Vietnam, we got into a real big fight. We were outnumbered at least ten to one. But I didn't know it. I had taken over 1st Platoon of B Company of the 12th Cav. We were up against a Viet Cong battalion. There may have been 300 to 400 of them. And they had just wiped out one of our platoons. At that time in the war, summer of 1966, it was a terrible loss. A bloody massacre.

I was an absolute rarity in Vietnam. A black West Pointer commanding troops. One year after graduation, I was very aggressive about my role and responsibilities as an Army officer serving in Vietnam. I was there to defend the freedom of the South Vietnamese government, stabilize the countryside, and help contain Communism. The Domino Theory was dominant then, predominant as a matter of fact. I was gung ho. And I thought the war would last three years at the most.

There weren't many opportunities for blacks in private industry then. And as a graduate of West Point, I was an officer and a gentleman by act of Congress. Where else could a black go and get that label just like that?

Throughout the Cav, the black representation in the enlisted ranks was heavier than the population as a whole in the United States. One third of my platoon and two of my four squad leaders were black. For many black men, the service, even during a war, was the best of a number of alternatives to staying home and working in the fields or bumming around the streets of Chicago or New York.

There were only a very few incidents of sustained fighting during my tours. Mostly you walked and walked, searched and searched. If you made contact, it would be over in thirty or forty minutes. One burst and then they're gone, because they didn't want to fight or could not stand up against the firepower we could bring with artillery and helicopter gunships.

I had a great deal of respect for the Viet Cong. They were trained and familiar with the jungle. They relied on stealth, on ambush, on their personal skills and wile, as opposed to firepower. They knew it did not pay for them to stand and fight us, so they wouldn't. . . .

. . . What was very clear to me was an awareness among our men that the support for the war was declining in the United States. The gung ho attitude that made our soldiers so effective in 1966, 67, was replaced by the will to survive. They became more security conscious. They would take more defensive measures so they wouldn't get hurt. They were more scared. They wanted to get back home.

Career officers and enlisted men like me did not go back to a hostile environment in America. We went back to bases where we were assimilated and congratulated and decorated for our performance in the conduct of the war.

Personally it was career-enhancing. A career Army officer who has not been to war during the war is dead, careerwise. I had done that. I received decorations. Two Silver Stars, five Bronze Stars, eleven Air Medals. . . . But in 1978 I decided I did not want to cool my heels for the next eight to ten years to become a general. . . . I resigned my commission, worked a year as a special assistant to the U.S. Secretary of Commerce, and joined General Motors as a plant manager.

The Anderson Platoon won both an Oscar and an Emmy. As time passes, my memory of Vietnam revolves around the film. I have a print, and I look at it from time to time. And the broadness and scope of my two-year experience narrows down to sixty minutes.

QUESTIONS

1. How do the experiences of this Vietnam veteran compare with those of black soldiers in World War II?
2. Why were African-American men attracted to military service? What benefits did they derive from the military, and what does their disproportionate representation suggest about social and economic conditions in black communities?

Source: "Captain Joseph B. Anderson Jr.," in Wallace Terry, *Bloods: An Oral History of the Vietnam War by Black Veterans.* New York: Ballantine Books, 1984, 219–228.

PROFILE

Muhammad Ali

Boxing is a brutal sport. During the 1960s and 1970s, Cassius Clay showed that boxing was also an art, that it could be beautiful, and that the boxer could become a symbol of racial pride, endearing wit, and even love. Born Cassius Marcellus Clay in 1942 in Louisville, Kentucky, Clay went to Rome in 1960 where he won a gold medal as a member of the U.S. Olympic boxing team.

Muhammad Ali declared himself "The Greatest" and for many African Americans he was the epitome of the uncompromised and proud black man.

Clay turned the boxing world on its head with audacious declarations of his own greatness as a boxer and beauty as a black man. His defeats of Floyd Patterson and Sonny Liston confirmed the first claim. On February 25, 1964, Clay pounded Liston to become the world heavyweight champion. The next day he announced that he had joined the Nation of Islam and had taken a new name, Muhammad Ali. Explaining his timing of the announcement, he said: "When I joined the Nation in 1961, I figured I'd be pressured if I revealed it, so I kept it quiet for about three years. . . . But after beating Sonny Liston, I was getting more recognition and more power. I revealed it after that fight."

Ali was a master at "playing the dozens," a boasting style that angered his opponents and annoyed white reporters covering his bouts. In 1967, however, it was his refusal to be drafted into the military that brought down on his head the wrath of the boxing establishment and white America. Ali argued that his religion was opposed to military service just as it was against civil rights activism and integration. Muhammad Ali was the new black man who refused to accept the white man's rules about how to behave. He embodied the assertive black consciousness that invaded all forms of social and cultural life in the 1960s and 1970s.

But most black people also adored Ali for other reasons recalled basketball player Kareem Abdul-Jabbar, who in 1971 discarded the name Lew Alcindor:

> When Ali announced his refusal to accept the draft, I thought it was a very brave stand. . . . A meeting to help Ali was called by black athletes back in 1967. We let black people around the country know that we supported Ali. I think by that time Black Americans understood that their presence in Vietnam was highly disproportionate to their percentage of the American population and that the front-line casualties were being absorbed by Black Americans in much greater numbers than they should have.

A federal court found Ali guilty of draft evasion, but he was released on bail pending his appeal. Ali immediately became a popular antiwar speaker. In June 1970 the United States Supreme Court overturned his conviction on the grounds that the FBI had placed an illegal wiretap on his telephone.

Actor Harry Belafonte described Ali in admiring terms:

> He brought America to its most wonderful and its most naked moment. "I will not play in your game of war. I will not kill in your behalf. What you ask is immoral, unjust, and I stand here to attest to that fact. Now do with me what you will," he said. I mean he was, in many ways, as inspiring as Dr. King, as inspiring as Malcolm. Cassius was a black, young American. Out of the womb of oppression he was our phoenix, he was the spirit of our young. He was our manhood. . . . He was the vitality of what we hoped would emerge. . . . the perfect machine, the wit, the incredible athlete, the facile, articulate, sharp mind on issues, the great sense of humor, which was out of our tradition.

In 1974 Ali fought George Foreman to regain his world heavyweight boxing title. Four years later he lost the title to Leon Spinks. He regained it, retired, then attempted a comeback that ended with his October 2, 1980, loss to Larry Holmes. He was elected to the Boxing Hall of Fame in 1987. In 1996 he lit the Olympic Flame to open the summer games in Atlanta.

King: Searching for a New Strategy

Like President Johnson, Martin Luther King was attacked on many fronts. Many white people considered him a dangerous radical, while black militants considered him an ineffectual moderate. His first response to the urban rebellions in 1965 and 1966 had been to move his campaign to the North to demonstrate the national range of the civil rights movement. In 1966, King and the SCLC set up operations in Chicago at the invitation of the Chicago Freedom Movement. King was confident that he would receive the support of the city's white liberals and the entire black community. James Bevel, King's Chicago lieutenant, declared, "We are going to create a new city. . . . Nobody will stop us." His optimism proved unwarranted.

Chicago's powerful, wily mayor Richard Daley viewed King suspiciously from the outset, but treated him with respect and cautioned the police not to use violence against King's civil rights demonstrators. Because King's movement depended on provoking confrontation, not much happened until King attempted to march into the white ethnic enclave of Marquette Park and the all-white suburb of Cicero.

The ensuing violence attracted the nation's television cameras. Chicago's white liberals joined with King and Daley in negotiating the Summit Agreement on housing, which amounted to a hasty retreat by King in the face of virulent white rage and black militancy. The Chicago strategy was a dismal failure.

But Chicago reinforced two important lessons for King. First, racial discrimination was more than a southern problem: In Chicago he witnessed an intensity of hatred and hostility that surpassed even that of Birmingham. Second, racial discrimination was inextricably intertwined with the country's economic structure. And so he began to think more critically about the need not only to eradicate poverty but to end systemic economic inequality. "What good is it to be allowed to eat in a restaurant," he remarked, "if you can't afford a hamburger?" In the fall of 1967, he announced plans for his most ambitious and militant project, an integrated, nonviolent "Poor People's Campaign" the following spring. According to the plan, tens of thousands of the nation's dispossessed would descend on Washington to focus attention on the disadvantaged members of American society. Among other things, King and his aides wanted a federally guaranteed income policy.

King on the Vietnam War

While planning the Poor People's Campaign, King began to attack the war in Vietnam.. King rejected what he considered the hypocrisy of the federal government's determination to send black and white men to Vietnam "to slaughter, men, women, and children," while failing to protect black American civil rights protesters in places like Albany, Birmingham, and Selma. His statements that the president was more concerned about winning in Vietnam than winning the "war against poverty" in America turned Johnson against him and further alienated King from many of Johnson's black supporters, including the more traditional civil rights leaders who supported the war in Vietnam. At the same time, the young militants in SNCC, who had already condemned the war, did not rush to embrace him. But King persisted, and by 1968 he had become one of the war's most trenchant critics.

King's Murder

His search for a new strategy led King to a closer involvement with labor issues. In February 1968, attempting to gain union recognition for municipal workers in Memphis, 1,300 members of a virtually all-black sanitation workers local went on strike and together with the local black community boycotted downtown merchants. But Memphis mayor Henry Loeb refused to negotiate. On March 18, 1968, responding to a call from James Lawson, a long-time civil rights activist and the minister of Centenary Methodist Church in Memphis, King went to Memphis to address the striking sanitation workers.

The occasion was marked by violence. Nevertheless, King returned to Memphis on April 3 and delivered his last and perhaps most prophetic speech:

> I would like to live a long life. Longevity has its place. But I'm not concerned about that now. I just want to do God's will. And He's allowed me to go up to the mountaintop, and I've looked over. And I've seen the promised land. I may not get there with you. But I want you to know tonight that we as a people will get to the promised land. So I'm happy tonight. I'm not worried about anything. I'm not fearing any man. "Mine eyes have seen the glory of the coming of the Lord."

The next day King was murdered by James Earl Ray as he stood on the balcony of the Lorraine Motel in Memphis. His assassination unleashed a torrent of civic rage in black communities. More than 125 cities experienced uprisings. By April 11, forty-six people were dead, 35,000 were injured, and more than 20,000 had been arrested.

In what seemed to many a belated gesture of racial reconciliation, within days of King's assassination, Congress passed the Civil Rights Act of 1968. Proposed by Johnson two years before, the act outlawed discrimination in the sale and rental of housing and gave the Justice Department authority to bring suits against such discrimination.

This photograph of the camp site of the Poor People's Campaign, taken on May 31, 1968, Resurrection City, shows its location near the Reflecting Pool and the Lincoln Memorial in the nation's capital. The campaign dramatized the plight of the nation's poor and attracted support across race, class, and gender lines.

King's assassination also boosted support for the SCLC's faltering Poor People's Campaign. The campaign began in May when more than 2,000 demonstrators settled into a shantytown they called Resurrection City in Washington, D.C. For more than a month, they marched daily to various federal offices and took part in a mass demonstration on June 19. On June 24, police evicted them, and the campaign ended, leaving an uncertain legacy.

The Black Arts Movement and Black Consciousness

The years between 1967 and 1975 witnessed some of the most intense political and cultural discussions in the history of the black freedom struggle. Black power stimulated debate about both the future of black politics in the post-civil rights era and the role of black art and artists in the quest for black liberation. Creative people revisited the long-standing issue of whether black art is political or aesthetic. For a decade, discussion about black culture and identity focused on the relationship between art and the artist, and the political movement within the black community. This period became known as the black arts movement. Among the outstanding poets who helped to shape the revolutionary movement, introducing new forms of black writing and delivering outspoken attacks on "the white aesthetic" while stressing black beauty and pride were Sonia Sanchez, Nikki Giovanni, and Don L. Lee (Haki Madhubuti). One of the best examples of Giovanni's militant poems is "The True Import of Present Dialogue, Black vs. Negro," which appeared in her first collection, a self-published volume entitled *Black Feeling, Black Talk* (1967). In a shocking opening line she asked, "nigger/Can you kill/Can you kill/Can a nigger kill/Can a nigger kill a honkie." The poem continues, "Can you kill the nigger/in you/Can you kill your nigger mind/And free your Black hands to/strangle." Sanchez also captured the violence and turbulence of the era. In 1970 she published a major collection of poetry entitled, *We a BaddDDD People.* Of equal significance in the development and evolution of this creative fluorescence was playwright and poet LeRoi Jones.

The formal beginning of the movement was the founding in 1965 of the Black Arts Repertory Theater by LeRoi Jones, who changed his name to Imamu Amari Baraka in 1967. Jones was the bridge that linked the political and cultural aspects of black power. He had been closely associated with the white avant-garde poets in New York in the 1950s and early 1960s, but began to change in 1965 from an integrationist to a black cultural nationalist.

The guiding ethos of the black arts movement was the determination of black artists to produce black art for black people and thereby to accomplish black liberation. Baraka declared, "The Black man must seek a Black politics, an ordering of the world that is beneficial to his culture, to his interiorization and judgment of the world. The Black Artist . . . is desperately needed to change the images his people identify with, by asserting Black feeling, Black mind, Black judgment." In 1968 he coedited with Larry Neal the anthology *Black Fire,* which revealed the extent to which black writers and thinkers had rejected the premises of integration in favor of a new black consciousness and nationalist political engagement.

Larry Neal, who was part of the revolutionary action movement, offered a succinct definition of this important dimension of the freedom struggle:

> The Black Arts Movement is radically opposed to any concept of the artist that alienates him from his community. Black Art is the aesthetic and spiritual sister of the Black Power concept. As such, it envisions an art that speaks directly to the needs and aspirations of Black Americans. In order to perform this task, the Black Arts Movement proposes a radical reordering of the western cultural aesthetic. It proposes a separate symbolism, mythology, critique, and iconography. The Black Arts and the Black Power concept both relate broadly to the Afro-American's desire for self-determination and nationhood. Both concepts are nationalistic. One is concerned with the relationship between art and politics; the other with the art of politics.

The black arts movement was criticized because of its celebration of black maleness, its racial exclusivity, and its homophobia. It was never a unified movement in the sense of all black artists speaking in one voice. There was creative dissent and competing visions of freedom. In 1970 Maya Angelou published an autobiographical novel, *I Know Why the Caged Bird Sings*, that unveiled her experience with sexual abuse and the silencing of black women within black communities. Other black women writers would follow suit and in the 1970s create a black women's literary renaissance. Still, prominent integrationist writers agreed with some of the black arts movement's fundamental tenets and were converted to its principles.

The works of Langston Hughes, Lorraine Hansberry, Gwendolyn Brooks, and James Baldwin linked the black cultural renaissances of the 1930s, 1940s, and 1950s to the black arts movement. Brooks, for example, stressed the commitment of artist to community and the importance of the relationship between the artist and her audience. She had consistently supported community-based arts programs, and it seemed natural that she should "convert" to a black nationalist perspective during the sixties and join forces with younger artists.

But the most popular black writer of the era, especially among white audiences, was James Baldwin. Baldwin was an integrationist. In his work he had resisted the simple inversion of racial hierarchies that characterized some parts of the black power and black arts movements. He wrote: "I think all theories are suspect, that the finest principles may have to be modified, or may even be pulverized by the demands of life, and that one must find therefore, and move through the world hoping that center will guide one aright." Yet in many ways, Baldwin was as alienated and angry as some of the artists identified with black arts.

In *The Fire Next Time* (1963), he concluded with a phrase that echoed through discussions of the rebellions in Watts, Newark, and Detroit. "If we do not now dare everything, the fulfillment of that prophecy, recreated from the bible in song by a slave, is upon us: 'God gave Noah the rainbow sign, No more water, the fire next time!'"

Baldwin was also an unflinching commentator on white racism and had a major impact on public discourse. At one point he told his white readers, "There appears to be a vast amount of confusion on this point, but I do not know many Negroes who are eager to be 'accepted' by white people, still less to be loved by them; they, the blacks, simply don't wish to be beaten over the head by the whites every instant of our brief passage on this planet." And in *No Name in the Street*, Baldwin declared: "I agree with the Black Panther position concerning black prisoners: not one of them has ever had a fair trial, for not one of them has ever been tried by a jury of his peers." He explained: "White middle-class America is always the jury, and they know absolutely nothing about the lives of the people on whom they sit in judgment: and this fact is not altered, on the contrary it is rendered more implacable by the presence of one or two black faces in the jury box."

Poetry and Theater

The black arts movement had its greatest and most significant impact in poetry and theater. The movement had three geographical centers: Harlem, Chicago and Detroit, and San Francisco.

The Chicago-based *Negro Digest/Black World*, edited by Hoyt Fuller and published by John Johnson, promoted many of the works of the new generation of creative artists. Fuller, a well-connected intellectual with an exhaustive command of black literature, became editor of the monthly magazine in 1961. In 1970 he changed the name of the magazine to *Black World* to signal the rejection of "Negro" and the adoption of "black" to designate people of African descent. The name change identified African Americans with both the African diaspora and Africa itself.

TRACK 40

TRACK 41

In Detroit, Naomi Long Madgett's Lotus Press and Dudley Randall's Broadside Press republished the previous generation of black poets, notably Gwendolyn Brooks, Margaret Walker, and Sterling Brown. In Chicago, poet and literary critic, Don L. Lee, who changed his name to Haki Madhabuti, launched Third World Press, which published many of the black arts poets and writers.

TRACK 42

The Chicago-Detroit publishing nexus promoted new poets like Nikki Giovanni, Etheridge Knight, and Sonia Sanchez. These and other poets produced some of the most accomplished and experimental work of the black arts movement. It resonated with the sounds of the African-American vernacular, combining the rhythmic cadences of sermons with popular music and black "street speech" into a spirited new form of poetry that was free, conversational, and militantly cool.

Theater was another prominent genre of the black arts movement. Playwright Ed Bullin edited a special issue of the journal *Drama Review* in the summer of 1968 that featured essays and plays by most of the major activists in black arts, including Sonia Sanchez, Ron Milner, and Woodie King, Jr. This volume became the textbook of black arts. In his plays Bullins, who was greatly influenced by Baraka, portrayed ordinary black life and explored the inner forces that prevented black people from realizing their own liberation and full potential. He showed how racism had deformed the

Poet Nikki Giovanni, a graduate of Fisk University was one of the major figures in the Black Arts Movement of the 1970s. She once declared "Writing is not who I am, it's what I do." In 1971 she published, *Gemini: An Extended Autobiographical Statement on My First Twenty-Five Years at Being a Black Poet.* It was nominated for a National Book Award.

black experience and consciousness. Across the country local black communities formed their own theater groups, including Val Gray Ward's Kuumba Workshop in Chicago and Baraka's Spirit House Theater in New Jersey. These groups reached out to people by hosting seminars, guest appearances, fashion shows, art exhibits, dance recitals, parades, and mass media parties.

On the West Coast, in 1969, Robert Chrisman and Nathan Hare launched *The Black Scholar*, the first serious journal to promote black studies. Chrisman compared the black arts movement with the renaissance in Harlem during the 1920s: "More so than the Harlem Renaissance, in which Black artists were always on the leash of white patrons and publishing houses, the Black Arts movement did it for itself. Black people going out nationally, in mass, saying we are an independent Black people and this is what we produce."

Music

The cultural nationalists in the black arts movement cultivated an appreciation for modern jazz musicians, making them icons of the quest for black freedom. Baraka argued that jazz and other black music was the language that black people developed to give uncensored accounts of their experiences. He and other cultural nationalists believed that music could promote black identity and encourage the pride that was vital for political struggle. The music of the jazzmen was often dense and austere, but it could also be powerfully primitive and dazzlingly complex. Above all, the music appeared to challenge western conceptions of harmony, rhythm, melody, and tone. In jazz you have to improvise, to create your own form of expression by using whatever information inspires you. The emphasis is not on the original, but on individual articulation.

Cultural nationalists perceived jazz to be a self-consciously engaged, economically independent, politically useful art form. Novelist Ralph Ellison put it most succinctly:

> True jazz is an art of individual assertion within and against the group. Each true jazz moment (as distinct from the uninspired commercial performance) springs from a contest in which each artist challenges all the rest; each solo flight, or improvisation, represents (like the successive canvases of a painter) a definition of his identity: as individual, as member of the collectivity and as a link in the chain of tradition.

This outlook explains why Miles Davis's legendary album *Kind of Blue* (1959), one of the most progressive jazz albums ever produced, also became one of the most popular. Davis showed that art could be accessible without sacrificing excellence and rigor. Davis, in the words of one admirer, was able to "dance underwater and not get wet." For black cultural nationalists, Davis projected an image of uncompromising and uncompromised black identity.

Among other intensely celebrated jazzmen were Charlie Parker, Archie Shepp, Ornette Coleman, Pharoah Sanders, Eric Dophy, Thelonious Monk, and John Coltrane. Playwright Ronald Milner described Coltrane as "a man who through his saxophone before your eyes and ears completely annihilates every single western influence." Coltrane also played the deep, and deeply political, blues of "Alabama" written in response to the Birmingham church bombings.

Jazz, however, tended to appeal to intellectuals. Most black people preferred rhythm and blues, gospel, and soul. During the height of the black consciousness movement, black popular musicians gave performances and concerts to raise funds and to assert racial pride. Aretha Franklin and Ray Charles, for example, allowed SNCC workers to attend their concerts free. Just as the freedom songs had done, the soul music of the black power era helped unify black people.

No history of the era would be complete without mentioning the performances of the "Godfather of Soul," James Brown, the "Queen of Soul," Aretha Franklin's powerful rendition of the song "R.E.S.P.E.C.T.," and the financial contributions of Berry Gordy of Motown. James Brown's "Say It Loud, I'm Black and I'm Proud" became an anthem for the era. Brown linked sound commercial marketing to social commentary, confronting American racism with racial pride and righteous indignation. He confessed, "I may not do as much as some other individuals who have made it big," but, "you can bet your life that

I'm doing the best I can. . . . I owe it to the black community to help provide scholarships, to help children stay in school, to help equip playgrounds and recreation centers, and to keep kids off the streets." Brown was "totally committed to black power, the kind that is achieved not through the muzzle of a rifle but through education and economic leverage."

Berry Gordy contributed to black freedom struggles both artistically and financially. To support King's Chicago movement, Gordy arranged for Stevie Wonder to give a benefit concert at Soldier Field in Chicago. He made cash contributions to black candidates, to the NAACP and its Legal Defense and Educational Fund, and to the Urban League.

With Gordy's encouragement, his performers flirted just enough with black radicalism to gain a patina of militancy. During the late 1960s and early 1970s the musical and lyrical innovations of the Temptations, Stevie Wonder, and Marvin Gaye reflected Motown's politicization. In an address to one of the sessions launching Jesse Jackson's People United to Save Humanity (PUSH) in 1971, Gordy declared, "I have been fortunate to be able to provide opportunities for young people. . . . Opportunities are supposed to knock once in a lifetime, but too often we have to knock for an opportunity. The first obligation we (as black businessmen) have is to ourselves and our own employees, the second is to create opportunities for others." The musician Curtis Mayfield, on the other hand, simply explained, "Our purpose is to educate as well as to entertain. Painless preaching is as good a term as any for what we do."

The Second Phase of the Black Student Movement

The most dramatic expression of militant assertiveness after 1968 occurred among black college students. The black power generation of students was committed to transforming society, although those on predominantly white campuses often, but not always, seemed to be more reformist than revolutionary. Some observers describe the period of activism between 1968 and 1975 as the "second phase" of the black students movement.

The Orangeburg Massacre

The first phase, in this view, was launched by students at southern black colleges in the early 1960s. It began with the sit-ins in Greensboro, North Carolina, and the Freedom Rides, and culminated in the Mississippi Freedom Summer of 1964. By 1968, however, many of the student organizations that had grown out of the civil rights movement, notably SNCC, were in decline. The massacre of black students at South Carolina State College in Orangeburg on February 8, 1968, marks the end of the first phase and the beginning of the second. Students attending the historically black institution had protested a local bowling alley's whites-only admission policy. When the tension and protests escalated, state officials deployed the highway patrol and National Guard. On the evening of February 8, the students assembled at the front of the campus and taunted the officers; some threw rocks, bricks, and bottles. One officer was hit by a piece of lumber. Later, without warning, nine highway patrolmen opened fire on the students with shotguns. The officers killed three young men and wounded twenty-seven. Most of them were shot in the back. All the officers involved were later acquitted, but a young black activist and SNCC leader, Cleveland Sellers, was convicted of rioting, and served nearly a year in prison. He was pardoned in 1993. On February 8, 2001 South Carolina Governor James Hodges apologized to a group of survivors who had assembled in Orangeburg.

Black Studies

The second phase owed much of its inspiration to the black power and black arts movements. It began when significant numbers of black students enrolled in predominantly white institutions for the first time. The black students at the white campuses demanded courses in black history, culture, literature, and art as alternatives to the "Eurocentric" bias of the average university curriculum. Many black students also formed all-black organizations, such as the Black Allied Students' Association at New York University and the Black Organization of Students at Rutgers University.

Black students understood that education was essential to empowerment. In 1967 black students accounted for only 2 percent of the total enrollment at predominantly white colleges and universities. This meant that only 95,000 African Americans were among the approximately five million full-time undergraduates at these schools. Rutgers University in New Jersey provides a case study. Out of twenty-four thousand baccalaureate degrees it awarded between 1952 and 1967, only about two hundred went to African Americans. Federal legislation—especially the Civil Rights Act of 1964 and the Higher Education Act of 1965—outlawed discrimination or segregation in higher education, and by instituting an array of financial aid programs, it spurred colleges and universities to take affirmative action to recruit black students. Where there had been about one hundred black undergraduates at Rutgers in 1965, there were more than four hundred by 1968, accounting for nearly 3 percent of the undergraduate enrollment.

On the national level, the overall status of black people in education reflected the accomplishments of the classic phase of the civil rights movement, but the black power generation was determined to make its own mark on the struggle. In 1960, only 227,000 black Americans attended the nation's colleges (including those at predominantly black institutions). By the end of the 1960s, enrollments had increased by 100 percent, and in 1977, 1.1 million black students attended America's universities. This was an almost 500 percent increase over 1960. There was wide political diversity among this generation of students, but they shared the sense of being strangers in a white-controlled environment. Many found the campuses hostile, alien places and discovered little there with which they could identify. They resolved to change this situation.

At San Francisco State College, Nathan Hare, formerly a professor at Howard University, and black students demanded not only curriculum changes, but the structural transformation of the college. In the 1966–1967 academic year the Black Student Union (BSU) orchestrated a strike that involved thousands of students of diverse ethnic and racial backgrounds. The students deliberately chose to strike, rather than take over buildings, so that they could circulate freely on the campus, increasing their support, and maintaining their momentum. Among their demands were the creation of an autonomous degree-granting black studies department and the admission of more black students. The college ultimately did create the first black studies department in 1968, with Hare as its head.

Black students also took over administration buildings at other institutions, demanding not only that the schools offer more black studies courses and programs and hire more black faculty, but often that classrooms and facilities also be made available to local black communities. The upheavals that shut down Columbia University in 1968, for example, began when black student members of the Students Afro-American Society and Students for a Democratic Society at Columbia University demonstrated to block plans to construct a university gymnasium in nearby Morningside Park. The demonstrators argued that the gym would impinge on one of the few parks located in Harlem and that it was being built over strenuous objections from the Harlem community.

In 1968, Yale University's Black Student Alliance sponsored a symposium to discuss the need, status, and function of Afro-American Studies. Conference organizer Armstead Robinson saw it as the first attempt to create a viable program of Afro-American Studies. In December 1968 the faculty voted to make Yale one of the first major universities in the country to institute a degree-granting African-American Studies program. In 1969 Harvard University created an Afro-American Studies Department, and other schools soon followed. In 1969, the Institute of the Black World in Atlanta conducted a project to define the methods and purpose of black studies and then sponsored a black studies director's seminar. Ron Karenga wrote what remains a major textbook for the new field, *Introduction to Black Studies.* By 1973 some two hundred black studies programs existed in the United States. By the late 1980s, several of the programs, such as those at Cornell, Yale, and UCLA offered master's degrees in African-American studies. In 1988 Temple University, under the leadership of Molefi Kete Asante, became the first university to offer a Ph.D. in African-American Studies.

Still, there was no universally accepted definition of black studies. James E. Turner, founder of Africana Studies at Cornell, viewed it as a collective, interdisciplinary scholarly approach to the experiences of people of African descent throughout the world. History, in black studies, constituted the foundation for the analysis of common patterns of life that reflected the social conditions of black people. Africana studies or black studies theoreticians have generally agreed on four goals for this new scholarly field. (1) It should develop solutions to the problems facing black people in the African diaspora. (2) It should provide analysis of black culture and life that challenge and replace preexisting Eurocentric models. (3) It should promote social change and educational reform throughout the academy. And (4) it should institutionalize the study of black people as a field with its own theories, methods, ideologies, symbols, language, and culture. In short, the first generation of advocates envisioned black studies as being a revolutionary, historically grounded educational reform movement that sought to make the study of African descendants—their culture, problems, worldviews, and spirituality—a serious scholarly endeavor with practical implications for improving black peoples' lives.

The Election of 1968

In the presidential campaign of 1968, the Democrats provided the excitement but lost the election. In late 1967, Senator Eugene McCarthy of Minnesota entered the race as the antiwar alternative to Lyndon Johnson, but few politicians took him seriously, even though he won several primaries. Robert Kennedy, U.S. senator from New York, was taken seriously, even though by the time he entered the race in mid-March, most of the convention delegates were already pledged to Johnson, and, after Johnson's withdrawal, quickly transferred their allegiance to Vice President Hubert Humphrey. Whether Kennedy could have gained the nomination will never be known because—in the second traumatic assassination of 1968—he was murdered in June. Grief over his death, bitterness over the war, and personal rivalries spilled over to produce the most tumultuous political convention in modern American history, with Chicago policemen clubbing and gassing antiwar demonstrators.

In November, Republican Richard Nixon narrowly defeated Humphrey 43.1 percent to 42.7 percent in the popular vote and 301 to 191 in the electoral vote. George Wallace, the segregationist ex-governor of Alabama, in his first serious bid for the presidency, won 13.5 percent of the popular vote and forty-six electoral votes. Running as the candidate of the American Independent party, Wallace denounced civil rights legislation and court-ordered desegregation. He also endorsed the repression of demonstrators and rioters and promised to stamp out communism in Southeast Asia.

The Nixon Presidency

Of all modern presidents, Richard Nixon is probably the hardest to pin down with neat ideological labels. By the standards of the early twentieth-first century, much of his record seems progressive: He created the Environmental Protection Agency, endorsed an equal rights amendment to the Constitution that would have prohibited gender discrimination, and signed more regulatory legislation than any other president. His willingness to innovate in policy affecting African Americans can be illustrated by his naming of Daniel Patrick Moynihan, one of Johnson's experts on social policy, to be his domestic policy adviser. But Nixon also pursued a "Southern Strategy" that realigned the Republican party with the white southern backlash to civil rights and weakened the New Deal coalition.

The "Moynihan Report" and FAP

Moynihan first attracted national attention as assistant secretary of labor in the Johnson administration when a confidential memorandum he wrote—loosely organized and full of sweeping generalizations—was leaked to the press. It would later be published as "The Negro Family: The Case for National Action" and is popularly known as the "Moynihan Report." Moynihan's guiding assumption was that civil rights legislation, necessary as it was, would not address the problems of the inner city. There, he argued, the breakdown of the "lower-class" black family had led to the "pathology" of juvenile delinquency, illegitimacy, drug addiction, and poor performance in school. He attributed the vulnerability of the black family to "three centuries of almost unimaginable treatment" by white society: exploitation under slavery, the strain of urbanization, and persistent unemployment.

These forces, he argued, weakened the role of black men and resulted in a disproportionate number of dysfunctional, female-headed families. In the most-often repeated passage in the report, Moynihan declared that the black community had been forced into "a matriarchal structure, [which] because it is so out of line with the rest of American society, seriously retards the progress of the group as a whole, and imposes a crushing burden on the Negro male. . . . Obviously, not every instance of social pathology afflicting the Negro community can be traced to the weakness of family structure . . . [but] once or twice removed, it will be found to be the principal source of most of the aberrant, inadequate, or anti-social behavior that did not establish, but now serves to perpetuate the cycle of poverty and deprivation."

Though based on the work of earlier black scholars, such as E. Franklin Frazier, Moynihan's condemnation of "matriarchy" drew fire. Black social scientists, such as Joyce Ladner, Andrew Billingsley, and Carol Stack, countered that the structure of the black family reflected a functional adaptation that black people had made to survive in a hostile and racist American society. Historians Herbert Gutman and John Blassingame argued that Moynihan underestimated the prevalence of two-parent black families in the past. While many of the criticisms of the report were deserved, they diverted attention from its positive thrust. Moynihan wanted to eliminate poverty and unemployment in the black community and he recommended vigorous enforcement of the civil rights laws to achieve equality of opportunity.

Setting himself apart from other Johnson administration policy makers, Moynihan was one of the first to appreciate how white resentment of the Community Action Program (CAP) and the expansion of the welfare rolls would make both programs politically unfeasible.

Intrigued with Moynihan's independence, Nixon told him to develop a plan to assist poor families. Under the Family Assistance Plan (FAP) that Nixon unveiled in the summer of 1969, each family of four with no wage earner would receive an annual payment of $1,600 plus

$800 of food stamps. With its across-the-board guarantee of income, the plan eliminated an oppressive welfare bureaucracy and reduced the invidious comparison between "welfare recipients" and everyone else.

Had it passed, FAP would have preserved and promoted two-parent families by removing the prohibition against assistance to dependent children whose fathers were alive, well, and living at home. It would also have encouraged work by requiring able-bodied recipients to accept jobs or vocational training and by providing benefits to those accepting low-paying jobs. But although the House approved the plan, the Senate, under pressure both from conservatives who objected to any government programs for the poor and from welfare-rights advocates who complained that the payments were too low, killed it. Arguably, at least until President Clinton's failed health care plan in the 1990s, Nixon's FAP was the most significant failed initiative in the history of American social policy.

Busing

Yet however flexible he might have been on many issues, Nixon was acutely aware that he moved in a changed political environment and particularly in a far more conservative Republican party than he had when he ran against and lost to John F. Kennedy in 1960. Then, as a presidential candidate, he had had to appease Eastern, pro-civil rights liberals led by New York governor Nelson Rockefeller (1908–1979). But in 1968, an influx of southern segregationists whom Barry Goldwater had attracted to the Republican party in 1964 had to be appeased. Now Nixon chose to court closer relations with South Carolina senator Strom Thurmond, a Republican who had abandoned the Democratic party in 1964. Thurmond and his allies had demanded that if elected, Nixon would slow down the process of court-ordered school desegregation in the South. Finally, Nixon could hardly ignore George Wallace, with his racist appeals. In another three-way race in 1972, Wallace might ensure Nixon's defeat.

As a result of these pressures, the Nixon administration perfected its Southern Strategy and embarked upon a collision course with civil rights organizations, such as the NAACP, which supported busing to achieve school integration. Thus, the major battle over civil rights in the early 1970s was over the federal courts' willingness to implement desegregation goals by busing students across district lines. Nixon used the busing controversy to lure Wallace voters. In 1971 he had advised federal officials to stop pressing to desegregate schools through "forced busing." He argued that such efforts were ultimately "counterproductive, and not in the interest of better race relations."

Educational segregation in the North reflected residential segregation. In Boston, site of some of the most acrimonious busing protests, schools in black neighborhoods received less funding than their white counterparts. Buildings were derelict, seriously overcrowded, and deficient in supplies and equipment, even desks. In 1974 U.S. district judge W. Arthur Garrity ruled in favor of a group of black parents who had filed a class action suit against the Boston School Committee. The ruling found the school committee guilty of violating the equal protection clause of the Fourteenth Amendment. To achieve racial balance in the Boston schools, the judge ordered the busing of several thousand students between mostly white South Boston, Hyde Park, and Dorchester, and mostly black Roxbury.

White people who opposed busing organized demonstrations and boycotts to prevent their children from being bused into black communities and black children from being bused into white schools. During the first week of busing to achieve desegregation, white students and their mothers clashed with police officers outside South Boston High School. Violence and hostilities continued for weeks despite the arrests of dozens of people and the closing of bars and liquor stores. Sporadic violence persisted for another two years in Boston.

Nixon and the War

Meanwhile, the war in Vietnam seemed to drag on endlessly, with the peace negotiations that had begun in Paris in May 1968 making no apparent progress. Nixon realized that what most Americans disliked about the war was that it was killing their sons and husbands. So in 1969, he began to phase out direct U.S. involvement in the war. This "Vietnamization," he claimed, was made possible by the growing ability of the South Vietnamese to fight for themselves. What Nixon did not say was that another reason for troop withdrawals was that the morale of American soldiers was plunging rapidly. Drug abuse among troops was widespread, some soldiers had killed their officers, and some of those incidents had racial overtones. Along with his domestic record, Nixon's promise to "wind down the war" was widely popular and assured his reelection. In 1972 he defeated South Dakota senator George McGovern in a landslide.

Few in the Nixon administration, however, took South Vietnamese military capability seriously, and Nixon, just as much as Johnson, was unwilling to "lose" Vietnam. Between 1969 and 1971, Nixon stepped up the war. Even as American soldiers were being sent home, he escalated the air war dramatically. In the bombing of Cambodia in 1969–1970, for example—which was kept secret from Congress and the public—the United States dropped more bombs than it had on all of Asia in the Second World War.

But each time Nixon escalated the war—in the spring of 1970 with a joint American-South Vietnamese invasion of Cambodia, in the spring of 1971 with American air support for an invasion of Laos, in the spring of 1972 with the bombing of North Vietnam and the mining of its harbors—opposition to it grew. Antiwar demonstrations kept Nixon off balance and may have deterred him from further escalation.

The most dramatic response to Nixon's escalation in the Vietnam war came after the invasion of Cambodia in April 1970. The invasion triggered antiwar protests on many campuses. In one such protest, on May 4, Ohio National Guardsmen shot and killed four white students at Kent State University. The response of students across the country was electric: the first nationwide student strike in American history. Ten days later in Mississippi, the shooting and killing of two black students at Jackson State University attracted much less attention from either white students or the media. Three years later, at the beginning of 1973, the United States and North Vietnam signed a peace agreement. Congress then prohibited the reintroduction of American troops and the resumption of bombing, and in 1974 began cutting off military aid to the South Vietnamese government. The result of this loss of American support was predictable: in 1975 the Communists launched their final offensive, and South Vietnam collapsed.

Nixon's Downfall

If Nixon assumed the presidency in 1969 with any popular mandate, it was to restore law and order. The disorder that irritated the American public included many things: the inner-city riots, the antiwar demonstrations and campus protests, and the rise in crime. Responding to this mood, Nixon pushed legislation through Congress that gave local law enforcement officials expanded power to use wiretaps and enter premises without advance warning.

But Nixon's personality—a combination of paranoia and ruthlessness—pushed him beyond what the public would tolerate, and even beyond the law itself. He increasingly confused ordinary criminals with principled protesters and his political opponents, and decided to punish them all. One method was to create an extra-legal ring of burglars, operating out of the White House to gather incriminating information. In June 1972 they were discovered breaking into Democratic National Committee headquarters in the Watergate apartment complex in Washington. Full details emerged in a Senate investigation in 1973–1974, and on August 9, 1974, threatened with impeachment, Nixon resigned. His downfall, however, left no one of his stature or with his flexible attitude toward public policy to resist the takeover of the Republican party by more ideologically dogmatic conservatives. One early intimation of this was the difficulty Nixon's successor, Gerald Ford, had in securing the 1976 Republican presidential nomination against the right's new hero, former California governor Ronald Reagan.

The Rise of Black Elected Officials

Just as King searched for a new strategy after the victories of the early phase of the civil rights movement, other black leaders mobilized the newly enfranchised black electorate to win political office. After the adoption of the Voting Rights Act of 1965, Vernon Jordan, director of the Voter Education Project, coordinated registration drives and workshops across the South. As he explained, "Too many of these people have been alienated from the political process for too long a time . . . and so we have to . . . teach them what a local government is, how it operates, and try to relate their votes to the things they want."

By 1974 there were 1,593 black elected officials outside the South, and by 1980 the number had risen to 2,455. Although black people in northern cities had been able to vote for a century and had been slowly developing political muscle and winning representation in state legislatures and on municipal councils, they had not been able to command an equal voice in city governance. The rise of black power and the inspiration of the Voting Rights Act, however, signaled a new departure. People now eagerly engaged in the electoral process to achieve a political influence to which their numbers entitled them. In 1967 in Cleveland, where the black population had skyrocketed after World War II,

Carl Stokes became the first black mayor of a major American city, winning election with the support of white business leaders and the solid backing of the black community. In the same year prosecutor Richard G. Hatcher became mayor of Gary, Indiana, where the black population had also increased greatly after the war. Hatcher won by a mere 1,389 votes, garnering 96 percent of the black vote and 14 percent of the white vote.

The Gary Convention and the Black Political Agenda

These victories made possible one of the most significant events of recent black political history, the Gary convention of 1972. The three co-chairs of the convention were Detroit Congressman Charles Diggs, Hatcher, and writer and cultural nationalist Amiri Baraka of Newark, New Jersey. Political scientist Ronald Walters, who helped plan the convention, recalled that various ideological factions had to be placated to make the convention work: "The most important thing about 1972 was the fact that it was an election year, so it provided the environment for the politics taking place. So you had two groups of people who saw this as an opportunity to make some very important statements. One of these, of course, was the black nationalist movement led by Amiri Baraka, Maulana Karenga, and others at that time." The nationalists interpreted "black power" to mean that black people should control their own communities and create separate cultural institutions distinct from those of white society. These views clashed with the ideas espoused by the black elected officials represented by Stokes and Hatcher. According to Walters, "It was this body of people who really were contending for the national leadership of the black community in the early seventies. And in the seventies this new group of black elected officials joined the civil rights leaders and became a new leadership class, but there was sort of a conflict in outlook between them and the more indigenous, social, grass roots-oriented nationalist movement."

Hatcher observed that "people had come to Gary from communities all over the United States where they were politically impotent, but . . . they went back home and rolled up their sleeves and dived into the political arena." Approximately eight thousand people gathered to develop an agenda for black empowerment. The discussions about bloc voting, the efficacy of coalitions, and the feasibility of a third party inspired scores of individual African Americans to run for local office. The convention was not homogeneous, however, and no unified black consensus emerged.

Several discussions over strategies to secure common interests revealed deep-seated internal divisions that allowed ancillary issues to provoke even more impassioned disagreement. Coleman Young and other Michigan delegates walked out to protest a proposal calling for African Americans to reject "discriminatory" unions and form their own. Others walked out over a resolution condemning Israel for its "expansionist policy" toward the Palestinians. Others opposed "forced racial integra-

The National Black Convention Movement of the Black Power Era

1965	Maulena Karenga founds the US (as opposed to them) Organization in Los Angeles, California. Advocates cultural nationalism.
1966	Amiri Baraka founds Spirit House Movers and Players in Newark, New Jersey. Advocates cultural nationalism.
1966	Huey P. Newton and Bobby Seale found the Black Panther party
1966	Stokely Carmichael coins the term "black power."
1966	Representative Adam Clayton Powell, Jr. hosts the first Black Power Conference
1967	Second Black Power Conference, held in Newark, New Jersey, calls for partitioning the United States into separate black and white nations.
1968	Third Black Power Conference is held in Philadelphia, Pennsylvania.
1969	National Black Economic Development Conference held in Detroit, Michigan.
1969	Last Black Power Conference, held in Bermuda, ends in disarray.
1970	Congress of Afrikan Peoples, led by Amiri Baraka, is organized in Atlanta, Georgia. Adopts the slogan, "It's nation time."
1971	The Reverend Jesse Jackson founds People United to Save Humanity (PUSH) in Chicago, Illinois.
1972	National Black Political Convention is held in Gary, Indiana.
1973	National Black Feminist Organization is founded by Eleanor Holmes Norton and Margaret Sloan.
1974	Last National Black Political Convention is held in Little Rock, Arkansas.

tion of schools" through busing, arguing that such practices insulted black students and would cost black teachers their jobs.

The Gary convention was important because it signaled a shift in the political focus of the black community toward electoral politics and away from mass demonstrations and protest measures. Unity continued to elude subsequent conventions, however, and delegates attending the last National Black Convention at Little Rock, Arkansas, in 1974 abandoned the idea of a black political party. Deep ideological differences and institutional cleavages precluded coalitions and cooperation between black nationalists and the rising numbers of black elected officials. These same differences prevented some nationalists and elected officials from taking seriously the 1972 Democratic party presidential bid of New York congresswoman Shirley Chisholm.

Black People Gain Local Offices

Despite the demise of the National Black Convention movement, African Americans continued to register impressive gains in electoral politics. A few statistics indicate the success of black politicians. When the leaders first convened the Gary convention, there were thirteen African-American members of Congress; by 1997 there were forty. In 1972 there were 2,427 black elected officials; by 1993 there were 8,106. An amendment to the Voting Rights Act in 1975 enabled minorities to mount court challenges to at-large voting practices that diluted the impact of bloc voting; this helped increase the number of black elected officials. Districts were redrawn with race as the predominant factor in their reconfiguration. On November 5, 1985, State Senator L. Douglas Wilder was elected lieutenant governor in Virginia, making him the first African-American lieutenant governor in a southern state since Reconstruction. In 1989 he was elected governor, making him the first black governor of any state since Reconstruction.

Between 1971 and 1975, the number of African-American mayors rose from 8 to 135, leading to the founding of the National Conference of Black Mayors in 1974. In 1973, Coleman Young in Detroit and Thomas Bradley in Los Angeles became the first African-American mayors of cities of more than a million citizens. Bradley won in Los Angeles even though black people made up only 15 percent of the city's electorate. Ten years later, in 1983, Chicago swore in its first black mayor, Harold Washington. The era of the black elected official had arrived.

Economic Downturn

The 1970s were a decade of recessions and economic instability. Many black people experienced this economic downturn as a depression. During the 70s, as the gap between the incomes of the upper 20 percent of African Americans and their white counterparts narrowed, the gap between black men and women at the bottom of the economic ladder and their counterparts expanded. Poor black people were losing ground. In 1969, approximately 10 percent of white men and 25 percent of black men earned less than $10,000 (in 1984 constant dollars). In 1984 about 40 percent of black men between twenty-five and fifty-five earned less than $10,000 compared with 20 percent of comparable white men. Put a different way, between 1970 and 1986, the proportion of black families with incomes of less than $10,000 grew from 26.8 to 30.2 percent. Still, there were some improvements. The black middle class grew. In 1970, 4.7 percent of black families had incomes of more than $50,000; by 1986 the number had almost doubled to 8.8 percent. But in general, the relative economic status of black workers did not improve.

Black Americans and the Carter Presidency

In 1976 the United States celebrated its bicentennial. Flags flew from every flagpole, and fire hydrants were painted red, white, and blue. Tall ships sailed into New York harbor from around the world, and there were more parades than anyone could count. For African Americans, it was an important year, but for another reason. For the first time since 1964, the man most of them voted for was elected president—Jimmy Carter, a former governor of Georgia. Ninety percent of African-American voters favored the soft-spoken, religious Georgia Democrat over incumbent president Gerald Ford. As in 1960, their votes were crucial; without them, Carter could not have even carried his native South.

Black Appointees

Carter acknowledged his debt to the black electorate by appointing African Americans to highly visible posts. He named Patricia Harris secretary of Housing and Urban

PROFILE

Eleanor Holmes Norton

Eleanor Holmes was born in Washington, D.C. on April 8, 1938 to Coleman and Vela Holmes. Her father worked in the housing department of the District of Columbia and earned a law degree. Her mother was a teacher. Holmes attended Dunbar High School and, Antioch College in Yellow Springs, Ohio. In 1963 and 1964 she earned an MA in American Studies and a law degree from Yale University. While clerking for a federal judge in Philadelphia, she met her husband, Edward Norton and married him in October 1965. From that time to the present she would combine marriage, career, and motherhood with a commitment to social struggle for justice and equity for workers, women, and minorities. She has two children, Kathrine (who was born with Downs Syndrome) and John.

District of Columbia Delegate Eleanor Holmes Norton (1937–) speaks at a news conference in 1998 concerning Supreme Court decisions on issues of sexual harassment in schools and in the work place. She served as Chair of the Equal Employment Opportunity Commission during the Carter administration.

After completing her clerkship she became an advocate for human rights, beginning with a stint as the assistant legal director of the American Civil Liberties Union. Norton also placed her expertise at the service of the Mississippi Freedom Democratic party when it challenged the all-white Mississippi delegation at the Democratic National Convention of 1964.

Committed to preserving constitutional guarantees of the freedom of speech for all Americans, she represented Vietnamese War protesters, activists from civil rights organizations and even white klansmen. Norton was also able to put aside her personal feeling and successfully defend Alabama Governor George Wallace's rights to express his racist ideas in public facilities in New York City as the candidate of the American Independent party. Her defense of Wallace attracted both critics and admirers. In 1970, Mayor John V. Lindsay appointed her chair of New York's Human Rights Commission, the city's most powerful antidiscrimination agency. In 1974 Mayor Abraham D. Beame renewed her appointment. Again she impressed people with her mastery of legal questions and articulate commitment to battle racism and sexism, and to preserve free speech.

At a news conference she declared: "As commissioner, I will attempt to see that no man is judged by the irrational criteria of race, religion, or national origin. And I assure you that I use the word "man" in the generic sense, for I mean to see that the principle of nondiscrimination becomes a reality for women as well." In keeping with her vows, Norton, in 1973, helped to cofound the National Black Feminist Organization, to mobilize black women against the interwoven race, class, and sex exploitation and discrimination that they face in finding employment. In 1975 she coauthored *Sex Discrimination and the Law: Causes and Remedies.*

Jimmy Carter named Norton head of the Equal Employment Opportunity Commission (EEOC). From 1977 to 1982 she was largely responsible for enforcement of Title VII of the Civil Rights Act of 1972 and the Equal Employment Act of 1972. She cut the backlog of cases in half and increased the productivity of EEOC area offices by 65 percent. Norton firmly supported affirmative action. She declared: "Affirmative action is the most important modern anti-discrimination technique ever instituted in the United States. It is the one tool that has had a demonstrable effect on discrimination. No one who knows anything about the subject would say it hasn't worked. It has certainly done something, or else it wouldn't have provoked so much opposition. In just one decade—the 1970s—the number of sales, technical and professional jobs Blacks hold increased by 50 percent. Affirmative action, by all statistical measures, has been the central ingredient to the creation of the Black middle class." (Quotes from "Eleanor Holmes Norton, (1938–)" *Notable Black American Women,* Jessie Carney Smith, editor (1992), 809–12.)

In 1990, after serving as professor of law at the Georgetown University Law Center, Norton was elected the nonvoting representative to Congress from the District of Columbia.

Development, making her the first black woman to serve in the Cabinet. Carter appointed Andrew Young, former congressman from Georgia and a long-time political ally, ambassador to the United Nations. (Young was forced to resign in 1979.) Clifford Alexander, Jr. became the secretary of the Army. Eleanor Holmes Norton became the first woman to chair the Equal Employment Opportunity Commission (EEOC). Ernest Green, who had been one of the nine students to desegregate Little Rock's Central High School, was appointed assistant secretary of the Department of Labor. Wade McCree was appointed solicitor general in the Justice Department. Drew Days III became assistant attorney general for civil rights. Historian and former University of Colorado chancellor Mary Frances Berry was appointed assistant secretary for education. Carter also named Louis Martin his special assistant, making him the first African American in a position of influence on the White House staff.

Carter's Domestic Policies

There are many ways to judge the significance of the Carter presidency to African Americans. Carter's black appointments were practically and symbolically important. Never had so many black men and women occupied positions that had direct and immediate impact on the day-to-day operations of the federal government. Carter also helped to cement gains for civil rights. When Congress passed legislation to stop busing for school children as a means of integrating the schools, Carter vetoed it. He tried to improve fair employment practices by strengthening the enforcement powers of the EEOC. His Justice Department chose cases to prosecute under the Fair Housing Act that involved widespread discrimination, to make the greatest possible impact.

Yet Carter's overall record proved unsatisfactory to most African Americans. Despite a Public Works Employment Act that directed 10 percent of public works funds to minority contractors and helped spur the creation of 585,000 jobs, Carter failed to help Democrats in Congress pass either full-employment or universal health care bills. He also cut social welfare programs in an attempt to balance the budget, including school lunch programs and financial aid to black students.

Although the sluggish economy undermined Carter's popularity, the event that proved his undoing was the Iran hostage crisis that began in the fall of 1979. For many black people, however, Carter had become a disappointment long before that. They believed that he had done little to help them achieve social justice and economic advancement. Still the nomination of the conservative Ronald Reagan by the Republicans left black voters no alternative to Carter. In the election of 1980, 90 percent of black voters again supported him, but this time they could not prevent his defeat. Carter pulled down scores of Democrats with him, and the Republicans regained the Senate for the first time since 1954.

Conclusion

The civil rights movement's victories changed African-American life in particular and American culture in general. The black power and black arts movements continued the struggle for freedom in northern and western urban areas where housing segregation, rising unemployment, and persistent police brutality sparked rebellions that resulted in many deaths and widespread destruction in Watts, Newark, Detroit, and other cities. The black political convention movement did not create a black third party. But one of the most enduring legacies of the era was the rise of black elected officials. Black student militancy persisted despite the destruction of the Black Panther party. Throughout the late 1960s and 1970s, black students fought to create and institutionalize black studies as a new academic field. The black arts and black consciousness movement opened up new avenues for the expression of black unity and positive black identity. A new generation of black poets, dramatists, and musicians found receptive audiences.

The legislative successes of the early phase of the civil rights movement illuminated how much more needed to be done to achieve a truly egalitarian society. Poor people, black and white, needed jobs, housing, medical care, and education. To varying degrees, Presidents Johnson, Nixon, and Carter attempted to address these needs. Their efforts produced mixed results in the face of a disastrous war in Vietnam and a massive white backlash. In the 1980s Republicans would reap the benefit of the Democratic party's disarray, and the plight of the poor would deteriorate.

Still, some black intellectuals chose a long view in their assessment of the significance of the post-World War II decades of struggle. Historian and theologian Vincent Harding put it most eloquently:

> It may be that the greatest discovery . . . was the fact that there is no last word in the human struggle for freedom, justice, and democracy. Only the continu-

Timeline

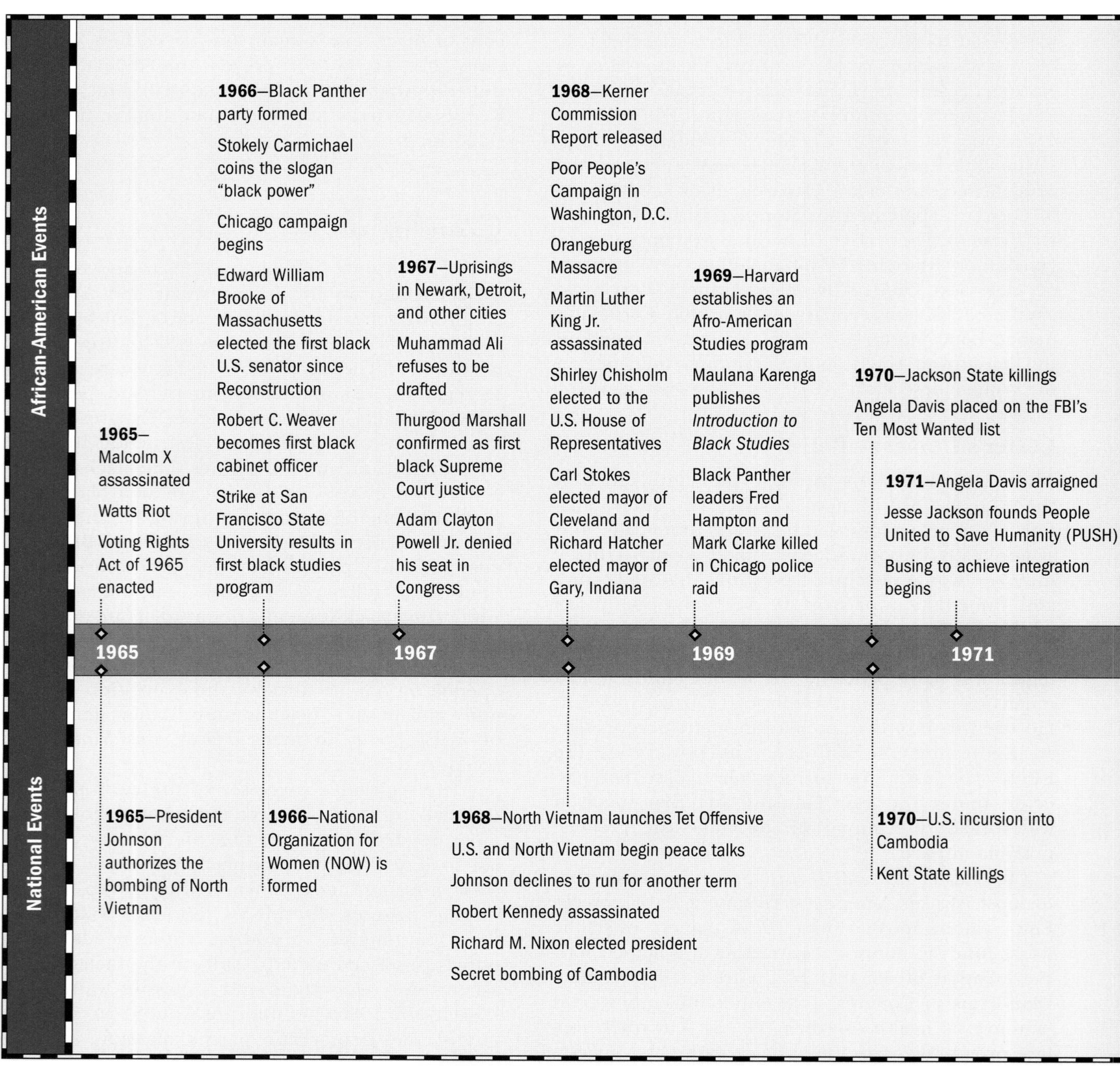
African-American Events
1965–Malcolm X assassinated
Watts Riot
Voting Rights Act of 1965 enacted
1966–Black Panther party formed
Stokely Carmichael coins the slogan "black power"
Chicago campaign begins
Edward William Brooke of Massachusetts elected the first black U.S. senator since Reconstruction
Robert C. Weaver becomes first black cabinet officer
Strike at San Francisco State University results in first black studies program
1967–Uprisings in Newark, Detroit, and other cities
Muhammad Ali refuses to be drafted
Thurgood Marshall confirmed as first black Supreme Court justice
Adam Clayton Powell Jr. denied his seat in Congress
1968–Kerner Commission Report released
Poor People's Campaign in Washington, D.C.
Orangeburg Massacre
Martin Luther King Jr. assassinated
Shirley Chisholm elected to the U.S. House of Representatives
Carl Stokes elected mayor of Cleveland and Richard Hatcher elected mayor of Gary, Indiana
1969–Harvard establishes an Afro-American Studies program
Maulana Karenga publishes *Introduction to Black Studies*
Black Panther leaders Fred Hampton and Mark Clarke killed in Chicago police raid
1970–Jackson State killings
Angela Davis placed on the FBI's Ten Most Wanted list
1971–Angela Davis arraigned
Jesse Jackson founds People United to Save Humanity (PUSH)
Busing to achieve integration begins
1965
1967
1969
1971
National Events
1965–President Johnson authorizes the bombing of North Vietnam
1966–National Organization for Women (NOW) is formed
1968–North Vietnam launches Tet Offensive
U.S. and North Vietnam begin peace talks
Johnson declines to run for another term
Robert Kennedy assassinated
Richard M. Nixon elected president
Secret bombing of Cambodia
1970–U.S. incursion into Cambodia
Kent State killings

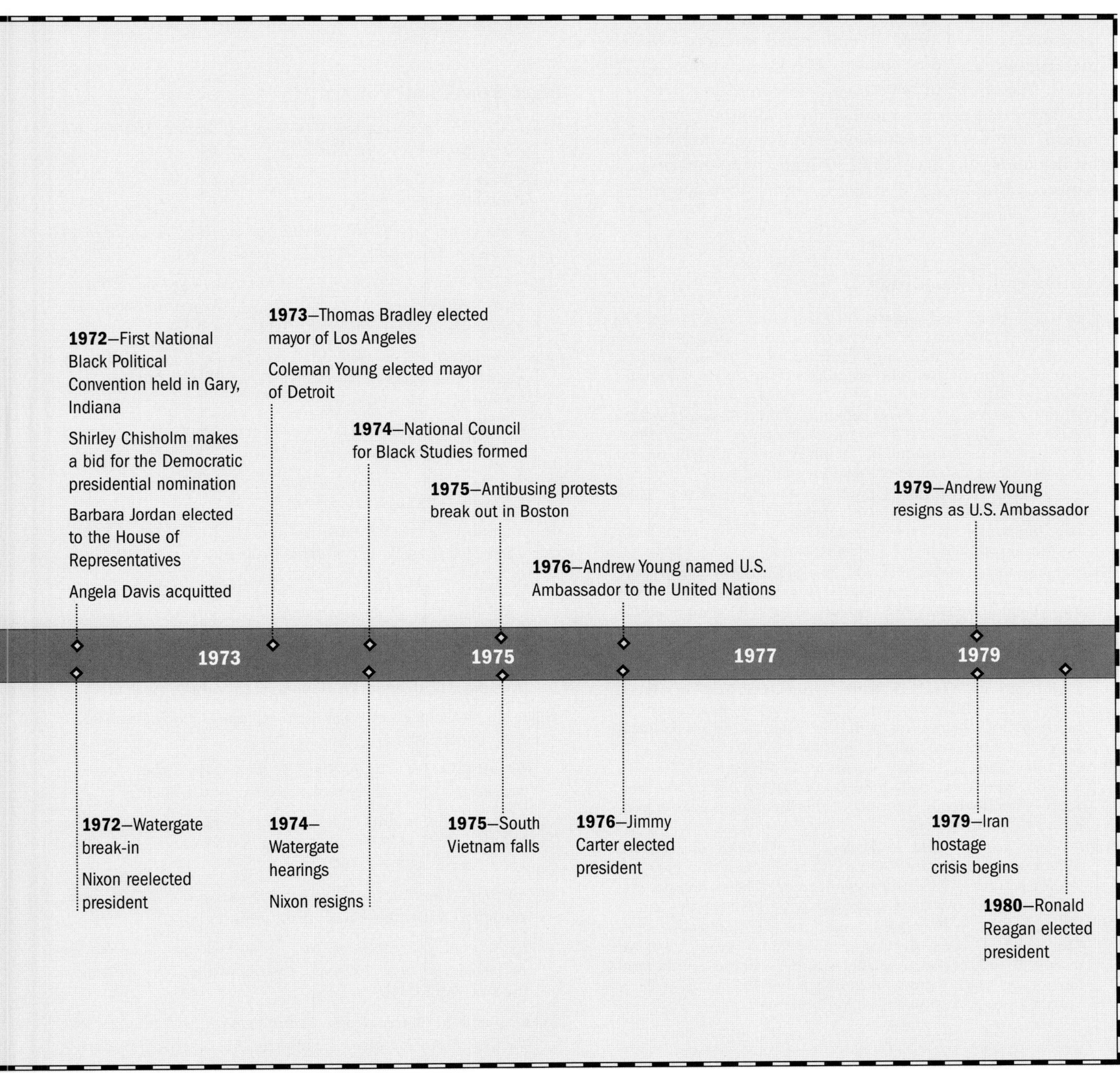
1972–First National Black Political Convention held in Gary, Indiana
Shirley Chisholm makes a bid for the Democratic presidential nomination
Barbara Jordan elected to the House of Representatives
Angela Davis acquitted
1973–Thomas Bradley elected mayor of Los Angeles
Coleman Young elected mayor of Detroit
1974–National Council for Black Studies formed
1975–Antibusing protests break out in Boston
1976–Andrew Young named U.S. Ambassador to the United Nations
1979–Andrew Young resigns as U.S. Ambassador
1973
1975
1977
1979
1972–Watergate break-in
Nixon reelected president
1974–Watergate hearings
Nixon resigns
1975–South Vietnam falls
1976–Jimmy Carter elected president
1979–Iran hostage crisis begins
1980–Ronald Reagan elected president

ing word, lived out by men, women, and children who dance and rest, who wrestle with alligators and stand firm before tanks, and presidents, and drug lords and deep, deep, fears. We learn again that the continuing word remains embedded in those who determined not to be moved, who know, against all odds, that they will overcome, will continue to create a more perfect union, a more compassionate world. The world remains with those who discover, in the midst of unremitting struggle, deep amazing powers within their own lives, power from, power for, the planet.

Recommended Reading

Stokely Carmichael and Charles V. Hamilton. *Black Power: The Politics of Liberation in America.* New York: Vintage Books, 1967. One of the most important books of the era of black power, by Carmichael, who popularized the slogan, and political scientist Hamilton.

Theodore Cross. *The Black Power Imperative: Racial Inequality and the Politics of Nonviolence.* New York: Faulkner Books, 1984. Provides a useful critique of the black power movement and explores the persistence of racial inequality.

Robert Dalleck. *Flawed Giant: Lyndon B. Johnson and His Times 1961–1973.* New York: Oxford University Press, 1998. A definitive biography of President Lyndon Johnson with fresh insights, grounded in exhaustive research.

Henry Hampton and Steve Fayer, eds. *Voices of Freedom: An Oral History of the Civil Rights Movement from the 1950s through the 1980s.* New York: Bantam Books, 1990. Contains the recollections of all the key participants in the critical battles and movements of the three decades that transformed race relations in America.

Robert C. Smith. *We Have No Leaders: African Americans in the Post-Civil Rights Era.* New York: State University of New York Press, 1996. A thoughtful critique of the successes and failures of black politics beginning with the National Black Political Convention in Gary, Indiana, in 1972.

Wallace Terry. *Bloods: An Oral History of the Vietnam War by Black Veterans.* New York: Ballantine Books, 1984. One of the best sources for firsthand accounts of the Vietnam War as experienced by black soldiers.

Brian Ward. *Just My Soul Responding: Rhythm and Blues, Black Consciousness, and Race Relations.* Berkeley, CA: University of California Press, 1998. An excellent study of black popular culture during the civil rights and black power movement era.

Craig Hansen Werner. *Playing the Changes: From Afro-Modernism to the Jazz Impulse.* Urbana, IL: University of Illinois Press, 1994. An insightful study of the gospel, blues, and jazz impulse in the writings of key black writers, including James Baldwin and Leon Forrest, during the post-civil rights movement era.

Additional Bibliography

Black Panthers

Philip S. Foner, ed. *The Black Panther Speaks.* Philadelphia: Lippincott, 1970.

Toni Morrison, ed. *To Die for the People: The Writings of Huey P. Newton.* New York: Writers and Readers Publishing, 1995.

Kenneth O'Reilly. *Racial Matters: The FBI's Secret File on Black America, 1960–1972.* New York: Free Press, 1989.

Robert Scheer, ed. *Eldridge Cleaver: Post-Prison Writings and Speeches.* New York: Random House, 1969.

Black Power and Politics

Robert L. Allen. *Black Awakening in Capitalist America.* Trenton, NJ: Africa World Press, Inc., 1990.

Elaine Brown. *A Taste of Power: A Black Woman's Story.* New York: Pantheon, 1992.

James H. Cone. *Martin & Malcolm & America: A Dream or a Nightmare.* Maryknoll, NY: Orbis, 1991.

Sidney Fine. *Violence in the Model City: The Cavanagh Administration, Race Relations and the Detroit Riot of 1967.* Ann Arbor, MI: University of Michigan Press, 1989.

James F. Finley, Jr. *Church People in the Struggle: The National Council of Churches and the Black Freedom Movement, 1950–1970.* New York: Oxford University Press, 1993.

Frye Gaillard. *The Dream Long Deferred.* Chapel Hill, NC: University of North Carolina Press, 1988.

B. I. Kaufman. *The Presidency of James E. Carter, Jr.* Lawrence, KS: University of Kansas Press, 1993.

Steven Lawson. *In Pursuit of Power: Southern Blacks and Electoral Politics, 1965–1982.* New York: Columbia University Press, 1985.

C. Eric Lincoln, *The Black Muslims in America.* Boston: Beacon Press, 1961.

J. Anthony Lukas. *Common Ground.* New York: Knopf, 1985.

John T. McCartney. *Black Power Ideologies: An Essay in African-American Thought.* Philadelphia, PA: Temple University Press, 1992.

William B. McClain. *Black People in the Methodist Church.* Cambridge: Schenkman, 1984.

Larry G. Murphy. *Down By the Riverside: Readings in African American Religion.* New York: New York University Press, 2000.

William E. Nelson, Jr. and Philip J. Meranto. *Electing Black Mayors: Political Action in the Black Community.* Columbus, OH: Ohio State University Press, 1977.

Gary Orfield. *Must We Bus? Segregated Schools and National Policy.* Washington, DC: Brookings Institution, 1978.

Robert A. Pratt. *The Color of Their Skin: Education and Race in Richmond, Virginia, 1954–89.* Charlottesville, VA: University Press of Virginia, 1992.

James R. Ralph Jr. *Northern Protest: Martin Luther King, Jr., Chicago, and the Civil Rights Movement.* Cambridge, MA: Harvard University Press, 1993.

Diane Ravitch. *The Great School Wars.* New York: Basic Books, 1974.

Wilbur C. Rich. *Coleman Young and Detroit Politics.* Detroit, MI: Wayne State University Press, 1989.

Bobby Seale. *Seize the Time.* New York: Random House, 1970.

James Melvin Washington. *Frustrated Fellowship: The Black Baptist Quest for Social Power.* Macon, GA: Mercer University Press, 1986.

Delores S. Williams. *Sisters in the Wilderness: The Challenge of Womanist God-Talk.* Maryknoll, NY: Orbis, 1993.

Gayraud S. Wilmore. *Black Religion and Black Radicalism.* New York: Anchor Press, 1973.

Black Studies and Black Students

Talmadge Anderson, ed. *Black Studies: Theory, Method, and Cultural Perspectives.* Pullman, WA: Washington State University Press, 1990.

Jack Bass and Jack Nelson. *The Orangeburg Massacre.* Cleveland, OH: Word Publishing, 1970.

William H. Exum. *Paradoxes of Protest: Black Student Activism in a White University.* Philadelphia, PA: Temple University Press, 1985.

Richard P. McCormick. *The Black Student Protest Movement at Rutgers.* New Brunswick, NJ: Rutgers University Press, 1990.

Cleveland Sellers, with Robert Terrell. *The River of No Return: The Autobiography of a Black Militant and the Life and Death of SNCC.* New York: William Morrow, 1987.

Class and Race

Jack M. Bloom. *Class, Race, and the Civil Rights Movement.* Bloomington, IN: Indiana University Press, 1987.

Martin Gilens. *Why Americans Hate Welfare: Race, Media, and the Politics of Antipoverty Policy.* Chicago: University of Chicago Press, 1999.

Michael Katz. *The Undeserving Poor: From the War on Poverty to the War on Welfare.* New York: Pantheon Books, 1989.

Bart Landry. *The New Black Middle Class.* Berkeley, CA: University of California Press, 1987.

William Julius Wilson. *The Truly Disadvantaged: The Inner City, the Underclass, and Public Policy.* Chicago: University of Chicago Press, 1987.

Black Arts and Black Consciousness Movements

William L. Andrews, Frances Smith Foster, and Trudier Harris, eds. *The Oxford Companion to African American Literature.* New York: Oxford University Press, 1997.

James Baldwin. *Notes of a Native Son.* New York: Dial Press, 1955.

_____. *Nobody Knows My Name.* New York: Dial Press, 1961.

_____. *The Fire Next Time.* New York: Dial Press, 1963.

_____. *No Name in the Street.* New York: Dial Press, 1972.

Imamu Amiri Baraka. *Dutchman and the Slave, Two Plays by LeRoi Jones.* New York: William Morrow, 1964.

Samuel A. Hay. *African American Theater: An Historical and Critical Analysis.* Cambridge, MA: Cambridge University Press, 1994.

LeRoi Jones and Larry Neal, eds. *Black Fire: An Anthology of Afro-American Writing.* New York: William Morrow, 1968.

LeRoi Jones. *Blues People: Negro Music in White America.* New York: William Morrow, 1963.

Frank Kofsky. *Black Nationalism and the Revolution in Music.* New York: Pathfinder Press, 1970.

Larry Neal. *Visions of a Liberated Future: Black Arts Movement Writings.* New York: Thunder's Mouth Press, 1989.

Leslie Catherine Sanders. *The Development of Black Theater in America: From Shadow to Selves.* Baton Rouge, LA: Louisiana State University Press, 1988.

Suzanne E. Smith. *Dancing in the Streets: Motown and the Cultural Politics of Detroit.* Cambridge, MA: Harvard University Press, 2000.

Autobiography and Biography

Imamu Amiri Baraka. *The Autobiography of LeRoi Jones.* New York: Freundlich Books, 1984.

Dennis C. Dickerson. *Militant Mediator: Whitney M. Young, Jr.* Lexington, KY: University Press of Kentucky, 1998.

James Farmer. *Lay Bare the Heart: An Autobiography of the Civil Rights Movement.* New York: Arbor House, 1985.

Jimmie Lewis Franklin. *Back to Birmingham: Richard Arrington, Jr., and His Times.* Tuscaloosa, AL: University of Alabama Press, 1989.

Elliott J. Gorn, ed. *Muhammad Ali: The People's Champ.* Urbana, IL: University of Illinois Press, 1995.

Charles V. Hamilton. *Adam Clayton Powell, Jr.: The Political Biography of an American Dilemma.* New York: Atheneum, 1991.

Hil Haygood. *King of the Cats: The Life and Times of Adam Clayton Powell, Jr.* Boston: Houghton Mifflin Co., 1993.

David Remnick. *King of the World: Muhammad Ali and the Rise of an American Hero.* New York: Random House, 1998.

Mary Beth Rogers. *Barbara Jordan: American Hero.* New York: Bantam Books, 1998.

Kathleen Rout. *Eldridge Cleaver.* Boston, MA: Twayne Publishers, 1991.

Bobby Seale. *Seize the Time.* New York: Random House, 1970.

Nancy J. Weiss. *Whitney M. Young, Jr., and the Struggle for Civil Rights.* Princeton, NJ: Princeton University Press, 1989.

Retracing the Odyssey

Motown Museum, 2648 West Grand Boulevard, Detroit, Michigan. (313) 875-2264. Sunday and Monday, Noon to 5:00 P.M. Tuesday through Saturday, 10:00 A.M. to 5:00 P.M. Birthplace of Berry Gordy's Motown Record Corporation, founded in 1957. The "Motown Sound" exemplified the music of such performers as The Jackson Five, Gladys Knight and the Pips, Marvin Gaye, Stevie Wonder. A sign hangs on the front of the structure, "Hitsville U.S.A." acknowledging the importance of this state historic site. The museum is composed of two adjoining houses filled with memorabilia of gold record awards, album covers, costumes, and musical instruments. Visitors are able to view in Studio A the original control booth where many hits such as "My Girl," "Baby Love," and "Please Mr. Postman," by the Temptations, Supremes, and other artists were recorded.

DuSable Museum of African-American History, 740 East 56th Place, Chicago, Illinois. Monday through Saturday, 10:00 A.M. to 4:00 P.M. Sunday, Noon to 4:00 P.M. Artist Margaret Goss Burroughs opened, in 1961, in her home the Ebony Musuem which moved in 1973 to its present location at Washington Park. It is now one of the nation's major museums of black history, life and culture. It houses an extensive collection of artifacts, art, books, and civil rights documents. It sponsors a diverse array of cultural and educational programs. The DuSable Museum is named in honor of Jean Baptiste Pointe DuSable, a Haitian-born immigrant who arrived in Chicago in 1779 and was the first non-Indian to settle in the area.

Southern Poverty Law Center Civil Rights Memorial, 400 Washington Avenue, Montgomery, Alabama 36104. The Civil Rights Memorial captures the history of the freedom struggle while ensuring that we do not forget the costs so many paid in the ongoing struggle against racism and social inequality.

The Martin Luther King, Jr. National Historic Site, 526 Auburn, NE, Atlanta, Georgia. (404) 331-3919. The district is composed of Martin Luther King's birthplace and gravesite. The Ebenezer Baptist Church where three generations of King men served as pastors, along with an informative National Park Service Visitors Center provides a detailed overview of King's life. Also in the district is the Martin Luther King, Jr., Center for Non-Violent Social Change, which contains King's personal papers and the records of the Southern Christian Leadership Conference in addition to an oral history collection.

REVIEW, RESEARCH & INTERACT

REVIEW QUESTIONS

1. Why did African-American residents of Watts, Newark, and Detroit rebel in 1965–1966? What did these rebellions suggest about the value of the civil rights movement victories?
2. How did the visions and ideals, successes and failures of Martin Luther King, Jr. compare with those of Lyndon B. Johnson? Why were these men at odds with each other?
3. What role did African Americans play in the Vietnam War?
4. In what ways can the presidency of Richard Nixon be considered progressive? Which reforms initiated by President Lyndon B. Johnson did Nixon advance once he took office?
5. What were the major ideological concerns of the artists of the black arts movement? To what extent did Baldwin and Amiri Baraka have similar views about art, consciousness, aesthetics, and politics?
6. What factors prevented African Americans from forming a third political party? What was the significance of the rise of black elected officials?
7. Why were African Americans disappointed with the presidency of Jimmy Carter?

Research Navigator.com RESOURCES FOR COLLEGE RESEARCH ASSIGNMENTS **www.researchnavigator.com**

Chapter 22 explores the evolution of black political consciousness in the wake of the civil right's movement. For further research on African American politics in the late 1960s and 1970s, use the tools available to you in Research Navigator.

As you investigate this topic, consider this question: "What were the key positions of advocates of the black power movement?"

- **ContentSelect:** Search in the History database using the search term *Malcolm X.*
- **Links Library:** Access the History: U.S. History database and explore the links for *Johnson, Lyndon* and *Vietnam War.*
- **New York Times on the Web:** To find out more, search the History database using the search term *Vietnam War.*

DOCUMENTS AND ACTIVITIES IN AFRICAN-AMERICAN HISTORY

Documents

22-1 Stokely Carmichael and "Black Power," 1966
22-2 Martin Luther King, Jr., "Conscience and the Vietnam War," 1967
22-3 "Our Nation Is Moving Toward Two Societies, One Black, One White—Separate and Unequal": Excerpts from the Kerner Report, 1968
22-4 Civil Disorders
22-5 "The Bottom of the Economic Totem Pole": African American Women in the Workplace
22-6 Affirmative Action in Atlanta, "Can Atlanta Succeed Where America Has Failed?"
22-7 Presidential candidate Jimmy Carter speaks of growing up behind an Invisible Wall of Racial Segregation," Los Angeles, CA, June 1, 1976
22-8 Toi Derricotte, Black in a White Neighborhood, 1977–1978

23

Modern Black America, 1980 to Present

Prolific writer, accomplished actress, and renowned poet, Maya Angelou (1928–) read an original poem, "On the Pulse of the Morning" at President Clinton's first inauguration in 1993. In 1970 she published her now classic autobiography, *I Know Why the Caged Bird Sings,* that describes her childhood in Stamps, Arkansas. She is the Reynolds Professor of American Studies at Wake Forest University in Winston-Salem, North Carolina.

MANY were lost in the struggle for the right to vote: Jimmie Lee Jackson, a young student, gave his life; Viola Liuzzo, a White mother from Detroit, called nigger lover, had her brains blown out at point blank range; [Michael] Schwerner, [Andrew] Goodman and [James] Chaney—two Jews and a Black—found in a common grave, bodies riddled with bullets in Mississippi; the four darling little girls in a church in Birmingham, Alabama. They died that we might have a right to live.

Dr. Martin Luther King Jr. lies only a few miles from us tonight. Tonight he must feel good as he looks down upon us. We sit here together, a rainbow, a coalition—the sons and daughters of slavemasters and the sons and daughters of slaves, sitting together around a common table, to decide the direction of our party and our country. His heart would be full tonight.

We meet tonight at the crossroads, a point of decision. Shall we expand, be inclusive, find unity and power; or suffer division and impotence?

Address by the Reverend Jesse Louis Jackson to the Democratic National Convention, July 19, 1988

CHAPTER OUTLINE

Progress and Poverty
- The Growth of the Black Middle Class
- The Persistence of Black Poverty

Ronald Reagan and the Conservative Reaction
- Dismantling the Great Society
- Black Conservatives
- The Thomas–Hill Controversy
- Debating the "Old" and the "New" Civil Rights
- Affirmative Action
- The Backlash

Black Political Activism in the Age of Conservative Reaction
- The King Holiday
- TransAfrica and the Antiapartheid Movement

Jesse Jackson and the Rainbow Coalition

Policing the Black Community
- Human Rights in America
- Police Director Hubert Williams of Newark

The Election of 1992
- "It's the Economy, Stupid!"
- Clinton Signs the Welfare Reform Act

African-American Cultural and Intellectual Movements at the End of the Millennium
- Black Feminism
- Black Intellectuals
- Afrocentricity
- Louis Farrakhan and the Nation of Islam
- The Million Man March
- The Million Woman March
- Black Christianity on the Front Lines
- The Hip-Hop Nation

2000 and Beyond
- The 2000 Census and Black America
- Reparations
- September 11, 2001

Conclusion

The civil rights movement succeeded in dismantling legal and political barriers to black freedom, but as the seventies ended, profound divisions within the black community emerged. For centuries, slavery, racism, and the relentless struggles to end them had bound black American communities together, burying many differences. Now, however, rifts expanded between the interests of the black middle class, which had grown considerably during the preceding decades, and those left to languish in impoverished inner-city neighborhoods. At the same time, heated debates erupted among advocates of different ideologies—integrationism, assimilationism, and nationalism. As in American society as a whole, the quest for gender equality increased tensions between black men and women. For better or worse, in recent decades it has become more difficult to speak of a united African America than at any time in the past.

But the need for solidarity did not diminish with the destruction of state-sanctioned segregation. Racism remains powerful in American politics and society. One of the driving forces behind the conservative resurgence of the 1980s was a reaction to the gains of black Americans. Now the whole edifice of laws and court cases that was built at such cost during the 1960s has come under attack. The need to counter this assault and to solve the problems of economic deprivation and continued discrimination remains.

Progress and Poverty

During the 1960s an increasing number of African Americans began to share in the wealth enjoyed by other Americans. Some became famous or wealthy, and most, for the first time, emerged from the extreme poverty and deprivation that had been the lot of nearly every African American in the past. Many, however—a far greater proportion than among white Americans—persisted in poverty.

The years after 1970 witnessed the consolidation of black economic, civic, and political progress. In part, this was exemplified by the rising prominence of such visible African Americans as entertainer Oprah Winfrey, Secretary of Commerce Ronald Brown, General and later Secretary of State Colin Powell, and basketball star Michael Jordan. These people, joined by many others, countered notions of white supremacy by rising to the top of their fields.

The very rich remained rare in the black community, but their numbers did grow. Oprah Winfrey, Bill Cosby, Michael Jackson, and Michael Jordan numbered among those few fortunate enough to acquire immense fortunes in the entertainment industry. Others, such as Reginald Lewis, made enormous sums in business. In the mid-1980s Lewis was, by some accounts, the wealthiest black American. Armed with a law degree from Harvard University Law School, this prodigious businessman first purchased the $55 million McCall Pattern Company in a leveraged buyout, and then in 1987 he purchased an international packaged goods company, Beatrice Foods, for $2.5 billion. At that time, it was the largest leveraged buyout in U.S. history. Before his untimely death in 1993, Lewis demonstrated an understanding of the need to give back to the community by donating millions to Harvard Law School, Howard University, and the NAACP.

Table 23–1
Median Income of Black and White Households, 1992 and 1997

	1992	1997	Change	Percent Change
White	$36,846	$38,972	$2,126	5.8
Black	$21,455	$25,050	$3,595	16.8

Source: U.S. Census Bureau Study of Income Data, 1997.

The Growth of the Black Middle Class

The achievements of the most successful African Americans are impressive, but more significant is the growth of the black middle class. In 1940 only 5.2 percent of black men and 6.4 percent of black women worked in white-collar occupations. By 1990 those figures had risen to 32 percent for black men and 58.9 percent for black women. Although still, on average, below that of white families, black family income has also increased dramatically. In 1940 only 1 percent of black families, compared with 12 percent of white families, had income at least twice as high as the government's poverty line; by 1995 almost 49 percent of black families did, compared with 75 percent of white families. Income in relation to white families also improved. In 1960, for example, two-parent black families earned 61 percent as much as two-parent similar white families, but by 1995 they earned 87 percent as much. This figure is even more impressive when one considers that a larger proportion of black people live in the low-wage South than do white people.

The economic boom of the Clinton years was particularly beneficial for black people. Although the median income of black families remains substantially below that of white families, it has risen at a greater rate (see Table 23–1). Black women now make 94 percent of what white women earn. In 1992, 39.1 percent of black households earned less than $15,000 annually; by 1997, the percentage had declined to 31 percent. The overall black poverty rate in 1997 was 26.5 percent, the lowest on record. In real terms, approximately 1.7 million black Americans went off the poverty rolls between 1992 and 1998. The decline in the poverty rate corresponds to increasing employment, although many of the jobs working-poor

PROFILE

Oprah Winfrey: World's Richest Black Woman

"Communicating with people is how I always developed any kind of value about myself. All my life," Oprah Winfrey recounts, "I've always known I was born to greatness." She remembers being two years old and speaking in church and hearing people say to her grandmother: "Hattie Mae, that child sure can talk. That is one talking child."

Oprah Winfrey with Michael Jordan on her television show in 1996.

Winfrey was born to a young unmarried woman, Vernita Lee, in Kosciusko, Mississippi, on January 29, 1954; she was raised by her maternal grandmother, Hattie Mae, and her father, Vernon Winfrey. Educated at Tennessee State University, she overcame the barriers that confront young, poor, black women in America to become one of the most admired and revered women in the country.

In 1984 Winfrey took over the ailing television talk show "A.M. Chicago." Within one month her ratings matched those of her formidable competitor, Phil Donahue, and within three months she was trouncing him. In less than a year, "A.M. Chicago" expanded to one hour and was renamed "The Oprah Winfrey Show." Winfrey, who always wanted to be an actress, but had no professional experience, then landed a role in Steven Spielberg's 1985 cinematic adaptation of Alice Walker's *The Color Purple* as the character Sofia. For her movie performance, Winfrey scored an Oscar nomination for best supporting actress. In 1986, The Oprah Winfrey Show was nationally syndicated. Winfrey formed her own production company, Harpo ("Oprah" spelled backward), and in 1989, bought her own television and movie production studio. She won thirty-two Emmy Awards—seven for outstanding talk show host—and the Emmy Lifetime Achievement Award (1998). In 2000 Winfrey launched the phenomenally successful women's magazine named "O." Even more influential has been the Oprah Book Club. The books it selects are virtually guaranteed a spot on the *New York Times* best-sellers list. Clearly one of the most powerful people in show business, Winfrey is also one of the richest women in America and one of the few African Americans on the Forbes 1998 list of the top 40 entertainers in the American entertainment industry.

Winfrey has forged a powerful connection with the viewing public with revelations about her private life. She has told of being the victim of incest, of having a stillborn child when only a child herself, of her promiscuous adolescence, and of her struggles with an eating disorder.

During her two decades on national television, Winfrey has developed an astonishing influence over American society and culture. She can focus attention on important problems in the black community and American society at large. She has also helped rid mass entertainment of the negative stereotypes it had imposed on black women since slavery.

African Americans are finding are in the low-paying service industry. In 1997, with the nation's overall unemployment rate at 4.6 percent, the lowest since 1970, black unemployment dropped below 10 percent for the first time in almost twenty-five years.

The increasing affluence of many black people rested not only on the removal of racial barriers to their employment and the implementation of affirmative action programs, but also on increased educational attainment. Many more black youths graduate from high school than ever before. In 1960, only 37.7 percent of African Americans between the ages of twenty-five and twenty-nine had completed high school, but by 1995, 86.5 percent had, almost exactly

DATA EXPLORATION
To explore this data, go to http://www.prenhall.com/hine/table23.2

Table 23–2
Black and White Children and the Conditions Contributing to Poverty

Children Living in Households Headed by Their Mothers, 1960–1990

Year	Black	White	Black Percentage as Multiple of White Percentage
1960	19.9%	6.1%	3.26
1970	29.4%	7.8%	3.78
1980	43.9%	12.9%	3.43
1990	58.1%	16.1%	3.61

Children with Unmarried Mothers, 1960–1990

Year	Black	White	Black Percentage as Multiple of White Percentage
1960	2.1%	0.11%	19.1
1970	4.6%	0.22%	20.9
1980	13.2%	0.73%	18.1
1990	33.1%	2.91%	11.4

Infant Mortality Rates (Deaths per 1,000 Births), 1960–1990

Year	Black	White	Black Percentage as Multiple of White Percentage
1960	43.9	22.9	1.92
1970	32.6	17.8	1.83
1980	21.4	11.0	1.95
1990	17.0	7.7	2.21

Location of Households Headed by Women, 1990

Location	Black	White
Central Cities	60.9%	27.7%
Suburbs	24.3%	49.5%
Nonmetropolitan Areas	14.8%	22.8%

Source: Adapted from Andrew Hacker, *Two Nations: Black and White, Separate, Hostile, Unequal* (New York: Ballantine Books, rev., 1995), p. 256. Reprinted with the permission of Scribner, a division of Simon & Schuster, Inc.

the same proportion (87.4 percent) as for white Americans. Black enrollment in college also rose from a mere 136,000 in 1960 to nearly 1,300,000 in 1990. Although the college completion rate for African Americans remains well below that for white Americans, statistics like these suggest that the number of African Americans trained for higher paying jobs has increased greatly since the 1960s.

The Persistence of Black Poverty

Nonetheless, despite the emergence of a substantial black middle class, many African Americans remain mired in poverty. The 26.5 percent of African Americans living below the poverty line in 1997 translates into more than nine million people. The black poverty rate is slightly lower than that of Hispanic Americans (27.1 percent), but more than twice that of non-Hispanic white Americans (11 percent). Most poor black people are trapped in devastated inner-city neighborhoods plagued by gang warfare, drug addiction, and high rates of HIV infection and are cut off from meaningful participation in the social and economic life of the nation.

The high rate of poverty in the black community disproportionately affects children. More than half of all African Americans under the age of eighteen live in families with only one parent, almost always the mother (see Table 23–2). Partly for this reason, the poverty rate for black children in 1997 was much higher—39 percent—than the overall black poverty rate. Female-headed single-parent families suffer from limited earning capacity, meager public assistance, poor housing, and inferior education. These conditions can handicap children for the rest of their lives, helping to perpetuate poverty.

Ronald Reagan and the Conservative Reaction

Beginning in the late 1970s American politics took a hard turn to the right. This shift profoundly affected African Americans, particularly the poor. With the election of Ronald Reagan to the presidency in 1980, the executive branch ceased to support expanded civil rights. It also sought to reduce welfare programs, and it staffed key agencies and the federal judiciary with opponents of affirmative action. The now overwhelmingly white Republican party became increasingly entrenched in the South, ending the Democratic party's long dominance in that region.

Ronald Reagan's defeat of Jimmy Carter in the 1980 presidential election marked the emergence of the New Right as the dominant force in American politics. Reagan possessed charm and the ability to communicate his vision to the American people. His election was, however, the result of more than personal charisma. Over the previous decade, many groups unhappy with the changes of the 1960s had developed powerful political organizations that found a home in the Republican party. These groups included those opposed to equal rights for women, to abortion rights, to the Supreme Court's decisions protecting the rights of the accused and banning compulsory prayer from the public schools, and a whole range of other issues.

White Southerners opposed to the changes wrought by the civil rights movement and white Northerners angry at school busing, affirmative action programs, and the tax burden they associated with welfare were a key part of this coalition.

Dismantling the Great Society

One of the New Right's key goals was to reverse the growth of social welfare programs created during and after the New Deal. To this end, from 1981 to 1993 Reagan and his Republican successor George Bush cut federal grants to cities in half and terminated programs crucial to the stability of many black families. As the federal government slashed funds earmarked toward redeveloping inner cities and constructing public housing between 1980 and 1992, the percentage of city budgets derived from the federal government declined from 14.3 percent to 5 percent. As a result, inner-city neighborhoods, where 56 percent of poor residents were African American, became more unstable.

Reagan advanced a "trickle-down" theory of economics. He believed that if the financial position of the wealthiest Americans improved, their increased prosperity would percolate through the middle and working classes to the poor. Unemployment statistics soon challenged this theory. By December of 1982, the unemployment rate had risen to 10.8, and the rate for African Americans was twice that of white Americans. The real income of the highest paid 1 percent of the nation, meanwhile, increased from $312,206 to $548,970 during the 1980s.

Reagan and Bush often cloaked their intent to undermine rights-oriented policies by appointing black conservatives to key administrative positions. Reagan chose William Bell, for example, to replace the effective Carter appointee Eleanor Holmes Norton as chair of the Equal Employment Opportunity Commission (EEOC). Because Bell was a conservative with few qualifications for the post, civil rights leaders and organizations immediately protested his appointment. Reagan simply replaced Bell the following year with yet another black conservative, Clarence Thomas, who strongly opposed affirmative action. Thomas reduced the commission's staff and allowed the backlog of affirmative action cases to grow to 46,000 and processing time to increase to ten months.

Reagan similarly tried to change the direction of the U.S. Commission on Civil Rights (CCR), but in this case he met with resistance. Since its creation in 1957 the commission had served as a civil rights watchdog, with no real enforcement powers, but with considerable influence on public opinion. Soon after Reagan took office, the CCR began to issue reports critical of his civil rights policies. Reagan responded by trying to load the commission with members sympathetic to his perspective. He replaced the commission's chair, Arthur S. Flemming, who was white, with a black Republican, Clarence Pendleton, former executive director of the San Diego Urban League. The vice chair, however, was Mary Frances Berry, a well-respected, long-time civil rights activist and historian who had been appointed by Carter and who frequently clashed with the new president. In 1984, Reagan tried to remove Berry from the Commission on Civil Rights, but she resisted, suing in court to retain her position. When her suit was successful, she became known as "the woman the president could not fire." Even with Berry, however, the Commission on Civil Rights declined to virtual insignificance under Pendleton during the Reagan years.

Black Conservatives

Men like Bell, Thomas, and Pendleton were part of a vocal cadre of black, middle-class, conservative intellectuals, professionals, and politicians who gained visibility and prominence during the Reagan years. To augment their influence in the Republican party, these conservatives cultivated a small, well-educated, articulate group of black men and women intellectuals in addition to black politicians. Prominent black proponents of conservative ideology include Thomas Sowell, Walter Williams, Shelby Steele, Armstrong Williams, Ward Connerly, and, until he broke with the others in the late 1990s, Glenn Loury. There was a critical difference, however, between elite black Republicans and the black politicians in the Democratic camp: black Republican politicians rarely exercised meaningful power within the party. They were expected to embrace the existing values and goals set down by the white party leaders. In contrast, elite black Democratic politicians could, and often did, make their influence felt. Moreover, they represented a large and essential constituency within the party.

The Thomas–Hill Controversy

The role of black conservatives acquired its greatest visibility when, in 1991, President George Bush nominated Clarence Thomas to the United States Supreme Court. Thomas was born in 1948 in rural Georgia. He graduated from Holy Cross College and Yale Law School. The symbolism of Thomas, who opposed the expansion of civil rights, replacing Thurgood Marshall, the greatest civil rights lawyer of the twentieth century, could not have been more dramatic.

George Bush's nomination of Thomas precipitated the most public exposure of gender conflict within the black community in history. Marshall had been one of the Court's great liberals and a staunch defender of civil rights. Thomas was a black conservative whose record on civil rights did not endear him to white liberals or for that matter, to many within the black community. His credentials for the position were also open to question: He had served only fifteen months as an appellate court judge. However, he was a black man, and the black community was loath publicly to contest his nomination or to challenge the cynical tokenism of the Bush administration. Still, civil rights organizations expressed grave reservations about the Thomas nomination. The Urban League declared, "We welcome the appointment of an African-American jurist to fill the vacant seat left by Justice [Thurgood] Marshall. Obviously, Judge Thomas is no Justice Marshall. But if he were, this administration would not have appointed him. We are hopeful that Judge Thomas' background of poverty and minority status will lead him to greater identification with those in America who today are victimized by poverty and discrimination. And [we] expect the Senate, in the confirmation hearings, to explore whether he is indeed likely to do so."

The anticipated easy confirmation process derailed when black law professor Anita Hill agreed to appear before the Senate Judiciary Committee, which heard testimony on Thomas's confirmation. Hill accused Thomas of sexually harassing her when she worked for him at the Equal Employment Opportunity Commission.

Both Anita Hill and Clarence Thomas were conservative Republicans, and both had earned law degrees at Yale. Hill did not volunteer to testify about Thomas's sexual harassment of her. She had answered questions put to her in a confidential investigation. When her answers were leaked to the press, she agreed to appear before the committee. Some senators questioned her own character and integrity. Thomas countered her charges with charges of his own. He declared that he was a victim of a "high-tech lynching" in the media and that Hill's accusations were false. Although many in the black community supported Thomas, progressive feminists, white liberals, and some black people supported Hill. Activist black women were especially incensed by the treatment that Hill received from the Senate and were determined to voice their opposition to Thomas's political views. Despite the opposition, Clarence Thomas won confirmation to the United States Supreme Court by a narrow 52–48 majority. On the Court, Thomas has proved to be an arch-conservative.

Debating the "Old" and the "New" Civil Rights

The Reagan and Bush administrations distinguished between what might be called the "old civil rights law," which they claimed to support, and the "new civil rights law," which they opposed. Developed in the decade between the *Brown* decision and the Voting Rights Act of 1965, the old civil rights law prohibited intentional discrimination, be it legal segregation in the schools, informal discrimination in the workplace, or racially biased restrictions on voting. The new civil rights law is concerned with discriminatory outcomes, as measured by statistical disparities, rather than with discriminatory intent. If, for example, black children overall are disproportionately in all-black schools, or if the workforce in a given firm, compared with the community in which it is located, is disproportionately white (or male), or if elected officials in a multiracial state or municipality are disproportionately white, then discrimination is assumed.

The remedies for such historic discrimination, collectively labeled "affirmative action," tend to be statistical in nature. They include increasing the number of minority pupils, minority employees, or (by redrawing the districts from which they were elected) minority elected officials to correspond to the percentage of the relevant minority population. In employment (and in admissions to colleges and universities), the methods used in reaching these goals became known as affirmative action "guidelines." Sometimes guidelines were imposed by court order; more often they were the result of voluntary efforts by legislatures, government agencies, business firms, and colleges and universities to comply with civil rights laws and court rulings.

Affirmative Action

Few civil rights policies in the twentieth century have proved more persistently controversial than affirmative action. Many white Americans oppose affirmative action, arguing that it runs contrary to the concept of achievement founded on objective merit and amounts to reverse racial or sexual discrimination. Ironically, because gender discrimination in employment was made illegal in the 1964 Civil Rights Act, prompting federal agencies to scrutinize the percentage of women in a given workforce, white women have been

VOICES

Black Women in Defense of Themselves

Within days after Anita Hill appeared before the Senate Judiciary Committee, a group of black women led by Elsa Barkley Brown, Barbara Ransby, and Deborah King raised more than $50,000 to purchase a three-quarter-page ad in the New York Times *to print this statement, "In Defense of Ourselves." Appearing on November 17, 1991, it was signed by 1,603 black women. Five black newspapers—the* San Francisco Sun Reporter, *the* Los Angeles Sentinel, *the* New York City Sun, *the* Atlanta Inquirer, *and the* Chicago Defender*—also published the statement:*

As women of African descent, we are deeply troubled by the recent nomination, confirmation and seating of Clarence Thomas as an Associate Justice of the U.S. Supreme Court. We know that the presence of Clarence Thomas on the Court will be continually used to divert attention away from the historic struggles for social justice through suggestions that the presence of a Black man on the Supreme Court constitutes an assurance that the rights of African Americans will be protected. Clarence Thomas's public record is ample evidence that this will not be true. Further, the consolidation of a conservative majority on the Supreme Court endangers the working class people and the elderly. The seating of Clarence Thomas is an affront not only to African American women and men, but to all people concerned with social justice.

We are particularly outraged by the racist and sexist treatment of Professor Anita Hill, an African American woman who was maligned and castigated for daring to speak publicly of her own experience of sexual abuse. The malicious defamation of Professor Hill insulted all women of African descent and sent a dangerous message to all women who might contemplate a sexual harassment complaint.

We speak here because we recognize that the media are now portraying the Black community as prepared to tolerate the dismantling of affirmative action and the evil of sexual harassment in order to have any Black man on the Supreme Court. We want to make clear that the media have ignored and distorted many African American voices. We will not be silenced.

Many have erroneously portrayed the allegations against Clarence Thomas as an issue of either gender or race. As women of African descent, we understand sexual harassment as both. We further understand that Clarence Thomas outrageously manipulated the legacy of lynching in order to shelter himself from Anita Hill's allegations. To deflect attention away from the reality of sexual abuse in African American women's lives, he trivialized and misrepresented this painful part of African American people's history. This country, which has a long legacy of racism and sexism, has never taken the sexual abuse of Black women seriously. Throughout U.S. history Black women have been sexually stereotyped as immoral, insatiable, perverse, the initiators in all sexual contacts—abusive or otherwise. The common assumption in legal proceedings as well as in the larger society has been that Black women cannot be raped or otherwise sexually abused. As Anita Hill's experience demonstrates, Black women who speak of these matters are not likely to be believed. In 1991, we cannot tolerate this type of dismissal of any one Black woman's experience or this attack upon our collective character without protest, outrage, and resistance.

As women of African descent, we express our vehement opposition to the policies represented by the placement of Clarence Thomas on the Supreme Court. The Bush administration, having obstructed the passage of civil rights legislation, impeded the extension of unemployment compensation, cut student aid and dismantled social welfare programs, has continually demonstrated that it is not operating in our best interests. Nor is this appointee. We pledge ourselves to continue to speak out in defense of one another, in defense of the African American community and against those who are hostile to social justice no matter what color they are. No one will speak for us but ourselves.

QUESTIONS

1. Why did the African-American women who signed this letter feel the need to defend themselves?
2. Why did they oppose the confirmation of Clarence Thomas to the Supreme Court?
3. Why were they unsympathetic to Thomas's claim that he had been a victim of a "high-tech" lynching?

Source: *The New York Times,* November 17, 1991, pg. 53.

Supreme Court Cases on Affirmative Action in Employment

1979	*United Steelworkers v. Weber* upholds preferential treatment in hiring and training by private firms
1980	*Fullilove v. Klutznick* upholds government programs that reserve places for minorities
1984	*Memphis Firefighters v. Stotts* rejects a judicial order for retaining less-senior black employees over white employees during layoffs
1986	*Wygant v. Jackson Board of Education* rejects school board's plan for laying off white teachers while retaining less senior black teachers, but also rejects Reagan administration position that affirmative action be limited to actual victims of discrimination, thus broadly upholding affirmative action
1986	*Local 93 of International Association of Firefighters v. City of Cleveland* upholds promotion of minorities ahead of white applicants with higher test scores and greater seniority
1986	*Local 28 of Sheet Metal Workers v. EEOC* upholds order that union meet minority quota for membership
1987	*U.S. v. Paradise* upholds judicial order imposing racial quotas in hiring and promotions of Alabama state troopers
1987	*Johnson v. Transportation Agency of Santa Clara County* upholds plan that promoted women over men
1987	*American Tobacco Co. v. Patterson* upholds seniority plans in place before 1964 unless discriminatory intent can be shown
1989	*Martin v. Wilks* rules that employees may challenge affirmative action plan after it has gone into effect. This decision is overruled by Congress in the Civil Rights Act of 1991
1989	*Richmond v. J. Croson and Co.* rules that Fourteenth Amendment prohibits set-asides for minority contractors, thus going against spirit of *Weber* and against the letter of *Fullilove v. Klutznick* and implying that all such plans face "strict scrutiny"
1990	*Metro Broadcasting v. FCC* upholds affirmative action plan increasing minority broadcasting owners, returning to *Fullilove*
1995	*Adarand Constructors v. Pena* strikes down a congressional statute requiring 10 percent of federal highway money to go to minority contractors and broadly asserts that any such programs using racial classifications are constitutionally suspect

among the major beneficiaries of affirmative action. But the major advocates of affirmative action have been African Americans, most of whom see it as a remedy for centuries of discrimination. The debate over affirmative action has thus, inevitably, led to racial polarization, and it even divided the black community.

The term "affirmative action" was first used by President Lyndon Johnson in a 1965 executive order that required federal contractors to "take affirmative action" to guarantee that job seekers and employees "are treated without regard to their race, color, religion, sex, or national origin." Much of the credit for compliance with affirmative action belongs to conservative Republican president Richard Nixon. In 1969, Arthur A. Fletcher, a black assistant secretary of labor in the Nixon administration, developed the "Philadelphia Plan," in which firms with federal government contracts in the construction industry would have to set and meet hiring goals for African Americans or be penalized. The plan became a model for subsequent "set-aside" programs that reserved some contracts for minority-owned businesses or that favored the hiring of women and minorities. The process of setting goals and timetables to achieve full compliance with federal civil rights requirements appealed to large corporations and accounted for the early success of affirmative action initiatives.

The Backlash

Though it has produced more litigation, the issue of affirmative action in employment has been less controversial than that of affirmative action in college and university admissions. State higher education institutions have been at the center of the controversy both because they are narrowly bound by the Fourteenth Amendment's prohibitions on racial discrimination and because they represent, far more than do elite private institutions, the gateways to upward mobility for millions of Americans, white and black. As the 1970s progressed, in the interest both of aiding disadvantaged minorities and of increasing racial and cultural diversity on campus, admissions offices began using different criteria for white and minority admissions.

In the late 1970s reaction to affirmative action set in. The case of *Regents of the University of California v. Bakke* was a key part of this backlash. The medical school at the University of California, as a form of affirmative action, had set aside sixteen of its one hundred places in each entering class for disadvantaged and minority students. They were considered for admission in a separate system. A white male student named Alan Bakke sued the university for discrimination after it rejected his application for admission. In 1976, the California Supreme Court ruled that he should be admitted to the university, but the university appealed the ruling to the U.S. Supreme Court, which also ruled in Bakke's favor in 1978. Of the nine justices, five agreed that the university violated Bakke's rights. However, other related legal issues were involved, and the court split without a majority on nearly every one of them. Only one justice declared that affirmative action cases should be judged on the same strict level of scrutiny that was applied to "invidious" discrimination. All the other justices stated that race-conscious remedies could be used in some circumstances to correct past discrimination.

California remains the center of the affirmative action storm because of its multiracial population. In 1995 Republican Governor Pete Wilson ended affirmative action in state employment. In 1996 California voters approved Proposition 209, the so-called California Civil Rights Initiative, which banned all state agencies from implementing affirmative action programs. The campaign for the proposition was led by Ward Connerly, a conservative black entrepreneur. Born in 1939 in rural Louisiana, he had earned a B.A. from Sacramento State College and had received over $140,000 from state contracts set aside for minority businesses. Nonetheless, Connerly maintained that affirmative action exacerbated the negative stereotyping of African Americans. He and his supporters insisted moreover that affirmative action had failed to address problems of poverty, unemployment, and inadequate education that beset the truly disadvantaged. Instead, it had merely elevated to higher status those least in need of assistance, especially middle-class white women. Finally, Connerly accepted the broader argument that affirmative action assaulted the concept of individual merit and violated core American values of equality and opportunity.

Fifty-four percent of California voters agreed with Connerly, and after the U.S. Supreme Court upheld Proposition 209, it went into effect. Its effect and that of similar laws or court rulings around the nation are now known. The number of African Americans and other protected minorities admitted to the whole University of California system dropped since the proposition was upheld by the U.S. Supreme Court, and the numbers at Berkeley, U.C.'s most prestigious campus, fell precipitously. In both California and Texas, which abandoned affirmative action in its university system after a court challenge, administrators have attempted to assure a diverse student body by other means. Both states now offer admission to their top schools to all students in the top ranks of their high school class. Whether this strategy will succeed in providing access to underrepresented groups remains to be seen.

Black, Asian, Hispanic, and white women protest in support of affirmative action at a meeting of the University of California's board of trustees at UCLA in 1994.

Black Political Activism in the Age of Conservative Reaction

Presidents Reagan and Bush did not completely reverse the advancement of the civil rights agenda. The increased participation of black men and women in the upper echelons of the Democratic party reflected the extent to which they had overcome political exclusion. In 1964 there were only 103 black elected officials in the nation; by 1994 there were nearly 8,500. Forty-one African Americans were serving in Congress by 1996. In

1988, Representative William H. Gray of Pennsylvania became chair of the House Democratic caucus, making him the first African American to reach the top ranks of congressional leadership. In June 1989, Gray became majority whip of the House of Representatives. In February 1989, Ronald H. Brown became the first African American to lead a major national political party when he was elected chairman of the Democratic party. That same year, David Dinkins was elected the first black mayor of New York City. In 1990, Sharon Pratt Dixon (Kelly) was elected mayor of Washington, DC, becoming the first woman and the first District of Columbia native to serve in that position. By the mid-1990s black men and women held the mayor's office in four hundred towns and cities. Clearly, the days of black political powerlessness have ended.

During the Reagan–Bush era, one house of Congress—and often both—was in the hands of the Democratic party. Reflecting the importance of African-American voters to the party, that house used its power to pass many equal rights laws. Among the most important of these statutes were the Voting Rights Act of 1982, the Civil Rights Restoration Act of 1988, and the Fair Housing Act of 1988. The Civil Rights Restoration Act of 1988 authorized the withholding of federal funds from an entire institution if any program within it discriminated against women, racial minorities, the aged, or the handicapped. The Fair Housing Act of 1988 provided for enforcing fair housing laws. It stipulated that either an individual or the Department of Housing and Urban Development (HUD) could bring a complaint of housing discrimination and authorize administrative judges to investigate housing complaints, issue injunctions and fines, and award punitive damages. With both laws, Congress was responding to Supreme Court decisions that had narrowed the scope of earlier legislation. The Civil Rights Act of 1991 was likewise a response to a spate of restrictive Supreme Court decisions. In it, Democrats secured the protection of many of the defenses of civil rights the court had called into question.

The King Holiday

Many African Americans invested symbolic importance in an effort to make Martin Luther King, Jr.'s birthday a national holiday, elevating him to the stature of Presidents George Washington and Abraham Lincoln, both of whom are honored with a holiday. At first Reagan resisted the effort, but he eventually gave in to pressure from African Americans and their white allies. On November 2, 1983, Reagan signed a law designating the third Monday in January to honor the great civil rights leader. On January 20, 1985, the United States officially observed Martin Luther King, Jr. Day for the first time. In 1988, more than 60,000 people made the pilgrimage to Washington, DC, to commemorate the twenty-fifth anniversary of the 1963 March on Washington and to remember Martin Luther King, Jr.'s "I Have a Dream" speech.

TransAfrica and the Antiapartheid Movement

Black activism persisted on the international as well as the national front. Much of this effort focused on ending the oppressive conditions of apartheid—the complete, social, political, and economic isolation of black people—in South Africa. A particularly detestable aspect of apartheid was its glorification of white racial supremacy, an ideology reminiscent of Adolf Hitler's Germany and the American South in the early 20th century.

Activist Randall Robinson, a native of Richmond, Virginia, and a graduate of Harvard Law School who had worked as an assistant for Michigan congressman Charles Diggs, sought to link African-American liberation struggles with those waged by Africans in South Africa and elsewhere. In 1977 he founded TransAfrica to lobby for black political prisoners in South Africa, chief among them Nelson Mandela. In 1984, Robinson was joined by Mary Francis Berry of the U.S. Commission on Civil Rights, Eleanor Holmes Norton, and others for a yearlong series of sit-ins at the South African Embassy in Washington, DC, during which hundreds were arrested.

The antiapartheid movement became a major priority for African-American activists. They were able to enlist the sympathy and help of white Americans on college campuses and to pressure many universities into divesting their investments in South Africa. Similar pressures were put on corporations, especially those vulnerable to consumer boycotts. In 1986 the Black Congressional Caucus persuaded their colleagues to enact a U.S. trade embargo against South Africa and sustain it over President Reagan's veto.

In 1990, bowing to international pressure and a souring domestic economy, South African President F.W. deKlerk removed the ban on the African National Congress, the key opposition party, and a few days afterward ended the twenty-eight-year prison term of its leader, Nelson Mandela. Soon thereafter, South Africa was transformed into a multiracial democracy, and Mandela was elected its president.

Jesse Jackson and the Rainbow Coalition

As Reagan's first term ended, Jesse Jackson made history by announcing that he would campaign for the presidency of the United States. The first African American to seek the presidential nomination of a major political party was congresswoman Shirley Chisholm, in 1972. Chisholm had little money and only a small campaign organization and was never taken as a serious candidate by her male competitors or the press. Her campaign had nonetheless helped raise the visibility of African-American voters. She captured more than 150 votes on the first ballot at the Democratic National Convention. In the thoroughly male world of presidential politics, however, a black man was a more credible contender.

Jesse Jackson's preparation for political battle was not the traditional climb from one elective office to another. Rather, he came up through the ranks of the civil rights movement, working alongside Martin Luther King, Jr., in the Southern Christian Leadership Conference (SCLC) and heading Operation Breadbasket, an organization that attempted to mobilize Chicago's black poor. After King's death, Jackson founded People United to Save (later Serve) Humanity (PUSH). This Chicago-based organization induced major corporations with large markets in the black community to adopt affirmative action programs. PUSH—EXCEL, which focused on education, succeeded in raising students' test scores and was given a large grant by the Carter administration.

In 1983, angered by the effects of Reagan's social welfare and civil rights rollbacks, Jackson and PUSH began a successful drive to register black voters. Jackson's charismatic style engendered enthusiasm, especially as the Democratic party searched for a presidential candidate who could challenge Reagan's popularity.

In November 1983, Jackson declared his candidacy for the Democratic nomination and honed an already highly effective style of grassroots mobilization. He began by appealing to what he would call a "rainbow coalition" of people who felt politically marginalized and underrepresented. The Rainbow Coalition was composed of diverse groups, including black people, white workers, liberals, Latinos, feminists, students, and environmentalists. Jackson developed a comprehensive economic policy focusing on tax reform, deficit reduction, industrial policy, and employment. The centerpiece of his plan was "Rebuilding America," a program to coordinate government, business, and labor in a national industrial policy. The Jackson platform was well within the tradition of American liberal reform, but was nonetheless far more progressive than anything his competitors proposed. In January 1984, Jackson gained credentials in international affairs when he traveled to Syria to plead for the release of United States Air Force pilot Robert Goodman, who had been held captive there for a year after being shot down in Syrian-controlled airspace. Jackson returned to America in triumph with the freed pilot.

Jackson eventually garnered almost one-fourth of the votes cast in the Democratic primaries and caucuses and one-eighth of the delegates to the convention. His speech to the convention cemented his position as a voice for progressive change and a spiritual heir to both Martin Luther King, Jr., and Robert Kennedy. Walter Mondale, Jimmy Carter's vice president, who won the nomination, broke new ground when he made Geraldine Ferraro his running mate and the first woman on a major party's presidential

In 1988, the Reverend Jesse Jackson (1941–) addressed the Democratic National Convention. He made two unsuccessful bids for the White House (1984, 1988) but remained a powerful force in the Democratic party because of his tremendous zeal in registering voters and building coalitions.

ticket. But many Jackson supporters had hoped that Mondale would pick Jackson.

In November 1984, black voters again overwhelmingly favored the Democratic ticket, but Reagan nonetheless won by a landslide with 59 percent of the popular vote. Mondale carried only his home state of Minnesota and the largely black District of Columbia. Clearly, most white Americans backed Reagan's conservative policies. Undeterred by defeat, Jackson worked to build his Rainbow Coalition, reaching out to a variety of constituencies, including the unemployed, militant trade unionists, small farmers, and gay people. He criticized the Democratic party's timid opposition to Reagan. Perhaps most important, he continued to promote voter registration and indeed inspired the registration of enough new voters to affect several races in the 1986 midterm elections. Democrats held onto control of the House and regained a majority in the Senate.

By the time Jackson announced that he would again run for president in October 1987, he had become a serious contender. He won fifteen presidential primaries and caucuses and garnered seven million votes, one-third of all those cast. His Rainbow Coalition, however, never materialized. His victories in the primaries were based on mobilizing his black supporters; almost all his white support tended to come from college towns and the highly educated. Michael Dukakis, governor of Massachusetts, won the 1988 Democratic nomination.

Despite Jesse Jackson's voter registration drive and the hopes of the black community, Reagan's vice president, George Bush, triumphed in the 1988 election. Bush's call for "a kinder, gentler America" was belied by the most memorable feature of his campaign, a polarizing ad that featured Willie Horton, a black convict who had raped a white woman while on furlough from a Massachusetts prison as part of a program approved by Dukakis and his Republican predecessor as governor. Jackson and other black leaders criticized the ad as a blatant appeal to white racism, but Bush would not renounce it.

Policing the Black Community

In March 1991, Los Angeles police pulled Rodney Glen King from his car after a high-speed chase and beat him with nightsticks. A bystander, George Holliday, captured the incident on videotape, which television newscasts broadcast repeatedly, increasing long-simmering anger over police brutality among African Americans in Los Angeles. When a jury of eleven white Americans and one Hispanic American acquitted the four police officers involved in the incident of all but one of the charges brought against them, south-central Los Angeles burst into flames of protest. The verdict highlighted the gulf between the perceptions of white and black Americans about the police and the criminal justice system. Where the mostly white jury had seen the police imposing justice and maintaining law and order, black Americans saw proof of injustice, police repression, and racism. Fifty-two people were killed in the outbreak that followed the verdict. Arsonists and looters devastated much of the community. Thousands of people were injured, four thousand were arrested, and an estimated one-half billion dollars worth of property was damaged or destroyed. The four officers were later retried in federal court on charges of violating King's civil rights. This time juries found two of them guilty and acquitted the other two. Meanwhile, a jury in King's civil suit ordered the city of Los Angeles to pay him $3.8 million in damages.

The Rodney King episode resonated with many black men across the country. Writer Earl Ofari Hutchinson suggested why:

> Black professionals or business owners still tell harrowing tales of being spread-eagle over the hoods of their expensive BMW's or Porsches while the police ran makes on them and tore their cars apart searching for drugs. In polls taken after the Rodney King beating, blacks were virtually unanimous in saying that they believed any black person could have been on the ground that night being pulverized by the police. These were eternal reminders to the "new" black bourgeoisie that they could escape the hood, but many Americans still considered them hoods.

Several such high-profile cases focused public attention on the relation of black communities to white police authorities throughout the 1980s and 1990s. In a sense the issue of police repression, a long-festering cause of tension and hostility that had been behind many of the riots of the 1960s, remained a constant. On November 16, 1992, two Detroit police officers were formally charged with the murder of Malice Green, a 35-year-old resident of the city. In the late 1990s the issue exploded into national consciousness with three cases. In 1997 a Haitian immigrant, Abner Louima, was beaten and sodomized while in custody at a Brooklyn police station. In 1999, New York police shot Amadou Diallo, a West African immigrant, forty-one times when they mistook his reaching for a wallet for going for a gun. A jury in Albany acquitted the four police officials charged in the Diallo killing. Finally, also in 1999, Patric Dorismond (a Haitian

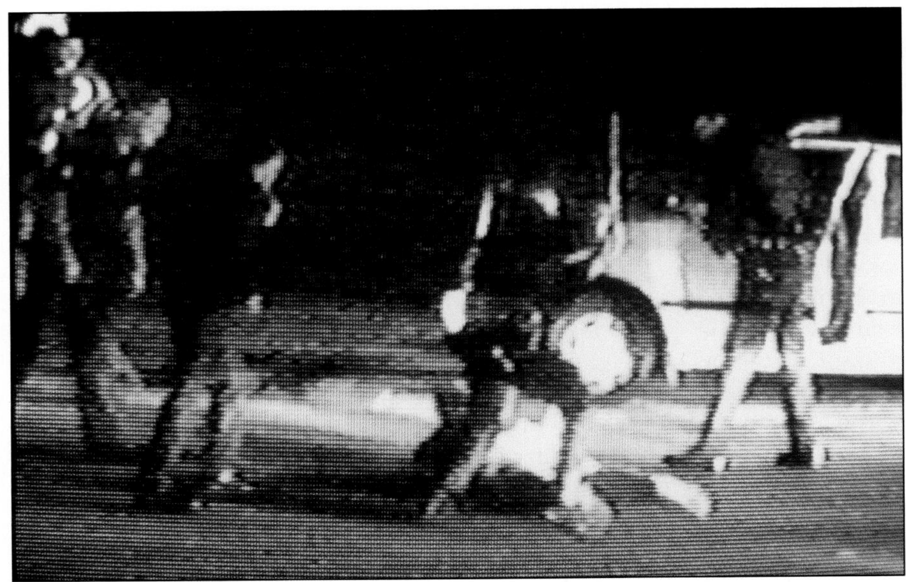

The videotaped beating of Rodney King by Los Angeles police—shown repeatedly on national television—bolstered charges by African Americans in Los Angeles that they were frequent victims of police brutality. Despite the graphic evidence, the officers were acquitted of using excessive force.

immigrant) was shot and killed after he refused to purchase drugs from, and got into an argument with, a team of undercover antinarcotic police officers. In each instance an enraged black community protested the police profiling as one more instance of biases towards black men and one that targeted other minorities for illegal detention.

Human Rights in America

In October 1998, the human rights group Amnesty International, known for its condemnation of human rights abuse in countries with repressive governments, published a report on police brutality in the United States. The report covered the actions of local and state police, the Federal Bureau of Investigation, the Immigration and Naturalization Service, and the prison system. Its contents came as no surprise to most black Americans or, indeed, to anyone who lived in America's poor, urban neighborhoods. The report detailed violations of the United Nations Code of Conduct for Law Enforcement Officials and the United Nations Basic Principles on the Use of Force and Firearms. Among the violations reported were the following:

- the shooting of unarmed suspects fleeing a minor crime scene
- excessive force used on mentally ill or disturbed people
- multiple shootings of a suspect, sometimes after the suspect was apprehended or disabled
- the beating of unresisting suspects
- the misuse of batons, chemical sprays, and electroshock weapons

These violations all involved the misuse of force during arrests, traffic stops, searches, and so forth. This was by far the greatest area of concern. The report also cited sexual abuse of prisoners and the denial of food and water to them. One of the most important points in the Amnesty International report was that most victims of American law enforcement abuse were members of racial and ethnic minorities, while most police officers were white.

It is far too easy to interpret these findings as showing that American police officers, as a group, are racists who purposefully use their authority to oppress people they don't like. In fact, the issue of police brutality is not nearly so simple. Police officers are under tremendous pressure and live dangerous lives, in part because of the wide availability of guns in American society. No one can be expected to have perfect judgment about using force, and the cumulative effect of years of dealing with violence can destroy a person's sense of perspective and moral equilibrium.

Neither is the problem of crime by black Americans a simple one. The level of crime in black communities is extremely high. The murder rate, for example, for African Americans in 1997 was seven times that of whites, and black victims accounted for 49 percent of all those murdered, even though African Americans make up only 12 percent of the population. Over 90 percent of those who murder, rape, and assault black people are black people themselves. The murder rate for young black men between the ages of fourteen and seventeen tripled between 1976 and 1993. Although this rate, like the rate of violent crime in the country in general, fell in the 1990s, the security of many African Americans remains imperiled.

Crime has devastated black neighborhoods. High crime rates raise the costs of business, driving jobs and investment dollars out of those areas most in need of them. Fear of violence leads many in the inner cities to barricade themselves inside their homes. The result has been a transformation of once vibrant neighborhoods into virtual ghost towns where the silence of the streets is punctuated only by the sound of gunfire. Filmmaker Spike Lee was shocked when he returned to the Brooklyn neighborhood in which he had grown up to shoot his film *Crooklyn*. He found that the streets had become so unsafe that the local children he used as extras had to be taught how to play the games he had played growing up in the 1970s because they had never been allowed to play outside. "Nowadays," Lee reflected after completing the film in 1994, "these kids, they'll shoot you dead in a second and not even think about it. The two big problems are crack and how accessible guns are. And also, you're talking about what Reagan did during his eight years. If I was a parent, I'd be terrified anytime my children left my sight. When I was growing up, I just had to be home by dark." Even Rosa Parks, heroine of the civil rights movement, has not been immune to the urban crime wave. In 1994 she was beaten and robbed in her Detroit home by a twenty-eight-year-old unemployed black man. Her assailant recognized Parks, but assaulted her anyway.

Being disproportionately the victims of crime, most African Americans have looked to the nation's police departments for aid. Because of their growing political power they have sought, not always successfully, to make the police both responsive to crime and fair in enforcing the laws. One key device for changing the behavior of law enforcement officials has been the appointment of black police chiefs.

Police Director Hubert Williams of Newark

Black mayor Kenneth Gibson appointed Hubert Williams as the police director in Newark, New Jersey, and Williams served from 1974 to 1985. He had earned a law degree from Rutgers University Law School and a master's in public administration from the City University of New York. A native of Georgia, Williams served for twelve years on Newark's police force before his appointment as police director.

Upon assuming command, Williams demoted and transferred several entrenched deputy chiefs and captains. He implemented a 911 system to increase police response to citizens' calls for assistance and placed police decoys on city streets to thwart muggers. Among the many innovations that the reform-minded Williams introduced were police sweeps of high-crime sections, roadblocks to deter drunken drivers, a truancy task force to discourage teenage crime, and police storefronts to foster the image of law enforcement officers as community service workers. Williams also acknowledged that he would use "color-conscious" policies in promoting and assigning officers. He argued that in a city where black people made up more than 50 percent of the population, it was good policy to assign detectives and administrators who reflected the racial composition of specific neighborhoods.

Williams received high marks for his performance, and soon white mayors in other cities also began appointing black officers—like Benjamin Ward in New York City; Lee P. Brown in Houston; William H. Moore in Pittsburgh, Pennsylvania; and Reuben Greenberg in Charleston, South Carolina—to head their police departments. By 1982 there were black police chiefs in fifty American cities, and in the 1990s the number increased to more than 130.

The Election of 1992

During his first campaign for the presidency, the personable, saxophone-playing Democratic party candidate, Arkansas governor Bill Clinton, was welcomed by black Americans into their churches, schools, and homes. They warmly embraced his bid for the presidency against incumbent George Bush, who had done little to win their loyalty, nominating conservatives to the federal courts and attacking civil rights legislation. White Americans, too, were dissatisfied with the Bush presidency. Although he enjoyed high approval ratings in early 1991 following American military success in evicting Iraq from Kuwait in the Gulf War, by early 1992 his ratings had slumped in the face of an economic downturn.

Politically, Clinton was a centrist. Undeterred by charges of womanizing, draft evasion, and marijuana smoking, he sharply attacked Bush's record and promised to make government more responsive. Clinton won in November 1992 with just 43 percent of the popular vote to Bush's 38 percent and third-party candidate H. Ross Perot's 19 percent. However, Clinton garnered 78 percent of the black vote and 39 percent of the white vote in key states including New Jersey,

Michigan, New York, Illinois, and California. The election did not present the Democrats with a clear mandate. While maintaining control of Congress, they gained no seats in the Senate and lost seats in the House. Republicans would use the ambiguous outcome to oppose most of Clinton's economic programs.

During his tumultuous presidency, most black people considered Clinton, despite major disappointments, the best president on race issues since Lyndon Johnson. Writer Toni Morrison called Clinton the first black president, and in some circles he was called the first woman president because of his support for equal rights for all women, both black and white. During the campaign, he visited riot-torn ruins of south-central Los Angeles and played the saxophone on Arsenio Hall's television show. In Clinton, black Americans had a friend. Indeed, he named his black friends to the transition team. Members included highly successful Washington, DC, attorney Vernon Jordan as cochair of the team, and Warren M. Christopher, Barbara Jordan, William Gray, III, and Marian Wright Edelman, founding president of the Children's Defense Fund. Clinton created a cabinet that mirrored the diversity of the American population—in some cases, such as Hazel O'Leary as Secretary of the Department of Energy and Ron Brown as Secretary of Commerce, appointing black people to posts that had nothing to do with race. He appointed many African-American judges, and he was the first American president to visit Africa.

"It's the Economy, Stupid!"

In 1996 Clinton became the first Democratic president to win a second term since Franklin Roosevelt. Throughout his two terms in office, Clinton focused attention on the economy, a strategy that won grudging support from moderate Republicans. His objectives were to strengthen the economy and to make more opportunities available for black Americans and other previously excluded groups. Toward these ends, in a significant departure from the policies of his predecessors, he supported a new tax bill that increased the taxes of higher income Americans. He also advocated expansion of the earned income tax credit to help improve the lives of working-poor and very poor Americans. His college student-aid program made available increased federal loan benefits. The economy boomed during the Clinton presidency, and when he left office in 2001, the country had the lowest poverty rate in 20 years. The Congressional Black Caucus (CBC) provided critical support for his economic programs. In 1993, CBC chairman Representative Kweisi Mfume of Maryland and the highest-ranking black congressman, Representative John Lewis, delivered the caucus vote that saved Clinton's $500 billion economic budget in both the House and Senate. In return, black congressmen gained financial support for inner city neighborhood development, poor families, children, and the elderly. Representative Mfume credited the CBC, for example, for saving the $2.5 billion allocation for food stamps that the Senate phased out and $3.5 billion for empowerment zones in cities and rural areas.

Unemployment plummeted from 7.2 percent when Clinton took office to 5.5 percent in 1995 and continued to decline in ensuing years. American businesses created 10 million new jobs, and many black people who feared they would never gain a foothold

President William Jefferson Clinton seen here with members of the Little Rock Nine who, as teenagers, defied hostile mobs to desegregate Central High School in Little Rock, Arkansas in 1957. African Americans claimed Clinton as being the first black president given his comfort around black people and the number of African Americans he considered to be friends.

in the economy found jobs, some for the first time. Reduced federal spending and the 1993 tax increase helped to cut the annual federal deficit in half. As interest rates fell and the stock market soared, optimistic Americans increased their consumer spending.

Clinton Signs the Welfare Reform Act

Shortly before his reelection, in August 1996, Clinton signed the Personal Responsibility and Work Opportunity Reconciliation Act, a welfare reform bill. This disappointed many African Americans and political progressives in general. The legislation combined Clinton's own ideas with others espoused in the Republicans' "Contract with America" blueprint for conservative changes. The Republicans had used this platform to win control of both houses of Congress in 1994. The main target of the Personal Responsibility Act was Aid to Families of Dependent Children (AFDC), a program created in 1935 as part of the Social Security Act to prevent children from suffering because of the poverty of their parents. Critics claimed that AFDC stipends discouraged poor mothers from finding work, that it was responsible for the breakdown of the family among the nation's poor, and that it did little to reduce poverty. Proponents of the welfare reform bill also insisted that the states did not have enough flexibility in administering welfare. The conservative welfare "reform" measure ended guarantees of federal aid to poor children, turning control of such programs over to the states along with allocations of block grants. The act denied benefits to legal immigrants, called for drastic reductions in food stamp appropriations, and limited families to five years of benefits. The law also required most adult welfare recipients to find employment within two years.

There were good reasons to believe that the welfare reform bill would not accomplish its sponsors' purposes. Most of the people who would be "encouraged to find work" by having their benefits reduced or cut entirely were among the least employable people in the labor force. A study of people terminated from general assistance in Michigan, for example, revealed that as many as two-thirds remained unemployed. As for the bill's effect on families, it is true that most women on welfare had their first children when they were unmarried teenagers, but there is little evidence that cutting welfare will prevent teenage pregnancies, and there is evidence that reforms targeted at improving the collection of child support payments for divorced mothers would reduce welfare costs far more effectively and humanely.

Clinton's support of the welfare act was consistent with his centrist ideology, and it was politically

A resplendent Spike Lee stands at the pinnacle of fame. Admired for his provocative and bold films, often he ignites controversy with his revealing explorations of some of the interior dynamics of black life and culture. Lee's most recent film, "Bamboozle" (2001), is a powerful satire about the minstrel components of modern black television shows.

PROFILE

Spike Lee, a Voice of Protest

Shelton "Spike" Jackson Lee, the son of composer and bassist Bill Lee and schoolteacher Jacqueline Lee, was born March 20, 1957, in Atlanta, Georgia, the eldest of six children.

Spike Lee is the most productive and influential black filmmaker in America today. He completed undergraduate studies at Morehouse College, and in 1982 he earned a degree from New York University Film School. His films appeal to the hip-hop generation because they grapple with many of the same issues that affect their lives, such as police brutality, racism, and a yearning for black empowerment. Between 1986 and 1998, Spike Lee wrote, produced, directed, and starred in more than ten films that examined a variety of controversial subjects: interracial love in *Jungle Fever*; a black woman's sexuality in *She's Gotta Have It*; color discrimination and sexism in the black fraternities in *School Daze*; and the deep fissures of race and class in American society in *Do the Right Thing*. He made a film about Malcolm X's life and documentaries about a cross section of men who attended the Million Man March and the death of four girls in the bombing of the 16th Street Baptist Church, in Birmingham, Alabama, in 1963.

In 1986, *She's Gotta Have It* won critical and commercial success. The film looks at black relationships in the 1980s from the perspective of one woman, Nola Darling. She juggles sexual relations with three black men: a narcissist, a violent middle-class overachiever, and a bicycling homeboy from the neighborhood, played by Lee. About this last character, Lee confided, "For me, Mars [the character] represented black youth, hip-hop, but he doesn't take or sell drugs or rape and mug people, ya know what I'm talkin' 'bout. He's funny." The movie shatters stereotypes—like the conventional wisdom that men shun commitment while women yearn for it—with humor and insight. Shot in approximately twelve days for $175,000, the film signaled the emergence of Lee's prodigious talent. It netted $8.5 million at the box office and won the Prix de Jeunesse Award at the film festival in Cannes, France. About the film, Lee said, "I think it's important young people know that there is no such animal as overnight success. I made that movie asking friends for donations."

Three years later, in 1989, Spike Lee scored another success with *Do the Right Thing*, a compelling look at racial and generational conflict in a Brooklyn neighborhood. The film probes the way some white people are simultaneously attracted to and repelled by black people, worshipping black stars and athletes, for example, while despising poor black people. The film also explores the explosiveness of racial confrontation across class lines. The movie grossed more than $27 million at the box office and earned an Oscar nomination for best screenplay.

Lee's combination of storytelling, cinematographic craft, and social comment has paved the way for a new generation of black filmmakers. "African American cinema, as far as Hollywood's concerned, is in its infancy," according to Lee, and has not produced "any Michael Jordan, Duke Ellington, James Baldwin, [or] Toni Morrison. We will, but it's gonna take time."

astute. His stance on the Welfare Reform Act immunized him from Republican attacks on the issue and had little impact on his support among African Americans. The president easily defeated his Republican opponent, Senator Robert Dole of Kansas, in the election of 1996.

The preliminary results of the new welfare reform strictures indicated that within a couple of years half of those who had taken jobs had returned to lives of unemployment, poverty, and quiet desperation. As the economy took a downturn in the closing months of Clinton's second term, conditions of poor mothers and children deteriorated steadily. The debate over welfare policy receded to the back burner during the 2000 election campaign and disappeared completely after George W. Bush took office, superseded by the emphasis on tax cuts for the wealthy.

African-American Cultural and Intellectual Movements at the End of the Millennium

The most positive developments for black Americans during the 1980s and 1990s came in the realm of culture. Beginning in the 1980s, a cultural renaissance emerged in every American community with a substantial African-American presence. Black consciousness institutions proliferated and flourished. They included black history and culture museums, festivals, expositions, publishing houses, bookstores and boutiques, concerts, theaters, and dance troupes. In 1996, *Publishers Weekly* reported that bookstores specializing in African-American books had increased from a dozen a few years earlier to more than two hundred. By 1994, there were seventy-five African-American publishing companies. In 1998 the National Literary Hall of Fame for Writers of African Descent opened at Chicago State University.

Black painters used outdoor murals to celebrate and cultivate positive images of the black experience. Playwrights such as August Wilson, Charles Fuller, and George C. Wolfe helped revitalize American theater, and the musician Prince's film *Purple Rain* (1984) broke new ground in African-American rock cinematography. Wilson won two Pulitzer prizes for his plays—*Fences* in 1987 and *The Piano Lesson* in 1990. In 1987 PBS aired Henry Hampton's "Eyes on the Prize," a six-part documentary on the civil rights movement. Spike Lee changed the status of black filmmakers in Hollywood with films such as *Do the Right Thing* and *Malcolm X.* Wynton Marsalis became a leading figure in American jazz. The Rodney King case inspired two important works: a symphony entitled *56 Blows,* by Alvin Singleton, and a one-woman docudrama entitled "Twilight: Los Angeles, 1992," by Anna Deavere Smith.

The new cultural renaissance differed from the black arts movement of the 1960s and 1970s. The contemporary fluorescence was more inclusive and more appreciative of women artists. It also included the work of openly gay and lesbian artists, such as documentary filmmaker Marlon Riggs, dance choreographer Bill T. Jones, and novelist E. Lynn Harris. Whereas poets and dramatists dominated the earlier movement, novelists—particularly women—hold sway in the new cultural renaissance. And much of the new work appeals to white as much as to black audiences, providing new insights into the lives of people of African heritage in a predominantly European society.

There were signs of this new trend as early as 1977, when Toni Morrison's *Song of Solomon* became a Book-of-the-Month Club selection, the first by a black author since Richard Wright's *Native Son* in 1940. Then Barbara Chase-Riboud made waves with *Sally Hemings* (1979), a fictional treatment of a woman who was both slave to and mistress of President Thomas Jefferson. In 1980, Toni Cade Bambara won the American Book Award for *The Salt Eaters.* At least as significant as these individual books was the founding in 1981 of a new publishing house, Kitchen Table: Women of Color Press. Then, in 1982, Alice Walker won the Pulitzer prize and the American Book Award for *The Color Purple,* which was later made into a movie by director Steven Spielberg, with Whoopi Goldberg in the starring role. In 1987, poet Rita Dove won the Pulitzer prize for poetry. In 1993 she became America's poet laureate, and in the same year Toni Morrison became the first African American to win the Nobel prize for literature. President Bill Clinton invited Maya Angelou to read one of her poems during his first inauguration ceremony in 1993.

Critics were not the only ones to take an interest in these works. In 1992 novels by three African-American women—Morrison, Walker, and Terry McMillan—made the *New York Times* best-seller list at the same time. This literary flowering reflected a new point of view that Alice Walker labeled "womanism" and others called black feminism. In 2001 the works of four African Americans made the *Times* best-seller list and revealed the expanding readership and growing appreciation of black literature across the racial spectrum. Publishers recognized and capitalized on the appeal of black novelists and the work of spiritual and personal development writers such as Iyanla Vanzant, who advised her readers to "value your ideas, your energy and your time. Value what you feel. Value yourself enough not to put yourself into situations or in the company of people who openly devalue you. Fill your mind with information you value and that will make you more valuable to yourself and to the world. When you set the standards of your own value, others will treat you accordingly." Throughout the late 1990s and into the early twenty-first century, black writers and entrepreneurs organized and attended black expos in Chicago, New York, Cincinnati, and Indianapolis, and conventions in Atlanta and Durham, North Carolina; a series of conferences targeted for specific segments of the black population and others focused on race attracted international audiences. Black writers were widely publicized, and some established themselves first by publishing their own work.

Black Feminism

The woman's rights movement first blossomed in the 1970s in the wake of the civil rights struggles and the antiwar protests of the 1960s. The National Organization for Women (NOW), founded in 1966, spearheaded efforts to end job discrimination against women, to legalize abortion, and to secure federal and state support for child care. One of the movement's early successes was Title IX of the Educational Amendments Act of 1972, which required colleges and universities to take affirmative action to ensure equal opportunity for women. Another was the Supreme Court's decision in *Roe v. Wade* legalizing abortion.

Modern feminism at first seemed to hold little appeal for most black women, yet affected them nonetheless. But later in the 1970s, many black women writers and activists, disillusioned with the attitudes of their male counterparts in the civil rights, black power, and black arts movements, sought to make the struggle against sexism as important as the struggle against racism. Between 1973 and 1975 the National Black Feminist Organization articulated many of the concerns specific to black women, from anger with black men for dating and marrying white women, to internal conflict over skin color, hair texture, and facial features, to the differences between the mobility of white and black women. Black feminists also attacked the myth of the black matriarchy and stereotypical portrayals of black women in popular culture, like the television show called "That's My Mama," featuring an overweight black woman as a domineering mother. Although the organization was short lived, it did break the silence imposed on black women by black liberation movements and on misogyny within black communities. Black feminists helped others to talk openly about domestic violence, rape, and sexual harassment in employment.

Black feminists started journals such as *SAGE* and organizations such as the Association of Black Women Historians, founded by Rosalyn Terborg-Penn and Eleanor Smith. Gradually, their scholarly, literary, historical, and polemical works found readers in the general public and a place in women's studies curricula. The work of visual artists like Faith Ringgold appeared in museums and community centers. As more black women enrolled in college, courses with titles like "Black Women Writers" and "Black Women's History" became part of college black studies curricula. By the early 1990s there were more black women in higher education, graduate, and professional degree programs than there were black men.

Within academia, the field of black women's history has grown rapidly: scholarly monographs, reference works, anthologies, conferences, and exhibitions have been produced, all devoted to the contribution black women have made to the political struggles and artistic accomplishments of African Americans. These historians have productively explored the role of race, class, and gender in the oppression of marginalized people in American society.

Black Intellectuals

An important part of the recent black cultural renaissance has been the rise to national prominence of black public intellectuals. These individuals go beyond their roles as scholars to participate in public debate and discourse about major issues.

In the past, most public intellectuals were white males. Among the few exceptions were the formidable W. E. B. Du Bois and novelists Richard Wright, James Baldwin, and Ralph Ellison. Within the past two decades, however, many of the most prominent public intellectuals to emerge have been African Americans. Among them are Cornel West, Henry Louis Gates, Jr., William Julius Wilson, Michele Wallace, Ishmael Reed, Stanley Crouch, Charles Johnson, Patricia Williams, John Edgar Wideman, Manning Marable, Robin D. G. Kelley, Michael Eric Dyson, Nell Irvin Painter, and bell hooks. Their views range from Marxist to extreme conservative, but they all desire to redefine black identity in this country and to explore how race is involved in its social and political workings. Historian Kelley put it well when he declared, "Culture and questions of identity have been at the heart of some of the most intense battles facing African Americans at the end of the century. . . . Not only has globalization continued to transform black culture, but it has also dramatically changed the nature of work, employment opportunities, class structure, public space, the cultural marketplace, the criminal justice system, political strategies, [and] even intellectual work." The emergence of these figures and the acclaim accorded them mark the end of America's long refusal to acknowledge the intellectual accomplishments of African Americans. In 1991 Henry Louis Gates assumed the leadership of both the Afro-American Studies Department and the W. E. B. Du Bois Institute at Harvard University. He lured philosopher Cornel West from Princeton and sociologist William Julius Wilson from the University of Chicago to create one of the strongest black studies departments in the country.

Afrocentricity

In the 1980s and 1990s a philosophy of culture referred to as "Afrocentricity" or "Afrocentrism" captured widespread media and academic attention. Although the philosophy and practice of Afrocentricity had been a prominent feature of black studies courses for more than a decade, the emergence of Temple University professor Molefi Kete Asante gave it a presence and a personality. In 1980 Asante published *Afrocentricity*, in which he argued that an African-centered perspective was needed to challenge

Artist Faith Ringgold (1934–) in *Tar Beach* (1988) uses quilts to explore critical cultural themes like family, leisure, love, creativity. Her quilts are reminiscent of Harriet Power's *Bible* quilts and as such make powerful use of a traditional woman's art form.

the dominance of Eurocentric values in education. Other leading Afrocentrists include Asa Hillard and John Henrik Clarke.

Many black educators enthusiastically embraced Afrocentricity as a way to celebrate and reclaim a positive African identity and to find unity with other peoples of the African diaspora. Afrocentrists rejected the idea of America as a melting pot. Assimilation, they argued, meant a rejection of their African cultural heritage. At the heart of this position is a strong indictment of American ideals and institutions for their complicity in the long oppression of black people.

Afrocentrists vigorously defended their perspective. Asante explained to his critics, "Afrocentricity is a terribly maligned concept. Afrocentricity is the idea that African people and interests must be viewed as actors and agents in human history, rather than as marginal to the European historical experience—which has been institutionalized as universal." Similarly, Tsehloane Keto declared that black scholars had to challenge the Eurocentric paradigm that "interpret[ed] the roles of African Americans through the invisible person model, the Ghetto model, the spook who sat by the door model, and the Sambo model." Black historians and social scientists, Afrocentrists argued, had to place Africa and its descendants at the center of their studies to increase appreciation of the contributions of black people in world history.

Many black people, however, vehemently rejected Afrocentricity, insisting that it was regressive and would foster self-segregation. Writer Earl Ofari Hutchinson conceded that Asante's idea merited attention while expressing skepticism about the claims of some Afrocentrist academics: "In their zeal to counter the heavy handed 'Eurocentric' imbalance of history, some have crossed the line between historic fact and fantasy. They've constructed groundless theories in which Europeans are 'Ice People,' suffer 'genetic defects,' or are obsessed with 'color phobias.' They've replaced the shallow European 'great man' theory of history with a feel good interpretation of history." White writers, notably historian Arthur Schlesinger, Jr., in *The Disuniting of America*, weighed in with blistering attacks. White and black critics alike cautioned that the Afrocentrist desire to fabricate "a glorious past" for black people did a disservice to the truth. Harvard University philosophy professor Cornel West assessed both the positive and negative value of Afrocentrism in 1993:

> Afrocentrism, a contemporary species of black nationalism, is a gallant yet misguided attempt to define an African identity in a white society perceived to be hostile. It is gallant because it puts black doings and sufferings, not white anxieties and fears, at the center of discussion. It is misguided because—out of fear of cultural hybridization and through silence on the issue of class, retrograde views on black women, gay men, and lesbians, and a reluctance to link race to the common good—it reinforces the narrow discussions about race.

Louis Farrakhan and the Nation of Islam

Beginning in the 1980s, the Nation of Islam's Minister Louis Farrakhan became a potent source of racial division in the nation. Farrakhan was the younger of two sons of immigrant parents from the West Indies. He became known as Minister Louis X when he assumed leadership of the Boston Temple of the Nation of Islam. As a young man, Farrakhan attended a black teachers' college in Winston-Salem, North Carolina, but dropped out to become a Calypso singer known as the Charmer. In 1955, while performing in Chicago, he heard Elijah Muhammad preach at the Nation of Islam's mosque. This marked a turning point in his life. Farrakhan joined the Nation and quickly ascended within its hierarchy in the wake of Malcolm X's rupture with Elijah Muhammad and subsequent murder in February 1965. Farrakhan became minister of the Harlem Mosque No. 7 and Muhammad's national representative. When Elijah Muhammad died in 1975, he designated his son, Wallace Deen Muhammad, or Warith, as he renamed himself, to be his successor. Warith sought to distance the Nation of Islam from the more far-fetched teachings of his father and to bring it more in line with actual Islamic teachings. He renamed the group the World Community of al-Islam in the West (WCIW) and in 1985 changed it again to the American Muslim Mission (AMM), after which it disbanded.

Farrakhan opposed Warith's decisions and within three years of Elijah Muhammad's death established himself as the leader of the Nation of Islam. In 1982 he purchased a building to publish a newspaper, *The Final Call*, and in 1985 he bought and moved into Muhammad's mansion in Chicago. Under Farrakhan's direction, and with $5 million in start-up capital from the Libyan dictator Colonel Muammar Qaddafi and subsequent federal government contracts, the Nation developed a number of economic enterprises, including media ventures, restaurants, clothing stores, and companies to provide security for apartment buildings, distribute soap and cosmetics, and manufacture pharmaceuticals. Farrakhan recruited among poor and marginalized urban African Americans and within the black prison population. The conservatism of the Reagan era complemented the reconstituted Nation's conservative social ideals, which harked back to those advanced by Booker T. Washington at the turn of the century. Farrakhan downplayed the struggle for civic and political rights. In 1985 he declared:

> God wants us to build a new world order: A new world order based on peace, justice and equality. Where do we start? . . . Physical separation is greatly feared [by whites], and it is not now desired by the masses of black people, but America is not willing to give us eight or ten states, or even one state. Let's be reasonable. . . . What we propose tonight is a solution that is in between two extremes. If we cannot go back to Africa, and America will not give us a separate territory, then what can we do here and now to redress our own grievances? . . . We propose that we use the blessings that we have received from our sojourn in America to do for ourselves what we have been asking the whites in this nation to do for us.

Until 1984, most Americans were barely aware of Farrakhan's existence. In that year, however, he broke the Nation of Islam's long-standing tradition of abstaining from politics to support Jesse Jackson's bid for the Democratic presidential nomination and soon ignited a firestorm of controversy. When some Jews took offense at Jackson's off-the-record reference to New York as "Hymietown" during a conversation with two African-American reporters, Farrakhan, whose Fruit of Islam provided security for Jackson's campaign, rose to his defense and made matters worse. On the February 24, 1984, "CBS Evening News," Farrakhan warned, "I say to the Jewish people, who may not like our brother: It is not Jesse Jackson you are attacking. . . . When you attack him, you are attacking the millions who are lining up with him. You're attacking all of us. . . . Why dislike us? Why attack our champion? Why hurl stones at him? It's our champion. If you harm this brother, what do you think we should do about it?"

In 1984, as in the past, Farrakhan's verbal assaults against Jews, whom he called a principal enemy of African Americans, attracted support from ultra-right-wing, anti-Semitic forces and condemnation from Jewish Americans and the Anti-Defamation League. Dredging up anti-Semitic shibboleths reminiscent of Hitler's Germany, Farrakhan blamed Jews for many of the ills plaguing African Americans. Jewish Americans, many of whom had been among the principal allies of African Americans during the civil rights movement, called on African-American organizations and leaders to repudiate Farrakhan and his rhetoric of "Jewish domination and control."

Several hundred thousand black men gathered in Washington, DC, on October 16, 1995, for the Million Man March. The event was conceived by Louis Farrakhan, the charismatic, but controversial, leader of the Nation of Islam.

The Million Man March

A major event during Farrakhan's tenure at the helm of the Nation of Islam was the Million Man March in Washington, DC, on October 16, 1995. Farrakhan called this a "Holy Day of Atonement and Reconciliation," to "reconcile our spiritual inner beings and to redirect our focus to developing our communities, strengthening our families, working to uphold and protect our civil and human rights, and empowering ourselves through the Spirit of God, more effective use of our dollars, and through the power of the vote."

While the Million Man March had its detractors, and the actual number of men who attended it were in dispute, it was a symbolic success and generated positive coverage even in the mainstream media. It inspired many black men to become more engaged with their communities and to speak out more forcefully against oppression. On this occasion, the Nation's conservative philosophy of religion, self-respect, family values, community responsibility, and "bootstrap capitalism" found a responsive audience.

Yet the goodwill dissipated when, three months after the march, Farrakhan embarked on a World Friendship Tour to some twenty countries in Africa and the Middle East. To the consternation of many, he met with the leader of the brutally repressive military regime in Nigeria, General Sani Abacha. At home, Farrakhan's intemperate rhetoric continued to attract attention. In the wake of the Million Man March, he failed to forge a coherent strategy to resolve African America's continuing social problems.

Several black intellectuals have made known their objection to or displeasure with Farrakhan, none more effectively than political scientist Adolph Reed. According to Reed, Farrakhan "weds a radical oppositional style to a program that proposes private and individual responses to social problems; he endorses moral repressiveness; he asserts racial essentialism; he affirms male authority; and he lauds bootstrap capitalism. . . . His focus on self-help and moral revitalization is profoundly reactionary and meshes perfectly with the victim-blaming orthodoxy of the Reagan/Bush era."

The Million Woman March

The success of the Million Man March inspired black women, and later black youths, to organize similar demonstrations. Initiated by two Philadelphia women—Phile Chionesu, a small-business owner, and Asia Coney, a public housing activist—on October 25, 1997, well over half a million black women gathered in Philadelphia to listen to speeches by California congresswoman and president of the Congressional Black Caucus Maxine Waters, rapper Sister Souljah, and South African activist Winnie Mandela. The march was a celebration, a call to unity, and a forum for black women to speak out against domestic violence, inadequate access to quality health care and educational opportunities, and the proliferation of drugs and violence in their communities. The march did not garner nearly as much media attention as had the Million Man March, perhaps because its organizers were relatively unknown. The march nonetheless symbolized the ongoing struggle of black women to be seen and heard in American society and to counter negative stereotypes and derogatory images of black womanhood. The 2000 census reported that women owned 38 percent of African American-owned businesses, a larger percentage than that of any other minority group and more than the nation's business community as a whole, of which women owned only 26 percent. Still, the census reveals that minority firms account for only 15 percent of all businesses in the nation.

Black Christianity on the Front Lines

By the 1990s, black Baptists constituted the fourth-largest U.S. religious group, with 8.7 million members. The numbers of black Roman Catholics grew to nine percent of that denomination. Likewise, the large numbers of Caribbean immigrants increased the numbers of black Episcopalians to ten percent of that church's 2.4 million members. Throughout the closing decade of the twentieth century, black people made significant strides in many denominations. George A. Stallings was consecrated a bishop of the American Roman Catholic Church in 1991, and two years later Pope John Paul II apologized for the Catholic Church's support of slavery. In 1990, in an address at the Riverside Church in New York City, Nelson Mandela thanked American churches for their support during South Africa's struggle against apartheid.

In the 214-year history of the African Methodist Episcopal Church, no woman had ever been appointed a bishop. But in July 2000, Vashti Murphy McKenzie broke the barrier when she was named bishop of the 18th Episcopal District in Southeast Africa (composed of approximately 200 churches and 10,000 members in Lesotho, Botswana, Swaziland, and Mozambique). Her

With the support of the Delta Sigma sorority, family, and the Baltimore, Maryland church community, Vashti Murphy McKenzie broke through "the stained-glass ceiling" (her words) to become the first woman to be appointed a Bishop in the history of the A.M.E. Church. She is a graduate of the University of Maryland, and earned a Master of Divinity from Harvard University's Divinity School and a doctorate in ministry at the United Theological Seminary in Dayton, Ohio.

four-year appointment followed a successful ten-year stint as a pastor of Baltimore, Maryland's Payne Memorial Church, during which time she increased the membership from 300 to more than 1,700. Upon assuming her post, Bishop McKenzie declared, "One of the things we're looking to do is to respond to the numbers of children who are being abandoned [because] of AIDS. . . ." She pledged to concentrate on programs for grass-root economic development, construction of schools, and expanded health care delivery.

Faced with the problems of the black community in the United States and with a changing population, African-American Christians in both traditional and nontraditional religious institutions developed outreach programs to create supportive communities for the embattled and vulnerable. An example of a modern religious reformer is the Reverend Eugene Rivers, founder, along with like-minded former students at Harvard University of the small Azusa Christian Community in a crime-plagued neighborhood in Boston. An evangelical Christian, Rivers believes that "the church is the last best hope that black people have." He turned a former crack house into a Christian settlement named Ella J. Baker House. Its primary goal, Rivers says, is to keep children from killing one another. He and fellow black clergy formed the 10-Point Coalition and entered into a partnership with the police. The collaboration helped eliminate juvenile murders for two-and-a-half years. Rivers advocates a pragmatic black nationalism aimed at developing a rich, viable black civil society centered on the church.

The Hip-Hop Nation

TRACK 43

Just as black feminists used the novel and black arts nationalists used poetry, a younger generation of African Americans, collectively known as the hip-hop nation, uses rap music to express its concerns. Rap is a form of rhythmic speaking in rhyme; "hip-hop" refers to the backup music for rap, which is often composed of a collage of excerpts, or "samples," from other songs. "Hip-hop" also refers to the culture of rap.

The first rap hit, "Rapper's Delight" by the Sugar Hill Gang, came out in 1979; it popularized the term "hip-hop." Rap's first superstars were Grandmaster Flash and the Furious Five. In the group's album, "The Adventures of Grandmaster Flash on the Wheels of Steel" (1981), Flash used the disk jockey technique of "scratching"—moving a record back and forth underneath a needle to produce a rhythmic, jarring sound. Flash is also credited with an innovative technique that involved hooking two turntables to the same set of speakers and manipulating different records on the turntables, switching quickly from one to the other to create a third, original composition.

N.W.A., a California group, created "gangsta rap" with their 1989 release of "Straight Outta Compton." In 1991, rapper Ice-T costarred in a box-office smash film, *New Jack City*. This film, along with *Boyz N the Hood* and *Menace II Society*, ushered in a new genre of black urban films that depicted the violence and alienation of many inner-city youths.

Rap draws inspiration from earlier black musical forms—rhythm and blues, soul, jazz, and gospel. Its rhythmic commentary on life in America's black communities draws on earlier black poets and messages of past and present political activists such as Martin Luther King, Jr., Malcolm X, and Lewis Farrakhan. Rap lyrics call attention to the dangers of drug use, AIDS, teenage pregnancy, and dropping out of school. As Grandmaster Flash and the Furious Five's lead vocalist Melle Mel rapped, "It's like a jungle sometimes, it makes me wonder, how I keep from going under."

When it first appeared, critics called rap music a fad. They were wrong: After two decades, in February 1999, *Time Magazine* signaled the coming of age of this genre of black music with an eleven-page cover story featuring the most celebrated rap performers and producers of the past twenty years. Hip-hop performer Lauryn Hill, twenty-three years old and nominated for an unprecedented ten Grammy Awards in 1999 (she won five), graced the cover of the issue.

Rap lyrics, the rap lifestyle, and rap artists have all aroused the consternation of older African Americans. The post–civil rights, black power, and black feminist elders have criticized rappers for their offensive, misogynist language, gang warfare, and violence against women. In 1995, for example, Black Women for Political Action pressured Time Warner to sell its rap label. The white media pilloried Ice-T for his antipolice lyrics.

2000 and Beyond

Within the American electorate, the election of 2000 revealed fault lines of culture, geography, race, class, and gender. A gender gap of about 11 percent reflected the fact that men strongly supported Republican, and women favored Democratic, candidates. The middle of the country and the South voted for Republican Texas Governor George W. Bush, while

Democratic candidate Vice President Albert Gore, Jr. carried the states of the Upper Midwest (Iowa, Minnesota, Wisconsin, Illinois, and Michigan), the Northeast, and the Pacific Coast. Gays and Lesbians voted 70 percent for Gore, while those who identified themselves as conservative Christians voted 80 percent for Bush. The campaign focused largely on economic issues—Social Security, taxes, health care (HMO reform and a prescription-drug benefit for seniors), and education.

Black community leaders and organizations worked hard to register voters and to increase turnout for the 2000 election. The NAACP, for example, spent $9 million dollars on Operation Big Vote. Its organizers even registered more than 11,000 prisoners in county jails in the South.

Although Gore did not effectively address the many concerns of black voters, especially those concerns connected to the criminal justice system, racial profiling by police, and the great disparities in sentencing for drug-related offenses, African Americans gave him ninety percent of their votes. Their support was not enough to ensure victory, however. In a hotly contested election, the outcome finally hung on one state: Florida. In the end, the U.S. Supreme Court, in a 5-to-4 ruling [*Bush v. Gore*, 121 S.Ct. 525 (2000)] decided the issue by halting the recount of ballots in Florida. The Court's majority based its ruling on the Fourteenth Amendment's prohibition of states denying citizens equal protection of the law. The Court insisted that the recount had to be stopped because the Florida Supreme Court, which had authorized it, had failed to provide uniform standards for determining the intent of the voters.

African Americans reported serious discrimination and interference with their voting in Florida. A group of political leaders in Jacksonville, Florida, filed a lawsuit claiming that many of their votes were thrown out as "undervotes" or "overvotes," especially in four city council districts with the highest concentration of African Americans in the state. According to the lawsuit, 26,000 ballots were not counted in Duval County, and more than 9,000 of those were cast in largely African-American precincts where Gore had captured more than 90 percent of the vote. Indeed, the U.S. Civil Rights Commission found that tens of thousands of African Americans were disfranchised in Florida. In a draft report, it declared, "African American voting districts were disproportionately hindered by antiquated and error-prone equipment like the punch card ballot system." This meant that more black and low-income voters, who tended to vote Democratic, had their ballots invalidated.

The Chair of the Commission, Mary Frances Berry, wrote in an essay in *The Journal of American History* (Vol. 88, no. 2, September 2001), "The United States Supreme Court helped undermine the pursuit of equal opportunity by African Americans for most of our history. . . . *Bush v. Gore* was so striking, in part, because the 5–4 majority has been assiduous about deference to state courts and states' rights in general. What the Court has done is to remind us that judges have social and political views that are reflected in their decisions. Each side has used the equal protection clause of the Fourteenth Amendment to convey its policy preferences. But, unlike the majority, in cases involving African American voting and the outcome of the 2000 election, the justices in dissent have remained consistent."

The 2000 Census and Black America

The 2000 United States census counted 281,421,906 Americans, a 13.2 percent increase from 1990. The numbers recorded the greatest diversity in the nation's history within the population. The census data revealed that the populations of southern and western states had grown significantly. Texas surpassed New York to become the second-most-populous state, following California. One of the most important changes in the 2000 census form was the listing of six racial categories instead of the usual two. Each citizen could thus choose any combination of two or more races, a mind-numbing selection of sixty-three possible racial classifications. Approximately 6.8 million people, 2.4 percent of the total population of the United States, identified themselves as belonging to more than one race. For the first time in U.S. history, African Americans were no longer the largest minority group: According to the 2000 census the nation's population consists of 35.3 million Hispanics, 34.7 million African Americans, and 1.8 million Americans who consider themselves to be a mixture of black and some other race, such as American Indian, Asian, Pacific Islander, or white.

Reparations

In 1969 James Foreman, in his "Black Manifesto," called on America's churches and synagogues to collect $500 million as "a beginning of the reparations due us as a people who have been exploited and degraded, brutalized, killed, and persecuted." While Foreman's call was widely publicized, churches made no serious effort to respond to his demand. Four years later, Boris

Timeline

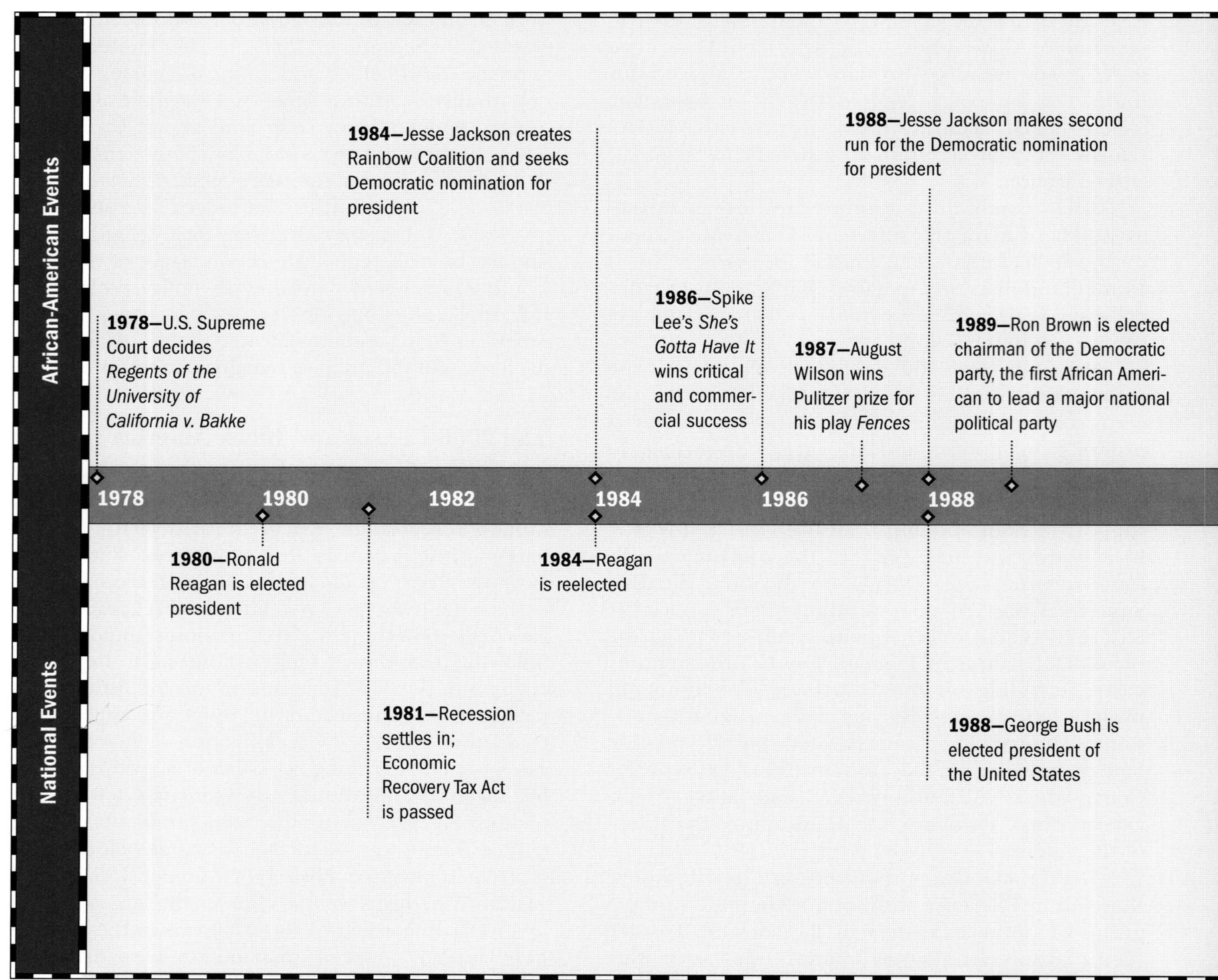

Bittker, a Yale Law School professor, raised the issue again and argued in *The Case for Black Reparations* that slavery and the persistence of government-sanctioned racial discrimination justified the creation of a program to provide compensation to black Americans. Since 1993, John Conyers, a black Democratic congressman from Detroit, has introduced a bill in every session of congress—not to pay reparations, but to establish a federal commission to investigate slavery and the legacy of racial discrimination. The bill has never come to the floor of the House of Representatives for a vote.

In 2000, the issue of reparations for slavery was resurrected and finally received widespread attention when Randall Robinson, founder and president of TransAfrica and a graduate of Virginia Union University and the Harvard Law School published *The Debt: What America Owes to Blacks.* Robinson reasoned that since Jews and Japanese-Americans have been compensated for the indignities and horrors that they experienced in World War II, African Americans were also due financial indemnification for slavery, for "246 years of an enterprise murderous

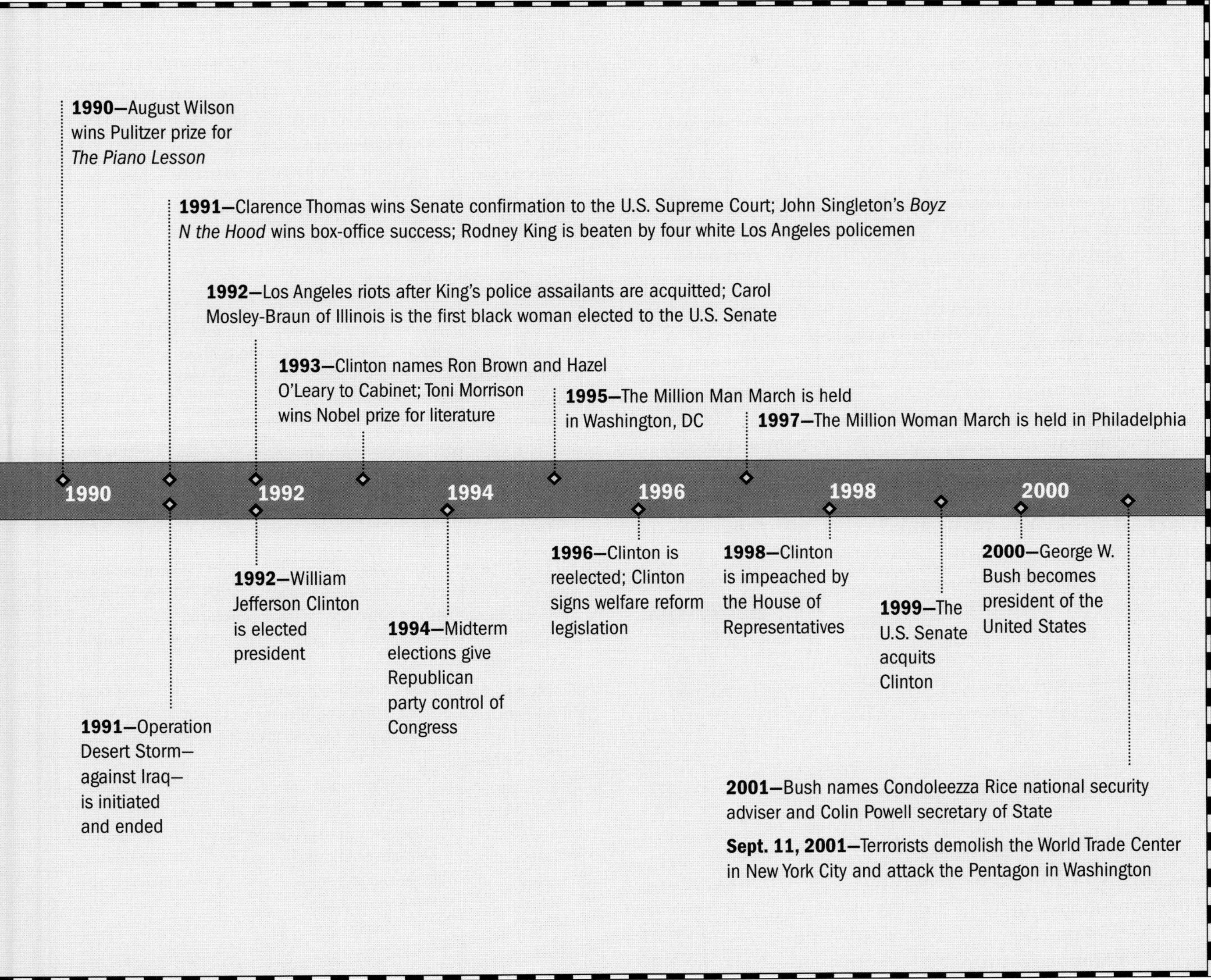

both of a people and their culture." Robinson maintained that many African Americans still bear the scars of slavery in terms of poor housing, inadequate health care, and insufficient educational opportunities. He insists that reparations would remedy the effect of such inequalities.

Some black writers and journalists adamantly reject arguments that reparations are a realistic resolution of the nation's slave and racist legacy. Two black journalists, William Raspberry and Juan Williams, object to the very idea of reparations. Instead, Raspberry favors a greater investment in education for African Americans, "not because of debts owed to or incurred by our ancestors, but because America needs its citizens to be educated and productive." Williams declared that "The suffering of long-dead ancestors is not a claim check for a bag full of cash. I don't want any money that belongs to any slave. That is obscene. The struggle of African-Americans for civil rights is not about selling out for a check."

September 11, 2001

Americans of virtually every racial, religious, and ethnic background were stunned and saddened on a Tuesday morning in September, 2001, when four commercial airliners were commandeered by terrorists and crashed into New York's World Trade Center, the Pentagon in Washington, and rural Pennsylvania. Several hundred African Americans perished among the 3,000 people who died that day.

Leonard Pitts, Jr., a black syndicated columnist for the *Miami Herald*, captured the feelings of many Americans when he wrote a rousing defense of the United States and its people against an unknown adversary. "Did you want to tear us apart?" he asked. "You just brought us together. Let me tell you about my people. We are a vast and quarrelsome family, a family rent by racial, cultural, political and class division, but a family nonetheless. We're frivolous, yes, capable of expending tremendous emotional energy on pop cultural minutiae, a singer's revealing dress, a ball team's misfortune, a cartoon mouse. . . . Some people—you, perhaps—think that any or all of this makes us weak. You're mistaken. We are not weak. Indeed, we are strong in ways that cannot be measured by arsenals."

If the debate over reparations dramatized the separate pasts that black and white Americans have experienced, then the tragedy of September 11, 2001, served to remind Americans of every background of the bond and the history that we all share.

Conclusion

New forms of music, art, literature, dance, and film reflect the divisions and the strengths of contemporary black America. Without a unifying movement, various black constituencies developed their own strategies to secure the resources to advance their interests. Black women organized feminist groups, welfare mothers joined welfare rights organizations, black professionals created caucuses and networked, students fought for the institutionalization of black studies programs at colleges and universities, and artists founded museums and publishing concerns and launched aesthetic movements. Meanwhile, politicians forged national caucuses and local associations. Writers produced trenchant commentaries about black life in America and penned memoirs and autobiographies that placed their private pains in the collective consciousness of the nation. Black gays and lesbians focused attention on their struggle to eradicate homophobia.

Jesse Jackson, whose Rainbow Coalition of the 1980s reflected this creative fragmentation, a quest for unity amidst diversity, asked at the 1988 Democratic convention, "Shall we expand, be inclusive, find unity and power; or suffer division and impotence?" His question remains unanswered as the black odyssey toward freedom and the transformation of American society continues into the next millennium.

Recommended Reading

Cathy J. Cohen. *The Boundaries of Blackness: AIDS and the Breakdown of Black Politics.* Chicago: University of Chicago Press, 1999. A black political scientist provides a sophisticated and provocative exploration into the social, political, and cultural impact of the AIDS epidemic on the African-American community.

Patricia Hill Collins. *Black Feminist Thought: Knowledge, Consciousness, and the Politics of Empowerment.* Boston: Unwin Hyman, 1990. A classic text in the study of black feminist theory and practice at the intersection of race, class, and gender by one of black studies' foremost sociologists.

Robin D. G. Kelley. *Yo' Mama Is DysFunkshional!* Boston: Beacon Press, 1998. Insightful essays about America's culture wars and an excellent critique of social science scholarship about black working-class culture and aesthetics by one of this generation's finest historians.

Ismael Reed. *Airing Dirty Laundry.* Reading, MA: Addison-Wesley Publishing Company, 1993. A collection of provocative, iconoclastic, and entertaining essays written by one of America's most insightful cultural critics.

Deborah Gray White. *Too Heavy a Load: Black Women in Defense of Themselves, 1894–1994.* New York: W. W. Norton, 1998. A brilliant study by a black woman historian of black women and the organizations they founded to fight for the ballot, against segregation, and against the sexism and misogyny of black nationalism in the contemporary era.

Additional Bibliography

Black Culture Studies

Brian Cross. *It's Not about a Salary . . . Rap, Race and Resistance in Los Angeles.* London: Verso, 1993.

Michael Eric Dyson. *Between God and Gangsta Rap: Bearing Witness to Black Culture.* New York: Oxford University Press, 1996.

Patricia Liggins Hill, general ed. *Call and Response: The Riverside Anthology of the African American Literary Tradition.* New York: Houghton Mifflin, 1999.

bell hooks. *Outlaw Culture: Resisting Representations.* New York: Routledge, 1994.

Robin D. G. Kelley. *Race Rebels: Culture, Politics, and the Black Working Class.* New York: Free Press, 1994.

Terry McMillan. *Five for Five: The Films of Spike Lee.* New York: Stewart, Tabori & Chang, 1991.

Joan Morgan. *When Chickenheads Come Home to Roost: My Life as a Hip-Hop Feminist.* New York: Simon & Schuster, 1999.

Tricia Rose. *Black Noise: Rap Music and Black Culture in Contemporary America.* Hanover, NH: Wesleyan University Press, 1994.

Greg Tate. *Flyboy in the Buttermilk.* New York: Fire-side, 1992.

Deborah Willis, *Reflections in Black: A History of Black Photographers, 1840 to the Present.* New York: W.W. Norton, 2000.

Black Politics and Economics

Andrew Billingsley. *Climbing Jacob's Ladder: The Enduring Legacy of African-American Families.* New York: Simon & Schuster, 1993.

Barry Bluestone and Bennett Harrison. *The Deindustrialization of America: Plant Closings, Community Abandonment, and the Dismantling of Basic Industry.* New York: Basic Books, 1982.

Martin Carnoy. *Faded Dreams: The Politics and Economics of Race in America.* Cambridge, U.K.: Cambridge University Press, 1994.

Robert Dallek. *Ronald Reagan: The Politics of Symbolism.* Cambridge, MA: Harvard University Press, 1984.

W. Avon Drake and Robert D. Holsworth. *Affirmative Action and the Stalled Quest for Black Progress.* Urbana, IL: University of Illinois Press, 1996.

Robert Gooding-Williams, ed. *Reading Rodney King: Reading Urban Uprising.* New York: Routledge, 1993.

Lani Guinier. *Tyranny of the Majority: Fundamental Fairness and Representative Democracy.* New York: Free Press, 1995.

Andrew Hacker. *Two Nations: Black and White, Separate, Hostile, Unequal.* New York: Ballantine Books, rev., 1995.

Charles P. Henry. *Jesse Jackson: The Search for Common Ground.* Oakland, CA: Black Scholar Press, 1991.

Anita Faye Hill and Emma Coleman Jordan, eds. *Race, Gender, and Power in America: The Legacy of the Hill–Thomas Hearings.* New York: Oxford University Press, 1995.

Douglas S. Massey and Nancy A. Denton. *American Apartheid: Segregation and the Making of the Underclass.* Cambridge, MA: Harvard University Press, 1993.

Adolph Reed, Jr. *The Jesse Jackson Phenomenon: The Crisis in Afro-American Politics.* New Haven, CT: Yale University Press, 1986.

Andrea Y. Simpson. *The Tie That Binds: Identity and Political Attitudes in the Post–Civil Rights Generation.* New York: New York University Press, 1998.

William Julius Wilson. *The Bridge over the Racial Divide: Rising Inequality and Coalition Politics.* Berkeley, CA: University of California Press, 1999.

Identity Studies

Molefi Kete Asante. *The Afrocentric Idea.* Philadelphia: Temple University Press, 1987.

Martin Bernal. *Black Athena: The Afroasiatic Roots of Classical Civilization: The Fabrication of Ancient Greece, 1785–1985.* New Brunswick, NJ: Rutgers University Press, 1987.

F. James Davis. *Who Is Black? One Nation's Definition.* University Park, PA: Pennsylvania State University Press, 1991.

Tsehloane Keto. *Vision, Identity and Time: The Afrocentric Paradigm and the Study of the Past.* Dubuque, IA: Kendall/Hunt Publishing Co., 1995.

Wilson Jeremiah Moses. *Afrotopia: The Roots of African American Popular History.* Cambridge, MA: Cambridge University Press, 1998.

Arthur M. Schlesinger, Jr. *The Disuniting of America.* New York: W. W. Norton, 1992.

Clarence Walker. *You Can't Go Home Again.* New York: Oxford University Press, 2001.

Cornel West. *Race Matters.* Boston: Beacon Press, 1993.

Liberation Studies

Derrick Bell. *Faces at the Bottom of the Well: The Permanence of Racism.* New York: Basic Books, 1992.

Michael C. Dawson. *Behind the Mule: Race and Class in African-American Politics.* Princeton, NJ: Princeton University Press, 1994.

W. Marvin Dulaney. *Black Police in America.* Bloomington, IN: Indiana University Press, 1996.

Henry Hampton and Steve Fayer. *Voices of Freedom: An Oral History of the Civil Rights Movement from the 1950s through the 1980s.* New York: Bantam Books, 1990.

Randall Robinson. *The Debt: What America Owes to Blacks.* New York: Plume, 2000.

Race, Gender, and Class

Michael Awkward. *Negotiating Difference: Race, Gender, and the Politics of Positionality.* Chicago: University of Chicago Press, 1995.

Paul M. Barrett. *The Good Black: A True Story of Race in America.* New York: Dutton, 1999.

Lois Benjamin. *The Black Elite: Facing the Color Line in the Twilight of the Twentieth Century.* Chicago: Nelson-Hall Publishers, 1991.

Ellis Cose. *The Rage of the Privileged Class.* New York: HarperCollins, 1993.

Douglas G. Glasgow. *The Black Underclass: Poverty, Unemployment, and Entrapment of Ghetto Youth.* New York: Random House, 1981.

Lawrence Otis Graham. *Our Kind of People: Inside America's Black Urban Class.* New York: HarperCollins, 1999.

Stanlie M. James and Abena P. A. Busia, eds. *Theorizing Black Feminisms: The Visionary Pragmatism of Black Women.* New York: Routledge, 1993.

Christopher Jencks. *Rethinking Social Policy: Race, Poverty, and the Underclass.* Cambridge, MA: Harvard University Press, 1992.

Jonathan Kozel. *Savage Inequalities: Children in America's Schools.* New York: Crown, 1991.

Haki R. Madhubuti. *Black Men—Obsolete, Single, Dangerous? Afrikan American Families in Transition: Essays in Discovery, Solution, and Hope.* Chicago: Third World Press, 1990.

Leith Mullings. *On Our Own Terms: Race, Class, and Gender in the Lives of African American Women.* New York: Routledge, 1997.

Jill Nelson. *Voluntary Slavery: My Authentic Negro Experience.* Chicago: Noble Press, 1993.

Black Conservatives

Thomas Sowell. *Preferential Policies: An International Perspective.* New York: William Morrow, 1990.

Shelby Steele. *A Dream Deferred: The Second Betrayal of Black Freedom in America.* New York: HarperCollins Publishers, 1998.

Shelby Steele/CCC. *The Content of Our Character: A New Vision of Race in America.* New York: St. Martin's Press, 1990.

Autobiography and Biography

Amy Alexander, ed. *The Farrakhan Factor: African-American Writers on Leadership, Nationhood and Minister Louis Farrakhan.* New York: Grove Press, 1998.

Marshall Frady. *Jesse: The Life and Pilgrimage of Jesse Jackson.* New York: Random House, 1996.

Randall Robinson. *Defending the Spirit: A Black Life in America.* New York: NAL/Dutton, 1998.

Retracing the Odyssey

The *Amistad* Research Center. Tilton Hall, Tulane University, New Orleans, LA 70118. (504) 865-5535. Monday–Saturday 9:00 A.M. to 4:30 P.M. The *Amistad* Center contains manuscripts and art that illuminate the history and culture of diverse ethnic groups and race relations in the United States. Approximately 90 percent of the Center's holdings document the history and records of African Americans' community organizations and struggles. The Center also houses records related to religious denominations—Protestant, Catholic, and Jewish. Its art gallery frequently exhibits the work of early black artists, such as Aaron Douglas.

Harpo Studios. 1058 W. Washington Blvd., Chicago, Illinois. (312) 591-9222. Harpo Studios is the complex created by Oprah Winfrey, perhaps the best-known television talk show host and media mogul in America. Harpo Studios are a state-of-the-art film production facility, the first and only such multimedia complex owned and operated by an African-American woman.

Rock and Roll Hall of Fame and Museum. One Key Plaza, Cleveland, Ohio 44114. (888)-764-Rock. Daily, 10:00 A.M. to 5:30 P.M. Opened in 1995 to document and celebrate the history of Rock and Roll performers. Among the museum's permanent collection of the 500 songs that shaped this musical genre are ones that range from the early blues singers to Otis Redding, Chuck Berry, James Brown, Ray Charles, Sam Cook, Marvin Gaye, and, of course, Aretha Franklin.

REVIEW, RESEARCH & INTERACT

REVIEW QUESTIONS

1. To what extent and in what key areas did the Reagan and Bush presidencies nullify or dismantle much of the Great Society legislation? How did African Americans respond to the era of Republican conservative reform?
2. What was the significance of Jesse Jackson's campaigns for the Democratic presidential nomination? What explains the chasm between black and white America over Minister Louis Farrakhan?
3. What factors contributed to the gulf between black middle-class Americans and poor African Americans in the inner city?
4. Why do so many Americans associate welfare with black people?
5. Why did affirmative action become one of the most contested issues of the 1990s? What are the differences between the old civil rights and the new civil rights? How did affirmative action in the workplace differ from affirmative action in education?
6. How did the Rodney King case illuminate the different perceptions black and white Americans have of the police and the justice system?
7. What were some of the major issues or concerns of black women in the 1990s? What factors gave rise to black feminism? What is the black women's literary renaissance?
8. What are the reasons for the increased attention devoted to identity and culture issues by black intellectuals?

Research Navigator.com **www.researchnavigator.com**

Chapter 23 looks at the recent history of African Americans. For further research on contemporary black life, use the tools available to you in Research Navigator.

As you investigate this topic, consider this question: "What role did racism play in the politics of the 1980s?"

- **ContentSelect:** Search in the History database using the search term *Jesse Jackson.*
- **Links Library:** Access the History: U.S. History database and explore the links for *Clinton, Bill* and *Reagan, Ronald.*
- **New York Times on the Web:** To find out more search the History database using the search term *Million Man March.*

DOCUMENTS AND ACTIVITIES IN AFRICAN-AMERICAN HISTORY

Documents

23-1 William Julius Wilson, *The Urban Underclass*
23-2 Richard Viguerie, Why the New Right Is Winning, 1981
23-3 Jesse Jackson, Address before the Democratic National Convention, July 18, 1984, Wednesday
23-4 Thurgood Marshall, Remarks on the Bicentennial of the Constitution, 1987
23-5 Jessie Jackson, Common Ground, 1988
23-6 Elaine Bell Kaplan, "Talking to Teen Mothers"

Interactive Table

Black and White Children and the Conditions Contributing to Poverty, p. 580
http://www.prenhall.com/hine/table23.2

EPILOGUE

"A Nation Within a Nation"

Since the first Africans were brought to these shores in the seventeenth century, black people have been a constant and distinct presence in America. During the prolonged course of the Atlantic slave trade, approximately 600,000 Africans were sold into servitude in what became the United States. By the outbreak of the Civil War in 1861 there were nearly four million African Americans in this country. Today black people number over 30 million and make up slightly over 10 percent of the nation's population.

Initially regarded merely as an enslaved labor force to produce cash crops and not as a people who would or could enjoy an equal role in the political and social affairs of American society, African Americans constituted a separate ethnic, racial, and cultural group. For more than two centuries they remained outcasts.

People of African descent developed decidedly ambivalent relationships with the white majority in America. Never fully accepted and never fully rejected, black people relied on their own resources as they created their own institutions and communities. In 1852 Martin Delany declared, "We are a nation within a nation." A half century later W. E. B. Du Bois observed that the black man wanted to retain his African identity and to be an American as well. "He would not Africanize America, for America has too much to teach the world and Africa. He would not bleach his Negro soul in a flood of white Americanism, for he knows that Negro blood has a message for the world. He simply wishes to make it possible for a man to be both a Negro and an American, without being cursed and spit upon by his fellows, without having the doors of Opportunity closed roughly in his face."

Sometimes in desperation or disgust, some black people have been willing to abandon America or reject assimilation. The slaves who engaged in South Carolina's 1739 Stono rebellion attempted to reach Spanish Florida. As early as 1773, slaves in Massachusetts pledged to go to Africa after emancipation. From the 1790s to the start of the Civil War, visions of nationhood in Africa attracted a minority of African Americans. During the 1920s, Marcus Garvey and the Universal Negro Improvement Association glorified Africa while seeking black autonomy in the United States. By the 1950s, Elijah Muhammad, Malcolm X, and the Nation of Islam attracted black people by emphasizing a separate black destiny.

Yet in spite of the horrors of slavery, the indignity and cruelty of Jim Crow, and the unrelenting violence and discrimination inflicted on people of color, most African Americans have not rejected America but worked and struggled to participate fully in the American way of life. African slaves accepted elements of Christianity, and their descendants found solace in their spiritual beliefs. Black Americans have embraced American principles of brotherhood, justice, fairness, and equality before the law that are embedded in the Declaration of Independence and the Constitution. Again and again, African Americans have insisted that America be America, that the American majority live up to its professed ideals and values.

The nation within a nation has never been homogeneous. There have been persistent class, gender, and color divisions. There have been tensions and ideological conflicts among black leaders and organizations as they sought strategies to overcome racial inequities and white supremacy. Some leaders, such as Booker T. Washington, have emphasized self-reliance and economic advancement while others, including W. E. B. Du Bois and leaders of the NAACP, have advocated full inclusion in the nation's political, economic, and social fabric.

Furthermore, African Americans have been far more than victims, than an exploited labor force, than the subjects of segregation and stereotypes. They have contributed enormously to the development and character of American society and culture. As slaves, they provided billions of hours of unrequited labor to the American economy. Black people established churches, schools, and colleges that continue to thrive. Black people demonstrated a willingness to fight and die for a country that did not fully accept or appreciate their sacrifices. African Americans have made remarkable and innovative contributions to art, music, folklore, science, politics, and athletics that have shaped and enriched American society.

America is no longer what it was in 1700, 1800, or 1900. Chattel slavery ended in 1865. White supremacy is no longer fashionable or openly acceptable. Legal segregation was prohibited a generation ago. The capacity and willingness of Americans of diverse backgrounds and origins to live together in harmony has vastly improved in recent decades. Though we are now in the twenty-first century, the long odyssey of people of African descent has not ended nor will it end in the immediate future. Black people will continue to help mold and define this society, and they will continue to be "a nation within a nation."

Appendix

The Declaration of Independence

When in the course of human events it becomes necessary for one people to dissolve the political bands which have connected them with another and to assume, among the powers of the earth, the separate and equal station to which the laws of nature and of nature's God entitle them, a decent respect to the opinions of mankind requires that they should declare the causes which impel them to the separation.

We hold these truths to be self-evident, that all men are created equal; that they are endowed by their Creator with certain unalienable rights; that among these are life, liberty, and the pursuit of happiness. That, to secure these rights, governments are instituted among men, deriving their just powers from the consent of the governed; that, whenever any form of government becomes destructive of these ends, it is the right of the people to alter or to abolish it, and to institute a new government, laying its foundation on such principles, and organizing its powers in such form, as to them shall seem most likely to effect their safety and happiness. Prudence, indeed, will dictate that governments long established should not be changed for light and transient causes; and, accordingly, all experience hath shown that mankind are more disposed to suffer, while evils are sufferable, than to right themselves by abolishing the forms to which they are accustomed. But when a long train of abuses and usurpations, pursuing invariably the same object, evinces a design to reduce them under absolute despotism, it is their right, it is their duty, to throw off such government and to provide new guards for their future security. Such has been the patient sufferance of these colonies, and such is now the necessity which constrains them to alter their former systems of government. The history of the present King of Great Britain is a history of repeated injuries and usurpations, all having, in direct object, the establishment of an absolute tyranny over these States. To prove this, let facts be submitted to a candid world:

He has refused his assent to laws the most wholesome and necessary for the public good.

He has forbidden his governors to pass laws of immediate and pressing importance, unless suspended in their operation till his assent should be obtained; and, when so suspended, he has utterly neglected to attend to them.

He has refused to pass other laws for the accommodation of large districts of people, unless those people would relinquish the right of representation in the legislature, a right inestimable to them and formidable to tyrants only.

He has called together legislative bodies at places unusual, uncomfortable, and distant from the depository of their public records, for the sole purpose of fatiguing them into compliance with his measures.

He has dissolved representative houses, repeatedly for opposing, with manly firmness, his invasions on the rights of the people.

He has refused, for a long time after such dissolutions, to cause others to be elected; whereby the legislative powers, incapable of annihilation, have returned to the people at large for their exercise; the state remaining, in the meantime, exposed to all the danger of invasion from without and convulsions within.

He has endeavored to prevent the population of these States; for that purpose, obstructing the laws for naturalization of foreigners, refusing to pass others to encourage their migration hither, and raising the conditions of new appropriations of lands.

He has obstructed the administration of justice by refusing his assent to laws for establishing judiciary powers.

He has made judges dependent on his will alone for the tenure of their offices and the amount and payment of their salaries.

He has erected a multitude of new offices and sent hither swarms of officers to harass our people and eat out their substance.

He has kept among us, in time of peace, standing armies, without the consent of our legislatures.

He has affected to render the military independent of, and superior to, the civil power.

He has combined with others to subject us to a jurisdiction foreign to our Constitution and unacknowledged by our laws, giving his assent to their acts of pretended legislation—

For quartering large bodies of armed troops among us;

For protecting them, by mock trial, from punishment for any murders which they should commit on the inhabitants of these States;

For cutting off our trade with all parts of the world;

For imposing taxes on us without our consent;

For depriving us, in many cases, of the benefit of trial by jury;

For transporting us beyond seas to be tried for pretended offences;

For abolishing the free system of English laws in a neighboring province, establishing therein an arbitrary government, and enlarging its boundaries, so as to render it at once an example and fit instrument for introducing the same absolute rule into these colonies;

For taking away our charters, abolishing our most valuable laws, and altering, fundamentally, the powers of our governments.

For suspending our own legislatures and declaring themselves invested with power to legislate for us in all cases whatsoever.

He has abdicated government here by declaring us out of his protection and waging war against us.

He has plundered our seas, ravaged our coasts, burnt our towns, and destroyed the lives of our people.

He is, at this time, transporting large armies of foreign mercenaries to complete the works of death, desolation, and tyranny already begun with circumstances of cruelty and perfidy scarcely paralleled in the most barbarous ages, and totally unworthy the head of a civilized nation.

He has constrained our fellow citizens, taken captive on the high seas, to bear arms against their country, to become the executioners of their friends and brethren, or to fall themselves by their hands.

He has excited domestic insurrections amongst us and has endeavored to bring on the inhabitants of our frontiers, the merciless Indian savages, whose known rule of warfare is an undistinguished destruction of all ages, sexes, and conditions.

In every stage of these oppressions, we have petitioned for redress in the most humble terms; our repeated petitions have been answered only by repeated injury. A prince whose character is thus marked by every act which may define a tyrant is unfit to be the ruler of a free people.

Nor have we been wanting in attention to our British brethren. We have warned them, from time to time, of attempts made by their legislature to extend an unwarrantable jurisdiction over us. We have reminded them of the circumstances of our emigration and settlement here. We have appealed to their native justice and magnanimity, and we have conjured them, by the ties of our common kindred, to disavow these usurpations, which would inevitably interrupt our connections and correspondence. They, too, have been deaf to the voice of justice and consanguinity. We must, therefore, acquiesce in the necessity which denounces our separation, and hold them, as we hold the rest of mankind, enemies in war, in peace, friends.

We, therefore, the representatives of the United States of America, in general Congress assembled, appealing to the Supreme Judge of the world for the rectitude of our intentions, do, in the name and by the authority of the good people of these colonies, solemnly publish and declare, that these united colonies are, and of right ought to be, free and independent states: that they are absolved from all allegiance to the British Crown, and that all political connection between them and the state of Great Britain is, and ought to be, totally dissolved; and that, as free and independent states, they have full power to levy war, conclude peace, contract alliances, establish commerce, and to do all other acts and things which independent states may of right do. And, for the support of this declaration, with a firm reliance on the protection of Divine Providence, we mutually pledge to each other our lives, our fortunes, and our sacred honor.

Proposed clause on the slave trade omitted from the final draft of the Declaration

He has waged cruel war against human nature itself, violating its most sacred rights of life and liberty in the person of a distant people who never offended him; captivating and carrying them into slavery in another hemisphere, or to incur miserable death in their transportation thither. This piratical warfare, the opprobrium of infidel powers, is the warfare of the Christian king of Great Britain. Determined to keep open a market where men should be bought and sold, he has prostituted his negative for suppressing every legislative attempt to prohibit or restrain this execrable commerce.

The Constitution of the United States of America

(with clauses pertaining to the statue of African Americans highlighted)

We the people of the United States, in order to form a more perfect union, establish justice, insure domestic tranquility, provide for the common defense, promote the general welfare, and secure the blessings of liberty to ourselves and our posterity, do ordain and establish this Constitution for the United States of America.

Article I

SECTION 1. All legislative powers herein granted shall be vested in a Congress of the United States, which shall consist of a Senate and House of Representatives.

SECTION 2. 1. The House of Representatives shall be composed of members chosen every second year by the people of the several States, and the electors in each State shall have the qualifications requisite for electors of the most numerous branch of the State legislature.

2. No person shall be a representative who shall not have attained to the age of twenty-five years, and been seven years a citizen of the United States, and who shall not, when elected, be an inhabitant of that State in which he shall be chosen.

3. Representatives and direct taxes[1] shall be apportioned among the several States which may be included within this Union, according to their respective numbers, which shall be determined by adding to the whole number of free persons, including those bound to service for a term of years, and excluding Indians not taxed, three fifths of all other persons.[2] The actual enumeration shall be made within three years after the first meeting of the Congress of the United States, and within every subsequent term of ten years, in such manner as they shall by law direct. The number of representatives shall not exceed one for every thirty thousand, but each State shall have at least one representative; and until such enumeration shall be made, the State of New Hampshire shall be entitled to choose three, Massachusetts eight, Rhode Island and Providence Plantations one, Connecticut five, New York six, New Jersey four, Pennsylvania eight, Delaware one, Maryland six, Virginia ten, North Carolina five, South Carolina five, and Georgia three.

4. When vacancies happen in the representation from any State, the executive authority thereof shall issue writs of election to fill such vacancies.

5. The House of Representatives shall choose their speaker and other officers; and shall have the sole power of impeachment.

SECTION 3. 1. The Senate of the United States shall be composed of two senators from each State, chosen by the legislature thereof,[3] for six years; and each senator shall have one vote.

2. Immediately after they shall be assembled in consequence of the first election, they shall be divided as equally as may be into three classes. The seats of the senators of the first class shall be vacated at the expiration of the second year, of the second class at the expiration of the fourth year, and of the third class at the expiration of the sixth year, so that one third may be chosen every second year; and if vacancies happen by resignation, or otherwise, during the recess of the legislature of any State, the executive thereof may make temporary appointments until the next meeting of the legislature, which shall then fill such vacancies.[4]

3. No person shall be a senator who shall not have attained to the age of thirty years, and been nine years a citizen of the United States, and who shall not, when elected, be an inhabitant of that State for which he shall be chosen.

4. The Vice President of the United States shall be President of the Senate, but shall have no vote, unless they be equally divided.

5. The Senate shall choose their other officers, and also a president pro tempore, in the absence of the Vice President, or when he shall exercise the office of the President of the United States.

6. The Senate shall have the sole power to try all impeachments. When sitting for that purpose, they shall be on oath or affirmation. When the president of the United States is tried, the chief justice shall preside: and no person shall be convicted without the concurrence of two thirds of the members present.

[1] See the Sixteenth Amendment

[2] See the Fourteenth Amendment

[3] See the Seventeenth Amendment

[4] See the Seventeenth Amendment

7. Judgment in cases of impeachment shall not extend further than to removal from office, and disqualification to hold and enjoy any office of honor, trust or profit under the United States: but the party convicted shall nevertheless be liable and subject to indictment, trial, judgment and punishment, according to law.

SECTION 4. 1. The times, places, and manner of holding elections for senators and representatives, shall be prescribed in each State by the legislature thereof; but the Congress may at any time by law make or alter such regulations, except as to the places of choosing senators.

2. The Congress shall assemble at least once in every year, and such meeting shall be on the first Monday in December, unless they shall by law appoint a different day.

SECTION 5. 1. Each House shall be the judge of the elections, returns and qualifications of its own members, and a majority of each shall constitute a quorum to do business; but a smaller number may adjourn from day to day, and may be authorized to compel the attendance of absent members, in such manner, and under such penalties as each House may provide.

2. Each House may determine the rules of its proceedings, punish its members for disorderly behavior, and, with the concurrence of two thirds, expel a member.

3. Each House shall keep a journal of its proceedings, and from time to time publish the same, excepting such parts as may in their judgment require secrecy; and the yeas and nays of the members of either house on any question shall, at the desire of one fifth of those present, be entered on the journal.

4. Neither House, during the session of Congress, shall, without the consent of the other, adjourn for more than three days, nor to any other place than that in which the two Houses shall be sitting.

SECTION 6. 1. The senators and representatives shall receive a compensation for their services, to be ascertained by law, and paid out of the Treasury of the United States. They shall in all cases, except treason, felony, and breach of the peace, be privileged from arrest during their attendance at the session of their respective Houses, and in going to and returning from the same; and for any speech or debate in either House, they shall not be questioned in any other place.

2. No senator or representative shall, during the time for which he was elected, be appointed to any civil office under the authority of the United States, which shall have been created, or the emoluments whereof shall have been increased, during such time; and no person holding any office under the United States shall be a member of either House during his continuance in office.

SECTION 7. 1. All bills for raising revenue shall originate in the House of Representatives; but the Senate may purpose or concur with amendments as on other bills.

2. Every bill which shall have passed the House of Representatives and the Senate, shall, before it become a law, be presented to the President of the United States; if he approves he shall sign it, but if not he shall return it, with his objections, to that House in which it shall have originated, who shall enter the objections at large on their journal, and proceed to reconsider it. If after such reconsideration two thirds of that House shall agree to pass the bill, it shall be sent, together with the objections, to the other House, by which it shall likewise be reconsidered, and if approved by two thirds of that House, it shall become a law. But in all such cases the votes of both Houses shall be determined by yeas and nays, and the names of the persons voting for and against the bill shall be entered on the journal of each House respectively. If any bill shall not be returned by the President within ten days (Sundays excepted) after it shall have been presented to him, the same shall be a law, in like manner as if he had signed it, unless the Congress by their adjournment prevent its return, in which case it shall not be a law.

3. Every order, resolution, or vote to which the concurrence of the Senate and the House of Representatives may be necessary (except on a question of adjournment) shall be presented to the President of the United States; and before the same shall take effect, shall be approved by him, or being disapproved by him, shall be repassed by two thirds of the Senate and House of Representatives, according to the rules and limitations prescribed in the case of a bill.

SECTION 8. The Congress shall have the power

1. To lay and collect taxes, duties, imposts, and excises, to pay the debts and provide for the common defense and general welfare of the United States; but all duties, imposts, and excises shall be uniform throughout the United States.

2. To borrow money on the credit of the United States;

3. To regulate commerce with foreign nations, and among the several States, and with the Indian tribes;

4. To establish a uniform rule of naturalization, and uniform laws on the subject of bankruptcies throughout the United States;

5. To coin money, regulate the value thereof, and of foreign coin, and fix the standard of weights and measures;

6. To provide for the punishment of counterfeiting the securities and current coin of the United States;

7. To establish post offices and post roads;

8. To promote the progress of science and useful arts, by securing for limited times to authors and inventors the exclusive right to their respective writings and discoveries;

9. To constitute tribunals inferior to the Supreme Court;

10. To define and punish piracies and felonies committed on the high seas, and offenses against the law of nations;

11. To declare war, grant letters of marque and reprisal, and make rules concerning captures on land and water;

12. To raise and support armies, but no appropriation of money to that use shall be for a longer term than two years;

13. To provide and maintain a navy;

14. To make rules for the government and regulation of the land and naval forces;

15. To provide for calling forth the militia to execute the laws of the Union, suppress insurrections and repel invasions;

16. To provide for organizing, arming, and disciplining the militia, and for governing such part of them as may be employed in the service of the United States, reserving to the States respectively, the appointment of the officers, and the authority of training the militia according to the discipline prescribed by Congress;

17. To exercise exclusive legislation in all cases whatsoever, over such district (not exceeding ten miles square) as may, by cession of particular States, and the acceptance of Congress, become the seat of the government of the United States, and to exercise like authority over all places purchased by the consent of the legislature of the State in which the same shall be, for the erection of forts, magazines, arsenals, dock-yards, and other needful buildings; and

18. To make all laws which shall be necessary and proper for carrying into execution the foregoing powers, and all other powers vested by this Constitution in the government of the United States, or any department or officer thereof.

SECTION 9. 1. The migration or importation of such persons as any of the States now existing shall think proper to admit, shall not be prohibited by the Congress prior to the year one thousand eight hundred and eight, but a tax or duty may be imposed on such importation, not exceeding ten dollars for each person.

2. The privilege of the writ of habeas corpus shall not be suspended, unless when in cases of rebellion or invasion the public safety may require it.

3. No bill of attainder or ex post facto law shall be passed.

4. No capitation, or other direct, tax shall be laid, unless in proportion to the census or enumeration herein-before directed to be taken.[5]

5. No tax or duty shall be laid on articles exported from any State.

6. No preference shall be given by any regulation of commerce or revenue to the ports of one State over those of another: nor shall vessels bound to, or from, one State be obliged to enter, clear, or pay duties in another.

7. No money shall be drawn from the treasury, but in consequence of appropriations made by law; and a regular statement and account of the receipts and expenditures of all public money shall be published from time to time.

8. No title of nobility shall be granted by the United States: and no person holding any office of profit or trust under them, shall, without the consent of the Congress, accept of any present, emolument, office, or title, of any kind whatever, from any king, prince, or foreign State.

SECTION 10. 1. No State shall enter into any treaty, alliance, or confederation; grant letters of marque and reprisal; coin money; emit bills of credit; make any thing but gold and silver coin a tender in payment of debts; pass any bill of attainder, ex post facto law, or law impairing the obligation of contracts, or grant, any title of nobility.

2. No State shall, without the consent of the Congress, lay any imposts or duties on imports or exports, except what may be absolutely necessary for executing its inspection laws: and the net produce of all duties and imposts laid by any State on imports or exports, shall be for the use of the treasury of the United States; and all such laws shall be subject to the revision and control of the Congress.

3. No State shall, without the consent of the Congress, lay any duty of tonnage, keep troops, or ships of war in time of peace, enter into any agreement or compact with another State, or with a foreign power, or engage in war, unless actually invaded, or in such imminent danger as will not admit of delay.

Article II

SECTION 1. 1. The executive power shall be vested in a President of the United States of America. He shall hold his office during the term of four years, and, together with the Vice President, chosen for the same term, be elected, as follows:

[5] See the Sixteenth Amendment

2. Each State shall appoint, in such manner as the legislature thereof may direct, a number of electors, equal to the whole number of senators and representatives to which the State may be entitled in the Congress: but no senator or representative, or person holding any office of trust or profit under the United States, shall be appointed an elector.

The electors shall meet in their respective States, and vote by ballot for two persons, of whom one at least shall not be an inhabitant of the same State with themselves. And they shall make a list of all the persons voted for, and of the number of votes for each; which list they shall sign and certify, and transmit sealed to the seat of the government of the United States, directed to the president of the Senate. The president of the Senate shall, in the presence of the Senate and House of Representatives, open all the certificates, and the votes shall then be counted. The person having the greatest number of votes shall be the President, if such number be a majority of the whole number of electors appointed; and if there be more than one who have such majority, and have an equal number of votes, then the House of Representatives shall immediately choose by ballot one of them for President; and if no person have a majority, then from the five highest on the list the said House shall in like manner choose the President. But in choosing the President, the votes shall be taken by States, the representation from each State having one vote; a quorum for this purpose shall consist of a member or members from two thirds of the States, and a majority of all the States shall be necessary to a choice. In every case after the choice of the President, the person having the greatest number of votes of the electors shall be the Vice President. But if there should remain two or more who have equal votes, the Senate shall choose from them by ballot the Vice President.[6]

3. The Congress may determine the time of choosing the electors, and the day on which they shall give their votes; which day shall be the same throughout the United States.

4. No person except a natural born citizen, or a citizen of the United States, at the time of the adoption of this Constitution, shall be eligible to the office of President; neither shall any person be eligible to the office who shall not have attained to the age of thirty-five years, and been fourteen years a resident within the United States.

5. In case of the removal of the President from office, or of his death, resignation, or inability to discharge the powers and duties of the said office, the same shall devolve on the Vice President, and the Congress may by law provide for the case of removal, death, resignation or inability, both of the President and Vice President, declaring what officer shall then act as President, and such officer shall act accordingly until the disability be removed, or a President shall be elected.

6. The President shall, at stated times, receive for his services a compensation which shall neither be increased nor diminished during the period for which he shall have been elected, and he shall not receive within that period any other emolument from the United States, or any of them.

7. Before he enter on the execution of his office, he shall take the following oath or affirmation:—"I do solemnly swear (or affirm) that I will faithfully execute the office of president of the United States, and will to the best of my ability, preserve, protect and defend the Constitution of the United States."

Section 2. 1. The President shall be commander in chief of the army and navy of the United States, and of the militia of the several States, when called into the actual service of the United States; he may require the opinion in writing, of the principal officer in each of the executive departments, upon any subject relating to the duties of their respective offices, and he shall have power to grant reprieves and pardons for offenses against the United States, except in cases of impeachment.

2. He shall have power, by and with the advice and consent of the Senate, to make treaties, provided two thirds of the senators present concur; and he shall nominate, and by and with the advice and consent of the Senate, shall appoint ambassadors, other public ministers and consuls, judges of the Supreme Court, and all other officers of the United States, whose appointments are not herein otherwise provided for, and which shall be established by law; but the Congress may by law vest the appointment of such inferior officers, as they think proper, in the President alone, in the courts of laws, or in the heads of departments.

3. The President shall have power to fill up all vacancies that may happen during the recess of the Senate, by granting commissions which shall expire at the end of their next session.

Section 3. He shall from time to time give to the Congress information of the state of the Union, and recommend to their consideration such measures as he shall judge necessary and expedient; he may, on extraordinary occasions, convene both houses, or either of them, and in case of disagreement between them with respect to the time of adjournment, he may adjourn them to such time as he shall think proper; he shall receive ambassadors and other public ministers; he shall take care that the laws be faithfully executed, and shall commission all the officers of the United States.

[6] See the Twelfth Amendment

Section 4. The President, Vice President, and all civil officers of the United States, shall be removed from office on impeachment for, and conviction of, treason, bribery, or other high crimes and misdemeanors.

Article III

SECTION 1. The judicial power of the United States shall be vested in one Supreme Court, and in such inferior courts as the Congress may from time to time ordain and establish. The judges, both of the Supreme and inferior courts, shall hold their offices during good behavior, and shall, at stated times, receive for their services, a compensation, which shall not be diminished during their continuance in office.

SECTION 2. 1. The judicial power shall extend to all cases, in law and equity, arising under this Constitution, the laws of the United States, and treaties made, or which shall be made, under their authority;—to all cases of admiralty and maritime jurisdiction;—to controversies to which the United States shall be a party;[7]—to controversies between two or more States;—between a State and citizens of another State;—between citizens of different States;—between citizens of the same State claiming lands under grants of different States, and between a State, or the citizens thereof, and foreign States, citizens or subjects.

2. In all cases affecting ambassadors, other public ministers and consuls, and those in which a State shall be party, the Supreme Court shall have original jurisdiction. In all the other cases before mentioned, the Supreme Court shall have appellate jurisdiction, both as to law and fact, with such exceptions, and under such regulations as the Congress shall make.

3. The trial of all crimes, except in cases of impeachment, shall be by jury; and such trial shall be held in the State where the said crimes shall have been committed; but when not committed within any State, the trial shall be such place or places as the Congress may by law have directed.

SECTION 3. 1. Treason against the United States shall consist only in levying war against them, or in adhering to their enemies, giving them aid and comfort. No person shall be convicted of treason unless on the testimony of two witnesses to the same overt act, or on confession in open court.

2. The Congress shall have power to declare the punishment of treason, but no attainder of treason shall work corruption of blood, or forfeiture except during the life of the person attained.

[7] See the Eleventh Amendment

Article IV

SECTION 1. Full faith and credit shall be given in each State to the public acts, records, and judicial proceedings of every other State. And the Congress may by general laws prescribe the manner in which such acts, records and proceedings shall be proved, and the effect thereof.

SECTION 2. 1. The citizens of each State shall be entitled to all privileges and immunities of citizens in the several States.[8]

2. A person charged in any State with treason, felony, or other crime, who shall flee from justice, and be found in another State, shall on demand of the executive authority of the State from which he fled, be delivered up to be removed to the State having jurisdiction of the crime.

3. No person held to service or labor in one State under the laws thereof, escaping into another, shall, in consequence of any law or regulation therein, be discharged from such service or labor, but shall be delivered up on claim of the party to whom such service or labor may be due.[9]

SECTION 3. 1. New States may be admitted by the Congress into this Union; but no new State shall be formed or erected within the jurisdiction of any other State, nor any State be formed by the junction of two or more States, or parts of States, without the consent of the legislatures of the States concerned as well as of the Congress.

2. The Congress shall have power to dispose of and make all needful rules and regulations respecting the territory or other property belonging to the United States; and nothing in this Constitution shall be so construed as to prejudice any claims of the United States, or of any particular State.

SECTION 4. The United States shall guarantee to every State in this Union a republican form of government, and shall protect each of them against invasion; and on application of the legislature, or of the executive (when the legislature cannot be convened) against domestic violence.

Article V

The Congress, whenever two thirds of both Houses shall deem it necessary, shall propose amendments to this Constitution, or, on the application of the legislatures of two thirds of the several States, shall call a convention for proposing amendments, which

[8] See the Fourteenth Amendment, Sec. 1

[9] See the Thirteenth Amendment

in either case shall be valid to all intents and purposes, as part of this Constitution, when ratified by the legislatures of three fourths of the several States, or by conventions in three fourths thereof, as the one or the other mode of ratification may be proposed by the Congress; Provided that no amendment which may be made prior to the year one thousand eight hundred and eight shall in any manner affect the first and fourth clauses in the ninth section of the first article; and that no State, without its consent, shall be deprived of its equal suffrage in the Senate.

Article VI

1. All debts contracted and engagements entered into, before the adoption of this Constitution, shall be as valid against the United States under this Constitution, as under the Confederation.[10]

2. This Constitution, and the laws of the United States which shall be made in pursuance thereof; and all treaties made, or which shall be made, under the authority of the United States, shall be the supreme law of the land; and the judges in every State shall be bound thereby, any thing in the Constitution or laws of any State to the contrary notwithstanding.

3. The senators and representatives before mentioned, and the members of the several State legislatures, and all executive and judicial officers, both of the United States and of the several States, shall be bound by oath or affirmation to support this Constitution; but no religious test shall ever be required as a qualification to any office or public trust under the United States.

Article VII

The ratification of the conventions of nine States shall be sufficient for the establishment of this Constitution between the States so ratifying the same.

Done in Convention by the unanimous consent of the States present the seventeenth day of September in the year of our Lord one thousand seven hundred and eighty-seven, and of the independence of the United States of America the twelfth. In witness whereof we have hereunto subscribed our names.

Articles in addition to, and amendment of, the Constitution of the United States of America, proposed by Congress, and ratified by the legislatures of the several States, pursuant to the fifth article of the original Constitution.

[10] See the Fourteenth Amendment, Sec. 4.

Amendment I [First ten amendments ratified December 15, 1791]

Congress shall make no law respecting an establishment of religion, or prohibiting the free exercise thereof; or abridging the freedom of speech, or of the press; or the right of the people peaceably to assemble, and to petition the government for a redress of grievances.

Amendment II

A well regulated militia, being necessary to the security of a free State, the right of the people to keep and bear arms, shall not be infringed.

Amendment III

No soldier shall, in time of peace be quartered in any house, without the consent of the owner, nor in time of war, but in a manner to be prescribed by law.

Amendment IV

The right of the people to be secure in their persons, houses, papers, and effects, against unreasonable searches and seizures, shall not be violated, and no warrants shall issue, but upon probable cause, supported by oath or affirmation, and particularly describing the place to be searched, and the persons or things to be seized.

Amendment V

No person shall be held to answer for a capital or otherwise infamous crime, unless on a presentment or indictment of a grand jury, except in cases arising in the land or naval forces, or in the militia, when in actual service in time of war or public danger; nor shall any person be subject for the same offense to be twice put in jeopardy of life or limb; nor shall be compelled in any criminal case to be a witness against himself, nor be deprived of life, liberty, or property, without due process of law; nor shall private property be taken for public use, without just compensation.

Amendment VI

In all criminal prosecutions, the accused shall enjoy the right to a speedy and public trial, by an impartial jury of the State and district wherein the crime shall have been committed, which district shall have been previously ascertained by law, and to be informed of the nature and cause of the accusation; to be confronted with the witnesses against him; to have compulsory process for obtaining witnesses in his favor, and to have the assistance of counsel for his defense.

Amendment VII

In suits at common law, where the value in controversy shall exceed twenty dollars, the right of trial by jury shall be preserved, and no fact tried by a jury shall be otherwise reexamined in any court of the United States, than according to the rules of the common law.

Amendment VIII

Excessive bail shall not be required, nor excessive fines imposed, nor cruel and unusual punishments inflicted.

Amendment IX

The enumeration in the Constitution of certain rights shall not be construed to deny or disparage others retained by the people.

Amendment X

The powers not delegated to the United States by the Constitution, nor prohibited by it to the States, are reserved to the States respectively, or to the people.

Amendment XI [January 8, 1798]

The judicial power of the United States shall not be construed to extend to any suit in law or equity, commended or prosecuted against one of the United States by citizens of another State, or by citizens or subjects of any foreign State.

Amendment XII [September 25, 1804]

The electors shall meet in their respective States, and vote by ballot for President and Vice President, one of whom, at least, shall not be an inhabitant of the same State with themselves; they shall name in their ballots the person voted for as President, and in distinct ballots, the person voted for as Vice President, and they shall make distinct lists of all persons voted for as President and of all persons voted for as Vice President, and of the number of votes for each, which lists they shall sign and certify, and transmit sealed to the seat of the government of the United States, directed to the President of the Senate;—The President of the Senate shall, in the presence of the Senate and House of Representatives, open all the certificates and the votes shall then be counted;—The person having the greatest number of votes for President, shall be the President, if such number be a majority of the whole number of electors appointed; and if no person have such majority, then from the persons having the highest numbers not exceeding three on the list of those voted for as President, the House of Representatives shall choose immediately, by ballot, the President. But in choosing the President, the votes shall be taken by States, the representation from each State having one vote; a quorum for this purpose shall consist of a member or members from two thirds of the States, and a majority of all the States shall be necessary to a choice. And if the House of Representatives shall not choose a President whenever the right of choice shall devolve upon them, before the fourth day of March next following, then the Vice President shall act as President, as in the case of the death or other constitutional disability of the President. The person having the greatest number of votes as Vice President shall be the Vice President, if such number be a majority of the whole number of electors appointed, and if no person have a majority, then from the two highest numbers on the list, the Senate shall choose the Vice President; a quorum for the purpose shall consist of two thirds of the whole number of Senators, and a majority of the whole number shall be necessary to a choice. But no person constitutionally ineligible to the office of President shall be eligible to that of Vice President of the United States.

Amendment XIII [December 18, 1865]

Section 1. Neither slavery nor involuntary servitude, except as punishment for crime whereof the party shall have been duly convicted, shall exist within the United States, or any place subject to their jurisdiction.

Section 2. Congress shall have power to enforce this article by appropriate legislation.

Amendment XIV [July 28, 1868]

Section 1. All persons born or naturalized in the United States, and subject to the jurisdiction thereof, are citizens of the United States and of the State wherein they reside. No State shall make or enforce any law which shall abridge the privileges or immunities of citizens of the United States; nor shall any State deprive any person of life, liberty, or property, without due process of law; nor deny to any person within its jurisdiction the equal protection of the laws.

Section 2. Representatives shall be apportioned among the several States according to their respective numbers, counting the whole number of persons in each State, excluding Indians not taxed. But when the right to vote at any election for the choice of electors for President and Vice President of the United States, representatives in Congress, the executive and judicial officers of a State, or the members of the legislature thereof, is denied to any of the male inhabitants of such State, being twenty-one years of age, and citizens of the United States, or in any way abridged, except for participating in rebellion, or other crime, the basis of representation there shall be reduced in the proportion which the number of such male citizens shall bear to the whole number of male citizens twenty-one years of age in such State.

SECTION 3. No person shall be a senator or representative in Congress, or elector of President and Vice President, or hold any office, civil or military, under the United States, or under any State, who having previously taken an oath, as a member of Congress, or as an officer of the United States, or as a member of any State legislature, or as an executive or judicial officer of any State, to support the Constitution of the United States, shall have engaged in insurrection or rebellion against the same, or given aid or comfort to the enemies thereof. But Congress may by a vote of two thirds of each House, remove such disability.

SECTION 4. The validity of the public debt of the United States, authorized by law, including debts incurred for payment of pensions and bounties for services in suppressing insurrection or rebellion; shall not be questioned. But neither the United States nor any State shall assume or pay any debt or obligation incurred in aid of insurrection or rebellion against the United States, or any claim for the loss or emancipation of any slave; but all such debts, obligations, and claims shall be held illegal and void.

SECTION 5. The Congress shall have the power to enforce, by appropriate legislation, the provisions of this article.

Amendment XV [March 30, 1870]

SECTION 1. The right of citizens of the United States to vote shall not be denied or abridged by the United States or by any State on account of race, color, or previous condition of servitude.

SECTION 2. The Congress shall have power to enforce this article by appropriate legislation.

Amendment XVI [February 25, 1913]

The Congress shall have power to lay and collect taxes on incomes, from whatever source derived, without apportionment among the several States, and without regard to any census or enumeration.

Amendment XVII [May 31, 1913]

The Senate of the United States shall be composed of two senators from each State, elected by the people thereof, for six years; and each senator shall have one vote. The electors in each State shall have the qualifications requisite for electors of the most numerous branch of the State legislature.

When vacancies happen in the representation of any State in the Senate, the executive authority of such State shall issue writs of election to fill such vacancies: Provided, That the legislature of any State may empower the executive thereof to make temporary appointments until the people fill the vacancies by election as the legislature may direct.

This amendment shall not be so construed as to affect the election or term of any senator chosen before it becomes valid as part of the Constitution.

Amendment XVIII[11] [January 29, 1919]

After one year from the ratification of this article, the manufacture, sale, or transportation of intoxicating liquors within, the importation thereof into, or the exportation thereof from the United States and all territory subject to the jurisdiction thereof for beverage purposes is thereby prohibited.

The Congress and the several States shall have concurrent power to enforce this article by appropriate legislation.

This article shall be inoperative unless it shall have been ratified as an amendment to the Constitution by the legislatures of the several States, as provided in the Constitution, within seven years from the date of the submission hereof to the States by Congress.

Amendment XIX [August 26, 1920]

The right of citizens of the United States to vote shall not be denied or abridged by the United States or by any State on account of sex.

Congress shall have the power to enforce this article by appropriate legislation.

Amendment XX [January 23, 1933]

SECTION 1. The terms of the President and Vice President shall end at noon on the 20th day of January and the terms of Senators and Representatives at noon on the 3d day of January, of the years in which such terms would have ended if this article had not been ratified; and the terms of their successors shall then begin.

SECTION 2. The Congress shall assemble at least once in every year, and such meeting shall begin at noon on the 3d day of January, unless they shall by law appoint a different day.

---

[11] Repealed by the Twenty-first Amendment.

SECTION 3. If, at the time fixed for the beginning of the term of president, the President-elect shall have died, the Vice President-elect shall become President. If a President shall not have been chosen before the time fixed for the beginning of his term, or if the President-elect shall have failed to qualify, then the Vice President-elect shall act as president until a President shall have qualified; and the Congress may by law provide for the case wherein neither a President-elect nor a Vice President-elect shall have qualified, declaring who shall then act as President, or the manner in which one who is to act shall be selected, and such person shall act accordingly until a President or Vice President shall have qualified.

SECTION 4. The Congress may by law provide for the case of the death of any of the persons from whom, the House of Representatives may choose a President whenever the right of choice shall have devolved upon them, and for the case of the death of any of the persons from whom the Senate may choose a Vice President whenever the right of choice shall have devolved upon them.

SECTION 5. Sections 1 and 2 shall take effect on the 15th day of October following the ratification of this article.

SECTION 6. This article shall be inoperative unless it shall have been ratified as an amendment to the Constitution by the legislatures of three-fourths of the several States within seven years from the date of its submission.

Amendment XXI [December 5, 1933]

SECTION 1. The Eighteenth Article of amendment to the Constitution of the United States is hereby repealed.

SECTION 2. The transportation or importation into any State, Territory, or possession of the United States for delivery or use therein of intoxicating liquors in violation of the laws thereof, is hereby prohibited.

SECTION 3. This article shall be inoperative unless it shall have been ratified as an amendment to the Constitution by conventions in the several States, as provided in the Consitution, within seven years from the date of the submission thereof to the States by the Congress.

Amendment XXII [March 1, 1951]

No person shall be elected to the office of the President more than twice, and no person who has held the office of President, or acted as President, for more than two years of a term to which some other person was elected President shall be elected to the office of the President more than once.

But this article shall not apply to any person holding the office of President when this article was proposed by the Congress, and shall not prevent any person who may be holding the office of President, or acting as President, during the term within which this article becomes operative from holding the office of President or acting as President during the remainder of such term.

This article shall be inoperative unless it shall have been ratified as an amendment to the Constitution by the legislatures of three-fourths of the several States within seven years from the date of its submission to the States by the Congress.

Amendment XXIII [March 29, 1961]

SECTION 1. The District constituting the seat of Government of the United States shall appoint in such manner as the Congress may direct.

A number of electors of President and Vice President equal to the whole number of Senators and Representatives in Congress to which the District would be entitled if it were a State, but in no event more than the least populous State; they shall be in addition to those appointed by the States, but they shall be considered, for the purposes of the election of President and Vice President, to be electors appointed by a State; and they shall meet in the District and perform such duties as provided by the twelfth article of amendment.

SECTION 2. The Congress shall have power to enforce this article by appropriate legislation.

Amendment XXIV [January 23, 1964]

SECTION 1. The right of citizens of the United States to vote in any primary or other election for President or Vice President, for electors for President or Vice President, or for Senator or Representative in Congress, shall not be denied or abridged by the United States or any State by reason of failure to pay any poll tax or other tax.

SECTION 2. The Congress shall have power to enforce this article by appropriate legislation.

Amendment XXV [February 10, 1967]

SECTION 1. In case of the removal of the President from office or of his death or resignation, the Vice President shall become President.

SECTION 2. Whenever there is a vacancy in the office of the Vice President, the President shall nominate a Vice President who shall take office upon confirmation by a majority of both Houses of Congress.

SECTION 3. Whenever the President transmits to the President pro tempore of the Senate and the Speaker of the House of Representatives his written declaration that he is unable to discharge the powers and duties of his office, and until he transmits to them a written declaration to the contrary, such powers and duties shall be discharged by the Vice President as Acting President.

SECTION 4. Whenever the Vice President and a majority of either the principal officers of the executive departments or of such other body as Congress may by law provide, transmit to the President pro tempore of the Senate and the Speaker of the House of Representatives their written declaration that the President is unable to discharge the powers and duties of his office, the Vice President shall immediately assume the powers and duties of the office as Acting President.

Thereafter, when the President transmits to the President pro tempore of the Senate and the Speaker of the House of Representatives his written declaration that no inability exists, he shall resume the powers and duties of his office unless the Vice President and a majority of either the principal officers of the executive departments or of such other body as Congress may by law provide, transmit within four days to the President pro tempore of the Senate and the Speaker of the House of Representatives their written declaration that the President is unable to discharge the powers and duties of his office. Thereupon Congress shall decide the issue, assembling within forty-eight hours for that purpose if not in session. If the Congress, within twenty-one days after receipt of the latter written declaration, or, if Congress is not in session, within twenty-one days after Congress is required to assemble, determines by two-thirds vote of both houses that the President is unable to discharge the powers and duties of his office, the Vice President shall continue to discharge the same as Acting President; otherwise, the President shall resume the powers and duties of his office.

Amendment XXVI [June 30, 1971]

SECTION 1. The right of citizens of the United States who are eighteen years of age or older to vote shall not be denied or abridged by the United States or by any State on account of age.

SECTION 2. The Congress shall have power to enforce this article by appropriate legislation.

AMENDMENT XXVII[12] [May 7, 1992]

No law, varying the compensation for services of the Senators and Representatives, shall take effect until an election of Representatives shall have intervened.

---

[12] James Madison proposed this amendment in 1789 together with the ten amendments that were adopted as the Bill of Rights, but it failed to win ratification at the time. Congress, however, had set no deadline for its ratification, and over the years—particularly in the 1980s and 1990s—many states voted to add it to the Constitution. With the ratification of Michigan in 1992 it passed the threshold of ¾ of the states required for adoption, but because the process took more than 200 years, its validity remains in doubt.

The Emancipation Proclamation

By the President of the United States of America:

Whereas, on the twenty-second day of September, in the year of our Lord one thousand eight hundred and sixty-two, a proclamation was issued by the President of the United States, containing, among other things, the following, to wit:

> That on the first day of January, in the year of our Lord one thousand eight hundred and sixty-three, all persons held as slaves within any State or designated part of a State, the people whereof shall then be in rebellion against the United States, shall be then, thenceforward, and forever free; and the Executive Government of the United States, including the military and naval authority thereof, will recognize and maintain the freedom of such persons, and will do no act or acts to repress such persons, or any of them, in any efforts they may make for their actual freedom.
>
> That the Executive will, on the first day of January aforesaid, by proclamation, designate the States and parts of States, if any, in which the people thereof, respectively, shall then be in rebellion against the United States; and the fact that any State, or the people thereof, shall on that day be, in good faith, represented in the Congress of the United States by members chosen thereto at elections wherein a majority of the qualified voters of such State shall have participated, shall, in the absence of strong countervailing testimony, be deemed conclusive evidence that such State, and the people thereof, are not then in rebellion against the United States.

Now, therefore I, Abraham Lincoln, President of the United States, by virtue of the power in me vested as Commander-in-Chief, of the Army and Navy of the United States in time of actual armed rebellion against the authority and government of the United States, and as a fit and necessary war measure for suppressing said rebellion, do, on this first day of January, in the year of our Lord one thousand eight hundred and sixty-three, and in accordance with my purpose so to do publicly proclaimed for the full period of one hundred days, from the day first above mentioned, order and designate as the States and parts of States wherein the people thereof respectively, are this day in rebellion against the United States, the following, to wit:

Arkansas, Texas, Louisiana, (except the Parishes of St. Bernard, Plaquemines, Jefferson, St. John, St. Charles, St. James Ascension, Assumption, Terrebonne, Lafourche, St. Mary, St. Martin, and Orleans, including the City of New Orleans), Mississippi, Alabama, Florida, Georgia, South Carolina, North Carolina, and Virginia, (except the forty-eight counties designated as West Virginia, and also the counties of Berkley, Accomac, Northampton, Elizabeth City, York, Princess Ann, and Norfolk, including the cities of Norfolk and Portsmouth), and which excepted parts, are for the present, left precisely as if this proclamation were not issued.

And by virtue of the power, and for the purpose aforesaid, I do order and declare that all persons held as slaves within said designated States, and parts of States, are, and henceforward shall be free; and that the Executive government of the United States, including the military and naval authorities thereof, will recognize and maintain the freedom of said persons.

And I hereby enjoin upon the people so declared to be free to abstain from all violence, unless in necessary self-defense; and I recommend to them that, in all cases when allowed, they labor faithfully for reasonable wages.

And I further declare and make known, that such persons of suitable condition, will be received into the armed service of the United States to garrison forts, positions, stations, and other places, and to man vessels of all sorts in said service.

And upon this act, sincerely believed to be an act of justice, warranted by the Constitution, upon military necessity, I invoke the considerate judgment of mankind, and the gracious favor of Almighty God.

In witness whereof, I have hereunto set my hand and caused the seal of the United States to be affixed. Done at the City of Washington, this first day of January, in the year of our Lord one thousand eight hundred and sixty-three, and of the Independence of the United States of America the eighty-seventh.

By the President: Abraham Lincoln

William H. Seward, Secretary of State.

Key Provisions of the Civil Rights Act of 1964

An Act

To enforce the constitutional right to vote, to confer jurisdiction upon the district courts of the United States to provide injunctive relief against discrimination in public accommodations, to authorize the Attorney General to institute suits to protect constitutional rights in public facilities and public education, to extend the Commission on Civil Rights, to prevent discrimination in federally assisted programs, to establish a Commission on Equal Employment Opportunity, and for other purposes.

Be it enacted by the Senate and House of Representatives of the United States of America in Congress assembled, that this Act may be cited as the "Civil Rights Act of 1964."

TITLE I—VOTING RIGHTS

SECTION 101 . . .(2) No person acting under color of law shall—

(A) In determining whether any individual is qualified under State law or laws to vote in any Federal election, apply any standard, practice, or procedure different from the standards, practices, or procedures applied under such law or laws to other individuals within the same county, parish, or similar political subdivision who have been found by State officials to be qualified to vote;

(B) deny the right of any individual to vote in any Federal election because of an error or omission on any record or paper relating to any application, registration, or other act requisite to voting, if such error or omission is not material in determining whether such individual is qualified under State law to vote in such election;

(C) employ any literacy test as a qualification for voting in any Federal election unless (i) such test is administered to each individual and is conducted wholly in writing, and (ii) a certified copy of the test and of the answers given by the individual is furnished to him within twenty-five days of the submission of his request made within the period of time during which records and papers are required to be retained and preserved pursuant to title III of the Civil Rights Act of 1960 (42 U.S.C. 1974–74e; 74 Stat. 88): Provided, however, That the Attorney General may enter into agreements with appropriate State or local authorities that preparation, conduct, and maintenance of such tests in accordance with the provisions of applicable State or local law, including such special provisions as are necessary in the preparation, conduct, and maintenance of such tests for persons who are blind or otherwise physically handicapped, meet the purposes of this subparagraph and constitute compliance therewith.

TITLE II—INJUNCTIVE RELIEF AGAINST DISCRIMINATION IN PLACES OF PUBLIC ACCOMMODATION

SECTION 201. (a) All persons shall be entitled to the full and equal enjoyment of the goods, services, facilities, and privileges, advantages and accommodations of any place of public accommodation, as defined in this section, without discrimination or segregation on the ground of race, color, religion, or national origin. (b) Each of the following establishments which serves the public is a place of public accommodation within the meaning of this title if its operations effect commerce, or if discrimination or segregation by it is supported by State action:

(1) any inn, hotel, motel, or other establishment which provides lodging to transient guests, other than an establishment located within a building which contains not more than five rooms for rent or hire and which is actually occupied by the proprietor of such establishment as his residence;

(2) any restaurant, cafeteria, lunchroom, lunch counter, soda fountain, or other facility principally engaged in selling food for consumption on the premises, including, but not limited to, any such facility located on the premises of any retail establishment; or any gasoline station;

(3) any motion picture house, theater, concert hall, sports arena, stadium or other place of exhibition or entertainment;

(4) any establishment (A)(i) which is physically located within the premises of any establishment otherwise covered by this subsection, or (ii) within the premises of which is physically located any such covered establishment, and (B) which holds itself out as serving patrons of such covered establishment. . . .

(d) Discrimination or segregation by an establishment is supported by State action within the meaning of this title if such discrimination or segregation

(1) is carried on under color of any law, statute, ordinance, or regulation; or

(2) is carried on under color of any custom or usage required or enforced by officials of the State or political subdivision thereof; or

(3) is required by action of the State or political subdivision thereof. . . .

SECTION 202. All persons shall be entitled to be free, at any establishment or place, from discrimination or segregation of any kind on the ground of race, color, religion, or national origin, if such discrimination or segregation is or purports to be required by any law, statute, ordinance, regulation, rule, or order of a State or any agency or political subdivision thereof.

SECTION 203. No person shall (a) withhold, deny, or attempt to withhold or deny, or deprive or attempt to deprive, any person of any right or privilege secured by section 201 or 202, or (b) intimidate, threaten, or coerce, or attempt to intimidate, threaten, or coerce any person with the purpose of interfering with any right or privilege secured by section 201 or 202, or (c) punish or attempt to punish any person for exercising or attempting to exercise any right or privilege secured by section 201 or 202.

SECTION 204. (a) Whenever any person has engaged or there are reasonable grounds to believe that any person is about to engage in any act or practice prohibited by section 203, a civil action for preventive relief, including an application for a permanent or temporary injunction, restraining order, or other order, may be instituted by the person aggrieved and, upon timely application, the court may, in its discretion, permit the Attorney General to intervene in such civil action if he certifies that the case is of general public importance. Upon application by the complainant and in such circumstances as the court may deem just, the court may appoint an attorney for such complainant and may authorize the commencement of the civil action without the payment of fees, costs, or security. . . .

SECTION 206. (a) Whenever the Attorney General has reasonable cause to believe that any person or group of persons is engaged in a pattern or practice of resistance to the full enjoyment of any of the rights secured by this title, and that the pattern or practice is of such a nature and is intended to deny the full exercise of the rights herein described, the Attorney General may bring a civil action in the appropriate district court of the United States by filing with it a complaint

(1) signed by him (or in his absence the Acting Attorney General),

(2) setting forth facts pertaining to such pattern or practice, and

(3) requesting such preventive relief, including an application for a permanent or temporary injunction, restraining order or other order against the person or persons responsible for such pattern or practice, as he deems necessary to insure the full enjoyment of the rights herein described. . . .

TITLE III—DESEGREGATION OF PUBLIC FACILITIES

SECTION 301.(a) Whenever the Attorney General receives a complaint in writing signed by an individual to the effect that he is being deprived of or threatened with the loss of his right to the equal protection of the laws, on account of his race, color, religion, or national origin, by being denied equal utilization of any public facility which is owned, operated, or managed by or on behalf of any State or subdivision thereof, other than a public school or public college as defined in section 401 of title IV hereof, and the Attorney General believes the complaint is meritorious and certifies that the signer or signers of such complaint are unable, in his judgment, to initiate and maintain appropriate legal proceedings for relief and that the institution of an action will materially further the orderly progress of desegregation in public facilities, the Attorney General is authorized to institute for or in the name of the United States a civil action in any appropriate district court of the United States against such parties and for such relief as may be appropriate. And such court shall have and shall exercise jurisdiction of proceedings instituted pursuant to this section. The Attorney General may implead as defendants such additional parties as are or become necessary to the grant of effective relief hereunder. . . .

TITLE IV—DESEGREGATION OF PUBLIC EDUCATION

Definitions

Section. 401. As used in this title—. . . .
(b) "Desegregation" means the assignment of students to public schools and within such schools without regard to their race, color, religion, or national origin, but "desegregation" shall not mean the assignment of students to public schools in order to overcome racial imbalance. . . .

Survey and Report of Educational Opportunities

Section 402. The Commissioner shall conduct a survey and make a report to the President and the Congress, within two years of the enactment of this title, concerning the lack of availability of equal educational opportunities for individuals by reason of race, color, religion, or national origin in public educational institutions at all levels in the United States, its territories and possessions, and the District of Columbia. . . .

TITLE V—COMMISSION ON CIVIL RIGHTS . . .

Duties of the Commission

Section 104. (a) The Commission shall—

(1) investigate allegations in writing under oath or affirmation that certain citizens of the United States are being deprived of their right to vote and have that vote counted by reason of their color, race, religion, or national origin; which writing, under oath or affirmation, shall set forth the facts upon which such belief or beliefs are based;

(2) study and collect information concerning legal developments constituting a denial of equal protection of the laws under the Constitution because of race, color, religion or national origin or in the administration of justice;

(3) appraise the laws and policies of the Federal Government with respect to denials of equal protection of the laws under the Constitution because of race, color, religion or national origin or in the administration of justice;

(4) serve as a national clearinghouse for information in respect to denials of equal protection of the laws because of race, color, religion or national origin, including but not limited to the fields of voting, education, housing, employment, the use of public facilities, and transportation, or in the administration of justice;

(5) investigate allegations, made in writing and under oath or affirmation, that citizens of the United States are unlawfully being accorded or denied the right to vote, or to have their votes properly counted, in any election of presidential electors, Members of the United States Senate, or of the House of Representatives, as a result of any patterns or practice of fraud or discrimination in the conduct of such election; . . .

TITLE VI—NONDISCRIMINATION IN FEDERALLY ASSISTED PROGRAMS

Section 601. No person in the United States shall, on the ground of race, color, or national origin, be excluded from participation in, be denied the benefits of, or be subjected to discrimination under any program or activity receiving Federal financial assistance.

Section 602. Each Federal department and agency which is empowered to extend Federal financial assistance to any program or activity, by way of grant, loan, or contract other than a contract of insurance or guaranty, is authorized and directed to effectuate the provisions of section 601 with respect to such program or activity by issuing rules, regulations, or orders of general applicability which shall be consistent with achievement of the objectives of the statute authorizing the financial assistance in connection with which the action is taken. No such rule, regulation, or order shall become effective unless and until approved by the President. Compliance with any requirement adopted pursuant to this section may be effected

(1) by the termination of or refusal to grant or to continue assistance under such program or activity to any recipient as to whom there has been an express finding on the record, after opportunity for hearing, of a failure to comply with such requirement, but such termination or refusal shall be limited to the particular political entity, or part thereof, or other recipient as to whom such a finding has been made and, shall be limited in its effect to the particular program, or part thereof, in which such non-compliance has been so found, or

(2) by any other means authorized by law:

Provided, however, that no such action shall be taken until the department or agency concerned has advised the appropriate person or persons of the failure to comply with the requirement and has determined that compliance cannot be secured by voluntary means. In the case of any action terminating, or refusing to grant or continue, assistance because of failure to comply with a requirement imposed pursuant to this section, the head of the federal department or agency shall file with the committees of the House and Senate having legislative jurisdiction over the program or activity involved a full written report of the circumstances and the grounds for such action. No such action shall become effective until thirty days have elapsed after the filing of such report. . . .

TITLE VII—EQUAL EMPLOYMENT OPPORTUNITY . . .

Discrimination Because of Race, Color, Religion, Sex, or National Origin

Section 703. (a) it shall be an unlawful employment practice for an employer—

(1) to fail or refuse to hire or to discharge any individual, or otherwise to discriminate against any individual with respect to his compensation, terms, conditions, or privileges of employment, because of such individual's race, color, religion, sex, or national origin; or

(2) to limit, segregate, or classify his employees in any way which would deprive or tend to deprive any individual of employment opportunities or otherwise adversely affect his status as an employee, because of such individual's race, color, religion, sex, or national origin.

(b) it shall be an unlawful employment practice for an employment agency to fail or refuse to refer for employment, or otherwise to discriminate against, any individual because of his race, color, religion, sex, or national origin, or to classify or refer for employment any individual on the basis of his race, color, religion, sex, or national origin.

(c) it shall be an unlawful employment practice for a labor organization—

(1) to exclude or to expel from its membership, or otherwise to discriminate against, any individual because of his race, color, religion, sex, or national origin;

(2) to limit, segregate, or classify its membership, or to classify or fail or refuse to refer for employment any individual, in any way which would deprive or tend to deprive any individual of employment opportunities, or would limit such employment opportunities or otherwise adversely affect his status as an employee or as an applicant for employment, because of such individual's race, color, religion, sex, or national origin; or

(3) to cause or attempt to cause an employer to discriminate against an individual in violation of this section.

(d) It shall be an unlawful employment practice for any employer, labor organization, or joint labor-management committee controlling apprenticeship or other training or retraining, including on-the-job training programs to discriminate against any individual because of his race, color, religion, sex, or national origin in admission to, or employment in, any program established to provide apprenticeship or other training. . . .

Other Unlawful Employment Practices

Section 704. (a) It shall be an unlawful employment practice for an employer to discriminate against any of his employees or applicants for employment, for an employment agency to discriminate against any individual, or for a labor organization to discriminate against any member thereof or applicant for membership, because he has opposed any practice made an unlawful employment practice by this title, or because he has made a charge, testified, assisted, or participated in any manner in an investigation, proceeding, or hearing under this title.

(b) It shall be an unlawful employment practice for an employer, labor organization, or employment agency to print or publish or cause to be printed or published any notice or advertisement relating to employment by such an employer or membership in or any classification or referral for employment by such a labor organization, or relating to any classification or referral for employment by such an employment agency, indicating any preference, limitation, specification, or discrimination, based on race, color, religion, sex, or national origin, except that such a notice or advertisement may indicate a preference, limitation, specification, or discrimination based on religion, sex, or national origin when religion, sex, or national origin is a bona fide occupational qualification for employment.

Equal Employment Opportunity Commission

Section 705. (a) There is hereby created a Commission to be known as the Equal Employment Opportunity Commission, which shall be composed of five members, not more than three of whom shall be members of the same political party, who shall be appointed by the

President by and with the advice and consent of the Senate. One of the original members shall be appointed for a term of one year, one for a term of two years, one for a term of three years, one for a term of four years, and one for a term of five years, beginning from the date of enactment of this title, but their successors shall be appointed for terms of five years each, except that any individual chosen to fill a vacancy shall be appointed only for the unexpired term of the member whom he shall succeed. The President shall designate one member to serve as Chairman of the Commission, and one member to serve as Vice Chairman. The Chairman shall be responsible on behalf of the Commission for the administrative operations of the Commission, and shall appoint, in accordance with the civil service laws, such officers, agents, attorneys, and employees as it deems necessary to assist it in the performance of its functions and to fix their compensation in accordance with Classification Act of 1949, as amended. . . .

TITLE VIII—REGISTRATION AND VOTING STATISTICS

SECTION 801. The Secretary of Commerce shall promptly conduct a survey to compile registration and voting statistics in such geographic areas as may be recommended by the Commission on Civil Rights. Such a survey and compilation shall, to the extent recommended by the Commission on Civil Rights, only include a count of persons of voting age by race, color, and national origin, and determination of the extent to which such persons are registered to vote, and have voted in any statewide primary or general election in which the Members of the United States House of Representatives are nominated or elected, since January 1, 1960. Such information shall also be collected and compiled in connection with the Nineteenth Decennial Census, and at such other times as the Congress may prescribe. The provisions of section 9 and chapter 7 of title 13, United States Code, shall apply to any survey, collection, or compilation of registration and voting statistics carried out under this title: Provided, however, that no person shall be compelled to disclose his race, color, national origin, or questioned about his political party affiliation, how he voted, or the reasons therefore, nor shall any penalty be imposed for his failure or refusal to make such disclosure. Every person interrogated orally, by written survey or questionnaire or by any other means with respect to such information shall be fully advised with respect to his right to fail or refuse to furnish such information.

Key Provisions of the Voting Rights Act of 1965

An Act

To enforce the fifteenth amendment to the Constitution of the United States, and for other purposes.

Be it enacted by the Senate and House of representatives of the United States of America in Congress assembled, That this Act shall be known as the "Voting Rights Act of 1965."

Section 2. No voting qualification or prerequisite to voting, or standard, practice, or procedure shall be imposed or applied by any State or political subdivision to deny or abridge the right of any citizen of the United Sates to vote on account of race or color.

Section 4. (a) To assure that the right of citizens of the United States to vote is not denied or abridged on account of race or color, no citizen shall be denied the right to vote in any Federal, State, or local election because of his failure to comply with any test or device in any State with respect to which the determinations have been made under subsection (b)... (1) demonstrate the ability to read, write, understand, or interpret any matter, (2) demonstrate any educational achievement or his knowledge of any particular subject, (3) possess good moral character, or (4) prove his qualifications by the voucher of registered voters or members of any other class. ...

Section 10. (a) The Congress finds that the requirement of the payment of a poll tax as a recondition to voting (i) precludes persons of limited means from voting or imposes unreasonable financial hardship upon such persons as a precondition to their exercise of the franchise, (ii) does not bear a reasonable relationship to any legitimate State interest in the conduct of elections, and (iii) in some areas has the purpose or effect of denying persons the right to vote because of race or color. Upon the basis of these findings, Congress declares that the constitutional right of citizens to vote is denied or abridged in some areas by the requirement of the payment of a poll tax as a precondition to voting.

Section 11. (a) No person acting under color of law shall fail or refuse to permit any person to vote who is entitled to vote under any provision of this Act or is otherwise qualified to vote, or willfully fail or refuse to tabulate, count, and report such person's vote.

(b) No person, whether acting under color of law or otherwise, shall intimidate, threaten, or coerce, or attempt to intimidate, threaten, or coerce any person for voting or attempting to vote, or intimidate, threaten, or coerce, or attempt to intimidate, threaten, or coerce any person for urging or aiding any person to vote or attempt to vote, or intimidate, threaten, or coerce any person for exercising any powers or duties under section 3 (a), 6, 8, 9, 10, or 12 (e).

Executive Order 13050 (13 June 1997)

By the authority vested in me as President by the Constitution and the laws of the United States of America, including the Federal Advisory Committee Act, as amended (5 U.S.C. App.), and in order to establish a President's Advisory Board on Race, it is hereby ordered as follows:

SECTION 1. Establishment. (a) There is established the President's Advisory Board on Race. The Advisory Board shall comprise 7 members from outside the Federal Government to be appointed by the President. Members shall each have substantial experience and expertise in the areas to be considered by the Advisory Board. Members shall be representative of the diverse perspectives in the areas to be considered by the Advisory Board.

(b) The President shall designate a Chairperson from among the members of the Advisory Board.

SEC. 2. Functions. (a) The Advisory Board shall advise the President on matters involving race and racial reconciliation, including ways in which the President can:

(1) Promote a constructive national dialogue to confront and work through challenging issues that surround race;

(2) Increase the Nation's understanding of our recent history of race relations and the course our Nation is charting on issues of race relations and racial diversity;

(3) Bridge racial divides by encouraging leaders in communities throughout the Nation to develop and implement innovative approaches to calming racial tensions;

(4) Identify, develop, and implement solutions to problems in areas in which race has a substantial impact, such as education, economic opportunity, housing, health care, and the administration of justice. . . .

(b) The Advisory Board also shall advise on such other matters as from time to time the President may refer to the Board.

(c) In carrying out its functions, the Advisory Board shall coordinate with the staff of the President's Initiative on Race.

SEC. 3. Administration. (a) To the extent permitted by law and subject to the availability of appropriations, the Department of Justice shall provide the financial and administrative support for the Advisory Board.

(b) The heads of executive agencies shall, to the extent permitted by law, provide to the Advisory Board such information as it may require for the purpose of carrying out its functions.

(c) The Chairperson may, from time to time, invite experts to submit information to the Advisory Board and may form subcommittees or working groups within the Advisory Board to review specific matters.

(d) Members of the Advisory Board shall serve without compensation but shall be allowed travel expenses, including per diem in lieu of subsistence, as authorized by law for persons serving intermittently in the Government service (5 U.S.C. 5701-5707).

SEC. 4. General. (a) Notwithstanding any other Executive order, the functions of the President under the Federal Advisory Committee Act, as amended, except that of reporting to the Congress, that are applicable to the Advisory Board shall be performed by the Attorney General, or his or her designee, in accordance with guidelines that have been issued by the Administrator of General Services.

(b) The Advisory Board shall terminate on September 30, 1998 unless extended by the President prior to such date.

William J. Clinton
The White House
June 13, 1997

Historically Black Four-Year Colleges and Universities

Institution and Location	Year Founded	Land-Grant, Public, or Church Affiliated Denomination
Alabama A&M University, Normal, Alabama	1875	Land-grant
Alabama State University, Montgomery, Alabama	1867	Public
Albany State University, Albany, Georgia	1903	Public
Alcorn State University, Lorman, Mississippi	1871	Land-grant
Allen University, Columbia, South Carolina	1870	AME
Arkansas Baptist College, Little Rock, Arkansas	1884	Baptist
Barber-Scotia College, Concord, North Carolina	1904	Presbyterian
Benedict College, Columbia, South Carolina	1870	Baptist
Bennett College, Greensboro, North Carolina	1873	United Methodist
Bethune-Cookman College, Daytona Beach, Florida	1904	United Methodist
Bluefield State College, Bluefield, West Virginia	1895	Public
Bowie State University, Bowie, Maryland	1865	Public
Central State University, Wilberforce, Ohio	1887	Public
Cheyney University, Cheyney, Pennsylvania	1837	Public
Claflin College, Orangeburg, South Carolina	1869	United Methodist
Clark Atlanta University, Atlanta, Georgia	1988	United Methodist
Concordia College, Selma, Alabama	1922	Lutheran
Coppin State University, Baltimore, Maryland	1900	Public
Delaware State University, Dover, Delaware	1891	Land-grant
Dillard University, New Orleans, Louisiana	1930	Congregational/ United Methodist
Edward Waters College, Jacksonville, Florida	1866	AME
Elizabeth City State University, Elizabeth City, North Carolina	1891	Public
Fayetteville State University, Fayetteville, North Carolina	1867	Public
Fisk University, Nashville, Tennessee	1866	United Church of Christ
Florida A&M University, Tallahassee, Florida	1887	Land-grant
Florida Memorial College, Miami, Florida	1879	Baptist
Fort Valley State College, Fort Valley, Georgia	1895	Land-grant
Grambling State University, Grambling, Louisiana	1901	Public
Hampton University, Hampton, Virginia	1868	Private
Harris-Stowe State College, St. Louis, Missouri	1857	Public
Howard University, Washington, DC	1867	Public
Huston-Tillotson College, Austin, Texas	1952	United Church of Christ/ United Methodist
Jackson State University, Jackson, Mississippi	1877	Public
Jarvis Christian College, Hawkins, Texas	1913	Disciple of Christ Christian Church
Johnson C. Smith University, Charlotte, North Carolina	1867	Presbyterian
Kentucky State University, Frankfort, Kentucky	1886	Land-grant
Knoxville College, Knoxville, Tennessee	1875	Presbyterian
Lane College, Jackson, Tennessee	1882	Christian Methodist Episcopal
Langston University, Langston, Oklahoma	1897	Land-grant
LeMoyne-Owen College, Memphis, Tennessee	1870	United Church of Christ
Lincoln University, Jefferson City, Missouri	1866	Land-grant
Lincoln University, Lincoln, Pennsylvania	1854	Public
Livingstone College, Salisbury, North Carolina	1879	AME
Miles College, Birmingham, Alabama	1908	Christian Methodist Episcopal
Mississippi Valley State University, Ita Bena, Mississippi	1946	Public

Institution and Location	Year Founded	Land-Grant, Public, or Church Affiliated Denomination
Morehouse College, Atlanta, Georgia	1867	Baptist
Morgan State University, Baltimore, Maryland	1867	Public
Morris Brown College, Atlanta, Georgia	1881	AME
Morris College, Sumter, South Carolina	1908	Baptist
Norfolk State University, Norfolk, Virginia	1935	Public
North Carolina A&T St. U, Greensboro, North Carolina	1892	Land-grant
North Carolina Central University, Durham, North Carolina	1909	Public
Oakwood College, Huntsville, Alabama	1896	Seventh Day Adventist
Paine College, Augusta, Georgia	1882	United Methodist
Paul Quinn College, Dallas, Texas	1872	AME
Philander Smith College, Little Rock, Arkansas	1877	United Methodist
Prairie View A&M University, Prairie View, Texas	1878	Land-grant
Rust College, Holly Springs, Mississippi	1866	United Methodist
Saint Augustine's College, Raleigh, North Carolina	1867	Episcopal
Saint Paul's College, Lawrenceville, Virginia	1888	Episcopal
Savannah State College, Savannah, Georgia	1890	Public
Selma University, Selma, Alabama	1878	Baptist
Shaw University, Raleigh, North Carolina	1865	Baptist
Sojourner-Douglass College, Baltimore, Maryland	1980	Private
South Carolina State University, Orangeburg, South Carolina	1896	Land-grant
Southern University and A&M College, Baton Rouge, Louisiana	1880	Land-grant
Southern University at New Orleans, New Orleans, Louisiana	1956	Public

Institution and Location	Year Founded	Land-Grant, Public, or Church Affiliated Denomination
Southwestern Christian College, Terrell, Texas	1949	Church of Christ
Spelman College, Atlanta, Georgia	1876	Presbyterian
Stillman College, Tuscaloosa, Alabama	1876	Presbyterian
Talladega College, Talladega, Alabama	1867	United Church of Christ
Tennessee State University, Nashville, Tennessee	1912	Land-grant
Texas College, Tyler, Texas	1894	Christian Methodist Episcopal
Texas Southern University, Houston, Texas	1947	Public
Tougaloo College, Tougaloo, Mississippi	1869	United Church of Christ/United Missionary Society
Tuskegee University, Tuskegee, Alabama	1881	Land-grant
University of Arkansas at Pine Bluff, Pine Bluff, Arkansas	1873	Land-grant
University of the District of Columbia, Washington, DC	1977	Public
University of Maryland, Eastern Shore, Princess Anne, Maryland	1886	Land-grant
University of the Virgin Islands, St. Thomas, United States Virgin Islands	1962	Public
Virginia State University, Petersburg, Virginia	1882	Land-grant
Virginia Union University, Richmond, Virginia	1865	Baptist
Voorhees College, Denmark, South Carolina	1897	Episcopal
West Virginia State College, Institute, West Virginia	1891	Public
Wilberforce University, Wilberforce, Ohio	1856	AME
Wiley College, Marshall, Texas	1873	United Methodist
Winston-Salem State University, Winston-Salem, North Carolina	1892	Public
Xavier University of New Orleans, New Orleans, Louisiana	1925	Roman Catholic

Presidents and Vice Presidents of the United States*

1. George Washington (1789)
   John Adams (1789)
2. John Adams (1797)
   Thomas Jefferson (1797)
3. Thomas Jefferson (1801)
   Aaron Burr (1801)
   George Clinton (1805)
4. James Madison (1809)
   George Clinton (1809)
   Elbridge Gerry (1813)
5. James Monroe (1817)
   Daniel D. Tompkins (1817)
6. John Quincy Adams (1825)
   John C. Calhoun (1825)
7. Andrew Jackson (1829)
   John C. Calhoun (1829)
   Martin Van Buren (1833)
8. Martin Van Buren (1837)
   Richard M. Johnson (1837)
9. William H. Harrison (1841)
   John Tyler (1841)
10. John Tyler (1841)
11. James K. Polk (1845)
    George M. Dallas (1845)
12. Zachary Taylor (1849)
    Millard Fillmore (1849)
13. Millard Fillmore (1850)
14. Franklin Pierce (1853)
    William R. King (1853)
15. James Buchanan (1857)
    John C. Breckinridge (1857)
16. Abraham Lincoln (1861)
    Hannibal Hamlin (1861)
    Andrew Johnson (1865)
17. Andrew Johnson (1865)
18. Ulysses S. Grant (1869)
    Schuyler Colfax (1869)
    Henry Wilson (1873)
19. Rutherford B. Hayes (1877)
    William A. Wheeler (1877)
20. James A. Garfield (1881)
    Chester A. Arthur (1881)
21. Chester A. Arthur (1881)
22. Grover Cleveland (1885)
    T. A. Hendricks (1885)
23. Benjamin Harrison (1889)
    Levi P. Morton (1889)
24. Grover Cleveland (1893)
    Adlai E. Stevenson (1893)
25. William McKinley (1897)
    Garret A. Hobart (1897)
    Theodore Roosevelt (1901)
26. Theodore Roosevelt (1901)
    Charles Fairbanks (1905)
27. William H. Taft (1909)
    James S. Sherman (1909)
28. Woodrow Wilson (1913)
    Thomas R. Marshall (1913)
29. Warren G. Harding (1921)
    Calvin Coolidge (1921)
30. Calvin Coolidge (1923)
    Charles G. Dawes (1925)
31. Herbert C. Hoover (1929)
    Charles Curtis (1929)
32. Franklin D. Roosevelt (1933)
    John Nance Garner (1933)
    Henry A. Wallace (1941)
    Harry S. Truman (1945)
33. Harry S Truman (1945)
    Alben W. Barkley (1949)
34. Dwight D. Eisenhower (1953)
    Richard M. Nixon (1953)
35. John F. Kennedy (1961)
    Lyndon B. Johnson (1961)
36. Lyndon B. Johnson (1963)
    Hubert H. Humphrey (1965)
37. Richard M. Nixon (1969)
    Spiro T. Agnew (1969)
    Gerald R. Ford (1973)
38. Gerald R. Ford (1974)
    Nelson A. Rockefeller (1974)
39. James E. Carter Jr. (1977)
    Walter F. Mondale (1977)
40. Ronald W. Reagan (1981)
    George H. Bush (1981)
41. George H. Bush (1989)
    James D. Quayle III (1989)
42. William J. Clinton (1993)
    Albert Gore (1993)
43. George W. Bush (2001)
    Richard B. Cheney (2001)

* Year of inauguration

Supreme Court Justices

Name*	Years on Court	Appointing President
JOHN JAY	1789–1795	Washington
James Wilson	1789–1798	Washington
John Rutledge	1790–1791	Washington
William Cushing	1790–1810	Washington
John Blair	1790–1796	Washington
James Iredell	1790–1799	Washington
Thomas Johnson	1792–1793	Washington
William Paterson	1793–1806	Washington
JOHN RUTLEDGE†	1795	Washington
Samuel Chase	1796–1811	Washington
OLIVER ELLSWORTH	1796–1800	Washington
Bushrod Washington	1799–1829	J. Adams
Alfred Moore	1800–1804	J. Adams
JOHN MARSHALL	1801–1835	J. Adams
William Johnson	1804–1834	Jefferson
Brockholst Livingston	1807–1823	Jefferson
Thomas Todd	1807–1826	Jefferson
Gabriel Duval	1811–1835	Madison
Joseph Story	1812–1845	Madison
Smith Thompson	1823–1843	Monroe
Robert Trimble	1826–1828	J. Q. Adams
John McLean	1830–1861	Jackson
Henry Baldwin	1830–1844	Jackson
James M. Wayne	1835–1867	Jackson
ROGER B. TANEY	1836–1864	Jackson
Philip P. Barbour	1836–1841	Jackson
John Catron	1837–1865	Van Buren
John McKinley	1838–1852	Van Buren
Peter V. Daniel	1842–1860	Van Buren
Samuel Nelson	1845–1872	Tyler
Levi Woodbury	1845–1851	Polk
Robert C. Grier	1846–1870	Polk
Benjamin R. Curtis	1851–1857	Fillmore
John A. Campbell	1853–1861	Pierce
Nathan Clifford	1858–1881	Buchanan
Noah H. Swayne	1862–1881	Lincoln
Samuel F. Miller	1862–1890	Lincoln
David Davis	1862–1877	Lincoln
Stephen J. Field	1863–1897	Lincoln
SALMON P. CHASE	1864–1873	Lincoln
William Strong	1870–1880	Grant
Joseph P. Bradley	1870–1892	Grant
Ward Hunt	1873–1882	Grant
MORRISON R. WAITE	1874–1888	Grant
John M. Harlan	1877–1911	Hayes

* Capital letters designate Chief Justices

† Never confirmed by the Senate as Chief Justice

Supreme Court Justices *(continued)*

Name*	Years on Court	Appointing President
William B. Woods	1881–1887	Hayes
Stanley Matthews	1881–1889	Garfield
Horace Gray	1882–1902	Arthur
Samuel Blatchford	1882–1893	Arthur
Lucious Q. C. Lamar	1888–1893	Cleveland
MELVILLE W. FULLER	1888–1910	Cleveland
David J. Brewer	1890–1910	B. Harrison
Henry B. Brown	1891–1906	B. Harrison
George Shiras, Jr.	1892–1903	B. Harrison
Howell E. Jackson	1893–1895	B. Harrison
Edward D. White	1894–1910	Cleveland
Rufus W. Peckham	1896–1909	Cleveland
Joseph McKenna	1898–1925	McKinley
Oliver W. Holmes	1902–1932	T. Roosevelt
William R. Day	1903–1922	T. Roosevelt
William H. Moody	1906–1910	T. Roosevelt
Horace H. Lurton	1910–1914	Taft
Charles E. Hughes	1910–1916	Taft
EDWARD D. WHITE	1910–1921	Taft
Willis Van Devanter	1911–1937	Taft
Joseph R. Lamar	1911–1916	Taft
Mahlon Pitney	1912–1922	Taft
James C. McReynolds	1914–1941	Wilson
Louis D. Brandeis	1916–1939	Wilson
John H. Clarke	1916–1922	Wilson
WILLIAM H. TAFT	1921–1930	Harding
George Sutherland	1922–1938	Harding
Pierce Butler	1923–1939	Harding
Edward T. Sanford	1923–1930	Harding
Harlan F. Stone	1925–1941	Coolidge
CHARLES E. HUGHES	1930–1941	Hoover
Owen J. Roberts	1930–1945	Hoover
Benjamin N. Cardozo	1932–1938	Hoover
Hugo L. Black	1937–1971	F. Roosevelt
Stanley F. Reed	1938–1957	F. Roosevelt
Felix Frankfurter	1939–1962	F. Roosevelt
William O. Douglas	1939–1975	F. Roosevelt
Frank Murphy	1940–1949	F. Roosevelt
HARLAN F. STONE	1941–1946	F. Roosevelt
James F. Brynes	1941–1942	F. Roosevelt
Robert H. Jackson	1941–1954	F. Roosevelt
Wiley B. Rutledge	1943–1949	F. Roosevelt
Harold H. Burton	1945–1958	Truman
FREDERICK M. VINSON	1946–1953	Truman
Tom C. Clark	1949–1967	Truman
Sherman Minton	1949–1956	Truman
EARL WARREN	1953–1969	Eisenhower

* Capital letters designate Chief Justices

Supreme Court Justices *(continued)*

Name*	Years on Court	Appointing President
John Marshall Harlan	1955–1971	Eisenhower
William J. Brennan, Jr.	1956–1990	Eisenhower
Charles E. Whittaker	1957–1962	Eisenhower
Potter Stewart	1958–1981	Eisenhower
Byron R. White	1962–1993	Kennedy
Arthur J. Goldberg	1962–1965	Kennedy
Abe Fortas	1965–1970	L. Johnson
Thurgood Marshall	1967–1991	L. Johnson
WARREN E. BURGER	1969–1986	Nixon
Harry A. Blackmun	1970–1994	Nixon
Lewis F. Powell, Jr.	1971–1987	Nixon
William H. Rehnquist	1971–1986	Nixon
John Paul Stevens	1975–	Ford
Sandra Day O'Connor	1981–	Reagan
WILLIAM H. REHNQUIST	1986–	Reagan
Antonin Scalia	1986–	Reagan
Anthony Kennedy	1988–	Reagan
David Souter	1990–	Bush
Clarence Thomas	1991–	Bush
Ruth Bader Ginsburg	1993–	Clinton
Stephen Breyer	1994–	Clinton

* Capital letters designate Chief Justices

Ethnic composition of the United States in 1790, by Region

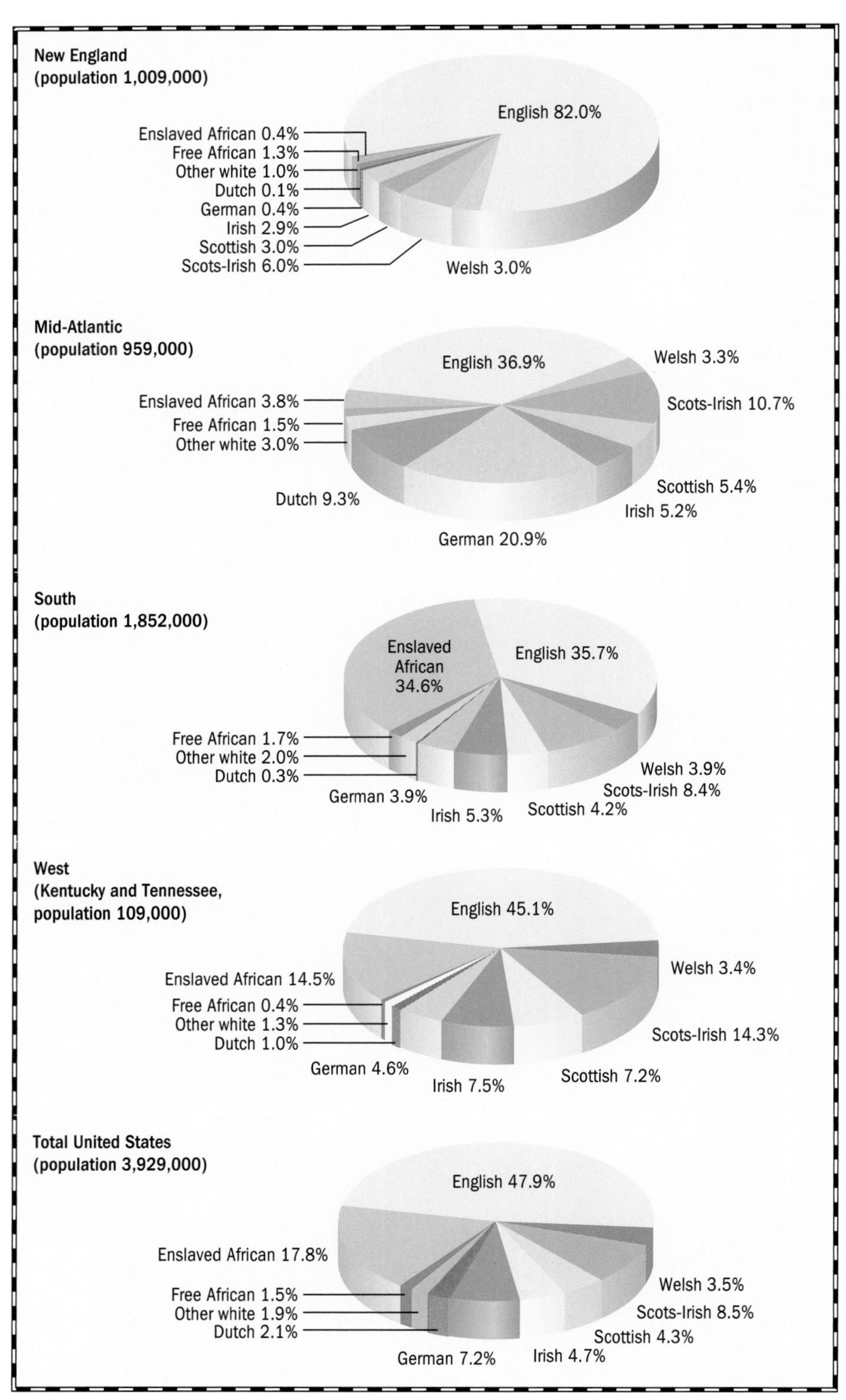

Admission Into the Union

State	Slave Status (before 1860)	Date of Admission	State	Slave Status (before 1860)	Date of Admission
1. Delaware	Slave	December 7, 1787	26. Michigan	Free	January 26, 1837
2. Pennsylvania	Free	December 12, 1787	27. Florida	Slave	March 3, 1845
3. New Jersey	Free	December 18, 1787	28. Texas	Slave	December 29, 1845
4. Georgia	Slave	January 2, 1788	29. Iowa	Free	December 28, 1846
5. Connecticut	Free	January 9, 1788	30. Wisconsin	Free	May 29, 1848
6. Massachusetts	Free	February 6, 1788	31. California	Free	September 9, 1850
7. Maryland	Slave	April 28, 1788	32. Minnesota	Free	May 11, 1858
8. South Carolina	Slave	May 23, 1788	33. Oregon	Free	February 14, 1859
9. New Hampshire	Free	June 21, 1788	34. Kansas	Free	January 29, 1861
10. Virginia	Slave	June 25, 1788	35. West Virginia	NA	June 20, 1863
11. New York	Free	July 26, 1788	36. Nevada	NA	October 31, 1864
12. North Carolina	Slave	November 21, 1789	37. Nebraska	NA	March 1, 1867
13. Rhode Island	Free	May 29, 1790	38. Colorado	NA	August 1, 1876
14. Vermont	Free	March 4, 1791	39. North Dakota	NA	November 2, 1889
15. Kentucky	Slave	June 1, 1792	40. South Dakota	NA	November 2, 1889
16. Tennessee	Slave	June 1, 1796	41. Montana	NA	November 8, 1889
17. Ohio	Free	March 1, 1803	42. Washington	NA	November 11, 1889
18. Louisiana	Slave	April 30, 1812	43. Idaho	NA	July 3, 1890
19. Indiana	Free	December 11, 1816	44. Wyoming	NA	July 10, 1890
20. Mississippi	Slave	December 10, 1817	45. Utah	NA	January 4, 1896
21. Illinois	Free	December 3, 1818	46. Oklahoma	NA	November 16, 1907
22. Alabama	Slave	December 14, 1819	47. New Mexico	NA	January 6, 1912
23. Maine	Free	March 15, 1820	48. Arizona	NA	February 14, 1912
24. Missouri	Slave	August 10, 1821	49. Alaska	NA	January 3, 1959
25. Arkansas	Slave	June 15, 1836	50. Hawaii	NA	August 21, 1959

Racial Composition of the Population (IN THOUSANDS)

Year	White	African American	American Indian	Hispanic	Asian	Year	White	African American	American Indian	Hispanic	Asian
1790	3,172	757	(NA)	(NA)	(NA)	1930	110,287	11,891	(NA)	(NA)	(NA)
1800	4,306	1,002	(NA)	(NA)	(NA)	1940	118,215	12,866	(NA)	(NA)	(NA)
1820	7,867	1,772	(NA)	(NA)	(NA)	1950	134,942	15,042	(NA)	(NA)	(NA)
1840	14,196	2,874	(NA)	(NA)	(NA)	1960	158,832	18,872	(NA)	(NA)	(NA)
1860	26,923	4,442	(NA)	(NA)	(NA)	1970	178,098	22,581	(NA)	(NA)	(NA)
1880	43,403	6,581	(NA)	(NA)	(NA)	1980	194,713	26,683	1,420	14,609	3,729
1900	66,809	8,834	(NA)	(NA)	(NA)	1990	205,710	30,486	2,065	22,354	7,458
1910	81,732	9,828	(NA)	(NA)	(NA)	1996	219,749	30,503	2,288	28,269	9,743
1920	94,821	10,463	(NA)	(NA)	(NA)	2000	211,461	34,658	2,476	35,306	10,641

Source: U.S. Bureau of the Census, U.S. Census of Population: 1940, vol. II, part 1, and vol. IV, part 1; 1950, vol. II, part 1; 1960, vol. I, part 1; 1970, vol. I, part B; and Current Population Reports, P25-1095 and P25-1104; Statistical Abstract of the United States (1997); and unpublished data.; Population Estimates Program, Population Division, U.S. Census Bureau, January 2001.

U.S. Work Force

Year	Total Number Workers (1000s)	Farmers as % of Total	Women as % of Total	% Workers in Unions
1810	2,330	84	(NA)	(NA)
1840	5,660	75	(NA)	(NA)
1860	11,110	53	(NA)	(NA)
1870	12,506	53	15	(NA)
1880	17,392	52	15	(NA)
1890	23,318	43	17	(NA)
1900	29,073	40	18	3
1910	38,167	31	21	6
1920	41,614	26	21	12
1930	48,830	22	22	7
1940	53,011	17	24	27
1950	59,643	12	28	25
1960	69,877	8	32	26
1970	82,049	4	37	25
1980	108,544	3	42	23
1990	117,914	3	45	16
2000	140,900	5.5	47	18.6

Source: *Historical Statistics of the United States* (1975); *Statistical Abstract of the United States* (1991 and 1996); Population Estimates Program, Population Division, U.S. Census Bureau, April 2001.

Vital Statistics

(PER THOUSAND)

Year	Births	Deaths	Marriages	Divorces
1800	55	(NA)	(NA)	(NA)
1810	54.3	(NA)	(NA)	(NA)
1820	55.2	(NA)	(NA)	(NA)
1830	51.4	(NA)	(NA)	(NA)
1840	51.8	(NA)	(NA)	(NA)
1850	43.3	(NA)	(NA)	(NA)
1860	44.3	(NA)	(NA)	(NA)
1870	38.3	(NA)	9.6 (1867)	0.3 (1867)
1880	39.8	(NA)	9.1 (1875)	0.3 (1875)
1890	31.5	(NA)	9.0	0.5
1900	32.3	17.2	9.3	0.7
1910	30.1	14.7	10.3	0.9
1920	27.7	13.0	12.0	1.6
1930	21.3	11.3	9.2	1.6
1940	19.4	10.8	12.1	2.0
1950	24.1	9.6	11.1	2.6
1960	23.7	9.5	8.5	2.2
1970	18.4	9.5	10.6	3.5
1980	15.9	8.8	10.6	5.2
1990	16.7	8.6	9.8	4.7
2000	14.8	8.8	8.5	4.1

Source: *Historical Statistics of the United States* (1975); *Statistical Abstract of the United States* (1999) CDC 2000 National Vital Statistics Report, Vol. 49, No. 6, 8/22/01.

Photo and Text Credits

Chapter 12: Photos: The Granger Collection, 258; Library of Congress, 261; Harper's Weekly, A. R. Waud, 262; Christie's Images, SuperStock, Inc., 266 top; Courtesy of Library of Congress, 266 middle; Moorland-Spingam Research Center, 269; The Granger Collection, 270; The Granger Collection, 275; Library of Congress, 279. Text: Map 12-2, *The Atlas of African-American History and Politics*, 1/E by A. Smallwood and J. Elliot. © The McGraw-Hill Companies. Reprinted with permission of the McGraw-Hill Companies.

Chapter 13: Photos: The Granger Collection, 284; The Granger Collection, 286; The Granger Collection, 288; Photographs and Prints Division, Schomburg Center for Research in Black Culture, The New York Public Library, Astor, Lenox, and Tilden Foundations, Chicago Mosher, 289; The New York Public Library, Research Libraries, 292; University of North Carolina, Southern Historical Collection, 294 left; Rutherford B. Hayes Presidential Center, 294 right; Courtesy of the Library of Congress, 296; E. Sachse and Company, "The Shackle Broken by the Genius of Freedom," Baltimore, MD; 1874. Chicago Historical Society, 298; Thomas Nast/Library of Congress, 301. Text: Table 13-1, Eric Foner, *Freedom's Lawmakers: A Directory of Black Officeholders during Reconstruction* (1993), xiv; The Statistics of the Population of the United States, Ninth Census (1873), xvii, 287.

Chapter 14: Photos: © Collection of the New-York Historical Society, 308; Courtesy of the Library of Congress, 321; The Granger Collection, 322; Solomon D. Butcher Collection, Nebraska State Historical Society, 324; Corbis, 325; Courtesy of the Library of Congress, 328. Text: Benjamin Mays. (1971). Excerpt from *Born to Rebel: An Autobiography*. Athens: University of Georgia Press. Reprinted by permission, 326.

Chapter 15: Photos: Henry Ossawa Tanner, "The Banjo Lesson" 1893. Oil on canvas. 49 × 35½". Hampton University Museum, Hampton, Viriginia, 334; Courtesy of Hampton University Archives, 338; The Granger Collection, 339; The Granger Collection, 342; Courtesy of the Library of Congress, 344; Frederic Remington, Frederic Remington Museum, 346; The Granger Collection, New York, 349; National Park Service, Maggie L. Walker National Historic Site, 352; Cook Collection/ Valentine Museum Library, 354; © 2000 Bettman/Corbis, 357; Erwin E. Smith, "Part of a Parade of the Negro Fair in Bonham, Texas." Home Town of the Photographer. Bonham, Texas, nitrate negative, 1910–1915. LC.S611.790. The Erwin E. Smith Collection of the Library of Congress on deposit at the Amon Carter Museum, Fort Worth, Texas, 358.

Chapter 16: Photos: Jacob Lawrence, "The Migration of the Negro," Panel No. 1, 1940–1941. Tempera on masonite, 12 × 18 in. (30.5 × 45.7 cm.) Acquired 1942. The Phillips Collection, Washington, DC, 364; Brown Brothers, 368; Photographs and Print Division, Schomburg Center for Research in Black Culture, The New York Public Library, Astor, Lenox and Tilden Foundations, 371; The Granger Collection, 373; Courtesy of the Library of Congress, 375; Schomburg Center for Research in Black Culture, 375; Courtesy of the Library of Congress, 382; Library of Congress, 386. Text: Voices, page 390, "A Migrant to the North Writes Home:" Leslie H. Fishel, Jr. and Benjamin Quarles, *The Negro: A Documentary History* (Glenview, IL: Scott, Foresman Co., 1967) pp. 398–399, and Winthrop D. Jordan and Leon F. Litwack, The United States, 6/e. (Englewood Cliffs, NJ: Prentice Hall, 1987), p. 601. Jordon and Litwack cite Emmett J. Scott, ed., "Letters of Negro Migrants of 1916–1918," Journal of Negro History, IV (July 1919), pp. 290–340. Map 16–3 adapted from *The Harlem Renaissance* by Steven Watson, copyright © 1995 by Steven Watson. Used by permission of Pantheon Books, a division of Random House, Inc., p. 394.

Chapter 17: Photos: Aaron Douglas, "Aspects of Negro Life: From Slavery Through Reconstruction, 1934," oil on canvas, 60 × 139", Schomburg Center for Research in Black Culture, Art & Artifacts Division, The New York Public Library, Astor, Lenox, and Tilden Foundation, 400; The Granger Collection, 403; The Granger Collection, 406; New York Daily News, 409; Betsy E. Reyneau. A. Phillip Randolph. National Archives, 413; The Beinecke Rare Book and Manuscript Library, Yale University, 415; Frank Driggs/Corbis, 418; Frank Driggs Collection, 419. Text: Langston Hughes. "I, Too" from *Collected Poems* by Langston Hughes. Copyright © 1994 by the Estate of Langston Hughes. Used by permission of Alfred A. Knopf, a Division of Random House, Inc., 401; Langston Hughes. "Red Silk Stockings" from *Collected Poems* by Langston Hughes. Alfred A. Knopf, a Division of Random House, 416.

Chapter 18: Photos: Isaac Soyer (1907–1981), "Employment Agency," 1937. Oil on canvas, 34¼ × 45 in. (87 × 114.3 cm.), Collection of the Whitney Museum of American Art, New York, 428; Margaret Bourke-White/LIFE Magazine © Time Pix, 432; Doris Ulmann, Schomburg Center for Research in Black Culture, 433; Corbis, 435; Corbis, 438; Scurlock Studios, 439; Courtesy of the Library of Congress, 440; Courtesy Mary McLeod Bethune Council House National Historic Site, Washington, DC, 444; Corbis, 446. Text: Table 18–1, "The Negro Problem and Modern Democracy" by Gunnar Nydrol. © 1944, 1962 by Harper & Row Publishers, Inc. Reprinted by permission of HarperCollins

Publishers, Inc., 431; Excerpt of letter from a sharecropper to the National Association for the Advancement of Colored People, June 21, 1934. The publishers wish to thank The National Association for the Advancement of Colored People for the use of this work., 436; Ralph Ellison. Excerpt from "Perspective of Literature," from *Collected Essays of Ralph Ellison.* Copyright © 1986 by Ralph Ellison. Reprinted by permission of Random House, Inc., 449.

Chapter 19: Photos: Archibald Motley, Jr., "Barbeque," 1934. Oil on canvas, 36¼ × 40⅛ in. The Howard University Gallery of Art, 454; Corbis, 457; Frank Driggs Collection, 458; Getty Images, Inc., 462; Winold Reiss, Portrait of Langston Hughes (1902–1967 Poet) ©1925. National Portrait Gallery, Washington, DC, USA, Art Resource, NY, 464; © David Lees/CORBIS, 468; Getty Images, Inc., 469; © CORBIS/ Bettman, 473. Text: Margaret Walker. Excerpt from "On Being Female, Black, and Free," from *On Being Female, Black, and Free: Essays by Margaret Walker, 1932–1992,* edited by Maryemma Graham, (1997). Reprinted by permission of Maryemma Graham, 467; Langston Hughes. "The Negro Speaks of Rivers," from *Collected Poems* by Langston Hughes. Copyright © 1994 by the Estate of Langston Hughes. Used by permission of Alfred A. Knopf, a Division of Random House, Inc., 464; Lewis Allan. "Strange Fruit." © 1939 (Renewed) by Music Sales Corporation (ASCAP), words and music by Lewis Allen. International copyright secured. All rights reserved. Reprinted by permission, 469.

Chapter 20: Photos: Courtesy of the Library of Congress, 480; Courtesy of the Library of Congress, 484; Horace Pippin (1888–1948), "Mr. Prejudice," 1943. Oil on canvas, 18 × 14 inches. Philadelphia Museum of Art, gift of Dr. and Mrs. Matthew T. Moore. Photo by Graydon Wood, 486; Courtesy of the Library of Congress, 492; National Archives and Record Administration, 493; © Robert Maass/CORBIS, 496; Michael Barson, 497; UPI/Corbis, 501; CORBIS, 502; AP/Wide World Photos, 503. Text: William H. Hastie. Excerpt from "Why I Resigned," *Chicago Defender,* February 6, 1943. Reprinted by permission of the Chicago Defender., 488.

Chapter 21: Photos: Romare Bearden, "Watching the Trains Go By," 1964. Photograph by Sharon Goodman. © Romare Bearden Foundation/Licensed by VAGA, New York, N.Y., 512; Corbis, 515; © AFP/CORBIS, 518; AP/Wide World Photos, 522; John G. Moebes, Greensboro News & Record, 523; UPI/Corbis, 525; Steve Schapiro/Black Star, 528; AP/Wide World Photos, 531; © Flip Schulke/CORBIS, 534; ©1976, Matt Herron/Take Stock–Images of Change, 536. Text: Martin Luther King, Jr. Excerpts of Birmingham bus boycott speech given on December 5, 1955. Reprinted by arrangement with the Estate of Martin Luther King, Jr., c/o Writers House, Inc. as agents for the proprietor. Copyright Martin Luther King, 1963, copyright renewed 1991 Coretta Scott King, 513 and 519; From *Daybreak of Freedom: The Montgomery Bus Boycott* by Stewart Burns. Copyright © 1997 by The University of North Carolina. Used by permission, 517; Bernice Johnson Reagon. Excerpt from "We'll Never Turn Back," from *Everybody Says Freedom: A History of the Civil Rights Movement in Songs and Pictures,* by Pete Seeger and Bob Reiser. Copyright © 1989 by Pete Seeger and Bob Reiser. Reprinted by permission of W. W. Norton and Company, Inc., 528; Martin Luther King, Jr. Excerpts of "I have a dream. . ." speech given on August 28, 1963. Reprinted by arrangement with the Estate of Martin Luther King, Jr., c/o Writers House, Inc. as agents for the proprietor. Copyright Martin Luther King, 1963, copyright renewed 1991 Coretta Scott King, 531.

Chapter 22: Photos: Elizabeth Catlett, *Malcolm X Speaks For Us,* 1969. Lithograph, 95 × 70 cm. Elizabeth Catlett/Licensed by VAGA, New York, NY, 542; Leonard Freed/Magnum Photos, Inc., 547; AP/Wide World Photos, 550; Getty Images, Inc., 552; Mark Jury, *The Vietnam Photo Book,* 553; Frank Johnston/ Black Star, 556; © Bettman/Corbis, 558; Prentice Hall, 560; AP/Wide World Photos, 568. Text: Wallace Terry. Excerpt, "Captain Joseph B. Anderson, Jr." from *Bloods, An Oral History of the Vietnam War by Black Veterans* by Wallace Terry. Copyright © 1984 by Wallace Terry. Used by permission of Random House, Inc., 555.

Chapter 23: Photos: CORBIS, 576; Steve Green/AP Wide World Photos, 579; Damian Dovarganes/AP/Wide World Photos, 585; Paul Conklin, PhotoEdit, 587; Rob Crandall/Stock Boston, 589; © AFP/CORBIS, 591; Chrvstvna Czajkowsky/ AP/Wide World Photos, 594; Faith Ringold, "Tar Beach," 1988. Acrylic pieced and printed fabric, 74 × 69 in. Collection: Solomon R. Guggenheim © Faith Ringold, Inc., 596; James Nubile/The Image Works, 598; AP/Wide World Photos, 599. Text: Table 23–2: Reprinted with the permission of Scribner, a division of Simon & Schuster, Inc. from TWO NATIONS, BLACK AND WHITE, SEPARATE, HOSTILE, UNEQUAL. Expanded and updated edition by Andrew Hacker. Copyright © 1992, 1995 by Andrew Hacker, 580; (1991). "African-American Women In Defense of Ourselves," advertisement in *New York Times,* November 17, 1991, p. 53, 583.

INDEX

A

Abacha, Sani, 598
Abbott, Robert S., 392
Abdul-Jabbar, Kareem, 556
Abernathy, Ralph, 520; Albany movement, 529; Birmingham confrontation, 529–530; Freedom Rides, 525
Abraham Lincoln Battalion, 483
Abyssinian Baptist Church, 393
Ackerman, Amos T., 297
Actors/actresses, 461–463
Adams, Henry, 302
Addams, Jane, 372
Adventures of Grandmaster Flash on the Wheels of Steel, 600
Affirmative action, 568, 582–584
Africa: Garvey's Universal Negro Improvement Association (UNIA) and the return to, 402, 407–410; Pan-Africanism, 410–411
African-American Edison Pioneer, 377
African Legionnaires, 409
African Methodist Episcopal (AME) Church, 266, 340, 341, 344, 474, 599
African Methodist Episcopal Zion Church, 341, 393, 474
Afro-American League (Chicago), 369, 372
Afro American Realty Co., 392
Afrocentricity, 595–597
Agricultural Adjustment Act (AAA), 434–435
Agriculture: *See also specific crops*; Carver, work of, 379; crop liens, 325–326; farmer alliances, 313; farmer discontent following Reconstruction, 311–313; land issues following Civil War, 261–262; New Deal and impact on, 434–435, 436; peonage, 326; renters, 325; sharecropping, 264, 265, 324–325; World War II, effects of, 493
Aguinaldo, Emilio, 351
Aid to Families of Dependent Children (AFDC), 592
Aiken, William, 266
Alabama: Birmingham confrontation, 529–530; bombing of 16th St. Baptist Church, 531; desegregation in, 514; disfranchisement in, 315; Freedom Rides in Anniston, 525; Montgomery bus boycott, 515–521; Tuskegee Study in Macon County, 448–449; violence against black voters, 300; Voting Rights Act of 1965 and Selma, 535–536
Alabama Christian Movement for Human Rights (ACMHR), 529
Alabama Dry Dock and Shipbuilding Co., 494
Albany movement, 528–529
Alcindor, Lew. *See* Abdul-Jabbar, Kareem
Alcorn, James L., 289, 290
Alcorn A&M College, 289, 339
Alert, The (Remington), 346
Alexander, Clifford, Jr., 569
Alfa Suffrage Club, 322
Alfred A. Knopf publishers, 417
Algebra Project, 526
Ali, Muhammad, 556
All God's Chillun Got Wings (O'Neil), 420
Allen, Lewis, 469, 532
Allen University, 340, 356
Along the Way (Johnson), 406
Alpha Kappa Alpha, 378
Alpha Phi Alpha, 378
Alston, Charles, 440
Amalgamated Meatcutters Union, 392
American Baptist Home Mission Society, 269, 340
American Bar Association (ABA), 356, 359
American Citizens' Equal Rights Association of Louisiana, 316
American Dilemma, An, 437
American Federation of Labor (AFL), 353–354, 411, 412, 413, 430, 441, 444, 494
American Federation of Musicians, 456–457
American Medical Association, 355
American Missionary Association, 269, 292, 340
American Muslim Mission (AMM), 597
American Negro Academy, 372, 376–378, 414
American War College, 485
American West Indian News, 443
American Woman's Suffrage Association, 292, 376
Ames, Adelbert, 300, 323
Amherst College, 356, 359
Amnesty International, 589
Amos 'n' Andy Show, 460–461
Amsterdam News, 393
Anderson, Charles, 372
Anderson, E.D., 350
Anderson, Eddie, 461, 489
Anderson, Joseph B., Jr., 555
Anderson, Marian, 437, 467
Anderson, Sherwood, 417
Anderson, William G., 528
Anderson Platoon, The, 555
Angelou, Maya, 559, 576, 594
Anniston, Alabama, 525
Anson, Adrian Constantine "Cap," 359
Antiapartheid movement, 586
Anti-Lynching bill: in 1921 and 1922, 372, 405–407; in 1935, 439
Antioch Baptist, 456
Apaches, 345
Apollo Theater, 457, 459
Arizona (ship), 486
Arkansas: disfranchisement in, 315; Elaine riot (1919), 387; Little Rock, 522
Armed Forces Nurse Corps, 491
Armstrong, Lillian Hardin, 465
Armstrong, Louis, 419, 420, 457, 465, 467, 469
Armstrong, Samuel Chapman, 338
Army Air Corps: treatment of blacks, 488, 489; Tuskegee Airmen, 491–492
Army Reorganization Act (1869), 345
Art: black arts movement (1965–1975), 558–561; Harlem Renaissance, 413–418; New Deal programs, 440–441; in the 1930s and 1940s, 470; in the 1980s and 1990s, 592–594
Arthur, Chester, 328
Artis, William, 441
Arts and Crafts Guild (Chicago), 470
Asante, Molefi Kete, 562, 595–596
Ashley, James M., 276
Associated Publishers, 414
Association for the Study of Negro Life and History, 414, 437
Association of Black Women Historians, 595
Atlanta: Cotton States Exposition (1895), 339, 365, 367, 369; riot of 1906, 384–385; sit-ins, 524; Washer Women's Association, strike by, 354–355
Atlanta *Constitution*, 320, 384
Atlanta Life Insurance Co., 353, 432
Atlanta University, 405, 406
Attica prison, 549
Augusta, Georgia, Ware High School, 337
Autobiography of an Ex-Colored Man, The (Johnson), 406
Autobiography of Malcolm X (Haley), 545
Avery College, 269
Azor (ship), 323
Azusa Christian Community (Boston), 600

B

Bachelor-Benedict Club, 378
Baker, Ella, 431, 443–444, 495, 520, 524
Baker, George. *See* Divine, Father Major Jealous
Baker, Josephine, 420
Baker, Willoughby Alva, 500
Bakke, Alan, 585
Bakke decision, 584–585
Baldwin, James, 418, 471–472, 559, 595
Baldwin, William H., 339, 367
Ballou, Charles C., 382
Baltimore, Charles W., 386, 387
Bambara, Toni Cade, 594
Banjo Lesson, The (Tanner), 334, 414
Banking, 352, 392; Depression and, 432
Baptist churches, 258, 266, 341; Women's Day in, 342–343
Baraka, Amiri, 566
Barber, Ed, 267
Barnett, Ferdinand, 322
Barnett, Ross, 527
Barrow, Joe Louis. *See* Louis, Joe
Barry, Marion, 524
Barthe, Richmond, 440
Baseball, 359, 420–421, 473
Basie, Count, 457, 467
Basketball, 359
Bates, Ruby, 446, 447
Bates College, 337
Beame, Abraham D., 568
Bearden, Romare, 512
Beasley, Mathilda, 345
Beavers, Louise, 461, 462
Bebop, 458, 459
Beck, William J., 350
Beckwith, Byron de la, 530
Belafonte, Harry, 556
Bell, Alexander Graham, 377
Bell, Derrick, 503
Bell, Rieves, 486
Bell, William, 581
Belle, Cool Papa, 473
Belle of the Nineties (film), 461
Benedict College, 269, 546
Bennett College, 269, 340
Benson, Al, 465
Berea College, 269
Berea Presbyterian, 456
Berry, Chuck, 456
Berry, Mary Frances, 569, 581, 586, 601
Bethel Literary and Historical Association, 374
Bethune, Mary McLeod, 437, 438, 491
Bethune Cookman College (Cookman Institute), 353, 412, 438
Beulah (film), 462
Bevel, James, 524, 530, 557
Bible Quilt, The (Powers), 342
Bicycling/bicycle racing, 359
Biddle University (Johnson C. Smith University), 359, 421
Big Brother movement, 374
Big Sea, The (Hughes), 464
Big Sister movement, 374
Billingsley, Andrew, 563
Billups, Kenneth, 456

Binga, Jesse, 432
Binga Bank, 432
Biology, blacks in, 379
Biology of the Cell Surface (Just), 378
Birdland, 458
Birmingham, Alabama: bombing of St. Baptist Church, 531; confrontation, 529–530
Birth of a Nation, The (film), 403–404
Bishop College, 359
Bittker, Boris, 601–602
"Black," adoption of term, 559
Black Allied Students' Association (NYU), 561
Black arts movement (1965–1975), 558–561
Black Arts Repertory Theater, 558
"Black Cabinet," 437, 439
Black Christian Nationalism (Cleage), 544
Black churches. See Churches; *specific church name*
Black codes, 274, 275
Black Congressional Caucus, 586
Black convention movement, 274–276
Black Cross Nurses, 409
Black Feeling, Black Talk (Giovanni), 558
Black feminism, 376, 594–595, 600
Black Feminist Theology, 544
Black Fire (Baraka and Neal), 558
Black Manhattan (Johnson), 406
"Black Manifesto," 547, 601
Black Man's Burden Association, 351
Black Messiah, The (Cleage), 544
Black Methodists for Church Renewal, 546–547
Black Organization of Students (Rutgers), 561
Black Panther Party for Self-Defense, 546–549, 551
Black power, 543, 546–547: King's view of, 543, 546; Randolph's view of, 544
Black Presbyterian United, 547
Black Scholar, The, 560
Black Star Line, 409, 410
Black Student Union (BSU), 562
Black studies, 561–562
Black Theology, 544
Black Theology and Black Power (Cone), 544
Black Thunder (Bontemps), 463
Black Women for Political Action, 600
Black World, 559
Blackbirds, 420
Blacker the Berry..., The (Thurman), 417
Blair, Ezell, Jr., 523
Blake, Eubie, 420, 467
Blakeslee, Clarence, 501
Blakey, Art, 458
Blassingame, John, 563
Blease, Coleman, 321, 338
"Bloody Sunday," 535, 536
Blues, the, 357–358, 419
Bond, Horace Mann, 406
Bond, Julian, 524
Bontemps, Arna, 463
Booker T. Washington Sanatorium, 491
Booker T. Washington (ship), 409
Boston: Azusa Christian Community, 600; busing in, 564
Boston *Guardian*, 369
Boston Riot (1903), 369
Bouey, Harrison N., 323
Boulé, 378
Boxing, 358–359, 473, 556
Boycotts: Montgomery bus, 515–521; of streetcars, 318
Boynton, Amelia P., 535
Boyz N the Hood (film), 600
Braddock, James J., 473
Bradford, David H., 481
Bradley, Aaron A., 273
Bradley, Joseph, 298
Bradley, Mamie, 515
Bradley, Thomas, 567
Bravo, Wellman, 418
Brawley, Benjamin, 416, 417
Breeden, James, 546
Breedlove, Sarah, 353
Brewster, Willie Wallace, 532
Briggs v. *Elliott*, 503
Broadside Press, 559
"Bronx Slave Market, The," 431
Bronzeville, 465
Brooke, Edward W., 551
Brooklyn Dodgers, 359, 473
Brooks, Gwendolyn, 559
Brooks, Sara, 393–394
Brooks, Van Wyck, 417
Brotherhood of Sleeping Car Porters (BSCP), 402, 406, 412–413, 445
Brotherhood of Timber Workers, 354
Brown, Charlotte Hawkins, 438
Brown, Elsa Barkley, 583
Brown, Henry, 317, 318
Brown, Hubert G. "H. Rap," 546
Brown, James, 560–561
Brown, Lee P., 590
Brown, Pat, 550
Brown, Ray, 459
Brown, Ronald H., 578, 586, 591
Brown, Sterling, 559
Brown, William Wells, 272
Brown II, 514–515
Brown University, 421
Brown v. *Board of Education of Topeka, Kansas*, 443, 500–506
Brownsville Affair (1906), 346–347, 375, 378
Bruce, Blanche K., 287, 288, 312
Bryan, William Jennings, 368
Bryant, Carolyn, 515
Buffalo soldiers in combat, 346, 349
Bullin, Ed, 559–560
Bunche, Ralph, 437, 498, 536
Bureau of Refugees, Freedmen, and Abandoned Lands, 262–264
Burke, Richard, 293
Burke, Selma, 470
Burkhead, L.S., 266
Burks, Mary Frances Fair, 516
Burns, Tommy, 358
Burroughs, Nannie Helen, 342–343, 461
Bush, George, 581, 582, 588, 590
Bush, George W., 553, 592, 600–601
Bush v. *Gore*, 601
Business and industry: collapse of, in the Depression, 431–433; following Civil War, 291, 351–353
Busing, 564
Buy, Edna, 466

C

Cabin in the Sky, 468
Cain, Richard H., 267, 272, 312, 323
California: affirmative action in, 584–585; *Bakke* decision, 584–585; black arts movement in, 559; Los Angeles riot (1991), 588; migration to, 391, 493–494; Watts riot (1965), 550
California Civil Rights Initiative (Proposition 209), 585
Caliver, Ambrose, 437, 439
Calloway, Cab, 418, 457, 489
Cane (Toomer), 416
Capra, Frank, 462, 489
Cardozo, Francis L., 272, 287
Carey, Archibald, 404
Carmichael, Stokely, 543, 544, 545–546, 547
Carnegie, Andrew, 336, 339, 367
Carnegie Corp., 437
Carnegie Foundation for the Advancement of Teaching, 355
Carnera, Primo, 473
Carney, Harry, 418
Carpetbaggers, 286
Carrier, Aaron, 388
Carrier, Sarah, 388
Carrier, Sylvester, 388
Carter, Jimmy, 526, 567–569, 580
Carter, Robert, 504
Carter, Samuel, 388
Carver, George Washington, 379, 380
Cary, Mary Ann Shadd, 376
Case for Black Reparations, The (Bittker), 602
Catlett, Elizabeth, 470, 542
Cato, Will, 320
Cavalry: Ninth regiment, 345–350; Seventh regiment, 346; Tenth regiment, 345–350, 380–381
Cayton, Horace R., 465, 492
Census (2000), 601
Central Intercollegiate Athletic Association (CIAA), 359
Central Tennessee Law School, 356
Chamberlain, Daniel H., 301
Chaney, James, 532, 533, 577
Charles, Ray, 560
Charles, Robert, 319–320
Chase, W. Calvin, 367, 371
Chase-Riboud, Barbara, 594
Cheatham, Henry P., 311, 312
Check and Double Check (film), 460–461
Chestnutt, Charles W., 414
Cheyenne, 345
Chicago: art workshops in, 470; black arts movement in, 559, 560; dance and song in 1930s and 1940s, 466–470; first black mayor of, 567; gospel in, 466; jazz in, 465–466; migration to (1910–1920), 392; Renaissance, 463–470; riot of 1919, 387
Chicago American Giants, 421
Chicago Conservator, 322
Chicago *Defender*, 387, 388, 392, 413, 421, 460, 464, 465, 488
Chicago Freedom Movement, 557
Chicago Unions, 359
Chicago White Stockings, 359
Child, Lydia Maria, 268
"Children's crusade" (Birmingham, 1963), 530
Childress, Alvin, 461
Chionesu, Phile, 599
Chisholm, Shirley, 567, 587
Chocolate Dandies, 420
Chrisman, Robert, 560
Christian Methodist Episcopal Church, 474
Christopher, Warren M., 591
Church, Mary. *See* Terrell, Mary Church
Church of God in Christ, 343, 474
Churches, 258, 341–345: *See also specific church name or denomination*; in Chicago, 392; from 1890–1900, 341–345; gospel in Chicago, 466; in Harlem, 393; Holiness Movement and the Pentecostal Church, 343; music, 342, 456–457; in the 1930s and 1940s, 474–475; Reconstruction and, 264–267; as solace and escape, 343
Cities. *See* Urban areas; *specific cities*
City-Wide Young People's Forum, 443
Civilian Conservation Corps (CCC), 435
Civil rights: crusade for, during Reconstruction, 272; NAACP as advocate for, 441; Reconstruction and role of black politicians, 290
Civil Rights Act: of 1866, 276, 277; of 1875, 298, 299, 343; of 1957, 521–522, 551; of 1960, 551; of 1964, 531–533, 552, 561, 582; of 1968, 557; of 1972, Title VII of, 568; of 1991, 586
Civil Rights Commission, U.S., 601
"Civil Rights Juba," 356
Civil rights movement (1955–1965): *See also specific people involved*; Albany movement, 528–529; Brown II, 514–515; Freedom Rides, 524–525, 527; Kennedy administration and, 527; Little Rock, Arkansas, 522; lynching of Emmett Till, 515; major events of, 516; march on Washington, 530–531; Mississippi Freedom Democratic party, 533–535; Mississippi Freedom summer, 533; Montgomery bus boycott, 515–521; prosperity and prejudice in the 1950s, 514; sit-ins in Greensboro, Nashville, and Atlanta, 523–524; Southern Christian Leadership Council (SCLC), 521; Student Nonviolent Coordinating Committee (SNCC), 524, 525, 526; violence, list of dates and events, 532;

voter registration projects, 527–528; Voting Rights Act of 1965 and Selma, 535–536; white resistance to, 514–515; women in, 443–444
Civil rights movement (1965–1980): Black Panther party, 546–549; black power and Stokely Carmichael, 543, 544, 545–546; black student movement, 561–562; busing, 564; Carter administration and, 567–569; innercity rebellions, 549–551; King's assassination, 557–558; Malcolm X, 410, 459, 542, 545; National Council of Churches and, 546; Nixon administration and, 563–565; prison reform movement in 1970s, 549; rise of black elected officials, 565–567; white backlash and black nationalism, 544–547
Civil rights movement (1980–), 577–607: affirmative action, 582–584; Clinton administration and, 590–592; debate of the "old" and the "new," 582; growth of the black middle class, 578–580; persistence of poverty, 580; political activism, 585–586; Rainbow Coalition and Jesse Jackson, 587–588; Reagan/Bush administrations and, 580–585; timeline, 602–603
Civil Rights Restoration Act (1988), 586
Civil War, violence following, 271–272
Civil Works Administration (CWA), 435
Claflin College, 269, 290, 340
Clansman, The (Dixon), 403
Clarence, Thomas, 491
Clark, James G., 535
Clark, Kenneth, 504, 549
Clark, Mark, 549
Clark, Septima, 336–337
Clarke, John Henrik, 596
Clarke, Kenny, 459
Class, social. *See* Social classes
Clay, Cassius Marcellus. *See* Ali, Muhammad
Cleage, Albert, Jr., 544
Cleaver, Eldridge, 547
Clergymen, 341, 342, 343
Cleveland: art workshops in, 470; first black mayor of, 565–566; housing in, 392
Cleveland, Grover, 353
Cleveland Indians, 473
Clinton, Bill, 328, 590–592, 594
Clothes/dress, bebop, 459
Club movement (1870s–1890s), 374–376
Clutchette, John, 549
COFO. *See* Council of Federated Organizations (COFO)
Cold War, 482, 497–500: anticommunism at home, 497, 498; desegregating the Armed Forces, 499–500; Du Bois and Bunche, 498; Robeson, 498–499; Wallace and the 1948 presidential election, 499
Cole, James F., 350
Cole, Robert, 406
Coleman, Ornette, 560
Colleges/universities, 269–270, 289–290, 337, 339–341, 345; *See also specific colleges/universities*; black student movement, 561–562; fraternities and sororities, 378; graduate and professional schools, 442–443; land-grant, 289–290, 338, 339–340; in the 1920s, 415; in the 1990s, 580; protest in 1940s, 495–496; sit-ins by students in Greensboro, Nashville, and Atlanta, 523–524; sports at, 359, 421; Title XI of Educational Amendments Act, 595
Collins, Addie Mae, 531, 532
Color Purple, The (Walker), 579, 594
"Color Struck" (Hurston), 417
Colorado, women's suffrage in, 376
Colored American, 348
Colored Farmers' Alliance, 313
Colored Methodist Episcopal (CME) church, 266–267
Colored Normal, Industrial, Agricultural and Mechanical College of South Carolina, 340
Colored Tennessean, 260
Colored Woman in a White World, A (Terrell), 375
Colored Women's League, 372, 374, 375
Coltrane, John, 560
Columbia University: Alpha Phi Alpha, 378; Law School, 501; upheavals in 1968, 562
Colvin, Claudette, 517, 518, 520
Comics, 460
Comiskey, Charles, 420
Commission on Civil Rights (CCR), 581
Committee for Industrial Organization (CIO), 444–445, 494
Committee on Civil Rights, 499
Communism, Cold War era and, 497, 498
Communist party: Herndon, role of, 446; NAACP versus, 447–448; National Negro Congress and, 448; reasons blacks joined, 445, 446; Scottsboro case, 445–447
Community Action Programs (CAPs), 552, 563
Compromise of 1877, 301–302
Cone, James H., 544
Coney, Asia, 599
Congregational churches, 267
Congress: Great Society and, 554; members in (1867–1900), 311, 312; members in (1996), 586; rise of black elected officials, 566–567; women in, 568
Congress of Racial Equality (CORE), 495, 496, 527, 544, 546; Mississippi Freedom summer, 533
Congressional Black Caucus (CBC), 591
Conner, Douglas, 492–493
Connerly, Ward, 581, 585
Connie's Inn, 418–420
Connor, Eugene T., 529, 530
Conservatives, black, 581
Consolidated Bank and Trust Co., 352
Constitution, The (Atlanta), 320, 384
Constitutional conventions (1867–1868), 286–287
Convict lease system, 329–330
Conyers, John, 518, 551, 602
Cook, Mercer, 527
Cooke, Marvel, 431
Cookman Institute (Bethune Cookman College), 353, 412, 438
Coolidge, Calvin, 410
Cooper, Ann Julia, 376, 377
Cooper, E.E., 348
"Cordelia the Crude" (Thurman), 417
CORE. *See* Congress of Racial Equality (CORE)
Cornell University: Alpha Phi Alpha, 378; black studies at, 562
Correll, Charles, 460
Cortor, Eldzier, 470
Cosby, Bill, 578
Cosmos Club, 378
Cotton Club, 418
Cotton States Exposition (1895), 339, 365, 367, 369
Council of Federated Organizations (COFO), 526, 533, 544
Council of Women of the Darker Races, 352
Counterintelligence Program, FBI's (COINTELPRO), 548–549
Courts. *See* Legal issues/lawsuits; U.S. Supreme Court
Cowboys, 347
Crawford, Anthony, 327–329
Crawford, George, 501
"Creation: A Negro Sermon, The" (Johnson), 406
Crime in black communities, 589–590
Crisis, The, 372–373, 383, 403, 414, 416, 418, 431, 441, 442, 487, 494, 495, 502–503
Crooklyn (film), 590
Crop liens, 325–326
Crouch, Stanley, 595
Crum, William D., 368
Crummel, Alexander, 376, 377
Cuba, black soldiers in, 347–351
Cuban Stars, 421
Cuban X Giants, 359
Cullen, Countee, 415, 416, 417, 418
Culture, black: *See also* Art; Education; Literature; Music; Religion; Sports; Black Chicago Renaissance, 463–470; industry, American racism and, 457; popular, for the masses, 460–463; in St. Louis, 456–457
Cumming v. *Richmond County [Georgia] Board of Education*, 337

D

Dabney, John, 353
Dahmer, Vernon, 532
Daley, Phyllis, 490
Daley, Richard, 557
Dana, Charles A., 276
Dance: at Connie's Inn, 420; in the 1930s and 1940s, 466–470
Daniels, Jonathan, 532
Darrow, Clarence, 372, 407
Dartmouth College, 289
Darwin, Charles, 336
Daughters of the American Revolution, 437
Davis, Angela, 549
Davis, Benjamin, Jr., 446
Davis, Benjamin O., Jr., 483, 491–492
Davis, Ellabelle, 467
Davis, John P., 448
Davis, Miles, 458, 560
Day, Leon, 473
Days, Drew III, 569
Daytona Educational and Industrial Institute for Training Negro Girls, 438
Debt: What America Owes to Blacks, The (Robinson), 602
Dee, Henry Hezekiah, 532
Defense Worker (Thrash), 470
deKlerk, F.W., 586
DeLaine, Joseph A., 503
Delany, Martin R., 263, 292, 301, 310, 323
DeLarge, Robert C., 312
Delaware, desegregation in, 514
Delta Sigma Theta, 378
Democratic national convention, of 1988, 577
Democratic party: in the 1880s, 310, 311–312; first black elected chairman, 586; Mississippi Freedom Democratic party, 533–535; in the 1920s, 407; in 1934–1936, 439–440; Rainbow Coalition, 587–588; reestablishment after Reconstruction, 300
Depression (1929–1933), 428–434: *See also* New Deal; collapse of black businesses, 431–433; failure of relief, 433–434; impact on blacks, 430–433; protest during, 441–444; unemployment statistics, 430–431
DePriest, Oscar, 392, 439
Desegregation. *See* Civil rights movement
Detroit: art workshops in, 470; black arts movement in, 559; first black mayor of, 567; riot of 1943, 494–495; riot of 1967, 550–551
Detroit Housewives' League, 444
Dewey, Thomas, 499
Diallo, Amadou, 588
Diamondback Club, 378
Diet: on farms, 324; of soldiers, 345
Diggs, Charles, 566
Dill, G.W., 293
Dinkins, David, 586
Discrimination, challenges in courts, 442–443
Discrimination, military: in the Army, 345–346, 381–383; costs of, 486–487; protests against, 487, 488
Diseases/health: from 1860–1900, 355–356; farm life and, 324
Disfranchisement, 314–315
Disuniting of America, The (Schlesinger), 597
Divine, Annie, 533
Divine, Father Major Jealous, 474–475
Dixiecrats, 499
Dixie to Broadway, 420
Dixon, George, 358
Dixon, Sharon Pratt, 586
Dixon, Thomas, 403
Do the Right Thing (film), 592, 593
Doby, Larry, 473

Dodds, Mattiwilda, 467
Dodson, Ben, 260
Dodson, Betty, 260
Dole, Robert, 592
Dophy, Eric, 560
Dorismond, Patric, 588–589
Dorsey, Thomas, 466
Douglas, Aaron, 400, 415, 416, 417, 418, 440, 470
Douglass, Frederick, 272; Freedmen's Savings and Trust Company and, 297; migration and views of, 324; women's suffrage and, 376
Dove, Rita, 594
Dowling, William E., 494
Doyle, Pauline (Lobo), 491
Drake, St. Clair, 465, 492
Drama Review, 559
Draper, Elizabeth, 352
Dred Scott decision, 277
Drew, Timothy, 474
Drumgo, Fleeta, 549
Drums at Dusk (Bontemps), 463
Du Bois, W.E.B. (William Edward Burghardt), 340–341, 365, 377, 405, 418, 429, 455, 462–463, 595; *Birth of a Nation* and, 403; clergymen, view of, 342; Cold War and, 498; Communist party and, 448; *The Crisis* and, 372–373; Garvey and, 410; Harlem Renaissance and, 414, 416, 417; House Un-American Activities Committee (HUAC) and, 498; NAACP and, 366, 372, 441–442; Niagara Movement, 366, 369, 371–372; Pan-Africanism and, 410, 498; racial issues and, 365–366, 369–371; relations with Washington, 369–371; riot of 1906 (Atlanta) and, 385; riot of 1917 (East St. Louis) and, 386; Wilson, support for, 378–380; World War I and, 381, 383
Dubuclet, Antoine, 288
Ducksworth, Roman, Jr., 532
Dukakis, Michael, 588
Dunbar, Paul Laurence, 377, 414
Duncan, Todd, 467
Dunham, Katherine, 466–468
Dupree, Jack, 293
Dyer, Leonidas, 372
Dyer Anti-Lynching bill (1921, 1922), 372, 405–407
Dyson, Michael Eric, 595

E

Eastland, James O., 514
East St. Louis riot (1917) (Illinois), 385–386, 406
Ebony, 465
Eckerd, Elizabeth, 522
Eckstine, Billy, 458
Economic Opportunity Act (1964), 552
Economy: in the Carter administration, 569; in the Clinton administration, 591–592; Depression (1929–1933), 428–434; downturn in the 1970s, 569; growth of the black middle class in the 1990s, 578–580; in the 1950s, 514; in the 1960s, 549–550; Panic of 1873, 271, 297; persistence of poverty (1960s–1990s), 580; prior to World War II, 481, 483; Reagan's trickle-down economics, 581; Reconstruction, 289–290; War on Poverty, 551, 552; white resentment of black success, 320–321, 327–329
Edelman, Marian Wright, 591
Edison, Thomas, 377
Education: *See also* Colleges/universities; Afrocentricity, 595–597; black student movement, 561–562; black teachers, 267–269, 336–337; *Brown* v. *Board of Education of Topeka, Kansas*, 443, 500–506; busing, 564; from 1880–1900, 336–341; fraternities and sororities, 378; graduate and professional, 442–443; Hampton model, 338; Head Start, 552; land-grant colleges, 289–290, 339–340; Little Rock, Arkansas, 522; medical schools, 355; in the 1920s, 415; in the 1990s, 579–580; private academies and high schools, 337–338; Reconstruction, 267–271, 288–290; segregated, 337–338; Washington and Tuskegee model, 338–341; white southern response to black, 270–271; of women, 271, 595
Education Act, 552
Education Amendments Act (1972), Title IX of, 595
Edwards, Thyra, 483
Edwards, Willie, Jr., 532
Eight Box Law (1992), 314
Eighteenth Amendment, 418
8th Illinois, 348, 349
Eisenhower, Dwight, 514, 521, 522, 532
Elaine, Arkansas riot (1919), 387
Election(s), 287; of 1876, 300–302; of 1936, 439–440; of 1948, 499; of 1960, 525–527; of 1964, 544; of 1968, 562–563; of 1984, 587–588; of 1988, 588; of 1992, 590–592; of 1996, 592; of 2000, 600–603; rise of black elected officials, 565–567
Elijah Muhammad, 474, 545, 597
Elite, black, 376–378: *See also* Social classes; conservatives, 581; during the Depression, 431–432; Four Hundred, 375; fraternities and sororities, 378; Talented Tenth, 366, 371, 375, 376, 410; upper class, 378
Ella J. Baker House, 600
Ellington, Edward K. "Duke," 418, 457, 461, 465, 467, 469
Elliott, R.W., 503
Elliott, Robert Brown, 298, 299, 312
Ellison, Ralph, 449, 472, 560, 595
Emperor Jones, The (O'Neil), 420, 462
Employment: affirmative action, 582–584; black workers by major industrial group in the 1920s, 411; in the Clinton administration, 591; Depression, impact of, 430–433; Fair Employment Practices Committee (FEPC), 485, 494; in labor (from 1860–1900), 353–355; New Deal, 435, 437, 440; in the 1920s, 411–413; in the 1950s, 514; in the 1960s, 549–550; in the 1980s, 581; in the 1990s, 578–579; in northern cities, 393; professional (1860–1900), 355–356; strikes during 1919–1920, 402; unemployment from 1925–1945, 430–431; World War II and working on the home front, 493–494
Employment Agency (Sayer), 428
Enforcement Acts (1870 and 1871), 296–297
Enterprise Railroad, 291
Entertainment: *See also specific types*; clubs, 418–420; Harlem Jazz Age, 418–420; in the 1930s and 1940s, 457–473; rent party, 420; song, dance, and stage in the 1920s, 420
Entrepreneurs, 351–353, 465
Episcopal churches, 267, 345
Episcopal Society for Racial and Cultural Unity, 547
Episcopal Union of Black Clergy and Laity, 547
Equal Employment Act of 1972, 568
Equal Employment Opportunity, Committee on, 527
Equal Employment Opportunity Commission (EEOC), 533, 568, 569, 581, 582
Equal Rights League, 387
Erwin, Sam, Jr., 514
Ethiopia, 483
Europe, Jim, 383
Evers, Medgar, 530, 532
Evers, Myrlie, 515
"Everybody's Protest Novel" (Baldwin), 471–472
Evy, Fred, 418
Executive Order #8802, 484, 485
Executive Order #9346, 494
Executive Order #9981, 500
Executive Order #11063, 527
Exile, The (film), 462
Exodusters, 323–324
Eyes on the Prize (Hampton), 592

F

Fagan, Sadie, 469
Fagen, David, 351
Fair Employment Practices Committee (FEPC), 485, 494
Fair Housing Act (1988), 569, 586
Fair Play Committee (FPC), 461–462
Falls, Robert, 260
Falwell, Jerry, 514
Family Assistance Plan (FAP), 563–564
Family life: during the Depression, 431; on farms, 324–329; impact of migrations on, 393–394; Moynihan Report, 563–564; reuniting families following Civil War, 260–261
Farad, Wali, 474
Fard, Wallace D., 474
Farmer, James, 495, 496, 524
Farrakhan, Louis, 597–598
Faubus, Orville, 522
Fauset, Jessie, 415, 416, 417, 418
Fax, Elton, 441
FBI (Federal Bureau of Investigation), 589; *See also* Hoover, J. Edgar; COINTELPRO, 548–549; Montgomery bus boycott and, 520–521; Ten Most Wanted list, first black woman on, 549
Federal Art Project, 440, 470
Federal Council of Churches, 546
Federal Council on Negro Affairs, 437
Federal Emergency Relief Administration (FERA), 435, 436
Federal Music Project, 440
Federal Theater Project, 440, 441
Federal Writers Project, 440
Fellowship of Reconciliation (FOR), 496
Feminism, black, 376, 594–595, 600
Fences (Wilson), 592
Ferraro, Geraldine, 587–588
Fetchit, Stepin, 461
Fields, Mamie Garvin, 375
Fifteenth Amendment, 295–296: ways of evading, 314
15th New York National Guard Unit, 383
56 Blows, 593
Filmmakers, 462–463, 590, 592, 593
Final Call, The, 597
Fine Clothes to the Jew (Hughes), 416
Fire, 417
Fire in the Flint, The (White), 416
Fire Next Time, The (Baldwin), 559
First African Baptist Church, 258, 352
Fisk University, 269, 340, 359, 400, 406; Jubilee Singers, 356
Flash and the Furious Five, Grandmaster, 600
Flemming, Arthur S., 581
Fletcher, Arthur A., 584
Flexner, Abraham, 355
Flint-Goodridge Medical College, 355
Flipper, Henry O., 328
Florida: disfranchisement in, 315; election of 2000, 601; first segregation laws in, 316; Rosewood riot (1923), 388
Florida A&M University, 289, 339, 359
Folsom, Jim, 514
Food, Tobacco, and Agricultural and Allied Workers of America, 445
Food, Tobacco, and Agricultural Workers Union, 445
Football, 359
For My People (Walker), 463, 467
Foraker, James B., 347
Ford, Gerald, 565
Ford, Henry, 393
Ford, James, 445
Ford Motor Co., 411
Foreman, Clark, 437
Foreman, George, 556
Foreman, James, 527, 547, 601
Forrest, Nathan Bedford, 293
Fort Des Moines, Iowa, officer training school at, 381
Forten, Charlotte, 267, 269
Fort Leavenworth, 345
Fortune, T. Thomas, 367, 385
Fort Valley High and Industrial School (Georgia), 338
48th Volunteer Regiment, 351
49th Volunteer Regiment, 351

Foster, Andrew "Rube," 421
Four Hundred, 375
Fourteenth Amendment, 277, 298, 310, 318, 447, 501; equal protection clause of, 442, 502, 564
Franco, Francisco, 483
Franklin, Aretha, 560
Franklin, John Hope, 406, 437, 504
Fraternities, 378
Frazier, E. Franklin, 406, 437, 441, 463, 563
Frederick Douglass Memorial Hospital and Training School, 355
Freedmen's Book, The (Child), 268
Freedmen's Bureau, 262–264, 267, 269, 272, 273, 344; bill of 1866, 276–277
Freedmen's Hospital, 355; School of Nursing, 491
Freedmen's Savings and Trust Company, 297
Freedom Farms Corporation, 534
Freedom movement. *See* Civil rights movement
Freedom Rides, 524–525, 527
Freedom Singers, 528
Free Speech and Headlight, 322
Frye, Theodore, 466
Fuller, Charles, 592
Fuller, Hoyt, 559
Furbish, W. Hines, 290

G

Gaines, Lloyd, 442
Gaines v. *Canada,* 442
Galloway, Abraham, 291
Gandhi, Mohandas, 495
Gardiner, Asa Bird, 328
Garnet, Henry Highland, 272
Garrity, W. Arthur, 564
Garvey, Marcus, 322, 402, 406, 407–411, 474
Gary, Indiana, first black mayor of, 566
Gary convention, 566–567
Gaskin, Leonard, 458
Gates, Henry Louis, Jr., 595
Gaye, Marvin, 561
Gayle, W.A., 517
Gayle v. *Browder,* 521
Gee, Jack, 419
General Electric/Westinghouse Board of Patent Control, 377
Georgia: Albany movement, 528–529; Atlanta riot of 1906, 384–385; Cotton States Exposition (1895), 339, 365, 367, 369; disfranchisement in, 315; education in, 337, 338; first segregation laws in, 318; sit-ins, 524; slave insurrection law and the Supreme Court, 446; Washer Women's Association, strike by, 354–355
Georgian, The (Atlanta), 384
Ghettoes, 391
Ghost Dance, 346
Gibbs, Jonathan C., 272, 289
Gibbs, Mifflin W., 289, 290
Gibbs, Thomas, 289
Gibson, Josh, 473
Gibson, Kenneth, 590
Gillespie, Dizzy, 458, 459
Gillespie, Frank L., 392
Gilpin, Charles, 420
Giovanni, Nikki, 558, 559, 560
Gish, Lillian, 403
Gleaves, Richard H., 310
"God's Trombones: Seven Negro Sermons in Verse" (Johnson), 406
Goldberg, Whoopi, 594
Golden State, 432
Goldwater, Barry, 534, 544, 564
Gompers, Samuel, 412
Gone with the Wind (film), 461
Goodman, Andrew, 532, 533, 577
Goodman, Robert, 587
Good Samaritan Building, 353
Gordon, Dexter, 458
Gordon, Eugene, 447
Gordy, Berry, 550, 560, 561
Gordy, Raynoma, 550
Gore, Albert, Jr., 600–601
Gosden, Freeman, 460
Gospel music, 466, 474
Government appointees, Carter administration and, 567–569
Governor, first black, 567
Grady, Henry, 309
Grandfather clause, 315, 368
Grange, 312–313
Granger, Lester, 487
Grant, Charlie, 420
Grant, Madison, 403
Grant, Ulysses S., 297, 300, 301
Graphic art, black, 470
Gray, Fred D., 449, 520
Gray, Victoria, 533
Gray, Wardell, 458
Gray, William H., 586, 591
Great Depression. *See* Depression (1929–1933)
Great migration. *See* Migration, great
Great Society, 551–552, 553, 554, 581
Green, Bennie, 458
Green, Ernest, 569
Green, Malice, 588
Green, Virginia C., 267–268
Green, William, 413
Greenberg, Jack, 504
Greenberg, Reuben, 590
Greene, Lorenzo, 437
Greener, Richard, 290
Greensboro, North Carolina, 523–524
Greer, Sonny, 418
Griffith, D.W., 403
Griffith, Thomas, 350
Griggs, Sutton E., 335, 351
Grimke, Francis, 377
Gruening, Martha, 386
Guihard, Paul, 532
Guinn v. *United States,* 372
Gulf of Tonkin (1964), 553
Gutman, Herbert, 563

H

Habeas corpus, 297
Haley, Alex, 545
Hall, Adelaide, 420
Hamburg Massacre, 300–301
Hamer, Fannie Lou, 527, 533, 534, 536
Hamilton, Alexander, 353
Hamilton, Charles V., 543, 544
Hammond, John, 468
Hammond, Samuel, Jr., 532
Hampton, Fred, 549
Hampton, Henry, 592
Hampton, Wade, 300, 301, 310
Hampton College, 269, 367, 421
Hampton Normal and Agricultural Institute, 338, 339, 359
Handy, W.C., 357
Hansberry, Lorraine, 559
Haralson, Jeremiah, 312
Harding, Vincent, 569–570
Hare, Nathan, 560, 562
Harlan, John Marshall, 317, 318
Harlem Artists Guild, 470
Harlem Art Workshop, 470
Harlem: black arts movement in, 560; Jazz Age, 418–420; migration to (1910–1920), 392–393, 394; music clubs in the 1930s and 1940s, 457–459
Harlem Community Art Center, 441, 470
Harlem Federal Theater Project, 441
Harlem Housewives Cooperative, 443
Harlem Property Owners' Improvement Corp., 392–393
Harlem Renaissance, 377, 413–418
Harmon, William E., 470
Harmon Foundation, 470
Harper, Frances Ellen Watkins, 272, 376
Harris, Abram, 437
Harris, Benny, 458
Harris, Blanche Virginia, 268
Harris, E. Lynn, 593
Harris, John T., 298
Harris, Louise, 445
Harris, Patricia, 567–569
Harvard Law School, 356
Harvard University, 359, 369, 562
Hastie, William H., 437, 439, 483, 487, 488
Hatch, Edward, 346
Hatcher, Richard G., 566
Havis, Ferdinand, 288
Hawes, Bessie, 356
Hayes, Arthur Garfield, 407
Hayes, Roland, 467
Hayes, Rutherford B., 301–302
Head Start, 552
Health. *See* Diseases/health
Hedgeman, Anna, 546
Henderson, Clarence, 523
Henderson, Fletcher, 457
Henderson, William, 315
Henry, Aaron, 533, 535
Herald Tribune, 414
Heritage House, 470
Herndon, Alonzo Franklin, 353, 432
Herndon, Angelo, 446
Higher Education Act of 1965, 561
Highwarden, Ethel, 379
Hill, Anita, 582, 583
Hill, Lauryn, 600
Hill, Sam, 323
Hill, T. Arnold, 487
Hill, W.R., 323
Hillard, Asa, 596
Hines, Earl, 458
Hip-hop generation, 593, 600
Historical Records Survey, 440
Hitler, Adolf, 473, 482
Hoboing, 449
Hodges, James, 561
Hoge, Solomon L., 328
Holden, William W., 295
Holiday, Billie, 459, 468–470
Holiday, Clarence, 469
Holiness movement, 343
Holliday, George, 588
Holmes, Coleman and Vela, 568
Holmes, Larry, 556
Holsey, M.A.L., 444
Home to Harlem (McKay), 415, 416
hooks, bell, 595
Hoover, Herbert, 430, 433
Hoover, J. Edgar: Black Panthers and, 548; Garvey and, 409; King and, 520–521
Hopkins, Charles T., 385
Hopkins, Harry, 437, 440
Horne, Lena, 469
Horse racing, 359
Horton, Willie, 588
Hospital and Training School for Nurses, 355
Hospital for Women and Children (Syracuse), 355
Hospitals, first black, 355
Hot Chocolates, 420
House Behind the Cedars, The (Chestnutt), 414
Houseman, John, 441
House Un-American Activities Committee (HUAC), 498
Housewives' leagues, 444
Housing: in Chicago, 392; in Cleveland, 392; Fair Housing Act (1988), 586; in Harlem, 393; Phillis Wheatley homes, 372, 374–376; renting by farmers, 325; rent party, 420; for soldiers, 345, 381
Houston, Charles Hamilton, 441, 442, 443, 501
Houston, Texas riot (1917), 386–387
Howard, Gertrude, 461
Howard, Oliver O., 262–264, 273

Howard College, 421
Howard University, 271, 359; Alpha Kappa Alpha, 378; Delta Sigma Theta, 378; law school at, 356, 442; Omega Psy Phi, 378, 379; Phi Beta Sigma, 378; School of Medicine, 355; sit-ins in the 1940s, 495–496; Zeta Phi Beta, 378
Howell, Clark, 373, 385
Howell, Robert P., 260
Hudson, Hosea, 446
Huggins, Ericka, 547
Huggins, Rachel, 500
Hughes, Charles Evans, 381, 447
Hughes, James, 464
Hughes, Langston, 389, 392, 401, 415, 416, 417, 418, 429, 456, 464, 465, 559
Human rights, 589–590
Humphrey, Hubert H., 534–535, 563
Hunter, Hezekiah, 268
Hunter, Jane Edna, 376, 389–390
Hunter, Jessie, 388
Hunton, Addie W., 438
Hurston, Zora Neale, 415, 416, 417, 418, 440
Huston, Adam, 350
Hutchinson, Earl Ofari, 588, 596–597
Hyman, John A., 312

I

I.N. Vaughn Co., 445
I, Too (Hughes), 401
Ice-T, 600
Ickes, Harold, 437
Idaho, women's suffrage in, 376
I Know Why the Caged Bird Sings (Angelou), 559, 576
I Wonder as I Wander (Hughes), 464
"If We Must Die" (McKay), 415
Illinois: black arts movement in, 559; Chicago Freedom Movement, 557; Chicago Renaissance, 463–470; Chicago riot (1919), 387; East St. Louis riot (1917), 385–386, 406; first black mayor of Chicago, 567; migration to Chicago (1910–1920), 392; Springfield riot (1908), 385
Illinois Record, 350
I'm No Angel (film), 461
Imitation of Life (film), 461, 462
Immigration and Naturalization Service, 589
Imperium in Imperio (Griggs), 335
"In Defense of Ourselves," 583
In Friendship, 520
Incandescent Lighting: A Practical Description of the Edison System (Latimer), 377
Independent Order of St. Luke, 352, 353
Indiana University, Kappa Alpha Psi, 378
Indianapolis University, Sigma Gamma Rho, 378
Industrial School for Colored Girls, 352
Industrial Workers of the World (IWW), 354
Institute of the Black World, 562
Institution for the Education of Colored Youth, 271
Insurance industry, during the Depression, 432–433
Integration, Malcolm X's views of, 545
Intellectuals, 595
International Congress of Women (Berlin, 1904), 375
International Labor Defense (ILD), 447
International Ladies Garment Workers Union, 445
International Mine, Mill, and Smelter Workers, 445
Interreligious Foundation for Community Organization, 547
Introduction to Black Studies (Karenga), 562
Inventors, 377
Invisible Man (Ellison), 449, 472
Iowa State University, 379
Islam, Nation of, 474, 545, 551, 555, 597–598

J

Jack, James W., 374
Jack Benny Show, The, 461
Jackson, George, 549
Jackson, Jesse Louis, 561, 597, 604; Democratic National Convention (1988), 577; Rainbow Coalition, 587–588
Jackson, Jimmie Lee, 532, 535, 577
Jackson, Jonathan, 549
Jackson, Juanita E. *See* Mitchell, Juanita
Jackson, Mahalia, 466
Jackson, Michael, 578
Jackson, Mississippi, 525; Evers murder, 531
Jackson, Rudy, 418
Jackson, Tony, 465
Jackson, W.T.S., 359
Jackson, Wharlest, 532
Jackson State University, 565
Jazz, 357, 592; black arts movement in, 560; in Chicago, 465–466; Harlem Jazz Age, 418–420
Jeffries, Jim, 358
Jesse Binga's State Bank, 392
Jet, 465
Jews: Farrakhan and, 597–598; relations between blacks and, 547
Jim Crow, origin of term, 316
Job Corps, 552
John F. Slater Fund, 339
John Paul II, Pope, 599
Johnson, Andrew, 264, 273, 274, 276–277, 338
Johnson, Bidd, 458
Johnson, Charles S., 437, 463, 595
Johnson, Gloria, 524
Johnson, Jack, 358–359
Johnson, James Weldon, 377, 404–407, 417, 418
Johnson, John, 465, 559
Johnson, John Rosamond, 405, 406
Johnson, Lyndon B., 527, 531, 534–535, 536, 543–544, 562; affirmative action, 584; Great Society, 551–552, 553, 554; Kerner Commission and, 551; Vietnam War and, 552–555; War on Poverty, 551, 552
Johnson, Prince, 327
Johnson, Sargent, 440–441
Johnson, Smith, 350
Johnson C. Smith University (Biddle University), 359, 421
Joint Committee on National Recovery (JCNR), 448
Jones, Bessie, 325
Jones, Bill T., 593
Jones, C.P., 343
Jones, Eugene Kinckle, 437, 439
Jones, Frederick, 342
Jones, LeRoi. *See* Baraka, Amiri
"Jones Family, The," 460
Joplin, Scott, 356, 467
Jordan, Barbara, 591
Jordan, Duke, 458
Jordan, Michael, 578
Jordan, Vernon, 565, 591
Josephson, Barney, 469
Journal, The (Atlanta), 384
Journal of Negro History, 414
Journey of Reconciliation (1947), 496
Julian, George W., 276
Jungle, The (Sinclair), 366
Jungle Fever (film), 593
Jurists, blacks as, 329
Just, Ernest Everett, 379
Just around the Corner (film), 461

K

Kanawha (ship), 409
Kansas, "Exodusters," 323
Kansas City Monarchs, 473
Kappa Alpha Psi, 378
Karamu House Artist Association, 470
Karenga, Maulana, 566
Karenga, Ron, 562
Katherine Dunham Dance Co., 466–468
Katherine Dunham School of Arts and Research, 468
Katzenbach, Nicholas, 535
Keaton, James Max, 491
Kee, Salaria, 483
Kelley, Robin D.G., 595
Kelly, Alfred, 504
Kennedy, John F., 527, 529, 530, 545
Kennedy, Robert F., 525, 527, 562–563
Kent State University, 565
Kentucky: desegregation in, 514; women's suffrage in, 376
Kerner, Otto, 551
Kerner Commission, 551
Keto, Tsehloane, 596
Kettle Hill, 349
Kimball Union Academy, 379
Kincaid, Nelson, 418
Kind of Blue, 560
King, A.D., 530
King, B.B., 467
King, Coretta Scott, 519, 527, 536
King, Deborah, 583
King, Ed, 535
King, Lonnie, 524
King, Martin Luther, Jr., 326, 496, 513, 543; Albany movement, 528–529; assassination of, 532, 557–558; Birmingham confrontation, 529–530; black power and, 544, 546; bombing of 16th St. Baptist Church, 531; Freedom Rides, 525, 527; holiday commemorating, 586; Hoover and, 520–521; "I Have a Dream" speech, 531; Kennedy and, 527; Mississippi Freedom Democratic party, 535; Montgomery bus boycott, 518, 519–521; Poor People's Campaign, 557, 558; Selma and voting rights, 535, 536; Southern Christian Leadership Council (SCLC) and, 521; Vietnam War and, 557
King, Rodney, 588, 592–593
King, Woodie, Jr., 559
Kipling, Rudyard, 336
Kitchen Table: Women of Color Press, 594
Klunder, Bruce, 532
Knight, Etheridge, 559
Knights of Labor, 353, 354
Knights of the White Camellia, 293
Knock on Any Door (Motley), 463
Ko-Ko, 465
Koppin Theater, 419
Korean War, 500
Ku Klux Klan, 273, 289, 529–530: *Birth of a Nation* and, 403–404; formation of, 293–295; Garvey and, 410; revival of, in the 1920s, 402, 404; violence in the 1960s, 529–530, 533
Ku Klux Klan Act (1871), 296–297
Kuumba Workshop, 560

L

Labor. *See* Employment
Ladner, Joyce, 563
Lady Sings the Blues (Holiday), 469
Lafayette, Bernard, 524
La Guardia, Fiorello, 484
La Menthe, Ferdinand J. *See* Morton, Jelly Roll
Lampkins, Daisy Adams, 438, 443, 444
Land-grant colleges, 289–290, 338, 339–340
Land issues/ownership: blacks as landowners, 326–327; crop liens, 324–325; following Civil War, 261–262, 264, 290–291; peonage, 326, 329; renting, 325; sharecropping, 264, 265, 324–325
Langston, Carrie, 464
Langston, John Mercer, 263, 311, 312
Langston University, 339
Latimer, Lewis H., 377
Law schools, challenges to segregation in, 442–443
Lawrence, Jacob, 364, 441, 470
Lawson, James, 524, 546–547, 557
Lawyers: blacks as (1860–1900), 356; blacks as (1940s–1955), 500–506; blacks as (1960s), 527, 554; blacks as (1990s), 581–582; first black woman, 271; women as, 271, 356, 500–502

Leadbelly, 467
League for Non-Violent Civil Disobedience Against Military Segregation, 500
League of Nations, 411
Lee, Bill, 593
Lee, Don L., 558, 559
Lee, George, 532
Lee, Herbert, 532
Lee, J. Oscar, 546
Lee, Jacqueline, 593
Lee, Johnny, 461
Lee, Robert E., 338
Lee, Spike, 590, 592, 593, 594
Lee, Walter L., 465
Legal issues/lawsuits: affirmative action cases, list of, 584; blacks as jurists, 329; *Briggs* v. *Elliott*, 503; *Brown* II, 514–515; *Brown* v. *Board of Education of Topeka, Kansas*, 443, 500–506; for civil rights, 290; convict lease system, 329–330; *Gayle* v. *Browder*, 521; *Guinn* v. *United States*, 372; *McLaurin* v. *Oklahoma*, 502; *Missouri ex rel. Gaines* v. *Canada*, 501; NAACP challenges racial discrimination in the courts, 442–443; *Nixon* v. *Herndon*, 407, 443; *Norris* v. *Alabama*, 447; *Plessy* v. *Ferguson*, 316–318, 521; *Powell* v. *Alabama*, 447; Scottsboro Boys, 445–447, 449; segregated justice, 329; *Sipuel* v. *Board of Regents of the University of Oklahoma*, 442, 502; *Smith* v. *Allwright*, 443, 500, 514; *Sweatt* v. *Painter*, 442–443, 502
Legend Singers, 456
Leonard Medical School, 355
"Letter from Birmingham Jail" (King), 529–530
Levey, Stan, 458
Levinson, Stanley, 520
Lewis, John, 524–525, 535, 591
Lewis, John E., 350
Lewis, John L., 444
Lewis, Norman, 441
Lewis, Reginald, 578
Lewis, Sinclair, 417
Lewis, William H., 356, 359, 368
Liberian Exodus Joint Stock Steamship Co., 323, 344
Liberty Insurance Co., 392
"Lift Every Voice and Sing" (Johnson), 404, 405
Lincoln, Abraham, on voting rights, 272
Lincoln, Robert, 328
Lincoln Temple Congregational Church, 375
Lincoln University (Lincoln Institute), 269, 376, 421, 456; law school, 442
Lindsay, John V., 491, 568
Liston, Sonny, 556
Literature: *See also specific authors*; black arts movement, 558–561; Chicago Renaissance, 463–465; Harlem Renaissance, 413–418; New Deal, 440; in the 1930s and 1940s, 470–472; in the 1980s and 1990s, 592–594; women writers, 292, 322, 415, 418, 559, 593–594
Little, Earl, 410
Little, Malcolm. *See* Malcolm X
Little Colonel, The (film), 461
Little Rock, Arkansas, 522
Littlest Rebel, The (film), 461
Liuzzo, Viola Gregg, 532, 577
Living Way, The, 322
Livingston College, 359, 421
Locke, Alain, 377, 414, 415, 416, 418
Lodge, Henry Cabot, 315
Loeb, Henry, 557
Loendi Club, 378
Long, Howard H., 382
Long, Jefferson H., 284, 312
Longshoremen's Protective Union, 354
Los Angeles: first black mayor of, 567; riot of 1991, 588; Watts riot of 1965, 550
Lotus Press, 559
Louima, Abner, 588
Louis, Joe, 473, 489
Louisiana: disfranchisement in, 315; farmers' alliance in St. Landry Parish, 313; first segregation laws in, 316; grandfather clause in, 315; labor strikes in, 354; New Orleans riot (1900), 319–320; violence against black voters, 300
Loury, Glenn, 581
Love, Earl, 419
Loveless, H.A., 353
Lowndes County (Mississippi) Freedom Organization (LCFO), 544, 547
Lunceford, Jimmie, 467, 489
Lynch, John R., 312, 323
Lynchings, 272, 293, 320–321, 322; Dyer Anti-Lynching bill (1921, 1922), 372, 405–407; of Emmett Till, 515; 1935 legislation against, 439; "Strange Fruit," 469
Lytle, Lutie A., 356

M

M Street Colored High School (Paul Laurence Dunbar High School), 376
Macbeth, 440, 441
McCain, Francis, 523
McCarthy, Eugene, 562
McCarthy, Joseph, 498
McCauley, James and Leona (Edwards), 518
McClendon, Rose, 441
McClennan, Alonzo, 355
McCree, Wade, 569
McDaniel, Hattie, 461, 462
McDuffy, J.D., 327
McGovern, George, 564
McGraw, John J., 420
McIntyre, George H., 292
McKay, Claude, 414–415, 416, 417
McKenzie, Vashti Murphy, 599–600
McKinley, William, 289, 348, 351, 368
McKissick, Floyd, 544
McLaurin, G.W., 502
McLaurin v. *Oklahoma*, 502
McMillan, Terry, 594
McNair, Chris, 531
McNair, Denise, 531, 532
McNeil, Joseph, 523
McQueen, Butterfly, 461
McRae, Carmen, 469
McShann, Jay, 458
Madden, Owney, 418
Madgett, Naomi Long, 559
Madhabuti, Haki, 558, 559
Maine, U.S.S., 348
Malcolm X, 410, 459, 542, 545
Malcolm X (film), 592
Malcolm X Speaks for Us (Catlett), 542
Mandela, Nelson, 586, 599
Mandela, Winnie, 599
Manly, Alex, 319
Mann Act, 358
"Many Thousand Gone" (Baldwin), 472
"Maple Leaf Rag," 357
Marable, Manning, 595
Marches: Million Man March (1995), 598; Million Woman March (1997), 599
March on Washington (1963), 530–531
March on Washington Movement (MOWM) (1941), 483–485
Marine Corps' treatment of blacks, 489
Marrow of Tradition, The (Chestnutt), 414
Marsalis, Wynton, 592
Marshall, Burke, 527, 530
Marshall, James F., 343
Marshall, Thurgood, 441, 442–443, 487, 503, 504–505, 527, 554, 581–582
Martin, Louis, 569
Maryland, desegregation in, 514
Mason, Charles Henry, 343
Mason, Charlotte Osgood, 417
Master Farad Muhammad, 474
Mather Academy, 338
Maybank, Burnet, 440
Mayfield, Curtis, 561
Maynor, Dorothy, 467
Mayors: first black, 566, 586; National Conference of Black Mayors (1974), 567
Mays, Benjamin E., 309, 319, 326, 336, 337, 338, 342, 343, 519
Medicine (1860–1900), 355–356
Meerpol, Abel, 469
Meharry Medical School, 355
Meigs, Montgomery C., 344
Melle Mel, 600
Memphis, Tennessee, King's assassination, 557–558
"Memphis Blues," 357
Menace II Society (film), 600
Meredith, James, 527, 532
Merrick, John, 432
Messenger, The, 412, 416
Methodist churches, 266, 340, 341; African Methodist Episcopal (AME) Church, 266, 340, 341; Colored Methodist Episcopal (CME) church, 266–267
Mexico, punitive expedition to, 380–381
Mfume, Kweisi, 591
Micheaux, Oscar, 462–463
Michigan: black arts movement in, 559; Detroit riot of 1943, 494–495; Detroit riot of 1967, 550–551; first black mayor of Detroit, 567
Middle class. *See* Social classes
Middleton, Delano, 532
Migration: Garvey's Universal Negro Improvement Association (UNIA) and return to Africa, 402, 407–410; World War II, impact of, 493–494
Migration, following Reconstruction: Exodusters, 323–324; Liberian Exodus, 323, 344; to the North, 323; within the South, 324
Migration, great, 388–394: to Chicago, 392; destinations, 390–391; to Harlem, 392–393, 394; impact on families, 393–394; map showing population distribution in 1920, 391; population growth in selected northern cities (1910–1920), 389; reasons for, 388–390
Migration of the Negro, Panel 1 (Lawrence), 364
Miley, Bubber, 418
Militancy, black, 546, 547–549: black student movement, 561–562
Military: Brownsville Affair (1906), 346–347; Buffalo soldiers in combat, 346, 349; civilian hostility, 346–347, 348; in Cuba, 347–351; desegregation of (1948), 499–500; discrimination in the Army, 345–346, 381–383; fighting Native Americans, 345, 346; Houston riot (1917) and, 386–387; Korean War, 500; Mexico, punitive expedition to, 380–381; in the Navy, 347; as officers, 348–349, 381; Persian Gulf War, 553; Philippine Insurrection, 344, 348, 351; Spanish-American War, 347–351; Vietnam War, 552–555; women in the Spanish civil war, 483; World War I, 381–383
Military, World War II: Army's Air Corps treatment of blacks, 488, 489; beginning of desegregation, 489–490; costs of military discrimination, 486–487; Executive Order #8802, 484–485; institutional racism, 485–486; March on Washington Movement (MOWM) (1941), 483–485; Marine Corps' treatment of blacks, 489; Navy's treatment of blacks, 485–486, 489; between 1939–1940, 483; protests by soldiers and civilians, 487, 488; transformation of black soldiers, 492–493; Tuskegee Airmen, 491–492; women in, 487, 490, 491
Miller, Dorie, 480, 485–486, 492
Miller, Kelly, 377, 390, 414
Miller, Thomas E., 311, 312, 314, 315, 340
Million Man March (1995), 598
Million Woman March (1997), 599
Mills, Florence, 420
Milner, Ronald, 559, 560
Miner, Myrtilla, 271
Ming, Robert, 504

Minor, Robert, 446
Minstrel shows, 356
Minton's Playhouse, 459
Mirror of the Times, The, 289
Mississippi: disfranchisement in, 314, 315; Freedom Rides in Jackson, 525; Freedom summer, 533; Lowndes Country Freedom Organization (LCFO), 544, 547; lynching of Emmett Till, 515; resistance to desegregation, 514; violence against black voters, 300
Mississippi Freedom Democratic party (MFDP), 533–535
Missouri, desegregation in, 514
Missouri ex rel. Gaines v. *Canada,* 501
Mr. Prejudice (Pippins), 486
Mitchell, Arthur W., 439
Mitchell, Clarence, 443
Mitchell, Joseph G., 350
Mitchell, Juanita (Juanita E. Jackson), 443
Mitchell, Maggie. *See* Walker, Maggie Lena
Mitchell, Margaret, 461
Mitchell, William, 352
Mondale, Walter, 587, 588
Monk, Thelonious, 459, 560
Monroe's Uptown House, 459
Montgomery, Olen, 445
Montgomery bus boycott, 515–521
Montgomery Improvement Association (MIA), 518, 519, 520
Montgomery Voters League, 516
Mood Indigo, 465
Moore, Aaron McDuffie, 432–433
Moore, Amzie, 526, 527
Moore, Charles Eddie, 532
Moore, George, 293
Moore, Oneal, 532
Moore, Tim, 461
Moore, William H., 590
Moore, William Lewis, 532
Moorish Science Temple of America, 474
Morehouse, Henry L., 340
Morehouse College, 269, 326, 359
Morgan, Richard, 419
Morrill Land-Grant Act: of 1862, 289, 339; of 1890, 339
Morris Brown College, 340, 344, 353
Morrison, Toni, 591, 594
Morrow, Juanita, 495
Morton, Jelly Roll, 357, 465–466
Moses, Robert Parris, 526, 527, 533
Moss, Thomas, 320–321, 322
Motley, Archibald, Jr., 441
Motley, Constance Baker, 500–502, 503, 504, 506
Motley, Joel, 501
Motley, Willard, 463
Motown, 550, 560
Movies: black filmmakers, 590, 592, 593; in the 1930s and 1940s, 461–463; rap, 600
Moynihan, Daniel Patrick, 563
Moynihan Report, 563–564
Muhammad, Elijah, 474, 545, 597
Muhammad, Wallace Deen, 597
Muhammad Speaks, 545
Mules and Men (Hurston), 418
Municipal Opera Co. (MUNY), 456
Murder rate, 589–590
Murphy, Curtis, 524
Murray, George W., 312
Murray, Pauli, 496
Musgrave, Marianne, 495
Music, 356–358: bebop, 458, 459; black arts movement in, 560–561; blues, 357–358; in Chicago, 465–466; church, 342, 466; classical, 456; freedom songs, 528; gospel, 466, 474; Harlem Jazz Age, 418–420; jazz, 357, 465, 560, 592; minstrel shows, 356; Motown, 550, 560; New Deal, 440; in the 1930s and 1940s, 457–460, 465–466; ragtime, 356–357; rap, 600; slave work songs, 356; soul, 560–561; spirituals, 356; swing, 459
Music Is My Mistress (Ellington), 465
Muslim Mosque, Inc., 545
Mussolini, Benito, 473, 482
Mutual aid societies, 352
Myers, Isaac, 278, 354
Myrdal, Gunnar, 437

N

N.W.A., 600
NAACP. *See* National Association for the Advancement of Colored People (NAACP)
Nabrit, James, 504
Naismith, James, 359
Nance, Lee, 293
Nanton, "Tricky Sam," 418
Nash, Charles E., 312
Nash, Diane, 524
Nashville, Tennessee, 524
Nast, Thomas, 301
Nation, The, 406, 416
Nation of Islam, 474, 545, 551, 555, 597–598
National Advisory Commission on Civil Disorders, 551
National American Woman's Suffrage Association, 322
National Association for the Advancement of Colored People (NAACP), 322, 372–374: attempt by southern states to destroy, 514–515; *Birth of a Nation* and, 403–404; civil rights struggles and, 441; Communist party versus, 447–448; The Crisis, 372–373, 383, 403, 414, 416, 418, 431, 441, 442, 487, 494, 495, 502–503; Du Bois and, 366, 372, 441–442; formation of, 366, 372; Garvey and, 410; James Weldon Johnson, role of, 404–407; Legal Defense and Educational Fund, 500, 501; military discrimination and, 487; Montgomery bus boycott and, 516, 519, 520, 521; in the 1920s, 404, 407; in the 1930s, 441–444; Operation Big Vote, 601; riots following World War I and, 386; Southern Christian Leadership Council (SCLC) and, 521; Spingarn Medal, 379, 491, 498, 518; voter registration projects and, 527; Washington versus the, 373–374; women in, 352, 353, 375, 443–444; during World War II, 495
National Association of Colored Graduate Nurses (NACGN), 355, 487, 491
National Association of Colored Women (NACW), 322, 372, 374, 375, 438
National Baptist Convention, Incorp., 474
National Baptist Convention of America, Unincorp., 474
National Bar Association, 356
National Black Convention (1864), 289
National Black Convention movement, 566–567
National Black Economic Development Conference (1969), 547
National Black Feminist Organization, 568, 595
National Colored Labor Union, 278, 354
National Colored Woman's League, 374
National Commission of Black Churchmen (NCBC), 546
National Conference of Black Mayors (1974), 567
National Council of Churches (NCC), 544, 546–547: Commission on Religion and Race, 546
National Council of Negro Women (NCNW), 438, 491
National Council of Women, 374
National Farmers' Alliance, 313
National Federation of Afro-American Women, 372, 374
National Industrial Recovery Act (NIRA), 435
National Labor Relations Act (NLRA), 439, 440, 444
National League on Urban Conditions among Negroes (Urban League), 372, 374, 412, 416
National Literary Hall of Fame for Writers of African Descent, 592
National Medical Association, 355
National Negro Business League, 369, 372, 444
National Negro Congress (NNC), 448; Sponsoring Committee of, 443
National Notes, 374
National Organization for Women (NOW), 594–595
National Recovery Administration (NRA), 435
National Urban League, 400; military discrimination and, 487
National Youth Administration (NYA), 438
Native Americans, blacks fighting, 345, 346
Native Son (Wright), 463, 471
Naval Academy, 347
Navy, 347, 480, 485–486, 489
Navy Cross, 486
Navy Nurse Corps, 490
Nazis (National Socialist party), 482; *See also* World War II
Neal, Grace, 406
Neal, Larry, 558
"Negro," rejection of term, 559
Negro American League, 473
"Negro Art Hokum, The" (Schuyler), 416
Negro Digest, 465
Negro Digest/Black World, 559
Negro Factories Corp., 409
"Negro Family: The Case for National Action, The," 563–564
Negro Fellowship League, 322
Negro History Bulletin, 414
Negro History Week, 414, 437
"Negro in American Culture, The" (Douglas), 470
Negro in Our History, The (Woodson), 414
Negro Leagues, 359
Negro National Anthem, 404, 405
Negro National League, 421, 473
Negro National News, 443
Negro Soldier, The (film), 462, 489
Negro Speaks of Rivers, The (Hughes), 464
Negro Women's Franchise League, 443
Negro World, 409
Negro Youth Conference (1937), 438
Newark, New Jersey: police director in, 590; riot of 1967, 550
New Careers program, 552
New Day, 475
New Deal, 434–441: *See also* Depression (1929–1933); abuse by agencies, 434–435, 436; black officials in, 435–437, 439; black social scientists and, 437; first (1933–1935), 434–438; second (1936–1943), 439–441
New Era Club, 372, 374
New Jack City (film), 600
New Jersey: black arts movement in, 560; Newark riot of 1967, 550
New Negro, The, 414, 416
New Negro Art Theater Dance Co., 466
New Orleans: riot (1900), 319–320; Storeyville section, 357
New Orleans (film), 469
New Right, 580, 581
New York Age, 367, 393, 406, 447
New York City: art workshops in, 470; black arts movement in, 560; first black mayor of, 586; Harlem Jazz Age, 418–420; Harlem Renaissance, 413–418; migration to Harlem (1910–1920), 392–393; music clubs in the 1930s and 1940s, 457–459
New York *Evening Post,* 372
New York Medical College and Hospital, 355
New York News, 393
New York University, 561
Newspapers: *See also specific papers*; comics, 460; first black, 289; in Harlem, 393
Newton, Huey P., 547, 548–549
Niagara Movement, 366, 369, 371–372
Nicodemus, Kansas, 323
Nigger Heaven (Van Vechten), 417
Nillin, Margrett, 259
Nineteenth Amendment, 376
92nd Division: 368th Infantry Regiment of, 381–382; 369th Infantry Regiment of, 382–383; 371st Infantry Regiment of, 383; 372nd Infantry Regiment of, 383
9th Battalion, Ohio's, 348
Ninth Cavalry Regiment, 345–350

Nixon, E.D., 516, 517, 519, 520
Nixon, Richard, 527, 563–565, 584
Nixon v. *Herndon*, 407, 443
No Name in the Street (Baldwin), 559
No Time for Prejudice: A Story of the Integration of Negroes in Nursing in the United States (Staupers), 491
Nobel Drew Ali, 474
Nobel Peace Prize, first African American to receive, 498
Nobel Prize for literature, 594
Norfolk Red Stockings, 359
Norris, Clarence Willie, 445, 447
Norris v. *Alabama*, 447
North Atlantic Treaty Organization (NATO), 497
North Carolina: disfranchisement in, 315; resistance to desegregation, 514; sit-in in Greensboro, 523–524; Wilmington riot, 319
North Carolina Mutual Life Insurance Co., 432–433
Northern communities, 391–393
Norton, Edward, 568
Norton, Eleanor Holmes, 568, 569, 581, 586
Not Without Laughter (Hughes), 465
Nurses, black, 355–356: in World War II, 487, 490, 491
Nursing schools, 355–356

O

Oberlin College, 375, 376
Odd Fellows and Pythians, 369
Of Booker T. Washington and Others (Du Bois), 370
O'Hara, James E., 312
Ohio, Kent State University killings, 565
Ohio State University, Alpha Phi Alpha, 378
Oklahoma: desegregation in, 514; "Exodusters," 323; Tulsa riot (1921), 387–388
O'Leary, Hazel, 591
Olivet Baptist Church, 392
Olympics (1936), 472–473
Omega Psi Phi, 378, 379
O'Neill, Eugene, 417, 420
Operational Breadbasket, 587
Opportunity, 400, 416, 418, 437, 487
Oprah Winfrey Show, 579
Orangeburg Massacre (1968), 561
Organization for Afro-American Unity, 545
Othello (Shakespeare), 420
Owen, Chandler, 412
Owens, Jesse, 472–473
Oxley, Lawrence W., 437

P

Paige, Satchel, 473
Painter, Nell Irvin, 595
Palmer, A. Mitchell, 402
Pan African Conference (London, 1900), 376
Pan-Africanism, 410–411, 498, 547
Panic of 1873, 271, 297
Parham, Charles Fox, 343
Paris, Treaty of (1898), 351
Parker, Charlie, 458, 459, 467, 560
Parker, John J., 433, 441
Parker, Mack Charles, 532
Parks, Raymond, 518
Parks, Rosa, 495, 517–519, 590
Parsons, C.L., 323
Passing of the Great Race, The (Grant), 403
Patrons of Husbandry, 312–313
Patterson, Floyd, 555
Patterson, Haywood, 445
Patterson, John, 525
Patterson, Robert, 485, 490
Patti, Black, 467
Paul Laurence Dunbar High School (M Street Colored High School), 376
Paul Quinn College, 340, 359
Payton, Benjamin, 546
Payton, Philip A., 392
Peace Mission Movement, 474–475
Peake, Mary, 267
Pearl Harbor, 486
Peck, Fannie B., 444
Peck, William H., 444
Pendleton, Clarence, 581
Penn, Lemuel, 532
Pentagon, terrorist attack on (Sept. 11, 2001), 603
Pentecostal Church, 343
Peonage, 326, 329
People's Grocery Co., 320–321
People's party. *See* Populist party, formation of
People United to Save/Serve Humanity (PUSH), 561, 587
Perot, H. Ross, 590
Perry, Benjamin F., 279
Perry, Lincoln Theodore Monroe (Stepin Fetchit), 461
Pershing, John J., 349, 380, 381
Persian Gulf War, 553, 590
Personal Responsibility and Work Opportunity Reconciliation Act (1966), 592
Phi Beta Sigma, 378
Philadelphia, Million Woman March (1997), 599
Philadelphia Independent, 460
"Philadelphia Plan," 584
Philippine Insurrection, 344, 348, 351
Phillis Wheatley clubs, 372, 374–376
Phoenix, South Caroline riot (1898), 319
Physicians, black, 355–356
Piano Lesson, The (Wilson), 592
Pickens, Francis W., 273
Piedmont Tuberculosis Sanitarium for Negroes, 352
Pike, James S., 293
Pinchback, P.B.S., 287
Pippins, Horace, 486
Pitts, Leonard, Jr., 603
Pittsburgh Courier, 388, 439, 448, 461, 483
Plains Indians, 345, 346
Plantation Review, 420
Plessy, Homer A., 316–318
Plessy v. *Ferguson*, 316–318, 337, 521
Plummer, Clifford, 371
Poetry, black arts movement, 559
Police: black police directors, 590; brutality, in the 1990s, 588–590; following Reconstruction, 329; repression, 547–549
Politics (1867–177): *See also specific political parties*; black leaders, 287–288, 289, 291; civil rights, 290; constitutional conventions, 286–287; economic issues, 290–291; educational and social welfare issues, 288–290; elections, 287, 300–302; land issues, 290–291; opposition, 291–293; Reconstruction, 272, 273, 278; timeline, 304–305; women politicians, 292
Politics (1875–1900), 310–314: black congressmen, 311, 312; Colored Farmers' Alliance, 313; Democrats and farmer discontent, 311–313; disfranchisement, 314–315; Populist party, 313–314
Politics (1900–): blacks in government positions, 392; Kennedy administration and the civil rights movement, 527; Mississippi Freedom Democratic party, 533–535; National Black Convention movement, 566–567; 1936 election, 439–440; 1948 election, 499; 1960 election, 525–527; 1968 election, 562–563; 1992 election, 590–592; 1996 election, 592; political activism (1980s–1990s), 585–586; Rainbow Coalition, 587–588; rise of black elected officials, 565–567; 2000 election, 600–603; Wilson, support for, 378–380; women politicians (1970s), 567, 587
Pollard, Frederick Douglass "Fritz," 421
Pool, Elijah. *See* Elijah Muhammad
Poor People's Campaign, 557, 558
Populist party, formation of, 313–314
Porgy and Bess (Gershwin), 420
Port Royal Experiment, 262, 327
Potter, Tommy, 458
Poverty: *See also* Economy; Social classes; persistence in 1980s–1990s, 580; War on Poverty, 551, 552
Powell, Adam Clayton, Jr., 487, 500, 554
Powell, Adam Clayton, Sr., 393
Powell, Bud, 459
Powell, Colin, 578
Powell, Ozie, 445
Powell, Rodney, 524
Powell, Ruth, 495, 496
Powell v. *Alabama*, 447
Powers, Harriet, 342
Prairie View A&M, 359
Presbyterian churches, 267, 341
Presbyterian Interracial Council, 547
"Pretty Baby," 465
Price, Cecil, 533
Price, Leontyne, 467
Price, Victoria, 447
Pridget, Gertrude, 357
Prince, 592
Princeton Theological Seminary, 289
Prioleau, George W., 348
Prison life, 329–330: reform movement in 1970s, 549
Pritchett, Laurie, 528–529
Professionals, black, 355–356: education of, 442–443
Progressive movement, 366
Progressive National Baptist Convention, 474
Progressive party, 378
Project 100,000, 553–554
Proposition 209 (California Civil Rights Initiative), 585
Prostitution, 393–394
Provident Hospital and Training Institute, 355, 392
Public Works Administration (PWA), 435
Public Works Employment Act, 569
Pulitzer Prizes, 592, 594
Pullman, George, 412
Pullman Palace Car Co., 308, 412, 413, 445
Purple Rain (film), 592
PUSH-EXCEL, 587
Putnam, Caroline Remond, 376

Q

Qaddafi, Muammar, 597
Quaker's Institute for Colored Youth, 292
Quayle, Dan, 553
Quarles, Benjamin, 437

R

Racial etiquette, 318–319
Racism, in the 1920s, 402–404: *See also* Civil rights movement; *Birth of a Nation, The*, 403–404; Ku Klux Klan, 404; scientific, 403–404
Radical Republicans: Freedmen's Bureau bill and Civil Rights bill, 276–277; Johnson's vetoes, 276–277; members of, 276; proposals, 276
Radio, 460–461
Ragtime, 356–357
Railroads: black porters and attendants, 308; Brotherhood of Sleeping Car Porters (BSCP), 402, 406, 412–413, 445; segregation on, 316–318
Railway Labor Act, 445
Rainbow Coalition, 587–588
Rainey, Gertrude "Ma," 419
Rainey, Joseph H., 287, 297, 312
Rainey, Ma, 357, 467
Rainey, William "Pa," 357
Randall, Dudley, 559
Randolph, A. Philip, 406, 448; black power and, 544; Brotherhood of Sleeping Car Porters (BSCP) and, 412–413, 445; Garvey and, 410; League for Non-Violent Civil Disobedience Against Military Segregation, 500; March on Washington Movement, 483–485, 530; military discrimination and, 487
Randolph, Benjamin K., 293
Ransby, Barbara, 583
Ransier, Alonso J., 312
Ransom, Leon A., 502–503
Rapier, James T., 299, 312
Rap music, 600

Rapper's Delight, 600
Raspberry, William, 602
Ray, Charles B., 271
Ray, Charlotte Augusta Burroughs, 271
Ray, Charlotte E., 271, 356
Ray, James Earl, 557
Reagan, Ronald, 544, 565, 569, 588; conservative reaction in administration of, 580–585; King holiday, 586
Reagon, Bernice Johnson, 528
Reagon, Cordell, 528
Reason Why the Colored American Is Not in the Columbian Exposition, The (Wells), 322
Rebecca of Sunnybrook Farm (film), 461
Reconstruction (1865–1868), 258–305: churches, 264–267; civil rights, 272, 276, 290; economic issues, 290–291; education, 267–271, 288–290; end of, 299–302, 310; Freedmen's Bureau, 262–264; freedom, what it meant, 259, 263; under Johnson, 274, 276; land, issues of, 261–262, 264, 290–291; legislation, 276–277; politics in, 272, 273, 278; radical, 277–279; reaction of white Southerners, 278–279; reactions of former slaves, 260; reuniting of black families, 260–261; sharecropping, 264, 265; timeline, 280–281; violence, 271–272
Reconstruction Act, First (1867), 277–278
Reconstruction Finance Corp., 433
Red Scare, 402
Red Shirts, 301
"Red Silk Stockings" (Hughes), 416
Redcross, Bob, 458
Redding, Louis, 504
Reeb, James, 532, 535
Reed, Adolph, 598
Reed, Ishmael, 595
Reed, Paul, 320
Reese, Frederick, 535
Reese, John Earl, 532
Reid, Ira De A., 437
Religion: *See also specific churches and faiths*; Black Theology, 544; from 1890–1900, 341–345; gospel music in Chicago, 465–466; Holiness Movement and the Pentecostal Church, 343; National Council of Churches, 544, 546–547; Nation of Islam, 474, 545, 551, 555, 597–598; in the 1930s and 1940s, 474–475; in the 1990s, 599–600
Remington, Frederic, 346
Renting versus sharecropping, 325
Rent party, 420
Reparations, 601–602
Republican party: *See also* Radical Republicans; blacks in (1880s), 310–311; during the Depression, 433; factionalism, 291, 293, 378; in the 1920s, 407
Resurrection City, 558
Revels, Hiram, 287, 288, 289, 312
Revue Nègre, 420
Reynolds, Ellsworth, 418
Reynolds, Grant, 500
Rice, Thomas "Daddy," 316
Richardson, George, 385
Richmond, David, 523
Rickey, Branch, 473
Riggs, Marlon, 593
Ringgold, Faith, 595, 596
Riots, 383–388: Atlanta, Georgia (1906), 384–385; Chicago, Illinois (1919), 387, 392; Detroit, Michigan (1943), 494–495; Detroit, Michigan (1967), 550–551; East St. Louis, Illinois (1917), 385–386, 406; Elaine, Arkansas (1919), 387; following King's assassination, 557–558; Houston, Texas (1917), 386–387; inner-city, in the 1960s, 549–551; Los Angeles, California (1991), 588; Newark, New Jersey (1967), 550; Phoenix, South Carolina (1898), 319; prison, in the 1970s, 549; during Reconstruction, 272; Rosewood, Florida (1923), 388; Springfield, Illinois (1908), 372, 385; Tulsa, Oklahoma (1921), 387–388; Watts, California (1965), 550; Wilmington, North Carolina (1898), 319
Rising Tide of Color, The (Stoddard), 403
Rivers, Eugene, 600
Rivers, Eunice, 448
Rivers, Prince, 272
RJ Reynolds, 445
Roach, Max, 458, 459
Roberson, Lizzie Woods, 343
Roberts, H.K., 295
Robertson, Carole, 531, 532
Robertson, Willie, 445
Robeson, Paul, 420, 421, 462, 489, 498–499
Robinson, Armstead, 562
Robinson, Bill "Bojangles," 420, 461, 489
Robinson, Jackie, 359, 391, 473, 527
Robinson, Jo Ann, 516, 517, 518, 520
Robinson, Mallie, 391
Robinson, Randall, 586, 602
Robinson, Ray, 489
Robinson, Spottswood, 504
Rockefeller, John D., 336
Rockefeller, Nelson, 564
Roe v. *Wade*, 594
Roger, Albert, 320
Rogers, J.A., 483
Rollin, Charlotte, 292
Rollin, Frances, 292
Rollin, Katherine, 292
Rollin, Lottie, 376
Rollin, Louise, 292
Rollin, William, 292
Roman Catholic Church, 267, 345, 547, 599
Romney, George, 551
Roosevelt, Eleanor, 435–437, 439, 484, 487
Roosevelt, Franklin D., 375, 432, 483, 491; Executive Order 8802, 484, 485; Executive Order 9346, 494; March on Washington Movement and, 484–485; New Deal and, 434–435, 437, 439, 470; World War II and, 482–483
Roosevelt, Theodore, 347, 349, 350, 368, 375, 378, 406
Roper, Daniel, 437
Rosenwald, Julius, 367, 392
Rosewood, Florida riot (1923), 388
Ross, Diana, 469, 550
Ross, Malcolm, 494
Rough Riders, 349, 350
Rowan, Carl, 527
Rowland, Dick, 387
Ruffin, Josephine St. Pierre, 374
Rust College, 269, 340
Rustin, Bayard, 495, 496, 520, 524, 530, 535, 536
Rutgers University, 421, 561–562

S

Sacco, Nicola, 402
SAGE, 595
St. Augustine College, 269
St. Louis, in the 1930s and 1940s, 456–457
St. Louis American, 456
St. Louis Argus, 456
"St. Louis Blues," 357
St. Louis Symphony, 456
St. Luke Herald, 352
St. Luke's Penny Savings Bank, 353
St. Mark's Episcopal Church (Harlem), 393
St. Mark's Protestant Episcopal Church (Charleston), 267
St. Paul College, 269
St. Philip's Protestant Episcopal Church, 393
Sally Hemings (Chase–Riboud), 594
Salt Eaters, The (Bambara), 594
Sam Houston College, 359
Sanchez, Sonia, 558, 559
Sanders, Pharoah, 560
San Francisco State College, 562
San Juan Hill, 349, 350
Savage, Augusta, 441, 470
Savage School of Arts and Crafts, 441
Savage Studios, 441
Savannah Educational Association, 267
"Say It Loud, I'm Black and I'm Proud," 560
Sayer, Issac, 428
Scalawags/scoundrels, 286
Schlesinger, Arthur, Jr., 597
Schmeling, Max, 473
Schnetzler, Maid Hedwig, 379
Schomburg, Arthur, 377
School Daze (film), 593
Schools. *See* Education
Schuyler, George, 416, 443, 448
Schwerner, Michael, 532, 533, 577
Scientific racism, 403–404
SCLC. *See* Southern Christian Leadership Council (SCLC)
Scott, Emmett J., 367
Scott, Marie, 321
Scott, Robert K., 294
Scottsboro Boys, 445–447, 449, 518
Sea Islands, 327
Seabrook, Joseph, 267
Seale, Bobby, 547, 548
Second Reconstruction, use of term, 513
Secret Ritual of the Nation of Islam, The (Fard), 474
Segregation: *See also under specific topic, e.g. Education*; educational, after Reconstruction, 288; educational, challenges to, 442–443; of federal agencies and buildings, 380; following Reconstruction, 315–318; in military, 381; segregated justice, 329; streetcar, 318; use of term, 316
Sellers, Cleveland, 561
Selma, Alabama, 535–536
Separate but equal doctrine, 317, 318, 337, 502, 506; challenging constitutionality of, 442
September 11, 2001, 603
Seventh Cavalry Regiment, 346
Sex Discrimination and the Law: Causes and Remedies (Norton), 568
Sexual harassment, 582, 583
Seymour, William J., 343
Shabazz, El-Hajj Malik El-, 545
Sharecropping, 264, 265, 324–325
Shaw, Nate, 446
Shaw College, 269, 359
Shaw University, 355, 524
She's Gotta Have It (film), 593
Shepp, Archie, 560
Sheridan, Philip H., 272
Sherman, William Tecumseh, 261, 264, 327
Sherrod, Charles, 529
Shotgun Policy, 300
Showboat, 420, 462
Shuffle Along, 420
Shuttlesworth, Fred, 520, 525, 529
Sigma Gamma Rho, 378
Sigma Pi Beta, 378
Simmons, William J., 404
Simms, Willie, 359
Simpson, Theodosia, 445
Simpson College, 379
Sinclair, Upton, 366
Singers/singing: Bessie Smith, 419; freedom songs, 528; gospel, 465–466; Legend Singers, 456; of the 1920s, 418, 419, 420; of the 1930s and 1940s, 466–470; of the 1960s, 550; rap, 600
Singleton, Alvin, 593
Singleton, Benjamin "Pap," 323
Sioux, 346
Sipuel, Ada Lois, 442, 501–502
Sipuel v. Board of Regents of the University of Oklahoma, 442, 502
Sissle, Noble, 420
Sisters of Blessed Sacrament, 345
Sit-ins, 522–524: in Greensboro, Nashville, and Atlanta, 523–524; in the 1940s, 495–496; Reconstruction, 278; at South African Embassy, 586
16th St. Baptist Church, 531, 532

Slavery, in America: end of, 260–261; reparations for, 601–602
Smalls, Robert, 272, 288, 290, 312, 315, 324
Smith, Anna Deavere, 593
Smith, Bessie, 419, 467
Smith, Billy, 523
Smith, Carter, 350
Smith, Eleanor, 595
Smith, Ellison D., 440
Smith, Henry, 532
Smith, Hoke, 385
Smith, Lamar, 532
Smith, Mary Louise, 520
Smith, Miranda, 445
Smith, Ruby Doris, 524
Smith, Willie Mae Ford, 466
Smith v. *Allwright*, 443, 500, 514
SNCC. *See* Student Nonviolence Coordinating Committee (SNCC)
Social classes: *See also* Elite, black; fraternities and sororities, 378; growth of the middle class in the 1990s, 578–580; persistence of poverty (1960s–1990s), 580; upper (1860s–1920s), 378
Social Darwinism, 336, 402
Social scientists and the New Deal, 439–441
Social Security Act (SSA), 439, 440
Social welfare: *See also* New Deal; Clinton administration and, 592; Great Society, 551–552, 554; Great Society, dismantling of, 581; organizations, 374–376; Reconstruction, 290
Soledad Brothers, 549
Song of Solomon (Morrison), 593
Sororities, 378
Soul music, 560–561
Soul on Ice (Cleaver), 547
Soule, Charles, 263
Souljah, Sister, 599
Souls of Black Folk, The (Du Bois), 365, 369–370, 455
South: migration within the, 324; segregated schools in the, 337–338
South Africa, 586
South Carolina: disfranchisement in, 315; education in, 337, 338, 340; Eight Box Law (1992), 314; Ku Klux Klan in, 294, 295; Phoenix riot, 319; segregated schools in, 337; state land commission, 290; violence against black voters, 300–301
South Carolina State College, 337, 379; Orangeburg Massacre (1968), 561
South Side Writers Group, 463
Southeastern Conference, 359
Southern Christian Leadership Council (SCLC), 521, 527, 557; Birmingham confrontation and, 529–530; Carmichael's SNCC versus, 544; Voting Rights act of 1965 and Selma, Alabama and, 535–536
Southern Farmers' Alliance, 313
Southern Homestead Act (1866), 264
"Southern Manifesto, The," 514, 551
Southern Regional Council (SRC), 495, 527
Southern University, 339
Southside Community Art Center, 470
Southwestern Athletic Conference, 359
Sowell, Thomas, 581
Spain, civil war in, 483
Spanish-American War, 347–351
Sparks, Lee, 387, 388
Spaulding, Charles Clinton, 432–433
Special Field Order 15, 261–262, 264, 273, 327
Speese family, Moses, 324
Spencer, Herbert, 336
Spicer, Laura, 260–261
Spielberg, Steven, 594
Spingarn, Amy, 417
Spingarn, Joel E., 372, 383, 406
Spingarn, Medal, 379, 491, 498, 518
Spinks, Leon, 556
Spirit House Theater, 560
Sporting Life, 359
Sports, 358–359: baseball, 359, 420–421, 473; basketball, 359; boxing, 358–359, 473, 556; college, 359, 421; football, 359; in the 1920s, 420–421; in the 1930s and 1940s, 472–473; track, 472–473
Springfield, Illinois riot (1908), 372, 385
Stack, Carol, 563
Stallings, George A., 599
Staupers, Mabel K., 438, 487, 490, 491
Steele, Shelby, 581
Stephens, John W., 293
Stephenson, D.C., 404
Stephney, Haywood, 492
Stevens, Thaddeus, 276
Stewart, T. McCants, 315
Stoddard, Lothrop, 403–404
Stokes, Carl, 566
Storey, Moorfield, 372
Straight Outta Compton, 600
"Strange Fruit," 469
Streetcar segregation, 318
Strikes: labor, 354–355; in 1919–1920, 402; in 1939, 445; Reconstruction, 278
Student Nonviolence Coordinating Committee (SNCC), 524–528, 544, 546, 547; Mississippi Freedom summer, 533; women and, 534
Suffrage, 344; first black women's organizations, 322; in the 1900s, 376
Sugar Cane, 420
Sugar Hill Gang, 600
Sumner, Charles, 276, 298
Sumner, William Graham, 336
Sumner High School, 456
Supreme Life, 432
Survey Graphic, 416
Sweatt, Herman, 442–443, 502
Sweatt v. *Painter*, 442–443, 502
Sweet, Ossian, 406, 407
Sweet Honey in the Rock, 528
Swing music, 459
Symphony in Black (film), 469
Syphilis, Tuskegee Study of, 448–449

T

Taft, William Howard, 356, 368, 375, 378
Talented Tenth, 366, 371, 375, 376, 410
Talladega College, 340
Taney, Roger, 277
Tanner, Henry Ossawa, 334, 414
Tar Beach (Ringgold), 596
Taylor, Alrutheus, 406, 437
Taylor, Fannie, 388
Taylor, Geo., 350
Taylor, John G., 392–393
Taylor, Libby, 461
Taylor, Marshall W. "Major," 359
Teaching for the Lost-Found Nation of Islam in a Mathematical Way (Fard), 474
Temple, Shirley, 461
Temple university, 562
Temptations, 561
Tennessee: disfranchisement in, 315; first segregation laws in, 316; King's assassination in Memphis, 557–558; sit-ins in Nashville, 524; women's suffrage in, 376
10-Point Coalition, 600
Tenth Cavalry Regiment, 345–350, 380–381
Terborg-Penn, Rosalyn, 595
Terrell, Mary Church, 316, 372, 373, 374, 377, 438
Terrell, Robert H., 375
Terrell Law (1923), 443
Terry, Neely, 343
Tet Offensive in Vietnam, 554
Texas: affirmative action in, 585; Brownsville Affair (1906), 346–347; disfranchisement in, 315; Houston riot (1917), 386–387; Terrel Law (1923), 443; violence in Washington County, 319
Theater: black arts movement, 558, 559–560; New Deal, 440, 441
Their Eyes Were Watching God (Hurston), 418
There Is Confusion (Fauset), 416
3rd Alabama, 348
Third World Press, 559
Thirteenth Amendment, 273
Thomas, Clarence, 581–582, 583
Thomas, John W.E., 392
Thompson, "Big Bill," 404
Thrash, Dox, 470
Thurman, Wallace, 415, 416–417, 418
Thurmond, Strom, 499, 564
Tilden, Samuel J., 301
Till, Emmett Louis, 515, 532
Tillman, Benjamin R., 315, 368
Time-Warner, 600
Title IX of Education Amendments Act, 595
Title VII of the Civil Rights Act of 1972, 568
To Secure These Rights, 499
Tobacco industry, 445
Tobacco Workers Organizing Committee, 445
Tolton, Augustus, 345
Tompkins, Frank, 381
Toomer, Jean, 415, 416
Tougaloo University, 269, 340
Towne, Laura, 267
TransAfrica, 586
Travis, Dempsey, 486
Triggs, Clarence, 532
Trotter, William Monroe, 369, 370, 371, 378–380, 383
Truman, Harry S, 498, 499, 500
Trumball, Lyman, 276
Truth, Sojourner, 376
Tucker, Earl "Snakehips," 420
Tulsa, Oklahoma riot (1921), 387–388
Turé, Kwame, 547
Turner, Benjamin S., 284, 312
Turner, Henry McNeal, 319, 340, 343, 344, 351, 367
Turner, James E., 562
Turner, Mary, 321
Tuskegee Airmen, 491–492
Tuskegee Institute, 339–340, 353, 359, 367, 368–369, 379
Tuskegee Study, 448–449
Twenty-fifth Infantry Regiment, 345, 346–347, 351
Twenty-fourth Infantry Regiment, 345, 348, 349, 351
23rd Kansas, 348, 349
Twilight: Los Angeles, 593

U

Ugly Fishing Club, 378
Uncle Tom's Children (Wright), 463
Unemployment. *See* Employment
Union Bethel Church, 344
Union Leagues, 278
Unions: from 1860–1900, 353–355; in the 1920s, 411–413; in the 1930s and 1940s, 444–445; strikes, 354–355, 445; women in, 445; World War II and the impact on, 494
United Automobile Workers, 494
United Farm Equipment and Metal Workers, 445
United Methodist Church, 547
United Mine Workers (UMW), 354, 444
United Nations Basic Principles on the Use of Force and Firearms, violations of, 589
United Nations Code of Conduct for Law Enforcement Officials, violations of, 589
United Presbyterian Church, 547; Commission on Religion and Race, 546
U.S. Army Nurse Corps, 487, 490
U.S. Department of Labor, Division of Negro Economics, 412
United States Electric Lighting Company, 377
U.S. Employment Service (USES), 483
U.S. Public Health Service (USHS), 448
U.S. Supreme Court, 368, 554; affirmative action cases, list of, 584; on Alabama's segregation laws, 518; *Bakke* decision, 584–585; *Briggs* v. *Elliott*, 503; *Brown* II, 514–515; *Brown* v. *Board of Education of*

U.S. Supreme Court, (*continued*)
Topeka, Kansas, 443, 500–506; *Bush* v. *Gore*, 601; on Civil Rights Act of 1875, 343; *Cumming* v. *Richmond County [Georgia] Board of Education*, 337; Dred Scott decision, 277; Fourteenth Amendment interpretation, 310; *Gaines* v. *Canada*, 442; *Gayle* v. *Browder*, 521; Georgia's slave insurrection law and, 446; *Guinn* v. *United States*, 372; *McLaurin* v. *Oklahoma*, 502; *Missouri ex rel. Gaines* v. *Canada*, 501; *Nixon* v. *Herndon*, 407, 443; *Norris* v. *Alabama*, 447; *Plessy* v. *Ferguson*, 316–318, 337, 521; *Powell* v. *Alabama*, 447; "separate but equal" doctrine, 317, 318, 337, 442, 502, 506; *Sipuel* v. *Board of Regents of the University of Oklahoma*, 442, 502; *Smith* v. *Allwright*, 443, 500, 514; *Sweatt* v. *Painter*, 442–443, 502
Universal Negro Improvement Association (UNIA), 322, 402, 407–410
University of Alabama, 359, 527
University of California, affirmative action and, 584–585
University of Michigan, Alpha Phi Alpha, 378
University of Mississippi, 527
University of Oklahoma: *McLaurin* v. *Oklahoma*, 502; *Sipuel* v. *Board of Regents of the University of Oklahoma*, 442, 502
University of South Carolina, 290
University of Texas (Austin), *Sweatt* v. *Painter*, 442–443, 502
University of Vermont, 359
Up from Slavery (Washington), 259, 407
Uptown Art Laboratory, 441
Upward Bound, 552
Urban areas: *See also specific cities*; black migration within South to, 324; inner-city rebellions in the 1960s, 549–551
Urban League (National League on Urban Conditions among Negroes), 372, 374, 412, 416
Utah, women's suffrage in, 376

V

Van Vechten, Carl, 417
Vandervall, Isabella, 355
Vann, Robert L., 439, 461, 487
Vanzant, Iyanla, 594
Vanzetti, Bartolomeo, 402
Vardaman, James K., 384
Vaughan, Sarah, 458, 469
Veiled Aristocrats (film), 462
Victorio, Chief, 346
Vietnam War: Johnson administration and, 552–555; Nixon administration and, 564–565
Villa, Francisco "Pancho," 380
Villard, Oswald Garrison, 372, 373
Violence: *See also* Riots; against black voters, 300–302; civil rights movement and, list of dates and events, 532; crime in black communities, 589–590; following Reconstruction, 319–322; following World War I, 383–388; King's assassination, 532, 557–558; of Ku Klux Klan, 293–295, 529–530, 533; lynching. *See* Lynchings; Mississippi Freedom summer, 533; Orangeburg Massacre (1968), 561; police brutality in the 1990s, 588–590; rape, 321; over the Vietnam War, 565; in Washington County, Texas, 319
Virginia: disfranchisement in, 315; resistance to desegregation, 514
Virginia Union University, 269, 352, 359
Voice from the South by a Black Woman of the South, A (Cooper), 376
Voice of Missions, 344
Volstead Act, 418
Volunteers in Service to America (VISTA), 552
Voter Education Project, 565
Voting rights: disfranchisement, 314–315; Eight Box Law (1992), 314; Fifteenth Amendment, 295–296, 314; grandfather clause, 315, 368; Lincoln on, 272; Mississippi Freedom summer, 533; in the 1950s, 514; in the 1960s, 527–528, 533; Radical Republicans and, 276; *Smith* v. *Allwright*, 443, 500, 514; universal manhood suffrage, 278; violence against black voters, 300–302, 532; women's suffrage, 322, 376
Voting Rights Act: of 1965, 534, 535–536, 552, 565; of 1975, 567; of 1982, 586

W

Wade, Benjamin, 276
Wald, Lillian, 372
Walker, A'Lelia, 417–418
Walker, Alice, 594
Walker, Armstead, 352
Walker, Charles Joseph, 353
Walker, Fleetwood, 473
Walker, Frank, 419
Walker, Madam (Sarah Breedlove), 353, 418
Walker, Maggie Lena, 352, 353
Walker, Margaret, 463, 467, 559
Walker, Moses Fleetwood, 359
Walker, Weldy Wilberforce, 359
Wallace, Daniel Webster, 327
Wallace, George, 447, 527, 544, 563, 564, 568
Wallace, Henry, 499
Wallace, Henry C., 379
Wallace, Michele, 595
Waller, Thomas "Fats," 418–420
Walls, Josiah T., 284, 300, 312
Walters, Ronald, 566
Ward, Benjamin, 590
Ward, Theodore, 463
Ward, Val Gray, 560
Ware, Virgin Lamar, 532
Ware High School, 337
Warfield, William, 467
Warith, 597
War on Poverty, 551, 552
Warren, Earl, 505–506
Washington, Booker T., 259, 338–340, 341, 345, 379, 407; Atlanta riot of 1906 and, 385; Brownsville Affair (1906), 347; clergymen, views on, 342; influence of, 367–368; NAACP and, 373–374; Niagara Movement and, 371; opposition to, 369; Philippine Insurrection and, 351; racial issues and, 365, 366–369; relations with Du Bois, 369–371; Terrell and, 375; Tuskegee Institute, formation of, 339–340, 367, 368–369
Washington, D.C.: first black mayor of, 586; march on (1963), 530–531; Million Man March (1995), 598; Resurrection City, 558
Washington, Fredi, 461
Washington, Harold, 567
Washington, Margaret Murray, 374, 375
Washington, Mary Ellen, 393
Washington and Jefferson College, 421
Washington and Lee University, 421
Washington Bee, 367
Washington County, Texas, 319
Watching the Trains Go By (Bearden), 512
Watergate, 565
Waters, Ethel, 420, 489
Waters, Maxine, 599
Watson, Henry, 327
Watson, Thomas, 313–314
Watts rebellion (1965), 550
Ways of White Folks, The (Hughes), 416
Weary Blues, The (Hughes), 464
Weaver, George L.P., 527
Weaver, James B., 313
Weaver, Robert, 437, 439, 527
Webster, Milton, 413
Weems, Charlie, 445
Welfare Reform Act (1996), 592
Wells, Ida Barnett, 321, 322, 372
Wells, Mary, 550
Wells-Barnett, Ida, 374, 376, 377
Wesley, Cynthia, 531, 532
West, Charles, 421
West, Cornel, 595, 597
West Point, 328
Wheatley, Phillis, 374–376
Whipper, Leigh, 292
Whipper, William, 292, 315
White, Ben Chester, 532
White, Charles, 470
White, George H., 311, 312, 319, 392
White, Walter, 405, 416, 417, 433–434, 441, 442, 443–444, 487, 494
White Brotherhood, 293
White Citizens' Councils, 514
White League, 300
White supremacy, 336; *See also* Ku Klux Klan; in the 1950s, 514; racism in the 1920s, 402–404
White supremacy, challenges to (1860–1915), 334–363: black professionals, 355–356; in business, 351–353; in churches, 341–345; in education, 336–341; in labor, 353–355; in military, 345–351; in music, 356–358; in sports, 358–359; timeline, 360–361
White supremacy in late nineteenth century, 308–333: African Americans and southern courts, 329–330; black farm families and, 324–329; disfranchisement and, 314–315; migration and, 323–324; politics and, 310–314; racial etiquette and, 318–319; segregation and, 315–318; timeline, 330–331; violence and, 319–322
Whitecaps, 293
Whiteside, Charles, 267
Whittaker, Johnson C., 328
Wicker, Tom, 549
Wideman, John Edgar, 595
Wilberforce University, 369
Wilder, L. Douglas, 567
Wiley College, 359
Wilkins, Roy, 485, 495, 551
Willard, Jesse, 359
William E. Harmon Awards for Distinguished Achievement among Negroes, 470
Williams, Armstrong, 581
Williams, Daniel Hale, 355, 392
Williams, Eugene (Chicago riot, 1919), 387
Williams, Eugene (Scottsboro Boys), 445
Williams, Henry Sylvester, 410
Williams, Hosea, 535, 536
Williams, Hubert, 590
Williams, James H., 350
Williams, Joe, 465
Williams, Juan, 602
Williams, Mary Lou, 458
Williams, Nancy, 265
Williams, Patricia, 595
Williams, Spencer, Jr., 461
Williams, Walter, 581
Williams-Jones, Pearl, 466
Willis, Dorsie, 347
Wilmington, North Carolina riot (1898), 319
Wilmore, Gayraud S., 546
Wilson, August, 592
Wilson, Henry, 276, 345
Wilson, James, 379
Wilson, Pete, 585
Wilson, William Julius, 595
Wilson, Woodrow, 378–380, 381, 403–404: Fourteen Points, 410–411
Winfield, Hemsley, 466
Winfrey, Oprah, 578, 579
Wint, Theodore J., 350
Winter, Leon, 327
Wolfe, George C., 592
Woman's Era, 374
Women: in the 1990s, 578; actresses, 461–462; black feminism, 594–595, 600; business owners, 352, 353; in civil rights movement, 443–444; club movement, 374–376; dancers/singers of the 1920s, 419; dancers/singers of the 1930s and

1940s, 466–470; Depression and impact on, 431; education of, 271, 595; employment as domestics during World War I, 393; FBI's Ten Most Wanted list, first black woman on, 549; in government positions, 438, 567–569; lawyers, 271, 356, 500–502; lynching of, 321; mayors, 586; migration within South to urban areas, 324; Million Woman March (1997), 599; Montgomery bus boycott and role of, 516–519; in NAACP, 352, 353, 375, 443–444; as nurses, 355–356, 487, 490, 491; as physicians, 355; politicians (1970s), 567–569, 587; politicians (Reconstruction), 292; prostitution, 393–394; rape of, 321; religious leaders, 343; sexual harassment, 582, 583; singers (blues), 357, 419; singers (Motown), 550; sit-ins and role of, 495–496; SNCC and, 534; in the Spanish civil war, 483; suffrage, 322, 376; teachers, 266, 267; in unions, 445; World War II (as nurses), 487, 490, 491; World War II (working on the home front), 493, 495; writers, 292, 322, 415, 418, 559, 593–594
Women's Army Auxiliary Corps (WAACs), 490
Women's Day Workers and Industrial League, 443
Women's International League for Peace and Freedom, 375
Women's Political Council (WPC), 516, 517, 518, 519
Women's rights movement, 292; black feminism, 594–595, 600
Wonder, Stevie, 561
Woodson, Carter G., 377, 414, 437, 447
Woodson, George H., 356
Woodward, C. Vann, 504
Woolworth, sit-in at, 523–524
Work, Monroe, 437
Working Girls' Home Association, 376
Works Progress Administration (WPA), 437, 439, 440, 443, 470
World Community of al-Islam in the West (WCIW), 597
World's Fair (1893), 322
World Trade Center, terrorist attack on (Sept. 11, 2001), 603
World War I, 381–383
World War II, 480–509: on the eve of (1936–1941), 482–485; on the home front, 493–496; transition to peace after, 497
World War II, blacks in the military: Army's Air Corps treatment of blacks, 488, 489; beginning of desegregation, 489–490; costs of military discrimination, 486–487; Executive Order 8802, 484, 485; institutional racism, 485–486; March on Washington Movement (MOWM) (1941), 483–485; Marine Corps' treatment of blacks, 489; Navy's treatment of blacks, 485–486, 489; between 1939–1940, 483; protests by soldiers and civilians, 487, 488; transformation of black soldiers, 492–493; Tuskegee Airmen, 491–492; women in, 487, 490, 491
Wright, Ada, 447
Wright, Andy, 445
Wright, Jonathan J., 272, 285, 287, 290
Wright, Mose, 515
Wright, Richard, 463, 471, 595
Wright, Roy, 447
Writers: *See also specific writers*; Black Chicago Renaissance, 463–465; Harlem Renaissance, 413–418; women, 292, 322, 415, 418, 559
Wyoming, women's suffrage in, 376

X

Xavier University, 345

Y

Yale University: Alpha Phi Alpha, 378; black studies at, 562; Law School, 359
Yarmouth (ship), 409, 410
YMCA, 392, 406
Young, Andrew, 319, 569
Young, Charles D., 348, 380–381, 382
Young, Coleman, 492, 566
Young Communist League, 496
Younge, Samuel, Jr., 532
Young Negroes' Cooperative League, 443
YWCA, 443

Z

Zeta Phi Beta, 378